art in chicago

1945–1995

art in chica 1945– 1995

*Thames and
Hudson*

*Museum of
Contemporary Art
Chicago*

Organized by
Lynne Warren

Essays by
Jeff Abell
Dennis Adrian
Staci Boris
John Corbett
Kate Horsfield

Barbara Jaffee
Judith Russi Kirshner
Carmela Rago
Franz Schulze
Peter Selz
Bill Stamets
and Lynne Warren

With contributions
from
Monique Meloche
and Dominic Molon

contents

Art in Chicago, 1945–1995 was prepared on the occasion of the exhibition of the same name originated by the Museum of Contemporary Art, Chicago, and on view there from November 16, 1996 through March 23, 1997.

"Art in Chicago" is a multipart project that includes a historical exhibition, "Art in Chicago, 1945–1995"; a scholarly catalogue; and a survey exhibition, "Time Arts Chicago," with accompanying live performances.

The exhibition "Art in Chicago, 1945–1995" is generously sponsored by PHILIP MORRIS COMPANIES INC.

"Time Arts Chicago" exhibition and performances are generously sponsored by SARA LEE FOUNDATION

Major support of the research, exhibitions, and project catalogue has also been provided by THE HENRY LUCE FOUNDATION.

Additional support has been provided by the National Endowment for the Humanities and by a grant from the Illinois Arts Council, a state agency.

First published in the United States of America in 1996 by Thames and Hudson, 500 Fifth Avenue, New York, New York 10110

First published in Great Britain in 1996 by Thames and Hudson Ltd., London

Library of Congress Catalog Card Number 96-60369

British Library Cataloguing-in-Publication data

A catalogue record for this book is available from the British Library

ISBN 0-500-23728-X

Produced by the Publications Department of the Museum of Contemporary Art: Donald Bergh, Director, and Amy Teschner, Associate Director

Publication Coordinator and Editor: Terry Ann R. Neff

Design and Typography: studio blue

Jacket photographs: Joe Ziolkowski

Printed and bound in Hong Kong

Stephanie French
Vice President,
Corporate Contributions
and Cultural Programs
Philip Morris Companies Inc.

For nearly thirty years the Museum of Contemporary Art in Chicago has been presenting exciting and provocative work by the most influential artists of our time. Since the very beginning of its exhibition program, the museum's leadership has championed artists from the hometown vicinity, beginning with the retrospective of the Chicago artist H. C. Westermann in 1969.

It is fitting that in the inaugural year of exhibitions at the MCA's new building, the museum has looked to its community's artistic richness and organized an exhibition that will bring to the public, for the first time, a sweeping view of the breadth and depth of Chicago's artistic vision from the postwar era to the present day. To continue this vision, the museum will be instituting a series of exhibitions featuring the work of Chicago artists.

At Philip Morris, we have shown a consistent commitment to the arts for nearly forty years. Our support of "Art in Chicago, 1945–1995" reflects our long-standing support of contemporary art, and our involvement in encouraging creativity and innovation in all the arts. With our Chicago-based food company, Kraft Foods, we join in celebrating the opening of this major new cultural center and in saluting the Chicago artists who have influenced the art of our times.

sponsors'
forewords

This decade represents a defining time for Chicago. A comparison is often made with a time about a century ago—the 1890s—when the World's Columbian Exposition was the great catalyst for creating the first art and cultural boom in our city. It is probably more than just a coincidence that the last decades of the nineteenth and twentieth centuries are so culturally significant. Many people believe that preparing for a new century can energize a community.

The new Museum of Contemporary Art is a beautifully and distinctively designed building, with its sculpture garden and magnificent view of Lake Michigan. And with its completion, the city's cultural landscape is enhanced and Chicago's artistic life made even more vibrant.

Sara Lee Corporation is delighted to be associated with this landmark occasion. Throughout its fifty-seven years, Sara Lee has supported cultural endeavors as part of our commitment to enhancing the communities in which we operate. And I believe Chicago is the one American city that can be defined most of all by the cultural and artistic life that it offers its people. Sara Lee is proud to call Chicago our corporate home.

John H. Bryan
Chairman and
Chief Executive Officer
Sara Lee Corporation

Kevin E. Consey
Director and Chief Executive Officer

foreword

"For a city that is probably one of the best analyzed, most carefully described, and incessantly invoked in the western world, Chicago's art history remains a closely guarded secret." These provocative words were written in 1988 by Professor Neil Harris of the University of Chicago in reference to Chicago's prewar art history, but they are no less true of the postwar half-century, the period covered by "Art in Chicago, 1945–1995."

Furthermore, what has been known of the fifty years that have passed since Chicago's art world was transformed by GIs returning from war, has been refracted by myth and legend to cast a distorted or cloudy picture. Although the stereotypes that have resulted hold some truth, they are also sadly weary and stale, long overdue for a fresh look.

To continue Professor Harris's observation ("The Chicago Setting," *The Old Guard and the Avant-Garde: Modernism in Chicago, 1910–1940* [Chicago: The University of Chicago Press, 1990] ,p. 3), what is it about a city whose "geography, architecture, politics, and social pathology, like its industrial and merchandising innovations and literary currents, have provoked a scholarship that is the envy of larger rivals," yet whose art history has been so thoroughly ignored? There is no "basic text" on Chicago art, a fact that has mystified generations of out-of-town visitors to our museum's bookstore, a text, revealingly, never requested by locals either hardened by the indifference often shown to home-grown visual arts over the years or simply unaware that our city has had a long, interesting, multifaceted art history.

To some extent, a city that has led the world in so many arenas—architecture, sociology, journalism, transportation, manufacturing, and more recently, sports and improvisational theater and comedy—may understandably fail to pay attention to other arenas. Lack of serious, critical attention, however, can quickly and unfortunately lead to the self-fulfilling prophecy of a lesser status. The infamous "Second City syndrome" that has plagued all areas of Chicago life has nowhere had such a deleterious

effect as in the visual arts. For many years, to quote Walter Sherwood writing in 1929, "as soon as a Chicago artist won his spurs he packed his paint kit and took a fast train to New York" ("Chicago's Place in the Fine Arts," *Chicago: The World's Youngest Great City* [Chicago: American Publishers, 1929] , p. 35).

The Museum of Contemporary Art (MCA) has traditionally exhibited and collected the works of locally based artists along with national and international figures. With the maturing in the 1980s of the Chicago arts community (in typical Chicago style, largely through the arenas of merchandising and education—the international art expos and the boom in higher education in the arts) and the maturing of the MCA as symbolized by its recent move to new, expanded quarters, it is timely and appropriate to undertake a serious treatment of the distinctive and diverse art history of Chicago. Furthermore, because of the unique circumstances of this great American city—often cited as the prototypical American city—it is even more appropriate that this history be viewed within the larger cultural, social, and political life of the city. Although in the 1990s this type of approach is fashionable, to approach Chicago's visual-arts history in any other way would be simply to leave out a good deal of the story. While the "city that works" has often overshadowed the "city that creates," the creative community in Chicago has long been sensitive to the larger issues of the role of art in the life of the community.

This book and the exhibition it accompanies are the result of five years of research, planning, and community involvement. The project began under the auspices of a major research grant from The Henry Luce Foundation, whose primary interest in American art, its documentation, and study allowed the MCA to assemble a project team led by Curator, Special Projects, Lynne Warren. Ms. Warren's long history in the Chicago community (she arrived here in 1971) allowed her a first-person view of half of the period in question, and her long tenure at the MCA (she joined the staff in 1978) as both exhibitions and collections curator allowed significant, sustained contact with the Chicago community.

What quickly emerged was that this exhibition would be a very different one from those Chicagoans are accustomed to. For years the only game in town was The Art Institute of Chicago's Annual Exhibition by Artists of Chicago and Vicinity shows, and expectations ran high that the MCA should pick up the ball in presenting a juried competition of local talent—an impulse that ran counter to the MCA's desire to present a baseline history. As well, research revealed that the story of Chicago's art history was larger, broader, and more diversified than previously known, even by those few experts in the field.

Thus the MCA invited leading arts administrators, historians, and patrons to serve on an advisory committee. René H. Arceo, Arts Director, Mexican Fine Arts Center Museum, Chicago; Don Baum, artist and curator; Barry Blinderman, Director, University Galleries, Illinois State University, Normal; Amina J. Dickerson, former Director of Elizabeth F. Cheney Center for Education and Public Programs, Chicago Historical Society; Joyce Fernandes, Program Director of Sculpture Chicago; Ronne Hartfield, Executive Director of Museum Education, The Art Institute of Chicago; Ruth Horwich, collector and Honorary Chairperson of the Hyde Park Art Center, Chicago; Gregory Knight, Director of Visual Arts, City of Chicago, Department of Cultural Affairs; Robert Pincus-Witten, art historian and writer; Victor Alejandro Sorell, art historian and Special Assistant to the Dean, College of Arts and Sciences, Chicago State University; Peter Taub, former Executive Director, Randolph Street Gallery, Chicago; Martha Ward, art historian, University of Chicago; and James Yood, art historian and critic, Northwestern University, Evanston, Illinois; as well as the essayists who contributed to this book, were all generous with their time and expertise. The MCA also convened a series of five community roundtables for artists, critics and writers, dealers and collectors, educators and community activists, and other interested parties. We sought

counsel from our advisory committee about what we would like to do and disseminated our intentions at roundtables. The response to these meetings was extraordinary: numerous individuals came forward with information and materials, as well as concerns and advice, for which the MCA is deeply grateful.

A major result of the research phase was the recognition that although a major historical exhibition and book would be invaluable, an even more comprehensive product would be of great value to the community. Thus the MCA committed itself to building an Archive of Art in Chicago, and received, in 1995, another major grant from The Henry Luce Foundation to start up this unique resource. In this way the MCA will continue its efforts to support and preserve the local production beyond the "Art in Chicago, 1945–1995" exhibition itself. We are not only extremely grateful to The Henry Luce Foundation for making this possible, but to the many individuals who have contributed or pledged to contribute to this repository.

As the project developed and major support for the survey exhibition was received from Philip Morris Companies Inc. and for the "Time Arts Chicago" exhibition from the Sara Lee Foundation, the "Art in Chicago" team, now expanded to include education staff, began exploring how best to present this history to the public. Recognizing the broader importance of this history, the decision was to apply to the National Endowment for the Humanities for support, the first time the MCA had applied for a special exhibitions grant. The mission of this agency to disseminate scholarly research to wide audiences and the MCA's own goals to become a major participant in the cultural life not only of Chicago and the region but of the nation dovetailed, and in 1994 we were elated to receive a planning grant from this agency. We have also been fortunate to receive support for this project from the Illinois Arts Council, a state agency.

"Art in Chicago, 1945–1995," as broad and thoroughly researched as it is, cannot be all things to all people. There are inevitably omissions, areas that warrant further detail, artists and movements that bear reexamination. Our hope is that "Art in Chicago," in its presentation and especially in the form of this book, will provide a focal point for the intense commitment and passion Chicagoans bring to their city, their culture, and their aspirations, now and in the future.

acknowledgments

Lynne Warren
Project Director, Art in Chicago

"Art in Chicago, 1945–1995" is one of the most ambitious, sustained projects the Museum of Contemporary Art has undertaken, and such a project would not have been possible without the extraordinary commitment of the entire institution, its staff and board of trustees.

I wish particularly to acknowledge the role of Director Kevin E. Consey, who, when he arrived from Southern California at the MCA in 1989, brought an abiding interest in how local communities function and how cities affect their artists and vice versa. It was Kevin Consey who initially suggested that the MCA explore his adopted community's art history in a significant way, and without his ceaseless support and the many resources the institution has put toward the "Art in Chicago" project, this exhibition and book simply would not exist in this form. I must also thank James W. Alsdorf Chief Curator Richard Francis, who, arriving at the MCA from England in 1993 during the project's initial research phase, brought his unique experience of the London and Liverpool communities to serve as an excellent sounding board and occasional provocateur. His passionate desire to involve the art community as fully as possible resulted in the series of roundtable discussions and in the tapping of our community's deep well of arts professionals to form a distinguished advisory committee: René H. Arceo, Don Baum, Barry Blinderman, Amina J. Dickerson, Joyce Fernandes, Ronne Hartfield, Ruth Horwich, Gregory Knight, Robert Pincus-Witten, Victor Alejandro Sorell, Peter Taub, Martha Ward, and James Yood, and Dennis Adrian, Barbara Jaffee, Judith Russi Kirshner, Franz Schulze, and Peter Selz, who also served as essayists. Also serving as catalogue essayists for the time arts section were John Corbett, Kate Horsfield, Carmela Rago, and Bill Stamets, and especially Jeff Abell who contributed his own essay and served as editor for this section.

The invaluable counsel of this knowledgeable and dedicated group has allowed us to create a visual and written record that while inevitably not complete, will serve as a comprehensive basic text on the subject. We would also like to thank the over 200 members of the arts community—artists, dealers, collectors, writers, and others—who participated in our five community roundtable discussions. The insights of the participants and the good will we felt during these public forums were tremendous motivators.

As well as being one of the most ambitious projects ever undertaken by the MCA, "Art in Chicago" constitutes a model of how exhibitions and publications are best realized in today's rapidly changing climate. "Art in Chicago" was truly a team effort and, simply, I had the "dream team": Staci Boris, Assistant Curator, served as an enthusiastic collaborator. Fresh from assisting on the complicated "Art at the Armory" project, she often dazzled me with her competence and analytic ability. The intelligence and insight she brought to this complex and often overwhelming process forged a sophisticated and fruitful professional relationship. While serving virtually as an equal partner on every aspect of the project, Ms. Boris researched and realized the timeline that gives structure to this book and the exhibition; this alone is a major contribution to scholarship on Chicago.

Monique Meloche, Project Assistant, seasoned by her years of ably coordinating the MCA's Benefit Auction and working with the registrar's office, came to the team as the compleat assistant—able to discharge her duties of coordinating the involved administration of "Art in Chicago" while also making major contributions, especially in the nitpicking, often thankless, pursuit of handling the over one hundred loans, and obtaining accurate checklist information and the images that illustrate this book. As this is the first comprehensive scholarly book and exhibition on the topic, it was imperative that we "get it right," and Ms. Meloche's attention to detail allowed me the luxury of delegating extraordinary responsibility to her. She assumed a crucial part of the team's work, visiting studios, writing artists' biographies, and curating the "Black Light" special section of the exhibition.

Dominic Molon, Research Assistant, Time Arts, came to the team from the State University of New York at Stony Brook, but he was no stranger, having served with me in the late 1980s as a curatorial intern. Mr. Molon was charged with the difficult task of becoming "the" expert on time arts in Chicago, which he did with enthusiasm, long, long hours, and penetrating intellectual analysis. Working closely with many members of this community, he coordinated the time arts section of the book and the "Time Arts Chicago" exhibition, and authored numerous biographies for this book.

Finally on the curatorial team—and without whose contributions this project would have been woefully understaffed—are the many interns who carried out ceaseless research and fact-checking: we thank Joree Adilman, Amy Bero, Steve Clark, Anna Friedman, Krishna F. Knabe, Megan H. Mack, Courtenay E. Smith, Sheldon Krasnow, Laura Stoland, Michelle Tirado, Lance Warren, and Elizabeth K. Whiting, most of whom are also contributors to the artists' biographies section.

The "Art in Chicago" project team also included education personnel Wendy Woon, Director of Education; Margaret Farr, Assistant Director of Education; Marie Shurkus, Manager of Public Programs; Rhonda Brown, Education Coordinator of Special Projects; and Pablo Helguera, Education Assistant. Jason Koziara, Community Outreach Assistant and Public Ally, and Erika Varricchio, Coordinator, Outreach Programs, also part of the education team, along with Ms. Farr, contributed artists' biographies. In weekly meetings in which concepts for the effective presentation of the huge body of material we had amassed were developed, the education personnel suggested and planned thorough, exciting, and innovative interpretive programs.

While the whole MCA staff must be acknowledged for their enthusiasm and support, other key members of the project team were Don Bergh, Director of Design and Publications, and Amy Teschner, Associate Director of Publications; Lela Hersh, Manager, Collections and Exhibitions, who also wrote several artists' biographies, and her staff Chandra King, Associate Registrar, and Deborah Peterson, Assistant Registrar, and Juliet Nations-Powell, Photo Archive Assistant. Jim Prinz and Joe Ziolkowski served as Staff Photographers. Don

Meckley, Chief Preparator, and Mykl Ruffino, Preparator, ably managed the exhibition construction and installation of the hundreds of items that make up the show; and Dennis O'Shea, Technical Supervisor, was an invaluable resource in planning and realizing the audio-visual aspects of the exhibition. I am also grateful to Carolyn Stolper Friedman, Director of Development, and Ann Shillinglaw, Director, Foundation and Government Relations, for their efforts on behalf of fundraising for the project, and to Lori Kleinerman, Director of Marketing, Maureen King, Director of Public Relations, and Mike Thomas, Assistant Director of Public Relations, for their roles in "getting the word out." Former MCA staff members Grant Samuelsen and Nadine Wasserman provided artists' biographies for the catalogue. Librarians Amanda Kaiser and Emily Gage provided critical research support.

During the research phase, the project was also supported by community members giving of their valuable time to meet in ad hoc committees that reviewed our research in light of the larger civic history of Chicago; we thank artist and social activist Lionel Bottari; Dr. Charles Branham, senior historian, DuSable Museum of African American History; artist and educator Mario Castillo; Richard Christiansen, chief art critic, *Chicago Tribune*; MCA Trustee Richard Cooper; Leon Despres, fomer Hyde Park Alderman; Susanne Ghez, Director of The Renaissance Society at the University of Chicago; artist and peace activist Pearl Hirshfield; Doris Holleb, professor of Urban History, University of Chicago; attorney and MCA Trustee Marshall Holleb; economist and teacher Sarah Peters; writer, critic, and performance artist Carmela Rago; George Roeder, Chairman of Undergraduate Division and professor in the Liberal Arts Department at The School of The Art Institute of Chicago; Don Rose, former press secretary to Martin Luther King, Jr., and political analyst and consultant; art critic Jerry Saltz; and artist and mural historian John Pitman Weber.

Many, many people stepped forward or furnished us with resources and/or assistance above and beyond the normal call of duty, and to these we are particularly thankful: George Adams; Jones Alk-Cullinen; Edith Altman; Lucius Armstrong; at The Art Institute of Chicago: former Archivist John Smith and current Archivist Bart H. Ryckbosch, Courtney Donnell, Associate Curator, and Daniel Schulman, Assistant Curator, in the Department of Twentieth Century Painting and Sculpture, and Pam Stuedemann, Photo Rights Coordinator, Imaging and Technical Services; Raye Bemis; Howard Becker; Jerry Blumenthal and Gordon Quinn of Kartemquin Films; Wayne and Eleanor Boyer; Tom Brand; Kenneth Burkhardt; Mwata Bowden of the AACM; at the Center for Creative Photography, The University of Arizona: Archivist Amy Rule; Carolyn Chavez at the Cole Taylor Bank; at the Chicago Artists Coalition, Arlene Rakoncay and Jeff Abell; at the Chicago Historical Society, Eileen Flanagan, Prints & Photographs Department; the staff at Color Wizard; Sharon Couzin; Joan Dickinson at Randolph Street Gallery; Jeff Donaldson; Dzine; Stan Edwards; Carol Ehlers; Beverly Ellstrand; Sally Fairweather; Barton Faist; at The Field Museum of Natural History, Photographic Department, Nina Cummings; Allan Frumkin; Leon Golub; James R. Grossman; Neil Harris; Jo Hormuth and John Phillips; Mary Jane Jacob; Leigh Jones; Dr. Jerome Kavka, Archivist, Institute for Psychoanalysis; John Kearney; Wesley Kimler; Blanche M. Koffler; Phil Krone; Ellen Lanyon; June Leaf; Judith Burson Lloyd, Illinois Art Gallery; Jack Ludden; Ed Maldonado; Lou and Dawn Mallozzi; Heather McAdams; Tom McCormick; Pat Murphy; Claes Oldenburg; Lorenzo Pace; Tom Palazzolo; Jerry Peart; Frank Piatek; Marcos Raya; Helen Roberson of the North Shore Art League, Winnetka; Mark Rogovin; Alejandro Romero; Carol Rosofsky; at The School of The Art Institute of Chicago: Robert Loescher, professor and Goldabelle, McComb, Finn Honorary Chair in Art History, and Mindy Faber and Chris Bratton at the Video Data Bank; Andy Soma; Nancy Spero; Bill Stamets; Tom Strobel; Bibiana Suarez; Ken Thompson at *P-Form*; Michael S. Thompson; Michael Topol of Swell Pictures, Inc.; Irene Tsatsos; at the University of Illinois at Chicago: Dan Sandin, Tom DeFanti, and Maxine Brown at the Electronic Visualization Laboratory, Karen Indeck, Director of Gallery 400, School of Art and Design, Westin Thorn, Special Collections, and Mary Ann Bamberger, Assistant Special Collections Librarian; Hamza Walker, Director of Education, The Renaissance Society at the University of Chicago; Brenda Webb; Susan Weininger; Ann Weins, Editor, *New Art Examiner*; and Maurice Wilson.

The following furnished us with formal interviews as well as other help: Jerry Blumenthal and Gordon Quinn, Lynn Book, Phyllis Bramson, Fred Camper, George Cohen, Camille Cook, Marianne Deson, Brendan deVallance, Dominick Di Meo, Sharon Evans, Allan Frumkin, Richard Feigen, Ellen Fisher, Leon Golub, Ilona Granet, Richard Gray, James Grigsby, John Grimes, Bruce Gunderson, Robert Heinecken, Hudson, Bud Holland, Tom Jaremba, Tom Kalin, Vera Klement, Ellen Lanyon, Nathan Lerner, Lewis Manilow, Shirley Mordine, Pat Murphy, Linda Novak, Darinka Novitovic, Tom Palazzolo, Carmela Rago, Miroslaw Rogala, Dan Sandin and Tom DeFanti, Jean Sousa, Nancy Spero, Larry Steger, Barbara Sykes-Dietze, Alene Valkanas, and Michael Zerang. To all we are grateful.

It was a pleasure and extremely good fortune to work on this complex and word-full book with Terry Ann R. Neff, who served as Publication Coordinator and Editor. I have produced catalogues under Ms. Neff's guidance and sharp eye before and never has one of my projects required more expertise and experience than this. Kathy Fredrickson and Cheryl Towler Weese of studio blue designed and produced the book, with the assistance of Gail Wiener; it was a pleasure to work with designers who had an instinctive feel for the material as well as creativity and diligence.

Other consulting personnel include Miroslaw Rogala, Darrell Moore, and Mac Rutan who produced the CD-ROM prototype that will structure how we carry the dissemination of material on Chicago's visual culture into the future with our Archive of Art in Chicago, and Ed Rankus and Hans Schaal who produced the video that is the centerpiece of the "1968" special section of the exhibition.

The exhibition and book would not have been possible without the generosity of the over 120 lenders to the exhibition. We are in their debt, yet know that through the assembling of so many significant objects, lenders will see their works anew in light of the compelling story that is told. And, as with all MCA projects, it is the artists who must be thanked. It is their dedication, hard work, and perseverance, often through difficult times, that allows us to have any exhibition, especially an exhibition of such quality and originality.

Finally, during the course of the "Art in Chicago, 1945–1995" project, our community has lost many significant voices. Some we were able to hear before their passing in interviews, and all of them left extraordinary legacies: Serge Chermayeff, Constance Teander Cohen, Bud Holland, Joseph Goto, Henry Hanson, Shirley Hardin, Sam Koffler, Christina Ramberg, Aaron Siskind, Steven J. Urry, and Claire Zeisler. Just as this book was going to press, Joseph Randall Shapiro, extraordinary patron, collector, wise man, and the founder and inspiration behind the MCA, died. Art in Chicago will never be the same. It is in memory of these friends that we offer this book.

Franz Schulze

art in chicago: the two traditions

In this essay Franz Schulze, who has been a shaping force within the Chicago art community for close to forty years, provides an overview of the last fifty years of artistic development in Chicago. Schulze is probably best known in Chicago for his seminal book *Fantastic Images: Chicago Art Since 1945* (1972) and as the critic who coined the terms "The Monster Roster" and "Imagism"; the latter term, which originally referred to artists of the immediate postwar generation, came to define the generation of artists who emerged in the late 1960s. More recently Schulze has turned his attention to architecture and has authored the distinguished biographies *Mies van der Rohe: A Critical Biography* (1985), and

Philip Johnson: Life and Work (1994). Schulze is currently the Betty Jane Hollender Professor of Art at Lake Forest College, Illinois, where he has taught since 1953. LW

when a.j.

Liebling's famous essay "The Second City" was published in *The New Yorker* in 1952,[1] it caused the Chicagoans who read it no end of embarrassment. Liebling's portrait of their city as backward, unsophisticated, and past whatever prime it may once have boasted seemed to many of them typical of the New York literary condescension they loved to hate. Still, it had the ring of truth. In the immediate post-World War II years, Chicago was an urban giant but no world city, having long since failed to realize the commercial and cultural ambitions it set for itself at the time of the World's Columbian Exposition roughly a half-century earlier.

It is worth recalling that Liebling wrote his article exactly as New York was entering its own high halcyon phase, a period now remembered with pride, and wistfulness, by all Americans, not just Manhattanites. The arts, especially painting and sculpture, were flourishing in New York during the years following World War II—moreover, in an environment as overall livable as it was intellectually invigorating. Talk focused on names like Jackson Pollock, Willem de Kooning, Mark Rothko, and Robert Motherwell: chief inventors of an idiom commonly called Abstract Expressionism that seemed not only new to the history of art, but bolder and more daring than anything going on at the time in Europe. If New York, in New York's eyes, had overtaken Paris, where did that leave Chicago but 800 miles inland, worth reaching most appropriately by the back of Liebling's hand?

Indeed in Chicago during the same postwar period, there was no art press, gallery community, or company of specialized art institutions to compare with counterparts in New York. There was the Art Institute, to be sure, a towering tree of so many branches—museum, school of art, school of drama, theater, forum for the showing of contemporary art—that little else could grow in its shade, least of all the local artists' plantings.

As for the city as a cultural whole, it had several excellent museums of science and history, a respectable symphony orchestra but no resident opera or ballet, a couple of first-rate universities, and a notoriously sluggish theater world. In the production of original work in the so-called high arts, it had fallen into the habit of generating surges of startling creativity in certain fields, especially in literature and architecture, that somehow were never sustained; either the leading creative spirits died or, more commonly—it had the same effect—left Chicago for places presumably more appreciative of them. Chief among these was New York, by 1945 the destination not only of pilgrims stateside but of an army of eminent European refugees in all the arts and sciences. Piet Mondrian, Max Ernst, Hans Hofmann, Jacques Lipchitz, and André Breton only begin the long list of foreigners whose decision to settle in Manhattan was a major source of inspiration to the rising native painters and sculptors. In Chicago only two Europeans of historical distinction took up residence—Ludwig Mies van der Rohe, who in 1938 assumed the chair of the School of Architecture at Armour Institute of Technology—later Illinois Institute of Technology (IIT)—and László Moholy-Nagy (**plate 3**), the founder a year earlier of The New Bauhaus (later the Institute of Design [ID]) on the Near North Side (**see Selz essay**). And Mies and Moholy, nursing grudges dating back to their European days, did not like each other.

Moreover, by the end of 1946, Moholy was dead and Mies had built nothing in Chicago outside the campus of IIT. The city had little to show in outward form for the nearly ten years the two men had lived there. Liebling was more truthful than cruel when he later defined most of what he saw beyond the limits of downtown as "a boundless agglutination of streets, dramshops, and low buildings without urban character," while the Loop itself "is like Times Square and Radio City set down in the middle of a vast Canarsie [**fig. 1**]."[2] People old enough to remember may have forgotten how appalling and how visible Chicago's slums were in the later 1940s—those being the days prior to urban renewal—although they may recall that what seemed to thrive most in Chicago was its inventively corrupt political system.

SECOND CITY

III~THE MASSACREE

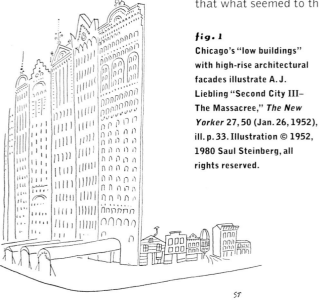

fig. 1
Chicago's "low buildings" with high-rise architectural facades illustrate A.J. Liebling "Second City III– The Massacree," *The New Yorker* 27, 50 (Jan. 26, 1952), ill. p. 33. Illustration © 1952, 1980 Saul Steinberg, all rights reserved.

to the chicagoans
the figure
was no liability at all,
but an expressive asset
of the first order,

demonstrably the most nearly
universal metaphor
by which humans had
confronted and
accounted for
experience since the
dawn of history

all this is the downside.

Among more than a few things Liebling did not see, because he could not or chose not to look past stereotypes that came easily to him as a New Yorker, was that Chicago's art and architecture worlds were shaking off their latest languor even as he wrote. They did so together and separately, for reasons both unique to each and common to their origins in Chicago.

The change was already underway in 1948. In that year Mies undertook the commission for his first buildings in downtown Chicago, while, more manifestly, a group of students at The School of The Art Institute of Chicago (SAIC) and the Institute of Design assembled the first of a series of activities that consolidated the creative energies of an exceptional postwar Chicago generation. Exhibition Momentum, as its organizers called themselves, grew out of a demonstration against the decision of the Art Institute to forbid students from entering its juried Annual Exhibition by Artists of Chicago and Vicinity (C&V). With so few alternative exhibition possibilities in town, the Chicago show had long been the only event that provided local artists an opportunity to put their work before a reasonably well-informed public.

The passion of the students' protest was largely a factor of their age. Most of them were GI Bill veterans already in their twenties, old and impatient enough to chafe at being classified as unworthy of competing with either professionals or local Sunday painters.

Nothing was more remarkable about the early history of Momentum than the tense union it forged between two constituencies naturally ill-disposed toward one another. The ID students were idealists in the Bauhaus tradition, sworn to accept the real world even as they sought to redesign it, from spoons to skyscrapers to the social order. The SAIC crowd was indebted to a no less Modernist outlook, but to one which, deploring the spiritual dysfunction of society in its contemporary form, took refuge in a deeply inward, stubbornly personal, artistic vision. The intensity with which the two groups clung to their opposing views generated both the

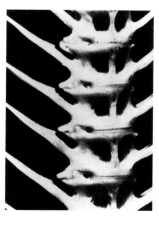

fig. 2
Artworks as reproduced in *Momentum 1950* exhibition portfolio. Left to right: Franz Schulze, Louis Kriesberg, Robert Hall, and Edward Bedno. Museum of Contemporary Art, Chicago, Archive of Art in Chicago.

mutual respect and the hostile exchanges that motivated their organization of a series of more or less annual exhibitions intended as countersalons to the C&V show. Thus they published exhibition catalogues that contained statements of sharply contrasting opinions. Here is SAIC student Leon Golub, writing in the 1950 catalogue: "The contemporary artist is a law unto himself. His inverted, fragmented concept of reality rarely coincides with that of others. He needs endlessly pursue his identity and question the validity of his actions. But he remains thrust aside, alienated, and a solitary."[3] In retort, ID student Alex Nicoloff declared: "Do you [implicitly Golub] forget that creativity extends itself into the events of every day, into the social relationships we form or cannot? To plant and cultivate seed, design a better chair or table, a better living or working area, and relate these to a more adequate communal organization, this is to better life."[4]

At a distance of nearly fifty years, both statements are instructive not only of the ways in which a younger generation was thinking about the creative act in Chicago in the wake of a great war, but of the directions eventually taken by the fine and utilitarian arts that Golub and Nicoloff respectively stood for (**fig. 2**). Each statement had the sound of a manifesto, and in fact the two groups comprising Momentum shared a yearning for revolution, for a radically new way of artistic behavior that grew from a corollary dissatisfaction with much that had gone on before, especially in Chicago. Those were the years following a global cataclysm; they called for responses of equivalent force and dimension. Whatever their personal differences, Mies and Moholy eventually proved to be among the seminal figures who imposed European Modernism on American architecture and design, casting out Art Deco and the remains of the Beaux-Arts, and raising up the aesthetic of the International Style and the Bauhaus. Meanwhile, just as the painters of New York rejected the Social Realists, the Ben Shahns, Jack Levines, William Groppers, et al., who were the measure of much American art in the 1930s and early 1940s, their counterparts in Chicago—the youthful SAIC alumni—pointedly separated themselves from the regionalists and other prewar Midwesterners, from Grant Wood and John Steuart Curry to Francis Chapin and Ivan Albright (**plate 1**).

it took postwar chicago

painting longer to make a national name for itself than it did Chicago architecture—and even so a lesser one—and the difference can be accounted for by the interaction of personalities and institutions with the city's cultural history and tradition. Not until the Chilean Matta (Roberto Matta-Echaurren) was appointed to the SAIC faculty in 1954 did students there enjoy a sustained encounter with a painter (or sculptor) of international reputation (**fig. 3**). The generation of the late 1940s, on the other hand, grew up in a world that seemed to bear out many of A.J. Liebling's flintier observations. Since SAIC was the only place of size and consequence to study studio fine art in Chicago, and since for years its program had been more content than not with a midwestern domestication of international Modernism, the young ex-GIs found only a handful of faculty who would encourage the ambitions they had become seasoned enough to entertain. Among the few instructors with an educated sympathy for European Modernism were Kathleen Blackshear, Texas-born; and Paul Wieghardt, a native of Germany who had once studied with Paul Klee. Yet neither Blackshear nor Wieghardt nor their few similarly minded colleagues commanded the authority to marshal their students into a united or vigorous following.

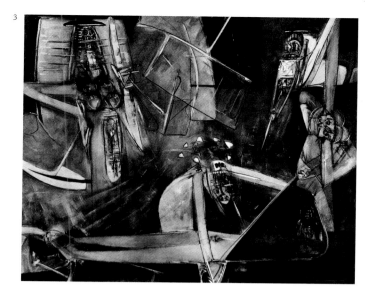

At least two of the younger Chicagoans, Golub (**plates 23, 25, and 40**) and George Cohen (**plate 21**), who together went on to wield substantial influence on postwar Chicago painting, spent a portion of their student days at another Chicago academic institution, this one of unimpeachable international standing: the University of Chicago. While the university under President (later Chancellor) Robert Maynard Hutchins had earlier fashioned an iron clad curriculum that favored philosophy over the sensuous arts and the word over the image, Golub and Cohen employed that bias to their advantage by learning the history of art from a distinguished faculty composed mainly of German émigré scholars, thus increasing their own awareness of a world far beyond the horizon of prewar Chicago art and art students. Once enrolled at SAIC, they and their classmates—several of them already comparably well educated—gained more from the Art Institute's library and permanent collection of painting, superb as the latter was in the modern period (though less so in its holdings of Old Masters), than from their studio instructors.[5] And they profited comparably from another important Chicago repository, The Field Museum of Natural History, whose collections included some exemplary art from ancient, Asian, and tribal cultures (**fig. 4**).

This, then, is the sum of the principal assets and liabilities of a generation of artists who came of age in a world and a city vastly altered by war: Their country had been the chief victor in that war, gaining dominion over Western civilization at the cost of the more parochial worldview that seemed sufficient to the prewar years. Thus conditioned, the artists found themselves undertaking their educations and careers in a major American metropolis that was blessed with cultural institutions of front rank, but accustomed to offering little sustenance to the practitioners of the very arts these artists had chosen to pursue. They knew that virtually no painters or sculptors living in Chicago had risen to fame in the same way as writers like Carl Sandburg, Sherwood Anderson, and Ben Hecht, or architects like John Wellborn Root, Louis Sullivan, and Frank Lloyd Wright. Moreover, while they knew about the attractions of New York as they might have read at length about Paris, in the 1940s they could not afford to leave the city most of them had come of age in. Chicago was good fortune qualified, with no alternative.

Out of this context came the art of Don Baum (**plates 58 and 107**), Cosmo Campoli (**plate 15**), Theodore Halkin (**plate 45**), June Leaf (**plates 22 and 28**), Evelyn

Statsinger (**plate 10**), and H.C. Westermann (**plates 31, 33, 35, and 36**), as well as
Cohen and Golub and several others of the 1940s/50s generation—an art notable for a collective preoccupation with dark and sequestered states, fantasies, and iconic archaisms
that reflect little interest in normative material reality. The New York painters had followed a
somewhat similar route, abandoning their prewar interest in political subject matter and
turning inward, to an exploration of myth and the content of their own psyches.

But New York grew increasingly committed to the formal vehicle of abstraction, while
Chicago never abandoned a preference for the figural image. One must account for this difference to some degree by the New Yorkers' literally close and inspiriting contact with the
European Modernists and the Chicagoans' distance from them. New York seized the opportunity to learn from the Europeans and their well-developed sympathy for abstraction, while
Chicago, like most of the rest of the United States, remained attached to more conservative
idioms, that is, to figurative art as a whole. Nevertheless, the Chicagoans found a generative
compensation in their independence, actively dismissing the Manhattan aesthetic and ratio-
nalizing abstraction as an absence rather than a presence, as a loss of something, not a
gain (**fig. 5**). To the Chicagoans the figure was no liability at all, but an expressive asset of
the first order, demonstrably the most nearly universal metaphor by which humans had
confronted and accounted for experience since the dawn of history. This view, it should be
qualified, did not extend to an identification with postmedieval Western art, most of which
was seen as imprisoned by material fact. Probing beneath surface appearance to a presumably
deeper reality was imperative, thus recourse was taken to the values and the art of ancient
and so-called primitive societies. Another qualification: this Chicago rationale, based on a
substantial knowledge of the history of art, was both serious and unironic in intent. The
celebration and mimicking of naïve, so-called "outsider" art is a preoccupation of later
Chicagoans, hardly of the 1950s group.[6]

In fact, of further relevance to the latter generation is Liebling's comment on the special
allure Chicago intellectuals of the 1950s found in the "Great Books" and in psychoanalysis.
It was an accurate perception, traceable to programs associated with the University of

Chicago, especially its highly public intellectuals Hutchins and Mortimer Adler, as well as with the Institute for Psychoanalysis and its charismatic director, the Hungarian émigré Franz Alexander (**fig. 6**). Many of the artists themselves were carried along with this current, if not by reading Aristotle or Milton or Montaigne, surely by delving into Franz Kafka, Ferdinand Celine, Djuna Barnes, and Margaret Mead—or by taking to the couch themselves. Moreover, psychoanalysis, with its emphasis on the importance of the dream state, seemed further justification for the expressive use of narrative and icon, since dream imagery is figurative, not abstract.

One cannot help inferring from all of this some measure of the origin of Chicago's reputation as a city whose art world has been devoted to Surrealism. Even so, that taste originated less with the postwar artists, most of whom preferred Expressionism to Surrealism, than with the city's new generation of collectors, who in the 1950s found it more affordable to purchase the work of rising Surrealist stars like Victor Brauner, Joseph Cornell, and Paul Delvaux than that of established, and expensive, textbook figures like Picasso and Matisse.

Apropos taste, one of the more remarkable and seldom noted instances of it was the interest Mies van der Rohe took in the work of several of the Chicago figurative artists. On first impression nothing might seem more alien to the reasoned geometry of his architecture than the fey imagery of Evelyn Statsinger and the magically irrational constructions of H.C. Westermann. Yet the fact that Mies bought their work is less implausible when one recalls that the art he collected in Europe (Klee, mostly [**fig. 7**]) and the public sculpture he proposed for his buildings (Lehmbruck, Kolbe, Maillol) tended to be figurative and poetically evocative rather than either geometric or otherwise abstract. Mies, it would seem, regarded paintings and sculptures ideally as counterfoils to architecture, not imitations of it. Nor is it surprising that the students of Momentum, from both The School of The Art Institute of Chicago and the Institute of Design, returned the favor in the form of their deep and abiding admiration of him. They invited him to serve on the jury of the 1950 show.

6

7

fig. 6
Franz Alexander, director of the Institute for Psychoanalysis, Chicago (1932–56). Photo: Joseph Merante, courtesy Institute for Psychoanalysis.

fig. 7
Ludwig Mies van der Rohe in his Chicago apartment with a painting by Paul Klee and a sculpture by Pablo Picasso, c. 1960. Photo courtesy Franz Schulze, Lake Forest, Illinois.

chicago was created,
to begin with,
by commerce and
industry,
with the arts

treated most hospitably
when they produced
work that appealed to
the city's
positivist personality

at that
very time
Mies

was beginning the ascent that carried him without interruption to a level of unmatched influence in world architecture. In 1951, three years after he began designing them, he completed the pair of apartment towers at 860–880 Lake Shore Drive (*fig. 8*), his first major work realized in America outside the IIT campus and, as it turned out, the most identifiable single model for the form of high-rise buildings anywhere in the world during the 1950s and early 1960s. While 860–880 had the effect of launching Mies's public American career, he had in fact been in Chicago and teaching at IIT long enough that his students—together with a company of local disciples, not least among them Herbert Greenwald, the developer of 860–880—had a firm notion of his importance and a corresponding belief in it. By the time 860–880 was finished, his followers were mature enough to conceive and complete their own designs, at a time, moreover, when the national economy was at last strong enough to address the need for new buildings that had grown urgent in the course of the Depression and World War II.

Thus the Miesian style was transformed into a School. The city itself cooperated. Building is an activity it has traditionally understood with more natural ease—or cared about, or even paid attention to—than it has the more rarefied issues debated by painters, sculptors, and art critics. Chicago was created, to begin with, by commerce and industry, with the arts treated most hospitably when they produced work that appealed to the city's positivist personality. The ideal art is architecture, for it is constructed as well as imagined, and more and more as the 1950s wore on, local firms like Loebl, Schlossman & Bennett; Naess & Murphy; Perkins & Will; and Skidmore, Owings & Merrill grew, usually with Mies in the forefront of their consciousness, while scholars and journalists remembered that some other great architects had worked in town in an earlier day—Adler & Sullivan, Burnham & Root, Holabird & Roche, William LeBaron Jenney, the young Frank Lloyd Wright: the so-called Chicago School.

By 1960 the arts of painting and architecture as played out in Chicago shared a dedication to the Modernist aesthetic and a preoccupation with achieving the goal of national and even international recognition. Otherwise, their tempers were as dissimilar as those of the two wings of Momentum in its early days. While the habit of painters is normally to work alone, in Chicago the practice of the breed was strikingly hermetic, certainly by contrast with its counterpart in New York, where a larger, more assured community of colleagues and supporters was a fact of every artist's life. Some Chicagoans literally kept their studios in the back bedrooms and porches of family two-flat apartments, working in steadfast solitude.[7] The most profitable contact with the world beyond their tight little cubicles was with a small group of commercial galleries, notably Allan Frumkin, Richard Feigen, and Holland-Goldowsky, each likewise of postwar vintage, that had been successful enough in the 1950s to offer qualified hope for the future of the city's best painters and sculptors. But such progress was not sufficient to halt the Chicago artist's ancient urge to leave town, to make it in New York, that is, where it counted. By 1960 Golub, Leaf, Spero, and Westermann had moved away. The Wells Street Gallery, which sought during the 1950s to establish an Abstract Expressionist beachhead in Chicago, closed after a couple of seasons, ignored by nearly everyone but its own co-op membership.[8] New York itself meanwhile took only sporadic note of Chicago

fig. 8
Ludwig Mies van der Rohe,
860–880 Lake Shore Drive,
Chicago (1948–51), 1951.
Photo: Hedrich-Blessing,
courtesy Chicago Historical
Society (HB-14545-B).

artists, and not always cordially, since the Chicago tilt toward the figure seldom made an affirmative impression on a city where abstraction reigned. When ex-Chicagoan Peter Selz, lately appointed to the curatorial staff of The Museum of Modern Art, New York (MOMA), included Campoli, Golub, and Westermann in a 1959 exhibition called "New Images of Man," a substantial number of Manhattan critics hammered it and morale in Chicago went into sharp decline.[9] Nor did it rebound when, three years later, MOMA invited Cohen, Golub, and Robert Barnes to participate in another show, "Recent Painting USA: The Figure," that took a similar hiding from the critics.

Chicago architecture, contrarily, sailed into the 1960s under full throttle. The 1950s had been boom years, especially in the building of residential projects, and if the new decade brought with it an emphasis on commercial structures, the shift only added to the city's architectural momentum. By the end of the 1960s, in fact, Chicago could look back on one of the most fertile periods in its architectural history. Although Mies never finished his plan for the IIT campus as he originally intended it,[10] he did leave his best single contribution to it until the last: the School of Architecture building, S.R. Crown Hall (**fig. 9**). In fact, one of the reasons IIT relieved him of his commission for the campus plan was that he was being distracted by clients all over the world, for whom he produced such historic works as the Seagram Building in New York (1958) and the Neue Nationalgalerie in Berlin (1967).

During the same years, Chicago's big firms left behind a comparably illustrious list of works, including the Inland Steel Building (1957) and John Hancock Center (1969) by Skidmore, Owings & Merrill; Lake Point Tower (1968) by Schipporeit & Heinrich; The Daley Civic Center (1965) and McCormick Place I (1971) by C.F. Murphy (earlier Naess & Murphy); The First National Bank Building (1969) by Perkins & Will and C.F. Murphy; and Marina City (1967) by Bertrand Goldberg Associates (**fig. 10**).[11]

Collectively these buildings were notable for a rational, declarative expression of the structural frame, an architectural abstraction that the students of the old ID would have understood and applauded. Commentators beyond the city limits were explicit in their agreement; they talked of a Second Chicago School. Few among them doubted that the city had estab-

fig. 9
Ludwig Mies van der Rohe, S.R. Crown Hall, Illinois Institute of Technology, Chicago (1950–56), c. 1956. Photo: Hedrich-Blessing, courtesy Chicago Historical Society (HB-18506-Q4).

fig. 10
Bertrand Goldberg Associates, Marina City, Chicago (1959–67), c. 1965. Photo: Hedrich-Blessing, courtesy Chicago Historical Society (HB-23215-A5).

9

10

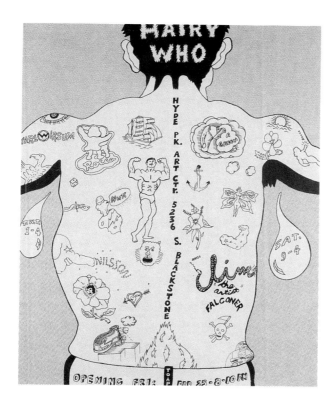

fig. 11
Hyde Park Art Center,
Chicago, "Hairy Who" exhibi-
tion poster, 1966. Offset lith-
ograph, 28 7/8 x 22 5/16 in.
Museum of Contemporary
Art, Chicago, Archive
of Art in Chicago, Gift of
Don Baum.

lished itself as the premier metropolis of modern architecture. If a measure of the Bauhaus legacy was immanent in the spare rectilinearity of the new building, its palpable muscularity was arguably more nearly native to the city. At the close of the 1960s, the architects and painters of Chicago—even if some of them knew and respected one another—occupied radically different public positions and professional environments. The irony is obvious: each group had striven heroically to rebel against the past and to impose its new worldview on the culture around it, yet each proved to be more controlled than it realized by the very history it sought to be free of. Painting had been traditionally the city's orphan child, architecture its cherished princeling, and very little had altered that relationship.

yet if painting at the outset

of the 1960s was in a depressed state, by the end of the decade both its fortunes and disposition had brightened perceptibly. A new generation had sprung up—quite suddenly, it seemed—replacing the previous group, so many of whom had in any case already left town. One can even pinpoint the source of the revival, the Hyde Park Art Center (HPAC), a slightly tattered, not-for-profit, store-front gallery a few blocks from the University of Chicago, or more than six miles from the main downtown gallery district. The year is also identifiable, 1966, and the players in the drama were the exhibition coordinator Don Baum, a veteran of the Momentum wars, and six young painters who, affecting the habit of the rock groups of the day, called themselves The Hairy Who (**fig. 11**). James Falconer, Art Green, Gladys Nilsson (**plate 66**), Jim Nutt (**plates 59, 68, 86, and 156**), Suellen Rocca (**plate 57**), and Karl Wirsum (**plates 49 and 64**) had all come of age in the decade of Pop art, and the subjects they pulled up from the lower depths of the American visual vernacular showed it. Yet, as if to resist the model set by New York, they tended toward an especially impudent coarseness and vulgarity in their work. This was skateboard Pop; by contrast such Manhattan stars as Warhol and Rosenquist were sleekly uptown, high-style, and urbane. Baum followed his first presentation of the Who with group exhibitions by several other artists of the same generation and kindred stylistic inclinations, most memorably Ed Paschke (**plates 67, 87,**

103, and 161) and Roger Brown (*plates 83, 84, 90, and 134*). The majority of these painters were SAIC graduates, and even if an overtone of mocking irony distinguished their work from the earnestness of the 1940s/50s group and the brooding lyricism of later fantasts like Barnes and Irving Petlin, their persistent reliance on the figure, especially the frontal image, led some observers to discern a connection among the generations and to suggest that there was a Chicago School in painting as surely as in architecture.[12] The term Imagism, coined to embrace the whole postwar figural phenomenon, was later taken over by dealers, writers, and collectors close to the Hyde Park Art Center and made to apply only to artists associated with it.[13] The appropriation, if in large part factionally self-serving, proved spectacularly successful: during the late 1960s and the 1970s and even beyond, the later Imagists,[14] dissociated (some would say liberated) from the early ones, became the most celebrated Chicago art movement of the century, winning the national attention so long yearned for locally, so long withheld.

the momentum of the late 1960s

only accelerated during the 1970s, but the mood changed from more or less simple good cheer, much of it associated with the HPAC successes, to something more complicated, finally more contentious. In retrospect it could have been no other way; the 1970s, reacting to the ambitions mounted during the previous decades, were a period of rising expectations and as such they yielded all the rewards and frustrations that such a condition is bound to lead to. The later Imagists had no sooner made their lively emergence than other artists sensed and acted on the possibility of gaining greater public attention for themselves. The Participating Artists of Chicago (PAC), formed in 1966, staged a variety of exhibitions and events over the next several years, all of them without the help of any regular institutional sponsorship. Yet in 1967, and partly in response to the growing collective pressure within the art community, the long-discussed hopes for a new museum in Chicago materialized in the form of the Museum of Contemporary Art (*fig. 12*).

These various developments unfolded at the same time the national political conflict aroused by the Vietnam War and the civil rights movement approached its climax early in the 1970s. Even though the Chicago gallery world's response to the crisis was confined to a few shows of pointedly politicized art that amounted to more gesture than action,[15] the passions of the moment worked themselves out more substantively in a spate of new programs, new organizations, new movements, and more exhibitions of more art in more forums by more artists of more varied stylistic persuasions. The most vital political art came from the mural movement, which began with William Walker's *Wall of Respect* on the South Side and led to a multitude of wall paintings throughout the city, nearly all of them politically hortatory in content (*see Warren and Boris, pp. 85–86*). Another former Momentumite, Ellen Lanyon (*plate 46*), was the chief force in the Chicago founding of the West East Bag (WEB), a women artists' group that eventually inspired the creation of the women's galleries ARC and Artemisia. The S. W. and B. M. Koffler Foundation was organized, with an advisory board responsible for assembling a collection of art done exclusively by Chicago artists. The Twelfth Bienal of São Paulo featured "Made in Chicago," a selection of work by the later Imagists.[16] The local gallery world expanded—more nearly exploded—as old walkups and store-fronts west of the traditional glitter of Michigan and Ontario turned West Hubbard Street into an "alternative district [*fig. 13*]." Added to this commercial growth was the installation of the new, municipally funded Chicago Cultural Center in the big, high-ceilinged rooms that were left free when the city decided to move the Chicago Public Library to a new building, completed in 1992 at the south edge of the Loop.

In terms of sheer volume and variety of production, the art world of Chicago in the 1970s set an unprecedented pace. Yet if this was a condition common to most locales in an increasingly art-conscious America, in Chicago it was marked by a special vexation, the ancient habit of the city's painters and sculptors to measure themselves against the model of New York, thus to question and urgently debate their own identity. Los Angeles, universally expected to become the new Second City, did not seem to bear such a burden, probably because California was far enough away from Manhattan—and home in any case to another monumental arts industry, the movies (with its own abundance of talent and money)—that it could bask in its year-round sunshine and awesome rate of growth and think of itself as an independently sovereign American culture. Nor was the sense of being overtaken by another city the extent of the Chicago artists' insecurities. There was all that powerhouse architecture in their very midst; people came daily from all over the world to look at the great towers of downtown Chicago or to stroll the Frank Lloyd Wright neighborhoods of the western suburbs. Only rarely did those tourists visit the galleries, which were not what drew them to the city in the first place.

These conditions and a consequently defensive posture in the local art world help to explain why the Museum of Contemporary Art strove so hard in its early days and ever since to be taken seriously as an institution with an international horizon. While its first director, Jan van der Marck, allotted more space to Chicago art than he is usually remembered for, he was after all a native European with a cosmopolitan background and wide-ranging ambitions, and he never shied from admitting that he found the Chicago Surrealist bias a retardataire taste and the Imagists its provincial outgrowth.[17]

fig. 12
237 East Ontario Street, Chicago. Left: office building at time of purchase by the Museum of Contemporary Art from Hugh Hefner, Playboy Enterprises, 1967. Right: Museum of Contemporary Art, 1967–68. Photos courtesy Museum of Contemporary Art, Chicago.

fig. 13
The building at 9 West Hubbard Street housing N.A.M.E. and Artemisia galleries, 1984. Photo: Tom Van Eynde, Oak Park, Illinois.

at the end of the
century
the signs of a
uniqueness of style or
expressive temper—

a unitary identity
that many of the city's
culture specialists
have made a habit of
yearning for—

are less evident
than ever

fig. 14
New Art Examiner 1, 3 (Dec.
1973), ill. p. 12. Illustration
by Larry Kowalski.

Nevertheless, the city continued to beat out its own rhythm. The later Imagists were shown in so many venues and treated to so much press coverage in the 1970s[18] that the city's other artists spent the decade in a feverish effort to prove that there was more to Chicago art than The Hairy Who and their close relatives. They were right, of course, as the activities of a growing number of abstract painters and electronic and Conceptual artists attest in retrospect. N.A.M.E. Gallery, one of the major alternative spaces, was tirelessly devoted to demonstrating the variety of work done in 1970s Chicago.[19] But the reputation of a Johnny-One-Note town seemed fixed, especially when the New York press began paying attention, as it usually does to news coming out of Chicago, by isolating one apparently unique trait (in this case Imagism) while ignoring everything else that wore no obvious hometown label.[20]

Writing about art, in fact, became one of the focused issues of the 1970s, along with all the others. There was next to no serious art criticism in Chicago in the years immediately following World War II, and it was not until the 1960s that something approaching it appeared, mostly in the city's newspapers. Several attempts at putting together an art journal had failed before the *New Art Examiner* was first published in 1973.[21] Palpably a shoestring operation over most of its history, and testy and ill-tempered at times, the *Examiner* has nevertheless proven itself one of the most gratifying additions to the Chicago art world of the past half-century. It grew out of the quarrelsome mood that filled the air everywhere in America at the turn of the 1970s, and among its early targets were the Imagists and their supporters, whom the *Examiner* identified and assailed as an entrenched local elite (**fig. 14**).[22] In the last twenty years, that mission has largely faded from its pages, as from the minds of many, especially the youngest, Chicagoans, but the magazine remains the single local press instrument accessible to any writer with an idea and the tolerable ability to express it.

Has the level of Chicago criticism risen during the past several decades? Most observers would say yes, but only a few of them would argue that the city has produced any critic worthy of comparison with the best of late twentieth-century art writers. Until the 1970s verbal exchange more formal than badinage in the back rooms of galleries was not Chicago's style. Lectures or formal round tables were rare among critics, dealers, and curators, rarer still among artists. Insofar as Chicago was perceptibly disinclined toward art talk, it could not have been less like New York.

In the meantime, however—the 1980s and 1990s—a preoccupation with theory has taken command of the international worlds of art and architecture alike, with the result that discussion has not only come alive, but often seemed to replace the stuff it is supposed to be about. This has not guaranteed a better overall grade of published writing either in Chicago or elsewhere; on the contrary, theoretical thinking has led all too easily, and globally, to intellectual maundering expressed in impenetrable prose.

Several questions follow: Has Chicago art been uninspiring of good criticism or have the critics failed to measure up to the art? If one blames the art more than the critics, how does one account for the wide gap between the demonstrable excellence of Chicago architecture and the earnest but overall modest record of Chicago architectural criticism over the past several generations?[23] The appearance in the 1980s of a brace of adventurous young architectural theoreticians, mostly at the University of Illinois at Chicago (UIC), and all of them enthusiastically fluent in the most arcane Postmodernese—one thinks of Catherine Ingraham, Mitchell Schwarzer, Robert Somol—has not been accompanied by any noticeable improvement in the critical prose in the local public prints. That group seems to have reserved most of their energies for communication with their own kind, in national, not local, publications.

Clearly, the press belongs to New York, and where the press is, is not only critical discourse but cultural power. That has long been obvious in the world of painting. It is now evident in architecture too, since that art has, if anything, been in the very forefront of the theory-oriented strike force that returned national architectural attention to New York and the East Coast over the past quarter-century. Verbally adroit architects like Robert Venturi, Robert A.M. Stern, and Peter Eisenman have been as effective in negotiating this shift as the host of critics and theoreticians who thrive in the word-rich atmosphere of Manhattan.

15

It is about that same quarter-century ago that Mies died, and only a slight oversimplification to suggest that the internationally special position of the building art in Chicago passed with him. The Sears Tower (1974) by Skidmore, Owings & Merrill is arguably the last important Modernist building to be erected in downtown Chicago by a Chicago architectural firm. Postmodernism, with its ironies and renewed devotions to history, took over American architecture in the 1970s and most of the 1980s. Yet Chicago has a record of only middling achievement during phases—the 1920s was another—dominated by historical styles. Whatever the cause, the city has failed to produce a major Postmodernist architect; indeed more buildings put up in the city during the 1970s and 1980s were designed by non-Chicago firms than at any time in the past century. Worse still, for the outward look of the city, only a handful of these, like 333 West Wacker (**fig. 15**), by the New York office of Kohn Pedersen Fox, were successful. One is tempted to take seriously the concept of the genius loci, that tutelary

16

fig. 15
Kohn Pedersen Fox, 333
West Wacker Drive, Chicago
(1983). Photo: Bill Engdahl,
Hedrich-Blessing, Chicago
(SN825-G8).

fig. 16
River North gallery district,
Chicago, 1987. Photo © Bill
Stamets, Chicago.

deity said to govern the look of a place independent of the conscious minds that try to assemble or reassemble it. Certainly gloss has seldom managed to look good in a Chicago setting, and the aggressively shiny objects imposed on Wacker Drive during the 1980s included almost consistently disappointing works by such normally respectable architects as Ricardo Bofill (The R.R. Donnelley Building) and Kevin Roche (The Leo Burnett Building). It is as if the terrain resisted all efforts to dress it up in unnaturally satiny clothing.

But glitz became the way of the world in the 1980s, not just in architecture, but in gallery and museum art as well. It was a Lucullan decade, an era of unbounded appetite and unremitting deference to it, with developers commissioning architects ("signature architects") to put up vastly more buildings than the economy could absorb and art dealers doing much the same with the prices of everyone they handled, from dead Masters to postpubescent art-school graduates. The whole structure came crashing down at last, in the late 1980s, with architectural offices laying off legions of staff, galleries closing en masse, and artists obliged to adjust not only their prices but their critical expectations.

These misfortunes unfolded in Chicago as surely as anywhere. Some national vogues did not catch on there: a trifling amount of Bad Painting got painted, even less of the new decorativism, and only a little more of the designer angst so common to Neo-Expressionism. Even so, there was just as much industrialization of art and preening among collectors, artists, and dealers in Chicago as in Düsseldorf or San Francisco. Many of the veterans of the 1970s, recalling how hard they had worked to coax seed to grow in an arid landscape, resented the offspring of the 1980s for assuming the feast now laid before them was their deserved inheritance. On the other hand, it can be argued the young made the most of what was given them. No other generation since World War II did more to relieve Chicago of its reputation as a city locked in a spastic figural embrace.

Circumstance helped. The high-flying art market was enough by itself to draw attention to any and all new currents in the local art scene. Older galleries, like Richard Gray and William Struve, opened spaces in the now-flourishing River North district, joining pioneers like Jan Cicero, Rhona Hoffman, Donald Young, and Zolla/Lieberman (**fig. 16**). Still later firms were added, notably CompassRose, Feature, and Robbin Lockett. The sheer physical size of the River North exhibition lofts, most of them made over from the interiors of old warehouses, was a measure of the confidence that infused the gallery scene. Meanwhile, led by the alternative space Randolph Street Gallery, other new showcases spun centrifugally into older, meat-and-potatoes neighborhoods like Pilsen and Wicker Park that once seemed altogether alien to an activity like contemporary art.

The artists, themselves responding to the gentrification process of the 1980s, had moved earlier to these districts, finding quarters that were tolerably cheap and more than tolerably livable. With the table set so abundantly, a generation of artists including Jeanne Dunning (**plate 149**), Hirsch Perlman (**plate 137**), Dan Peterman (**plate 140**), and Tony Tasset (**plate 145**) proceeded to produce and exhibit a body of work that was mostly abstract in form but influenced strongly by Conceptualism, with some Minimalism and Pop thrown in. They talked more about "objects" than about art; materials and materiality counted for more in their work than something as time-worn as emotional association. It is hard to imagine their making a mark without the groundwork done in the 1970s by such Chicago Conceptualists as Phil Berkman (**plate 81**), Robert C. Peters (**plate 112**), and Charles Wilson (**plate 91**), but indebtedness did not deprive them of a sense of their own distinctiveness. They were an uncommonly cool lot, quite at home in a thriving Chicago art world and inclined either to be unconscious of the old Imagists, or to ignore them, or, now and then, to nod appreciatively to them for having laid the foundation of patronage so effectively in Chicago.

Further impetus to this group and their latter-day kin in installation and performance art, film, video, and electronics was provided by several local institutions. The Terra Museum of American Art, itself an addition of the 1980s, staged an exhibition, "Surfaces: Two Decades of Painting in Chicago," that included many of the new breed of Chicago artists. The latter were already making their presence felt on the faculty of the art department of the University of Illinois at Chicago, a school that gradually took on a position of influence in local art education comparable to that of the School of the Art Institute and the Institute of Design. Growth in the offerings in studio and theory occurred in other academic settings as well: at Northwestern University, the University of Chicago, DePaul and Loyola universities. Nor did these institutions confine their activities to curricular reorientation. Some of the most brisk activities in the Chicago art world of the past generation have occurred in such newly added exhibition agencies as the Mary and Leigh Block Gallery at Northwestern and The David and Alfred Smart Gallery (later Museum) at the University of Chicago. Yet another evidence of shifting local priorities can be discerned in the record of women in the operation of these various organizations. The first curator at the Block Gallery was Kathy Foley, while Susanne Ghez has supervised the programs at The Renaissance Society at the University of Chicago since 1974. At various times in the history of the Museum of Contemporary Art, Mary Jane Jacob and Judith Russi Kirshner have occupied the chief curatorship, and Kirshner now heads the art department at the University of Illinois at Chicago.

The ambitious and self-sure mood of the 1980s reached into all constituencies of the Chicago scene. One of the standard litanies in reviews of the local art world that appear regularly in the national press is that no group, not the artists, the dealers, the critics, or the museum people, has represented itself more impressively over the past half-century than the private collectors, on whose walls the art created and midwifed by others ends up—until it is given at last, mostly, to the museums. While such reports are invariably laced with journalistic flattery, there is no denying that a combination of toughness, intelligence and generosity has been demonstrably characteristic of Chicago collecting since World War II (**see Adrian essay**). The tradition begun in the 1940s and 1950s by the Maurice Culbergs, Morton Neumanns, Joseph Randall Shapiros, and Edwin Bergmans was sustained in the 1960s by the Robert Mayers and Albert Newmans and continued in later decades by Gerald Elliott, Stefan Edlis and Gael Neeson, Lewis and Susan Manilow, and Paul and Camille Oliver-Hoffmann. When buying, these collectors have shown a preference for twentieth-century art. When giving, they have tended to bestow their favors first on the Museum of Contemporary Art, later, as their personal reputations ripen and their possessions grow older, on the Art Institute.

no fact is more pertinent

to an account of the early 1990s than the sharp change in fortunes that began on the national economic and political level and proceeded into the cultural realm, leaving the arts in an unfamiliar state of defensiveness. The luxury of the 1980s left everyone touched by it unprepared for the recession late in the decade that eroded much of the self-assurance common to American visual culture as a whole since World War II. The open-handed clients of the 1980s faded from view, with both architecture and painting sustaining a serious loss of patronage.

On the heels of this ill fate, and to some extent growing out of it, was the revival of power
in the national political right wing, which made the most of the occasion to quicken its drum-
beat of hostility toward the more experimental arts. The National Endowment for the Arts
and the National Endowment for the Humanities, formerly taken for granted as sources of
funding for any and all endeavors self-designated as creative, found themselves not only
under critical fire, but threatened with outright elimination.

With the decade only half-completed, the crises remain unresolved. In Chicago there have
been recent signs of recovery in the gallery community and news of more commissions
awarded to the city's architects. Indeed, the spiritual curve of the art world could turn upward
again, although probably not so abruptly as it fell several years ago. With the future as
unpredictable as all futures normally are, it may be enough to summarize the present as it
seems manifest in the visual arts of Chicago.

At the end of the century the signs of a uniqueness of style or expressive temper—a unitary
identity that many of the city's culture specialists have made a habit of yearning for—are
less evident than ever. If pluralism has become a cliché applied to the description of all the
world's arts communities, it is because it fits the picture, simply and accurately. The spreading communication net that began with the invention of printing in the fifteenth century and
continues in the form of the current computer/information technological revolution, has
made a dizzying assortment of expressive options instantaneously open to artists everywhere,
while paradoxically reinforcing the freedom to rely on familiar stylistic habits. Radical formal inventions have emerged from such genres as installation and electronic art, while narrative content has been broadened by artists celebrating the heritage of various ethnic communities in media as old as painting.

Thus, as figural artists continue to work in Chicago, with no loss of following, the tides of
other manners and outlooks, each with its own champions, advance upon the city in unceas-
ing procession. The two most respected artists to work in Chicago during the 1980s are Ed
Paschke, a later Imagist painter, and Martin Puryear (**plates 119 and 125**), a sculptor of
abstractions totally free of any geographical school ties. Similarly, architects devoted to the
uncluttered structural "Chicago frame"—Ralph Johnson of Perkins & Will, for one—continue to find clients in the city and spaces on which to build—adjacent to the work of designers and planners whose own stylistic identities are as manifold as the globally far-flung
locales they represent.

The new Museum of Contemporary Art may be interpreted as a symbol of this multifaceted
condition. It was designed by a German, Josef Paul Kleihues, who has made a point of
acknowledging his own pluralist debt, to the Chicago architectural tradition on the one hand
and, on the other, to the works of his compatriot, the great nineteenth-century Romantic-
Classicist Karl Friedrich Schinkel. The museum is, in short, consciously conceived as a structure both international and local in scope and ambition. The extent to which Chicago itself
has gained the stature of a world metropolis in the fifty years covered by the works in this
exhibition remains to be seen. That achievement, judging from the character of the city's current art world, is what the last of this and the first of the next century are meant to serve.

notes

1 A.J. Liebling, "The Second City," *The New Yorker* 27, 48–50 (Jan. 12, 19, and 26, 1952)(in three parts).

2 Ibid., part one, "So Proud to be Jammy-Jammy," p. 29.

3 Leon Golub, "A Law Unto Himself" in *A Forum: 9 Viewpoints*, catalogue insert, *Momentum Nineteen-Fifty*, unpag.

4 Alex Nicoloff, "Article," in ibid.

5 The celebrated figures of Renaissance naturalism and Baroque high drama found few champions among the younger Chicagoans. Unsurprisingly, El Greco was admired, especially in his later, more visionary works, and Rembrandt enjoyed a measure of favor as well, mostly for the psychological depth of his portraits. Otherwise, little interest was shown in the Old Masters.

6 The earlier Chicagoans knew naïve art as well as the later ones did, and in fact acquainted themselves with artists "outside" the canon though not necessarily naïve. The *Bildnerei der Geisteskranken* (The Art of Psychotics), by the German psychiatrist of the 1920s Hans Prinzhorn, was known among the early Imagists, who also paid attention to such lesser known but altogether professional artists as the strange nineteenth-century Austrian portraitist Anton Romako and the eighteenth-century Swiss master of facial grotesquerie Franz Xavier Messerschmidt.

7 Theodore Halkin remembered this as true of himself and a number of his peers of the late 1940s and early 1950s. Conversation with the author, Sept. 14, 1995.

8 Principal figures of the Wells Street Gallery were Robert Natkin, Judith Dolnick, Donald Vlack, Jerry Van De Wiele, Ann Mattingly, and Ernest Dieringer. Most of them left Chicago for New York after the gallery closed.

9 See Dennis Raverty, "*Critical Perspectives* on New Images of Man," *Art Journal* 53 (Winter 1994), pp. 62–64.

10 Mies's first major American commission was the redesigning of the entire IIT campus, which was meant to create the first all-modern university campus in the United States. The plan was largely carried out, although in short steps, during the 1940s and most of the 1950s.

11 See Franz Schulze, "The New Chicago Architecture," *Art in America*, May–June 1968, pp. 60–70.

12 See Patrick T. Malone and Peter Selz, "Is There a New Chicago School?" *ARTnews* 54 (Oct. 1955), pp. 36–39; Franz Schulze, *Fantastic Images: Chicago Art Since 1945* (Chicago: Follett, 1972). Two group exhibitions also developed the theme: "New Chicago Painters and Sculptors," organized for Beloit College in 1956 by Allan Frumkin, and "The New Chicago Decade," organized for Lake Forest College in 1959 by Franz Schulze.

13 Central figures contributing to this redefinition were dealer Phyllis Kind, critics Dennis Adrian and Russell Bowman, and HPAC director Don Baum.

14 The names most prominently identified with this group are Ed Paschke, Jim Nutt, and Roger Brown.

15 Two reactions were the "Richard J. Daley" protest exhibition at Feigen Gallery, showing work by forty-seven Chicago and New York artists, and "Response" (Nov. 2, 1968), a one-day program organized by Chicago artists and galleries, including such activities as "Special Chicago Artists' Response" at 601 N. Fairbanks Court; Films by John Heinz and Tom Palazzolo at Allan Frumkin Gallery; and "A Funny Thing Happened on My Way to the Convention" at Lo Giudice Gallery.

16 Walter Hopps was in charge of the US entry, but the theme and contents of "Made in Chicago" were the responsibility of Don Baum.

17 Jay Jacobs, *Art Gallery*, Feb. 1970. Jacobs reported that van der Marck "will tell you [Surrealism] is still considered *modern* in Chicago."

18 E.g., "The Chicago School," Midwest Magazine, *Chicago Sun-Times*, June 12, 1972, p. 109; Ellen Edwards, "Nutt's Weirdos Grow on You," *Chicago Reader*, Apr. 19, 1974, pp. 2 and 10; Patricia Moore, "Art Made in Chicago Comes Home," *Chicago Daily News*, Jan. 10, 1975.

19 Exhibitions from N.A.M.E. Gallery included these examples: "Four Conceptual Artists" (Phil Berkman, Michael Crane, Angels Ribe, Francesc Torres), 1973; Performance: "Ses Mashees," by Gunderson and Clark, 1974; "Environmental Sculpture" (Lyn Blumenthal, Kate Horsfield, Dan Kaplan, Martin Long), 1974; "Wall/Floor Sculptures" (Pamela Burgess, Richard Keaveny, Pat Mangan), 1977.

20 This persistent dynamic, which has made Chicago a more comfortable environment for the Imagists and their stylistic cohorts (not to mention "Chicago-style" writers like Mike Royko and Studs Terkel), did little to keep such gifted local off-breeds of the 1950s, 1960s, and 1970s as Joyce Treiman, Kestutis Zapkus, and Andrea Blum from seeking audiences elsewhere.

21 *Midwest Art Reviews and Chicago Gallery Guide*, founded in 1965, folded in 1967. *Art Scene*, founded in 1967, folded in 1969.

22 See Frank Pannier, "A Painter Reviews Chicago," *New Art Examiner*, part one, Summer 1974, p. 3; part two, Oct.–Nov. 1974, pp. 2–3; Derek Guthrie, "Speakeasy," *New Art Examiner*, Oct. 1993, pp. 14–17.

23 *Inland Architect* magazine has had a sporadic existence since the late nineteenth century, alternately rising up and dying away over the years. It has been the best source in Chicago of informed criticism during that time, but its spasmodic ways have kept it from developing the sort of tradition that might encourage first-class writers to work for it. The best architectural literature coming out of Chicago has been that of academic scholars, who have historically preferred book format to periodicals.

Peter Selz

modernism comes to chicago: the institute of design

In this essay Peter Selz, a distinguished art historian and himself a former teacher at the legendary "Chicago Bauhaus" from 1949 until 1955, traces the history of this seminal institution and the impact of its visionary founder, the artist, educator, and theorist László Moholy-Nagy. The history is complex: after two incarnations, The New Bauhaus (1937–38) and the School of Design (1939–44), the Institute of Design (ID) became part of the Illinois Institute of Technology in 1949, where it continues to the present day.

Although its distinguished photography program produced internationally known photographers beginning in the late 1950s and lasting into the 1970s, ID's heyday was in the years 1939–48 when it stood as an independent school, fueled by Moholy-Nagy's vision. It was through the photography department that the visual arts have been most influenced, not only by the aesthetic visions of such figures as Harold Allen, Harry Callahan, Barbara Crane, Yasuhiro Ishimoto, Kenneth Josephson, and Aaron Siskind, but through the teaching methods many ID graduates carried to art schools and university art departments across the United States and around the world. In Chicago, however, ID's legacy has been little acknowledged until very recently. LW

the fact that

The New Bauhaus ($fig. 1$) took shape in Chicago was no mere accident. Chicago has a long and distinguished history of modern architecture and, with interruptions, to be sure, has continued to be at the forefront of avant-garde architecture (see Schulze essay). As early as 1897 an Arts and Crafts Society, based on the model of the pioneering London institution of Robert Morris and Walter Crane, was organized in Chicago. This was actually ten years earlier than the foundation of the comparable German Werkbund for which Walter Gropius designed his first pivotal building long before he established the Bauhaus. Born and bred in the Industrial Revolution, Chicago was the center of the production of farm machinery as well as meat packing and mail-order marketing. The Prairie City, surrounded by its gigantic steel mills, saw the potential of a new technology and its effect on the physical environment: technical exigencies were accepted as both necessary and desirable for a new century.[1]

The Art Institute of Chicago had been founded even earlier, in 1866, as an art school called the Academy of Design. In 1882 it was organized into The School of The Art Institute of Chicago (SAIC) and The Art Institute of Chicago (AIC), to be run by separate boards. In addition to fine-arts classes, the school offered courses in the commercial arts and design to instruct young men (and a few women) to make useful contributions to the growing industrial society. In keeping with its original mandate, in the late 1920s the Art Institute received funds from the Association of Arts and Industries (AAI, f. 1922), a local organization dedicated to "American production of original creative work of modern character."[2] The small department at the Art Institute labeled "School for Industrial Art" was under the direction of Alfonso Iannelli, who had visited the Bauhaus in 1924, and who, it seems, was at times its sole faculty member.

In 1935 Marshall Field's family offered the department store proprietor's large old house at 1905 South Prairie Avenue to AAI (**fig. 2**), which severed its connection to the Art Institute. When Iannelli resigned from his position in 1937, Norma K. Stahle, AAI's executive director, invited Walter Gropius to take over the new school planned for the premises. But Gropius, who had just accepted a professorship at Harvard, immediately recommended his old friend and former Bauhaus associate László Moholy-Nagy, who was in London at that time, for

the position. Moholy was offered the directorship in May 1937. He came to Chicago for an interview in July, and accepted the position of director of "The New Bauhaus—American School of Design" in Chicago.[3]

The climate in Chicago was favorable for Moholy's new experiment. At the University of Chicago, the philosopher and educator John Dewey was locating aesthetics in everyday life and insisted, furthermore, that any distinction between the fine and useful arts was absurd. His precepts were not very different from the tenets of the Bauhaus. He believed that the artist, like the philosopher, has an impact on life and can change it.[4]

The first impact of European Modernism was the highly controversial Armory Show, which came to Chicago from New York in 1913. In 1932 James Johnson Sweeney, a young *Chicago Daily News* critic who became an important curator and director in New York and later in Houston,[5] mounted the exhibition "Plastic Redirections in 20th Century Painting" at The Renaissance Society at the University of Chicago. The first exhibition of its kind

fig. 1
László Moholy-Nagy, *The New Bauhaus American School of Design*, 1937, cover. Photo courtesy Peter Selz, Berkeley, California, and The University of Illinois at Chicago, The University Library, Department of Special Collections, Institute of Design Collection.

fig. 2
Marshall Field residence, 1905 South Prairie Avenue, Chicago, home to The New Bauhaus (1936–39), c. 1906. Photo: Charles R. Clark, courtesy Chicago Historical Society (CRC-128-E).

3

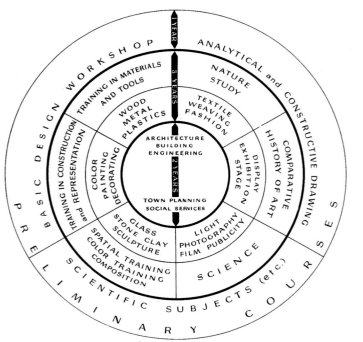

4

fig. 3
László Moholy-Nagy, *Light-Space Modulator* (originally titled *Light Prop for an Electric Stage*), 1923–30. Kinetic sculpture of steel, plastic, wood, and other materials, with electric motor, 59 1/2 x 27 1/2 x 27 1/2 in. Busch-Reisinger Museum, Harvard University Art Museums, Cambridge, Massachusetts, Gift of Sibyl Moholy-Nagy.

fig. 4
The New Bauhaus American School Design, 1937, chart of programs, p. 4. Photo courtesy The University of Illinois at Chicago, The University Library, Department of Special Collections, Institute of Design Collection.

in America, it included works by Hans Arp, Constantin Brancusi, Alexander Calder, Juan Gris, Jean Hélion, Fernand Léger, Joan Miró, Piet Mondrian, and Pablo Picasso.

Even the German Bauhaus was known to Chicagoans, thanks to lectures by one of its former students, Helmut von Erffa, and by Frank Lloyd Wright.[6] Moholy-Nagy himself was familiar to the advanced art world in Chicago through an exhibition organized by The Arts Club of Chicago (f. 1916) titled "The New Typology" (1931), and the publication *The New Vision* (1932), the English translation of his Bauhaus book *Von Material zu Architektur* (1930).[7]

Throughout this time Clarence J. Bulliet, writing for various dailies and weeklies during his long tenure as Chicago's leading art critic (1931–52), wrote informatively and sympathetically about modern art.[8] Although Bulliet always gave encouragement to Chicago's artists, he was also aware that they were "at the foot of the ladder" and "rated as dust on the sandals of New York."[9] It is important to realize that Chicago, the place where modern architecture and literature flourished—with writers such as Nelson Algren, Sherwood Anderson, James T. Farrell, and Ben Hecht, and poets Carl Sandburg and Harriet Monroe—did not give rise to many significant painters and sculptors in the first half of the century. Most of the Chicago artists of the time seemed preoccupied with romantic nostalgia, be it personal, regional, or social. It can be argued that Ivan Albright (**plate 1**) was the sole Chicago-based artist of the prewar period to reach a national reputation.[10] Indeed, Chicago was the site of the Society for Sanity in Art, founded in 1936 with the specific purpose of deriding Modernist art in all its forms.

Artists of the caliber of Moholy-Nagy and those he appointed to The New Bauhaus faculty filled an important gap in Chicago's prewar art world. A remarkable man whose own person and work synthesized the modern movement, Moholy-Nagy was convinced that rational and coherent art and design in collaboration with science and technology could bring about social change. As a member of MA, an organization of vanguard Marxist Hungarian artists, he issued a manifesto in 1922 called "Constructivism and the Proletariat," proclaiming, "There is no tradition in technology, no consciousness of class or standing. Everybody can be the machine's master or its slave....This is our century— technology, machine, socialism. Make your peace with it. Shoulder its task."[11] A year later Walter

Gropius invited him to join the faculty of the Bauhaus in Weimar. Moholy and Josef Albers were to teach the preliminary course, replacing Johannes Itten's Expressionist mysticism with Modernist rationalism; Moholy also directed the metal workshop and taught classes in photography.

Originally a painter, Moholy-Nagy continued painting throughout his life (**plate 3**). By the end of World War I, he was working in an abstract mode, influenced by Suprematism and Constructivism. He also developed a nonrepresentational syntax for photography and in 1921 produced the first photograms.[12] At the same time he made precise representational photographs and did highly original photomontages. In all media he was preoccupied with light, often using plastics to achieve transparency. Always exploring the possibilities of technology as well as the limitations of chance, he created—as early as 1927—several paintings by telephone, giving precise orders to a draftsman on the other end of the line. His work in three dimensions reached its apex in the *Light-Space Modulator* (**fig. 3**), a motorized sculpture in which the rotating steel, wood, and transparent plastic shapes create plays of light and shadow. This kinetic sculpture became the source for Moholy's film *Light Display: Black and White and Gray* (1930), in which the mobile creates a new cinematic vision of motion and change. In London in 1935–37, Moholy again used abstract light plays for Alexander Korda's film *The Shape of Things to Come*, based on the novel by H.G. Wells. Throughout this time he incorporated space, light, and motion into his painting and sculpture, his "Light Modulators" and "Space Modulators," respectively. He also continued producing exhibitions and working as a stage designer.

Above all, however, Moholy-Nagy was a teacher. He believed—a long time before Joseph Beuys made this into a tenet of his theories of art—that "Everybody is talented."[13] This principle formed the basis of Moholy's teaching, first at the Bauhaus in Germany and then in Chicago. Situated within the idealistic era of Modernism, Moholy saw the school as a place where artists and poets, philosophers, scientists, and technologists would work together to create a more vital civilization. Indeed, education was not to be sequestered within the studio or classroom. Students at The New Bauhaus and its successors were to look around them and see that forms have meaning and to understand that art should not be different from life, but within life.

The prospectus and chart (**fig. 4**) of The New Bauhaus clearly stated the five-year program:

We know that art itself cannot be taught, only the way to it. We have in the past given the function of art a formal importance, which segregates it from our daily existence, whereas art is always present where healthy and unaffected people live. Our task is, therefore, to contrive a new system of education which, along with a specialized training in science and technique, leads to a thorough awareness of fundamental human needs and a universal outlook. Thus, our concern is to develop a new type of designer, able to face all kinds of requirements, not because he is a prodigy but because he has the right method of approach. We wish to make him conscious of his own creative power, not afraid of new facts, working independently of recipes.

Upon this premise we have built our program.[14]

The beginning of The New Bauhaus was certainly auspicious. *The New York Times* published an interview with Moholy and soon thereafter pointed out that the United States gained enormously by "importing genius from Europe," naming Albert Einstein, Thomas Mann, and Walter Gropius, but also "Lazlo [sic] Moholy-Nagy, painter, sculptor and photographer [who] arrived here a few days ago to head a school in Chicago, to be known as The New Bauhaus."[15]

Moholy began to appoint a faculty. Hin Bredendieck, who had been his student at the Bauhaus in Dessau, was asked to formulate what

came to be known as the "Foundation Course."[16] Eventually Bredendieck would also be in charge of the Wood and Metal Workshop. Gyorgy Kepes, who had worked with Moholy in Berlin and London, was invited to take over the Light Workshop (photography); Henry Holmes Smith filled in until Kepes arrived in 1937.

Kepes became a major force in Chicago. The photographer Nathan Lerner (**plate 2**), one of the new school's first students and later an instructor, recalls Kepes as "an incredible mind and human being, who would explain ideas to students, make them comprehensible—someone whom you could truly trust."[17] In 1944, the year in which he published his pivotal book, *Language of Vision,* Kepes left Chicago for the Massachusetts Institute of Technology where he became the founding director of the Center for Advanced Visual Studies which explored the affinities of art, technology, and the natural world.

The Photography Department of The New Bauhaus and its successors, with instructors such as Nathan Lerner (at ID 1938–43 and 1945–49), Arthur Siegel (at ID 1946–54 and 1967–78), Harry Callahan (at ID 1946–61); Aaron Siskind (at ID 1951–70); and Arthur Sinsabaugh (at ID 1951–59), gave rise to a new generation of photographers whose work was closer to abstract art than to the observation and documentation that was dominant among the American sharp-focus artists. In accordance with

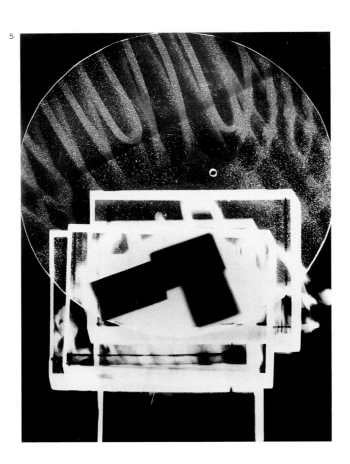

5

6

fig. 5
László Moholy-Nagy,
Photogram, 1922. Gelatin
silver print, 15 1/2 x 11 3/4 in.
Museum Ludwig, Cologne.
Photo: Rheinisches
Bildarchiv, courtesy Museum
Ludwig, Cologne, and
Hattula Moholy-Nagy.

fig. 6
Alexander Archipenko with
students at the Institute of
Design, Chicago, 1946.
Chicago Daily News,
February 6, 1946. Photo
courtesy Illinois State
Historical Library,
Springfield.

Moholy's assertion that "the enemy of photography is convention,"[18] experiments in distortion, solarization, and cliché verre were carried on, as well as in photograms (**fig. 5**) and photomontage.

Besides Moholy-Nagy, the most prominent member of the original faculty was Alexander Archipenko, a seminal figure in the development of Modernist sculpture (**fig. 6**). Archipenko had gone in 1890 from his native Kiev to Paris, where he experimented early on with the interrelationship of concave and convex forms, or positive and negative space, and also made mobile "sculpto-paintings." He immigrated in 1923 to the United States, where he exhibited widely and taught extensively. By the time he took charge of the Modeling Workshop at The New Bauhaus in 1937, his work had become rather stylized, but his understanding of the relationship of solids to voids became paradigmatic for some of the work done by the sculpture students, even if he did play the grand master, smashing work he did not like with his heavy cane.

Although not always successful, Moholy tried to seek out the best people to teach a wide range of disciplines.[19] David Dushkin was an excellent person to head the Music Workshop. In addition to playing music and studying musicology, students were encouraged to build innovative instruments and to investigate the sounds of various common materials such as wood, metal, and grasses. In 1937 Charles Morris offered a course called "Intellectual Integration" and dealt early on with the theory of signs and semantics. A young philosophy professor at the University of Chicago and a former student of the philosopher Rudolf Carnap, Morris believed that collaboration between artists and scientists was both possible and necessary. At The New Bauhaus, his scientific analysis of art was an important influence on the intellectual path of the school. With a view toward integrating science into this unique curriculum, the University of Chicago biologist

Ralph Gerard and the physicist Carl Eckart were appointed as part-time faculty.

Although space and money were in short supply, Moholy managed to bring two important exhibitions to the Marshall Field mansion. The first featured abstract sculpture by Naum Gabo, Barbara Hepworth, Henry Moore, and Alexander Calder, and paintings by Piet Mondrian and Moholy-Nagy himself. The second exhibition, organized by The Museum of Modern Art, New York, dealt with the first hundred years of photography.

Moholy's personality and his enthusiasm for Modernist art made an indelible impression on his students. Nathan Lerner recalls:

I first met Moholy-Nagy in 1937, on the day The New Bauhaus opened in Chicago. The walls of his offices were covered with paintings constructed of clear plastic sheets slightly raised above white panels. The sheets were scratched and painted as to cast shadows on the panels. I also saw surfaces covered with pins casting shadows; to my astonishment they seemed to move even as we talked. Overhead, suspended from the ceiling, thick twisted plastic shapes floated, catching and reflecting light as they moved. The meeting had lasting significance for me. I became aware for the first time that light itself, like clay or paint, could be a medium.[20]

Another testimony of an encounter with Moholy was recalled by Richard Koppe (at ID 1946–63), who was also in that first class at the Field mansion (**plate 6**). Koppe remembers Moholy showing his large collection of Bauhaus materials, captivating the students, who

were down on their hands and knees looking through the forest of table legs to illustrate a point he made about space.... In classes we were introduced to the photogram, photomontage, hand sculpture, the tactile chart, space modulators, light modulators, the paper problem, machine investigation... along with color theory, drawing, lettering, drafting... I have never seen so many and so varied results produced by any class within the scope of this curriculum. Perhaps a higher value was placed on inventive creativeness than on aesthetic consideration, though they were part and parcel of the same order.[21]

In addition to actual teaching and running the school, Moholy-Nagy had to persuade his new community of Chicago of the importance of his undertaking, seen by many as quite a radical one. And he was a very persuasive man. John Walley, who later became one of the most esteemed members of the ID faculty, remembers how Moholy brought The New Bauhaus into a "politically and economically

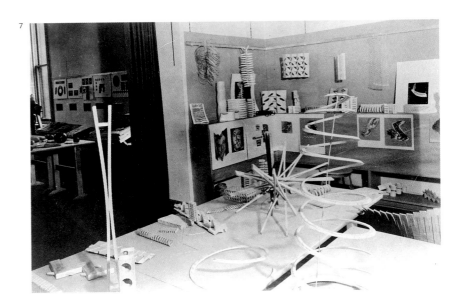

7

depressed" art scene, arriving at the headquarters of the Artists' Union "with a large movie projector, two slide projectors, films and large scale blow-ups. The shock, the impact of the new ideas created a turmoil in the artist group and turned into a marathon debate lasting well after midnight."[22]

The students involved in this new program were exploring all kinds of media and materials and may not have been aware that much of the work was clearly indebted to a Constructivist heritage. E.M. Benson, writing about the "Chicago Bauhaus" in an article in the *Magazine of Art,* warned that imitations of Alexander Archipenko and Moholy-Nagy are not that different from imitations of realist painters such as the popular Alexander Brook and Kenneth Hayes Miller.[23]

When the work of the first ID class was exhibited in the summer of 1938, Bulliet praised it in the *Chicago Daily News.* The reviewer in *Time* was a bit more dubious:

In Chicago this week visitors at the New Bauhaus found an exhibition of bewildering nameless objects: gadgets of wire, wood, sandpaper, linoleum, felt, rubber and ordinary paper, cut in odd accordion patterns [fig. 7]. These objects, which sometimes suggest the scraps left in cabinet maker's shops and sometimes the more outlandish contraptions of Rube Goldberg, represented part of the first year's work of the 70 students at the New Bauhaus....[24]

Some of the students with a good deal of art-school training were aware that the German Bauhaus had artists such as Wassily Kandinsky, Paul Klee, Lyonel Feininger, and Oskar Schlemmer on the faculty. They were disappointed that the Chicago school could claim no advanced work in painting and sculpture; art was considered a private affair to be pursued outside the school. They were not

enthralled with the Foundation Course, which required hands-on work with hand and machine tools. That, however, was only a minor problem in the debacle of The New Bauhaus. Almost from the beginning, Moholy felt a lack of real support from the industrialists on the board of the Association of Arts and Industries. Sibyl Moholy-Nagy, Moholy's wife and first biographer, remembered:

The big industrialists who formed the Board of Directors were glad to leave the functions of an executive committee to smaller people whose vanity was flattered by being sponsors to a cultural enterprise that had aroused international comment. They now offered an unending stream of criticism and naive advice to students, faculty maintenance personnel, founded on no more than the necromancy of the checkbook.[25]

AAI had expected the school to train specialists who would create tangible products for an American industry just beginning to recover from the Great Depression. Instead they saw this array of "bewildering nameless objects." AAI attempted to terminate Moholy, accusing him of "lacking balance, diplomacy, patience and teaching experience."[26] The faculty, however, unanimously signed a "Declaration of Loyalty," drafted by Charles Morris and addressed to Moholy and the board. However, alleging stock market reverses, AAI decided to close the school. Fall classes were canceled; the five-year contract with Moholy was abrogated. Greatly perturbed, but not relenting, Moholy sued AAI[27] and made immediate plans to start a new school of design in Chicago.

Moholy found quarters for the new "School of Design" in an abandoned bakery above the old Chez Paree nightclub at 247 East Ontario Street. Classes began in February 1939 with eighteen day students and twenty-nine enrolled for the evening classes; the faculty worked at first without pay. The school was financed partly by Moholy's earnings as a designer for the Parker Pen Company and Spiegel's mail-order house, and partly by Walter P. Paepcke, president of the Chicago-based Container Corporation of America and the school's major patron for many years (**fig. 8**). Paepcke was a truly enlightened capitalist, who also commissioned eminent artists, including Willem de Kooning, Fernand Léger, Richard Lindner, Henry Moore, Man Ray, Ben Shahn, and Rufino Tamayo, to create important innovations in graphic design. As well, he founded the Aspen Institute for Humanities and was involved in the Great Books program at the University of Chicago. Subsidies from the Carnegie Corporation and the Rockefeller Foundation were soon forthcoming. Moholy appointed a committee of sponsors that included Alfred Barr, John Dewey, Walter Gropius, Joseph Hudnut, and Julian Huxley. In the introduction to the catalogue for the comprehensive and highly influential exhibition "Bauhaus 1919–1928" at The Museum of Modern Art, Barr concluded that "Bauhaus designs, Bauhaus men, Bauhaus ideas, which taken together form one of the chief cultural contributions of modern Germany, have been spread throughout the world."[28] But as soon as the Nazis assumed power in Germany, they closed the school (in 1933).

The School of Design's curriculum differed little from that of its predecessor. The Basic Design (Foundation Course) and Product Design Workshop were taught by James Prestini, a former School of Design student and a consummate craftsman and designer, together with Charles Niedringhaus, an educator and furniture designer. The Light Workshop was under Kepes's direction, assisted now by continuing student Nathan Lerner and James T. Brown. The Painting Workshop was led by Robert J. Wolff, a

member of the American Abstract Artists group who was joined for a brief time by Johannes Molzahn, a well-known German abstract painter. There was also a Weaving Workshop, headed by former German Bauhaus student Marli Ehrmann, assisted by the Munich-trained weaver Else Regensteiner. During 1941–42, the young John Cage taught music at the school, experimenting with his students on his compositions including nonmusical sound and the total absence of sound. Cage also performed a few concerts using instruments that students had made as product-design problems. Additional lecturers from the University of Chicago, including the outstanding sociologist Lloyd Warner, augmented the students' education. Summer sessions were held, first in 1939 at the Paepcke estate in Somonauk, Illinois, and then in 1940 at Mills College in Oakland, California. The latter had a direct impact on art education in the San Francisco Bay Area.[29]

During the Second World War, the school contributed to the war effort by offering a course in camouflage under Kepes's direction. Expanding beyond the visual focus of the school, Moholy, who had been wounded in World War I, turned to his old friend from Budapest, the noted Chicago psychoanalyst Dr. Franz Alexander, to work toward an improved therapy for the rehabilitation of wounded veterans.

In 1944 the name of the school was upgraded to "Institute of Design" (ID) and a new board of directors was created; Walter P. Paepcke continued to serve as chair. At the end of the war, the school moved to temporary quarters at 1009 North State Street and then, in 1946, to its own building at 632 North Dearborn Street, a fine example of Richardsonian Romanesque designed by Henry Ives Cobb which had previously housed the Chicago Historical Society (**fig. 9**). An increasing inclination toward the tenets

9

8

of Modernism in America coupled with the availability of the GI Bill to pay college tuition caused enrollment to increase dramatically at ID. Almost 500 students were enrolled by the fall of 1945; a year later the day and evening students totaled almost 2,000. With increased revenue and a rather generous board, the school flourished and it became possible to come close to Moholy's ideal of education commensurate with "the need for a well-balanced social organization, an education for personal growth and not a mere training in skills for the purpose of profit; a social organization in which everyone is utilized to his highest capacity."[30]

As the school grew, so did the faculty. In 1945 Emerson Woelffer (at ID 1941–49; **plates 17 and 24**) joined the Painting Workshop. An early aficionado of jazz, Woelffer brought a new mode of artistic expression to the school through his painting and sculpture influenced by ethnic art and Surrealist imagery. His studio, noisy with jazz musicians, became a vital gathering place for teachers and students, and was severely missed when he left for Black Mountain College in North Carolina in 1949.

Also in 1945 Crombie Taylor was appointed secretary to the school and became a teacher of architecture, which was under the direction of Ralph Rapson from 1944 until 1947, when Rapson left, eventually to become dean of architecture at the University of Minnesota; he was an important architectural designer and city planner.

Supplementing the challenging curriculum and extraordinary faculty were prominent men and women from many disciplines, who, in a practice going back to the German Bauhaus, were invited as speakers and visitors. Among them were the architects Alvar Aalto, Walter Gropius, Richard Neutra, Paul Rudolph, José Luis Sert, and William Wurster; art historians Sigfried Giedion and Henry-Russell Hitchcock; artists and designers Herbert Bayer, Naum Gabo, Stanley William Hayter, Barbara Hepworth, Frederick Kiesler, Franz Kline, Fernand Léger, Matta, Henry Moore, and Man Ray; legendary comedian Charlie Chaplin; photographers Ansel Adams, Berenice Abbott, Helen Levitt, Frederick Sommer, and Paul Strand; and philosopher Rudolf Carnap.[31]

R. Buckminster Fuller, a visiting lecturer in 1948–49, was probably ID's most important guest instructor (**fig. 10**). One of the great innovators of the century, Fuller was interested in comprehensive

10

11

12

global strategies "to make man a success in the universe." At ID, Fuller lived in a trailer in a parking lot and taught survival skills. Aesthetics of the Bauhaus and, in fact, any stylistic considerations, seemed irrelevant to his larger concerns. He and twelve of his students constructed the first model of the geodesic dome, and then reerected it at Black Mountain College for further testing. During the summer of 1949, other current and former ID faculty also taught at Black Mountain, ID's sister institution. The ID students, however, found the Black Mountaineers easygoing, esoteric, and medita- tive, while the Black Mountain students thought the Chicago types were ambitious, aggressive, and businesslike.[32]

Fuller, however, did not overlap with Moholy- Nagy. Diagnosed with leukemia in 1945, Moholy lived for only another year, during which he contin- ued to work at an enormous rate, designing for commercial companies and lecturing around the country. He also created some of his finest work in painting, the "Leuk" series, named after his can- cer, and in Plexiglas sculpture. He persevered on what may be his greatest accomplishment, his book *Vision in Motion*, which perhaps summarizes the Modernist position better than any book written by an artist. Like the final paintings and sculptures, the book was created in Chicago and represents an essential aspect of this city's contribution to modern art. *Vision in Motion* was published by Paul Theobald in Chicago shortly after Moholy-Nagy's death in November 1946.

Nathan Lerner became acting director of ID. Lerner, like so many members of the rotating ID fac- ulty, was a man of great versatility. Head of the Light Workshop since 1945, he also functioned as head of Product Design.[33] Arthur Siegel, a former ID student, took over the Light Workshop, now renamed the Department of Photography. Siegel's

organization of the Symposium on Photography in 1946 was the first event of its kind and helped elevate the medium to a new level of seriousness. Among the participants were Berenice Abbott, Erwin Blumenfeld, Beaumont Newhall, Paul Strand, Roy Stryker, and Weegee. ID was one of the very few places in the United States where photography was taught as an academic discipline in which students could actually obtain accredited degrees in the field.

After her husband's death, Sibyl Moholy-Nagy, a self-educated woman of great intellect and critical flair, began teaching humanities, while also prepar- ing her discerning biography of Moholy, published in 1950. Myron Kozman, a painter and graphic designer who had been one of the five original students at The New Bauhaus almost ten years earlier, joined the staff in 1946 and taught in many capacities into the 1950s. Between 1945 and 1947, four additional painters also joined the ID faculty: John Walley, who began his career working as a cartoonist and mural- ist, was also a designer and an administrator, but above all, a teacher. During the Depression, as direc- tor of the Illinois WPA Design Workshop, he hired students from ID. After serving in the Air Force as a camouflage expert, he became the head of the Foundation Course. After a stint at Black Mountain College, he returned to ID where he rotated in many of its departments. Part of a generation of idealist Modernists and an individual of great personal warmth, Walley believed that the artist/designer could bring about a better and more humane world by planning for a more rational society. He talked about "personal space" and "body language" long before these concepts became fashionable.

Hugo Weber brought a full background in European culture to the school when he arrived in 1946 (**fig. 11**). Weber had studied with Johannes Itten at the Kunstgewerbeschule in Zurich, and was also a student of art history at the University of

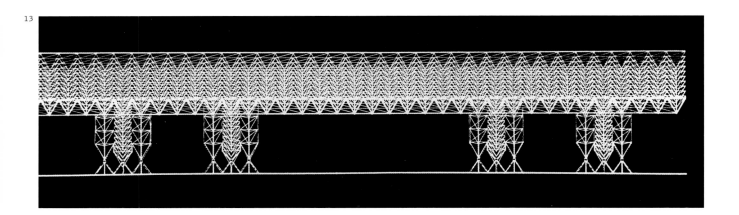

13

Basel, his native city. A friend or colleague of many leading artists such as Marino Marini, Alberto Giacometti, Aristide Maillol, and Hans Arp (with whom he collaborated), Weber brought new ideas to the Foundation Course, which he directed for nine years. As a teacher he would alternate long periods of silence with remarks of great cogency. In his own version of Abstract Expressionism, Weber made paintings with rhythmic energy related to automatism. Richard Koppe (**plate 6**) joined ID's staff as head of Visual Design. He had studied at the avant-garde St. Paul School of Art in Minnesota before joining the first class of The New Bauhaus, and had been one of the few abstract artists in the WPA.

The fourth artist to join ID in 1946 was Eugene Dana. Dana had also been a student at the St. Paul school, and was teaching at Brooklyn College when he was tapped by Serge Chermayeff, who had recently been appointed to succeed Moholy-Nagy.

Chermayeff arrived at ID in 1947. Born in Azerbaijan in the Caucasus, Chermayeff immigrated with his family to England when he was a child. Educated at Harrow and Cambridge, he spent several years as a professional ballroom dancer before turning first to interior design and then to architecture. In 1913, when Eric Mendelsohn arrived in England, the two architects established a partnership and executed a number of commissions. Chermayeff came to the United States in 1942; he was serving as the chair of Brooklyn College's design department when he received the ID appointment.

Chermayeff's personality was in great contrast to Moholy's (**fig. 12**). A superb and meticulous designer, he was rather authoritarian, even dictator-

ial, according to some students.[34] Chermayeff focused his greatest attention on the architecture program, bringing in the Swiss architect Otto Kolb who taught at ID in 1946–51. Gerhard Kallmann, who worked for *Architecture Review* in England after leaving his native Germany, also joined the ID faculty in 1949, but remained only one year. Later, in partnership with Michael McKinnell, Kallmann became well known for his design of Boston City Hall.

Most important for ID, however, was the appointment of Konrad Wachsmann, an eminent engineer as well as architect who had studied with Hans Poelzig in Berlin. He designed a summer house for Albert Einstein, who subsequently sought President Franklin D. Roosevelt's help in facilitating Wachsmann's emigration from Germany in 1941. In the United States, Wachsmann worked with Gropius on prefabricated housing and then with Chermayeff on "mobilar structures." As head of Advanced Building Research at ID, Wachsmann and his students developed a remarkable hangar for the US Air Force (**fig. 13**). This futuristic, experimental structure anticipated later buildings based on system analysis.

Chermayeff made other new appointments. Frank Barr, a highly innovative graphic designer, came to teach typography. Misch Kohn (at ID 1948–72) was the first figurative painter on the ID faculty. After working for the WPA in the 1930s, Kohn went to Mexico where he looked to José Clemente Orozco as a mentor and became associated with Taller de Graphica Popular. He was considered one of America's foremost printmakers when he was appointed to ID to teach graphic design in 1948. He then rotated with Richard Koppe as head of the Visual Design Department.

In the area of "Cultural Studies" at ID—a designation that seems to anticipate the 1990s— Margit Varro took over music instruction from David Dushkin. Born in Hungary and a friend of Bela Bartok's, Varro gave wonderful lectures and brilliant performances, teaching everything from ancient music to Bartok's use of the Fibonacci series.[35]

In 1949, while completing my doctorate on German Expressionism at the University of Chicago, I became the first art historian to teach at ID (**fig. 14**). I offered courses in the history of art (including architecture) that were tailored to the philosophy of the school. The program stressed the initial intuitive and psychological/perceptual insights on the part of the students. In 1952, when I introduced a graduate program in art education, it was clear that the country was ready for an actual teacher-training program based on Bauhaus-ID principles. The theories of John Dewey, Sigmund Freud, and especially Victor Lowenfeld's child development and visual expression studies were very relevant to this program.[36] Its purpose was to lead teachers away from rote activity toward experimentation with materials. It also stressed the importance of thoughtful looking at art on the part of students.[37] The program attracted not only elementary, high school, and college teachers, and art supervisors, but also many former ID students.

Quite a few of these students have become noted artists, such as Fred Berger (**plate 75**), June Leaf (**plates 22 and 28**), Robert Kostka, Norman Laliberte, Alex Nicoloff, and Irene Siegel. Elliot Eisner, a graduate student in the program, was able to carry it further as head of art education at Stanford University and as one of the leading art educators in the country. The Getty Center for Education in the Arts has recently promoted a similar approach toward the integration of aesthetics into the school curriculum.

In 1950 Elmer Ray Pearson, who had studied with Moholy at ID and then with Mies van der Rohe at the Illinois Institute of Technology (ITT), began his thirty-year teaching career at ID. He also became a chronicler of the school. In the same year Harold Cohen became a member of the teaching staff. Cohen saw John Walley as his mentor and recalls, "When I entered ID, my life started to have meaning—I found who I was."[38] Cohen tried to convey this attitude to his own students at ID (1950–55), and later as professor of architecture and environmental design at the State University of New York in Buffalo.

During Chermayeff's tenure other appointments ensured that ID's educational ideals would spread across the nation: Jesse Reichek, an ID student in the early 1940s, established a life-long friendship with Kepes and Prestini. After World War II, Reichek taught briefly at ID before spending a number of years in Paris, where he exhibited at the Galerie Cahiers d'Art. He returned to ID in 1951 to head the Product Design Department, but left in 1952 for the University of California, where, in cooperation with Charles Eames, he set up a Foundation Course for the department of architecture at Berkeley. Later joined by Prestini, he taught generations of students ID concepts as well as courses concerned with architecture and the political environment.

ID's vision was probably spread most widely in the arts by the many talented photographers who both taught at and graduated from the school. Arthur Siegel (**plate 19**) and Harry Callahan (**plates 7, 12, and 30**) were both on the faculty when Aaron Siskind (**plates 11 and 20**), a master of both abstract and documentary photography and a close friend of Franz Kline and other New York Abstract Expressionist painters, joined ID in

fig. 13
Konrad Wachsmann, *Structural System for Large Airplane Hangar* (detail), 1951. Photo from *50 Jahre New Bauhaus Bauhaus-Nachfolge in Chicago* (Berlin: Argon Verlag, 1987), p. 219.

fig. 14
Peter Selz in Illinois Institute of Technology/ Institute of Design parking lot, 632 North Dearborn Street, Chicago, 1953. Photo: unknown ID student, courtesy Peter Selz, Berkeley, California.

14

1951. During the same year, Arthur Sinsabaugh (**plate 52**), a former student who had studied with Moholy, Siegel, and Callahan, was added. It was, above all, the combination of Callahan's and Siskind's teaching that made ID the leading school for photography. Callahan left in 1961 for the Rhode Island School of Design, but Siskind remained at ID for twenty years, inspiring numerous photographers.

Never properly funded, the Institute of Design suffered financial difficulties for most of its existence. They increased with the drop in enrollment after the great influx of veterans under the GI Bill. Walter P. Paepcke, still the principal supporter, began to focus most of his interest on the Aspen Institute. In order to maintain ID, it was found necessary to affiliate with another solvent institution. Negotiations with the University of Chicago, Northwestern University, and the University of Illinois took place as early as 1948.[39] Although members of the University of Chicago faculty had been teaching at ID since its beginning, Robert Maynard Hutchins, the university's chancellor, told Chermayeff and Paepcke that "art had no room in a university."[40] Finally, the school turned to ITT, in spite of an early warning by Gropius that considerable antagonism against ID could be expected from Mies and his associates. But Henry Heald, the president of IIT and a prominent member of the Unity of Art and Science movement, welcomed the school and promised that it would retain its autonomy as the affiliation was announced at a special meeting of the board of directors on November 22, 1949.[41]

In addition to the external problems, there had always been controversies inside the school, which grew more pronounced after Moholy's death. By 1951 old disputes between Chermayeff and Wachsmann were so pronounced that the former suggested to President Heald that Wachsmann's Department of Advanced Building Research be separated from ID.[42] Asked by Chermayeff to intervene on his behalf, Gropius wrote to Heald, stating that "Wachsmann with all his charm is so egocentric a man that I believe he should not be a teacher."[43]

This controversy may well have been one reason for Chermayeff's resignation in 1951. Crombie Taylor, a man with meager leadership abilities, became acting director, facing a difficult faculty and student body. The search for a permanent director commenced at once. Among the twenty-five candidates considered and interviewed were architects and designers Charles Eames, Louis Kahn, George Fred Keck, Paul Rand, Ralph Rapson, and Paul Rudolph; art historians and educators

Robert Goldwater, Edgar Kaufman, Herbert Read, and James Thrall Soby; and artists Max Bill, Richard Lippold, Ernest Mundt, Harry Bertoia, Robert J. Wolff, and John Walley and Hugo Weber from within the faculty. But disagreement was rife and staff members shifted their positions constantly. Prior to his resignation from the school in 1953, John Walley wrote an open letter, "Crisis in Leadership at the Institute of Design," in which he speaks of the school's great international reputation under Moholy, the efforts of the faculty to maintain this standard, and the destructive attitude by the "leadership of Crombie Taylor, Hugo Weber and Konrad Wachsmann, demonstrating a philosophy of contempt for students and faculty."[44]

Clearly the situation had become untenable. It was not helped when, without consulting an admittedly divided faculty, IIT simply appointed a new director in 1955: Jay Doblin, a commercial designer with the firm of Raymond Loewy. The installation of a director coming from the marketing branch of design was repugnant to the ID faculty. Their internal battle forgotten, the faculty sent an anonymous letter to the IIT administration stating (in part): "certain fundamental tenets of our approach to education of the designer have been brought into serious jeopardy.... The designer must be more than stylist or decorator who caters to fashionable, or opportunistic needs. The designer must be an ethically responsible professional with a developed ability based on the most penetrating scientific and artistic insight of our time." The letter concluded: "This appointment represents a fundamental departure from our educational purpose."[45] The administration did not reconsider; Doblin, a well-meaning and able individual, remained with tenure. In protest Harold Cohen, Charles Forberg (who had been added to the architecture faculty shortly before), Crombie Taylor, Hugo Weber, and I tendered resignations; Arthur Siegel, who had rejoined the photography staff, and Konrad Wachsmann were told that their contracts would not be renewed.

With its greatly reduced faculty, the school moved to the basement of S.R. Crown Hall, the beautiful edifice Mies designed for IIT's architecture department and which formed the center of the campus. In the meantime, President Heald left IIT to become director of the Ford Foundation, and was succeed by John Rettaliata, an engineer. With ID now a department of an engineering school, Doblin's position was extremely difficult. After he himself left IIT in 1969, he recalled: "So there we were, the remains of the foremost school of experimentation (ID), the triumphant school of purism (Mies's Department of Architecture) and a commercial designer, all locked up in Crown Hall. Three divergent philosophies on a collision course."[46] It could very well have closed its doors like its sister institution, Black Mountain College, had done earlier, but ID continued with undergraduate and master's programs in Visual Design, Product Design, Photography, and Art Education. It is now located in a nineteen-story tower on Chicago's South Side at 3360 South State Street. There have been several directors since Doblin resigned in 1969.

Although as Sir Herbert Read observed in 1963, the Bauhaus idea "had spread throughout the world and is the active influence wherever any real advance in living is made,"[47] there were also inherent flaws in its program. The sculptor George Rickey, an ID student in the late 1940s, noted that its "method of teaching has spread all over the world and has changed every art school in Europe, here in America, and in Japan... but when the students went into typography or architecture, it's as though they never had that course."[48] Similarly, Jesse Reichek pointed out that "when the students went into Visual Design, Product Design, Architecture, or Photography, they entered into courses of instruction that actually differed little from what other institutions had to offer. The school was never able to build a curriculum beyond the Foundation Course."[49]

The lack of continuity was not the only problem. Probably more important was the collapse of the belief that better design would bring about a better world. Kepes concluded his penetrating analysis of art in the contemporary world by privileging advertising art, "which is not handicapped by traditional forms," as the art that could best prepare "the way for positive popular art, an art reaching everybody and understood by everyone."[50] But, as America and the rest of the industrial and postindustrial world turned increasingly toward a multinational plutocracy, and as the political and cultural climate in the 1940s grew increasingly corrupt, such a belief seemed absurd. Moholy's early idea that the artist-designer could gain control of the means of production turned out to be a grand illusion. In the early days of the modern movement, a new functional architecture created fine public housing for the middle and lower classes, but as developers began using debased Modernist designs for quick profits, the quality of design as well as its purpose became degraded. When, in 1963, Gropius, the model of integrity in modern architecture and the father of

the Bauhaus, became the principal designer of the Pan Am tower, a monstrous high-rise blocking New York's Park Avenue, faith in architecture as a vehicle for transformation toward a more humane society began to wane.

The high-rise building, one of the paradigms of Modernism, began to be viewed not as the solution to congestion, but as the culprit that destroys circulation in our cities, isolates its inhabitants, and actually helps destroy the urban landscape. Peter Blake, one of the leading protagonists of the modern movement both as a critic and architect, asserted in 1974: "We have seen and lived the future and it simply didn't work. The Modern Movement—the creed in which we were raised and to which we pledged allegiance throughout our professional lives—has reached the end of the road."[51]

ID also never resolved the obvious conflict between the fine arts, practiced by most of its teachers, and the design of marketable commodities. It placed its emphasis on experimentation, but wanted to leave the practice of art outside its walls. It prescribed that the designer in an industrial society create reproducible products, be they chairs, graphic designs, or photographs, not one-of-a-kind works of art. This position, however, was unsatisfactory to many students and went against the grain in Chicago, which despite—or perhaps because of—its industrial base was inclined toward Expressionism and Surrealism. ID's exclusion of art focused light on the other major Chicago art school of the era, the School of the Art Institute. As Franz Schulze discusses (see p. 21), the focus of SAIC students, while respectful of Bauhaus ideals and of Mies in particular, was quite different. SAIC students were engrossed with the indigenous and exotic art that they studied at the Field Museum of Natural History. They talked about Surrealist art, which they could also see in the emerging Chicago collections of the Culbergs, the Shapiros, and the Bergmans (see Adrian, pp. 71–73). The Surrealists' glorification of the absurd and the irrational seemed to them a coherent response to a world responsible for Auschwitz and Hiroshima. SAIC students saw the skills of industrial precision used for purposes of devastation, and they were disillusioned with the promise of the machine. Introspection might be more likely to produce meaningful results in a search for human values.

In the late 1940s the "rationalists" at ID encountered the romantic and irrational and subjective art by SAIC students in the arena of Exhibition Momentum, initially organized as a protest against the Art Institute's policy of excluding student work from their prestigious Annual Exhibitions by Artists of Chicago and Vicinity (**see Schulze, p. 17, and Jaffee, pp. 56-57**). Almost from the beginning, ID students and faculty were attracted to this new, progressive exhibition opportunity. Hugo Weber wrote a brief introduction to the first Momentum catalogue in 1948; Roy Gussow, an ID student, actually chaired the first exhibition. The 1950 catalogue was designed by Robert Nickle (**plate 43**), a teacher of Product Design; Alex Nicoloff, a Visual Design student, designed the 1952 catalogue; Burton Kramer was responsible for the 1954 effort (**fig. 15**).

In the mid-1950s attitudes began to change at ID, especially among those inclined toward art rather than design. Freud and Jung began to be discussed in the studios and hallways as vehemently as Buckminster Fuller. Some of the students, like their SAIC colleagues, explored a primitivist sort of expressionism with Surrealist overtones. Their incongruous figurations were confirmed by Jean Dubuffet's lecture "Anticultural Positions" at the Arts Club in 1951, in which the French artist emphasized passion and violence. His antirational stance became more acceptable to many young Chicago artists than the clear appeal to reason by Moholy and Kepes. In Chicago, as elsewhere, Existentialist concerns and issues of alienation became paramount.

When we think of Chicago artists of the postwar period, it is the idiosyncratic Imagists, once mislabeled the "Monster Roster," that come to mind: Robert Barnes, Don Baum (**plates 58 and 107**), Cosmo Campoli (**plate 15**), Dominick Di Meo (**plate 44**), George Cohen (**plate 21**), Leon Golub (**plates 23, 25, and 40**), Joseph Goto (**plates 18 and 27**), Theodore Halkin (**plate 45**), June Leaf (**plates 22 and 28**), Irving Petlin, Seymour Rosofsky (**plates 39 and 104**), Evelyn Statsinger (**plate 10**) and H.C. Westermann (**plates 31, 33, 35, and 36**). And then we think of their successors, the Hairy Who, the False Image, and the Non-Plussed Some groups and later individuals such as Ed Paschke (**plates 67, 87, 103, and 161**), among others, whose expressions, fantasies, and often raunchy vitality relate to the Second City in a manner forming a significant contrast to the utopian optimism of the Bauhaus tradition as exemplified in the Institute of Design.

fig. 15
Burton Kramer, *Momentum Midcontinental Exhibition 54*, 1954, cover. Photo courtesy Museum of Contemporary Art, Chicago, Archive of Art in Chicago.

notes

1 As early as 1901, Frank Lloyd Wright delivered a lecture at Jane Addams's Hull House which he called "The Art and Craft of the Machine." He asserted that the machine—the symbol of technology—was the "great forerunner of democracy" because it liberated the individual. Going far beyond his major European contemporaries, Wright proposed a machine aesthetic—later to be called "Functionalism"—at the very beginning of the century. Frank Lloyd Wright in Bruce Brooks Pfeiffer, ed., *Frank Lloyd Wright: Collected Writings* (New York: Rizzoli, 1992), vol. 1, p. 59.

2 For a discussion of the social and economic circumstances surrounding the formation of AAI, see Lloyd Engelbrecht, "László Moholy-Nagy in Chicago," in *Moholy-Nagy: A New Vision for Chicago* (Springfield: Illinois State Museum, 1990), pp. 24–26.

3 Ibid.

4 When the philosopher Charles Morris, who taught at both the University of Chicago and The New Bauhaus, first introduced Dewey to Moholy's educational concepts, the older man was very much impressed and eventually joined a group of patrons of the now-renamed School of Design.

5 Sweeney was director of paintings and sculpture at The Museum of Modern Art, New York, in 1945–46, director of the Solomon R. Guggenheim Museum, New York, in 1952–60, and director of the Museum of Fine Arts, Houston, in 1961–68.

6 "Glass Houses" (1931), sponsored by AAI.

7 It was in this pivotal book that Moholy first outlined the education principles of the Bauhaus, which served as the basis of his new school in Chicago.

8 In 1938 Bulliet was the first critic to give serious consideration to Buckminster Fuller and drew attention to Fuller's concept of "universal architecture." See Sue Ann Kendall, "C.J. Bulliet: Chicago's Lonely Champion of Modernism," *Archives of American Art Journal* 26, 2–3 (1986), pp. 21–31. In 1927 Bulliet wrote an extensive catalogue on Alexander Archipenko, pioneer of modern sculpture, who was to be on the original faculty of the School of Design, as The New Bauhaus was renamed in 1939.

9 C.J. Bulliet, *Chicago Daily News*, Feb. 6, 1937.

10 The history of the prewar era is dealt with in Sue Ann Prince, ed., *The Old Guard and the Avant-Garde: Modernism in Chicago, 1910–1940* (Chicago and London: The University of Chicago Press, 1990). This book is an edited collection of the proceedings of a 1988 symposium titled "The Coming of Modernism to Chicago, 1910–1940," organized by the Archives of American Art, Smithsonian Institution, and cosponsored by The Art Institute of Chicago.

11 László Moholy-Nagy, "Constructivism and the Proletariat," in *MA*, May 1922.

12 In the same year Man Ray also achieved photographs without a camera which he called "Rayographs." Christian Schad had made similar experiments earlier during his Dada years in Switzerland which are known as "Schadographs."

13 See László Moholy-Nagy, *Von Material zu Architektur*, Bauhaus Book 14 (Munich: Albert Langen Verlag, 1929); English trans.: *The New Vision* (New York: Brewer, Warren & Putnam, 1932), not to be confused with Moholy's posthumously published *Vision in Motion* (Chicago: Paul Theobald, 1946).

14 *The New Bauhaus American School of Design* (Chicago, 1937), p. 4.

15 Edward Alden Jewell, "Chicago's New Bauhaus," *The New York Times*, Sept. 12, 1937, sec. 11, p. 7.

16 This terminology became standard as well at the School of the Art Institute, where it is still in use today.

17 Nathan Lerner, Interview with Laura Stoland, Archive of Art in Chicago, Oral History Project, Museum of Contemporary Art, Chicago, Mar. 21, 1995.

18 Moholy-Nagy in Charles Traub, ed., *The New Vision* (New York: Aperture, 1982), p. 49.

19 It is interesting to wonder "what might have been" if Moholy had been successful in securing the services of all those he indeed invited to be on the first faculty. Jean Hélion, Herbert Bayer, and Xanti Schawinsky were invited to teach painting, typography, and display, respectively, but none managed to get an American visa in time. Moholy, considering architecture an essential element in The New Bauhaus curriculum, approached Frank Lloyd Wright. But the sage of Taliesin who had made such a decisive impact on modern architecture in Europe was not a friend of the "Functionalism" and the International Style associated with the Bauhaus, and furthermore, would certainly not teach at somebody else's school, especially as he just had set up his own apprenticeships at Taliesin. Moholy then turned to the Chicago Modernist George Fred Keck to teach architecture, but Moholy's proposal to establish a full-fledged architectural curriculum was discouraged by Gropius due to the difficulty of gaining accreditation for such a program. Furthermore, Moholy's attempt to coordinate The New Bauhaus's architectural program with that of Mies's program at the Armour Institute after he accepted that position in 1938 was discouraged both by Mies and The New Bauhaus's parent organization, AAI.

Similarly, Moholy's hopes to have courses in art history met with no immediate success. He had hoped that James Johnson Sweeney, a strong advocate of Modernism throughout his life, would teach The New Bauhaus courses on the history of art. But Sweeney had little faith in AAI and declined to join the new school. Moholy then turned to Sigfried Giedion, a Modernist Swiss art and architectural historian and close friend of the Bauhaus. Giedion, however, decided to remain in Zurich.

20 Nathan Lerner, "Memories of Moholy-Nagy and the New Bauhaus" in *The New Bauhaus/School of Design in Chicago* (New York: Banning + Associates, 1993), p. 13.

21 Richard Koppe, "The New Bauhaus," John Walley Papers (Box 3, Folder 5), The University of Illinois at Chicago, The University Library, Department of Special Collections, University Archives. I am greatly indebted to Laura Stoland for bringing these papers and a great deal of material on The New Bauhaus and ID to my attention.

22 John Walley, "The Influence of the New Bauhaus on Chicago 1938–1943," John Walley Papers (note 21).

23 E.M. Benson, "Chicago Bauhaus," *Magazine of Art* 31, 2 (Feb. 1938), p. 38.

24 "Bauhaus: First Year," *Time* 2, 2 (July 1938), p. 21.

25 Sibyl Moholy-Nagy, *Moholy-Nagy, Experiment in Totality* (New York: Harper & Brothers, 1950), p. 156.

26 Papers of The New Bauhaus, Bauhaus-Archiv, Berlin.

27 "New Bauhaus School Closes; Director Sues," *Chicago Sunday Tribune*, Oct. 16, 1938. The lawsuit was settled out of court and Moholy used his payment for the benefit of his new school.

28 Alfred H. Barr, Jr. in Ise Gropius, Walter Gropius, and Herbert Bayer,

eds., *Bauhaus 1919–1928* (Boston: C.T. Bramford Co., 1959), pp. 5–6.

29 In 1940 Professor Alfred Neumeyer, chairman of the art department at Mills College, invited Moholy-Nagy and a number of other members of the ID faculty (Kepes, Ehrmann, Niedringhaus, Prestini, and the painter Robert J. Wolff) to teach a summer session with courses in drawing, painting, photography, weaving, paper cutting, metalwork, modeling, and casting based on Bauhaus/ID principles. Simultaneously, the Mills College gallery mounted a large exhibition with paintings by Moholy and Wolff, photographs by Kepes, wooden bowls by Prestini, and a wall-hanging by Ehrmann. The summer session was attended by artists, art teachers, architects, and designers in the San Francisco Bay Area.

30 Moholy-Nagy, *Vision in Motion* (note 13), p. 11.

31 Most of this information is from an interview by the author with Robert Kostka, Berkeley, California, Dec. 12, 1993.

32 Mary Emma Harris, *The Arts at Black Mountain* (Annandale-on-Hudson, New York: Bard College, 1987), p. 160.

33 Lerner was a successful product designer; among his contributions is the bear-shaped, squeezable plastic "honey bear" bottle.

34 Alex Nicoloff, Interview with the author, Berkeley, California, Apr. 19, 1994.

35 For more on Varro, see Robert Kostka, "Remembering Mrs. Varro," unpublished manuscript, 1990.

36 Victor Lowenfeld, *Creative and Mental Growth* (New York: Macmillan, 1957).

37 Peter Selz and Richard Koppe, "The Education of the Art Teacher," *School Arts* 54 (1955), pp. 5–12. Reprinted in Hans M. Wingler, *Bauhaus* (Cambridge, MA: The MIT Press, 1969), pp. 209–210.

38 Harold Cohen, Talk at the Institute of Design Reunion, Chicago, Aug. 1, 1987.

39 Preface to the ID Papers, The University of Illinois at Chicago, The University Library, Department of Special Collections, Institute of Design Collection.

40 Ibid.

41 Special Meeting of the Board of Directors, Institute of Design, Nov. 22, 1949, ID Papers (note 39).

42 Letter from Serge Chermayeff to Henry Heald, Archives of the Institute of Design, Bauhaus-Archiv, Berlin.

43 Letter from Walter Gropius to Henry Heald, Archives of the Institute of Design, Bauhaus-Archiv, Berlin.

44 John Walley, "Crisis in Leadership at the Institute of Design," Archives of the Institute of Design, Bauhaus-Archiv, Berlin.

45 John Chancellor, "The Rocky Road from the Bauhaus," *Chicago*, July 1955.

46 Jay Doblin, "Chicago Bauhaus: Past, Present and Future," unpublished lecture, May 11, 1974.

47 Herbert Read in L. Hirschfeld-Mack, *The Bauhaus: An International Survey* (Croydon, Australia: Langmans, 1963), p. 53.

48 George Rickey in Jane Allen and Derek Guthrie, "Institute of Design," *Chicago Tribune*, Jan. 16, 1972.

49 Jesse Reichek, Interview with the author, Petaluma, California, May 1, 1994.

50 Gyorgy Kepes, *Language of Vision* (Chicago: Paul Theobald, 1944), p. 129.

51 Peter Blake, *Form Follows Fiasco* (Boston: Little Brown & Company, 1974), p. 167.

Barbara Jaffee

pride of place

The dilemma of working as an artist in Chicago yet not being typecast as a "Chicago artist" is a long-standing one. What might be described as a dismissive label when used by the national press has at times, within the city, been seen as a pejorative one. This identity dilemma has been exacerbated by the lack of historical awareness that has also long characterized Chicago's art community. Each generation has wrestled with its identity vis-à-vis this city with little knowledge of the previous generations' struggles; often the very stereotypes and myths artists wished to sweep away have been solidified. In this essay Barbara Jaffee, an artist, instructor of painting at The School of The Art Institute of Chicago, and PhD candidate in art history at the University of Chicago, examines what has always been a major concern for artists living in Chicago: how to define themselves in the face of the often limiting definitions afforded by geographical location, lack of resources, and lack of historical awareness. LW

in 1965

the inaugural issue of *Midwest Art Reviews and Chicago Gallery Guide* quoted a young painter voicing what was by then a familiar refrain: "Chicago is a nice place to live," he observed, "but I wouldn't want to work here." The regularity with which this and similar laments have been repeated could be described as a leitmotif of the story of art and artists in this city. Chicago *is* a great place to live. Why isn't it a great place to work? The obvious answer sounds flippant—*who* says it isn't? In fact, this is precisely the kind of question that needs to be asked. What counts as art in Chicago and why? Whose kind of town is Chicago, anyway?

For most of the nineteenth century, Chicago was a destination for artists, not a point of departure. This changed dramatically following the Great Chicago Fire in 1871. As architects and engineers descended upon the city, many of its painters and sculptors discreetly departed—for the duration of Chicago's reconstruction, or so they claimed. When artists spoke of leaving Chicago at the turn of the century, it was again simple economics. With its huge School of the Art Institute (SAIC), which had grown in tandem with the industrial expansion that transformed the city in the 1890s, Chicago had become a center of artistic training—a place that produced more young artists than any market could reasonably be expected to absorb. Economic imperative played a lesser role in 1924,

54

when aesthetic satisfaction was the reason cited by departing Modernist Raymond Jonson. Jonson, a pioneering advocate of an American abstract art, styled himself as a prophet of coming spiritual rebirth. He would go on to found the Transcendental Painters Group, a colony of like-minded abstract painters living and working in the New Mexico desert.

Jonson was at least twenty years ahead of his time. It would not be until the 1940s that a realignment of culture, patriotism, and patronage would awaken in American artists and audiences alike a hunger for an indigenous advanced style.[1] The creation of an avant-garde has proven itself since to be the single most important ingredient in the ecology of a healthy urban art world. The world of modern art spins in something of a vicious circle. Artists produce work ostensibly free of market considerations, but in reality must attempt to anticipate the desires of their often elusive audiences. Collectors, motivated by a love of objects or a desire to intervene in history, at the same time look cautiously to institutions for confirmation of their commitments. Museums are by nature conservative, yet compelled to court all manner of constituencies in order to fulfill their missions. In this world, originality and authenticity have been the prized characteristics for most of the past fifty years, measured against standards that assume the existence of some kind of collective identity. In practical terms, originality requires collectivity. This has meant that art in Chicago has had to become "Chicago Art" in order to survive.

The mechanism of this transformation is not always evident. In 1945 the world of contemporary art in Chicago was small, dominated by the once-controversial production of its prewar expressionists

(Modernists who came of age in the 1920s and 1930s).[2] But in the highly charged atmosphere of the immediate postwar era, the big news in Chicago's art world was the passing of what were described as "New York-type" galleries (small spaces showing only two-dimensional works), in favor of a new type—a commercial studio integrating art, architecture, and design (**fig. 1**).[3] This "Chicago-style" gallery took its cues from a synthesis of art and commerce with a long tradition here—from the arts-and-crafts practiced at Jane Addams's Hull House in the 1890s to the extension of the Bauhaus experiment begun under László Moholy-Nagy in 1937 (*see Selz essay*). At The Art Institute of Chicago (AIC), curator Katharine Kuh's preoccupations helped to position the city's major art museum as an advocate of the nonobjective art favored by this nascent avant-garde. AIC was, at the time, one of the most progressive museums of art in the country. Its curators and director, Daniel Catton Rich, shared a passionate vision of the role art could play in society, and were dedicated to an ideal of artistic freedom. They promoted abstract art because they believed that it embodied a timeless and transcendent social utility. They were, in a word, formalists— in the once-penetrating sense that insisted the aesthetic was a branch of knowledge, albeit intuitive. Kuh (**fig. 2**) in particular had the spirit of a social reformer, a taste she acquired early as a student enrolled in the University of Chicago's progressive Laboratory School.

Despite its beachhead in Chicago, wartime enthusiasm for nonobjective art was on the ebb in the early years of the Cold War, as many Americans were discovering that what they had so vigorously defended against the Fascists was not much to their

fig. 1
Baldwin Kingrey storefront, Diana Court Building, North Michigan Avenue at Ohio Street, Chicago, c. 1947. Photo: Berko, courtesy the Decorative and Industrial Arts Collection, Chicago Historical Society, and Kitty Baldwin Weese, Chicago.

liking after all. In 1948 the country's left and right wings clashed over the status of modern art, and the Art Institute found itself embroiled in controversy— a controversy with unexpected consequences for the formation of an identifiably Chicago art. When its Annual Exhibition of American Art opened on November 6, 1947, it was the fifty-eighth such survey of the state of art in America the museum had mounted. It was not a show like any other, however. The fifty-eighth annual took as its theme the pervasive phenomenon of abstract and Surrealist art by Americans from all over the country (**fig. 3**). Response to the show was immediate, and covered the spectrum of political opinion at the time. Conservatives, not surprisingly, condemned it. Moderates also decried the show's extremism. AIC had a great deal at stake in the uproar; it was, after all, among the first to advance such bold propositions about American art.[4]

The Art Institute's director of fine arts, Daniel Catton Rich (**fig. 4**), attempted to clarify the show's message. In a strongly worded argument, Rich defended what he described as the "Freedom of the Brush."[5] He noted that AIC curators Fred Sweet and Katharine Kuh had criss-crossed the American countryside without preconception, only to find that interest in nonrepresentational painting was on the rise—as compelling a force in "Walnut Creek, California, Muscoda, Wisconsin, [and] Lincoln, Nebraska" as in the large cities. Why this should be

was clear to Rich: nonrepresentational painting had a long history in the United States, beginning in 1913 with the shock of the Armory Show (which traveled from New York, to AIC, and later to Boston, introducing a generation of Americans to modern art), and nurtured over the years by the arrival of refugee artists and intellectuals. The present challenge for this broad and vital movement, according to Rich, came from what he described as "the growing conservatism in all fields of American taste." More disheartening was opposition from moderates. This group, Rich claimed, provided unwitting support to conservatives anxious to dismiss all modern art as subversive. This was bitter irony at best, he charged: "at the very moment when our abstractionists and surrealists are being attacked as Communists, the Communists themselves are accusing such artists of serving 'the selfish interest of the bourgeoisie' and, 'catering to their decadent and perverted tastes.'"

The Art Institute's board, one assumes, supported Rich's principled position the following year when, according to AIC archivist John W. Smith, he found himself accused in Congress of Communist leanings by Representative George A. Dondero of Michigan.[6] Yet the political pressures of the moment surely took their toll. Within months of the opening of its American Annual, AIC announced that undergraduate art students would no longer be invited to submit works for inclusion in the juried Annual

fig. 2
Katharine Kuh in her office at The Art Institute of Chicago, 1951. Photo: Stephen B. Lewellyn, © 1996, The Art Institute of Chicago, all rights reserved.

fig. 3
The Art Institute of Chicago, *Fifty-eighth Annual Exhibition of American Paintings and Sculpture: Abstract and Surrealist American Art*, 1947, cover. Photo © 1996, The Art Institute of Chicago, all rights reserved.

2

3

Exhibition by Artists of Chicago and Vicinity (C&V). This show, an established stepping stone to artistic success in Chicago, had, in its last two years, attracted considerable attention for some of its more provocative entries—particularly those submitted by a new generation of expressionists, many of whom began their training at SAIC during or after the war. Although AIC's decision was probably made in the hopes of avoiding future confrontation, this denial of access to younger artists was itself viewed as a provocation. Out of frustration emerged the artists' group Momentum, and a series of ambitious counter-salons were born (*see Schulze, p. 17*).

This tenuous combination of circumstance would have tremendous repercussions for the future of art in Chicago: the Art Institute's actions, however unwittingly, had started a ball rolling that would become a Chicago School. At first it was a largely subterranean movement, the interest of collectors like Joseph Randall Shapiro and dealers Allan Frumkin and Richard Feigen still some years away (*see Adrian, pp. 71–74*). Postwar prosperity had led to a remarkable surge in the number of art galleries in Chicago, and by 1951 those showing Chicago artists tended to support either the established prewar expressionists, or the abstractionists associated with Moholy-Nagy's surviving Institute of Design (ID). Over the next several years, a number of new galleries opened, and others expanded in size or began to include art by Chicagoans.[7] Outdoor art fairs exploded across the city and suburbs (*fig. 5*), the result of public relations efforts spearheaded by retail and real estate groups.[8] Yet younger expressionists, artists whose works both engaged and challenged traditional practices, continued to be hard-pressed to

find exhibition opportunities outside of Momentum's continuing efforts.

It is tempting to view, as a triumph, the reversal of fortune that led to the identification of these same struggling artists as a Chicago School, tentatively by Peter Selz and Patrick T. Malone in 1955 ("Is There a New Chicago School?" *ARTnews*, October 1955) and definitively by Franz Schulze in his now classic 1972 book, *Fantastic Images: Chicago Art Since 1945* (*fig. 6*). But this would be to obscure the reality that their triumph was equal parts struggle and serendipity. Although, retrospectively, the emergence of figurative expressionism as the preeminent postwar movement in Chicago art may seem inevitable, it required some dramatic shifts in local climate—shifts which made, in a manner of speaking, for a very bumpy ride. As the following will show, two crucial circumstances, the departure of AIC's Daniel Rich and Katharine Kuh (signaling a slow decline in the Art Institute's involvement with contemporary art) and the collapse of the integrity of Moholy-Nagy's Institute of Design legacy, both cleared and confused the way.

It is possible to imagine a very different image for Chicago art—one associated with such refinements as the exquisitely nonobjective aesthetic nurtured at ID. But the year 1954 was a turning point in the influence of ID on the fine arts in Chicago. Although a flurry of activity that year suggested that a Moholy-style marriage of the fine and industrial arts was still imminent, the Bauhaus vision that would be fulfilled in Chicago was that of the materialist Mies van der Rohe, not the spiritualist Moholy (*see Schulze, p. 23*). Behind this denouement were the massive urban renewal efforts that captured the imagination of the city's architecture and

fig. 6
Franz Schulze, *Fantastic Images: Chicago Art Since 1945*, 1972, book cover.

fig. 7
5364–5640 South Lake Park Avenue, Chicago, 1950. These stores and apartment buildings were constructed in the early 1890s in anticipation of the World's Columbian Exposition held in Jackson Park in 1893. They were eventually demolished as part of the Hyde Park Renewal Project. Photo: Mildred Mead, 1950, courtesy Chicago Historical Society (ICHi-06975).

design community, as federal funds, intended to resurrect the public housing programs of the 1930s, became available for inner-city development after 1949 (**fig. 7**).[9] Many of the figures prominent in the new collaborative design studio-galleries were caught up in this ambitious new arena. As a result, their confident commitment to the idealism of the immediate postwar period would find expression through Chicago's civic and commercial aspirations—in the optimism of International Style architecture and urban planning, and in a powerful language of advertising and design. The less obviously practical arts of painting and sculpture were cut adrift from their links to a synthesis of art, architecture, and design, and the once-promising "Chicago-style" gallery of the 1940s degenerated into an eclectic boutique—seen increasingly by artists and critics as regressive.[10]

Meanwhile, enthusiasm for abstraction continued unabated at the Art Institute even as commitment to the purpose of its C&V show was waning. For the years 1949 and 1950, the show was curated by AIC staff, and reflected their advocacy of nonobjective art. The catalogues were substantial, even lavish, but became little more than pamphlets after the reinstatement of the open-jury process (and reinclusion of student submissions) in 1951. In 1954 AIC eliminated the show altogether, intending to replace the yearly format with a biennial survey (the 1955 show was instead a reinauguration of the annual schedule, as the result of a vigorous protest by the Chicago branch of Artists Equity Association). Claiming that disarray from a building project

made housing a Chicago exhibition impossible, the Art Institute eliminated the C&V show entirely in 1957 and 1958. In its place, the Chicago Society of Artists and Mayor Richard J. Daley cosponsored an unjuried exhibition at Chicago's Navy Pier (**fig. 8**). Prizes usually awarded at the C&V show were given by a jury including Daniel Rich, Joseph Shapiro, and the artist John Walley. Chicago collector Arnold Maremont subsidized the exhibition. In 1959 the Chicago and Vicinity Show returned to the Art Institute, but by this time it had devolved from a premier showcase of Chicago artists to little more than an anachronistic curiosity.[11]

The growing internationalism of the art world in the 1950s almost certainly acted against the insistent parochialism of a Chicago show. Yet in 1948 moderates across the country had voiced concern that, despite its apparent victory, the progressive cause of modern art was still at risk. They promoted a Solomonic compromise: the best contemporary art (i.e., the contemporary art most likely to find a wide audience in the United States), they claimed, was stylistically advanced yet retained recognizably humanistic content.[12] This should have been good news indeed for Chicago's expressionists. But in the pre-McCarthy foment of the late 1940s, figurative expressionism would appear to partisans of avant-garde art as too closely aligned with reactionary forces. In the late 1940s and throughout the 1950s, The Art Institute of Chicago, like The Museum of Modern Art in New York, would stand unwaveringly behind only the most formally advanced, experimental, and abstract art, insisting that any compromise was a capitulation to isolationists and anti-Communists. A representational art, even the existentialist and ambivalent variety favored by a small coterie of Chicagoans, would have to be dismissed as counter-productive.

Not everyone agreed with the urgency of this cause. AIC's indifference to their efforts continued to spur many a young artist to heroic individual and group initiatives (*fig. 9*).[13] But others, particularly those who came of age under the patronage of the WPA, were unaccustomed to, or uneasy with, the competitiveness of the postwar era. They turned to professional organizations like the Artists League of the Midwest, and to the newly formed Chicago branch of Artists Equity Association, fraternal groups that promoted a sense of solidarity among artists which recalled, sentimentally perhaps, the idealized comforts of the New Deal. In 1950 the members of the Artists League voted to become part of Artists Equity, setting the stage for what might have been a new constellation of influence and support. Instead, Artists Equity's Chicago leadership chose to dissipate its energies in an almost quixotic assault on AIC policy. Although it would accomplish much of practical value for its membership over the

years, its relentlessly negative focus on AIC seems to have had exactly opposite the desired effect. By decade's end the Art Institute, for most of its long history an open forum for the airing of new ideas, was out of the advocacy business for good.[14]

Between 1959 and 1961 a succession of artist-run galleries opened and closed, as the most visible among their artists capitalized on their brief notoriety and moved on. Momentum leader Leon Golub's final departure from Chicago in 1959 was considered by many to be emblematic of a new level of discontent. The need to foster a sense of community among artists was apparent, but the consensus was that Chicago lacked the prestige of a major institution to validate new movements. Late that year a combination of circumstance and opportunity led local collector Joseph Shapiro to sponsor several young artists (Roland Ginzel, Richard Hunt, Miyoko Ito, Ellen Lanyon, John Miller, Kerig Pope, Seymour Rosofsky, and Vicci Sperry) in a venture called the Superior Street Gallery. Although Superior Street closed in September 1961, Shapiro's philanthropic appetite had been whetted for the larger project with which he would soon become associated, the movement for a Chicago museum of contemporary art.[15]

fig. 8
Navy Pier, Chicago, *1958 Chicago Artists Exhibition*, cover. Photo courtesy Museum of Contemporary Art, Chicago, Archive of Art in Chicago.

fig. 9
Meeting of artists involved in the Contemporary Art Workshop, Chicago, c. 1950. Photo courtesy Contemporary Art Workshop, Chicago.

1958 CHICAGO ARTISTS

EXHIBITION

Sponsored by
THE ART INSTITUTE
OF CHICAGO
AND
CHICAGO ART
ORGANIZATIONS
IN COOPERATION
WITH THE
HONORABLE RICHARD J. DALEY
MAYOR OF
THE CITY OF CHICAGO

FROM JUNE 14 THROUGH JUNE 29, 1958 · NORTH EXHIBITION HALL, NAVY PIER, CHICAGO, ILLINOIS

Chicago galleries map, 1966

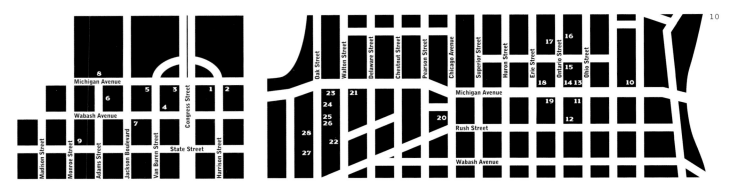

1 La Borie Gallery, 522 S. Michigan
2 Western European Gallery,
  600 S. Michigan
3 Guildhall Galleries Ltd.,
  404–06 S. Michigan
4 S. H. Mori Gallery, 83 E. Van Buren
5 Findlay Galleries, Inc., 320 S. Michigan
6 Florentine Gallery, 53 E. Adams
7 St. Benet Gallery, 300 S. Wabash
8 Art Institute of Chicago, Rental and Sales
  Gallery, Michigan at Adams
9 Galleria D'Arte, Palmer House,
  Monroe and State
10 William Findlay Gallery, 505 N. Michigan
11 Allan Frumkin Gallery, 620 N. Michigan
11 Richard Gray Gallery, 620 N. Michigan
11 K. Kazimir Gallery, 620 N. Michigan
12 Arts Club of Chicago, 109 E. Ontario

13 Devorah Sherman Gallery,
  619 N. Michigan
14 Fairweather-Hardin Gallery,
  141 E. Ontario
15 B. C. Holland Gallery, 155 E. Ontario
15 Galleria Roma, 155 E. Ontario
16 Ontario East Gallery, 235 E. Ontario
17 Goldwach Gallery, 226 E. Ontario
17 Richard Feigen Gallery, 226 E. Ontario
18 International Galleries, 645 N. Michigan
19 Main Street Gallery, 642 N. Michigan
20 Conrad Gallery, 46 E. Chicago
21 Benjamin Galleries, 900 N. Michigan
22 Royal Athena Gallery, 58 E. Walton
23 Kovler Gallery, 952 N. Michigan
24 Distelheim Galleries, 113 E. Oak
25 Frank J. Oehlschlaeger Gallery,
  107 E. Oak
26 Gilman Galleries, 103 E. Oak
27 Welna Gallery, 54 E. Oak
28 Culture's Gallery, 72 E. Oak

Others (not shown)
Center For Religious Art, 180 N. Wabash
Sergel Gallery of Original Prints,
86 E. Randolph
De Pierre Galleria, 221 N. LaSalle
Newcomb-Macklin, 400 N. State
Gallery 500d, 500 N. Dearborn

North
Gallery Mid-North, 2238 N. Lincoln
Black Door Gallery, Sedgwick

South
Contemporary Prints & Drawings,
5225 S. Harper
Fine Arts Faculty, 5211 S. Harper
Harper Galleries, 5210 S. Harper
Waller Gallery, 5300 S. Blackstone

Expectations were high on November 16, 1965, when the Adult Education Council of Chicago held a panel discussion on the topic of an educational gallery for contemporary art in Chicago. New galleries had opened, and there were two feisty young Chicago-based journals to track the progress during their short (and under-celebrated) runs: *Midwest Art Reviews and Chicago Gallery Guide* (renamed *Chicago Midwest Art*) (1965–67), and *Art Scene* (1967–69) (**fig. 10**). Local artists, aware that an effort to establish a contemporary art gallery had been underway for over a year, were anxious to hear concrete results. No longer the marginalized beatniks and bohemians of the 1950s, these artists were growing comfortable with the flexing of their collective muscle, as they had most recently in the organization of several large, group exhibitions.[16] Once ad hoc groups were incorporating as sophisticated not-for-profit foundations—the Poets and Writers in 1965 and the artists' PAC (Participating Artists of Chicago, formerly Phalanx) (**fig. 11**) soon after— and they understood the importance of their growing political and economic clout.[17]

Much of the discussion that night focused on the purpose of the proposed institution, with some arguing in favor of a kunsthalle (devoted to temporary exhibitions), and others for the greater prestige and permanence of a museum in which display would be one goal among others, such as procurement, care, and study. Not unreasonably, these issues figured into the choice of a name for the new institution, already incorporated as the Gallery of Contemporary Art. As late as spring 1966, one critic referred in print to the "institute of contemporary art," clearly agitating in favor of a name more appropriate for an organization intended to promote a cause.[18] Given their commitment to emerging art, the group might have opted for "institute" if it were not already in such prominent local use. Still, the change of name officially to Museum of Contemporary Art (MCA) in May 1966 was a curious one. Even thirty years later, it invites some reflection on the implications of this paradoxical coupling.

Chicago's new "museum" of contemporary art answered to a complicated charge. No single institution could have hoped to satisfy everyone, but the

Museum of Contemporary Art's inaugural exhibition in the fall of 1967, "Pictures to Be Read/Poetry to be Seen" was a remarkable effort. Its engaging theme provided the opportunity to juxtapose a startling variety of current approaches — from the unconventional to the idiosyncratic — and the effect was one of near seamless integration of local and broader interests. Over the next ten years, that balance would prove more elusive than expected, and the MCA struggled to define itself, its audience, and its mission. The young museum needed to demonstrate its support for an unequivocally home-grown movement, and, in 1969, artist and educator Don Baum was invited to produce a Chicago show. Several of the artists he selected had exhibited for the first time only a few years before, as part of the large group shows organized by Phalanx or by Don Baum at the Hyde Park Art Center between the early to mid-1960s. They had achieved widespread critical attention based on their resemblance to then-current Pop art idioms. The impresario of the theatrical "Don Baum Says: 'Chicago needs Famous Artists,'" installed in the museum's lower level "basement" and outfitted in a design that might best be described as an ironic spin on the Chicago-style gallery of the late 1940s (**fig. 12**), Baum began a process of identification for Chicago that was fixed definitively by his organization of the 1973 "Made in Chicago" (featuring many of the same artists), the US entry in the

Twelfth Bienal of São Paulo and an exhibition circulated throughout South America and Mexico.

"Made in Chicago" was an idea whose time had come. Baum's bold efforts to associate a spirited yet impertinent art with the character of its place of origin inspired artist and scholar Franz Schulze to retool his partisanship of the "Monster Roster" of expressionists associated with Momentum in the 1950s. Schulze, a one-time cochair of Momentum's exhibition committee, had entered the critical fray when he began writing regular reports on Chicago for *ARTnews* in September 1957. An articulate champion of Chicago's figurative expressionists, Schulze had long argued the existence of an indigenous Chicago imagery and Chicago paint technique. But for a November 1971 *ARTnews* special supplement on art in Chicago, Schulze fashioned something entirely new — a compelling saga of generations of Chicago artists, all exhibiting the aesthetic equivalent of a rare genetic flaw: a propensity towards expressionism of an introverted, spastic, apocalyptic kind. In place of the extroverted rhetoric of the 1950s, Schulze's characterization diagnosed at least three generations of Chicago artists as immersed, consciously or otherwise, in a kind of psychological malaise.[19] In the disaffected aftermath of political scandal and economic contraction, the return of a larger version of "Made in Chicago" to MCA in January 1975 (following exhibition at the National Collection of Fine Arts, Smithsonian

fig. 10
Chicago Midwest Art (formerly *Midwest Art Reviews and Chicago Gallery Guide*), Chicago Galleries Map, September 1966.

fig. 11
Al Lunak, Martin Hurtig, Roland Ginzel, Ellen Lanyon, Lawrence Salomon, and Jordon Davies at PAC's invitational show, "Reflections," at 2146 North Halsted Street, Chicago, 1967. Photo: Peter Holbrook, Redway, California.

fig. 12
Museum of Contemporary Art, Chicago, "Don Baum Says: 'Chicago Needs Famous Artists,'" 1969, "basement" installation view, including furnace, fake wood paneling, and brick wallpaper. Photo courtesy Museum of Contemporary Art, Chicago.

12

11

Institution, during October–December 1974) was very nearly triumphal.

Emerging out of twenty-five years of fits and false starts, the meaning of this belated institutional and critical validation for art in Chicago is both obvious and obscure. It is undeniable that the powerful identity forged between Chicago's veteran figure painters of the 1950s and the irreverent Imagists of the 1970s created an attractive and marketable image. For many artists, it made a career in Chicago a reality. Yet in exchange for its new notoriety, art in Chicago would no longer be figured as an actor within or upon the larger stage of world art production. Art in Chicago was isolated—reconfigured—into "Chicago Art," an idiosyncratic and insular tradition. The patina of this official history—with its deterministic diagnosis and overtones of pathology—would color the accomplishments of all artists in Chicago with more than a tinge of defensiveness, even as a polemic of "dueling" traditions (a reassertion of the refined geometricism that is Moholy-Nagy's enduring contribution) engendered a sense of identity and urgency that briefly invigorated the Chicago scene.[20] But the banner of avant-gardism would soar in other directions, thanks in part to the advent of government patronage. State and federal arts agencies established in 1965 began finally in 1972 to provide meaningful financial support for individual artists and arts organizations. New institutions, presenting organizations, and advocacy groups emerged, committed to the experimentation that had characterized art-making in the 1960s.[21] These "alternative spaces" were fundamentally different from their predecessors, in part because their new sources of revenue afforded them an unusual combination of independence and security. The more audacious among them (N.A.M.E. Gallery and its spin-off, Chicago Filmmakers, for example) were able to create an art world of their own, one that shared a language of relevancy based in the new media of film, video, performance, and installation.

The vigor of this alternative scene was also inspired by the more politicized notions of avant-gardism that emerged in Chicago during the 1960s—products of the deep divisions provoked by the struggle for civil rights and opposition to the war in Vietnam (**ʌᴇᴇ Warren and Boris, pp. 86–87, and Rago, pp. 113–114**). The indefatigable Chicago-based *New Art Examiner* has its origins in this milieu. Under founding editors Derek Guthrie and Jane Allen, the *Examiner* promised in 1973 to approach the business of art-writing with the critical and analytical tools of the cultural historian—a far cry from the formalisms then reigning in New York. Public funding for the arts encouraged greater inclusiveness, as the establishment of a variety of ethnically oriented art institutions in the early 1970s suggests.[22] In fact, government patronage brought into being a generation of Chicago artists that might otherwise never have existed. Interdisciplinary experimenters, women, ethnic minorities, even an urban underclass were exposed to possibilities and afforded opportunities that likely would have been beyond their reach. Yet this renaissance in public funding for the arts was linked, uncritically, with ambiguous schemes of urban revitalization. As one result, bureaucratic gestures in support of art's intrinsic value proved increasingly difficult to sustain.

The various programs consolidated under the Comprehensive Employment and Training Act (CETA) of 1973, are a case in point. CETA's predecessors (including the Model Cities program implemented through the Office of Economic Opportunity) had channeled funds into a succession of community-based antipoverty programs, many of which included vocational arts training for Chicago youth as early as 1965. CETA was designed to put more control over funds into the hands of local representatives. In Chicago this shift corresponded to the slow awakening of city officials to the economic impact of the arts. In 1975 a Chicago Council on the Fine Arts, first proposed in 1966, became a reality after the Mayor's Committee on Economic and Cultural Development mandated funding through a tax on local hotels designed to stimulate tourism. These same representatives, working with the Mayor's Manpower Advisory Planning Council, hit upon an ambitious plan to employ as well as train visual artists under CETA. A modest beginning (eight to ten artists employed for six months between April and September of 1975 at an hourly wage of $2.50 for the purpose of mounting a Chicago arts festival), blossomed into the allocation of over $1 million in CETA funds for Chicago arts organizations by that fall (part of $8 million used to create over 1,100 jobs in more than 100 nonprofit social and cultural agencies). Yet this validation of artists in the work force and, by extension, of art in society, was perceived as jarring by some. A sensationalized "exposé" in the *Chicago Sun-Times* towards the end of 1976 accused the city of supporting college-educated artists on the public dole. CETA funds for artists were quickly rechanneled into two separately administered tracks: an elite Artist-in-Residence program coordinated by the Chicago Council on Fine Arts, and a restricted job-training grant given directly to nonprofit organizations and functioning as an entitlement program for an underclass of the demonstrably disadvantaged. Neither art-for-art's sake nor art-for-work-relief's-sake would survive the federal budget cuts that put an end to CETA in 1981.

The precarious balancing act that Chicago artists and organizations performed in the 1970s was transformed in the 1980s, as the combination of a strong local economy and Chicago's higher national profile made it possible for an unprecedented number of artists to find a place for themselves within the social structure of the city's expanding art world. The process began in the late 1970s, when New York "discovered" Chicago and, in two essays back-to-back in the summer 1976 *Art in America*, celebrated America's Midwest as a land whose bounties included breathing space and a refreshing absence of orthodoxy.[23] Expressionisms of all persuasions were "in" as a national phenomenon, and critic Peter Schjeldahl's casual remark in the *Village Voice* referring to the "Chicagoization" of New York sent waves of excitement flowing through local establishments.[24] Outsider envy peaked in 1979, when the New York-based magazine *Art in America* sent editor Carrie Rickey to produce its semiannual survey of the state of development in the heartland. Rickey reported glowingly on Chicago's new district of "loft" galleries north of the river.[25] This new gallery district took off in the mid-1980s in response to President Ronald Reagan's "revolution," and the

success in May 1984 of the fifth Chicago International Art Exposition (**fig. 13**).

But the glamour of "Chicagoization" was short-lived. The end of the 1980s was either The End of History (when the Berlin Wall fell) or the end of the line as the art market contracted dramatically—symbolized nowhere more vividly than by the 1989 fire that destroyed the six-story complex of buildings that had once housed much of Chicago's "SuHu."[26] The gap between artistic haves and have-nots widened, and the question, alternative to what?— leveled at not-for-profit spaces when they seemed to be little more than farm operations for the commercial dealers in the late 1970s—acquired a new urgency. The expansion of the art market in the 1980s had enabled some nonprofits, notably Randolph Street Gallery, to refine their missions along reconstructive lines. Founded in 1979 to provide artists with exhibition space, Randolph Street Gallery was encouraged by funders to reconsider its direction and reorganize on a more corporate model. The gallery's board and the new director, Peter Taub (**fig. 14**), decided in 1986 that what Chicago needed most was not "wall space," but a self-conscious, socially conscious arena in which artists and audiences might meet as equals.[27] But performance art, popular in the 1980s as programmers learned to capitalize on its ambiguous status as a desirable yet supposedly unmarketable commodity, has provided in the 1990s a new spin on the old "alterna-

fig. 13
Chicago International Art Exposition, Vernissage party at Navy Pier, Chicago, 1984. Left to right: gallery owner Rhona Hoffman, Mayor Harold Washington, and Museum of Contemporary Art President Helyn D. Goldenberg. Photo © Bill Stamets, Chicago.

fig. 14
Peter Taub, director of Randolph Street Gallery, Chicago (1986–95), at work, 1987. Photo: Gwendolen Cates, Venice, California.

14

13

15

fig. 15
Uncomfortable Spaces:
Galleries Worth Looking For
1,1 (1992), exhibition
announcement/mailer.
Design by David Alexander.
Photo © Uncomfortable
Spaces, Chicago.

tive" notion: a loose coalition of four low-budget galleries opened with great expectations in the early 1990s, all proudly run for-profit. Known collectively as Uncomfortable Spaces (**fig. 15**), the four galleries (Beret International, Ten in One, Tough, and MWMWM) embrace fully the paradox of an art that is desirable in some measure precisely because of its willingness occasionally to tweak its audience.

Efforts to establish a critical, financial, and practical base of support have been mounted by generations of artists hoping to remain in Chicago—including some who yielded ultimately to the call of apparently greener pastures. During the 1950s, the compelling and contradictory style of figurative expressionism known today as the Chicago School effected a gradual journey from margin to center, displacing the refined products of ID design almost by default. At the same time, the Cold War imperatives which helped to launch Abstract Expressionism as an international avant-garde in 1959 reinforced broader sentiments unreceptive to figuration.[28] What would be characterized later as the "triumph" of New York School painting seemed to seal Chicago's fate as a regionalist satellite. Government funding went a long way towards leveling this playing field, but, in its own bureaucracy, public patronage mimicked rather than upset the established hierarchies of the private realm. The creation of an avant-garde "Chicago-style" in the 1970s led as much towards a tangled web of identity politics as it did towards market stability. Yet despite years in which the polarization of Chicago's Imagists

and abstractionists seemed to be an essential component of economic and aesthetic survival, the current generation of Chicago artists is arguably a pluralistic one (*see Schulze, p. 33*).[29] Artists today speak unapologetically about their commitment to living and working in Chicago; the sentiment compels neither challenge nor justification (*see Kirshner essay*).

Still, the most important circumstances affecting the shape of art in Chicago are surprisingly unchanged. Paranoia, patriotism, and free expression continue to produce volatile episodes, as highly publicized recent events in Chicago and elsewhere attest. Current debates over federal funding, in the absence of anything like a public airing on the value of art in a complex society, follow the same reactionary logic employed in the past. And what is known as "Chicago Art" remains less than the sum of art in Chicago. Once this litany might have been grounds for self-fulfilling prophecies about the viability of Chicago's art world. But not anymore.[30] The much-heralded death of avant-gardism in the mid-1980s has given artists in Chicago some room to maneuver. More and more, the tendencies dominating contemporary practice—multiculturalism, and community-based and socially responsive forms of expression—begin to look like what has found a home in Chicago all along. Interviewed by Franz Schulze in 1988, artist and critic Harold Haydon observed poignantly that Chicagoans of his generation (the 1930s and 1940s) said, "'Let them try to match Chicago. It's not that great in New York.' And they had hopes of making [Chicago] the artistic capital of the Midwest of the nation. But, later on, they discovered that the airplane took you right over to California and ignored Chicago…"[31] In an age of global communications, by contrast, Chicago's historic strength as a city of neighborhoods is remarkably in tune with the priorities and possibilities of the present. For its artists, this could be the best of all possible worlds.

notes

1 As Serge Guilbaut has demonstrated, one result of the abandonment by the United States government of its policy of isolationism in preparation for an eventual entrance into the European war was that the defense of culture and the survival of civilization became linked in public consciousness. See Guilbaut's *How New York Stole the Idea of Modern Art: Abstract Expressionism, Freedom, and the Cold War* (Chicago: University of Chicago Press, 1983), *passim* but especially pp. 49–99. In Chicago this linkage was promoted by several war-related exhibitions and installations, including "War Art," an exhibition demonstrating a continuous development from Cubism to camouflage at the University of Chicago's Renaissance Society, and a series of "little rooms" at the Art Institute, focusing on the interrelationship of the war and the cause of modern art.

2 These included artists who had been nurtured under the protective wing of the WPA in Illinois, 1935–43. Prominent among those who exhibited at centralized locations like the Art Institute, the Palmer House Galleries, the Chicago branch gallery of the Associated American Artists, and the Chicago Public Library Art Room were George Buehr, Francis Chapin, Eleanor Coen, Margo Hoff, Max Kahn, Arthur Osver, and Joyce Trieman. Outlying organizations including The Renaissance Society at the University of Chicago, the Evanston Art Center, and the North Shore Art League in Winnetka, offered additional exposure.

3 Principal among the new studios was Baldwin Kingrey. Backed by architect Harry Weese, the gallery opened in the summer of 1947 with a show of decorative arts and furniture design in combination with fine art. Architects Edgar Bartolucci and Jack Waldheim shared a studio-gallery with photographers Gen Idaki and Riley O'Suga, and textile designer Angelo Testa. This applied-arts tendency was continued by Boyd-Britton Associates, and epitomized by Richard Koppe's 1949 design for the interior of the Well of the Sea Restaurant in Chicago's Hotel Sherman. Other outlets included Ric Riccardo's Restaurant Gallery on Rush Street, and, after 1950, artist and interior designer Marguerite Hohenberg's Gallery of Non-Objective Painting at 102 East Oak Street.

4 The politics of the situation doubtless were exacerbated by the recent recall from Prague of a touring exhibition of American art organized by the US State Department. Well-received abroad, this survey was denounced at home as Communistic propaganda. Curators at the Art Institute were well aware of these circumstances. See Marilyn Robb, "Chicago," *ARTnews* 46 (Jan. 1948), p. 39.

5 Daniel Catton Rich, "Freedom of the Brush," *Atlantic Monthly*, Feb. 1948.

6 "In a speech delivered to the House of Representatives on August 16, 1949, Dondero quoted extensively from Rich's *Atlantic Monthly* article as evidence that Rich was an encourager of "international art thugs" who were set on destroying American art and principles" (John W. Smith, "The Nervous Profession: Daniel Catton Rich and The Art Institute of Chicago, 1927–1958," *Museum Studies* 19, [1993], p. 76).

7 Chicago's new bohemia was North Michigan Avenue, pioneered beginning in 1948 by Madeline Tourtelet's Gallery Studio, the reopened Benjamin Galleries, and the Esquire Theater's Gallery of Advanced Photography. The first two would close within a year, succeeded by the Frank J. Oehlschlaeger Studio (Oehlschlaeger had been director of Marshall Field's picture gallery) and later Elizabeth Nelson (taking over the exhibition schedule of the closing Associated American Artists Gallery). In 1949 Hyde Park got a

taste of the avant-garde when two of its newest galleries, Mary Louise Womer's Little Gallery and the Bordelon Gallery, became regular outlets for Momentum. In 1951 Chicago's venerable Arts Club (f. 1916) reopened again as an exciting venue for contemporary European art on the city's North Side. The Stevens-Gross Gallery and Werner's Bookstore Gallery both opened the same year. Between 1952 and 1953, Main Street Bookstore Gallery at 642 North Michigan began to integrate young, local artists into its schedule; Newman Brown opened at 15 East Grand (and reopened two years later with a huge space at 660–678 North Wabash); Stuart Brent opened his Seven Stairs Gallery; and Allan Frumkin and Sydney Rafilson opened "New York-type" galleries (white walls, painting only). The following year several others opened in quick succession: the House of Arts, the Frank Ryan Gallery, Ken Studios, La Boutique Fantasque, Holmes' Studio (closed almost immediately, but its artists joined the new Lantern Gallery), Charles Feingarten, Avant Arts, Kerrigan-Hendricks, Wells Design, Robert North Designs, Fairweather-Garnett in Evanston (later moved to Chicago as Fairweather-Hardin Gallery), Myrtle Todes Gallery in Highland Park, and Leonard Linn in Winnetka.

8 The Magnificent Mile Art Festival sponsored by the North Michigan Avenue Association, the 57th Street Art Fair organized by a community group, the Old Town Triangle Association's Old Town Holiday Fair, and the Avenue of Art sponsored by the North Shore Art League with the Highland Park Chamber of Commerce. This paradigm continues today in the hugely popular, multimedia annual Around the Coyote, begun in Chicago's gentrifying Bucktown-Wicker Park neighborhood in 1990.

9 These included initially private programs such as Mies's new campus for the Illinois Institute of Technology, the expansion of Michael Reese (then the largest private hospital in Chicago), and the Lake Meadows, Prairie Shores, and South Commons housing complexes. Eventually, the city would contribute additional funds, for public schools, parks, housing, and later, for the Stevenson Expressway extension. The most celebrated, if not the largest, urban-renewal program in the United States took place in Hyde Park-Kenwood, the home of the University of Chicago. There, a huge undertaking requiring city, federal, and local resources on an unprecedented scale, resulted in the completion of basic planning by 1955, and in the investment of $24 billion in public funds (and millions in institutional and private funds) within five years.

10 A. James Speyer, a Mies-trained architect, teacher, and collector, began reporting on art in Chicago for *ARTnews* in September 1955. Reviewing works by Italian painter Guido La Regina at the Myrtle Todes Gallery, Speyer noted, "It is difficult to have looked at this work in a gallery which emphasizes furniture and fashionable accessories and fits painting between home furnishings. The paintings were superior to the competitive paraphernalia, and yet they were disturbingly too comfortable there...." Speyer's comments take on added significance when one considers his future impact as curator of twentieth-century painting and sculpture at the Art Institute, a post to which he was appointed in 1961.

11 The Annual Exhibition by Artists of Chicago and Vicinity limped on into the 1960s and 1970s, instigating some artistic agitation in 1964 (cf. n. 17) and briefly igniting controversy in 1967, when a painting in which some sexual acts were depicted was first declared the top prize-winner by the show's judges, and then rejected by AIC for inclusion in the

actual exhibition. At the same time, a construction by Roy Schnackenberg was included only after modification by the artist, in compliance with AIC's specific request that the depiction of an American flag (which covered a life-size pair of lovers) be altered by removal of the bunting's characteristic stars. (The public censure anticipated but narrowly avoided by AIC in 1967 would descend with a vengeance in the late 1980s, when first a controversial depiction of Chicago's late Mayor Harold Washington and then a provocative installation involving an actual American flag prompted a paroxysm of outraged opinion and even more outrageous behavior. Ultimately, however, debate has focused, rightly, on the issue of censorship.) It was decided in the 1980s that the C&V show would no longer be held at the Art Institute itself. In 1990, the show's final installment to date, the renamed Chicago Show opened at the Chicago Public Library Cultural Center. Much like the reviled Navy Pier Show of the late 1950s, the 1990 edition was riddled by controversial decisions over who and what would be included—a sound and fury signifying nothing, to gauge by the indifferent public response.

12 Howard Devree, "Forces of Reaction: Outside Attacks on Modern Movements Bolstered by the Work of Extremists," *The New York Times*, Jan. 18, 1948, sec. 2. Devree's article mentions AIC's 1947–48 American annual by name.

13 In 1950 artists John Alquith, Cosmo Compoli, Ray Fink, Leon Golub, and John Kearney opened the Contemporary Art Workshop—a gallery, workshop, and studio for emerging artists. In 1953 Roland Ginzel, Ellen Lanyon, Arthur Levine, Aaron Roseman, and Janet Ruthenberg founded the Graphic Art Workshop, a nonprofit printmaking studio. Artists Eugene Bennett and John Miller began to manage the new 414 Art Workshop Gallery that same year.

14 A crusader for modern art since 1927, Daniel Rich was battle-wearied on several fronts by the late 1950s—his administrative duties overwhelming the curatorial, and his board of trustees less and less supportive of his programs. He resigned his position in 1958 to become director of the Worcester Art Museum in Massachusetts. Katharine Kuh left the following year, moving to New York to became an independent curator and art correspondent for the *Saturday Review.*

15 Shapiro's involvement with the founding of the Museum of Contemporary Art is well known. Drawn into the circle promoting the idea of a new museum in 1964, Shapiro was instrumental in securing the building on East Ontario Street where the museum opened in 1967. He served as its president until 1974.

16 A pseudonymous Virginia Redheart challenged her fellow artists through a privately distributed artists' newsletter to demand their fair share of the income they generated for others, not only through the sale of their works but through their participation in high-profile exhibitions and events.

17 Two shows in the spring of 1964, "Seven and Up" at DePaul's downtown campus (inspired by the Art Institute's stipulation that no works larger than seven feet could be submitted to the C&V show), and a survey, "The Sunken City Rises," at IIT's Herman Hall, led to the institution of an annual autumn salon the following four years: "Eye on Chicago," "Phalanx 3," "Phalanx 4," and "Phalanx 5," all at IIT. Following their incorporation as PAC, the 150 artist-members formed a fundraising group (Friends of PAC), that enabled them to lease exhibition space at 2146 North Halsted. PAC mounted a dozen exhibitions and film programs on Halsted and elsewhere before losing their gallery to urban renewal. Meanwhile, a tradition of large, juried shows was ending at the Hyde Park Art Center which, chased by urban renewal, had landed recently at 5236 South Blackstone. Director of Exhibitions Don Baum celebrated the center's new home with the retrospective "Hyde Park Art—Past and Present" in 1962. Within a few years Baum would put HPAC on the map, with a series on Chicago art and artists (1964–65) and large thematic group shows in 1965–66. Experimental film found outlets, under the direction of John Heinz at HPAC, and as part of the Phalanx exhibitions as well. Camille Cook began organizing film programs for the Society of Typographic Arts, a group long known for its unusual exhibitions at the Normandy House Restaurant; she went on to found the Film Center at SAIC in 1972 (cf. n. 21).

18 Franz Schulze, "Report from Chicago," *Art in America*, Mar.–Apr. 1966, p. 121.

19 This essay turned out to be a foreshadow of the fully fleshed historical theory Schulze presented in *Fantastic Images*, in which the notion of ephemeral allegiances and shared influences—all unique to Chicago—again dominated. The impact of these assertions was reinforced by the critic Max Kozloff in "Inwardness: Chicago Art Since 1945" (a less celebratory evaluation of the Chicago neurosis than Schulze's), in the October 1972 issue of *Artforum.*

20 The controversy emerged publicly in the summer of 1974 when a Chicago painter, Frank Pannier, raised his voice against conventional wisdom to argue in the *New Art Examiner* that an alternative existed to the Chicago tradition with ties to both Cubism (through SAIC instructor Paul Wieghardt) and to the Bauhaus. Later, when the MCA hosted the larger version of "Made in Chicago," a contingent of local abstractionists and their advocates responded with a countersalon, "The Other Tradition," that ran concurrently at Michael Wyman Gallery. The MCA mounted its own survey of abstract art in 1976, a striking amalgamation of Bauhaus-derived and more eccentric forms of abstraction that had emerged in Chicago (especially in art by women) during the 1970s. Unfortunately, this failed to appease partisans, many of whom felt Chicago's "true" abstract artists had been slighted. The suspicion that their efforts as abstract artists were destined for a regionalist ghetto seemed confirmed. The ensuing dispute has proved more burden than blessing—for artists more prescriptive than descriptive, and for critics and art historians more demanding of daring rhetorical gymnastics.

21 For a history of alternative spaces, see Lynne Warren, *Alternative Spaces: A History in Chicago* (Chicago: Museum of Contemporary Art, 1984). Significant changes occurred in local art schools and departments of art during the same period. SAIC underwent a painful transformation in the mid-1960s from a declining Beaux-Arts-style academy to a more flexible and responsive program. Eventual reforms resulted in a stronger voice for faculty in school policy, the hiring of artists and teachers from outside the heretofore closed circle of the Art Institute community, and the securing of external studio space as the first stage of an ambitious building campaign. Electronics, kinetics, sound, and video all entered the curriculum in the early 1970s, and the new work found an outlet in SAIC's Wabash Transit Gallery at 218 South Wabash (1969–76). Chicago's other "academies of the new" included the University of Illinois Chicago Circle, where new media triumphed: in the studio with a redesigned program emphasizing art in the service of ideas, and in the laboratory, where physicist Dan Sandin designed and built the Image Processor, which enabled artists to manipulate special video effects.

Jack Burnham, author of *Beyond Modern Sculpture*, was an eloquent advocate of new art forms while on the faculty of Evanston's Northwestern University in the late 1960s and early 1970s. Even the University of Chicago hosted a pioneering performance art festival in 1977. Schools and universities provided a variety of public venues for new art (or new histories of art): at the University of Chicago, The David and Alfred Smart Museum and The Renaissance Society; at Northwestern University, the Mary and Leigh Block Gallery of Art; at Columbia College, The Museum of Contemporary Photography; and, at SAIC, the Film Center and the Video Data Bank.

22 New institutions that opened in the early 1970s to serve a diversified public include the Ukrainian National Museum, the Ukrainian Institute of Modern Art, the Balzekas Museum of Lithuanian Culture, the Polish Museum of America, and the Spertus Museum of Judaica.

23 Peter Schjeldahl, "Letter from Chicago," pp. 52–58, and Donald B. Kuspit, "Regionalism Reconsidered," pp. 64–69; both in *Art in America* 64 (July–Aug. 1976).

24 The Chicago "effect" was enhanced by the emergence of an East Village-like scene here (Michael Leonhart, "The Art Party in Chicago: Ritual of the New Wave," *New Art Examiner*, Mar. 1981, p. 13). Within a few years this "New Wave" of Chicago expressionists would come to national attention, under the proud patrimony of earlier Chicago traditions (Dan Cameron, "A New Generation of Chicago Artists," *ARTnews*, Oct. 1984, pp. 110–116).

25 Carrie Rickey, "Chicago," *Art in America* 67 (July–Aug. 1979), pp. 47–56.

26 See Jean Fulton and Allison Gamble, "Trial by Fire: Nine Chicago Gallery Spaces Destroyed," *New Art Examiner* (June 1989), pp. 38–39.

27 Sculpture Chicago, founded in 1983 for the advocacy of public sculpture through the presentation of biennial programs, has followed Randolph Street Gallery's example, committing its considerable resources to increasingly experimental and interactive forms of public art.

28 See Eva Cockcroft, "Abstract Expressionism: Weapon of the Cold War," *Artforum* 12 (June 1974), pp. 39–41.

29 Chicago's art world has embraced most recently a variety of practices best described as Postmodernist. At the same time, it appears, from the vantage point of the present, that reconstructive approaches to Modernist practices also emerged quietly on several fronts in Chicago in the late 1970s and early 1980s. One of these was a reactivation of a poet-and-painter dialogue of long standing, through the launching in 1978 of a new magazine, *White Walls*, an investigation into words and images coedited by Buzz Spector and Reagan Upshaw. On another front is a group of artists engaged in a more private conversation, inspired by a panel discussion at N.A.M.E. Gallery on the work of feminist artist Mary Beth Edelson in 1982. Calling themselves the Artists Discussion Circle, this diverse group has sustained a lively debate over topics such as archetypal symbols, occult meanings, the moral responsibility of the artist, and the role of ritual in human development. As a group, they have created only one public work, the monumental installation *Labyrinth*, at ARC Gallery in 1985. The community-based collective Chicago Public Art Group, a multi-ethnic, multiracial artists' cooperative, continues the work begun by the muralists of the 1960s. On the city's near South Side, the ideals of the 1960s also guide the activities of the

artists of Pros Arts Studio. Pilsen also is home to The Mexican Fine Arts Center Museum, established in 1986 as a vehicle through which the Mexican community might begin to participate more fully in and contribute more visibly to the cultural life of Chicago. Elsewhere, Sapphire and Crystals, a network of black women artists, meets regularly to motivate, encourage, and organize exhibitions for its membership. And the list goes on. (See Warren and Boris essay.)

30 This difference is reflected in the more "boosterish" activities of today's artist-run advocacy organizations compared with those of the past. Two prominent examples are the Chicago Artists' Coalition (f. 1975), with its newsletter and numerous publications, a slide registry, job referral service, discounts, and endorsed health insurance plans; and the Near Northwest Arts Council, formed in 1984 to help develop a local environment conducive to the arts, and to involve artists directly in issues of gentrification and community development. The council has devoted particular effort to a project of developing cooperative housing for artists.

31 Franz Schulze and Harold Haydon, *Harold Haydon Interview: October 10, 1988*, unpublished transcript, Archives of American Art, p. 37.

Dennis Adrian

private treasures,
public spirit

Chicago's legendary collectors and patrons of the arts have received considerable attention both within and outside of the city. From the Potter Palmers who acquired the masterpieces of Impressionism and Post-Impressionism that formed the Art Institute's core of masterpieces in the early part of the century to the present-day collectors in all areas who are consistently rated among the "Top 100" in annual surveys in the art press, Chicago's collectors have been a vital force in shaping the culture of the city. In this essay, curator, critic, and teacher Dennis Adrian, himself a serious and important collector, surveys significant Modernist collections of the 1940s and 1950s and the impact they had on the developing contemporary art scene in Chicago during these decades. He looks to more recent times—the 1960s to the present—to outline the synergies among the creative activities of Chicago artists and the activities of their patrons in collecting, institution building, and promoting Chicago as a vital artistic center. LW

private collecting

in Chicago—often varied and unpredictable—has had a major impact on the city's artistic life since the beginning of the twentieth century. While the riches bestowed upon this city by The Art Institute of Chicago's legendary nineteenth- and early twentieth-century patrons are outside the focus of this essay, it is important to note that much of what they collected was acquired at a time when this material was contemporary or at least recent art, setting a precedent of adventurousness that was emulated in the postwar period and that continues to characterize Chicago collectors.

During the hiatus in activity occasioned by the Second World War, Old Establishment Chicago to some degree continued collecting (largely in the northern suburbs) with the acquisition of Impressionist and related material, mostly paintings, but with interesting deviations into Degas drawings and the like.[1] But many of these private collections were not widely seen by the public, nor were they visible during charity-organized house and collection tours, as many collections formed in Chicago proper came to be.

In the 1950s one or two major collections evinced a continuum of artistic interests from the Old Masters to the present. The collection of Leigh and Mary (Lasker) Block ranged from Jean Baptiste Siméon Chardin and Jean-Honoré Fragonard to recent Braque

fig. 1
Morton Neumann with
works by Wesselmann,
Thiebaud, Warhol, and oth-
ers in the stairwell of his
Chicago town home, 1968.
Photo: Frank Lerner,
New York.

fig. 2
Joseph and Jory Shapiro at
their home in Oak Park,
Illinois, 1968. Photo: Frank
Lerner, New York. The flavor
of Surrealism dominated the
Shapiro collection, but was
tempered with aspects of
Cubism, Futurism, the early
abstraction of Franticek
Kupka, and extended up to
Nicolas de Staël, Enrico Baj,
Morris Graves, and a diver-
sity of younger American
and European artists.

and Picasso. Other splendors in this collection included major works by van Gogh, Gris, Gauguin, Bonnard, Henri Rousseau, and Matisse. While the Block collection was not always easy to visit in situ, it was occasionally available to artists and students, and because the Blocks lent generously to many exhibitions, the nature and quality of their collection were well known. Equally impressive was the collection of Samuel and Florene (May) Marx (later Mrs. Wolfgang Schoenborn). Here were a stupendous series of early Matisses, works by Brancusi, Léger, Modigliani, and Picasso, and a group of Colima and Nayarit pre-Columbian objects. The collection of Mr. and Mrs. Nathan Cummings also bridged the gap from Impressionism to living masters of Modernism, including Picasso, Morandi, and others alongside Degas and Cézanne. Other collectors, such as Mr. and Mrs. James Alsdorf, were by the early 1950s also extending the Chicago practice of a combination of interests in older and modern things. This collection presented Renaissance bronzes, Far Eastern antiquities, and distinguished older decorative arts and furniture along with paintings by Picasso, Léger, and de Chirico, to name only a few.

Perhaps the best-known Chicago collection that coalesced in the early 1950s and that extended from what we now regard as classic Modernism up to and including very recent art is that of Mr. and Mrs. Morton G. Neumann, now the Morton G. Neumann Family Collection (**fig. 1**). At first their collection had focused in the areas of rare books and Huguenot and eighteenth-century English silver.

Contact with major Modernist dealers such as Pierre Loeb, Curt Valentin, and Pierre Matisse, along with trips to Europe and New York, stimulated in the Neumanns an energetic interest in and appreciation of modern art. By the end of the 1950s, the Neumanns' remarkable collection ranged from major early Cubist and later Picassos through Dada, Surrealism (especially Miró), with stops at Constructivism (Mondrian), and Futurism (Severini, Balla, Duchamp-Villon), to Kandinsky, Léger, Ernst, Arp, Magritte, and Matta, on to Rothko, Kline, and Rauschenberg, and forward to the various directions of the 1960s through the 1980s.[2] Also, carrying on a direction first dramatically charted by the Chicago collector Maurice Culberg in an assemblage of more than sixty works by Dubuffet before the collector's death in 1951, the Neumanns put together a fierce group of early Dubuffets.

The Neumann collection, formed out of personal contacts with artists by the open and engaging personalities of Morton, Rose, and their sons, Arthur and Hubert, presented a vivid continuity of many of the major threads of modern and contemporary art in Europe and America. A tour of the collection generated unforgettable exhilaration, and the Neumanns' hospitality to countless visitors is legendary. This openness, shared by many other major Chicago collectors, is an extremely important factor in the evolution of artistic understanding and production in Chicago.

An equally exciting artistic variety and interaction existed in the collection of Mr. and Mrs. Joseph Randall Shapiro (**fig. 2**). There the themes of

2

1

3

fig. 3
Claire Zeisler at her Lake
Shore Drive residence in
Chicago with African cap
and necklace, gourd box
from the Cameroons, and
paintings by Victor Brauner,
Paul Klee, and Max Ernst,
1981. Photo: Alexas Urba,
Chicago, courtesy Joan
Binkley, Lake Bluff, Illinois.
At its height, the Zeisler
collection contained impor-
tant sculptures, paintings,
and other works by Nevelson,
Calder, Brauner, Ernst, Kline,
Miró, Albers, Rauschenberg,
Bridget Riley, William
Wiley, Jenny Holzer, and of
Chicago artists, Westermann,
Lostutter, and Nutt.

classic Modernism (Chagall, Dubuffet, Bacon, Giacometti, Ernst, Klee, Miró, Balthus, Tanguy, Magritte, Gorky) intermingled with works by Maryan, H.C. Westermann (**plates 31, 33, 35, and 36**), Don Baum (**plates 58 and 107**), and Richard Hunt (**plates 29 and 38**). For many of these latter artists, Joseph Shapiro's patronage was among their earliest encouragements and was an important impetus in their careers.[3]

In addition to the collection, the hospitality of the Shapiro home was unequaled; for generations the Shapiros welcomed artists, scholars, students, and collectors from around the world for evenings of discussion, analysis, and recollection. This inviting spirit very likely did more over a longer period to encourage and support modern artistic activity after 1950 in Chicago than any other single factor. Although Jory Shapiro died in 1993, still today, Joseph Shapiro fascinates his visitors with his irrepressible enthusiasm for art in all its manifestations.

The Shapiros, like many other Chicago collectors of the first rank, were and remain generous in their benefactions to museums and other cultural institutions, public and private. There is not a single museum, university, cultural center, or other artistic institution in the Chicago area that has not benefited in some way, usually materially and directly, from the Shapiros' extraordinary supportive involvement. Some of their methods were ingenious: the Shapiros established a system whereby University of Chicago students could lease first-rate graphic works by major artists. This program provided the opportunity to learn about art by living with it—an experience

essential to any deep or enduring involvement with the field. It also planted the notion of the benefits of collecting and the responsibility of making one's holdings available to others. Many artists and collectors found a Shapiro loan to be a catalyst in their cultural development.[4]

Another enduring manifestation of the Shapiros' dedication to the artistic life of Chicago was their participation in the creation of a modern art museum for the city: Joseph Shapiro became the prime founder and first president of the Museum of Contemporary Art (MCA). He has continued to enlist the involvement of numerous other benefactors and has also continued to champion MCA's responsive engagement with the artistic production of its own locale, as well as with the international art world.

The extraordinary development of Chicago's private collections during the 1950s has special significance as well in the example of Muriel Kallis Newman (Mrs. Jay Steinberg and later Mrs. Albert Newman). Her own training as an artist led Muriel Newman to Abstract Expressionism in its first great flowering around 1950. Becoming a friend and patron of many practitioners of Abstract Expressionism, she came to acquire major works. Muriel Newman's collection was the product of her own special and rare qualifications: her considerable intelligence, shrewdness, and wit, along with her art training made her an intimate participant in the New York avant-garde during one of its most consequential phases. With the possible exception of Katharine Kuh, the curator of painting and sculpture at The Art Institute of Chicago (AIC) in the 1950s, there was probably no one else in Chicago with the degree of acuity of Muriel Newman.[5]

The other figure of comparable interest during this period and until her death in 1992 was Claire Zeisler (Mrs. Ernest Zeisler). Whereas Muriel Newman had moved from artist to collector, Claire Zeisler's progression was in the opposite direction. She began as a collector in the 1930s, and by the end of the 1960s had become an artist of international stature and influence in fiber sculpture, a field that in many ways she invented (**plate 65**). Still, she never abandoned her idiosyncratic and remarkable collecting practice. She had gathered important Modernist works by Burri, Klee, Picasso, Moore, Gleizes, and others when such interests were not common. She then moved into Native American tribal art, especially baskets; African and Oceanic objects; Chinese, Egyptian, Etruscan, and Greek antiquities; Mayan shell carvings; ropes of coral and amber; and an indescribable variety of other fascinatingly beautiful and rare things (**fig. 3**).

Being an artist, Claire Zeisler understood the importance of making her collection available. The experience of the visitor was significant not only because of the quality and diversity of the collection, but for the way in which Mrs. Zeisler lived with her things. The environment was aesthetically charged and emotionally satisfying. Instead of staging a theatrical display, Mrs. Zeisler succeeded in arranging her home so that the artworks reverberated with one another on many levels—formally, coloristically, materially, emotionally, artistically, and spiritually. Perhaps only the dense Oceanic and Northwest Coast American tribal art installations at The Field Museum of Natural History during the 1950s even paralleled the intensely exciting ambiance experienced in viewing the Zeisler collection in its compelling setting.

Another highly personal accumulation of modern art during the 1950s, a collection ranging from Forest Bess, Stanley Spencer, and Kurt Seligman to Matta and Willem de Kooning, was put together by the advertising executive Earle Ludgin and his wife, Mary. Thanks to the generosity of their family, a great portion of this collection has come to benefit visitors to the Art Institute, the Museum of Contemporary Art, and The David and Alfred Smart Museum of Art, The University of Chicago.

The second half of the decade of the 1950s also saw the beginnings of other collections that shared some directions, particularly Surrealism, with the Shapiro, Neumann, Newman, and Zeisler collections: those of Mr. and Mrs. Edwin A. Bergman and Mr. and Mrs. Leonard J. Horwich (**fig. 4**).

Each of these collections developed a major emphasis within wide-ranging collecting activities. The Bergmans' unparalleled group of works by Joseph Cornell—over one hundred of them, half of which are now gifts to AIC—and the Horwiches' nearly forty Calder mobiles, sculptures, drawings, and prints—a number of which will come to MCA—constitute very significant modern art legacies in this city. Furthermore, both these and other collectors continued the policies of generosity and hospitality that were such special hallmarks of the Shapiros and Neumanns, Claire Zeisler, and that is still such a welcome feature of Muriel Newman's, Ruth Horwich's, and Lindy Bergman's personalities.

These are but a few of the most noteworthy collections of this era. Thus, by the early and mid-1950s, the Chicago art world already was home to private collections that were first-rate, intelligent, and filled with unsurpassed masterworks of modern art. Postwar prosperity and optimism infused this scene with a sense of ferment and excitement that provided a very dynamic atmosphere of involvement with art in the city. Various other interactive factors contributed to this energized climate: the develop-

fig. 4
Ellen Lanyon, *Portrait of Ruth and Leonard Horwich*, 1968. Graphite on paper, 71 1/2 x 47 1/4 in. Ruth Horwich, Chicago. Photo courtesy Museum of Contemporary Art, Chicago.

fig. 5
Kathleen Blackshear, c. late 1950s. Photo courtesy The Art Institute of Chicago, Archive, gift of Harold Allen.

5

4

ment of Abstract Expressionism in New York as
an American avant-garde could be glimpsed in AIC's
American shows, and Chicago artists were advanc-
ing their own points of view in events such as the
Momentum exhibitions (*see Schulze, p. 17, and
Jaffee, p. 56*). The Society for Contemporary
American Art (later The Society for Contemporary
Art), founded in 1940 as an AIC adjunct group,
provided means by which a skillful curator could
make acquisitions from the museum's annual
American shows. This was an important lever under
the hitherto dense indolence AIC had too often
displayed regarding opportunities to make significant acquisitions in this area.

The School of The Art Institute of Chicago
(SAIC) was experiencing an important influx of veterans which instilled a new level of maturity
and seriousness into the student body. SAIC instructors such as Kathleen Blackshear (*fig. 5*), Laura
van Papplendam, and Paul Wieghardt (and later,
others such as Whitney Halstead) reinforced an
already existing regard for Surrealism and for the
North and South American and Oceanic art in
the Field Museum as works of art and not merely
ethnographic curiosities. Such awareness gave
an important impetus to the collecting of African,
Oceanic, and pre-Columbian art in the city.[6]

The Arts Club of Chicago, in its new (1951) Mies
van der Rohe premises on East Ontario Street,
resumed the important Modernist exhibitions that
had distinguished it for many years. Among its pro-

grams was Jean Dubuffet's famous "Anticultural
Positions" lecture in 1951. Dubuffet's advocacy
of *l'art brut* precipitated interests and attitudes
already in the air among Chicago artists, and
focused greater attention upon tribal art and sowed
the seeds for the later appreciation of outsider art.[7]

Chicago in the 1950s also saw the appearance
of a new crop of serious younger art dealers.
Modernist art had had its promoters before World
War II, notably Katharine Kuh (before World
War II a dealer, later a curator at the Art Institute),
the Roulliers, and others (*see Jaffee, p. 55*),
but the war intervened and it took almost a decade
for the market to equal its earlier level. The most
interesting new dealers mixed European Modernism
(mostly Cubism and Surrealism) with younger
European, American, and Chicago artists. Some,
such as Allan Frumkin (*fig. 6*), even included
tribal arts.

This increased activity in Chicago was heightened
by developments on the national and international
art scenes. The critic Lawrence Alloway, during his
tenure as director of the Institute for Contemporary Art in London, visited Chicago in 1956 and 1957
in conjunction with preparations for a large Leon
Golub exhibition at the ICA that was mounted in
1957. He saw works by Cosmo Campoli (*plate 15*),
George Cohen (*plate 21*), Roland Ginzel (*plate
48*), Joseph Goto (*plates 18 and 27*), Theodore
Halkin (*plate 45*), Ellen Lanyon (*plate 46*),
June Leaf (*plates 22 and 28*), Evelyn Statsinger

(**plate 10**), and H. C. Westermann (**plates 31, 33, 35, and 36**) at the point when they were just beginning their careers. Alloway was one of the first internationally influential figures to see any significant representation of Chicago artists, and his sympathetic discussions of new directions in American art spread word of Chicago to England and elsewhere abroad.

A further integration of Chicago within the larger art scene took place in 1959 with the "New Images of Man" exhibition at The Museum of Modern Art in New York, curated by Peter Selz. An urbane European, Selz had received his doctorate in art history from the University of Chicago, and had written an important book about German Expressionism. His heterogeneous show in New York included works by Campoli, Golub, and Westermann alongside those of artists such as Appel, Dubuffet, Giacometti, and Richier. Although the Chicagoans fared poorly in New York's critical climate, the exhibition succeeded in positioning them within the context of an international show, thematic in character, with a serious catalogue, and held at what was the most important Modernist art venue in the world. As a result of this exhibition and the activities of the postwar generation of artists, a significant critical climate was beginning to emerge in the writings of Patrick Malone, Whitney Halstead, Franz Schulze, Peter Selz, and a few others in Chicago. This incipient critical focus on Chicago appeared in both local and national publications. The city was coming of age.

The late 1950s produced yet another wave of collectors. Among them, Lewis Manilow is an outstanding example. A young lawyer in the mid-1950s, he also was passionate about theater, music, and contemporary visual art, both locally and in New York, which he visited often. He responded to Abstract Expressionism and also to Chicago's counterpart, especially large-scale works by Leon Golub. His acquisition of Golub's huge *Reclining Youth* (1959) (**plate 40**) signaled that Chicago collectors were prepared to acquire significant Chicago works on a scale physically and financially comparable to New York. Lewis Manilow also collected an incomparable group of early Westermann sculptures, three of which, along with the Golub, are now in the collection of MCA (**plate 36**).

Lewis Manilow and his wife, Susan, have demonstrated an impressive range of collecting interests, from antique rugs and Edgar Degas to Julian Schnabel and Anselm Kiefer (**fig. 7**). His early response to figures such as Peter Saul,[8] critical to the directions of Chicago art in the 1960s and 1970s, helped define the connections among Chicago artists of several decades. One of the Manilows' special gifts has been their direct contacts with artists: an extremely fruitful period of Mark di Suvero's production in the late 1960s took place in and around Chicago, in large part due to the support and attention of Mr. Manilow.[9] His angeling of the Randolph Street Gallery during a transitional point in the mid-1980s very likely ensured its continued existence, and many other artistic associations and museums have been and continue to be aided by the Manilows' support.

fig. 8
Mr. and Mrs. Robert B. Mayer's Winnetka home with Peter Agostini's *Carousel* featured in the five-room gallery annex, c. 1968. Photo courtesy Museum of Contemporary Art, Chicago.

fig. 9
Sylvia Sleigh, *Nancy Spero,
Leon Golub and Sons
Stephen, Phillip and Paul*,
1973. Oil on canvas, 72 1/2 x
96 1/4 in. The David and
Alfred Smart Museum of
Art, The University of
Chicago, Gift of Leon Golub
and Nancy Spero. Photo:
Jerry Kobylecky, Museum
Photography, courtesy The
Smart Museum of Art,
Chicago.

fig. 10
June Leaf's passport photo,
issued in New York in 1948.
Photo courtesy June Leaf,
New York.

In the late 1950s the serious commitment to Modernism of the Nathan Cummings continued spectacularly in the vast modern and contemporary art collection of their daughter and her husband, Beatrice and Robert B. Mayer (**fig. 8**). In the late 1960s and early 1970s, the Mayers' collection of more than two thousand works of art constituted one of the major modern art resources not only in the Chicago area, but in the world.[10] These holdings were accessible quite frequently to both groups and individual scholars and artists.

The collections touched on above are by no means an exhaustive list of significant and accessible groups of modern and contemporary art in Chicago in the early 1960s, but they are perhaps the ones that played the largest roles for the longest times. Others to be mentioned, if briefly, are the collections of modern masters and Chicago artists by Mr. and Mrs. Sigmund Kunstadter, Dr. and Mrs. Irving Foreman, Mr. and Mrs. Bernard Nath, Mr. and Mrs. Walter Netsch, Mr. and Mrs. Kenneth Newberger, Mr. and Mrs. Michael Newbury; the Surrealist collection of Mr. and Mrs. Harold X. Weinstein; and the groups of works by Golub, Giacometti, Munch, and later, Jim Dine, formed by the Miesian architect Gene Summers. Mies van der Rohe's own extraordinary collection of many Schwitters collages, nearly a hundred prime Munch

graphics, more than twenty-five Klees, and small sculptures by Picasso stimulated many of the architects (George Danforth, for example) in Mies's office and classes to their own involvements with art. And it was Mies who made the first purchase of a Westermann object, a rope relief still in the possession of the architect's family. This single fact unites in yet another way the currents of international Modernism in twentieth-century art and its important manifestations by Chicago artists.

Common to the collections discussed is that they offered artists and interested others a wide and growing exposure to the major currents of modern art. On the whole, such access to collections is still easier in Chicago than in most other cities around the world. Cubism, Dada, Surrealism, Constructivism, and Abstract Expressionism could be seen in depth and variety in Chicago, and the idea of being an artist in this city was not considered a mad dream that would better be given up in favor of a remove to Europe or New York.

Such migrations did occur, and they were of powerful consequence for Chicago art. A change came in Chicago's artistic scene in the two or three years just before 1960—a change brought about by the departure of many major artists for other locations. Golub and his wife, the artist Nancy Spero (**plate 37**), followed up a period of Fulbright

9

10

11

CHICAGO AND V

fig. 11
Curator A. James Speyer checks the titling for The Art Institute of Chicago's "74th Annual Exhibition by Artists of Chicago and Vicinity," 1973. The painting is *The Twelve Zloty Balthus Commemorative* by Roy Schnackenberg, a $1,000 award winner. Photo: Mike Budrys, courtesy *Chicago Tribune*.

residence in Italy in the late 1950s by a long residence in Paris before settling in New York (**fig. 9**); June Leaf, also in Europe on a Fulbright in 1958, settled in New York into a new marriage in 1960 (**fig. 10**). Westermann's marriage in 1959 to the artist Joanna Beall led before long to their departure for California before they ultimately settled in Connecticut. Robert Barnes left for New York in the late 1950s, went to England (on a Fulbright) and the continent, settling finally in Bloomington, Indiana. And the Wells Street group—John Chamberlain, Judith Dolnick, Anne Mattingly, Robert Natkin (**plate 32**), Stanley Sourelis, Don Vlack, and Gerald Van De Wilde—having been priced out of their Old Town neighborhood, all left for New York by 1959. There was a kind of pause around 1960 in the level and variety of activity in the art scene and it was several years before the nature of ensuing developments began to be seen.

During this pause, however, a significant change occurred at The Art Institute of Chicago. In 1961 A. James Speyer became curator of twentieth-century art, bringing to AIC the assets of his training and association with Mies van der Rohe as an architect, his activities as a collector, his relative youth, and a wide experience of the European and American art worlds (**fig. 11**). Unlike Mrs. Kuh, he had few administrative responsibilities outside his own department. This staff change helped bring about a change in AIC's relationship with its community of artists: despite a number of ingenious strategies devised under Mrs. Kuh, AIC was revealed as inadequate to the task of accommodating the emerging art scene and found itself reviled for its best intentions and efforts. Acquaintances with artists in Chicago and elsewhere allowed Speyer to enlarge and improve relationships, and his annual American shows and the reformed Annual Exhibition by Artists of Chicago and Vicinity meant the Art Institute in the 1960s and 1970s usually mounted at least two major contemporary exhibitions in a season.

A new burst of energy emerged from an unexpected source: an ongoing series of exhibitions beginning in 1962 at the Hyde Park Art Center (HPAC) under the direction of the artist and teacher Don Baum. Established in 1939, HPAC had a history of

serving its community, the University of Chicago area, principally Kenwood and Hyde Park, on Chicago's South Side. With the support, involvement, and administrative assistance of collectors such as the Leonard Horwiches and Mr. and Mrs. Michael Braude, HPAC became an increasingly lively venue for events and activities that shaped art in Chicago during the decade of the 1960s and beyond. Indeed, the artists who were emerging at HPAC at this time would set the pace and form the centerpieces of collections, and for the first time in Chicago's collecting history, continue to be the cores of collections for which the primary focus was the local production.

Don Baum's genius (apart from his eminence as an artist) was and is in creating dynamic synergies by locating the right personalities—artists, critics, scholars, students, collectors, curators—with something to contribute to his entrepreneurial but disinterested concept, and then letting them make active contributions of ideas. Baum's role is not exactly that of curator or scholar whose exhibitions are usually manifestations of a series of ideas and concerns worked out in advance. His achievements have something of the unanticipated outcome of collaboration. Also, while all of Baum's projects are serious, they often are also very good-natured, with a sense of fun and discovery. Against the ponderous fatuity that was beginning fatally to infect the climate of art criticism in the 1960s, Baum's down-to-earth spirit was and is energizing and refreshing. Baum's

exhibitions (very often with artist participation
in the design and installation) were very lively and
dynamic. They were brightly colored and full of
works exacting in technique and larkily high-spirited
and intense in feeling.[11]

By the beginning of the 1970s, the exciting
developments at the Hyde Park Art Center were defining a new artistic spirit: indeed several new
directions had emerged. Signaled by HPAC's first
"Hairy Who" exhibition, what soon came to be
called "Chicago Imagism" began to unfold. What
has been often overlooked from the vantage point
of subsequent decades is that simultaneously a group
of painters and sculptors involved with biomorphic
abstraction of various kinds was developing. Many of
these artists, such as Sarah Canright, William
Conger (**plate 127**), Jordan Davies, Frank Piatek
(**plate 61**), David Sharpe (**plate 69**), and
Steven J. Urry (**plate 62**), were graduates of SAIC.
Their work occasionally echoed the directions of
their predecessors of the 1950s and early 1960s,
Miyoko Ito (**plate 42**), Ginzel, Statsinger, and
the early Kerig Pope (**plate 56**), all of whom had
been exhibited rather frequently and were actively
collected.[12] Yet while all of these latter artists still
remain in Chicago (with the exception of Ginzel;
Ito died in 1983), this direction is not well understood, perhaps because many of the younger generation who might have carried it forth soon left the

city—Canright (with her husband, the Imagist Ed
Flood) in 1972, Sharpe, Davies, and Urry all left
Chicago in the early 1970s. Unlike earlier artists
who had left yet continued to be shown and
"claimed" as Chicagoans long after their depar-
tures, different circumstances intervened with these
artists: Canright's style altered considerably, Flood
died prematurely after an abstract phase in New
York, Davies no longer paints, Sharpe moved towards
a highly personal figuration, Urry is no longer living.
While Piatek and Conger remained to produce
significant bodies of work of biomorphic abstraction,
the Imagists seemed to get the lion's share of attention, and soon dominated local collecting.

As the 1970s began, the situation with abstract
sculpture was more promising. Significant in the same
way as was the Manilow purchase of Golub's *Reclining
Youth* a decade earlier, Urry's 1968 commission to
execute a monumental outdoor sculpture for Loyola
University[13] was viewed as a sign that ambitions
taken for granted by New York artists might also
enjoy acceptance in Chicago. The new optimism on
the sculpture scene was a product of several factors, but the effect of Mark di Suvero's presence in
the city (1963 and 1968–69) cannot be overesti-
mated (**fig. 12**). His works could be seen at the Lo
Giudice Gallery on East Ohio Street, and one could
even participate in his projects in progress south of
the city at a location provided by Lewis Manilow.[14]

The assistance of the Manilows and other collectors such as the Bergmans in obtaining access to industrial equipment, transport, tools, and materials, especially aluminum and scrap steel, had benefits not only for di Suvero but also for Urry, John Henry (**plate 110**), and other sculptors who set up a foundry on North Halsted Street not far from Richard Hunt's former CTA power substation studio on Lill Street. Another factor was that the city itself was beginning to revive its municipal sculpture tradition, largely dormant since World War II.[15] Sculptures by Picasso, Chagall, Miró, Moore, and Tony Smith—all installed to considerable public dismay in the late 1960s and early 1970s—were soon to become familiar landmarks, and were joined by works by Henry, Hunt, Jerry Peart (**plate 82**), Tom Scarff, and others who have continued fruitful careers in Chicago to the present day.[16]

With a whole new generation reared on the international, national, and local developments in contemporary art being presented at the Art Institute, The Renaissance Society at the University of Chicago, The David and Alfred Smart Museum, the Arts Club, and, after 1961 the DuSable Museum, after 1967 the Museum of Contemporary Art, after 1980 The Mary and Leigh Block Gallery at Northwestern University in Evanston, among other venues, many responded to the interest and quality of the various aspects of Chicago Imagism and significant collections of this material began to be formed in the 1970s. Rolf Achilles, Ani and Ali Afshar, Mr. and Mrs. Larry Aronson, Robert

Bergman, Albert Bildner, Dr. and Mrs. Peter Broido, Mr. and Mrs. Henry Buchbinder, Dr. and Mrs. Peter Dallos, James Faulkner and John Jones, Tricia Johns and Kenneth Northcott, Dr. and Mrs. Jim Jones, Mr. and Mrs. Alan Koppel, William Plummer, Mr. and Mrs. Gerald Silberman, Dr. and Mrs. Orrin Scheff, Loretta Thurm, Wilbur and Linda Tuggle, Mr. and Mrs. Howard Tullman, and a great many others made important acquisitions from the local production. While the collecting interests of this new generation were diverse as were those of their predecessors in the earlier decades, several important collections served to span the 1950s and 1960s into the 1970s: the Bergmans, Neumanns, Manilows, Shapiros, Newmans, Braudes, Mrs. Zeisler, Mayers, Horwiches, and William J. Hokin (of a younger generation, but who had begun collecting in his teens) all combined the second wave of Chicago art not only with their earlier Chicago holdings, but also with a wide representation of various American and international Modernism, classic and recent. The support offered by this generation of collectors also allowed the second wave of Chicago artists to make significant careers while based in Chicago, and allowed as well a whole new generation of dealers whose primary focus was Chicago art, including Phyllis Kind, Sonia Zaks, Marianne Deson, Walter Kelly, Nancy Lurie, Zolla/Lieberman, and others, many of whom continue to the present day.

With the 1980s came another cycle in Chicago's collecting history. Perhaps responding to the opportunities presented by the hot market economy of the later 1970s and 1980s, other collectors

fig. 13
Michael Hurson, *Portrait of Gerald Elliott*, 1980. Pastel and gouache on tracing paper, 14 x 16 5/8 in. Museum of Contemporary Art, Chicago, Gerald S. Elliott Collection. The Gerald S. Elliott Collection was bequeathed to the Museum of Contemporary Art after his death in 1994. The gift numbered 105 works, with major concentrations in Conceptual photography and the work of Bruce Nauman, Jeff Koons, Donald Judd, Sol LeWitt, and Cindy Sherman.

13

put together large and important groups of both classic Modernism and contemporary art (*see Jaffee, p. 63*). The collections of Stefan Edlis and Gael Neeson, Donna and Howard Stone, Lynn and Allen Turner, Paul and Camille Oliver-Hoffmann, Ralph and Helyn Goldenberg, Frances and Thomas Dittmer, the late Gerald S. Elliott (*fig. 13*), and a great many others were and are continuations of the greatest traditions of Chicago collecting. The high visibility of their holdings, the generosity of their loans and gifts to museums, their support of a wide variety of artistic institutions and associations, along with their active involvement with artists and scholars, are factors of the greatest importance in the artistic life of the city.

The 1970s and 1980s saw a boom in institutions as well. Of particular importance, as they demonstrated the city's commitment to local artists, were two events: the opening in 1977 of The Chicago Public Library Cultural Center (now Chicago Cultural Center) and the founding of the Percent for the Arts program in 1978 which began an organized process for commissioning, collecting, and maintaining works of art in the city and in and on its properties and buildings.

Museums, by and large, follow the paths first forged by adventurous collectors: the history of public collections in Chicago exemplifies this very well, and it is clear that over the century it has been the private figures who were in advance of the understanding and taste of the institutions. In Chicago the collectors Mr. and Mrs. Samuel W. Koffler undertook to remedy this circumstance by their active participation (*fig. 14*). The Kofflers exemplified the finest traditions of Chicago collectors—response to quality work in the city, a wide interest in all forms of art, an interest in scholarship and study, and direct contact with and support of artists, institutions, and organizations. In the 1970s they formed a collection of recent Chicago art with the sole aim of presenting it to a museum. Their selections were guided by regular consultation of artists, critics, scholars, curators, and others whom the Kofflers appointed to the advisory board of the S.W. and B.M. Koffler Foundation. This collection entered the National Museum of American Art of the Smithsonian Institution, Washington, DC, in 1979.[17] With this gift the Kofflers planted the flag of postwar Chicago artistic achievement firmly within the nation's heritage, forming a superb example of the generous spirit and actions of the best Chicago collecting traditions—traditions that both create an environment in which art can come to exist and in which it is properly valued and appreciated as a prime achievement of human culture.

fig. 14
Ellen Lanyon, *Portrait of Sam and Blanche Koffler*, c. 1964. Oil on canvas, 37 3/4 x 33 3/4 in. Blanche M. Koffler, Chicago. Photo courtesy Museum of Contemporary Art, Chicago.

notes

1 Many of AIC's most famous masterworks came into its collections prior to World War I, such as the Helen Birch Bartlett Memorial Collection with Seurat's *Sunday on the Island of La Grande Jatte* (1884–86), a group of major van Goghs, several of the greatest Toulouse-Lautrecs, a prime Blue Period Picasso, *The Old Guitarist* (1903/4), and a group of Kandinskys that Arthur Jerome Eddy had acquired from the infamous Armory Show of 1913. Old Establishment Chicago collecting in the postwar years provided AIC important groups of prints and drawings by Lautrec, Gauguin, Redon, Whistler, and Zorn, as well as many Old Master graphics and Japanese prints, setting in place the foundation of the museum's current world-class collections in these areas.

2 The extent and quality of the Neumanns' collection cannot be detailed here, but special mention should be made of their enormous holdings of huge groups of fine graphic works by artists such as Klee, Giacometti, Picasso, and Miró, as well as their paintings. The collection is featured in *The Morton G. Neumann Family Collection* (Washington, DC: National Gallery of Art, 1980).

3 For further information on the Shapiro collection, see *Selections from the Joseph Randall Shapiro Collection* (Chicago: Museum of Contemporary Art, 1969) and *An Irrational Act: Selections from the Joseph Randall Shapiro Collection*, (Chicago: The Art Institute of Chicago, 1992).

4 Joel Snyder, professor and chair, Department of Art, University of Chicago, gave an eloquent testimonial to this aspect of Joseph Shapiro's patronage, in remarks at the first annual Joseph R. Shapiro Award Dinner benefiting The David and Alfred Smart Museum of Art, October 11, 1995. He cited his experience as a benefactor of the program while he was a University of Chicago student in 1958.

5 The Muriel Kallis Newman Collection was given to The Metropolitan Museum of Art in New York in 1980, to the considerable dismay of the Chicago art community.

6 Major collections of this material, such as that of Laura and Raymond Wielgus, were amassed along with this material being integrated into such collections as Muriel Kallis Newman's and Claire Zeisler's. The combination of tribal art with Modernist works had distinguished the collections of many European Surrealist artists and critics, especially in France, as has been documented in William Rubin, ed., *"Primitivism" in 20th Century Art* (New York: The Museum of Modern Art, 1984). Curiously, considering the connections between Surrealism, already a strong presence in Chicago collections, and outsider, folk, and naive art, interest in this work did not really develop until the 1960s.

7 Indeed the intermittent presence of major artists from both New York and Europe infused additional energy into the Chicago art of the 1950s. Some, such as Franz Kline, came to jury a Momentum exhibition. Others, such as the Chilean-born Surrealist Matta, came as visiting artists to SAIC. Matta's presence in 1956 was critically influential for a number of the city's emerging artists, especially Robert Barnes, Kerig Pope, and Irving Petlin. Besides Dubuffet, Marc Chagall, Wifredo Lam, and Alberto Burri made public and private visits to the city.

8 While Saul lived and worked in Europe exclusively during the decade 1955–65, he began to show in the United States in early 1961 in both Chicago and New

York at the Allan Frumkin Gallery. Frumkin's attention had been brought to Saul by Matta, who had encountered Saul's work in Paris.

9 "Through Joe Lo Giudice, I met Mark di Suvero, who came out and spent summers on our farm [now the site of Governors State University]. We built those big pieces and I bought di Suveros. John Chamberlain came out…we had all kinds of guests, Jan van der Marck, the young and the beautiful people…." Lewis Manilow, Interview with Lynne Warren, Archive of Art in Chicago, Oral History Project, Museum of Contemporary Art, Chicago, July 21, 1995.

10 See *Selections from the Collection of Mr. and Mrs. Robert B. Mayer* (Chicago: Museum of Contemporary Art, 1968). Much of the Mayer collection has been dispersed since the publication of this catalogue, however.

11 To some degree this flavor had appeared in Chicago in the works of Cohen, Statsinger, Leaf, Westermann, and others (including Baum himself), but a further and significant injection of a brash and irreverent spirit allied with an extremely knowledgeable and sophisticated artistic approach came in the works of Peter Saul (see note 8). Whether or not the high-voltage color and dynamic compositions of Saul as well as Maryan, also presented by Frumkin gallery in 1961 and acquired by many collectors, directly influenced young Chicago artists such as Paul Lamantia, Jim Nutt (who worked at Frumkin gallery), and Karl Wirsum, their works demonstrated some very provocative possibilities of what art could look like and be about.

12 Ito was part of the Superior Street group supported by Joseph Shapiro; Ginzel's *Abstract Painting* (1963) (plate 48) was one of the first works acquired by Dorie and Paul Sternberg, who went on to be major collectors of Twombly, Johns, and Marden; Statsinger was hailed in a 1954 article in *Time* magazine (April 12) as becoming "honored…among American abstractionists" and was supported by Katharine Kuh's purchases for

AIC's prints and drawings collection; and Pope was acquired early on by the Horwiches.

13 This work was *Headscape*; it was destroyed in 1970.

14 One of the results of di Suvero's time in Chicago is the monumental *For Lady Day* (1968–69), installed at the Nathan Manilow Sculpture Park at Governors State University, University Park, Illinois.

15 Much of Chicago's prewar outdoor sculpture (as differentiated from WPA-sponsored sculpture, which tended to be reliefs installed as part of the architecture of various public buildings) was realized through the Ferguson Fund of the Art Institute. The need to divert materials such as bronze to the war effort interrupted the commissions realized through this important fund.

16 For a complete listing of Chicago's public art, see Ira J. Bach and Mary Lackritz Gray, *A Guide to Chicago's Public Sculpture* (Chicago and London: The University of Chicago Press, 1983).

17 See Joshua C. Taylor, *Chicago Currents* (Washington, DC: The National Collection of Fine Arts, 1979). This collection also circulated throughout the State of Illinois in 1976; this tour was accompanied by Dennis Adrian, *Koffler Foundation Collection*, (Chicago and Springfield: Illinois Arts Council, 1976). The National Collection of Fine Arts is today known as the National Museum of American Art, one of the museums of the Smithsonian Institution.

Lynne Warren

Staci Boris

chicago: city of neighborhoods

Chicago has often been described as a "city of neighborhoods," a phrase that encapsulates both its strengths and weaknesses. Chicago's numerous ethnic neighborhoods provide stimulating, diverse environments; Chicago has also been called the most segregated city in America. In this essay the complicated issue of evolving definitions for artists and art-making is examined within the setting of Chicago as the city of neighborhoods, acknowledging both the positive and negative sides of this reality. For within the neglected topic of Chicago's art history is an arena that has been even more ignored by local chroniclers, that of art arising from impulses and histories other than those of the mainstream. Artists working in this arena have made dynamic, internationally recognized contributions; yet outside of their circles and communities, few in Chicago know of these contributions. Within the mainstream contemporary art community, the local tendencies toward humanistic content and the need for artists to take matters into their own hands to create exhibition opportunities nurtured an ethos of socially and politically aware art, which was often devalued by the New York press because it did not imitate the canons set by the New York art world. One might surmise that this experience would promote common cause among Chicago artists who labored in studios to produce art for exhibition in galleries and museums and those who worked out of social conscience to produce works that spoke to other audiences in various neighborhoods and ethnic enclaves. Yet this was not the case, and it is only recently that the achievements of these latter artists—many of them highly instructive in light of today's dialogue—are being acknowledged in Chicago. LW

chicago and

the topic of ethnicity are almost synonymous. In 1991 *National Geographic* magazine featured an article on this city under the heading: "Chicago: Welcome to the Neighborhood." Ethnic once referred to the various European groups—the Italians, Germans, Irish, Polish, Slovaks, Croats, and so on who formed the first waves of immigration and shaped Chicago politically and socially. But perhaps because of the international acclaim and scholarship afforded to that great figure in social work, Jane Addams, and her focus on community activities based within immigrant neighborhoods, the perception of Chicago by those outside often seems stuck in a time-warp—the mythic Chicago of roiling blue-collar masses, noxious stockyards, and Al Capone.[1]

Today ethnic has become a synonym for "multicultural," which indicates all peoples *other* than Europeans and is a term with great currency in the art world. A constant concern among arts professionals is to give every group its due and arrange opportunities for "neglected" groups upon the mainstream contemporary art stage.[2] This attitude ignores two important realities. Some "community-based"[3] artists—as they are often dubbed— do not want the contemporary art world as their stage. The contemporary art world may not only be too narrow, it may be shaped by theoretical or stylistic issues that obscure or distort perception of their efforts. In other words, the very nature of these artistic efforts tends to be in opposition to contemporary art practice, which historically has emphasized individuality and innovation. Of equal concern is that the well-intentioned impulse of wishing to offer exposure to "alternative" ways of working often highlights and ultimately reinforces the very hierarchies that community-based artists eschew, once again subsuming their art into a format that does not suit them well.

These ways of working may include creating public works, such as murals, but there must be no confusion between public art created within, for, and by a community that is directed by an artist (or group of artists) and other connotations of the term. Chicago is a city rich in public art, although much of it is invisible to inhabitants and visitors alike because the Picasso in the Richard J. Daley Center Plaza or the Calder in the downtown Federal Plaza is what usually springs to mind when this term is used, not murals on the walls of neighborhood centers, businesses, or other sites on the South, West, or North sides.

To make this situation even more complicated, many artists choose to work outside the mainstream contemporary art world for social, political, or ideological reasons, while producing work that could comfortably be contained by it. These artists, who often do utilize their heritages in creating their work, tend to be categorized as "community-based" merely because they oppose the established institutions and definitions of the art world.[4] Besides their important aesthetic contributions, what is frequently overlooked in their case are the influential support and distribution systems they set up.

The experience of the African-American community must begin this broad overview of contributions outside what has been the mainstream.[5] With roots deep in the Great Migration that began in 1916, this Chicago community has been a significant cultural force for the world in its blues and jazz music, and in the visual arts as well.[6] A pioneering organization is the DuSable Museum of African American History, founded in 1961 by Margaret Burroughs (**fig. 1**).

Artist, poet, and community activist, Burroughs is probably the most significant figure in the underdocumented interrelationship of art, artists, and activism in Chicago. An alumna of The School of The Art Institute of Chicago (SAIC), Burroughs forged her philosophy of art-as-weapon utilizing the ideol-

fig. 1
Margaret Burroughs. Photo courtesy DuSable Museum of African American History, Chicago.

ogy of the 1930s. She was a veteran of the campaign that resulted in the founding of the South Side Community Art Center (SSCAC) under the New Deal in 1941,[7] a moment of promise in which black and white artists worked together towards improving their situation, and from which emerged such nationally known figures as Archibald J. Motley, Jr. (**plate 8**) and Eldzier Cortor (**plate 5**). This promise was destroyed, as Barbara Jaffee has noted, by McCarthyism and the Communist witch hunts of the 1950s. Artists with interracial friendships were branded as Communist, putting to an end black and white solidarity. Burroughs worked to shift attention to a new context, founding the DuSable Museum as an intellectual extension of SSCAC.

Sculptor Marion Perkins (**plate 16**), associated with SSCAC and the founding of the DuSable Museum, was one such artist/social advocate who challenged the Western standards he felt were not relevant to the goals of the black artist — in his words, "Let us not forget that we are all in the same boat with all the Negro people piloting through the storm toward the same cherished goal — full democratic rights and first class American citizenship."[8] In a lecture he presented (c. 1960) at the first Black Artists Conference, held at Atlanta University, he proposed the renewal of links with Africa and promoted a black aesthetic based in realism that would combat and replace prevailing and crippling stereotypes of African-Americans and elevate their cultural achievements.

Chicago's black activism and the arts reached national prominence (and little local attention in the museum/gallery world of the North Side) in 1967 when members of the Organization of Black American Culture (OBAC, pronounced *obasi*, the Yoruba word for chieftain), including artist William Walker, began painting images of important leaders on a *Wall of Respect* at 43rd and Langley streets (**fig. 2**). The wall itself contained an implicit expectation for community action or response, directly illustrated by the incorporation of the poem "Calling All Black People" by LeRoi Jones (Amiri Baraka). This mural and those that followed are usually cited as the first of their kind, continuing in the heritage of the Mexican muralists[9] and the federally sponsored WPA projects of the 1930s, but motivated by the volatile political and social climate of the 1960s. This type of community-based mural painting spread from the predominantly black South Side to other working-class and ethnic neighborhoods of Chicago in 1968–70.

The example in the black community had
almost immediate impact in the now fast-growing
Latino community.[10] In 1968, a year of great
unrest in Chicago (and many other cities worldwide), artist Mario Castillo directed the painting of
the first collective youth mural in the primarily
Mexican-American neighborhood of Pilsen, an area
defined at that time by 16th Street on the north,
Ashland Avenue on the west, the Chicago River on
the south, and Lake Michigan on the east. Working with young men associated with the Neighborhood Improvement and Beautification Program
of the Chicago Committee on Urban Opportunity,
Castillo designed a mural, *Peace,* on the exterior
of the Urban Progress Center (**fig. 3**). Its aesthetic
was a fusion of pre-Columbian motifs, hippie
pop culture symbols, and anti-Vietnam War sentiment. Long incorrectly referred to as *Metafisica*,
Castillo's mural is considered the first Latino
public-art mural in the United States. Other artists
were encouraged to follow suit. What subsequently
occurred in Pilsen was a renaissance of sorts,
with constant mural production around the
neighborhood, including Castillo's next major
project, *The Wall of Brotherhood* (1969), and
murals by Ray Patlán and others on the interior

and exterior of Casa Aztlán, a community center in
Pilsen (**fig. 4**).

The year 1969 was indeed a banner one for
murals in Chicago. Fueled by the events surrounding
the 1968 Democratic Convention, rising antiwar
sentiments, and the urgency of the civil rights movement, such artists as Mitchell Caton, Eugene Eda,
Don McIlvaine, Mark Rogovin, and John Pitman
Weber, in addition to the artists already mentioned,
worked with neighborhood youths and community
members to produce a variety of murals in such
areas as Hyde Park, Lawndale, West Chicago, and
Cabrini Green. By the end of 1970, over thirty public
murals existed in Chicago.

Chicago's copious mural production captured
the attention, if only briefly, of the press and established art-world organizations.[11] Outside funding,
as well as contributions from local community organizations, became available, allowing the muralists
to increase the scale of their work.[12] William Walker
produced his enormous mural *Peace and Salvation,
Wall of Understanding* on Locust and Orleans streets
in 1970. The aforementioned artists, along with
others, including Caryl Yasko, James Yanagisawa,
Santi Isrowuthakul, and Marcos Raya, continued
the momentum, and by 1975, almost 200 walls had

been completed.[13] These and subsequent murals, the progeny of the original *Wall of Respect* and the Latino mural movement, have made Chicago the international model for contemporary muralism.[14]

While the beginning work on the pioneering murals was, from all accounts, spontaneous, organization soon followed. In 1970 John Pitman Weber and William Walker formed the Chicago Mural Group, an ethnically diverse coalition of artists, still in existence today as the Chicago Public Art Group (CPAG) (**fig. 5**). In 1972 Mark Rogovin opened the Public Art Workshop (PAW), a community art and mural center, with Lester Wickstrom, a WPA artist, in a predominantly African-American neighborhood on the West Side. The accumulation of banners, floats, street-theater props, and other political ephemera created by the members of PAW provided the impetus to establish Chicago's Peace Museum — the first US museum devoted to the promotion of peace — which Rogovin founded in 1981 (**fig. 6**).

Also inspired by the momentum and the effects of the early mural movement in Chicago, Jeff Donaldson (**plate 63**), a contributor to the *Wall of Respect*, along with other artists who had been part of the visual arts workshop of OBAC, organized the seminal African-American arts collective called AfriCobra (African Commune of Bad Relevant Artists) in 1968. Based on the principles of self-determination and social responsibility, AfriCobra brought together an eclectic group of African-American professional artists interested in giving visual expression to the goals of the Black Power movement. Members were committed to uniform aesthetic principles (such as using imagery accessible to those untrained in art) and a political agenda, more specific and defined than that of the mural painters.[15] AfriCobra promoted the interests of African-American artists nationally, forming a network of artists who exhibited (and are still exhibiting today) in New York, Houston, Boston, and

fig. 4
Exterior of Casa Aztlán, 1831 South Racine Avenue, Chicago, 1996, with murals by Marcos Raya and Salvador Vega. Photo © Cynthia Howe, Chicago, courtesy Marcos Raya, Chicago.

fig. 5
John Pitman Weber, *The Wall of Choices*, 1970, Christopher House, Chicago's North Side. Photo: John Pitman Weber, Chicago, courtesy Chicago Public Art Group.

Washington, DC, as well as in Chicago (**fig. 7**). These artists, though not exhibiting in public spaces, were concerned with using art as a tool for liberation and for reinforcing the importance of an African-American community and heritage.

This seminal organization, however, did not emerge solely "in the community." Jeff Donaldson was trained at the Institute of Design (ID) and held a professorship at Northwestern University. Ronne Hartfield in her tenure at SAIC (1974–81)[16] was a crucial conduit between the mainstream and the African-American community. A writer and activist who went on to work for Urban Gateways, Hartfield mentored the Multi-Cultural Student Organization.[17] The organization and painting instructor Emilio Cruz brought in such visiting artists as AACM musicians Muhal Richard Abrams and Fred Anderson. These contacts provided an avenue for exchange between white and black artists that had been ruptured in the 1950s, and influenced the founders of N.A.M.E. Gallery, including Othello Anderson (**plate 128**), to realize the artists' co-op as a cultural center supportive of music, dance, film, and art. Lorenzo Pace (**plate 96**), a SAIC student in the 1970s who was involved exhibiting at and curating for N.A.M.E. Gallery in the late 1970s and

early 1980s, made not only some of the city's first multimedia work—fusions of visual art, music, and performance—but some of the first work created out of an African heritage that was widely viewed by the mainstream art community (**fig. 8**). Keith Morrison, a painter and early theorist of Pan-Africanism, was also SAIC-trained and exhibited at N.A.M.E. (**plate 78**).

Other mainstream and black institutions provided a support system for the African-American arts community that emerged, invigorated by the political struggles of the mid- to late 1960s. Roosevelt University, with its arts and music programs, was an important institution for the training of black artists,[18] and Chicago State University, with its advanced degrees in African-American (as well as Hispanic) studies, provided educational and employment opportunities, as did Loop College (now Harold Washington College) and Malcolm X College—city colleges that offered training in the arts as well as faculty positions. Johnson Publications not only employed many significant black artists and designers, but collected African-American art and sponsored such shows as the annual Black Creativity festivals (begun in 1971) at the Museum of Science & Industry.

fig. 6
Mark Rogovin, 1986. Photo courtesy The Peace Museum, Chicago.

fig. 7
AfriCobra, 1970. Seated left to right: Barbara Jones-Hogu, Nelson Stevens, Jae Jarrell, Wadsworth Jarrell, Jr. Standing left to right: Gerald Williams, Sherman Beck, Napoleon Jones-Henderson, Carolyn Lawrence, Omar Lama, Jeff Donaldson, Wadsworth Jarrell. Photo: Omar Lama, courtesy Jeff Donaldson, Washington, DC.

8

9

fig. 8
Lorenzo Pace,
*Mummification Series
II with Sound*, 1980.
Performance at The School
of The Art Institute of
Chicago. Photo © Samuel
Muhammad, courtesy the
artist, Upper Montclair,
New Jersey.

fig. 9
Mexican Fine Arts Center
Museum, 1852 West 19th
Street, Chicago, 1996. Photo
courtesy Mexican Fine Arts
Center Museum.

This multifaceted development is echoed in the Latino community, illustrated by the creation of The Latino Institute in 1974 as an advocate for Chicago's Latino community.[19] In 1975 an exchange program called Movimiento Artistico Chicano (MARCH) was formed with the goal of strengthening ties with Mexican artists and increasing exhibitions and recognition of Chicanos; artists such as Mario Castillo and Jose Gonzalez, as well as art historian Victor Alejandro Sorell, were involved. The Mexican Fine Arts Center Museum was founded in 1982, and, since 1987, boasts a new facility on 19th Street in Pilsen, as well as an international profile (**fig. 9**). Several neighborhood galleries, such as the Tabula Rasa Gallery and Prospectus Art Gallery, have provided area artists from a variety of backgrounds an exhibition venue and forum. Pilsen has also been the site of an annual artists' open house for the past quarter-century. Discussions and plans for the construction of a Latin American Museum of Art in the largely Puerto Rican neighborhood of Humboldt Park (also home of the Humboldt Park Puerto Rican Institute for the Arts) have been underway for several years. The Latino Chicago Theater Company in Wicker Park and the Latino Experimental Theatre Company are two additional manifestations of these culturally specific efforts.

More recently, in the late 1980s, young "bombers"—teenage graffiti artists such as Dzine (Carlos Rolon)—who began their careers on the streets, are now able to find employment with Urban Gateways and other school-based programs to lead murals by youths at inner-city high schools such as West Town's Roberto Clemente High. Members of the loose collective Aerosoul (such as Dzine, Zorro, and Caspar), who use spraypaint as their primary medium[20] (**fig. 10**), have participated with the more traditional muralists associated with the Public Art Group, such as Olivia Gude, now the coordinator of art education for the University of Illinois at Chicago (UIC), in such projects as viaduct murals, under the sponsorship of the Puerto Rican Cultural Center and the Marwen Foundation, which reaches city youth through art-education programs.

Again SAIC played a role in the development of artists from various Latino communities. As with African-American artists, SAIC has historically attracted students from Latin America and Americans of Latino heritage. Since his appointment to the faculty in 1973, art-history professor Robert Loescher has advised and supported several generations of Latin American and Latino students who attended SAIC, prominently Arnaldo Roche Rabell (**plate 130**), Alejandro Romero (**plate 151**), and

Bibiana Suarez.[21] It is interesting to note that the first Day of the Dead exhibition to occur in a mainstream arts institution had its impetus at SAIC, inspired by visiting artist Filippe Ehrenberg. SAIC faculty member and sculptor Jim Zanzi, together with former SAIC student Clay Morrison, a collector of folk art, organized a Day of the Dead exhibition at the short-lived artists' co-op West Hubbard Gallery in 1981. Today, Day of the Dead exhibitions are an annual feature for many area galleries and museums, and many have now become familiar with this important Mexican holiday and the cultural customs it celebrates.

The *New Art Examiner* has also played an important role in supporting community-based efforts and ideas not currently significant in the mainstream art world. The magazine published Keith Morrison's "Art Criticism: A Pan-African Point of View" in 1979, as well as articles about muralism and Latino issues,[22] and regularly looked toward the larger political life of the city, as in "Which Way Will Byrne Turn?," a 1979 article that examined a number of grass-roots arts issues in light of a new mayoral administration.

Yet, even with the contributions of these institutions and the figures associated with them, the efforts and achievements of African-American and Latino artists and organizations received until recently very little attention in the mainstream contemporary art world of commercial galleries, museums, and the press in Chicago. It is somewhat inexplicable that some of Chicago's most important aesthetic contributions—the contemporary mural movement, the AfriCobra group and the philosophy of Pan-Africanism, and the contributions of the Institute of Design-trained photographers—are best known outside the city and least known here.[23] The Chicago community is just now becoming aware of the extraordinary figures it has had in its midst: in 1992 the Chicago Historical Society mounted a retrospective of Archibald J. Motley, Jr.; in 1995 the Illinois Art Gallery's exhibition and symposium "Healing Walls" examined Chicago's mural movements. One can only wonder how the Chicago arts community, its identity vis-à-vis issues of regionalism and stylistic predilections, and the dissemination of art created in Chicago, both to a larger local audience and to larger national and international audiences, may have developed had the experiences of its richly diverse artists been given the same attention accorded to, say, Imagism.

Such speculation is really intended only to introduce the notion that many recent developments in the international contemporary art world[24] deal with issues of cultural identity, cultural heritage, and cultural critique; the role of artists in society, particularly as social and political activists; and the nature of public art — all issues that have a long history in Chicago. For instance, the activity of mural-making in Chicago is now more or less institutionalized within a system that includes corporate, foundation, and government support in collaboration with agencies that often have outright social goals, such as reaching "at-risk" youth or battling gangs and graffiti.[25] Laura Weathered of the Near NorthWest Arts Council (NNWAC) (*fig. 11*) noted at the Healing Walls symposium[26] that in 1992, after many witnessed on television the race riots that resulted from the Rodney King affair, there was a surge of funding available from organizations who wanted to "make a difference." Many who might rush in to fund murals to give children an alternative to joining gangs may have little knowledge of the traditional aesthetic aims of muralists, which have more subtle political and social goals, such as community beautification, collective expression as an aid to empowerment, or the creation of culturally specific instructive "texts" for second-generation as well as immigrant populations. These issues are of great currency in the mainstream contemporary art dialogue, and few cities and arts communities offer an unbroken, almost thirty-year history in dealing with them as does Chicago.[27]

The career of leading painter and muralist and community activist Hector Duarte alone is extraordinarily instructive. Before coming to Chicago in 1985, Mexican-born Duarte worked for five years in Cuernavaca, Mexico, at the Siqueiros Mural Workshop, immersing himself in mural painting and printmaking. His large-scale Chicago murals employ the traditional compositional methods of the Mexican Master as well as symbols recognizable to the larger Latino community in order to address contemporary concerns of Latino life in the United States (*fig. 12*). Duarte has participated in over thirty-five mural projects, and, through teaching at local schools, passes on this updated art form to local youth. Fittingly, in 1988, exactly twenty years after Mario Castillo's first mural in Pilsen, Duarte collaborated with artists Roberto Valadez and Luis Montenegro on an 18th Street mural called *Peace*, continuing its predecessor's strategy of combining traditional and nontraditional elements. While still committed to art as a collective expression, Duarte also produces studio work which has been shown in numerous exhibition spaces, primarily in Chicago.

Equally instructive is the experience of the so-called "third wave" of muralists currently active in Chicago. Funding, always an obstacle for community-based projects, today includes satisfying funders who may have some "guidelines." Jon Pounds, the current director of the Chicago Public Art Group, highlights the dangers of the "teenagerization" of murals, where the professional muralist is looked upon less for his potential to create a meaningful, artistic vision and more for his role as a social worker with disadvantaged youth. Though the mentoring process is essential in continuing the mural tradition, artists appreciate the opportunity to produce works of art, either individually or collectively, outside the arena of arts education.[28]

As many artists around the country adjust to shifting expectations and categorizations by society-at-large, and struggle to reconcile their aesthetic aspirations with the new social utility placed on artworks, in Chicago there are numerous artists whose careers again are instructive. The recent phenomenon of multiculturalism has had the unfortunate effect of artists being seen first and foremost as representatives of their racial groups rather than primarily as individuals with unique visions to express, regardless of their personal philosophies of working. Chicago's African-American artists present many role models of artists working within the international contemporary art arena while mining their unique cultural heritages, from Archibald J. Motley, Jr. (*plate 8*) and Eldzier Cortor (*plate 5*) in the 1940s and 1950s, to Richard Hunt (*plates 29 and 38*) in the late 1950s to the present, to Martin

fig. 11
Banner installation by Jo Arne, 1992, for Near NorthWest Arts Council (NNWAC) on the Flat Iron Building, 1579 North Milwaukee Avenue, Chicago. Photo: Jo Arne, Chicago, courtesy NNWAC, Chicago. NNWAC was founded in 1985 by artists living in what was becoming the premier artists' neighborhood in Chicago, Wicker Park/Bucktown, and represents artist-advocate groups and neighborhood centers that are concerned with supporting artists and addressing community issues.

Puryear (*plates 119 and 125*) in the 1980s, and Kerry James Marshall (*plate 171*) in the 1990s.

At the same time, Afro-centric art, with its foundation in the tenets of AfriCobra, has numerous practitioners today in Chicago, from painter/muralist Calvin B. Jones (*plate 167*) to ceramist Marva Jolly (*plate 158*) to painter Maurice Wilson (*plate 163*). These artists feel it is important to remain physically and spiritually within their own communities and to communicate, project, and relate to their own cultures. The very act of choosing to work in this tradition implies activism, which these artists do not avoid—Jones leads community-based mural works and educational programs; Jolly mentors African-American youth in various educational programs and is a cofounder of Sapphire and Crystals, an artists' co-op for African-American women; and Yale-educated Wilson furthers his career outside a system he feels cannot adequately represent him.

Latino artists Paul Sierra (*plate 132*), Nereida García-Ferraz (*plate 142*), Arnaldo Roche Rabell (*plate 130*), and Iñigo Manglano-Ovalle (*plate 147*) also pursue international careers as artists who express in their works their unique cultural heritages—some more overtly, some less—while muralists and painters Alejandro Romero (*plate 151*) and Marcos Raya (*plate 162*) maintain close associations with their neighborhoods through community projects and activism. As definitions blur and stereotypes dissolve, neighborhood boundaries will no longer be barriers; one can hope that Chicago is entering an age wherein all of its citizens know of its rich heritage in the visual arts.

fig. 12
Recent Chicago murals by Hector Duarte include collaborations with Mariah deForest. From top to bottom: *Loteria*, 1992–94, on the Swap-O-Rama flea market at 4100 South Ashland Avenue, which is 425 feet long (detail); *Chicago Everyone's City*, 1991, on the Security Federal Savings and Loan building on Milwaukee Avenue, which displays four flags (Poland, Puerto Rico, Mexico, and the United States) to reflect the neighborhood's mixed heritage. Photos courtesy the artists, Chicago.

notes

1 The text from a biography of H.C. Westermann in the third edition of *Contemporary Artists* (Chicago and London: St. James Press, 1990) demonstrates this attitude: "Westermann was from Chicago, a curious American city set on a lake which is notable for its importance as a railroad center, its slaughter houses, its grain exchange, and its modern architecture.... Somehow all these things have helped to produce a very odd group of artists..." (p. 1024). This mythic past has recently been capitalized upon at least in the gangster area—an Al Capone museum (Capone's Chicago) complete with an animatronic Capone is a feature of the newly vitalized tourist district in River North, home to many of Chicago's galleries.

2 "Mainstream contemporary art" is defined as work created in the postwar era that has been shown in commercial galleries and arts institutions such as (in Chicago) AIC, MCA, university-associated venues such as the Renaissance Society, Smart Museum, and Block Gallery, as well as "alternative spaces" begun by artists graduated from established art schools such as SAIC or UIC who founded these galleries out of the perception that the above institutions were locking them out. In Chicago these include N.A.M.E. Gallery, Randolph Street Gallery, and the Feminist co-ops Artemisia and ARC. Some institutions function in the mainstream contemporary art world and in other arenas, notably HPAC, and more recently, the Mexican Fine Arts Center Museum, which while serving Latino artists, is also part of the international museum circuit for traveling exhibitions by major postwar artists of Mexico, Spain, and South America, such as Wifredo Lam. The mainstream contemporary art world also includes the art press, in Chicago, chiefly the *New Art Examiner*.

3 This phrase is becoming a euphemism for African-American, Latino, and Asian artists whose work is seen as being outside of the traditional aesthetic orientation of the mainstream contemporary art world. In this essay "community-based" is more strictly defined and is used only in reference to artists who describe themselves as active within their neighborhoods or communities and who use their artistic talents to organize, improve, or otherwise promote non-aesthetic aims within an aesthetic framework. In other words, a Mexican-American artist who primarily creates murals is considered a community-based artist; an easel painter who utilizes traditional Mexican aesthetic traditions and uses as his subject matter his identity as a Mexican-American is *not* considered a community-based artist.

4 For example, an increasingly voiced complaint is that many mainstream institutions program minority artists only in February and October—Black History and Hispanic Heritage months, respectively.

5 The first substantial arrival in Chicago of African-Americans from the South was in 1916 in what is now known as the Great Migration; by 1920 the African-American population exceeded 109,000, most within an area of the Near South Side called "the Metropolis" (after World War II, "Bronzeville," and now officially designated "The Black Metropolis"). By 1945, with more than 300,000 African-Americans, Chicago was the second largest black city in the United States, after New York. During 1950–60, the African-American population increased to 813,000. A November 1995 *Chicago* magazine article, "The Real Silent Majority," states that over "176,000 black households in the Chicago metropolitan area" can be defined as middle class, and that "Chicago has one of the largest populations of black homeowners in the nation" (p. 86).

6 As artist and educator Hamza Walker recently postulated at a panel discussion, "Confronting Abstract Painting in Chicago" at Thomas McCormick Works of Art, Chicago, September 17, 1995, despite the Chicago art community's historic and continuing self-belittlement, this city is capable of producing an avant-garde. In post-war Chicago it just so happened that this avant-garde was in music, namely the Association for the Advancement of Creative Music and their recording and performing arm, the Art Ensemble of Chicago. The synergies between the advanced music community and the fine-arts community is little explored, but John Corbett discusses it briefly in his essay "Sonic Shards" (p. 120).

7 It is interesting to note that in Chicago, the home of two of the greatest World's Fairs, the little-known 1940 American Negro Exposition, organized to coincide with the seventy-fifth year of emancipation, was an event around which activism (especially labor and civil rights activism) and cultural and fine-arts activities coalesced. Although primarily devoted to industrial and economic development, there were displays of African-American culture, fine arts, music, and literature. This exposition probably would not have come to fruition if not for the assistance of New Deal planners. Robert W. Rydell, *World of Fairs* (Chicago and London: University of Chicago Press, 1993), pp. 187–89.

8 Marion Perkins, *Problems of the Black Artist* (Chicago: Free Black Press, 1971), p. 3.

9 "Los Tres Grandes"—Diego Rivera, Jose Clemente Orozco, and David Alfaro Siqueiros.

10 In the 1950s Latinos formed one percent of the population of Chicago, but grew to nearly twenty percent by 1990. Specifically regarding the Mexican-American community, in 1943 federal legisla-tion, later extended to 1947, pro-vided for temporary agricultural laborers to the United States to aid the war effort in what was known as the "Mexican Bracero" pro-gram. In 1960, 56,000 Mexican immigrants resided in Chicago—a number that more than doubled during the subsequent decade; by 1990, 353,000 persons of Mexican descent were living in Chicago.

11 For examples, see Harold Haydon, "He Paints to Show Mankind's 'Dignity, Pride and Unity,'" *Chicago Sun-Times*, Dec. 13, 1970, sec. 5, p. 12; Marilynn Preston, "Chicago's Murals—Art for People's Sake," *Chicago Today Magazine*, Dec. 10, 1972, pp. 4–6; F. K. Plous, Jr., "Street Scenes: On City Stone Cries of Help—and Hope" and "A Chicago Mural Guide," *Chicago Sun-Times, Midwest Magazine*, Sept. 1, 1974, pp. 10–13; John (Pitman) Weber, "Chicago's Wall Paintings: An Artist Sounds Off," *Chicago Daily News, Panorama*, Mar. 15–16, 1975, p. 17; and Marion E. Kabaker, "The Walls of the City Blossom into a Museum of the Streets," *Chicago Tribune*, May 5, 1978, sec. 2, pp. 1–2. Though being accepted and honored by art institutions was not desired by many of these artists, muralist John Pitman Weber acknowledges the MCA's 1971 exhibition "Murals for the People" as an important occurence in the mural movement. Muralists Weber, Eda, Walker, and Caton were asked by then-President Joseph Shapiro to paint portable murals in the MCA's gallery while visitors observed and engaged the artists in conversation. This exhibition, the first to show-case muralists, provided the artists a rallying point. "[The exhibition] was actually somewhat instrumen-tal in helping to shape Chicago's movement by providing the pretext for the movement's first manifesto, 'The Artists' Statement,' which got shared around as far as the East and West Coasts." John Pitman Weber, correspondence with Lynne Warren, Mar. 22, 1995. Museum of Contemporary Art, Chicago, Archive of Art in Chicago.

12 Eva Cockcroft, John (Pitman) Weber, and John Cockcroft, *Toward a People's Art* (New York: E.P. Dutton & Co., Inc., 1977), p. 10.

13 Chicago's pioneering mural move-ment was artist-initiated and com-munity-based; it did not rely on governmental or institutional sup-port. Strong artists' groups were formed which provided training for new muralists. These characteris-tics allowed the high-quality mural production to continue to this day. For a comparison with the short-lived, but productive Summerthing program in Boston, see ibid., pp. 46–55.

14 For a larger discussion of the inter-national contemporary mural move-ment, specifically its relationship to other art forms and Chicago's significance within it, see ibid.; Alan W. Barnett, *Community Murals: The People's Art* (Philadelphia: The Art Alliance Press; New York and London: Cornwall Books, 1984); Volker Barthelmeh, *Street Murals* (New York: Alfred A. Knopf, 1982); Jacques Damase, ed., *L'Art Public, Peintures Murales Contemporaines, Peintures Populaires Traditionelles* (Caen, France: Atelier D'A, 1981); Robert Sommer, *Street Art* (New York: Links Books, 1975).

15 The emphasis was on innate and intrinsic creative components of African-American visual arts. AfriCobra artists identified these components to be "bright colors, the human figure, lost and found line, lettering and images which identified the social, economic, and political conditions of our ethnic group." AfriCobra also formulated a set of principles that empha-sized "awesome imagery, free sym-metry, 'shine' and kool-aid color in 'jam pack and jelly tight compo-sitions.'" From Amherst, Univer-sity Art Gallery, University of Massachusetts at Amherst, *AFRI-COBRA III*, text by Barbara Jones Hogu (Amherst, 1973), unpag. It is also interesting to note that this catalogue ends with a quotation from the First International Conference of Negro Writers and Artists in 1956, the same confer-ence that Marion Perkins referred to in his lecture over ten years

earlier (see note 8), which illustrates a continuum of these important ideas and goals in Chicago.

16 SAIC historically has been one of the few art schools that enrolled African-Americans. Many of the artists of the Harlem Renaissance were schooled at SAIC in the 1910s and 1920s when no other professional art training was available to them.

17 The Multi-Cultural Organization originated in 1968 as the Union of Black Students. It "opened its door" in 1972 to "students of Latino and American Indian backgrounds [and] in 1977, the organization opened its door to all students regardless of background." *Degree Catalog, 1980–81* (Chicago: The School of The Art Institute of Chicago, 1980), p. 72. SAIC also started a black studies program in the 1970s largely due to efforts by MCO members. In recent years, the MCO became Artists of Color United which as of 1995 is inactive. Other recent student groups include the Korean Student Organization, Thai Student Organization, Latino Student Organization, and LGBU (Lesbian/Gay/Bisexuals United).

18 Roosevelt's President Dr. Theodore Gross describes the university as the area's "first...self-consciously dedicated to social justice in an era [the postwar years] of educational discrimination." Roosevelt "opened their doors to the children of immigrants, minorities and the working poor." *River North News* (Chicago) 10, 18 (Jan. 27, 1996), p. 1. It is interesting to note that Roosevelt graduated many of Chicago's black politicians, including the late Mayor Harold Washington.

19 Its mission statement reads," The purpose of the Institute shall be to empower committed individuals and groups to obtain, for the Latino community, a fair share of public and private resources to improve the quality of life for the Latino community in the Chicago metropolitan area." *Latino Institute Press Packet*, 1974.

20 Chicago's discovery of "aerosol art" came roughly at the same time as New York's, in the late 1980s.

Aerosoul first showed in a fine-arts context at the Axe Street Arena (now closed) in the Logan Square neighborhood in 1988.

21 Robert Loescher was the first area art historian who specialized in Latin American and Latino art history; at SAIC he instituted courses on Precolumbian, Mexican, and Latin American art history. He has also been active curating exhibitions, such as a show at SAIC's Betty Rymer Gallery of former students who had returned to their native countries and become successful artists, and in leading student trips to Mexico, Spain, and Portugal.

22 Keith Morrison, "Art Criticism: A Pan-African Point of View," *New Art Examiner*, Feb. 1979, pp. 4–7. This article was joined by John Nunley's thoughtful examination of the issue in the April 1979 *New Art Examiner*, "Implications of the African Aesthetic Impulse for Pan-African Art" (pp. 4 and 9). An article by Holly Highfill, "MARCH (Movimiento Artistico Chicano)," *New Art Examiner*, June 1975, p. 4, appeared on the same page as Victor Sorell's review of the major exhibition "Mexposicion," a showcase of Mexico's more visible twentieth-century artists, which went virtually unnoticed by the press in Chicago. The *New Art Examiner* also has consistently written about the mural movements, including Carole Stodder's "Bill Walker: Major Mural in Progress," Dec. 1974, p. 3.

23 After the initial AfriCobra exhibitions in Chicago which took place between 1969 (WJ Studio— Wadsworth and Jae Jarrell's studio) and 1972 (Malcolm X College), AfriCobra artists have seldom been shown in the city of its inception. It is interesting to note, however, that AfriCobra members are still considered "Chicago artists," despite the fact that they have dispersed to New York, Atlanta, Boston, Amherst, Philadelphia, Baltimore, and Washington, DC. It is also important to mention for the record that Jeff Donaldson, while pursuing a PhD at Northwestern University, specializing in African-American art, organized the historical CON-

FABA conference in 1970, in which such noted African-American art scholars as Samella Lewis, David Driskell, and Barry Gaither participated. Jeff Donaldson, conversation and correspondence with Staci Boris, Dec. 1995. Museum of Contemporary Art, Chicago, Archive of Art in Chicago.

24 There is consensus in the national and international art world that something has changed. Like all gradual awakenings, this attitude shift is impossible to pinpoint as an event on a timeline. Yet such projects as Mary Jane Jacob's "Places with a Past: New Site-Specific Art at Charleston's Spoleto Festival" of 1991 and David Ross' appointment also in 1991 as director of the Whitney Museum of American Art, as well as the 1993 Whitney Biennial, were early indicators. In Chicago, Randolph Street Gallery, guided by Director Peter Taub who was appointed in 1986, was a harbinger of this new philosophy; the gallery's current slogan is "Join us at the intersections of art and society." Recent local indicators include Mary Jane Jacob's 1994 "Culture in Action" program for Sculpture Chicago (see Kirshner, p. 140); and Joyce Fernandes's 1995 "Chicago Portraits," organized for the Chicago Cultural Center, which traveled commissioned photographs of leaders of various ethnic communities to the community centers of these groups, enlarging not only the possible sources of artists' production, but potential exhibition venues for a wide variety of artists. The recent adoption of the term "cultural worker" as a synonym for artist by the *New Art Examiner*, historically a publication with a considerable political and social slant, is also worth noting.

25 A recent project of note is the Terra Museum of American Art's collaboration with the Openlands Project, an organization dedicated to maintaining and creating open space in the region; The Chicago Youth Centers, which work with economically disadvantaged youth; and the Marwen Foundation, which focuses on youth arts education, to sponsor artists Gregory Warmack

(Mr. Imagination, plate 155), David Philpot, and Kevin Orth to "reclaim" a vacant lot adjacent to the Elliott Donnelley Youth Center on south Michigan Avenue. Also significant are Ameritech's sponsorship of murals by talented high-school students; and the City of Chicago's Gallery 37, a hugely successful summer arts program aimed at elementary and high-school children which is serving as an international model. This last program earned Chicago a "Livability" award in 1994 from the US Council of Mayors.

26 "Engaging Community: Cultural Organizations and Community Development," a panel of the Healing Walls Symposium, Illinois Art Gallery, Chicago, Nov. 4, 1995. Ms. Weathered also noted that this generosity was short-lived and funding has since decreased.

27 In an October 1995 conversation with Staci Boris, Jennie Kiessling, director of Community-based Programs at SAIC (a department which was formalized in 1993 after nearly a decade of SAIC's involvement with community programs as part of the school's Division of Continuing Studies and Special Programs) pointed out the distinction between "outreach programs" that tend to be one-time efforts, and programs devised to be long-term. SAIC is currently involved in collaborations with neighborhood centers and organizations such as the Daniel S. Mellum Shelter on the South Side and the Marshall Square Boys and Girls Club in Little Village, a Mexican-American neighborhood on the Southwest Side for which ongoing enrichment programs are taught by artists. Programs range from the establishment of photography labs to writing, filmmaking, and printmaking in collaborations with artist-run organizations like Anchor Graphics. Although open and free to commu-

nity members of all ages, these classes usually face uncertain financial futures. This type of long-term collaboration in concert with mainstream institutions is intended to provide neighborhood teenagers with opportunities they may not otherwise have.

28 See note 26. On a related panel, "Representation and Appropriation: How Artists and People of Different Cultures Use Imagery and Symbolism," Marcos Raya asserted that regarding his mural production, he always "paid out of his own pocket," to avoid any threats to his vision.

Jeff Abell, editor

John Corbett

Kate Horsfield

Carmela Rago

Bill Stamets

time arts in chicago

The various genres grouped within the Chicago-coined rubric of "time arts"—experimental film, video, performance art, sound, and movement—have led a sort of outlaw existence in relation to the more traditional art forms. Because they may have been highly experimental when they first emerged, or may require expensive equipment and technology, or are collaborative in their very nature, the various time-based media have dictated a somewhat separate existence outside the mainstream.

This section is edited by Jeff Abell with additional contributions by four writers with expertise in specialized areas within the time arts. The authors explore how these media have flourished, thanks to the support of devoted artists, audiences, and institutions, while unfortunately remaining obscure to the general public and art world alike. The accomplishments of individuals and collaboratives are outlined, especially those who have achieved international recognition and those who have created technological advances and new aesthetic languages. Institutions that support the efforts of time-based artists—from video cooperatives, to film distributors, to dance and movement collaboratives, to performance spaces at artist-founded galleries, to departments within area colleges and universities—are also explored.

Of all the artistic genres, the time arts seem the most dependent on their medium as the definer of style. While any of the forms may weave in and out of the larger art history, each indeed has a history shaped by the unique demands of its medium. In an introductory essay, Abell discusses the development of Time Arts in Chicago in terms of artists' responses to politics, exhibition venues, and traditional art forms. Abell then examines the emergence of "dance-theater" in his history of movement and dance in Chicago. Bill Stamets surveys experimental and independent filmmaking and looks at the film scene in Chicago and the dedicated efforts of the city's filmmakers. Carmela Rago gives a decade-by-decade account of performance art in Chicago. John Corbett's overview of sonic art documents avant-garde activity ranging from free jazz to performance-based work. Finally, Kate Horsfield discusses the development of Chicago video from image processing to community-based and politically oriented work. LW

using the term

"time arts" in a conversation anywhere outside of Chicago is likely to draw some sort of bewildered or bemused response. (My personal favorite was, "Does that have something to do with Salvador Dali and those melting watches he painted?") The term was originally coined in the early 1970s at The School of The Art Institute of Chicago (SAIC), where it continues to be used to provide an administrative "corral" for the "broncos" of the art academy, namely, the time-based and interdisciplinary art forms that have become increasingly important over the last fifty years. The media of performance art, film, video, sound, as well as so-called multimedia (or intermedia) work that combines them with such things as sculpture and installation, may share elements in common, but can scarcely be thought of as a single, unified phenomenon.

The combination of access to necessary technology and the related change in perspective as to what constitutes a work of art brought visual artists into the realm of time arts. The increasing importance of conceptual matters in the art world over the past fifty years encouraged a sense of art as idea rather than a product of skilled handicraft. The attendant shifts of consciousness in American culture at this time, including the antiestablishment rhetoric of the 1960s and the increasingly focused cultural critique offered by Feminism, have further encouraged artists to make work that is not simply about the construction of salable objects, but instead often questions the ethics and politics of the art market. Phenomena like performance art are unthinkable without such shifts in ideology.[1]

Moreover, if we can appreciate the importance that the invention of photography had on the arts in the late nineteenth century, and the subsequent impact of motion pictures on the development of the arts in the first half of the twentieth century, then we can recognize the impact of time arts on the evolution of art since World War II. By using new technologies, and encouraging the spread and distribution of those technologies, time artists have helped shape the art world.

The proliferation and democratization of technology is one characteristic of this period. Technological advances often originate in the military sphere, an area that tends to receive consistent government support, especially in weapons and espionage development. Magnetic recording, first on metal wire and then on metallic oxides in plastic, was developed by Germany during World War II as an espionage tool. The proliferation of that technology into first recording studios (in the 1950s) and then gradually the home market (by the 1960s) greatly expanded the possibilities for artists to manipulate and use sound as part of their artistic expressions, as it simultaneously made American pop music known world-wide.

That same technology—storing magnetic signals on plastic—is basic to video as well. Although Kate Horsfield speaks of how important the invention of the first video porta-paks was to the development of independent video art (*see p. 124*), anyone who worked with them can verify those machines were hardly easy or lightweight. It would take another technological innovation, namely digital circuitry, for video to become both convenient and affordable to the general population. It is also no coincidence that in the postwar years, film cameras and equipment became simple and economical enough to enter the home market, and that so-called experimental film in America really began to take hold.

These changes have emphatically not been restricted to the better publicized coasts. Events such as the 1968 Democratic Convention, and the racial tensions that followed the assassination of Dr. Martin Luther King, Jr., helped to radicalize the local art world. Carmela Rago points out that political actions and guerrilla theater events were not uncommon in Chicago as long ago as the late 1940s (*see p. 113*). Indeed, Chicago has been in step with most of the key changes in artistic thinking during the past half-century, despite the lack of media attention from local and national publications and broadcasters.

The evolution of the time arts in Chicago can be credited both to nurturing organizations and institutions, and to strong-willed, determined individual artists. On a basic level, the real growth of the time arts in Chicago parallels the growth of the not-for-profit art scene. The Hyde Park Art Center (HPAC) was one of the first showcases for experimental or avant-garde film, as well as painting and sculpture (*see Stamets, p. 109*). N.A.M.E. (originally N.A.M.E. Gallery) was founded in the early 1970s by a group of young artists with strong Conceptualist leanings. Performance and other experimental media were among the consistent components of the gallery's programs from the beginning.[2] Similarly, the presence of two women's cooperative galleries, ARC and Artemisia, promoted the presentation of Feminist performances. The existence of nonprofit galleries, on many levels, made time-arts work possible.

The strongest model for such a synergy between organization and artistic production is probably Randolph Street Gallery. When Randolph Street moved to their Milwaukee Avenue loca-

fig. 1
Hudson performing
Sophisticated Boom Boom
at Randolph Street Gallery,
Chicago, 1984. Photo from
announcement card,
Randolph Street Gallery.

fig. 2
Karen Finley performing
Tales of Taboo at Cabaret
Metro, Chicago, 1987. Photo
© Susan Anderson, Chicago.

tion in 1982, they were the first organization with an official performance curator, Hudson[3] (**fig. 1**), and the first gallery with a dedicated performance space. For many years the gallery offered weekly programs of performance and new music, as well as experimental film and video screenings. The gallery also sponsored public art, including outdoor installations and billboard projects. In addition to bringing in a wide range of nationally known artists (from Rachel Rosenthal and John Gray to Tim Miller and Ron Athey), the gallery encouraged the wildest and most unpolished of the local artists to "do their thing." This slightly anarchistic sensibility ("grunge" before it was hip) inspired and encouraged a whole generation of local artists, including Karen Finley (**fig. 2**), who once quipped that she "wasn't cool enough" to present her work at N.A.M.E.,[4] though over the years she splashed chocolate, beet juice, and wild talk around Randolph Street.

In addition to the not-for-profit art galleries, the Museum of Contemporary Art (MCA), especially with the programming of Alene Valkanas, encouraged performance (**fig. 3**), video, and sound artists, acting as the principal sponsor of the New Music America Festival in 1982, for example. Although MoMing and The Dance Center of Columbia College focused on dance, they also provided venues for performance art, and encouraged the interaction of the dance and performance communities. The Goodman Theatre—forsaking for a moment the general hostility that seems to exist between performance artists and traditional theater people, at least in Chicago—has included the occasional blue-chip performance artist on its roster, and sometimes even local artists, such as Paula Killen, or Miroslaw Rogala (**fig. 4**).

fig. 3
The Museum of Contemporary
Art sponsored performances
by internationally recognized
figures such as Tom Marioni,
pictured here at Breens Bar in
Chicago with Phil Berkman
and then-MCA Director John
Hallmark Neff, 1981. Photo:
Tom Van Eynde, Oak Park,
Illinois.

fig. 4
Performance artists Werner
Herterich and Lynn Book in
Miroslaw Rogala's video
opera *Nature is Leaving Us* at
The Goodman Theatre,
Chicago, 1988. Photo: Joe
Ziolkowski, Chicago.

The strongest and most consistent impact on Chicago's time artists has been the local universities. As the essays here attest, the School of the Art Institute has encouraged sound,
film, video, and performance in substantial ways. But one needs also to remember that
Columbia College (especially its Interdisciplinary Arts Program), the University of Illinois at
Chicago (UIC), Northwestern University in Evanston, the University of Chicago, and even
Northern Illinois University in DeKalb have all encouraged various combinations of time
arts. Moreover, there has been a positive, synergistic exchange of students and faculty among
these institutions, resulting in a vivid intermarriage of ideas and styles.

The numerous schools in the area also provide a constant infusion of "new blood" to the
Chicago time-arts scene, as new BFA- and MFA-holders emerge each year, to participate in
the scene for a time, then go on to other places; some remain and become part of the local
scene. The Chicago "scene" remains curiously consistent over the years. The "Regulars"
(many now in their forties) have been attending experimental film screenings or performance-
art events for twenty years; supplementing them is a big crowd of constantly changing people
who always seem to be about twenty-three years old.

Chicago has also seen its fair share of collective action outside the walls of any particular
institution. Bill Stamets notes the number of film festivals the city supports, and Carmela
Rago sees community endeavor as crucial to the performance-art scene. There have also
been a certain share of "collectives" over the years, ranging from the Imperial Aces in the
early 1970s, to Horses, Inc., who in the late 1970s were actively generating large-scale environmental performances like *The Haller Family Reunion* in Grant Park, to the group SXPU
in the mid-1980s, who functioned as a slightly wacky, punked-out performance collective, to
Goat Island in the 1990s, with their commitment to collaborative group process in creating
highly charged movement theater.

The collectives, however, have typically taken a back seat to individuals in Chicago, especially in the performance community. In certain ways, the city seems to have a soft spot for the iconoclast (indeed, the city offers the curious phenomenon of a foundation to promote "outsider" art, as oxymoronic as that sounds).[5] Just as Oprah brings the injured, dysfunctional, and just plain weird to her Harpo Studios (just south of the gallery district), local galleries and performance venues have favored artists who are distinctly individualistic. As a result, one looks in vain for distinctive Chicago "trends" or "styles" that are consistent throughout the city. Considering that Laurie Anderson (**fig. 5**), Karen Finley, and Judy Tenuta all got their starts in Chicago, one begins to get a sense of how delightfully inconsistent performance is here. John Corbett's characterization of the sonic-arts scene here—"fragmentary, centerless, wildly varied"—could apply to Chicago performance as a whole.

One of the more interesting developments of the past decade has been the evolution of the cabaret revues, in which a (sometimes seemingly endless) string of performances would be shown, usually emceed by another performer, often in persona. Chief among these has probably been Millie's Orchid Show, with performer Brigid Murphy as the redoubtable Millie May Smithy, introducing acts that range from monologists to song stylists to an actress who balanced a spoon on her nose and recited Shakespeare (a recurring motif in the Orchid Shows, and an audience favorite). Similarly, Gurlene and Gurlette Hussey, a pair of wonderfully atrocious drag queens, hosted a long-running series of evenings[6] that featured local gay and lesbian performers, and developed a near-cult following in the community. They unleashed on Chicago the inimitable Joan Jett Blakk (**fig. 6**), the drag queen who gained national attention by running first for Mayor of Chicago, and then for President in 1992, and who has since gone on to host her own ongoing series of performance evenings in San Francisco.

Both the Orchid Show and the Hussey reviews helped to develop a "club scene" for local performance, which up until the late 1980s was almost exclusively tied to the art world. Lawrence Steger also encouraged that scene, presenting performances at the Metro nightclub, and developing his own persona as nightclub host (at times with a scary resemblance to Joel Grey in *Cabaret*). Key to these developments was Leigh Jones's Club Lower Links (**fig. 7**), which was "the" venue in town for many performers.

5

6

7

The tendency of local performance artists, and indeed time artists in general, to go their own way makes the process of generalization more difficult. Historical lines become unclear, as artists shift back and forth between categories, genres, and media. James Grigsby had dance and music training, became known as a performance artist, but for years taught art-educa-tion classes. Sharon Evans began as a student of art history, became a performance artist, and then opened her own theater and became a playwright. Sandra Binion developed and pre-sented a diverse range of performance, but currently works primarily in photography and film. Videographer Suzie Silver also presented a number of performance works. This list of genre-hopping individuals could be continued almost indefinitely.

Moreover, technological advances in such things as computer-interactive images, sound, lighting, and multimedia continue to be developed in Chicago. The Electronic Visualization Laboratory at UIC, that originally provided a base for Dan Sandin and the first Image Processor, continues to explore the interactions of artists and new technology. Just as the first invention of video equipment could not have predicted its proliferation today, it remains to be seen what kinds of real-time art will be made with computers in the years ahead. Chicago can be expected to be one of the leading centers in that process.

Providing a linear, definitive history of the Chicago time-arts scene would be a ridiculous, even pointless, task. As noted above, the time arts do not speak from a single point of refer-ence, but from a multiplicity of positions, delighting in the "undecidability" of their dis-course. The goal of this group of interconnected essays, then, is not to provide a singular, authoritative account of how these multiplicitous arts operate in Chicago, but rather to pro-vide an initial probing of what are for the most part uncharted waters. There are many "histories" of video, new music, experimental film, movement, or performance art in Chicago, but they exist within the memories of the people who have been the participants. This group of essays is intended to open a door to these histories.

movement and performance in chicago

Jeff Abell

The interaction of artists and dancers has led to some of the most significant collaborations in the twentieth century. Dancers, actors, musicians, and visual artists came together at New York's Judson Church in the 1960s to create some of the most innovative and provocative art-making of the decade. Some of these works are now recognized as influential examples of Postmodernism, including Yvonne Rainer's *Trio A*, a nonvirtuoso movement work that can, theoretically, be performed by anyone, and Carolee Schneemann's *Meat Joy*, a classic "happening" involving food, paper, and human bodies. The interactions of dancers (Rainer, Trisha Brown, Steve Paxton, David Gordon, and others) with visual artists (Claes Oldenburg, Robert Morris, Jim Dine) provoked the evolution of new forms and new ideas.

A similar, yet distinctive, synthesis has taken place in Chicago as well. Over the past few decades, key figures in the Chicago dance community have created a rich array of work that can be characterized as "dance theater," but might just as easily be called "performance art."[1] Some of the key individuals teaching and producing performance art in Chicago come from dance backgrounds, creating a kind of subtextual bias toward dance or movement in work created here. Because some of the individuals involved in creating movement-based performance have also been the central figures at presenting organizations and teaching institutions in the city, they have exerted an influence that is both overt and covert on a generation of artists.

Of course, since narrative—stated or implied—seems crucial to much Chicago art in all media, it should come as no surprise that the dance community has always shown an interest in narrative forms that might seem to have more in common with theater or performance art than traditional, abstract modern dance. Sixty years ago Ruth Page used dance and theater for her 1934 "ballet" *Hear Ye! Hear Ye!*, with an original score by Aaron Copland. The plot centered on a murder trial: as each witness testified, the dancers acted out the chain of events according to that witness' perceptions. Constructing

fig. 1
Scene from Tom Jaremba's performance *Orfée* at the State of Illinois Center, Chicago, as part of Performance Chicago, 1986. Pictured is performer Dani K. Photo: Jan Ballard, Chicago, courtesy Mary Brogger, Chicago.

fig. 2
Mordine & Company performing *Mahagonny Songspiel* at The Dance Center of Columbia College, Chicago, 1980. Left to right: Paula Frasz, Mary Wohl Haan, Shirley Mordine, and Jennifer Grant. Photo: Charles Osgood, Chicago, courtesy Shirley Mordine, Chicago.

fig. 3
Gundersen Clark (Bruce Gundersen and Bob Clark) performing *Radma Wad* at N.A.M.E. Gallery, Chicago, 1975–76. Photo courtesy Bruce Gundersen and Ellen Fisher, Brooklyn, New York. Gundersen Clark's intensely ritualistic performances incorporated movement in sculptural installations.

fig. 4
James Grigsby and Shirley Mordine performing *In One Year and Out the Other* at The Dance Center of Columbia College, Chicago, 1991. Photo © William Frederking, Chicago, courtesy Shirley Mordine, Chicago.

a dance to portray an elaborate story is consistent with nineteenth-century ballet, but staging the same sequence of events over and over with shifting points of reference seems to presage some of the key aspects of Postmodern performances. Page's studio continues to act as a center for teaching and performance.

In the late 1960s, two individuals essential in shaping the Chicago performance and dance scenes arrived in the city. Milwaukee-born Tom Jaremba (**fig. 1**) arrived in Chicago in 1962 to dance in Sybil Shearer's company, then moved to New York, where he worked with Alwin Nikolais and Murray Lewis. He returned in 1966 to Chicago, where he did social work for a year before being hired by The Goodman Theatre as a choreographer. It was there, in 1969, he met Shirley Mordine (**fig. 2**), originally from Northern California, who arrived here by way of Minneapolis in 1968. Over the next few years, Jaremba and Mordine became the leading figures in performance and dance, respectively, Jaremba as founder and chair of the performance department at SAIC, and Mordine as chair of the dance department and artistic director of The Dance Center of Columbia College.

It seems appropriate that these two should have known one another and worked together at the beginnings of their careers. In 1969 Jaremba participated in a work Mordine devised called *Journey*. This was a wildly progressing theatrical spectacle, which centered on four characters, and incorporated such things as Hitler's speech at the 1936 Olympics, interactive video that showed actions outside the actual performance space, and twenty people on stilts at a climactic moment in the piece. At one of

the performances, a man wandered onto the stage and began interacting with the dancers in "provocative" ways. By the time police arrived, the man could not be found, and the police found themselves onstage, arguing with audience members over whether the man was part of the performance or not. In the audience that night were two individuals who were to play important parts in the Chicago scene in the coming decades: Jim Self and Nana Shineflug.

Although Mordine and Jaremba did subsequently perform in a duet called *Double Play*, by the early 1970s their careers had taken very different directions. A number of the dancers in *Journey* became part of Mordine's first company, the Chicago Dance Troupe. It was through one of the Dance Troupe members, Donna Sugarman, that Columbia College would acquire the Dance Center on North Sheridan Road in 1972. Jaremba began teaching full-time at SAIC in 1971, where he helped to shape the curriculum of the school; he continues to teach performance today. The Dance Center provided Mordine with a base of operations for her work. Jaremba developed his studio, Lodge Hall, in the heart of the vital artists' enclave Wicker Park, as a space to present his own work and that of such important early performance artists as Gundersen Clark (**fig. 3**), Ellen Fisher, Jean Sousa, and others.

Jaremba continued to move in a "theatrical" direction. Inspired by Nikolais and the continuing impetus of improvisational theater in Chicago, he evolved a theater company called The Fourth Force, with Ted Serantos as codirector. Jaremba also pushed a connection between dance and theater by

fig. 5
Jim Self performing *More of the Same in a Different Place* at MoMing, Chicago, 1975. Photo: Richard Pearlman, Chicago, courtesy Bob Eisen, Chicago.

fig. 6
Bob Eisen, Carol Bobrow, and Charlie Vernon in front of Links Hall, Chicago, 1979. Photo: Charles Osgood, Chicago, courtesy Bob Eisen, Chicago.

staging experimental productions of plays, such as Jean Cocteau's *Orfée* and *Holy Terrors (Les Enfants terribles)* in the 1980s.

While Mordine's work became more "dancey" (her word) in the late 1970s, she has continued to pursue dance-theater works throughout her career, including a version of the Kurt Weill/Bertolt Brecht *Mahagonny Songspiel* in 1980, and *Cartoons* in 1981. In the late 1980s she collaborated with performance-artist James Grigsby (**fig. 4**) on a piece called *In One Year and Out the Other*, with sets and costumes designed by Hollis Sigler. (Grigsby is also at least partly a dancer, having taken classes with Phyllis Sabold, as did Mordine and many others.)

Mordine, her company, and the Dance Center have provided the springboard for numerous other institutions and performers. In 1974 some of the original members of Mordine's Chicago Dance Troupe left to create MoMing Dance and Art Center. (The list of actual founders varies depending on the source, but certainly included are Tem Horowitz, Susan Kimmelman, Jackie Radis, Donna Sugarman, and Eric Trules.) MoMing became an invaluable resource to the dance community, and from the outset included such things as new music and performance art as part of its programming.

One of the people involved in the early days of MoMing was Jim Self (**fig. 5**). He left MoMing in 1975, and in 1976 began renting space at Links Hall. When Self left Chicago to dance with Merce Cunningham, the space at Links came under the aegis of Bob Eisen, Carol Bobrow, and Charlie Vernon (**fig. 6**). Eisen is the one constant, having continued to develop Links as a rehearsal and presenting space, a haven for innovative work involving

movement, performance, and sound, especially after MoMing closed in 1990.

Another significant figure in the interaction of dance and performance art is Nana Shineflug (**fig. 7**). Shineflug had her own teaching studio for many years above the Biograph Theater, and her own company, the Chicago Moving Company. If Shineflug has not always had the involvement with dance-theater works that Mordine has had, her work in the 1980s certainly pushed in that direction, as early as 1981, with a piece called *60/80* created for MCA. In that piece, a dance was fragmented throughout the museum. In the mid-1980s, encouraged by James Grigsby, Shineflug began to create performance art, including the powerful, autobiographical *Spiral Jetty*, and dance-theater works, such as *Seeing* (1985) and *Sufi Tales* (1987). Also in the mid-1980s, Shineflug became involved in a project that she referred to as "body art," working out with weights and participating in bodybuilding contests. She actually won several trophies in such contests!

Shineflug's studio became a center for many artists who went on to pursue their own careers, including the late Poonie Dodson (**fig. 8**), who in the mid-1980s created exquisite dance-theater pieces at MoMing, before leaving Chicago to pursue a career as a model and performer in Paris. Another of Shineflug's former dancers, Maya Ward, joined forces with dancer/choreographers Tim O'Slynne and Brian Jeffery to form a virtuoso and intellectually daring ensemble called XSIGHT! (**fig. 9**). Indeed, the initial impetus for the group came from the very program at which Shineflug's *Seeing* was premièred. Ward had created a dance called *On Awakening* for that program, in which O'Slynne and Jeffery were included. According to Jeffery, "from then on, we were inseparable."[2]

Both O'Slynne and Jeffery were members of Mordine & Company when they first began work on XSIGHT!. In the summer of 1986, O'Slynne, with Ward and Jeffery, created *What Are We Going To Do With Mary?* which was subtitled "a murder mystery in two acts." The piece combined theatrical story-telling with expertly danced movement to generate an original dramatic form somewhere between movement and dance. This work would become the foundation of XSIGHT!. Ironically, some fifty years after Ruth Page had done so, a new dance drama about a murder was being created in Chicago.

XSIGHT! continued to evolve their own version of dance theater in a series of increasingly provoca-tive productions: *All You Can Eat and Other Human Weaknesses* (1989), which has a recurring "spy" motif connecting mixed dance works; *The Pope's Toe* (1990), a hilarious work mixing religion and sexual-ity; and *Who's Afraid of Virginia Woolf—The Dance* (1992), a dance version of Edward Albee's play (which had one performance before Albee's repre-sentatives shut it down). This was the last major pro-duction by the original team: Ward's decision to

move to Santa Fe in 1992 and O'Slynne's diagnosis of AIDS in early 1993 curtailed any further large-scale collaborations.

After O'Slynne's death in 1994, Jeffery reconsti-tuted XSIGHT! with two new dancer/performers, Peter Carpenter and Marianne Kim. This trio, along with dancer Holly Quinn, continues to explore the image-based dramas that characterized XSIGHT! at its best. Carpenter and Kim also continue to work as individuals, both creating their own provocative movement-theater works, Carpenter favoring gender-questioning texts and Kim incorporating aspects of Japanese Butoh-style slow-motion imagery.

Paralleling XSIGHT! in terms of time and form, but from a very different aesthetic perspective, is the collaborative trio Fluid Measure. Originally formed as the performance-art wing of N.A.M.E. Gallery, Fluid Measure eventually separated from the gallery, and focused on the work of Kathleen Maltese, Donna Mandel, and Patricia Pelletier. Each member of this trio produces work that combines movement with storytelling, sets, props, and other theatrical trappings, generating pieces that tell per-sonal stories in distinctive ways. Among Fluid Measure's most ambitious endeavors was *Three Who*

fig. 7
Nana Shineflug performing *Transformations 3: Paint* at Columbia College, Chicago, 1984. Photo: Gail Abbey-Zeddies, Chicago, courtesy Nana Shineflug, Glenview, Illinois.

fig. 8
Publicity photograph of Poonie Dodson, c. 1983. Photo courtesy Nicholas Sistler, Chicago.

fig. 9
XSIGHT! dance group per-forming *The Pope's Toe* at MoMing, Chicago, April 1990. Featured are Maya Ward (fallen figure), Brian Jeffery (holding Ward's hand), and Tim O'Slynne (right center). Photo: Sapien/Meza, Chicago.

8

7

9

Traveled, which combined Jungian psychology, fairy tales, and personal stories about family dynamics into an evening-length performance that was part dance, part performance art.

Another stimulant for dance-theater work in Chicago was dancer and choreographer Timothy Buckley. Buckley arrived from New York in the late 1980s, and soon began working with local dancers to evolve original pieces that were as much performance art or theater as dance. The group of dancers that Buckley assembled—Bryan Saner, Kay Wendt-LaSota, Lydia Charaf, and Jeanette Welp—eventually formed their own group, The Sock Monkeys, and collaborated on original movement-based performances. For several years, the ensemble created distinctive, funny, and poignant work before the members decided to break up to pursue individual projects.

A further incentive to the evolution of movement-based performance in Chicago came with Lin Hixson, who, like Buckley, arrived in Chicago in the 1980s, and formed a collective of performers to develop original work. Hixson, with her husband, Matthew Goulish, and Greg and Timothy McCain, formed the collective Goat Island in 1987 (**fig. 10**). In the group's first incarnation, it included performer Joan Dickinson, who provided a unique presence in the 1989 production *We Got A Date*. Dickinson was replaced in 1990 by Karen Christopher, who contributed to the subsequent productions *Can't Take Johnny to the Funeral* (1991) and *It's Shifting, Hank* (1993).

Unlike some of the other ensembles mentioned above, Goat Island is not made up of trained dancers. The performers, collaborating under Hixson's direction, create pieces that involve often extremely intense or difficult movements (the performer holding his or her head under water for a long time, or inching across a gymnasium floor on his or

her belly), interspersed with text, music, and "acting." The result is a visceral experience that evokes a range of ideas and emotions without stipulating a narrative "meaning." Hixson's position as a SAIC faculty member continues and enhances the long-standing connection between movement and the performance curriculum at the school.

Evidence of that connection can be found in the work of two recent SAIC graduates who have begun to evolve their own dance-theater work in Chicago. Under the group designation of Atlas/Axis, Ken Thompson and Ames Hall have created a series of pieces that seem self-consciously to examine the relation of dance to performance. This is certainly true in the duo's first two collaborations, *Pas de Fromage* (1991) and *Last Tango In...* (1992). The former begins as a parody of a ballet class, and gradually begins to explore the relation of language to body image, class, and gender. *Last Tango In...* explores issues of control and power, using the "cold passion" of the tango (which was originally developed by Argentinian sailors) as a metaphor for the relationship of masculinity to domination. *Permanent Record* (1993) found the duo using repetitive, almost masochistic movement to demonstrate the more bizarre aspects of American education.

The interaction of performance art and dance has been furthered by notable guest artists as well. Meredith Monk (**fig. 11**) visited in the early 1970s (and indeed is sometimes credited with inciting the creation of MoMing). Ping Chong also did residencies in the 1970s and 1980s that invigorated local artists, as did Joe Goode and Jeff McMahon in the late 1980s and 1990s. Bill T. Jones has also been a regular visitor to the city. While Chicago may not have an official acknowledgment like New York's Bessie Awards that connects the dance and performance art communities, the two continue to thrive and inspire each other in the Windy City.[3]

fig. 10
Goat Island rehearsal, 1994. Left to right: Matthew Goulish, Tim McCain, Greg McCain, Karen Christopher, and Lin Hixson. Photo © Bill Stamets, Chicago.

fig. 11
Meredith Monk performing at MoMing, Chicago, for the Museum of Contemporary Art, 1977. Photo courtesy Museum of Contemporary Art, Chicago.

10

11

fig. 1
John Heinz filming
ThomasTrismegistris,
Chicago, 1967. Photo
courtesy John Heinz,
Aurora, Illinois.

experimental film in chicago

Bill Stamets

Chicago is nowhere in the existing histories of avant-garde film. Is there really so little to report, or has Chicago simply been overlooked or ignored? In 1969 *Chicago Magazine* reported, "There are over thirty 'independent,' 'underground,' 'experimental' or 'new American' filmmakers in the Chicagoland area."[1] When the San Francisco Museum of Art presented "Art in Cinema, a symposium on the avant-garde film" in 1947, none of the fifty-eight films screened came from Chicago. "The Most Representative American Film Poets" listed by the New York journal *Film Culture* in 1955 included no Chicagoans. A study of "invisible films" and "alternative cinemas" of the 1960s cited 421 works—with four from Chicago. The American Museum of the Moving Image posted three Chicagoans on its roster of 117 filmmakers in "a sort of first draft of recent film history" covering 1978 to 1988. Finally, the 1989 International Experimental Film Congress showcased no Chicago films, but Chicago critic Fred Camper appeared at this historic Toronto gathering. His essay "The End of Avant-Garde Film," published in 1986, largely set the agenda for the eight-day congress. From 1946 to 1966, he argued, the avant-garde enjoyed its "individual period" of maverick creativity before entering its "institutional period" for the next two decades, when this "movement" calcified into a "genre."

During Camper's "individual period," Chicago lacked the critical mass of film artists then working in New York and San Francisco. Nevertheless, during the later "institutional period," a self-conscious scene of cinema artists arose here—complete with items about festival awards and police raids making the newspaper gossip columns.

The Documentary Film Group, founded in 1941 by University of Chicago students, was Chicago's first viable alternative-film institution. Its initial credo was: "For the realist study of our era via nonfiction films." Although avant-garde films were not the group's raison d'être, they were screened reg-

ularly, and visiting luminaries included Maya Deren in 1948. Now called Doc Films, this group started the short-lived Midwest Film Festival in 1962. This six-day Hyde Park affair billed itself as "Chicago's only film festival" and "the only strictly 16mm competition in the United States."[2] Among local entrants was Michael Kutza, who won no prizes from the 1963 jury, which included critics Pauline Kael and Arthur Knight.

In 1965 Kutza founded the Chicago International Film Festival. "I just wanted a festival where filmmakers in Chicago could show their work to the public," he recalled at the festival's tenth anniversary. "Back then, in the early 1960s, the only place in town that screened noncommercial film was an art gallery in Hyde Park. Otherwise, you had to go to a festival. I had been submitting a few of my own little films—abstract, impressionistic studies—to festivals in Europe, but then, I thought, why not Chicago?"[3]

Kutza plugged experimental films, but the *Chicago Daily News* called a batch of short works in his first festival "2½ hours of trivia."[4] Kutza's enthusiasm for the movement soon waned. Returning from the New York Film Festival, he told a reporter in 1966 such fare was "too far out" for Chicago. "We'll have some far out, experimental stuff, but we won't make a whole festival of it."[5] "It is shocking how poorly these avant-garde boys handle the medium," snipped *Chicago's American*.[6]

That lone venue for noncommercial cinema where Kutza once showed his own work—the Hyde Park Art Center—got a film programmer, John Heinz (**fig. 1**), in 1965. He unfurled his avant-garde banner in *Resist!*, a sardonic underground zine that

debuted with a diatribe: "The Chicago International Film Festival had an evening of experimental films in which half the entries were from commercial movie makers. Some underground!"

Heinz disdained the Magick Lantern Society film series that Camille Cook created in 1966 for the Society of Typographic Arts, a group of graphic-arts professionals. "They were the advertising crowd," he recalls today.[7] Their motives were suspect. "More and more of the best TV commercials today include ideas stolen from films being made by college students and other young experimenters," said Kutza at the time.[8]

While Heinz courted notoriety with billings like "Films to Tease the Bourgeoisie" (**fig. 2**), Cook took an accommodating approach. Soliciting the Museum of Contemporary Art, she wrote Director Jan van der Marck in 1969: "You know we take pains to put on a professional show and prepare program notes. You wouldn't have to apologize for us."[9] When the National Endowment for the Arts launched a regional media-arts program, it looked for alternative-film groups affiliated with respectable art museums. SAIC offered Cook space, so under the wand of federal funding—an $8,000 NEA grant—the Magick Lantern Society turned into the Film Center in 1973.

A year later *The Film Center Gazette* memorialized the late Abraham Teitel, whose World Playhouse first brought foreign films to South Michigan Avenue. "Belated thanks to you, Mr. Teitel, we're showing the movies across the street now. We

hope you approve."[10] The *Gazette's* first issue announced that "Personal Cinema, also called experimental, avant-garde or underground," would get only two shows per month.[11]

Bill Brand, a SAIC graduate student, handed Cook a list of Structuralist films he wanted shown. She declined, explaining that the Film Center had to build an audience carefully. So Brand and a few classmates started Filmgroup at N.A.M.E. Gallery to exhibit their kind of films, sharing space with the alternative gallery created by SAIC painters and sculptors. Brand's model was a filmmakers' cooperative he visited in London during an international avant-garde congress. Showing films and sharing equipment, the group became Chicago Filmmakers.

"There is no discernible Chicago 'school' of filmmaking, but within Chicago there is certainly a Columbia College style, a Northwestern style, a School of the Art Institute style," argued B. Ruby Rich, reviewing the Film Center's semiannual show of Chicago filmmakers in 1979.[12] Chicago's first full-time film professor was Jack Ellis, hired in 1956 by Northwestern University. He taught for thirty-five years, while Gregory Markopoulos, SAIC's first filmmaking teacher, hired in 1966, quit after a few months. Before resigning, Markopoulos told the student newspaper: "It's the fault of the students—I don't expect any disorder and just won't have it. Perhaps it exists because of the old complex of being in the Midwest. Everyone is trying too hard to be like New York or San Francisco."[13]

Two part-time SAIC teachers made lasting contributions far beyond the classroom. Tom Palazzolo taught himself filmmaking after receiving an MFA in photography from SAIC in 1965. Many a Chicago-made film owed its existence to his resourcefulness in locating inexpensive 16mm film stock. The essence of numerous Chicago art films owed a spiritual debt to Colorado filmmaker Stan Brakhage, a charismatic autodidact who delivered three-hour, idiosyncratic, lyrical lectures on film history that drew overflow crowds.

As a teenager in New York, Fred Camper was drawn into avant-garde film by a screening of Markopoulos's *Twice a Man*. He came to Chicago in 1976 to teach in the department Markopoulos had inauspiciously inaugurated, but left in 1982 after a bitter tenure struggle, charging that "Some students have in fact betrayed themselves as capable of being even more political than their instructors."[14]

The 1980s (**fig. 3**) were a period of intramural agitation within the SAIC filmmaking department. Teachers, students, and a few outside supporters formed a nonprofit group called the Experimental Film Coalition in 1983 that lobbied the Film Center and the Chicago International Film Festival to show more experimental work. "We feel that Chicago has a terrible lack of opportunities for people to show their films," a spokesperson told *Screen Magazine*. A coalition member wrote a *Chicago Reader* story to hype the coalition's first screening and discount Chicago Filmmakers' past decade of offerings.[15]

"[A]vant-garde film has, for the first time since its inception as a movement, almost no impact on the culture as a whole," wrote Camper in "The End of Avant-Garde Film." Critic Sheldon Renan dated the avant-garde's demise to 1931; its legacy "surprised nobody and changed nothing," he wrote in 1967.[16] Yet there is also a history of films upsetting people in Chicago. Leni Riefenstahl's movie *The Blue Light* (1932) drew protestors to its September 3, 1974 screening at the Film Center in a women directors series. Riefenstahl herself was slated to visit four days later, but the invitation was withdrawn when her hosts discovered demonstrators were coming too. "Using fascist tactics—last minute blackmail—a small group of self-determined 'anti-fascists' has denied Chicago film buffs a unique opportunity," wrote David Elliott in the *Chicago Daily News*.[17] A movie that drew pickets, bomb threats, and aldermen's ire was Jean-Luc Godard's *Hail Mary*, which played at Facets in 1986.

Citizen monitors of cinema were nothing new. The Better Film Council had been founded in 1932 to "promote morally sound and artistic motion pic-

tures." The topic for the January 20, 1967 meeting was "The Pros and Cons of Censorship." Earlier that week, the Aardvark Cinemathèque showcased seven films deemed obscene by the Chicago Police Censor Board. The Motion Picture Appeal Board overruled the censors, resulting in an overflow turnout.

Other screenings drew city notice. "If the police can get away with harassing the Art Institute they may next be breaking into church basements and seizing copies of *Nanook of the North*," wrote Heinz in a letter to the *Chicago Daily News* on February 27, 1967. He was right. On April 12, Chicago police raided a church during an unlicensed screening. In the middle of showing Palazzolo's film *O*, the Reverend James Shiflett was hauled off to jail.

In May aldermen debated exempting churches, colleges, and museums from permits for exhibiting educational and scientific films. "What about moral or aesthetic justifications for a film?" demanded Alderman Leon Despres, representing the fifth ward where John Heinz's screenings faced "threats of a police raid and the use of paramilitary force by the corporation counsel's office." Heinz scheduled one last screening to flaunt the law; no police came. "I felt we'd been snubbed, I was ready to be a martyr," he said.[18] In June he launched "The Floating Cinemathèque," a guerrilla venue without fixed address or set schedule. "We exist only a few steps ahead of Sergeant Murphy," he told gossip columnist Virginia Kay. "We are a desperate band of filmmakers and film-heads who are trying to keep our art alive in this city."[19] He fantasized dodging police censors by projecting movies aboard an off-shore barge on Lake Michigan.

As personified by Tom "Chicago" Palazzolo, the underground scene's press coverage crested in 1967. Roger Ebert spotted an "omen" when Palazzolo's film *O* won a $1,000 prize in a Seattle experimental festival. "New York and California are supposed to be the centers of progress in experimental films, but Chicago, in a quiet and unassuming way, is running rings around the new work from the coasts," he wrote.[20]

"It may pain us to admit it, but there's nothing like making it in New York to really make it here in Chicago," stated the *Chicago Daily News* a month later, reporting that Palazzolo was getting "an exclusive showing of his movies at New York's ultra-prestigious Museum of Modern Art."[21] Besides "making it" in New York, Palazzolo and his films made their way to the Middle East on a United States Information Agency tour.

Twenty-five years later, Palazzolo was honored at the first Chicago Underground Film Fest

fig. 2
Flyer for film program at the Hyde Park Art Center, 1966. Photo courtesy John Heinz, Aurora, Illinois.

fig. 3
Heather McAdams filming Elvis impersonator Trent Carlini, 1991. Photo © Bill Stamets, Chicago. Throughout the 1980s McAdams, like Tom Palazzolo, captured the zanier side of Chicago life on film.

fig. 4
Tom Palazzolo directing
Added Lessons, Chicago,
1990. Photo © Bill Stamets,
Chicago.

fig. 5
Allen Ross at Chicago
Filmmakers, 1990. Photo ©
Bill Stamets, Chicago. Ross,
an experimental filmmaker
in Chicago for many years,
was actively involved with
Filmmakers from 1976 to
1990.

fig. 6
Jerry Blumenthal and
Gordon Quinn of
Kartemquin Films, 1993.
Photo © Bill Stamets,
Chicago.

(**fig. 4**). In program notes, organizer Jay Bliznick wondered: "Is underground just a marketable catch phrase like 'grunge' or 'Spam?'" He categorized the "underground" filmmakers of the 1990s as "a group that doesn't want the government's money so they can make films about harp seals, being gay, dying relatives, or any other 'interesting' topic. Their films have blood, guts, S & M, dead things, wet things, and things that say 'fuck' a lot." In contrast to the anti-commercial pose of the 1960s underground, this two-year-old festival lined up over a dozen corporate sponsors, including Kodak, Continental Airlines, and Skyy Vodka.

Chicago shares with New York, San Francisco, and Toronto an alternative film culture that survives despite motion-picture market forces and art-world boundaries. Museum policies, police censorship, press coverage, gentrification, funding agencies, personality cults, and ideological rifts are factors common to each community. Grants from the government, tenure for teachers, and salaries to media centers' staff have prompted in-house quarrels over cultural independence. What sets Chicago's filmmakers and film centers apart may be their diversity and longevity.

Chicago Filmmakers (**fig. 5**), for example, has hosted the BlackLight, Women in the Director's Chair, Festival of Illinois Film & Video Artists, International Lesbian and Gay, and Onion City Experimental Film festivals. Michael Kutza started and ran his festival for thirty years. Other veterans—Jim Taylor and Margaret Caples at the Community Film Workshop, Barbara Scharres at the Film Center, Milos Stehlik at Facets Multimedia, and Brenda Webb at Chicago Filmmakers—have devoted over two decades to the cause.

Ironically, Kartemquin Films (**fig. 6**), begun as a leftist collective in 1967, reached Hollywood with *Hoop Dreams* light years ahead of other Chicago independents. *Goldstein*, an experimental feature with a Nelson Algren cameo, went to Cannes and won the Prix de Nouvelle Critique in 1964. Today the only Chicagoans going to Cannes are critics like the *Sun-Times*'s Roger Ebert and curators—Michael Kutza, Barbara Scharres, and Milos Stehlik.

Internationally, the most prominent Chicagoan on the experimental front may be Fred Camper, a filmmaker who rarely screens his work and reviews art exhibits more often than films. Meanwhile television celebrities Siskel and Ebert are our real movie mascots.

chicago performance

Carmela Rago

fig. 1
Leon Golub at the Beaux-
Arts Ball at The School of
The Art Institute of
Chicago, c. 1946. Photo
courtesy Ellen Lanyon,
New York.

The term "performance art" was originally coined by artists in the early 1970s to describe works in which the artist's body, instead of a crafted object, became the locus of the art experience.[1] Yet performance art turned out to be such a useful term that its meaning has always spiraled beyond the specifics of its origin. Ever since the term was coined, it has been used to describe a wide range of theatrical or performative events created by artists both before and after the early 1970s. In 1979 art-historian RoseLee Goldberg published a book on performance art that traced its history from the Futurists to the present.[2] Goldberg successfully excavated the Modernist roots for what appears at times to be the essential Postmodern art form.[3] Performance art, according to Goldberg, can trace its existence to a very specific time of birth: F.T. Marinetti's *Futurist Manifesto,* but Chicago performance did *not* emerge fully grown like Venus.[4] Chicago's performance art has grown out of myriad local socio-political and cultural influences that began back in the 1940s and culminated in the 1968 Democratic Convention. This event inspired seismic changes in the way artists, dancers, writers, and actors approached art-making, and engendered an incipient performance community in the 1970s. This pioneering community eventually inspired a full-blown explosion of local performance art in the 1980s and 1990s.

The development of a community of like-minded (and invariably young) artists has been essential to the evolution of local performance. The Momentum group of the 1950s, iconoclasts such as Ken Nordine, The Imperial Aces of the mid-1970s, the Conceptual performance artists of the early to late 1970s (Phil Berkman, Gundersen Clark, Mary Jane Dougherty), early monologists of the late 1970s (of which this writer was a part), Millie's Orchid Show, Lower Links' cabaret-style performers, queer performance, The Curious Theater Branch, Big Goddess Pow Wow, and the latest wave, the Neo-Conceptual performance artists of the mid-1990s, have all helped to create, form, and inspire many of the movements instrumental in the creation of Chicago's performance history.

Although "performance art" as we know it was not really operative between 1945 and 1965, a small group of Chicago's artists, like artists all over the world, were creating performance-oriented events, ranging from forms of street theater to art-world soirées (**fig. 1**). According to artist Ellen Lanyon, artists were involved in performative political actions as early as 1948, with Leon Golub , Nancy Spero, and Lanyon herself among the participants. Local artists and writers active in Chicago since the late 1940s cited numerous examples — including SAIC's Surrealist and Beaux-Arts balls (with their tableaux vivants of paintings in the Art Institute's collection), artists' studio soirées, Oxbow Summer School, and "happenings" at the Hyde Park Art Center — of a kind of undisciplined, Dada- and Surrealist-inspired performance scene here.[5]

During the 1950s and 1960s, the arts atmosphere in Chicago was rich with experimentation. Improvisation in the theater and jazz communities mirrored Abstract Expressionism in the visual arts, the poetry of the Beats, and even such improvisation-based comedians as Mike Nichols and Elaine May. Chicago artists attended Second City, Paul Sills's Dream Theater, The Gate of Horn, The Compass Theater, The Quiet Night, and coffee houses scattered throughout the city. "Word Jazz" pioneer Ken Nordine collaborated with jazz musicians Johnny Frigo and Dick Marx at a North Side spot known as the Leia Aloha, where he told stories and recited poetry. In the mid-1950s, Henry Rago, editor of *Poetry: A Magazine of Verse*, initiated "Poetry Day," an annual fall celebration of poetry which over the years brought major poets such as T.S. Eliot, Gwendolyn Brooks, Robert Frost, James Dickey, and Wallace Stevens to read from their works.

During the late 1960s events began to gather momentum. Andy Warhol's Exploding Plastic Inevitable appeared at Piper's Alley. The Museum of Contemporary Art, founded in 1967, presented happenings and exhibited performance documentation and ephemera, and in the process brought some of the world's most prominent performance and multidisciplinary artists to Chicago. These artists helped to generate interest in new forms at local colleges and universities, and inspired younger artists to express themselves in new ways. Some of the artists, such as Carolee Schneemann, John Cage, Nam June Paik and Charlotte Moorman, Meredith Monk, Laurie Anderson, and Tina Girouard, worked with

fig. 2
A view of a 1960s peace
rally protesting the war in
Vietnam. Pictured in the back-
ground is a banner by
Dominick Di Meo. Photo: Tom
Palazzolo, Oak Park, Illinois.

fig. 3
Ellen Fisher and Andy Soma
(pictured here in a still
from Tom Palazzolo's film
Caligari's Cure, 1982)
were key members of Chicago's
punk performance scene.
Photo courtesy Tom Palazzolo,
Oak Park, Illinois.

students and faculty from Columbia College, Northwestern University, and SAIC.

The 1968 Democratic Convention galvanized a large number of artists into action. The event was redolent with planned and spontaneous performative actions by citizens, Yippies, flower children, artists, and police. A pig named Pigasus was nominated for President, and subsequently arrested at the Civic Center. An artists' peace march (in which Tom Palazzolo, among many others, took part) was staged (**fig. 2**), with artists carrying painted skulls on sticks bringing up the rear of the demonstration. Flowers were stuck into rifles by flower children. Haskell Wexler continued to shoot his film *Medium Cool* around the events of the convention itself, and integrated his plot into the real-life drama unfolding. "The whole world is watching!" the crowds chanted in video footage shown around the globe.

These actions and spontaneous happenings encouraged artists to deconstruct and decommodify art as product. Orchestrating a happening was the ultimate antiestablishment statement; a happening defied both purchase and traditional modes of critique.

The 1970s was a vibrant time for the arts in Chicago, as it was throughout the United States. Increased funding spawned alternative galleries and spaces that hosted performance-art events. The punk movement first arrived, and places such as Lamer Viper, a punk-rock, dance club, and performance venue on Halsted Street, influenced performance artists such as Austé Peciura, Jeffrey Deutsch, and

even Ellen Fisher (**fig. 3**). N.A.M.E., Midway Studios at the University of Chicago, Artemisia, ARC, West Hubbard, Randolph Street Gallery, MoMing, and Tom Jaremba's Lodge Hall were born. In addition, the Museum of Contemporary Art sponsored Chicago happenings, experimental theater events, and performances.

The first performance class in Chicago was started by Tom Jaremba and John Kurtich at SAIC in 1973: "Expanded Media" was designed to encourage students to meld body movement with multimedia presentations. Other SAIC faculty also encouraged experimentation in multidisciplinary work: Emilio Cruz (painting), Phil Hitchcock (who taught a class entitled "Concepts, Proposals, Actions"), Jim Zanzi (sculpture), and James Grigsby (education). The form was new, and its possibilities seemed unlimited.

Much of the early 1970s performance work in Chicago was situational and Conceptual, and created by sculptors rather than self-identified "performance artists." For example, Robert C. Peters, in his performance *A Pinewood Derby*, created a situation in which the audience became the performers (**fig. 4**); Peters never even appeared at the gallery. The entire performance was comprised of a series of highly structured situations that threw the audience members back on themselves. Several $100 bills were tacked to the east wall. Coats were graciously taken at the door, then hung on a coat rack which, when full, was hoisted into the air. It hung near the ceiling until the performance was over, making virtual prisoners out of audience members who had surrendered their coats.

By the late 1970s, under the leadership of women artists, performance began to become more auto-biographical. In 1977 Ilona Granet performed at N.A.M.E. Gallery in a piece entitled *Ranting and Raving Is Almost in Season, Ripe for the Picking, I'm Sick of the Licking*, in which she addressed the fear and loathing she felt after being raped five times. In the process of the performance, she walked outside and danced by the windows of the gallery on Hubbard Street, to the accompaniment of an audio script played for the audience within. While this was happening, a car slowed down, its passengers taunting and beckoning her, an unplanned verification of her point.

In 1979 Linda Novak curated a show which she entitled "Perf-Doc," the first exhibition of local performance-art ephemera, photographs, scripts, audio tapes, video documentation, and costumes. This concept would later be reexamined at Randolph

Street Gallery in an exhibition in 1980, in the "Alternative Spaces" show at MCA in 1984, and a few years later in the "Detritus" show at MoMing Dance and Art Center.

During the next fifteen years, Chicago performance as a whole began to develop and refine itself. By this time, despite the fact that the press had begun to cover performance more regularly, performance was curated sporadically at best at MCA. The slack was taken up by ARC, Artemisia, Beacon Street Gallery, Cross Currents, The Dance Center of Columbia College, Links Hall, Nancy Lurie Gallery, MoMing, N.A.M.E., Randolph Street Gallery (**fig. 5**), SAIC, and West Hubbard Gallery. They nurtured the talents of the second wave of performers, which included Jeff Abell (**fig. 6**), Sandra Binion, Lynn Book, Nancy Forest Brown, Brendan deVallance (**fig. 7**), Sharon Evans, Karen Finley (who returned here in the early 1980s after completing graduate school at the San Francisco Art Institute), Woody Haid, William Harper, Werner Herterich, Robert Metrick, Michael Meyers, Jean Parisi, Patricia Pelletier, Andy Soma, and others.

The first wave who remained here, including Phil Berkman, Ellen Fisher, James Grigsby, Tom Jaremba, Robert C. Peters, E.W. Ross, Encarnacion Teruel, and this writer, continued to be active. Some began touring regularly outside of Chicago. By the mid-1980s, some of these artists would turn to object-making, and others would leave town.

Fluid Measure, a not-for-profit performance collective, conceived and named by N.A.M.E. curator and artist Jean Sousa, and originally under the auspices of N.A.M.E. Gallery, was begun with the noble purpose of producing performance in Chicago in order to expand interest. Meanwhile, Hudson had come to Randoph Street Gallery in the early 1980s, become the performance coordinator, curator, and programmer, and created a state-of-the-art performance venue out of a humble gallery space. He completed what Fluid Measure had begun.[6]

In 1986, with the establishment of the performance quarterly *P-Form* by Brendan deVallance and Peter Taub, the efforts of curatorial visionaries such as Hudson, Leigh Jones, James Grigsby, and Brigid Murphy (in 1987), and increased interest by Chicago audiences in performance art, performance began to receive serious notice in the mainstream press. Ironically, this recognition came just as deVallance formed *P-Form* to address the void of performance criticism. In any case, though performance criticism was neither regular nor always reliable, acknowledgment in the press was an important step in the creation of dialogue between critics, artists, and the public.

The opening of Lower Links (**fig. 8**) by Leigh Jones in 1988 helped reinforce a local cabaret scene here, injecting life, serious fun, and art-for-art's-sake into the performance community. This was a place where experimentation ruled, yet artists such as

fig. 4
Installation view from Robert C. Peters's performance with Tom Mapp and Nick Despota, *A Pinewood Derby*, at N.A.M.E. Gallery, Chicago, 1980. Photo courtesy Robert C. Peters, Lake Forest, Illinois.

fig. 5
Gregory Green's performances at Randolph Street Gallery, Chicago, regarding nuclear apocalypse were an outgrowth of his sculptural installation work. Photo courtesy Feigen Inc., Chicago.

fig. 6
Jeff Abell performing *You May Be Tested Later On This Material* at Noyes Cultural Center, Evanston, Illinois, April 27, 1985. Photo: Kevin Wolff, Chicago, courtesy the artist, Chicago.

Nancy Bardawil, deVallance, Dani K, Robert Metrick, Iris Moore, Matthew Owens, Suzie Silver, Lawrence Steger, Beth Tanner, and numerous others created visually and verbally complex work that sometimes belied the camp environment. Lower Links closed in 1992.

At just about the same time, a young artist by the name of Brigid Murphy (**fig. 9**) began programming performances under the guise of her alter ego, Millie May Smithy. "Millie's Orchid Show" showcased the talents of many local performance artists, but also added a crazy, vaudevillian twist to the whole business of curating, by including Elvis impersonators, rope twirlers, and dancers, creating a mix of high and low art unlike anything yet witnessed in this city.

Also, by the late 1980s a third wave of young artists emerged, made up of Christine Amundson, Jennifer Fink, Paula Killen, Julie Laffin, Iris Moore, Travers Scott, Rennie Sparks, Lawrence Steger (**fig. 10**), Chris Sullivan, Blair Thomas, Cheryl Trykv, Marcia Wilkie, and others, who specialized in sexually ambivalent, sometimes outrageous, performance. Some of the performance was "queer performance," though much of it was about claiming a sexual identity in art-making. Toward the end of the 1980s, Gurlene and Gurlette Hussey (the alter egos of Doug Stapleton and the late Randy Esslinger) were performing regularly at Lower Links, Randolph Street Gallery, and other venues.

Groups such as The Funky Wordsmyths, The Loofa Method, and Example None are representative of artists inspired by poetry or the spoken word, who have turned to performance as a way of integrating media, movement, installation, or music into their work. Their work can be seen at poet Marc Smith's Poetry Slam (**fig. 11**), as well as Millie's Orchid Show, the Big Goddess Pow Wow, or at Live Bait.

Another younger group of artists, who could be called the fourth wave, seem to have emerged. Almost in reaction to the more stylized monologist/vaudeville/cabaret-inspired work of the last fifteen years, these artists are creating work that is more Conceptual, less aggressive, and closer in its purity to work from the beginning of the 1970s than anything since. Among this group are artists Audrey Colby, Joan Dickinson, Marianne Kim, Dolores Wilber, Mathew Wilson, Mary Zerkel and Michael Thomas, and Joseph Zilovsky, to name a few.

Randolph Street Gallery continues to show the work of local artists, as do the Blue Rider Theater and the newly formed Lunar Cabaret. Brigid Murphy has rebounded after a serious bout with cancer and returned to graduate school (in film). She will continue to produce her Orchid Shows at The Park West.

There is more work happening in this city than ever before, and more room than ever for experimentation. Critics now are continually analyzing what is "good performance" and what may be just forgettable. Tom Jaremba puts it this way: "Once anything is established, then it becomes something that has a history and defines what we expect. Certainly the standards are higher now—performance has spread into other areas. Performance is the real cross-over between art and life—and people are at a point now in which they are insisting on work that is heartfelt."[7]

7

8

9

10

fig. 9
Brigid Murphy as "Millie May Smithy" in an early performance of "Millie's Orchid Show," the multifacted extravaganza that Murphy has produced in Chicago since the mid-1980s. Photo © Susan Anderson, Chicago. "Millie's Orchid Show" helped bring performers such as Eric Bogosian, the Blue Man Group, and David Cale to Chicago and gained performance art a wider audience in Chicago.

fig. 11
Marc Smith's Poetry Slam (held regularly at the Green Mill in Chicago's Uptown) has influenced similar series nationwide. Photo © Steven Gross, Chicago.

fig. 10
Lawrence Steger and Iris Moore performing *Rough Trade* in 1992. This performance featured a switch in gender roles and persona, with Steger's piece titled *Bliss* and Moore's titled *The Illusion of Conspiracy*. Photo: Debra Levie, Chicago.

11

sound shards: chicago's sonic arts

John Corbett

The best entrance into the fragmentary, centerless, wildly varied world of Chicago's sonic arts is perhaps through the signature sounds of the city itself. The "big shoulders" industrial fount has a range of distinctive aural aspects. Consider, for instance, its trains: the Gatling-gun rattle of the El is still an integral part of the city's soundscape, while the stockyards that once provided another set of rail noises have all but disappeared. Since the late 1950s, Chicago has been the site of the largest airport in the world, O'Hare International, and this, too, is woven into the metropolis's subconscious aural fabric.

Of course, Chicago's human inhabitants play a crucial role in its soundscape. There's the infamous hard, flat, nasal Chicago "a," or the "oh" of a Midwesterner's "horrible." With strong ethnic neighborhoods the norm, Chicago's popular music environment has developed into a bold patchwork of mariachi, merengue, polka, reel, reggae, rembetika, salsa, jig, gospel, jazz, and blues; these idioms influence Chicagoland radio, contributing to a particularly diverse electromagnetic spectrum. Of course, jazz has had a special place in Chicago since some of its most famous practitioners came from New Orleans in the teens; before 1910 Wilber Sweatman gained notoriety on the South Side for simultaneously playing multiple clarinets. The blues has been unquestionably the city's main claim to music-culture fame, since Muddy Waters, Howlin' Wolf, and Little Walter patented the urban blues here in the increasingly amplified fallout of World War II. Thanks to Frank Sinatra, there's a (seemingly inescapable) melody associated with "my kind of town." But amidst the merriment, Chicago's sonic memory banks are indelibly etched with the sounds of civil disobedience and rioting in the late 1960s and an endless struggle over race and power. The work of sound artists in Chicago has to be listened to and written about in situ.

Any discussion of the broad umbrella of activities conventionally lumped together as "audio art" quickly runs into a definitional problem: how is it distinguished from the category of sound-organization commonly referred to as "music?" Where the musical activities of composition and performance are largely instrument- or ensemble-oriented, and refer to one (or more) of many specialized music "languages," the tradition of audio art has tended to investigate concepts and ideas with currency in other areas, such as the visual, philosophical, plastic, and electronic arts. What music and audio art have in common (other than the fact that they both address the ear) is that they are quintessential "time arts"; without the ephemeral ingredient of time, neither art form would take place. But artists since the dawn of Modernism have used audio as a medium largely separate from music; these (often musically untrained) explorers have included various Futurists and Dadaists, Wassily Kandinsky, Marcel Duchamp, Jean Dubuffet, and Nam June Paik, among many others.

In the Chicago context it would be impossibly artificial to construct a history of one of these traditions separate from the other. Music and audio art in the Windy City are deeply connected, and have been ever since John Cage (**fig. 1**)—a figure whose work alone is enough to confound the rigid separation of music and audio art—was a faculty member at the Institute of Design in the early 1940s (*see Selz, p. 43*). During his first stay in the city in the mid-1930s, Cage also wrote music for the dance department at the University of Chicago.[1]

As a way of grouping and categorizing the many facets of sound inquiry, it is useful to break up the field into six (often overlapping) subcategories: new and experimental music, jazz and improvisation, installation, instrument invention, electronic music, and radio art.

New and experimental music. In March 1942 a headline in the *New York World-Telegram* announced: "They Break Beer Bottles Now To Make Music In Chicago." The night before, John Cage, his then-wife, Xenia, and an ensemble had performed one of Cage's early percussion pieces—replete with broken bottles—as part of a lecture at The Arts Club of Chicago; fifty years later, Cage gave his third and final appearance at the same venue as part of his eightieth birthday celebration. While Chicago has never been a new music center on a par with Paris, New York, Cologne, or Darmstadt, it contains several vital contemporary compositional communities. Indeed, long before Cage resided in Chicago, the important (though criminally under-recognized)

fig. 1
John Cage, 1948. Photo:
Hazel Larsen Archer.

fig. 2
Vera Klement, *Ralph
Shapey*, 1968. Oil on canvas,
76 x 69 3/4 in. Courtesy the
artist, Chicago. Shapey and
Klement were married at the
time of the painting.

fig. 3
Still from Robert Snyder's
Hard and Flexible Music,
1988. Photo courtesy Video
Data Bank, Chicago. Snyder's
work in video complements
his work with digital music
and sound.

innovator Ruth Crawford studied piano (beginning in 1921) at Chicago's American Conservatory of Music; in Chicago she composed the music that won her a Guggenheim Fellowship in 1930.

Naturally, much of Chicago's academic music has clustered around its numerous academic institutions. John J. Becker, a member of the so-called "American Five" avant-garde composers, taught at Barat College in Lake Forest from 1943 to 1957. Russian-born experimentalist Alexander Tcherepnin taught at DePaul University for fifteen years starting in 1949. Since 1964 composer Ralph Shapey (**fig. 2**)—a student of exiled German vanguardist Stefan Wolpe—has been in the music department at the University of Chicago, where microtonal innovator Easley Blackwood and Israeli-born haute-academic Shulamit Ran are also faculty. North of the city, Northwestern University in Evanston is home to composer Alan Stout (who studied with Henry Cowell and Wallingford Riegger), as well as younger composers Jay Alan Yim and Amnon Wolman. Cage's music-related archives are now housed at Northwestern's music library.

Peter Gena, who studied with Lejaren Hiller and Morton Feldman, taught in the 1970s at Northwestern before moving to SAIC. Indeed, the sound program at SAIC has included some of the most interesting members of Chicago's new and experimental music families: in the early 1970s, Richard Teitelbaum taught in the program, followed by Frederic Rzewski, and eventually composer and videomaker Robert Snyder (**fig. 3**), who was responsible for bringing in an EMU synthesizer and

modernizing the studios. Along with Snyder, who studied there, the active new music program at Roosevelt University produced William Russo (who has taught at Columbia College since 1965), and Frank Abbinati. Anthony Braxton was a librarian in Roosevelt's music library before leaving the city in the late 1960s.

Independent of academic support, a number of new music groups and events have flourished (and floundered) in Chicago as well. On the fringe of academia, composer Sheldon Atovsky with SAIC professor Shawn Decker had a working ensemble called Kapture. In the late 1970s Roosevelt's electronic-music professor Don Malone worked with a noteworthy group named Musica Menta, with Kent Kessler, David Noffs, Daniel Scanlan, and Michael Zerang. Paul Fromm, the influential new music patron who for many years funded the journal *Perspectives of New Music*, was Chicago-based. In 1982 the Museum of Contemporary Art sponsored the New Music America Festival jointly with the Mayor's Office of Special Events and (strangely enough) the *Chicago Tribune*; and for a period there existed a local chapter called New Music Chicago. The city's new music underground has traditionally been different from that of New York, where the influence of Minimalism and Postmodernism was so pervasive; in Chicago, the Modernist and avant-garde lineages have generally persisted.

Laurie Anderson performed in Ira Licht's "Bodyworks" exhibition at MCA in 1975, before her *Big Science* record and subsequent big success in New York. In the late 1970s and early 1980s, Bill

Harper created rock-influenced operas; in 1987
Robert Metrick and Marcia Biasello presented *The
Martha (A Possible Opera)* at Randolph Street
Gallery. Out of the performance-art lineage, Lynn
Book and Andy Lateis developed a highly theatrical
version of Dadaist Kurt Schwitters's sound poem
Ursonate, and in 1986 Jeff Abell produced a festival
called "Homage to Fluxus," the second half of which
featured Flux-oriented music by Paik, George
Brecht, and Brendan deVallance.[2]

Lou Mallozzi has created numerous tape-based
sound works related to musique concrète, often
investigating language and sometimes made in conjunction with musicians like bass clarinetist and
composer Gene Coleman. With his Ensemble
Noamnesia, Coleman has helped keep independent
new music alive into the 1990s, producing monthly
concerts called "Face The Music" (held at Hot
House and more recently at Chicago Filmmakers).
These events have featured local new music groups
like Cube and Walleye (as well as national and international artists) performing seldom-played compositions by American and European avant-garde and
experimental composers.

Jazz and improvisation. In the mid-1940s, jazz
music cashed in some of its commercial valence in
the name of the art of bebop. Although New York
had arguably displaced it as the jazz capital,
Chicago remained one of the most important jazz
spots on the globe, and places like the corner of
63rd Street and Cottage Grove sprouted legends like
weeds. Early experimentalist composer, keyboardist,
and self-proclaimed extraterrestrial Sun Ra
(**fig. 4**) spent the 1950s in Chicago; in the city's
active jazz ecosystem he amassed his big band,
the Arkestra, and began utilizing space imagery in
his floor shows, before relocating to New York in

1961. Ra's composition *El Is A Sound Of Joy* is
one of the most moving tributes to a city's public
transport system ever written. Other important post-
bop jazz figures of the time included pianists
King Fleming, Andrew Hill, and Muhal Richard
Abrams (**fig. 5**).

In fact, Abrams was a charter member of the
Association for the Advancement of Creative
Musicians (AACM), which formed in 1964 to foster
forward-looking music in the aftermath of Ornette
Coleman, John Coltrane, Albert Ayler, and Cecil
Taylor's free jazz revolution. This crucial organiza-
tion was a model for many protectionist creative
music groups worldwide, and over the course of
its three-decade existence the AACM has included
Abrams, Fred Anderson, the Art Ensemble of
Chicago, Mwata Bowden, Anthony Braxton, Ernest
Dawkins, Douglas Ewart, George Lewis, Steve
McCall, Maurice McIntyre, Roscoe Mitchell, Amina
Claudine Myers, Leo Smith, Henry Threadgill,
Rita Warford, Ed Wilkerson (**fig. 6**), and Philip
Wilson. Though many of the original members
have sought their fortunes elsewhere, a few, includ-
ing Fred Anderson, have remained in Chicago.
In 1979, at one of the frequent AACM events held
there, Anderson recorded *Dark Day* (Message
Records) at MCA (**fig. 7**).

Other innovative jazz musicians and improvisers have worked outside of the AACM, including
a free jazz group in the early 1960s led by saxophonist Joe Daley, which included bassist Russell
Thorne and drummer Hal Russell (**fig. 8**). With his
group, the NRG Ensemble, Russell (who doubled
on sax and trumpet later in life) was very active up
until his tragic death in 1992. Liof Munimula, a free
improvising trio of Michael Zerang (percussion),
Don Meckley (shortwave radio, etc.), and Dan
Scanlan (violin, guitar, cornet), has been in existence

since 1981, though its most productive period was in the mid-1980s.

As co-music director, with Leo Krumpholz, of Links Hall (initially opened for dance in 1978), Zerang produced concerts by international jazz and improvised music luminaries like British guitarist Derek Bailey and South African bassist Johnny Dyani. Links Hall was also the site of weekly "Clamdance" concerts: ad hoc free sessions with mixed groups of Chicago improvisers. Krumpholz's breakaway venue Southend Musicworks was an essential outlet and inlet for creative music until its demise in 1993. Other key clubs have included (the now defunct) Club Lower Links, Hot House, and, most recently, the Lunar Cabaret. Percussionists Kahil El Zabar and Hamid Drake work in a wide variety of settings. Since coming to Chicago in 1989, saxophonist and clarinetist Ken Vandermark has quickly become the town's most active free music exponent, while free improvising guitarist and accordionist Jim O'Rourke (**fig. 9**) — also an important young composer — is perhaps the city's most prominent export, performing frequently in Europe and Japan.

Installation. In the early 1970s, a set of gentle, metal, wind-driven sound sculptures called "sonambients" by Harry Bertoia were installed in front of the Standard Oil Building downtown; and another Bertoia was installed in a quieter spot at the Chicago Botanic Gardens in Glencoe, Illinois. In 1978 MCA commissioned Max Neuhaus to create an installation for its Ontario location, and he came up with *Sound Installation, 1979* (1979), an unmistakable low hum in the museum's stairwell; in fact, Neuhaus had already spent 1964–65 as artist-in-residence at the University of Chicago. Lief Brush, who was married in a performance/ceremony at MCA in 1969, actively investigated sound installation as a student at SAIC, and M. W. Burns has created a body of text-based public-service-style installation art pieces. In 1986 Experimental Sound Studio curated "The Sound Show" at Randolph Street Gallery, which featured sound installations by twelve Chicago-based artists (**fig. 10**).

Instrument invention. In 1958 the legendary composer, author of *The Genesis of a Music*, and instrument inventor Harry Partch collaborated with filmmaker Madeline Tourtelot in Evanston on her films *Music Studio* and *Windsong*. A few decades down the road, Don Meckley (also lead preparator at MCA) began constructing his own typewriter-kalimba, hydro-kalimba, and the instrument he is best known for, his radio-tar, a shortwave radio with guitar-neck tuner. In the late 1970s Sam Pappas created a uniquely holistic approach to music invention, sculpting his own instruments (using combinations of organic materials: metal, bone, wood, animal hide), and writing his own pieces on handmade paper, using an unorthodox notation system of his own design.

fig. 6
Ed Wilkerson performing with the group Eight Bold Souls at Chicago Filmmakers, 1984. Photo © Bill Stamets, Chicago.

fig. 7
Album cover of Fred Anderson's *Dark Day*, recorded at the Museum of Contemporary Art, Chicago, 1979. Album courtesy John Corbett, Chicago.

fig. 8
Hal Russell preparing for a concert at Chicago Filmmakers, 1985. Photo © Bill Stamets, Chicago.

6

7

fred anderson quartet

a.a.c.m., chicago

dark day

8

fig. 9
Publicity photograph of Jim
O'Rourke, 1994. Photo:
Bettina Herzner, courtesy
John Corbett, Chicago.

While in Chicago, saxophonist Henry Threadgill
invented the "hubcaphone," a rack of hubcaps used
for percussion. AACM-member Douglas Ewart
(**plate 115**) is a well-known shakuhachi-maker and
builds rain sticks. Together with musical sawist and
fellow-improviser Hal Rammel — inventor of such
instruments as the triolin, electro-acoustic sound
palette, and single-string snath (**fig. 11**) — Ewart
teaches a course on instrument building at SAIC.
Bill Close and Bill Wallace also build long-string
sculptures and percussion instruments that they use
in performance.

Electronic music. Chicago has no renowned center
for electronic music like Princeton University or
Massachusetts Institute of Technology, but in its own
scattered way it has been a hub of activity for many
years. Chicagoan Laurens Hammond contributed to
electronic music (and rib-tips-style jazz) by building
the first electric organ here in 1929. In 1954 the
first jazz synthesizer recording was made by Sun
Ra on a Solovox in his Chicago apartment. Early
experiments with computer music, including the first
composition using digital computer, Lejaren Hiller
and Leonard Isaacson's *Illiac Suite* (1955–57),
were carried out downstate at the University of
Illinois at Urbana-Champaign. Hiller's *An
Avalanche for Pitchman, Prima Donna, Player
Piano, Percussionist and Pre-Recorded Playback*
was performed at the Ravinia Music Festival in
Highland Park, Illinois, in July 1968.

Roosevelt University has long been an important
institution for electronic experimentation in Chicago,
in part simply because it had a Moog Synthesizer
as early as 1968. Ramon Zupko ran Roosevelt's studio before Don Malone took on the task. At DePaul,
Raymond Wilding-White and Phil Winsor ran
the electronic facilities. SAIC has also encouraged
electronic music, and current faculty include elec-

tronic and computer composers Robert Snyder,
Lauren Weinger, Peter Gena, and Shawn Decker. In
the late 1970s, the group La Boue, a duo consisting
of Jeff Thomas and Dave Cloud, mixed live electronics and acoustic percussion.

Radio art. In the 1950s Chicago-based commercial
voice-over artist Ken Nordine developed "word jazz"
spots for airplay, blending comedy, poetry, and audio
art. William Neil, who moved to Chicago in 1986 as
composer-in-residence at the Lyric Opera, produced
a multimedia event as the opening of New Music
Chicago Festival 1988 by connecting four discrete
events via radio broadcast. But the real center of
gravity for radio art in Chicago was galvanized in
1989, when Experimental Sound Studio (f. 1986)
(**fig. 12**) initiated "Sounds From Chicago,"
coordinated by Eric Leonardson (himself an accomplished radio artist and sound designer). This series
of thirty curated programs, distributed for airplay
internationally, includes work by Dani K, Bill Milosz
and Lanny Silverman, Iris Moore, Radio Dada,
Rita Warford, Rick Wocjik, and many other audio
artists, composers, performance artists, and poets.

While it represents an active field of artistic
investigation of its own, radio also serves as one of
the primary vehicles for other forms of audio art
and experimental music. Chicago's National Public
Radio-affiliate WBEZ has continued to broadcast
Ken Nordine's pieces and occasionally features
the work of contemporary composers, improvisers,
and audio artists on cultural programs. Ira Glass
also produces his multifaceted weekly program "The
Wild Room" for WBEZ. College stations, like
the University of Chicago's WHPK and Northwestern's WNUR (which recently adopted the motto
"Chicago's Sound Experiment," overtly advertising
its allegiance to the edge), regularly feature contemporary composition, experimental popular music,
and vanguard jazz. Northern Illinois University's
WZRD maintains free-form programming, a creative
approach that virtually disappeared since its
heyday in the 1970s.

By featuring new music and Conceptual sonic
works, these stations bridge the gap between the
smaller communities of creative audio audiences and
the broader public sphere. They connect the media-
marginalized producers of experimental music, creative jazz and improvisation, sound installation,
instrument invention, and electronic music with the
Chicago ears they seek to infiltrate.

11

10

fig. 10
Installation view of "The
Sound Show" held at
Randolph Street Gallery,
Chicago, July 1986. Left to
right: Gene Coleman,
N.O.W.H.E.R.E.; Dan
Richardson, *Untitled*; Lou
Mallozzi, *Oracle*;
Maria LoVullo, *No Evil*.
Photo courtesy
Experimental Sound
Studio, Chicago.

fig. 11
Hal Rammel, *Bibliolin*, 1990.
Wood, paper, and metal,
17 x 6 x 3 in. Photo courtesy
the artist, Cedarburg,
Wisconsin.

fig. 12
From left, Dawn Mallozzi,
Lou Mallozzi, and Eric
Leonardson at the
Experimental Sound Studio,
Chicago, 1991. Photo:
Marc PoKempner, Chicago,
courtesy Experimental
Sound Studio, Chicago.

12

towards a history of chicago video

Kate Horsfield

The "history" of video art exists primarily in the memories of those who were around at the time, and in bits and pieces of printed materials. This is true for all video, and especially for Chicago video. By most accounts, video art was officially launched in 1965 when Nam June Paik bought one of the first porta-paks (portable record and playback decks) that had just been released for sale in the commercial market. The availability of the porta-pak was extremely significant because this was the first television equipment sold for individual use outside the broadcast system. This meant that people could finally make television rather than just watch it.

Video art developed at a temporal crossroad of dramatic cultural and social change that began in the social activism of the 1960s. While this activism failed to dismantle the major institutions of our society—family, school, government, church, military—it did infuse the establishment with issues developed from activist treatises on economics, race, gender, community, and environment. At the center of this activism was a demand to open up the communications systems so the ideals and politics of the 1960s could speak out.

Radical Software, the voice of the radical video movement, was first published in July 1970. It laid out the agenda for what was later to become the media-arts field. Editors Phyllis Gershuny and Beryl Korot summed up the vision for an alternative television:

Power is no longer expressed in land, labor, and capital, but by access to information and the means to disseminate it. As long as the most powerful tools (not weapons) remain in the hands of those who would hoard them, no alternative cultural vision can succeed.... Our species will survive neither by totally rejecting nor unconditionally embracing technology... but by humanizing it; by allowing people access to the informational tools they need to shape and reassert control over their lives.[1]

Published by the Raindance Collective in New York, *Radical Software* was a mix of political manifesto,

visionary rhetoric, communications theory, science fiction, technical expertise, and community gossip. Even the simplest descriptions were packed with a vision for a democratic communication system. Paul Ryan, in his column "Techniques," described the politics of working on the street with a porta-pak:

It's the whole business of where the authority is, and the authority goes with the information structure. If the authority is in books, of course the teacher has got it all over them; but if the authority is in video, it's in the hands of the kids who have video.[2]

Video offered people a chance to describe their own reality rather than having it described for them by the corporate giants who control television.

In the early 1970s experimentation with video was spreading in arts and activist communities across the United States. The video produced by the main collectives was called "guerrilla television," after Michael Shamberg's 1971 book. "Guerrilla television" refers to a raw documentary style that expresses an urgency that paralleled the 1960s demand for social change. Video was used to record events that represented the countercultural perspective, particularly events that promoted inclusion of new voices in media: a speech at Attica prison after the riots, a Native American sit-in at Plymouth Rock on Thanksgiving Day, the first Gay Rights March in 1970. The poor image quality produced by the black-and-white porta-pak cameras and the loose hand-held quality of the video-vérité style made the footage look as though it came directly from the street, in contrast to the slick packaging of mainstream television reporting. It suggested a cheaper, more democratic, and decentralized medium that could be made by and for the people.

Video's social agenda required the formation of new types of alternative organizations that could provide access to video equipment to individuals and communities. These organizations created a network, a "field," for video, developing access centers, teaching video to kids and community groups, developing programs for cable and public television, screening tapes, organizing collections of video, creating an exchange of tapes from one video community to another.

During the early 1970s in Chicago, several organizations formed around the idea of community access: Videopolis was organized by Anda Korsts, Communications for Change by Ted William Theodore, and Community Television Network by Denise Zaccardi. Videopolis was Chicago's first community access center in which neighborhood people, grass-roots groups, and community organizers could come to make video. It had an archive of tapes, a small amount of portable 1/2-inch open-reel production equipment, and held workshops in which professional staff trained community users to work with the equipment.

Another workshop program, designed for urban youth, was developed by Denise Zaccardi at the Alternative Schools Network in 1974. This program later became the Community Television Network, and focused on teaching inner-city youth, mostly African-American and Latino, video production to help them achieve self-awareness, develop critical viewing skills, and present issues of concern to their communities. The kids worked together in workshops as production teams to produce video for *Hard Cover*, CTVN's access program.

Cable was just becoming available in the early 1970s. Communications for Change was trying to organize cable access in Chicago around George Stoney's Canadian model, Channels for Change. Ted William Theodore, along with several other Chicago videomakers—Tom Weinberg, Mirko Popadic, Tom McMahon, Jeanne Meyers, and Bob Hercules— organized a citizens' committee that fought for the creation of Chicago Access Corporation, which is now one of the premier cable access organizations in the United States.

Channels for Change also became the parent organization of the Chicago Editing Center. Gathering together several individuals who shared an interest in grass-roots video, in 1978 Weinberg teamed up with Scott Jacobs (a former journalist who had produced a series of commercials for Mayor Jane Byrne) and Ted William Theodore to form the Chicago Editing Center:

We called the Center "the demilitarized zone" in Chicago because it was the only place where independent video producers, in strong competition for equipment, dollars, jobs, grants, recognition, life, could come together in a common purpose and work towards common goals.[3]

The Chicago Editing Center (renamed the Center for New Television in 1980 and the Center for Communications Resources in 1995) became, under Joyce Bolinger's direction, one of the most important media centers in the Midwest. It was built around the concept of access—offering training workshops; equipment access for independents and nonprofits; a screening program, "Video Sea," that brought in important videomakers from other locations; and a publication, *SCAN*, that informed the local community about issues and events in video, public television, and public access.

Of the video-vérité reporting of the early 1970s, most notable was "Four More Years," a one-hour program produced by the collective TVTV (Top Value Television) at the Republican National Convention in 1972. "Four More Years" was one of the first independently produced experimental documentaries broadcast on and commissioned by PBS. It gave several different perspectives on the convention, bracketing "official convention coverage" with behind-the-scenes dramas, satirical commentary, and scenes of antiwar demonstrators outside the convention hall. With this work, TVTV created a new type of humanized, "point of view" television documentary. Anda Korsts and Tom Weinberg were part of the collective working on this project. Following in this tradition, they developed a series based on Studs Terkel's best seller *Working*. The series, called "It's A Living," featured people talking about the working conditions of their jobs; it was broadcast on public television in 1976.

In 1970 Dan Sandin, originally trained as a physicist, moved to Chicago to teach interactive art and kinetic sculpture at the University of Illinois at

fig. 1
Dan Sandin in the first "EVE" performance, University of Illinois at Chicago Circle, 1975. Photo courtesy Electronic Visualization Laboratory, University of Illinois at Chicago.

fig. 2
Still from Phil Morton's *General Motors*, 1976. Photo courtesy Video Data Bank, Chicago.

3

fig. 3
Kate Horsfield (left) and
Lyn Blumenthal (right) at
the Los Angeles Woman's
Building as part of the sum-
mer video program from
July to August 1976.
Photos: Sheila Ruth, Los
Angeles, courtesy
Otis/Parsons School of Art
and Design, Los Angeles.
Horsfield and Blumenthal
founded the Video Data
Bank at The School of The
Art Institute of Chicago and
were crucial members of the
women's movement in the
arts of the 1970s.

Chicago. Sandin became interested in kinetics, light shows, and photography while in graduate school in the late 1960s at the University of Wisconsin, Madison. Having worked on the production of slides used in light shows, Sandin became interested in generating images electronically (**fig. 1**). He began teaching himself electronics in order to design a visual equivalent to the Moog Synthesizer. Around 1971, with a $3,000 grant from the Illinois Arts Council, Sandin began building the first Image Processor (IP).

Completed in 1973, the IP became extremely important to videomakers because of its power to generate a variety of images. Video synthesizers manipulate the basic television signal, combining and enhancing effects to generate complex layers of abstract images, highly saturated with color, and often moving in oscillated patterns across the screen. Sandin teamed up with Tom DeFanti, another faculty member at UIC, who developed a micro-computer language, Z-Grass, which interfaced with the IP to create computer graphics.

The IP was often used as a performance instru-ment for live events. While "Inconsecration of New Space" (1973) was probably the first public event featuring the IP, two other events were equally important: "EVE I" (1975) and "EVE II" (1976), held at the Circle Graphics Habitat at UIC. These events featured homemade video equipment patched together into an interactive electronic environment. A "performer" played the IP, with elec-tronic music—sometimes played by composer Bob Snyder—improvised to the images. Live video allowed the audience to shoot processed pictures of themselves on an SX-70 camera. Here is a description of "EVE I" from the announcement for "EVE II":

It was three days of video/computer artists and synthesis musicians performing together live before capacity audi-ences, explaining and exploring their equipment and gen-erally jamming with each other.

The Circle Graphics Habitat is one of the few places where computers do not restrict creativity and freedom, but instead, provide new personal freedoms in communi-cation using visuals.[4]

While the importance of the event was its live aspects, several tapes were made of the perfor-mances. The tapes, "Re-Scanning of EVE-I" and "Eve-88," were so successful that they drew the interest of museums and television broadcasters, who also screened or broadcast the tapes, and Chicago-style video was officially launched. The Image Processor was so influential on local video-makers that from the 1970s to the mid-1980s, the term "image-processed" became synonymous with Chicago video.

Phil Morton (**fig. 2**), who was teaching ceram-ics at SAIC, sensed the growing importance of the new medium and convinced Dean Roger Gilmore that the school needed to offer courses in video. By 1972 the video department was fully orga-nized—only two years after the first publication of *Radical Software*. Morton also organized a small collection of student-produced video tapes that included tapes from the "Visiting Thinker—Visiting Artist" program, such as Baba Ram Dass, R. Buckminster Fuller, Gene Youngblood, Alvin Toffler, and Anais Nin. This collection was called the Video Data Bank, and it was based on the notion of a "cul-tural data bank" as outlined in "Alternatives for Alternate Media/Peoples Video Theater Handbook" by Ken Marsh in *Radical Software*. In 1976 two recent graduates of the video department, Lyn Blumenthal and this writer (**fig. 3**), were hired to reestablish the Video Data Bank collection in the school library.

Along with community-based documentary, the other important direction in early video was Feminist video. While film was considered the province of men, the "access" politics of video pro-vided women with a means of being taken seriously as "makers" while providing a link with Feminist dialogue coming from the coasts. The first festival of women's video in the city, Chicago Women's Video Festival, organized by Judy Hoffman, Anda Korsts, and Lilly Ollinger, was held in 1973 at the UIC campus. Works were screened and a video workshop was taught; this event was seminal in terms of bringing together as a force women and women's video collectives.

The local arena became a stimulating laboratory for creating a new visual medium. With Sandin and DeFanti at UIC, and Robert Snyder and Phil Morton at SAIC, the two institutions worked together in a powerful synergistic relationship. The Chicago video scene became well known as a vigorously creative arena for experimental video. By the mid-to-late 1970s, this energy was attracting younger videomakers, including Annette Barbier and Drew Browning, Lyn Blumenthal, Dan Klepper, John Manning (**fig. 4**), Ed Rankus, Robert Snyder, Barbara Sykes-Dietze (**fig. 5**), and Janice Tanaka (**fig. 6**). Each of these videomakers produced substantial bodies of work that continued to draw more interest to Chicago video.

Alternative art spaces in Chicago began to screen video during the mid-1970s. One important video exhibition, "Ladies Home Video," was organized for Untitled Gallery in 1976 by Annette Barbier, Catherine deJong, and Denise Kunkel. Fifty local videomakers were invited to show their videos

and the organizers of the exhibition set up a viewing installation that mimicked viewing situations in the typical American home, with Naugahyde chairs, leatherette pillows, rugs, and floral-patterned drapes to make the viewers comfortable in spite of the experimental video on the screens.

Four people in particular were important in terms of drawing attention to Chicago video in new ways. Christine Tamblyn and Barbara Latham worked almost in tandem to bring people in to see what was going on in Chicago. Tamblyn taught a graduate production seminar and brought several important people from other video scenes into SAIC. Before leaving Chicago in the 1980s to pursue a degree at the University of California, San Diego, Tamblyn wrote several important critical essays on Chicago video. Barbara Latham, chair of SAIC's video department in 1979–84, brought in Bill Viola (**fig. 7**), Barbara London (assistant curator at The Museum of Modern Art), Shigeko Kubota, and Nam June Paik. Lyn Blumenthal, as codirector of the

fig. 4
Still from Barbara Latham, John Manning, and Ed Rankus, *AlienNATION*, 1979. Photo courtesy Video Data Bank, Chicago.

fig. 5
Still from Barbara Sykes-Dietze, *Kaliyan*, 1986. Photo courtesy the artist, Chicago.

fig. 6
Still from Janice Tanaka, *Beaver Valley*, 1981. Photo courtesy Video Data Bank, Chicago.

4

6

5
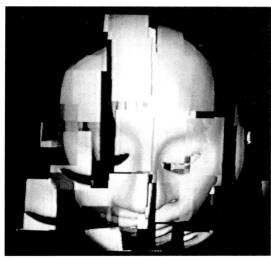

Video Data Bank, tirelessly promoted Chicago video in international video festivals, conferences, and screening venues. Tom Weinberg, as producer of the local PBS program "Image Union," was one of the first programmers to put Chicago video on public television. All of these efforts continued and heightened Chicago's reputation as an important center for experimental video.

Over the past quarter century, the Chicago video scene has continued to grow. It has produced many important videomakers, some of whom—Mindy Faber, Tom Kalin (**fig. 8**), Stashu Kybartus, Suzie Silver, David Simpson—have become internationally known. Many of the organizations founded in the 1970s have fulfilled a vital role in the local community and in the national media-arts arena. In 1976 the Video Data Bank contained 200 tapes; by 1995 the collection numbered over 3,000. Dan Sandin and Tom DeFanti are developing three-dimensional virtual reality at the Electronic Visualization Center at UIC. Youth at Community Television Network and two other local videomakers—Eric Scholl and Cindy Moran—recently had a program broadcast on

"P.O.V." on PBS. Tom Weinberg is developing a local public-affairs program for cable.

Street-Level Video (**fig. 9**), a new storefront video workshop for inner-city youth, was formed in 1992 by Iñigo Manglano-Ovalle, Paul Teruel, and Nilda Ruiz Pauley (*see Kirshner, p. 140*). In 1993 the group presented "Tele-Vecindario," an important new type of outdoor screening, as part of the "Culture in Action" project. More recently several accomplished videomakers—Chris Bratton, Vanalyne Green, Laura Kipnis, and Julie Zando—have been drawn to Chicago because local teaching institutions have created new positions teaching video and because of the vitality of the local scene.

The individual and group accomplishments of the first and second generation have created an invigorating climate for videomakers working in Chicago today. Ironically, while Chicago video is not well known among local film or art patrons, the video works produced here are critically acclaimed on a national and even international level. The reputation of this work continues to feed back into a climate of stimulating growth for Chicago video.

fig. 7
Bill Viola giving a lecture at The School of The Art Institute of Chicago, 1984. Photo: Eleftheria Lialios, Chicago, courtesy The Visiting Artists Department, The School of The Art Institute of Chicago.

fig. 8
Still from Tom Kalin, *Finally Destroy Us*, 1991. Photo courtesy Video Data Bank, Chicago.

fig. 9
Street-Level Video crew interviewing West Town residents, Chicago, 1993. Photo: Iñigo Manglano-Ovalle, Chicago, courtesy Sculpture Chicago.

notes

Abell, time arts in Chicago

1 Only in the past few years has this central position been articulated by such writers as Henry Sayre, in his book *The Object of Performance* (Chicago: University of Chicago Press, 1989). Sayre cites the unfixed, constantly changing nature of performance as its most significant quality, using Jacques Derrida's term "undecidability" as the best label for such work.

2 The reader is referred to some of the books produced by N.A.M.E., *Artbook 1,* 1977 and *Artbook 2,* 1980, that document these early works.

3 Originally from Ohio, Hudson created some of the first openly gay performance work in Chicago. He left Randolph Street in the mid-1980s to start a commercial gallery, Feature.

4 At a performance at N.A.M.E. in 1985.

5 The foundation, Intuit, publishes a magazine on outsider art as well.

6 Principally at Club Lower Links, but eventually at other clubs and non-profit galleries as well.

Abell, movement and performance

1 The term "dance theater" or *Tanztheater,* was originally used by the German choreographer Mary Wigman in the 1920s to define dramatic works that use movement as their principal mode of expression. This form regained currency in the 1970s largely due to the efforts of Pina Bausch.

2 Brian Jeffery, interview with the author, Chicago, Aug. 1995.

3 The author conducted interviews with Bob Eisen, Brian Jeffery, Shirley Mordine, and Nana Shineflug for this essay, and made use of an interview with Tom Jaremba by Dominic Molon, Archive of Art in Chicago, Oral History Project, Museum of Contemporary Art, Chicago, Mar. 8, 1995.

Stamets, experimental film

1 Joe Guzaitis, "Movies You Won't See at the Movies," *Chicago Magazine,* July 1969.

2 Midwest Film Festival press release, Documentary Film Group files, University of Chicago Library.

3 Michael Kutza, quoted by Gene Siskel, *Chicago Tribune,* Nov. 3, 1974.

4 Michaela Williams, "Anatomy of a Film Festival," *Chicago Daily News,* Nov. 27, 1965.

5 Ann Masters, *Chicago's American,* Nov. 7, 1966.

6 Ann Barzel, "Festival Buildup for a Flop," *Chicago's American,* Nov. 7, 1966.

7 John Heinz, telephone interview with the author, Chicago, Aug. 1995.

8 Michael Kutza, quoted by Clifford Terry, *Chicago Tribune,* Oct. 31, 1967.

9 Letter from Camille Cook to Museum of Contemporary Art, Chicago, July 30, 1969. Archive of Art in Chicago, Museum of Contemporary Art.

10 "Belated Thanks," *The Film Center Gazette* 2, 3 (May 1974).

11 "There is a Pattern," *The Film Center Gazette* 1, 1 (1973).

12 B. Ruby Rich, "A Chicago Film Sampler," *Chicago Reader,* Mar. 9, 1979.

13 Gregory Markopoulos, interview in *Momentum,* Nov./Dec. 1966.

14 "An Open Letter to the Faculty, Staff, and Students of The School of The Art Institute of Chicago," May 4, 1982. Posted on the SAIC Film Department bulletin board.

15 Harvey Nosowitz, "Experimental Film: New Development Corrects Underexposure," *Chicago Reader,* Jan. 27, 1984.

16 Sheldon Renan, *An Introduction to the American Underground Film,* (New York: Dutton, 1967).

17 David Elliot, quoted in *The Film Center Gazette* 2, 4 (Sept. 1974).

18 Heinz (note 7).

19 Virginia Kay, "Dateline Chicago," *Chicago Daily News,* June 14, 1967.

20 Roger Ebert, "Local Underground Edging Out Coasts," *Chicago Sun-Times,* Oct. 5, 1967.

21 "Panorama Pulse," *Chicago Daily News,* Nov. 1, 1969.

Rago, Chicago performance

1 Some of the original practioners, including Vito Acconci and Dennis Oppenheim, were Conceptual sculptors. To this day in some universities, the performance class is part of the sculpture department.

2 RoseLee Goldberg, *Performance: Live Art from the Futurists to the Present* (New York: Harry N. Abrams, Inc., 1979).

3 Performance studies, centered in anthropology and sociology, extend the theoretical range of performance to include a huge variety of cultural activities. For a sense of the range of this discourse, see Richard Schechner's *Performance Theory* (New York: Routledge, 1988 edition), pp. 252–53, where he provides a grid that covers everything from Aboriginal initiation rites to sandlot baseball.

4 *High Performance* magazine published two essays on Chicago performance art in the spring/summer
1982 issue. Christine Tamblyn, in
"Chicago Performance: An
Annotated Guide," dated the beginning of Chicago performance to
1973. In a parallel article called
"Sweet Home Chicago," Linda
Novak discussed performance work
back to 1968, specifically citing
the Democratic Convention as
its beginning.

5 The writer spoke to numerous indi-
viduals, including Jon Anderson,
RoseLee Goldberg, Tom Jaremba,
Ellen Lanyon, Richard Loving, Tom
Palazzolo, Joseph Parisi, Jean
Sousa, Christine Tamblyn, and Alene
Valkanas.

6 The name Fluid Measure eventually
passed to a performance collaborative separate from N.A.M.E., featuring Kathleen Maltese, Donna
Mandel, and Patricia Pelletier.

7 Tom Jaremba, interview with the
author, Chicago, Aug. 1995.

Corbett, sound shards

1 John Cage would make additional,
conspicuous visits to Chicago
over the years, including the 1982
New Music America Festival,
where special events honored his
eventieth birthday, as well as others
noted above.

2 Brendan deVallance contributed
"Homage to Nam June Paik,"
inspired by a work in which Paik had
dragged a violin along the ground on
a string. In his version, deVallance
tied a guitar to the back of a truck,
climbed aboard the guitar, and had
himself dragged around the block.

**Horsfield, towards a history of
Chicago video**

1 Phyllis Gershuny and Beryl Korot,
ed., "Masthead," *Radical Software*
1 (New York: Raindance Corporation, 1970).

2 Paul Ryan, "Techniques," in ibid.

3 Ted William Theodore, *SCAN* 10, 1
(Center for New Television, spring
1988), p. 1.

4 Press release announcing the second
"EVE" event, Video Department,
The School of The Art Institute of
Chicago, 1976.

Judith
Russi Kirshner

resisting
regionalism

Issues of identity and allegiance are complex and in Chicago, as Barbara Jaffee wrote in "Pride of Place," they are exacerbated by long-standing social and political realities within and outside of the arts community. Judith Russi Kirshner has served in a number of curatorial and education capacities in various Chicago arts institutions, including the Museum of Contemporary Art, the Terra Museum of American Art, The School of The Art Institute of Chicago, and currently as Director of the School of Art and Design at the University of Illinois at Chicago. In this essay she focuses on how for three decades the debates surrounding an identity for Chicago art have hovered in the background of deliberations by institutions, historians, critics, and the artists themselves. Celebrations and commemorations of the communal or historical aspects of the city's culture, including projects like "Art in Chicago," raise questions of stylistic definitions, of regionalism, of center and periphery. Those artists who believe the recognition of their merit should be independent from geographical location and who reject such categorization as convenience or convention have long been active participants in this debate. By examining the works and careers of some of these artists, Kirshner investigates issues such as the role of historical traditions or art-historical quotation; the use of found objects; the use of the image of the City of Chicago itself as subject matter, background, and source for personal investigation that underlie conventional discussions. In her rejection of regionalism as an organizing premise, she undermines crumbling stereotypes that are part of the politics of cultural identity at the end of the twentieth century. LW

"An art of place is concerned less with the phenomenal and geological aspects of a place than with the cultural, historical, ethnic, linguistic, political, and mythological dimensions of a site. To some degree, of course, site and place are matters of interchangeable perception. Thus, we see site-specific art transformed into a place-particular practice [. . .] a place, a condition, or an occasion is seen and worked as the materials of human or social exchange." — Jeff Kelley[1]

As I write this essay, wrestling with my own civic pride, I find myself longing for the comfort of a Chicago identity at a moment when issues of identity, whether political, sexual, or ethnic, are openly contested. This exhibition, at the end of the twentieth century, offers the first comprehensive attempt at tracing fifty years of artistic activity in a city once defined by regionalism, cultural isolation, and rebellion against the dominance of the New York art world. Like many similar endeavors, "Art in Chicago, 1945–1995" appears to me to be dependent on recollections of critics and curators who first developed the frameworks, the conditions of possibility, in a project that is characterized as much by memory as by history, by fiction as by fact. My contribution derives from my own institutional affiliations over the past twenty-some years in Chicago, beginning with my earliest impressions of the Imagists and the irreverent series of exhibitions staged brilliantly at the Hyde Park Art Center in the late 1960s.

A year after I first saw a Hairy Who comic book in 1969 in Rome, I moved to Chicago and soon joined the board at the Hyde Park Art Center (HPAC), working with Don Baum and Goldene Shaw on the 1976 "History of the Hyde Park Art Center" exhibition and catalogue. Although the HPAC experience was influential, I have always resisted the categorization that privileges colorful raunchy imagery, anti-intellectualism, and Pop cultural sources as sine qua non of a Chicago aesthetic. "Imagism," Franz Schulze's insightful label, proved to be an adhesive caption. His 1972 book legitimated the movement while also suggesting a figurative evolution from the "Monster Roster" and Momentum. Indeed there was a period when Chicago art and Imagism seemed coincident, if not synonymous, and a case can be made that the desire for collective identification exists in inverse proportion to the distance from the perceived center. Categories, like captions, are an efficient means to establish identity; too soon, however, a convenient label may engender stereotypes of regionalism, and other movements become counterpoints in a dynamic of negative comparisons. In Chicago, Imagism and figuration were pitted against abstraction and Conceptualism, movements not born or bred in the city. Although the rigidity of such categories now seems archaic — new work continues to dodge its interpreters and please new audiences — the debate over a Chicago style still flourishes as rumor and myth, and its scholarly bibliography over the past three decades is thin in comparison with its persistence and the resentment it provokes.

In this essay devoted to the 1970s, 1980s, and 1990s, I depart from a search for an overarching Chicago School, presenting a series of case studies of significant artists who refused the categorization and polarities that have thrived here. These artists' only shared characteristic is their resistance to being named Chicago artists. Because their artwork demonstrates a variety of strategies to negotiate or broker a relationship with the perceived image of Chicago's visual culture, they furnish a lens through which we learn about the whole and review the impact of regionalism, Feminism, Conceptualism, identity politics, and historicism on contemporary art. For example, Roger Brown's imagery of the region is posed against arguments for regionalism in a vision of the end of the world in Chicago (*plates 83, 84, 90, and 134*). Hollis Sigler has utilized the tactics of Feminism to locate her creativity in suburban domestic settings, intentionally distant from the center (*plate 111*). Hirsch Perlman's Postmodern analysis is a condition of Modernism (*plate 137*), while Iñigo Manglano-Ovalle's strategic interventions into the very premise of community and ethnicity offer opportunities for social activism in the 1990s (*plate 147*). And Tony Tasset works the art world as source and precedent, revealing its assumptions and his own identity in work that could be done anywhere, including Chicago (*plate 145*). These artists exemplify the lively multiplicity of styles that have flourished since the 1970s, when many of the artists who produced work in this city rejected group identity even as they searched for affinities and shared ideas with neigh-

fig. 1
Roger Brown, *Ablaze and Ajar*, 1972. Oil on canvas, 70 5/8 x 46 1/4 in. Mr. and Mrs. Bernard Nath, Highland Park, Illinois. Photo courtesy Phyllis Kind Gallery, Chicago.

fig. 2
Roger Brown, *City and Suburbs*, 1972. Oil on canvas, 70 1/2 x 96 in. Henry Buchbinder Family Collection, Chicago. Photo courtesy Phyllis Kind Gallery, Chicago.

bors. Now the dialogues take place on the internet—emblematic of communication where place is incidental—with strangers.

Of all the contemporary artists associated with Chicago, Roger Brown has most consistently represented the city, indeed, taken its architectural profile as signature of his own work. Transplanted from the South to Chicago as a student at the School of the Art Institute (SAIC), Brown positioned himself in his artwork as an anti-authoritarian outsider. Hailed for his regionalist vision, like Grant Wood, he established a reputation that depended on aesthetic and physical distancing. Repeatedly in a 1972 series, beginning with *Ablaze and Ajar* (**fig.1**) and concluding with *City and Suburbs* (**fig.2**), Brown anthropomorphized the city's modern skyscrapers and paradoxically became the standard bearer for Chicago Imagism—despite the fact that his work is basically not figurative like that of his peers Phil Hanson (**plate 77**), Gladys Nilsson (**plate 66**), Jim Nutt (**plates 59, 68, 86, and 156**), Ed Paschke (**plates 67, 87, 103, and 161**), Suellen Rocca (**plate 57**), Barbara Rossi (**plate 80**), and Karl Wirsum (**plates 49 and 64**)—and his is the only work expressive of geography or place. Critic Mary Mathews Gedo relates Brown's dramatic disaster series of the 1970s to the timing of his long relationship with architect George

Veronda, suggesting that the initiation of this positive alliance allowed the artist to examine earlier "disastrous" events and relationships in his life.[2] Gedo's psychological exploration of Brown's childhood spent with his grandparents in Alabama stays close to the artist's own observations, avoiding the conclusions made more easily by other critics, like Max Kozloff, who viewed the fantasies of Chicago Imagism as evidential grist for their psychological mills. By 1986 Donald Kuspit found the city's Modernist architecture a perfect foil for the expressive excesses of Chicago art, which he diagnosed as madness.[3]

Brown's *Autobiography in the Shape of Alabama (Mammy's Door)* (**plate 83**) resists self-indulgent revelation; however, there is genuine self-exposure and genealogy evident in the family photographs and correspondence he placed in this work dedicated to his great grandmother. Conflating minute details with dispassionate grand vistas, the artist synthesized current events with personal and political observations, and in *Autobiography* literally invoked the map as graphic description. Brown's landmarks—whether recognizable skyscrapers in topographical cityscapes or in panoramas such as *Greater Sprawling City* (**fig.3**) and *Thick Paint (Staying Clear of the Existential Smog)* (1983), which shows the John Hancock Center, Standard Oil Building, and Sears Tower—have dominated his dramatic silhouettes of Chicago since 1974.

Given Brown's idiosyncratic, ambivalent use of historical predecessors, *The Entry of Christ into Chicago in 1976* (**plate 90**) is an important example of his descriptive imagination. The painting is ten feet wide and introduces the city with one-story storefronts in the front plane; Michigan Avenue is in the background. Brown had not yet seen James Ensor's related painting of 1888 (the Ensor exhibition opened at the Art Institute after he had begun his own reprise of the masterpiece), but had heard about it from critic Dennis Adrian.[4] Not only a comic rejoinder to the tortured vision of Ensor, Brown's outrageous incongruousness—Jesus arrives on the back of a flat-bed truck to be greeted by dignitaries on a dais—celebrates a fantasy, making plausible and visible a faith derived from the artist's recollections of Southern revival-style religion.

fig. 3
Roger Brown, *Greater Sprawling City*, 1974. Oil on canvas, 85 x 60 in. Present location unknown. Photo courtesy Phyllis Kind Gallery, Chicago.

Brown is a preeminent voyeur, and if his undulating green fields and teethlike crevasses are analogies for body parts, his Freudian predilection is also apparent in his fulfillment of our desires as viewers to see into private spaces, behind public facades. On the other hand, the expansiveness of his vistas partakes of a cinematic vision nourished by the fantasy and romance of movies, often from a bird's-eye view. This distancing has been explained by his youthful activities as a stagehand for amateur theatricals and, indeed, the flattened landscapes and flanking elements recall stage designs and Brown's later sets for Mozart's *Cosi Fan Tutti* for the Chicago Opera Theater (1979). The move from the small theater as frame for his late 1960s narratives, first shown in the "False Image" exhibition of 1968, to his own real interest in artifice and theater, is pivotal. Brown's work, like that of his colleagues, has been explained and claimed by occasionally conflicting commentators who compare him with the Italian Surrealist Giorgio de Chirico and the lonely American Edward Hopper. In fact, he delighted in Nancy cartoons and children's illustrations, Japanese scrolls and the puns of René Magritte, whose 1966 Art Institute retrospective was influential. Legible as vernacular iconography, Brown's paintings, huge and complex, capture the span of Chicago's modern skyline for its nostalgic appeal and chronicle its underlying violence and hidden secrets as tiny tableaus illuminated in every window. His intricate patterning and isometric perspectives disguise a powerful gift for ironic documentation;

like a great satirist, he slips in an agenda that is critical to the very fabric of the American values he seems to celebrate.

In the 1970s the catchword for the sequence of mixed artistic styles and messages was "pluralism," and the exhibition histories of museums and alternative spaces ricocheted among Pattern and Decoration, Feminism, and Conceptualism. At the Museum of Contemporary Art (MCA) from 1976 to 1981, I participated in that history. Arriving as curator just after the 1976 exhibition "Abstract Art in Chicago," I organized exhibitions on the work of June Leaf (**plates 22 and 28**) and Claes Oldenburg, whose early careers took place in Chicago. A catalyzing moment in the cultural community took place in the 1980s, especially if one believes that history occurs in stops and starts, based on disruption rather than continuity. Not only was that decade marked by swollen commercial success with astronomical auction figures dominating headlines, so too did international imports flood the American art world. Larger agendas of Conceptual work by previously unrepresented individuals derailed the progression of Modernism, while academia embraced theories that undermined the conventions of formalist authority. If some of these theories were half-baked and half-understood, they presented new intellectual and aesthetic avenues for artists trained in Chicago. Swept away in the excitement of appropriation, simulation, and picture theory, Imagism lost its toehold when regional exhibitions like the hotly debated "Artists of Chicago and Vicinity" exhibitions were disbanded; the title of the 1980 traveling exhibition "Who Chicago?," with hindsight, sheds its irony to become a question of regionalism. As a Feminist writing away from the center in the 1980s, I developed my own voice, and attended to artists who had been relegated to secondary positions. As an educator (I began teaching at SAIC in 1981), I discovered that each semester brought challenges, as new ideas and trends inhibited any desire to fabricate a collective but encouraged constant exploration in a climate of diversity.

Hollis Sigler's Feminism, which she perhaps first developed in college and solidified later as an early member of Artemisia in 1973, is one example of the fracturing of a Chicago movement. In Chicago in the mid-1970s, both Artemisia and ARC provided exhibition opportunities for individuals and collectively supported ideas and work that were previously excluded. Sigler intensified the juxtaposition of personal with political, so that by 1993–94 in "The Breast Cancer Journal" (**fig. 4**), she shared her own illness and struggle for psychic and physical health with others who might be comforted by her imagery. But in the 1980s, Sigler's adept use of text, as in the more minimal paintings of Kay Rosen (**plate 123**), suggests that linguistic and Conceptual strategies had taken root in Chicago. Like Nancy Spero (**plate 37**),

Sigler painted subjective revelations and drew on traditional mediums for untraditional messages. She portrayed the city as backdrop to her own landscape, *Peopled By Phantoms Having No Homes* (**fig. 5**), a location in which she alternately domesticated and defined herself in opposition to its distant skyscrapers. By 1992, in *She Has Room of Her Own*, Sigler appropriated the city, Virginia Woolf's essay, and all the ideology that essay now signifies for her own representation. Operating from a marginal position, Sigler foregrounds her interiority in domestic settings and displaces the center, sometimes Chicago, to the edge.

In her jewel-colored paintings of interiors—vernacular, everyday suburban settings—she begins with a theatrical metaphor, a proscenium stage for hidden realities. Sigler often retains the curtained openings at each side of her stage-set-like compositions, but their scale suggests the up-close pleasures of the peep box, and her discursive intimacy, the liberties of a Feminist position. Her choice of style is motivated by a desire to emphasize content—the remarkable scope of emotions portrayed by unseen, never-pictured protagonists—over form or skill. By using language and loading her small canvases with ornamental details which become as disproportionately significant as language, she shifts from metaphor to allegory. Sigler resists the facile oppositions of sexual politics. With inscriptions that trans-

7

fig. 5
Hollis Sigler, *Peopled By
Phantoms Having No
Homes*, 1987 (detail). Oil
on canvas with painted wood
frame, 60 x 60 in. Present
location unknown. Photo
courtesy Carl Hammer
Gallery, Chicago.

fig. 6
Hollis Sigler, *Why Is Guilt
Part Of Temptation?*, 1985.
Oil on board, 12 x 17 in.
Private collection. Photo
courtesy Carl Hammer
Gallery, Chicago.

fig. 7
Hirsch Perlman, door from
exhibition space to vestibule
with balcony above, The
Renaissance Society at the
University of Chicago, 1988.
Photo: Tom Van Eynde,
Oak Park, Illinois, courtesy
the Renaissance Society,
Chicago.

form commentary into content, she animates and politicizes her uninhabited habitations. These titles, which fly in banners across the tops of her canvases or are inscribed on ornamental frames, spell out subjective responses to oppressive social structures and external situations, symbolic and sexual relations. Her sophisticated figures of speech position her creativity relative to continuously shifting sexual, social, and cultural networks, a strategy also adopted by other Feminist artists of the 1980s. Occasionally, her tone recalls romantic singers like Edith Piaf and Patsy Cline in laments such as "Her habits make her home," "She could never explain her pain," and "She's got them broken pearl blues."

A series of small paintings from 1985 have the emotional intensity of Frida Kahlo's condensed autobiographical icons and evoke the surreal landscapes and interiors of Gertrude Abercrombie (**plate 13**). In *You Keep Tampering With My Heart*, a dress with a bloody stain at the chest is spread-eagled like an offering on a table, while in *Why Is Guilt Part Of Temptation?* (**fig. 6**), flowers grow from a mound of earth unexpectedly settled on the bed. The complexities of love, or sexuality, the emotional costs of pleasure, are intertwined. In *Drawing from Life*, the bed is outdoors, surrounded by a vine-covered fence and bare trees. Bloody rivulets stain the white sheets in much the same way that the painter's marks sustain representation across the blank canvas. Camouflaged by a naïve style and primary-colored palette, which stand in contrast to her highly charged, gender-specific work, Sigler's radicality comes from her refusal to show herself, to be seen. Not only does she turn away from the mas-

culine gaze, she has excised the female body/figure from her narratives. Flesh made word, her characters are inscribed to perform in relationships with an unseen other woman, lover, mother, never absolutely identifiable. The idiosyncratic variety of the accessories of Sigler's suburban settings is matched by the multiple tones of the language—epigrammatic or discursive—and the range of moods and roles she assumes, from victim to heroine.

The perspectives adopted by Brown and Sigler also illustrate the gendered differences in their work and point to the intergenerational shifts from Modernism to Postmodernism. Brown's imagery—identical units of housing, clover-leaf highways, huge semis—the iconography of modernization in the 1970s, was often inspired by and seen from a distance on car trips. On the road, the artist depicted rural vistas, suburban housing developments—but always from a bird's-eye view, in contrast to the intimate interiors of Sigler. In the mid-1980s, when Sigler created her tiny bedroom series, or in *She was losing control of the Situation* (1988), an ominous tableau which shows a hose overflowing the inflatable pool and the barbecue burning out of control, Brown painted *Chicago Hit by a Bomb* (1985), and illustrated his architectural triad bursting into flames.

For Hirsch Perlman, there is no visual work, including his own photographs, that cannot be approached through language. His art, like much Conceptual work of the 1980s, dwells on the subtle distinctions between visual semiotics and textual connotations; architecture and documents yield evidence of power relations and become his subject matter. Inspired by Joseph Kosuth and Bruce Nauman, Perlman, along with Jeanne Dunning (**plate 149**), Tony Tasset (**plate 145**), Mitchell Kane, and Judy Ledgerwood, found support from galleries, particularly Feature and Robbin Lockett, and from critic Kathryn Hixson who consistently wrote about their work. This new generation of artists, students of Phil Hanson (**plate 77**) and Ray Yoshida (**plate 74**), perceived their work to belong to an art world whose center could be anywhere, New York or Zurich. If the Imagists embraced outsider artists, medieval and non-Western cultures for inspiration, this Conceptually oriented generation embraced the critical theories that were flooding art journals in the wake of Postmodernism. In a pumped-up atmosphere of possibility and even fame, they resisted the regional label as strenuously as did their Imagist predecessors. Their commercial and critical success was not limited to Chicago, and indeed was reinforced by the celebritization and economic highs of the moment. Chicago, already famous for significant Surrealist collections, was again stimulated by internationalism, which now brought German and Italian Neo-Expressionism to museums and private collections.

Trained as an undergraduate in architecture at Yale University, Perlman came to Chicago in 1984; he was already familiar with post-Structuralism, linking to representation allegory and other literary tropes of undecidability in language. In a 1990 interview published for an exhibition in Zurich, Perlman discussed his work as analogous to linguistic structures, and in so doing acknowledged his allegiance to important theoretical influences. "The exhibition as a whole," he stated, "is also still a narrative, a sentence or sentences. If it is a sentence, I have to look for the sense or nonsense of each work separately. Word, then stands for image here, and I can question the 'words' separately."[5] (As an example, he cites the word "library," which simultaneously is understood as a collection of books and as a construction built by an architect.) Perlman's self-doubt and linguistic misgivings had been made visual in his elegant and pristine installation for The Renaissance Society at the University of Chicago in 1988 (fig. 7). One of the city's preeminent locations for avant-garde art, the Renaissance Society has been identified as a home for Modernist experimentation since its inception in 1915. Perlman questioned this authority, producing slight architectural alterations to the vestibule and main gallery, as well as authorship, according to Postmodernist theo-

ries of language, placing the responsibility of understanding his work on the shoulders of his viewers/readers. At the same time that he resists the responsibilities of authorship, he also queries the so-called objectivity of documentary, in this case, architectural photographs.

The artist's deadpan photographs of actual buildings exhibited in conjunction with historical photographic reproductions paradoxically salvaged the past and disrupted the process of representation. Perlman juxtaposed blurry color photographs of modern monuments by Le Corbusier, Adolf Loos, and, in Chicago, Mies van der Rohe's Crown Hall at Illinois Institute of Technology (1950–56), Holabird and Root's Postmodern Chicago Historical Society (1987–88), and the Armory (now demolished for a new MCA) (plate 137), among others, with enlarged black-and-white photographs of details of Ludwig Wittgenstein's 1928 Stonborough-Wittgenstein House in Vienna. (The home Wittgenstein designed for his sister represents a critique of Modernist architecture, idealism, and ideology, by a philosopher whose subject was everyday language.) Unframed text panels adjacent to and larger than the framed photos described the details in the photographs, but reversed the usual pairing of text and image and, because of their placement in the gallery, became captions to that very space in which the viewer stood. No longer was the usual relationship between text and illustration trustworthy, but obviously relative and discon-

8

9

10

fig. 8
Dan Peterman, *Sulfur Cycle*,
1994. Installation at
Museum of Contemporary
Art, Chicago, 1994. Photo
courtesy Museum of
Contemporary Art.

fig. 9
Gordon Matta-Clark, *Circus
or The Caribbean Orange*,
1978. Interior view at
Museum of Contemporary
Art, Chicago, 1978. Photo
courtesy Museum of
Contemporary Art.

fig. 10
Iñigo Manglano-Ovalle,
Green Card, 1992.
Laminated computer print,
2 x 3 1/2 in., edition of 25.
Photo courtesy Feigen, Inc.,
Chicago.

tinuous. Perlman's vision of landmarks, in contrast to Brown's and Sigler's, subverted the powerful claims of Modernism, symbolic of progress and internationalism. His representation of Chicago assumed as subject matter the ideological implications of imaging the city, and produced an unexpected acknowledgment of the artist's own role in a larger institutional critique.

In the 1990s, reinforced by political debates over cultural entitlements, artists discovered alternative, hybrid practices; they ignored the politics and aesthetics of Modernism and invented new formats and cosmopolitan identities undermining restrictions that previously defined them as regional, marginal, or excluded. Still, there are many artists who continue, like Brown, to make their environment a central element in their work. Moving from the Northwest to Chicago in 1985, Julia Fish paints small canvases to provide a map of a natural world and lived experience (**plate 144**). She depicts the spaces she inhabits, but focuses so closely on her immediate surroundings—for example, views from her studio window—that they become abstract representations. Unlike Jim Lutes, another immigrant from the Pacific Northwest, whose earlier depictions of the city around Milwaukee Avenue provided the backdrop for the artist's personal ghosts and psychic fears (**plate 126**), Fish refines the distinctions among resemblance, realism, and representation. Lutes, on the other hand, is now entirely devoted to abstract painting. Another position is that of Kerry James Marshall (**plate 171**). Neither regionalist nor social realist, Marshall paints black heroines and heroes to depict the imagery and failure of garden projects in Chicago's inner city. The titles, *Many Mansions* and *Better Homes and Gardens* (both 1994), seem vestigial, even painful, reminders of an unrealized Modernist utopia, gardens whose capacity to grow is constrained by

the collapse of the social and economic infrastructure of American cities.

From a platform Cornel West has called "the new cultural politics," Dan Peterman (**plate 140**) works as an artist and activist on Chicago's South Side. Addressing environmental issues, Peterman does not limit his practice to the neighborhood he imaginatively works to improve. Using recycled materials, which he calls "postconsumer plastics," he has built casual-looking, site-specific sculptural installations in many European museums. *Sulfur Cycle* (**fig. 8**) incorporated stacks of synthetic gypsum wallboard, the manufacture of which diverted a ton of sulfur from the atmosphere, in advance of their being installed in the new MCA. This project, which included sulfur dioxide emission rights purchased on the Chicago Board of Trade market, also extended earlier installations that used the actual building of the former MCA as their material—projects by Christo, Gordon Matta-Clark (**fig. 9**), Michael Asher, and Charles Simonds.

Subsumed by the growing power of conservatism in the 1990s, symbolic and political debates have left an important legacy for artists in Chicago. Strategies of critique shift from representation to performance, from commodity to practice, and inspiration and identity have been drawn from an expanding spectrum of sexual, ethnic, racial, or economic positioning, as well as family, location, or nationality. Iñigo Manglano-Ovalle (**plate 147**), born in Spain, reared in Colombia, and educated in the United States, draws from his lived experiences of mixed nationality and frequent migrations to reach broader issues of self-definition and critical self-reflection in Chicago. Often mutable, such representations of race and difference are forged on smaller units that remain in flux, always unsettled, or unsettling, as in the case of gang membership. Using site as the condition to analyze structures of civic unity,

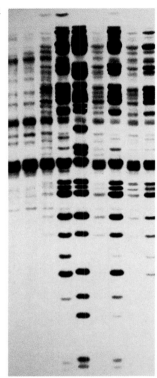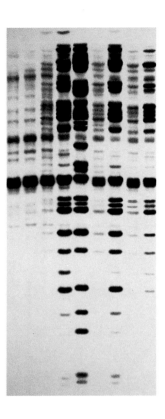

to represent the particularities of community and individual empowerment, Manglano-Ovalle demonstrates unequivocally how atomized, fragmented, and conflicted is the image of Chicago and his own selfhood. Chicago as landmark is broken down into its constituent, heterogeneous parts, which not only evade definitive pictorial representation but also resist mapping. Politicizing the definition of civic landmarks, Manglano-Ovalle's aesthetic occasions update the defining principles of cultural community and become metaphors for the struggle to define Chicago art. The issue of "turf," the claim to cultural property, is central to the dynamic of this work; the relativism of each definition nullifies any unified style and presents a hybrid vision of a collective group. Like other artists influenced first by Michel Foucault and more recently by postcolonial critique, in his work Manglano-Ovalle negotiates between subjectivity and politics, picturing the impact of colonialism and racial difference. In 1992, amidst mounting anti-immigrant sentiment, for an exhibition devoted to the celebration of the Quincentennial, he made a plastic identity card for the very first illegal alien, Christopher Columbus (**fig. 10**). For Manglano-Ovalle, the activities of surveillance, photography, and video present opportunities to implicate the viewer's

point of view as more than a point of departure, but the centrality of the individual in the frame, usually positioned on guard, achieves a level of immediacy that stands apart from the imaginative depictions of Sigler and Brown.

Manglano-Ovalle's work is informed by historic changes that have recast the political map of the world and altered urban populations and by the scientific imaging technologies that exist to test weapons or chart DNA patterns of his family (**fig. 11**). On occasion his artistic practice has also incorporated aspects of activism and collaboration. Working with a group of Latino youth in West Town, Manglano-Ovalle helped form Street-Level Video, an organization that continues without him today, as the permanent residue of the original project sponsored by "Culture in Action," Sculpture Chicago. Street-Level Video in 1993 shot and edited hundreds of videos documenting their stories, voicing their concerns about turf wars, drugs, housing, and gangs. Culminating in two ambitious projects, *Cul de Sac* and *Televecindario*, the dialogues encouraged and visualized in the work revealed the deep antagonisms and uncertainties of border definition, generational splits, and even some hope for reconciliation. These are issues that mark the culture wars of the 1990s and produce a vocabulary of political correctness, but which also have generated artwork specific to Chicago. But, for Manglano-Ovalle, recollections of evening walks with his grandfather inspired him; "The meeting of local residents could create a sense of place, ownership, and home; not just a 'site of critique,' but a 'site of possibility,' where productive change might be initiated."[6]

In *Televecindario*, an entire city block was the setting for ambitious video installations, graffiti painting, rap groups, and a one-day community celebration. On the evening of the block party, spectators mixed with performers, entered into the work the way one might enter a stage set. Beyond the limits of the museum, everyone was immersed in issues of the street, licensed to watch gang members discuss their own sophisticated verbal and visual codes, while seventy-five video monitors, linked by yellow cords connected to private homes, told a complicated and overlapping story—actually multiple stories—of a community's concerns. Based on interviews with residents, the video programs were dedicated to issues such as jobs, sexism, violence, and class demarcation. In every sense *Televecindario* was site-specific to the social, economic, racial, and political currents of one community, a particular unit, at a particular moment in the cultural life of the city. Yet in this project, the months of shooting and editing, the generative process and not just the end product, a one-night-only block party, were crucial. In the hands of Manglano-Ovalle's young collaborators, video provided the means to visualize their concerns and represent themselves; at the same time, it held out the possibility of continual transformation. In this work and others, from photo panels to orchestrated multimedia extravaganzas, Manglano-Ovalle challenges real political structures that allow viewers access or that separate one ethnic group from another.

Tony Tasset (**plate 145**) defined his career in the 1980s by rejecting a Chicago style in an overt embrace of Minimalism and Conceptualism, those very currents that had the slenderest history in the city. For the purposes of my argument, his rejection of place as defining and his use of precedents, albeit recent, make his work especially significant. Like other artists of his generation, he has critiqued and eventually capitalized on the glamorous surfaces of the media, which theorists of 1980s Postmodernism found philosophically and spiritually bankrupt. Rather than searching for the authentic, he has built a strong body of work on exteriority, on the meaning

of appearances. Using leather, fur, and animal skins instead of painted canvases, early in the 1980s Tasset composed elegant "domesticates"—his label for heavily framed surrogates for abstract paintings, Modernist icons (**fig. 12**). Beginning with the furniture of exhibitions—usually invisible containers, wrapping, and pedestals—he foregrounded their Minimal volumes, like his frames, as content. Seemingly untroubled by political critiques of consumerism or of the nostalgic recuperation of history, Tasset now produces overt homages to his predecessors and subverts the prevailing feminist and masculinist approaches to identity politics. Acknowledging the impossibility of originality, he attempts to supplement his prototypes, to be like them, or to be them, as seen recently in a photomural of the artist dressed in cowboy boots and posed as Robert Smithson against the Nevada desert. Audiences for Tasset's work appreciate this irony only if they know the history of Smithson, just as one must know Ensor to appreciate Roger Brown's version. Tasset's strategy, like that of Cindy Sherman, however, is the celebration of the counterfeit and Zelig-like impersonations. In the 1980s these attempts could be discussed as appropriations, but recently they suggest a more serious pathos, an attempt at self-fashioning independent of region and place.

fig. 11
Iñigo Manglano-Ovalle, *Twin*, 1995. Cibachrome of DNA analysis, two parts, each 61 x 25 in., edition 1/3. Susan and Lewis Manlow, Chicago. Photo courtesy Feigen, Inc., Chicago.

fig. 12
Tony Tasset, *Abstract Style II*, 1986. Cowhide, leather, suede, and painted wood frame, 37 x 40 x 2 in. Suzette and Timothy Flood, Chicago. Photo courtesy Rhona Hoffman Gallery, Chicago.

fig. 13
Tony Tasset, *I Peed in My Pants*, 1994 (detail). Cibachrome and frame, 83 1/4 x 38 1/4 x 2 in., edition 2/3. Refco Group, Ltd., Chicago. Photo courtesy Rhona Hoffman Gallery, Chicago.

13

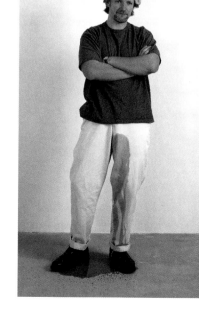

12

In Tasset's life-sized Cibachrome *I Peed in My Pants* (**fig. 13**), the bearded artist poses with arms crossed, legs apart, in T-shirt and khakis—a casual pose familiar from advertisements, themselves fashioned after artists' styles. This self-portrait is a peculiar construction of masculinity, somewhere between Robert Morris's *I-Box* (1962) and Jeff Koons's 1984 self-advertisements in national art magazines, as Tasset, with his pose and smugly confident look, almost taunts his viewers with his own self-staining. Amelia Jones best surveys the ways in which contemporary male artists address masculinity "as a negotiated system of identities that are accomplished through the ritual display of phallic attributes, specifically in relation to the masculinized function of the artist"—a function, she continues, "that could be said to exaggerate the attributes of masculinity affording power to the male subject in patriarchal culture."[7] Tasset's self-portrait sign subsumes the criticism of Jackson Pollock's masculine gestural emissions and the *Oxidation Paintings* of Andy Warhol, while demystifying volumes of heroicizing rhetoric and theoretical analysis into larger-than-life demonstration. He complicates the simple gender oppositions of Modernism by marking and mocking himself, staging this most banal admission of loss of control as a sovereign example of control. In 1994 Tasset again publicized his white-male identity in a work called

fig. 14
Tony Tasset, *My Parents*,
1994 (detail). Cibachrome
and frame, 52 x 72 in., edition 3/3. Ruttenberg Arts
Foundation, Chicago. Photo
courtesy Rhona Hoffman
Gallery, Chicago.

My Parents (**fig. 14**). As a billboard planned for downtown Chicago, this enormous portrait is humorous and horrific, remarkable for its ability to erase subjectivity, to conceal any trace of inner life by spectacularizing this American couple as poster parents. In what could be seen as a backlash against political correctness, such a facade shows all but tells nothing about a family, and more than ever masks the individual to project a full-scale advertisement for the white, middle-aged middle class. This time Tasset's predecessors are familial not artistic, yet the genealogical exposure paradoxically betrays no intimacies. Radiantly confident, dressed in their best, the couple are prosperous burghers, logical descendants of Grant Wood's *American Gothic* (1930), the famous icon in the Art Institute's collection. Tasset's billboard-sized Mom and Dad are complacent divinities, reassuring to some audiences, causing liberal discomfort to others, and finally, alien to many publics.

Roger Brown's double-sided map of Alabama (1974) projected his origins onto his home state and transferred private letters from his family into containers on the door of an autobiographical artwork. Two decades later Tasset has reversed this relationship, using his parents' image opportunistically, merely to signal his origins on a billboard. In the politics of racial and sexual difference, Tasset undermines geographical happenstance for an identity politics that is self-aggrandizing and placeless. Working against the grain of regionalism, restoring the prerogative of global heroism, he admits to artificiality and a never-ending fascination with the past. Tasset pits himself against history in such a close embrace that he simultaneously smothers the very idea of identity and individuality. His art presents flamboyant excursions in a complex visual culture, where the imagery of place, never static, changes over time according to social, economic, and political demands. Without attempting to define a school or movement, this essay points to individual accomplishments such as his as emblematic of major currents in three generations of art. My motivation in choosing these particular artists is born of a wish to situate significant ideas in the artistic milieu of Chicago, as the inception of a new museum demands a celebratory articulation of local culture.

notes

1 Jeff Kelley quoted in Claire F. Fox, "The Portable Border: Site-Specificity, Art, and the U.S.-Mexico Frontier," *Social Text* 41 (Winter 1994), p. 63.

2 For Brown, the skyscrapers in his paintings were characters in unfolding dramas, and he told Gedo that he wished "to depict buildings as isolated actors against a solid backdrop,...to have the buildings moving, rather than static as I had always presented them before." Mary Mathews Gedo, "Interviews with a Living Artist: The Art of Roger Brown," in John E. and Mary M. Gedo, *Perspectives on Creativity: The Biographical Method* (Norwood, NJ: Alex Publishing Corp., 1992), p. 168, n. 10.

3 Donald Kuspit, "The Madness of Chicago Art," *New Art Examiner* 13 (May 1986), pp. 22–26.

4 Montgomery, Alabama, Montgomery Museum of Fine Arts, *Roger Brown*, text by Mitchell Douglas Kahan with Dennis Adrian and Russell Bowman (Montgomery, 1980), p. 84.

5 Hirsch Perlman, interviewed by Renate Cornu and Harm Lux, in Zurich, Shedhalle Zürich, and Geneva, Halle Sud, *Hirsch Perlman* (Zurich, 1990), unpag.

6 Iñigo Manglano-Ovalle quoted in *Culture in Action* (Seattle: Bay Press, Inc., 1995), p. 83.

7 Amelia Jones, "Displaying the Phallus: Male Artists Perform Their Masculinities," *Art History* 17, 4 (Dec. 1994), p. 546.

The year 1945, marking the end of World War II, is widely acknowledged as starting a new era worldwide. In Chicago, 1945 not only demonstrates the great changes wrought by the war, but signals the end of the Social Realist style that Depression-era WPA programs had supported. A flood of returning GIs entered Chicago's art schools, subsequently creating distinctive styles of work that put Chicago on the international art map for the first time in the city's history. The mid-decade beginning point sets up an approximate rhythm for the next fifty years.

1945
1995

art
in chicago

1945–1956

a decade of momentum

Servicemen taking advantage of the GI Bill cause enrollment to explode at both the "Chicago Bauhaus"— László Moholy-Nagy's Institute of Design—and The School of The Art Institute of Chicago. The new aesthetic directions pursued by these students soon begin to overwhelm the established order when they win top prizes in The Art Institute of Chicago's long-standing Annual Exhibitions by Artists of Chicago and Vicinity. The Art Institute bans student work, creating a schism between the generations. In response, the younger generation founds a series of highly influential and successful *salons des refusés* known as Exhibition Momentum. This segment's title is both a play on these important exhibitions and a literal description of the tenor of the era. By the mid-1950s, however, this younger generation has itself become the established order. At the Institute of Design it is the end of an era when a new director abolishes fine-arts courses and significantly alters the nature of the institution. By 1956, the year ending this segment, many of the Young Turks who had prevailed against Chicago's art establishment had left the city in search of greener pastures.

1957–1965

the second city rises

Although no major event marks 1957 as a beginning point, a new aesthetic emerges with the first one-person exhibition of H.C. Westermann, whose enigmatic, personal imagery and highly finished craftsmanship becomes for many the prototypical "Chicago style." In 1959 artists associated with what is dubbed locally the "Monster Roster" are introduced to New York and the world via "New Images of Man," a controversial exhibition at The Museum of Modern Art, New York. Disheartened by the negative press given some of the Chicago artists, the new generation falters and institutional support dissipates. As well, in Chicago and across the country, a new, radical generation— the Baby Boom—is flexing its muscles, signaling the end of the Eisenhower years and the beginning of great societal change. The title for this segment of Chicago's art history is a play on an important exhibition at the Illinois Institute of Technology, "The Sunken City Rises," which referred to Chicago's origins in a swamp as well as its artists' attempts to redefine their historic secondary relationship with the New York art world.

1966–1976

the entry of the imagists into chicago

In 1966 a style explodes on the scene with the first of three exhibitions at the Hyde Park Art Center by a group of artists calling themselves The Hairy Who. Along with other young graduates from The School of The Art Institute of Chicago, they become collectively known as the Imagists. Their figurative style, with its emphasis on distortion, precise craftsmanship, and garish colors, and its sources in popular culture, quickly comes to define "Chicago art" to many within and outside the city. As the site of the 1968 Democratic Convention, Chicago is exposed to worldwide scrutiny. In reaction to the events surrounding the convention, some of Chicago's artists organize, protest, and create works in new media while others look only toward the art world. Financial support from the recently established National Endowment for the Arts (1965) enables the explosive growth of arts institutions, especially artist-run spaces. In 1973 the Imagists receive international exposure at the XII Bienal de São Paulo. In 1976 Imagist Roger Brown paints one of his best-known works, *The Entry of Christ into Chicago in 1976,* from which the title for this segment is taken.

1977–1985

the big picture

In 1977 the Chicago Cultural Center opens with a gallery devoted to showing a broad range of Chicago work. The City of Chicago's direct support of the visual arts signals a new time. Resentment of the Imagist style grows among young artists who perceive Imagism as dominating and defining Chicago art because of its high visibility at commercial galleries. Alternative spaces begin to falter by the beginning of the 1980s. Dissatisfaction with the status quo culminates in the founding of Feature, the first Chicago gallery to show Postmodern artists. The title of this segment refers both to an influential 1983 Hyde Park Art Center show, "The Big Pitcher: 20 Years of the Abstracted Figure in Chicago Art," and to the pluralistic nature of this period.

1986–1995

(un)assigned identities

In the mid-1980s, along with the rest of the country, Chicago experiences an art boom. A greatly expanded gallery scene emerges, with several new districts. The Art Institute of Chicago has built a new wing and is regularly presenting contemporary art for the first time in decades. Area institutions and the many university galleries present exhibitions of local artists at unprecedented rates. Randolph Street Gallery begins a new era of socially and politically informed shows curated by teams of artists, revolutionizing the way art is presented in Chicago. Controversy emerging around works of art energizes the community. Minority artists reassert their position in the Chicago art world, many addressing issues of cultural identity. By the early 1990s "Chicago Conceptualism," a Postmodern form enriched by theory and critical ideas, has emerged triumphant, and many Chicago-based artists are working in an international style with no particular "Chicago" quality. In acknowledgment of this new reality, the title of this segment is a play on a 1990 work by Iñigo Manglano-Ovalle, *Assigned Identities.*

1945–1956

*a decade
of momentum*

chicago

GI Bill (enacted
1944) significantly
increases enrollment
at art schools

Ivan Albright exhibits
with brother Malvin
(Zsissly) at The
Associated American
Artists Galleries,
New York

Johnson Publishing
Company launches
Ebony magazine

Midway Airport
handles 1.3 million
passengers annually

beyond

Television
manufacture begins

George Orwell's
The Animal Farm
published

Brooklyn Dodgers
announce signing of
Jackie Robinson

Charlie Parker and
Dizzy Gillespie
collaborations
embody bebop music

World War II ends

Nuremberg Trials
begin in Germany

President Franklin D.
Roosevelt dies; Harry
S. Truman succeeds

United Nations
formed

1 Ivan Albright. *The Temptation of St. Anthony*, 1944–45. Oil on canvas.

2 Nathan Lerner. *Eye on Window*, c. 1945. Gelatin silver print.

1946

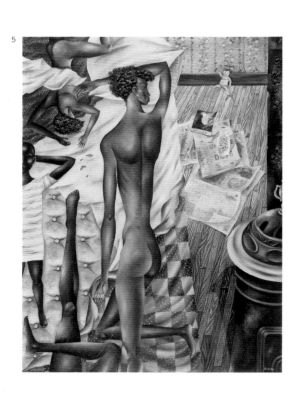

chicago	**beyond**
Benjamin Gallery opens on Superior Street	Salon des Réalités Nouvelles founded in Paris
Fairweather-Hardin Gallery opens in Evanston, Illinois	Alberto Giacometti first exhibits in New York
Triple "A" Gallery opens on Oak Street	Peggy Guggenheim closes Art of This Century Gallery and moves to Venice
AIC bans student work from its annual "Chicago and Vicinity" exhibitions	Art in Cinema established at the San Francisco Museum of Art
Chicago Chapter of Artists Equity founded	R. Buckminster Fuller builds the first geodesic dome
Serge Chermayeff becomes director of ID (until 1951)	Edwin Land invents the Polaroid Camera
László Moholy-Nagy's *Vision in Motion* published	Hungarian scientist Dennis Gabor describes holography (Nobel Prize in 1971)
The Chicago Land Commission created for slum clearance and urban renewal	Tennessee Williams's *A Streetcar Named Desire* premières in New York
Martin Kennelly elected mayor	The House Committee on Un-American Activities investigates the movie industry for Communist infiltration
Marshall Field III launches *Chicago Sun-Times*	India gains independence; Jawaharlal Nehru becomes the first Prime Minister

3 László Moholy-Nagy. *Nuclear II*, 1946. Oil on canvas.

4 Margo Hoff. *Murder Mystery*, 1946. Oil on casein on canvas board.

5 Eldzier Cortor. *Room No. 6*, c. 1946–49. Oil on gesso on board.

6 Richard Koppe. *Wall*, c. 1947. Oil on canvas.

7 Harry Callahan. *Eleanor*, 1947. Gelatin silver print.

6

7

8

9

8   Archibald J. Motley, Jr. *Gettin' Religion*, 1948. Oil on canvas.

9   Julia Thecla. *Confusion of Christmas*, 1948. Gouache with incising, graphite, and charcoal on cardboard.

10   Evelyn Statsinger. *In the Penal Colony*, 1949. Pen, ink, and crayon on paper.

11   Aaron Siskind. *Chicago 30*, 1949. Gelatin silver print.

12

12   Harry Callahan. *Chicago*, c. 1949.
     Gelatin silver print.

13   Gertrude Abercrombie. *The
     Courtship*, 1949. Oil on Masonite.

14   Vera Berdich. *Things to be
     Remembered*, 1949. Soft ground
     and photo etching with aquatint
     on paper.

13

14

chicago

Contemporary Art Workshop founded on Rush Street

The Renaissance Society begins annual summertime members' exhibitions (until 1963)

Chicago poet Gwendolyn Brooks is first African-American to win Pulitzer Prize for poetry

Muddy Waters releases the single "Rolling Stone"

Chicago's population reaches 3,621,000 (metropolitan area 5,600,000)

Dearborn Homes public housing project completed

beyond

Willem de Kooning, Arshile Gorky, and Jackson Pollock included in the US Pavilion at the Venice Biennale

Ralph Bunche becomes first African-American to win Nobel Peace Prize

Billy Wilder's *Sunset Blvd.* released

Charles Schulz's *Charlie Brown* debuts in seven newspapers

Korean War begins

Senator Joseph McCarthy investigates Communist activity in US State Department

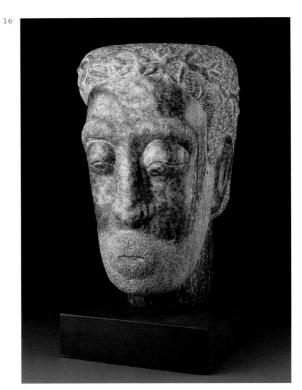

15 Cosmo Campoli. *Birth of Death*, 1950. Bronze, rock, wax, and steel.

16 Marion Perkins. *Man of Sorrows*, 1950. Marble.

17 Emerson Woelffer. *Untitled*, 1951. Oil and enamel on linen.

18 Joseph Goto. *Organic Form I*, 1951. Steel.

1951

chicago

AIC lifts student ban on "Chicago and Vicinity" exhibitions

"Harry Callahan: Photographs by Series" inaugurates AIC's new gallery for photography

Serge Chermayeff resigns as director of ID; Crombie Taylor succeeds (until 1955)

Aaron Siskind comes to teach photography at ID

Jean Dubuffet exhibition and "Anticultural Positions" lecture at the Arts Club

Goethe-Institut Chicago founded

860–880 Lake Shore Drive Apartments completed (Mies van der Rohe)

The Milwaukee Avenue, Lake Street, Dearborn Street Subway opens

Martin Kennelly reelected mayor

beyond

Robert Rauschenberg and Roy Lichtenstein have first solo exhibitions in New York

Harold Rosenberg coins the term "Action Painting"

The "Irascible 18" painters protest the antiabstract bias of The Metropolitan Museum of Art, New York

Akira Kurosawa's *Rashomon* introduces West to Japanese film

John Huston's *African Queen* released

J.D. Salinger's *The Catcher in the Rye* published

Jet magazine launched

Sugar Ray Robinson defeats Jake "Raging Bull" LaMotta for the middleweight championship

Ethel and Julius Rosenberg convicted of spying for the Soviet Union (executed 1953)

18

19

19 Arthur Siegel. *Untitled*, c. 1952.
    Color photograph.

20 Aaron Siskind. *Chicago 42*, 1952.
    Gelatin silver print.

21 George Cohen. *Emblem for an
    Unknown Nation #1*, 1954.
    Oil on Masonite.

22 June Leaf. *Red Painting*, 1954.
    Oil on canvas.

20

chicago

Allan Frumkin
Gallery opens on
Superior Street

Willem de Kooning's
painting *Excavation*
acquired by AIC

The Republican
National Convention
held in Chicago

beyond

John Cage's *4'3"* first
performed

Andy Warhol has first
solo exhibition in
New York

Aperture magazine
launched

Ralph Ellison's
Invisible Man
published

NBC premières the
"Today Show"

Lever House in New
York completed
(Gordon Bunshaft of
Skidmore, Owings &
Merrill)

US Congress passes
McCarran-Walter
Immigration and
Nationality Act

GI Bill extended to
Korean War veterans

US explodes the first
hydrogen bomb

Dwight D. Eisenhower
elected President

21

22

chicago

AIC opens Art Rental and Sales Gallery for Chicago-area artists (until 1987)

Matta is visiting professor at SAIC

The Lyric Theatre of Chicago opens (becomes Lyric Opera of Chicago, 1956)

Chicago metropolitan area produces one-quarter of the nation's total output of iron and steel

beyond

Frida Kahlo dies

Simon Rodilla completes *The Watts Towers* in Los Angeles

J.R.R. Tolkien's *The Fellowship of the Ring* published

Elia Kazan's *On the Waterfront* released

Swanson introduces the TV dinner

Bill Haley and the Comets record "Rock Around the Clock"

First Newport Jazz Festival in Rhode Island

Brown v. Board of Education of Topeka rules racial segregation in public schools unconstitutional

23

chicago

Crombie Taylor resigns as director of ID; Jay Doblin succeeds (until 1969)

Fairweather-Hardin Gallery opens in Chicago on Ontario Street

Article "Is There a New Chicago School?" by Patrick T. Malone and Peter Selz published in *ARTnews*

The Compass Players debuts (forerunners of The Second City)

The Prudential Building sets off new office construction

Chicago's Department of Urban Renewal created

Richard J. Daley elected mayor

Ray A. Kroc starts McDonald's in Des Plaines, Illinois

Chicagoan Esther Freedman becomes Ann Landers for the *Chicago Sun-Times*

beyond

First Documenta exhibition in Kassel, West Germany

Edward Steichen curates "The Family of Man" at MOMA

Allen Ginsberg reads "Howl" at Six Gallery in San Francisco

Nicholas Ray's *Rebel Without a Cause* released just after James Dean's death

Vladimir Nabokov's *Lolita* published

Chuck Berry's first hit "Maybelline" released

Rosa Parks refuses to give up her bus seat in Montgomery, Alabama

Alabama's bus segregation declared unconstitutional

AFL-CIO established

Jonas Salk's polio vaccine licensed

Disneyland opens in Anaheim, California

23 Leon Golub. *Hamlet*, 1954. Lacquer on Masonite.

24 Emerson Woelffer. *Morning Earth*, 1955. Oil and collage on canvas.

25 Leon Golub. *Siamese Sphinx II*, 1955. Lacquer on Masonite.

26 Harold Allen. *Church, Chilili, New Mexico*, 1955. Gelatin silver print.

27 Joseph Goto. *Untitled*, c. 1956. Steel.

28 June Leaf. *Arcade Women*, 1956. Oil on canvas.

29 Richard Hunt. *Construction N*, 1956. Cottonwood and steel.

26

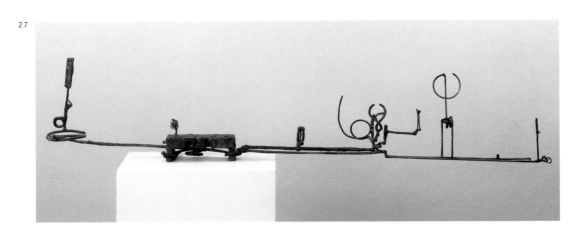

27

chicago

Don Baum becomes exhibitions chairman at HPAC (until 1973)

Allan Frumkin organizes "Chicago Imagist Painters and Sculptors" at Beloit College in Wisconsin

ID moves to present location, Mies van der Rohe's S.R. Crown Hall, IIT

O'Hare International Airport opens

The Eisenhower Expressway constructed

The Democratic National Nominating Convention held in Chicago

beyond

Jackson Pollock dies

First exhibition of British Pop art, Whitechapel Art Gallery, London

Cecil B. DeMille's *The Ten Commandments* and King Vidor's *War and Peace* introduce blockbuster films

Roger Vadim's *And God Created Women* stars Brigitte Bardot

Elvis Presley's "Heartbreak Hotel" released

Glenn Gould records Bach's "Goldberg Variations"

The Suez Crisis in the Middle East

Transatlantic telephone service inaugurated

The Federal Aid Highway Act authorizes US interstate highway system

Dwight D. Eisenhower reelected President

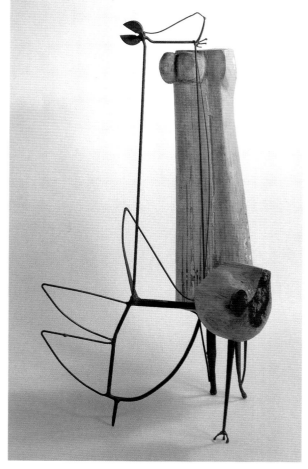

1957-1965

the second city
rises

30

31

chicago

"1957 Chicago Artists No Jury Exhibition" at Navy Pier

Richard Feigen Gallery opens on Superior Street

Exhibit A opens on Pearson Street (closes 1959)

Robert Natkin and Stanley Sourelis found Wells Street Gallery (closes 1959)

American Federation of Arts circulates "Abstract Photography: Aaron Siskind, Harry Callahan, Arthur Siegel, Arthur Sinsabaugh"

Inland Steel Building completed (Skidmore, Owings & Merrill)

The Old Town School of Folk Music opens on North Avenue

Edwin Berry, executive director of the Chicago Urban League, states Chicago is the most segregated city in the US

Life magazine calls Chicago police most corrupt in the nation

University of Chicago economist Milton Friedman's *A Theory of the Consumption Function* published

beyond

Situationniste Internationale formed by CoBrA and Lettrist members

Roland Barthes's *Mythologies* published

Jack Kerouac's *On the Road* published

Ingmar Bergman's *The Seventh Seal* released

Jean Genet's *The Balcony* premières in London

Soviet Union launches Sputnik

François "Papa Doc" Duvalier elected President of Haiti

Treaty of Rome establishes European Economic Community

President Eisenhower enforces desegregation in Little Rock, Arkansas

30 Harry Callahan. *Collage, Chicago*, 1957. Gelatin silver print.

31 H.C. Westermann. *Death Ship of No Port*, 1957. Pine, brass, metal wire, and enamel on fabric.

35

chicago

"1958 Chicago Artists No Jury Exhibition" at Navy Pier

Holland-Goldowsky Gallery opens on Ontario Street

The Jewish Federation of Metropolitan Chicago founded

The Chicago Housing Authority's Cabrini Extension Project completed

Chicago aldermen's terms increased from two to four years

beyond

Lawrence Alloway coins the term "Pop art"

Jasper Johns has solo exhibition at Leo Castelli Gallery in New York

John Cage's retrospective concert at New York's Town Hall

Truman Capote's *Breakfast at Tiffany's* published

Physicist William Higinbotham invents first video game (an ancestor of Pong)

First transatlantic passenger jet service from London to New York

36

32 Robert Natkin. *Honeymoon*, 1957. Oil on canvas.

33 H.C. Westermann. *The Old Eccentric's House*, 1956–57. Fir lath, birch-veneer plywood, and mirrors.

34 John Miller. *Seated Figure II*, 1957–58. Oil on canvas.

35 H.C. Westermann. *Mad House*, 1958. Douglas fir, metal, glass, and enamel.

36 H.C. Westermann. *Memorial to the Idea of Man If He Was an Idea*, 1958. Pine, bottle caps, metal, glass, enamel, and toys.

37

At their world, the wood which torture the sploat
The sick woman was turned into a corpse.
The corpse was hung from a stake.

M.S.

38

37 Nancy Spero. *At Their Word
    (The Sick Woman)*, 1957–58.
    Oil on canvas.

38 Richard Hunt. *Hero Construction*,
    1958. Steel.

39 Seymour Rosofsky. *Unemployment
    Agency*, 1958. Oil on canvas.

40

chicago

Superior Street
Gallery opens
(closes 1961)

"The New Chicago
Decade, 1950–60"
at Lake Forest
College, Illinois

"New Images
of Man" at MOMA
includes Chicago
artists

Franz Schulze
coins the term
"Monster Roster"

Allan Frumkin opens
a New York gallery

The Second City
opens on Wells Street

The poet Paul Carroll
launches *Big Table*,
a magazine for Beat
Generation writers

Richard J. Daley
reelected mayor

Queen Elizabeth II
visits Chicago

Pan-American Games
held in Chicago

Chicago White Sox
win pennant but lose
World Series

beyond

Allan Kaprow's first
"Happening"

Robert Frank's *The
Americans* published

Solomon R.
Guggenheim Museum
in New York
completed (Frank
Lloyd Wright)

Lorraine Hansberry
wins New York
Drama Critics Circle
Award for *A Raisin
in the Sun*

William S.
Burroughs's *Naked
Lunch* published

François Truffaut's *The
400 Blows* released

Berry Gordy launches
Motown

Buddy Holly, Richie
Valens, and Big Bopper
die in plane crash

Fidel Castro leads
revolution in Cuba and
assumes total power

Alaska and Hawaii
become US's 49th
and 50th states

1960

chicago

Allan Frumkin, Holland-Goldowsky, and Superior Street galleries sponsor "1st Chicago Invitational"

Population statistics indicate movement from city to suburbs

Scandal and reshuffling in Chicago Police Department

First televised presidential campaign debate (Kennedy-Nixon) broadcast from Chicago

McCormick Place opens

beyond

Yves Klein launches *Dimanche* magazine in Paris

The Nouveaux Réalistes group formed

Alfred Hitchcock's *Psycho* released

World's first birth control pill approved by US FDA

John F. Kennedy elected President

40 Leon Golub. *Reclining Youth*, 1959. Lacquer on canvas.

41 Yasuhiro Ishimoto. *Untitled* from the series "Chicago, Chicago," 1960. Gelatin silver print.

1961

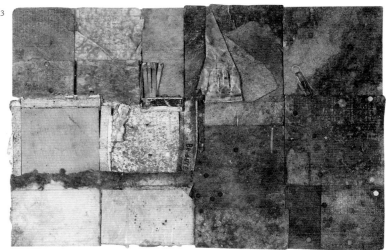

42 Miyoko Ito. *Monnongahela*, c. 1961. Oil on canvas.

43 Robert Nickle. *Untitled*, 1961. Paper collage.

44 Dominick Di Meo. *Torso/Landscape*, 1962. Plastic.

45 Theodore Halkin. *Lunar Perigee*, 1962. Mixed media on plywood.

44

1962

chicago

"Recent Painting in
the USA – The
Figure" at MOMA
includes George
Cohen and
Leon Golub

Korean American
Association of
Chicago founded

beyond

Andy Warhol paints
Marilyn Monroe and
Campbell's soup cans
and has his first
solo exhibition in
Los Angeles

Ed Ruscha produces
his first book of
photographs, *Twenty-
Six Gasoline Stations*

Marilyn Monroe dies

Vatican Council II
begins (ends 1965)

Telstar I satellite
allows global
communication links

Cuban Missile Crisis

US presidential
commission on the
status of women
established

45

171

46 Ellen Lanyon. *Fregene*, 1962.
Oil on canvas.

47 Michael Hurson. *Ballet of the Left-Handed Piano*, 1962.
Charcoal and oil on canvas.

48 Roland Ginzel. *Untitled*, 1963.
Oil on canvas.

49 Karl Wirsum. *Armpits*, 1963.
Oil and fur on canvas.

1962

46

47

1963

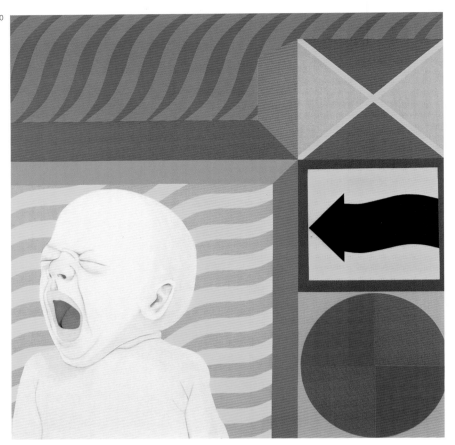

1964

chicago

"The Chicago School: 1948–1954" inaugurates Chicago series at HPAC

"The Sunken City Rises" and "Eye on Chicago" at IIT

"Seven & Up" at DePaul University

Ivan Albright retrospective at AIC, travels to New York

Marina City towers completed (Bertrand Goldberg Associates)

The Beatles perform in Chicago

Periodic severe rioting in African-American neighborhoods

beyond

"The Shaped Canvas" at the Solomon R. Guggenheim Museum, New York

Marshall McLuhan declares "the medium is the message" in *Understanding Media: The Extension of Man*

Susan Sontag's "Notes on Camp" published in *Partisan Review*

Nikita Khrushchev ousted as head of Soviet government

PLO organized

US Congress passes Civil Rights Act and Medicare Act

Malcolm X leaves Nation of Islam

US government issues landmark report on hazards of smoking

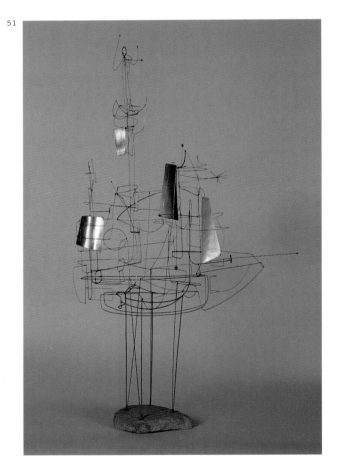

53

1964

54

50 Stan Edwards. *Infant in Altar IV*, 1964. Oil and acrylic on canvas.

51 Konstantin Milonadis. *Wave-Goer*, c. 1964. Stainless steel and stone.

52 Art Sinsabaugh. *Chicago Landscape #58*, 1964. Gelatin silver print.

53 Kenneth Josephson. *Chicago, 1964*, 1964. Gelatin silver print.

54 Gene Hedge. *Untitled*, 1964. Sisal lined industrial paper.

55

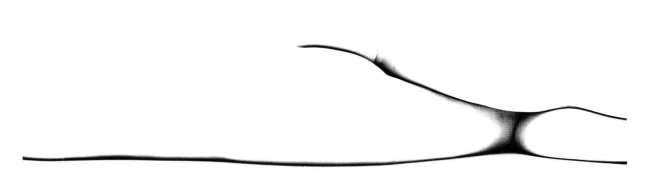

1965

55 Barbara Crane. *Human Form*, 1965–66/1993. Gelatin silver print.

56 Kerig Pope. *Two Children Observing Nature*, c. 1965. Oil on canvas.

57 Suellen Rocca. *Suellen's Corness Painting*, 1965. Oil on canvas.

58 Don Baum. *The Babies of della Robbia*, 1965. Plastic dolls, nylon, paint, wood, cloth, and paper.

57

56

58

1966 –1976

the entry of the imagists
into chicago

1966

59

60

59 Jim Nutt. *Miss E. Knows*, 1967. Acrylic on Plexiglas, aluminum, rubber, and enamel on wood frame.

60 Joseph Yoakum. *Mt. Baykal of Yablonvy Mtn. Range*, 1969 (?). Ballpoint pen, colored pencil, and ink on paper.

1967

61

62

61 Frank Piatek. *Herosagamos II (347th tube painting)*, 1967. Oil on canvas.

62 Steven J. Urry. *Blat*, 1967. Steel.

63 Jeff Donaldson. *A La Sango*, 1968. Mixed media on canvas.

64 Karl Wirsum. *Screamin' J. Hawkins*, 1968. Acrylic on canvas.

63

1968

chicago

"Six Formalists" at PAC

"Nonplussed Some," "Hairy Who III," and "False Image" at HPAC

"Richard Hunt" at AIC

"Richard J. Daley" protest exhibition at Feigen Gallery

Chicago artists and galleries respond to violence in society with one-day "Response"

"Violence in Recent American Art" at MCA

Mies van der Rohe retrospective at AIC

AfriCobra founded

Mario Castillo designs *Peace* mural in Pilsen

Live from Chicago opens on Clark Street (until 1970)

Mark di Suvero invited to Chicago by Joe Lo Giudice and Lewis Manilow

The Democratic National Convention held; antiwar protests and violent police response

Mayor Daley issues "shoot on sight" order to police during riots following Martin Luther King, Jr., assassination

beyond

Andy Warhol shot

Documenta IV devoted to Minimal and Op art

Bruce Nauman creates *First Hologram Series (Making Faces) (a-h)*

Stanley Kubrick's *2001: A Space Odyssey* released

Hair premières in New York

CBS debuts "60 Minutes"

Student riots in Paris

Martin Luther King, Jr., and Senator Robert F. Kennedy assassinated

Rep. Shirley Chisholm (D., New York) becomes first African-American woman elected to US Congress

Richard M. Nixon elected President

64

65

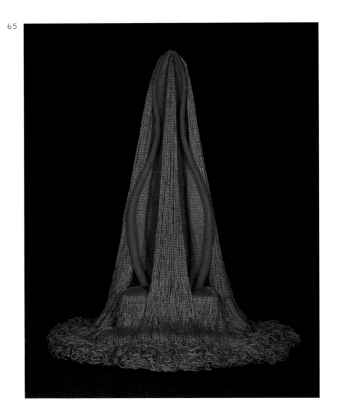

1969

66

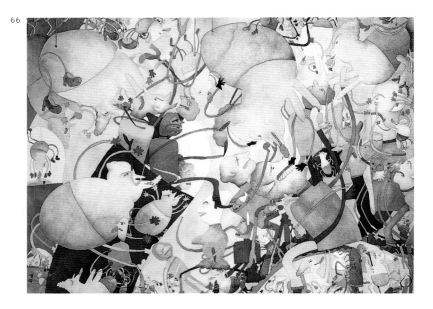

65 Claire Zeisler. *Red Preview*, 1969. Dyed jute.

66 Gladys Nilsson. *The Enterprize Encounterized By The Spydar People*, 1969. Watercolor on paper.

67 Ed Paschke. *Hophead*, 1970. Oil on canvas.

68 Jim Nutt. *Summer Salt*, 1970. Vinyl paint over plastic and enamel on wood and Masonite.

1970

69

69 David Sharpe. *Untitled*, 1970.
    Oil on canvas.

70 Edith Altman. *Obuli #23*, 1970.
    Birch wood.

71 Joseph Jachna. *Door County,
    Wisconsin*, 1970. Gelatin
    silver print.

70

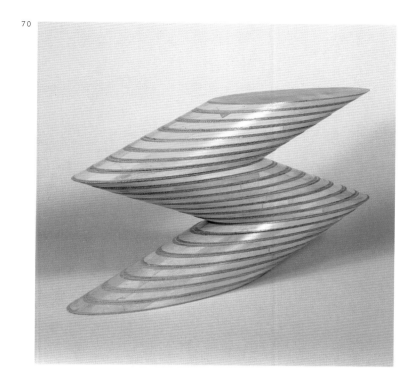

71

1971

72

73

74

75

72 Kazys Varnelis. *Untitled*, c. 1971.
    Acrylic on canvas.

73 Christina Ramberg. *Black Widow*,
    1971. Acrylic on Masonite.

74 Ray Yoshida. *Jizz and Jazz*, 1971.
    Acrylic on canvas.

75 Fred Berger. *A Flower; A Child;
    Will They Grow?*, 1971. Charcoal
    and crayon on paper.

1972

76

77

78

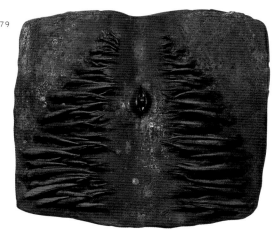

79

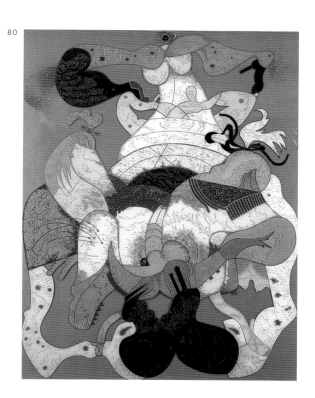

80

1972

76 Paul LaMantia. *Sorry Wrong Number*, 1972. Oil on canvas.

77 Phil Hanson. *Rousseau's Lily*, 1972. Acrylic on board.

78 Keith Morrison. *Under the El*, 1972. Oil on canvas.

79 Ruth Duckworth. *Untitled*, 1972. Glazed stoneware.

80 Barbara Rossi. *Brr'd and Baa'd*, 1972. Acrylic on Plexiglas, satin, human hair, and oil on wood frame (detail).

1973

81

82

81 Phil Berkman. *City security: Chicago*, 1973. Xeroxes on board. As published in "Anti-Object Art" issue, *Triquarterly* 32 (winter 1975).

82 Jerry Peart. *Escape*, 1973. Painted aluminum.

83 Roger Brown. *Autobiography in the Shape of Alabama (Mammy's Door)*, 1974. Oil on canvas, mirror, wood, hardware, Plexiglas, photographs, postcards, and cloth shirt.

84 Roger Brown. *Buttermilk Sky*, 1974. Oil on canvas.

chicago

Jim Nutt and Leon
Golub retrospectives
at MCA

Chicago Artists'
Coalition formed

Joseph Beuys lectures
at SAIC

Susanne Ghez
becomes director of
the Renaissance
Society

The David and Alfred
Smart Gallery
founded at the
University of Chicago

Marc Chagall's
mosaic *The Four
Seasons* unveiled at
First National Plaza

Alexander Calder's
Flamingo unveiled at
Federal Center Plaza

Sears Tower
completed (Skidmore,
Owings & Merrill)

Steppenwolf Theatre
Company opens in
Highland Park,
Illinois

The Joseph Holmes
Dance Company
founded

Latino Institute
founded

beyond

Jacob Lawrence
retrospective at the
Whitney Museum of
American Art,
New York

Lynda Benglis runs
sexually explicit ad in
Artforum

Hirshhorn Museum
and Sculpture
Garden opens in
Washington, DC

Roman Polanski's
Chinatown released

Stephen King's
first novel, *Carrie,*
published

Mikhail Baryshnikov
defects to the West

Oil embargo lifted

President Nixon
resigns; he is
pardoned by
President
Gerald R. Ford

Symbionese
Liberation Army
kidnaps Patty Hearst

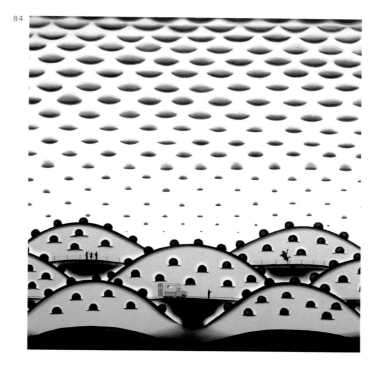

84

1974

85

1975

86

87

85 Henry Darger. *At Jennie Richee —Mabel introduces her Blengin sisters (three of them) to the little Vivians one p.m.*, date unknown. Carbon ink, pencil, tempera, and collage on paper.

86 Jim Nutt. *I'd Rather Stay (on the Other Hand)*, 1975–76. Acrylic on canvas and wood frame.

87 Ed Paschke. *Adria*, 1976. Oil on canvas.

1976

1976

88 Jane Wenger. *Untitled* from the "Self-Portrait" series, 1976. Gelatin silver print.

89 Dennis Kowalski. *Wedges*, 1976 (detail). Graphite on seven concrete wedges, this wedge installed at *New Art Examiner* offices, 230 East Ohio Street, Chicago.

90 Roger Brown. *The Entry of Christ into Chicago in 1976*, 1976. Oil on canvas.

1976

the big picture

1917

1985
TO
1991

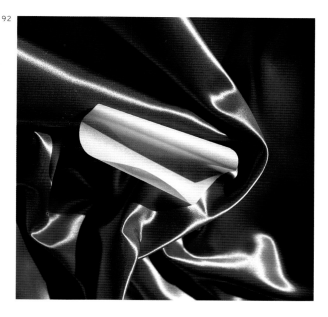

1977

chicago

The Chicago Public
Library Cultural
Center opens with
"Masterpieces of
Recent Chicago Art"

"The Photographer
and the City" at MCA

West Hubbard
Gallery founded as
East Hubbard
(until 1982)

"Europe in the
Seventies: Aspects of
Recent Art" at AIC

Claes Oldenburg's
Batcolumn erected at
the Social Security
Administration
Building on West
Madison Street

"Treasures of
Tutankhamun" at the
Field Museum

Byron Schaffer
converts factory on
West Belmont Avenue
into the Theatre
Building

Michael Bilandic
elected mayor

beyond

Richard Prince
introduces
"rephotography"

The New Museum of
Contemporary Art
founded in New York

Centre Georges
Pompidou opens
in Paris
(Piano & Rogers)

Marilyn French's
The Women's Room
published

George Lucas's
Star Wars released

Alex Haley's *Roots*
produced for
television

Elvis Presley dies

Mass exodus of "boat
people" from
Indochina

Stephen Biko dies in
police custody

US Senate approves
funding for the
neutron bomb

US Department of
Energy created

91 Charles Wilson. *Les Feux des Joie*,
1977. Chromogenic color prints
and text on paper. Installation at
N.A.M.E. Gallery, Chicago, 1977
(detail).

92 Thomas Kovachevich. *Caressing
You*, 1977. Tracing paper and
polyester.

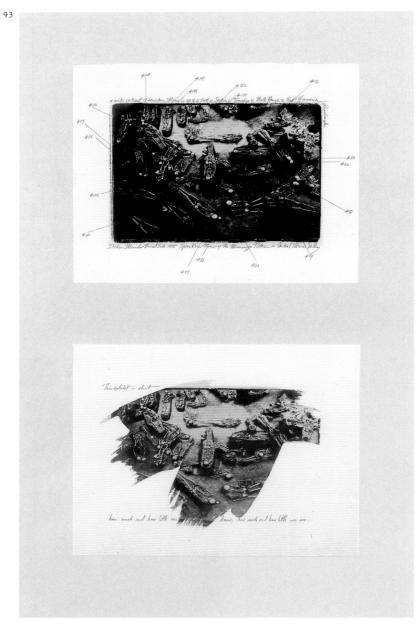

93 Esther Parada. *Overview #1* and
Overview #2 from the series
"Site Unseen," 1976/79.
Graphite and van Dyke brown
emulsion on Arches paper.

94 Daniel Ramirez. *TL-P 6.421*,
1976–77. Acrylic on canvas.

95 Ruth Thorne-Thomsen. *Plane
Crash*, 1977. Gelatin silver print.

1977

94

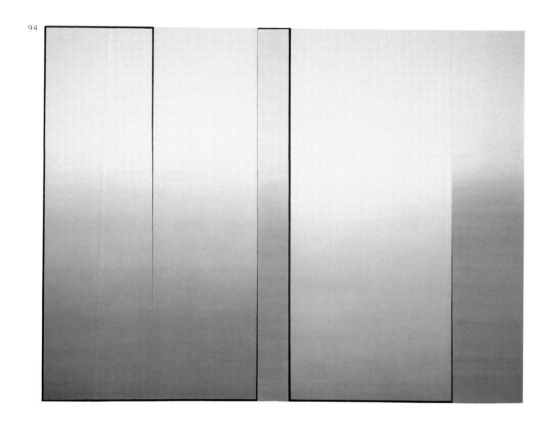

95

1977

1978

96

97

96 Lorenzo Pace. *Mummification Series VIII*, 1978. Wood, cord, sand, tape, and gauze.

97 Luis Medina. *Sons of the Devil, Chicago*, 1978. Silver-dye bleach print.

98 Jno Cook. *35mm Cockroach Camera*, 1978. Reclaimed materials.

99 Joyce Neimanas. *Don't Touch*, 1978. Ink, colored pencil, paper, staples, and safety pins on gelatin silver print.

98

99

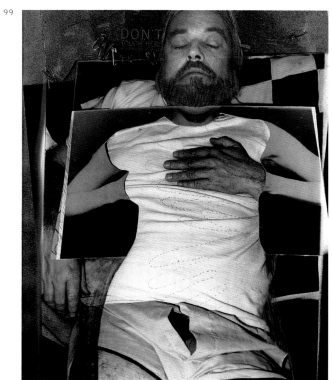

1978

1978

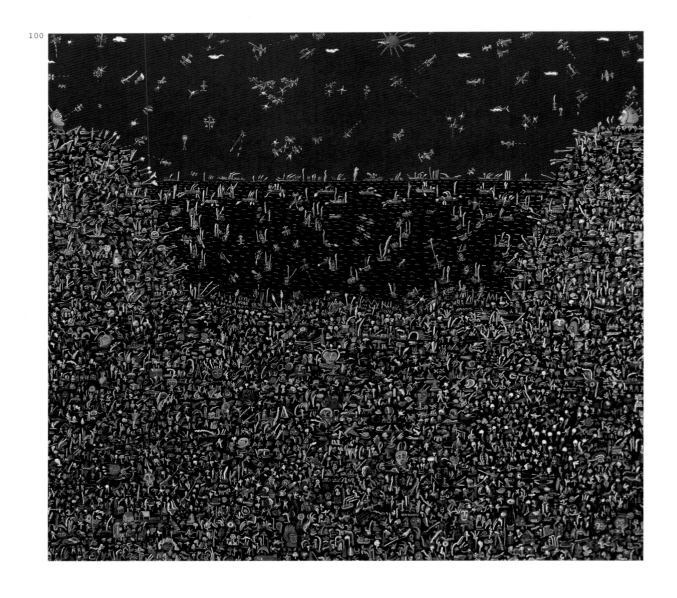

101

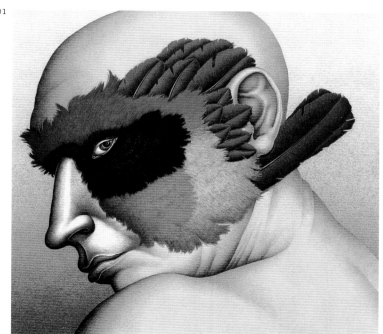

102

100   Robert Donley. *Invasion of the*   101   Robert Lostutter. *Red-Throated*
      Continent, 1978. Oil on canvas.   *Bee-Eater*, 1978. Watercolor
                                                        and graphite on paper.

                                             102   Margaret Wharton. *Morning*
                                                   Bed, 1978. Painted wood chair,
                                                   epoxy glue, glass, wire, and
                                                   wood dowels on concrete base.

1978

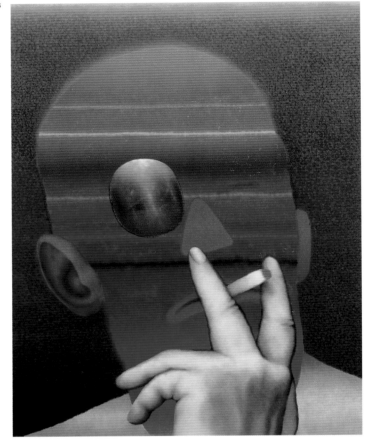

103

1979

103 Ed Paschke. *Fumar*, 1979.
Oil on linen.

104 Seymour Rosofsky. *Officer and
Lady*, 1979. Oil on canvas.

105 Richard Hull. *The Piano*, 1979.
Oil on canvas.

104

105

1980

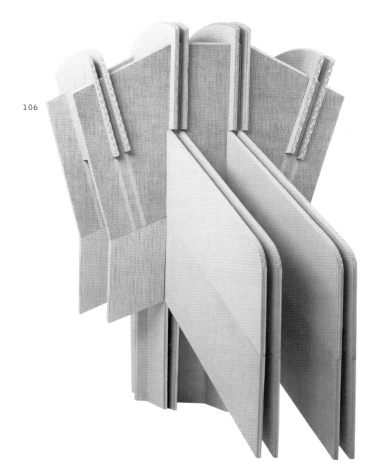

106

107

108

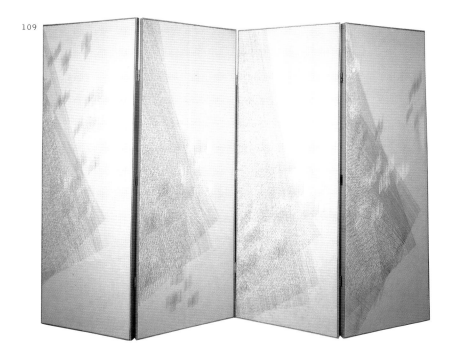

109

106 Diane Simpson. *Ribbed Kimono*, 1980. Colored pencil and crayon on corrugated archival board.

107 Don Baum. *Chinatown*, 1980. Wood, crushed metal cans, rulers, and glue.

108 Bob Thall. *Clark Street near Randolph Street, view west through State of Illinois Building construction site,* 1980. Gelatin silver print.

109 Michiko Itatani. *Untitled*, 1980. Acrylic on canvas, wood, and metal hinges.

110

chicago

"Roger Brown" at MCA

"Ruth Thorne-Thomsen" at AIC

"Margaret Wharton" at MCA

"Black Light-Planet Picasso" at Milwaukee Avenue loft of artists Jim Brinsfield and Darinka Novitovic

"The Morton G. Neumann Family Collection" at AIC following 1980 première at the National Gallery of Art, Washington, DC

Joan Miró's *Miró's Chicago* unveiled at Brunswick Plaza

Judy Chicago's *Dinner Party* on view in Printers Row

Mark Rogovin founds The Peace Museum on West Erie Street

The Chicago Blues Archive established at The Chicago Public Library

Mayor Jane Byrne temporarily takes up residence in Cabrini Green

beyond

Neo-Expressionism showcased in "A New Spirit in Painting" at the Royal Academy of Arts, London

Mary Boone and Leo Castelli share Julian Schnabel exhibition

Richard Serra installs *Tilted Arc* in Federal Plaza, New York (removed 1984)

"New York/New Wave" at P.S.1 in Long Island City

MTV introduced

IBM introduces the PC

Prince Charles and Lady Diana wed

Iran frees US hostages

Egypt's President Sadat assassinated

President Reagan survives assassination attempt

Sandra Day O'Connor is first woman appointed to the US Supreme Court

AIDS is recognized

1981

111

110　John Henry. *Lafayette '61*, 1981. Polished aluminum.

111　Hollis Sigler. *She Wants To Belong To The Sky, Again*, 1981. Oil on canvas with painted wood frame.

112　Robert C. Peters. *Chicago: Although Marco Polo Never Heard of Chicago, Its Story Really Begins with Him*, 1982. Loaves of bread, map, and text panels. Installation at Museum of Contemporary Art, Chicago, 1982 (detail).

113　John Phillips. *Space Shuttle*, 1981. Acrylic on canvas.

114　Mary Ahrendt. *A Guest*, 1982. Pigment on chromogenic color print.

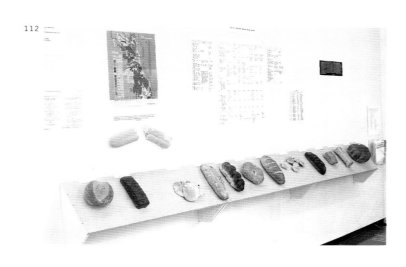

112

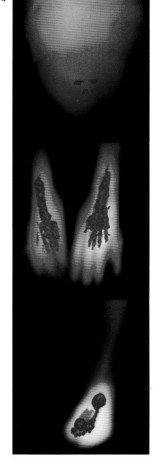

114

113

chicago

"Ed Paschke: Selected Works 1967–1981" at the Renaissance Society

"Selections from the Dennis Adrian Collection" at MCA

"Chicago Video" presented at MOMA and The Kitchen, New York

Mexican Fine Arts Center Museum founded

MCA organizes New Music America festival, cosponsored by the Mayor's Office of Special Events and the *Chicago Tribune*

Governor James R. Thompson cuts $1 million from Illinois Arts Council budget

Joseph Cardinal Bernardin appointed Archbishop of Chicago

Tylenol laced with cyanide kills seven Chicago residents

beyond

"Zeitgeist" at Martin-Gropius-Bau in Berlin

"Postminimalism" at The Aldrich Museum of Contemporary Art, Connecticut

Maya Lin's Vietnam War Memorial unveiled in Washington, DC

The first annual World of Music, Arts, and Dance festival (WOMAD), organized by Peter Gabriel in Shepton Mallet, England

Alice Walker's *The Color Purple* published

Steven Spielberg's *E.T.–The Extra-Terrestrial* released

Michael Jackson's *Thriller* released

The Falklands War

Equal Rights Amendment is defeated in US Congress

1982

1983

116

115

117

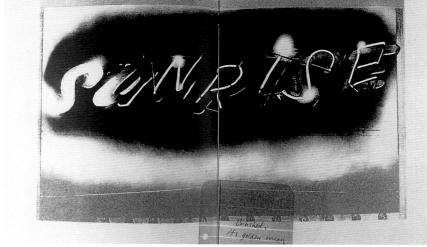

115 Douglas Ewart. *Wind Song*, 1983. Bamboo, steel, redwood, acrylic flutes, and brass chimes.

116 Lee Godie. *Untitled (Prince of a City)*, date unknown. Oil on window shade.

117 Ray Martin. *Acceptable Losses*, 1983. Cloth-bound book with lithographs, graphite, watercolor, and ink on paper (detail).

118 Barbara DeGenevieve. *Folie à Deux*, 1984. Photolinen.

119 Martin Puryear. *Greed's Trophy*, 1984. Steel rods and wire, hickory, ebony, rattan, and leather.

118

119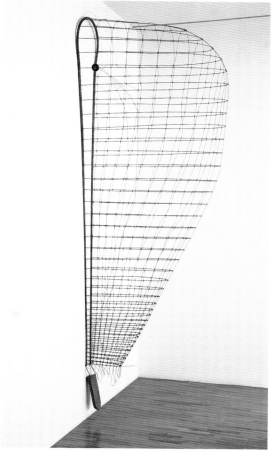

1984

120

120 James Valerio. *Night Fires*,
     1984. Oil on canvas.

121 Tom Czarnopys. *Untitled*, 1984.
     Oak and maple bark, poplar
     branch, and acrylic paint and
     matte medium on plastered
     gauze.

122 Buzz Spector. *Library*, 1984.
     Altered book pages, rocks,
     and wood.

123 Robert Heinecken. *Waking Up In
     News America*, 1984.
     Photolithograph on paper.

1984

121

122

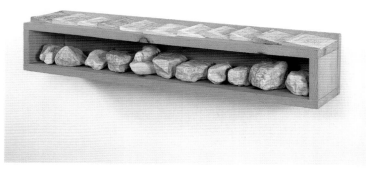

123

1984

1985

124

125

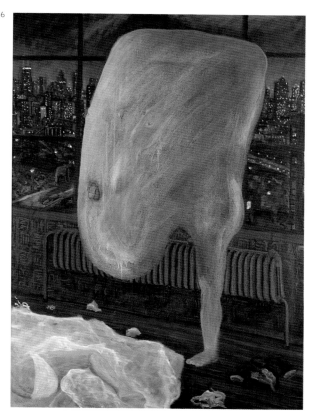

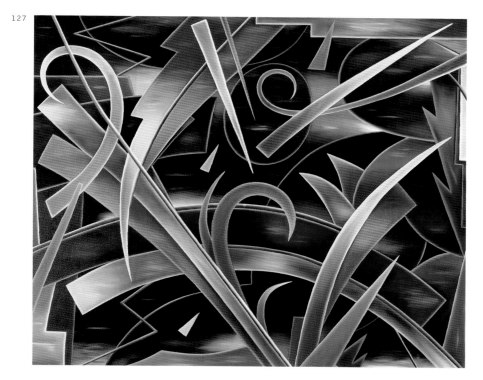

1985

124 Kay Rosen. *Various Strata*,
     1985/1996. Sign paint on
     museum board.

125 Martin Puryear. *Old Mole*,
     1985. Red cedar.

126 Jim Lutes. *The Evening of
     My Dysfunction*, 1985.
     Oil on canvas.

127 William Conger. *South Beach*,
     1985. Oil on canvas.

1986-1995

(un)assigned identities

128 **Othello Anderson and Fern Shaffer.** *Winter Solstice/Crystal Clearing Ceremony*, 1985 (detail). Documentary color photograph.

1986

129

1986

130

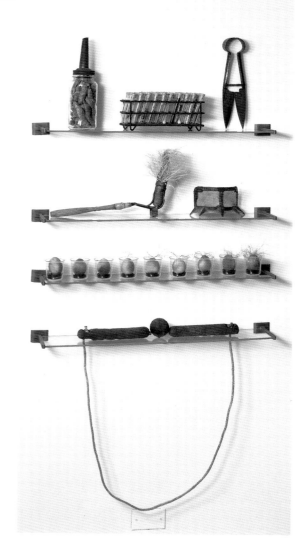

131

129 Richard Rezac. *Untitled*, 1986. Vermillion ink and acrylic medium on wood.

130 Arnaldo Roche Rabell. *You Have to Dream in Blue*, 1986. Oil on canvas.

131 Elizabeth Newman. *Untitled*, 1987. Cocoon jar, test tubes, test-tube rack, scissors, garden tool, root, calf-weaning device, hair, eggs, weighted cord, and ball.

1987

132 Paul Sierra. *Passing Storm*, 1987. Oil on canvas.

133 Anne Wilson. *Running in White Circles*, 1987. Synthetic felt, linen, and acrylic paint.

134 Roger Brown. *The Race to Make the World's Largest Painting*, 1988. Oil, straw, and pottery on canvas.

135 Rodney Carswell. *Tri-Color Cross, Encircled in 3 Gray Panels*, 1988. Oil and wax on canvas on wood.

134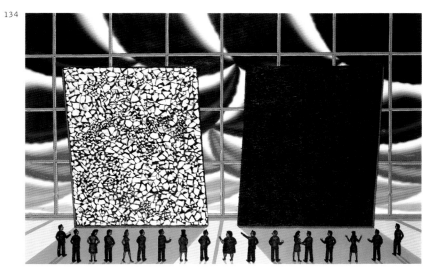

135

1988

136 Jin Soo Kim. *Untitled,*
    amputated, 1988. Mixed media.

137 Hirsch Perlman. *Untitled*
    (Armory), 1988. Chromogenic
    color print, Cor-x, frame,
    Plexiglas, laminated gelatin silver
    print, honeycomb board,
    and Sintra.

138 Joe Scanlan. *Untitled Candle*
    (8 oz. milk), 1988. Paraffin wax
    and cotton wick.

1988

137

138

1989

139

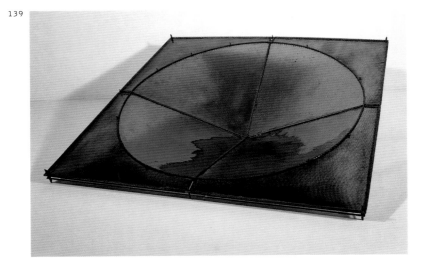

140

139 Frances Whitehead. *Cigale*, 1989. Shellac on steel.

140 Dan Peterman. *Small Change*, 1989. Densified, recycled aluminum cans.

141 Vera Klement. *Door to the River*, 1989. Oil and wax on canvas.

141

1989

1990

142

143
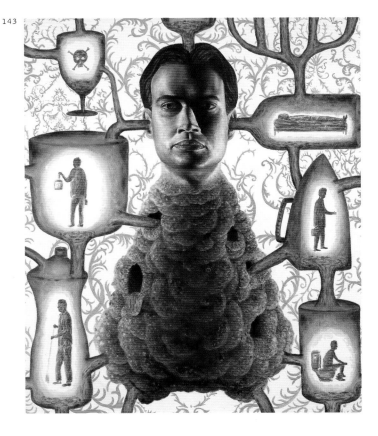

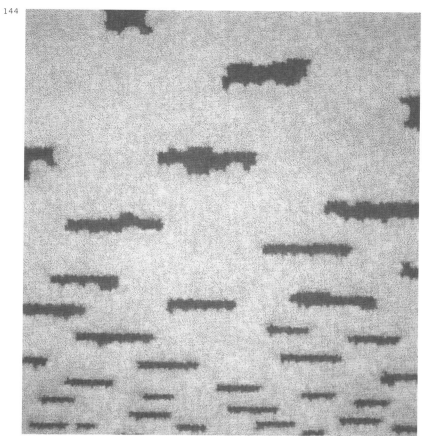

144

145

142 Nereida García-Ferraz. *Todo o nada*, 1990. Oil and wax on paper.

143 Ken Warneke. *The Tyranny of Everyday Life*, 1990. Oil and acrylic on Masonite.

144 Julia Fish. *Cumulous*, 1990. Oil on canvas.

145 Tony Tasset. *Abstraction with Wedges*, 1990. Plexiglas and poplar.

1990

148

146 Joe Ziolkowski. *No Title*, 1990. Gelatin silver print.

147 Iñigo Manglano-Ovalle. *Assigned Identities (Part 1)*, 1990. Laminated chromogenic color prints (detail).

148 Zhou Brothers. *Childhood Dream*, 1990. Oil and mixed media on canvas.

149 Jeanne Dunning. *Detail 8*, 1991. Laminated silver-dye bleach print.

150 (Art)ⁿ Laboratory: Stephan Meyers & Ellen Sandor. *The Equation of Terror: Chemical Terror, Arithmetic Operators I, Biological Terror, Arithmetic Relations, Economic Terror*, 1991. PHSColograms ®

1990

149

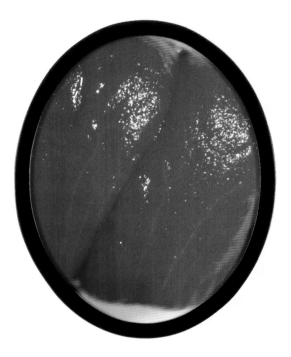

150

1991

229

151

152

151 Alejandro Romero. *Procession*,
     1991. Acrylic on canvas.

152 Richard Willenbrink. *Bacchus
     and His Attendants*, 1991.
     Oil on canvas.

153 Neil Goodman. *Triptych*, 1991.
     Bronze.

1991

1992

154

155

156

157

154 Gaylen Gerber. *Untitled*, not
dated. Oil on canvas. Installation
of twenty-five paintings at
The Renaissance Society at the
University of Chicago, 1992.

155 Gregory Warmack
(Mr. Imagination). *Throne and
Footstool*, 1992. Bottle caps,
velvet, buttons, and mixed media.

156 Jim Nutt. *Moat*, 1992. Acrylic
on linen and particle-board
frame (detail).

157 Phyllis Bramson. *Winter (again)*,
1992. Oil on canvas.

1992

"A Sequence of
Forms: Sculpture by
Illinois Artists" at
Chicago Cultural
Center and Illinois
Art Gallery

"Rodney Carswell" at
the Renaissance
Society

"Facts and Fables by
Luis Medina,
Photographer"
at AIC

"Artist—Lee Godie:
A 20-Year
Retrospective"
at Chicago
Cultural Center

Marshall Fields
launches a major arts
initiative with
Chicago schools

Three Art Expos
compete to be
Chicago's only expo

Michael Jordan
retires

"1993 Biennial
Exhibition" at the
Whitney Museum of
American Art is
devoted to art with
socio-political content

Louise Bourgeois
honored with a solo
exhibition at the
American Pavilion at
the Venice Biennale

Steven Spielberg's
Schindler's List and
Jurassic Park
released

Czechoslovakia
formally dissolved

Israel and the PLO
sign a peace accord

NAFTA ratified

ANC leader Nelson
Mandela and South
African President
F.W. de Klerk share
the Nobel Peace Prize

Ruth Bader Ginsburg
is the second woman
appointed to the US
Supreme Court

Siege of the Branch
Davidian cult
in Waco, Texas

Internet becomes the
"information
superhighway" with
its new enhanced
system

158

159

1993

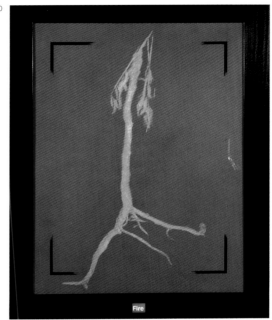

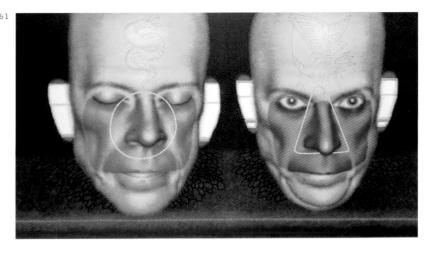

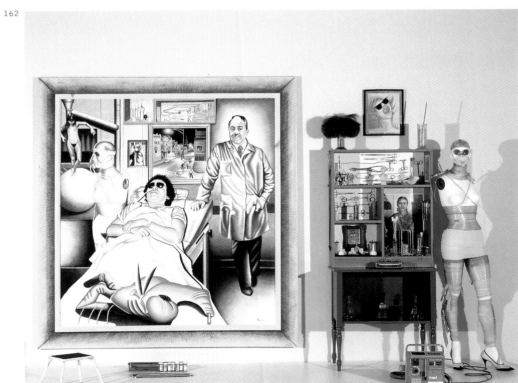

158 Marva Lee Pitchford Jolly.
     Alice from the series "Spirit
     Women," 1993. Pit-fired clay.

159 David Klamen. *Untitled
     (Vase)*, 1993. Oil on linen.

160 Miroslaw Rogala. *Trees are
     Leaving #2*, 1993. Chalk on
     paper, LCD-display color
     monitor, wood frame, video-
     tape, and VCR.

161 Ed Paschke. *The Decision*, 1993.
     Oil on linen.

162 Marcos Raya. *Night Nurse*,
     1993 (detail). Acrylic on canvas,
     cabinet, surgical instruments,
     mannequin, and found objects.
     Installation at the Mexican
     Fine Arts Center Museum,
     Chicago, 1993.

1993

163 Maurice Wilson. *Shock-O-Late and Nubian Head*, 1993. Acrylic and tar on burlap.

164 Paul Rosin. *Birth*, 1993. Oil on gelatin silver print.

165 Gary Justis. *Untitled*, 1993. Aluminum, brass, and motors.

166 Susanne Doremus. *Chicago*, 1994. Oil and linocut on canvas.

167 Calvin B. Jones. *Brilliant•as•the• Sun•Upon•the•World (Egungun)*, 1994. Mixed media on canvas.

1993

166

167

1994

168

168 Adelheid Mers. *American Beauties #19 (Flame)*, 1994. Ellipsoidal light fixture, aluminum templet, and color gel.

169 Steven Heyman. *Siblism*, 1995. Acrylic on canvas.

170 Indira Freitas Johnson. *Transformation* from the "Process of Karma" installation, 1995. Bark, stones, and plastic containers.

171 Kerry James Marshall. *Untitled (Altgeld Gardens)*, 1995. Acrylic and collage on canvas.

1994

169
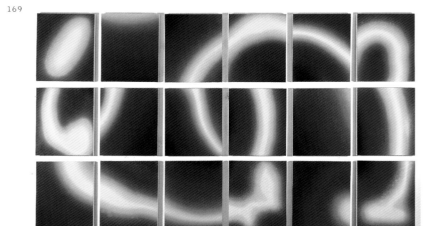

170

171

1995

239

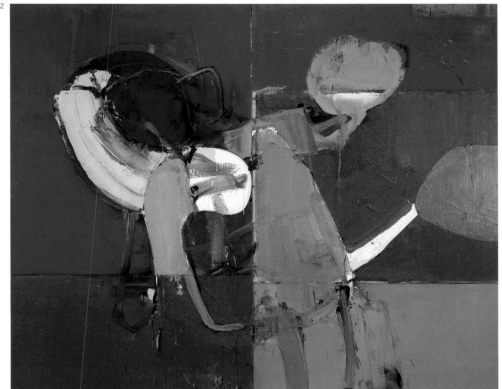

1995

172 Wesley Kimler. *Egmont*, 1995. Oil on canvas.

173 Tony Fitzpatrick. *Immigrant Flowers*, 1995. Chine collé etching on paper.

biographies

of the artists

The authors' names
are abbreviated as follows:

AB	**Amy Bero**	CES	**Courtenay E. Smith**
SB	**Staci Boris**	LS	**Laura Stoland**
MF	**Margaret Farr**	EV	**Erika Varricchio**
AF	**Anna Friedman**	LW	**Lynne Warren**
LH	**Lela Hersh**	NW	**Nadine Wasserman**
KFK	**Krishna F. Knabe**	EKW	**Elizabeth K. Whiting**
JK	**Jason Koziara**		
SK	**Sheldon Krasnow**		
MHM	**Megan H. Mack**		
MM	**Monique Meloche**		
DM	**Dominic Molon**		
SKM	**Sarah K. Mullen**		
GS	**Grant Samuelsen**		

Gertrude Abercrombie

(1909–1977) Gertrude Abercrombie, a painter of moody, highly personal paintings, was born in Austin, Texas, in 1909 to singers with a traveling opera company. Her parents resumed traveling shortly after her birth, relocating near Ravinia music park outside Chicago, where her mother became a prima donna in an opera company. As a young child, Abercrombie lived in Berlin for a year and Aledo, a small town in western Illinois, before her mother's opera career ended and the family put down roots in Chicago's Hyde Park, where Abercrombie was to spend her life. In 1929 Abercrombie graduated from the University of Illinois in Urbana-Champaign with a major in romance languages. She briefly studied art at SAIC and commercial art at the American Academy of Art in Chicago before taking a job as a commercial artist for a department store in 1931. She began painting seriously in 1932.

Although Abercrombie was not an "outsider artist," she was proud of her relative lack of art training and her paintings display some of the attributes associated with unschooled artists. Because of this, she is often cited in discussions of this genre. The artist's early life was to provide inspiration for her paintings, in which she cast herself in the role of the elongated, mysterious central figure in her autobiographical psychodramas. A confirmed Midwesterner who lived the majority of her life in urban surroundings, she nevertheless often depicted rural settings; some paintings are specifically titled as scenes from Aledo. Abercrombie's surreal scenes were drawn from her own mental landscape, no doubt expedited by her entering psychoanalysis in the 1950s with Dr. Franz Alexander, who founded the Institute for Psychoanalysis and was an important figure to such younger artists of the era as Leon Golub. Abercrombie's self-portraits show a stony-faced woman with a prominent chin and nose, thin lips, and dark brows over skeptical eyes; gloves, cats, owls, brooms, and other items associated with black magic or witchcraft appear.

During the Great Depression, Abercrombie began her regular appearances at Chicago's few, often short-lived, galleries, in art fairs, and in AIC's annual C & V exhibitions. She worked for the WPA in 1933–40. In the early 1940s, her successful showings in New York together with her 1944 solo exhibition in AIC's Chicago Room established her as a major local artist. Alone among the circle of artist-friends (such as Tud Kempf, Emil Armin, and Karl Priebe) with whom she had emerged, Abercrombie produced work of interest to successive generations in Chicago. She established a powerful persona as "the queen of the bohemian artists," having served as the model for the wild Eloisa Brace in James Purdy's novel *Malcolm*. Abercrombie also presided over legendary gatherings of artists, writers (including her close friend Thornton Wilder), and musicians such as classical composer Ned Rorem, bebop great Dizzy Gillespie, singer Sarah Vaughan, and such jazz legends as Sonny Rollins, Charlie Parker, and Max Roach; her house on Dorchester Street provided an important social hub for Hyde Park's many creative individuals. ·

Among the many visitors to her salon was Don Baum, who was to become an important artist as well as director of exhibitions at HPAC. The two became close friends, and he organized Abercrombie's 1977 HPAC retrospective shortly before her death, and as executor of her estate, placed many of her paintings in museums such as AIC, MCA, and especially the Illinois State Museum, Springfield. LW

Mary Ahrendt

(Born 1940) A Chicago native, Mary Ahrendt was born in 1940. Interrupting her education to marry and raise a family, she returned to school in the 1970s, obtaining her GED from Triton Junior College, River Grove, Illinois; her BA from UIC in 1978; and her MFA from SAIC in 1980. A skilled painter, Ahrendt began exhibiting while still in school, and was featured in a solo exhibition at the Feminist co-op Artemisia in 1978. At SAIC, however, she began experimentation with photography, chiefly the Polaroid SX-70 system, which had only recently been taken up as an artistic medium. She also began exhibiting at N.A.M.E. Gallery, Chicago, putting on several performance works in which she displayed parts of her body through cutouts in a large box placed in the gallery.

These two strands of experimentation came together in Ahrendt's first mature works, rephotographed SX-70s of herself and family members that accentuate the common deficiencies of this snapshot medium—overexposure, uneven development, unrealistic color, and close-focus distortion. Ahrendt then developed a unique working process. To achieve the basic image, she immersed herself in baths of various colors that exposed body parts (such as face, arms, and legs) above the water line, which she photographed with the SX-70 camera mounted on a tripod above her bathtub. These images were then rephotographed, blown up to large-scale Cibachrome prints, mounted on Masonite, and montaged together to create the final multipaneled pieces. This work, combining elements of performance, body art, and Feminist theory, has a silent, disturbing quality: the artist's body is a ghostly, fetuslike form in its deeply colored amniotic fluid. Extremely well received in the photographic community, these self-portraits were shown widely around the United States, including at the San Francisco Museum of Modern Art and the Indianapolis Museum of Art (both in 1982) and at the Just Above Midtown Gallery, New York (1983).

In the mid-1980s, Ahrendt began experimenting with the Duratrans medium—color positive films mounted in lightboxes that were beginning to be widely used for advertising purposes. In 1985 she installed one such piece in the recently dedicated Helmut Jahn–designed O'Hare CTA station by renting a commercial billboard space—an early example of a type of public art that became widespread in the 1990s.

After showing with Marianne Deson Gallery, Chicago, for a number of years, Ahrendt joined the Ehlers-Caudill Gallery, Chicago, in the late 1980s. In 1991 Ahrendt took her teaching certificate in order to work as an elementary-school art teacher in the Chicago Public Schools. She has devoted much of her energy to teaching during the 1990s. LW

Ivan Albright

(1897–1983) Although Ivan Le Lorraine Albright emerged as an important American artist prior to 1945, he was one of the few prewar Chicago artists who continued to have a significant career and impact upon the postwar art scene. His idiosyncratic, dizzyingly detailed paintings are often thought of as prototypically "Chicago" in their focus on the common man, everyday life, and extreme attention to detail.

Born into an artistic family in 1897 in North Harvey, Illinois, Albright moved as an infant to Edison Park, now a neighborhood on Chicago's Northwest Side, but then an outpost of log cabins. Albright came into the world with a twin, Malvin, who became a sculptor but never achieved his brother's fame. Their father had studied with Thomas Eakins, yet the twins (who were inseparable) came late to the decision to study art, wary of their father's less-than-distinguished reputation as a painter of sentimental pictures of children. Ivan Albright was in his mid-twenties when he began studying at SAIC, graduating in 1923. He immediately began to receive attention for his highly individualistic portraits. After travels and further study in Pennsylvania and New York, Albright settled in Warrenville, Illinois, in 1927, and began to paint in a studio shared by his father and his brother, who had taken up the nom de plume Zsissly in order to be distinguished from his twin, especially in exhibition catalogues where Ivan was often listed first. Albright married newspaper heiress Josephine Medill Patterson in 1946.

Although he quickly established himself as a major American painter, Albright received his greatest popular fame for *The Picture of Dorian Gray* (1943–44), painted for the movie based on Oscar Wilde's provocative novel about an evil, dissolute dandy who retains his youth and good looks while his blemishes and imperfections are transferred to a painting. (Malvin, with whom Ivan continued to be intimately associated, painted a "before" picture of a good-looking, youthful Dorian.) Albright continued into the 1970s to paint works characterized by overwhelming detail lavished on the surface qualities of skin, clothing, and other materials, often raked by an almost phosphorescent light. He also completed a number of landscapes and still lifes at various homes in Wyoming, Maine, and Vermont.

Albright was the subject of a retrospective organized by AIC in 1964, which traveled to the Whitney Museum of American Art in New York the following year. Around this time he dropped his middle name of Le Lorraine, after realizing the artist Claude Lorrain, after whom his father had named him, did not use an "e." In 1977 he received an Honorary Doctor of Fine Arts from SAIC. He died in 1983. Albright's works are in the permanent collections of many major US museums, but AIC is the chief repository. LW

Harold Allen

(Born 1912) Born in Portland, Oregon, in 1912, Harold Allen at age seven moved with his family to Blackfoot, Idaho, where he grew up as part of a largely Mormon farming and ranching community. Interested in art from early childhood, Allen began taking pictures at age twelve with a box camera. Leaving high school at the beginning of the Great Depression, he was forced to postpone college to help with the family potato business. In 1937, drawn to SAIC by the fact that Helen Gardner, author of *Art Through the Ages*, a book Allen had encountered in the public library, taught there, he finally began his higher education. SAIC's few photography course offerings, however, were commercially oriented, and in 1940 Allen took a night class at the School of Design (later ID), where he was exposed to the experimental ideas of László Moholy-Nagy and Gyorgy Kepes, who became lifelong influences. At this time he also became associated with Katherine Kuh through working as an assistant in her Diana Court gallery. In 1941 Allen was drafted into the Army. He was stationed in England and worked at the US Strategic Air Forces photo lab. At the war's end he returned to Chicago and assisted Helen Gardner with the third edition of her seminal art-history textbook, having photographed Stonehenge and other architecture as illustrations while in England. Upon Gardner's death in 1946, Allen took over the book's pro-

duction. Under the GI Bill in 1948, he enrolled in the art-history program at the University of Chicago (until 1954). Simultaneously he began teaching photography at SAIC, part-time (1948–60) and later full-time (1966–77), and became a beloved and influential teacher. In 1948 Allen also began a part-time career in AIC's Department of Oriental Art, where he worked with the Japanese print collection until 1966.

Allen is known primarily as an architectural photographer, particularly of churches of the Southwest and of Egyptian Revival architecture. He is also well known for his touching and often humorous photographs of funerary sculpture and architectural embellishments. His photographs are distinguished by their technical excellence; superb range of tone; and harmonious, yet never conventional, compositions.

Allen served as the official photographer for the Chicago Project of the Historic American Buildings Survey in 1964 and 1965. He has shown extensively in group exhibitions around the country, including "Chicago: The City and Its Artists, 1945–1978" at the University of Michigan Museum of Art, Ann Arbor. In 1984 Allen was the subject of a retrospective at AIC, which traveled to the Swen Parson Gallery at Northern Illinois University, DeKalb. He was awarded an honorary doctorate from SAIC in 1979. LW

Edith Altman

(Born 1931) Addressing issues of time, chance, and her past as a survivor of the Holocaust, Edith Altman has consistently reinvented her artistic struggle through the use of various media. Born Edith Hittman in 1931 in Altenberg, Germany, in 1939 she fled Nazi Germany with members of her family for the United States (settling eventually in Detroit). Her father was repeatedly interned at the Buchenwald concentration camp where his eight brothers and sisters perished; he later joined his family in the United States. Altman married her husband, Murray Altman, in 1950. She attended Wayne State University (1950–52, 1955) and Marygrove College (1956–57), both in Detroit. In 1967 the Altmans moved to Chicago.

Altman began showing in Chicago in 1971 with a solo exhibition at Feigen Gallery. Her sculptures from this period, entitled *Obuli* (from "oblique modular units"), are comprised of identical wooden elements stacked together in different geometrical configurations. After this series Altman's work went through various transformations—from the "Conceptual Placements" series (1973–82)—bundles of raw material

placed in deserted urban settings and photographed for documentary presentation—to obsessive ritual performances and mixed-media installations. The latter reflected a desire to enhance her analysis of the art object with elements of spirituality. These works were deeply influenced by her continuing study of the Kabbalah with a Hasidic rabbi.

In the 1982 installation *Der Kunstler Detektiv (The Artist Detective)*, Altman laid bare much of the victimization experienced by herself and her family, adopting the "information as art" style characteristic of artists such as Barbara Kruger and Jenny Holzer. A trip to Germany in 1983 to face the darker aspects of her experience as a Jewish refugee, and the death of her father the following year, spurred Altman to create installation pieces such as *When We Are Born We Are Given A Golden Tent, and All of Life Is the Folding and Unfolding of the Tent* (1987), a six-foot canvas tent laden with personal mementos, figurines, and protective symbols; and *Reclaiming the Symbol, Part Two* (1989), a history of the swastika representing it as both one of the most frequently used religious symbols and the emblem of the Nazi Party.

Altman was featured in important group shows in Chicago beginning in the 1970s. She appeared in AIC's C & V exhibition (1973), and showed at MCA in "Abstract Art in Chicago" (1976) and "New Dimensions: Time" (1980). She was given solo exhibitions at N.A.M.E. Gallery in 1987 and at the Rockford Art Museum and Chicago's Spertus Museum of Judaica in 1989. As part of the "Bridges and Boundaries" exhibition at the Spertus Museum in 1994, Altman worked with children to teach them about the Holocaust. Her presence as an artist has been complemented by her teaching experience at the Oxbow program of SAIC and at Notre Dame University, Indiana. DM

Fern Shaffer Othello Anderson

(Both born 1944) While continuing to paint individually, artists Othello Anderson and Fern Shaffer have chosen to collaborate in projects that address their mutual environmental concerns. Anderson, also known as a photographer, was born in 1944 in Charleston, Mississippi, and received a BFA (1973) and MFA (1974) from SAIC, while concurrently taking classes at the University of Chicago. He once again attended SAIC in 1987–88, participating in postgraduate study in twentieth-century art theory and criticism. Shaffer was born in 1944 in Chicago, and received a BFA from UIC (1981), followed by several years of graduate studies at both UIC and SAIC. She obtained an MA in interdisciplinary arts from Columbia

College, Chicago, in 1991. Both Anderson and Shaffer have been active in Chicago's "alternative spaces." Anderson was a founding member of N.A.M.E. Gallery in 1973, serving as its president in 1982–83; Shaffer was president of Artemisia Gallery from 1982 until 1992.

For over ten years Shaffer and Anderson have been performing and documenting a series of private sacred rituals, continuing the tradition of shamanistic practices utilized by ancient and tribal cultures. Their efforts are intended to encourage a return to spirituality and confront ecological crises brought about by technology and its waste products. The first projects of the early 1980s consisted of special ceremonies that marked the passage of seasonal equinoxes and solstices, but soon developed into rituals aimed at healing the earth, as the artists observed its declining ability to sustain life.

Scheduled for significant dates based on certain calendars or symbolic planetary alignments, the rituals take place in an area that is usually endangered or unhealthy. The artists designate the place sacred. Dressed in a garment created specifically for the ritual, Shaffer performs an energetic, trancelike ceremonial dance and offers prayers. Usually constructed of fibers, such as raffia or string, or recently bubble-wrap for an urban ritual, Shaffer's costumes enfold her body and establish a private place where she feels a spiritual transformation can occur. Anderson witnesses and documents the performance in a series of color photographs, which are often displayed next to the ceremonial garb and evocative objects taken from the site.

Shaffer and Anderson's projects have taken them to the frigid shores of Lake Michigan in winter; the Marching Bear Mounds in McGreggor, Iowa; a beach near a power plant in Indiana; northern and western regions of Illinois; a garbage dump in the center of Chicago; and Big Sur, California. Their collaborative works have been exhibited at Artemisia Gallery, Chicago (1986 and 1991); Centro Colombo Americano, Medellin, Colombia (1995); Julian Scott Memorial Gallery, Johnson State College, Vermont (1996); and Banco de la Republica, Bogotá (1996). Group exhibitions include those at Evanston Art Center, Illinois (1987); Sundered Ground, New York (1989); Charles A. Wustum Museum, Racine, Wisconsin (1990); R.A.W. Real Art Ways Gallery, Hartford (1994); and Thread Waxing Space, New York (1995). Their 1985 *Winter Solstice/Crystal Clearing Ceremony* is featured on the cover of Suzi Gablik's important book *The Reenchantment of Art* (1991). SB

Don Baum

(Born 1922) Don Baum has been a vital part of the art community in Chicago for close to fifty years as an artist, curator, and educator. While he has excelled in all his professions, it is as a curator that Baum has received particular renown. Baum's lively and often irreverent series of group exhibitions at HPAC, where he was director from 1956 to 1972, launched the careers of many Chicago artists, including those who became nationally and internationally known as the Imagists. Not afraid to show young or student artists, Baum organized the first shows for such figures as Frank Piatek and Suellen Rocca and included Jim Nutt, Roger Brown, Barbara Rossi, and many others in the now legendary group shows "Hairy Who," "False Image," "Non-plussed Some," and "Marriage, Chicago Style."

In 1969 Baum curated the first survey of Imagist art at MCA, "Don Baum Says: 'Chicago Needs Famous Artists.'" This title was in response to the departure of many of Chicago's older generation of artists to New York and elsewhere, and the need for local institutions to support the efforts of local artists. Baum's efforts were successful: the young artists he promoted were collected, written about, and picked up by dealers, especially Phyllis Kind Gallery, which led eventually to national attention. In 1973 Baum put together the US entry for the São Paulo Bienal, called "Made in Chicago," which featured many Imagist artists. This show, although somewhat controversial as it defied a boycott other American artists made of the Bienal in protest of Brazil's repressive military regime, traveled around Latin America and was mounted at the National Museum of American Art, Washington, DC, before returning to the MCA in Chicago.

Baum was born in Escanaba, Michigan, in 1922. After studying hotel management at Michigan State College in East Lansing, he took a hotel job in Chicago. In 1942 he enrolled at SAIC (from which he received an honorary doctorate in 1984). He also took classes at László Moholy-Nagy's School of Design and the University of Chicago. In 1948 Baum began teaching art at Roosevelt University in Chicago, serving as chairman of the Art Department from 1970 until his retirement in 1984; he also taught painting at HPAC (1955–65). Baum has also served on the Illinois Arts Council, the MCA's Board of Trustees, and the International Exhibitions Committee in Washington, DC.

In his studio work, Baum concentrates primarily on assemblage. His constructions fall generally into two series: assemblages that combine animal bones and/or plastic dolls with other found objects, and more recently, his "Domus"

sculptures. The works made with dolls from the 1960s are a particular signature of the artist's: stripped bare, exposing their sexlessness, they create disquieting tableaus. The Domus works are miniature houses created from all sorts of materials ranging from found wood and metal to linoleum and painted canvasboard and cardboard. Nonspecific, but following a typical model of a house, these works carry a nostalgic aura generated by the materials chosen for each. Baum's artwork has been featured in numerous solo exhibitions, including those at HPAC (1961 and 1981) and the Madison Art Center in Wisconsin (1988). His work has been featured in group exhibitions at HPAC, AIC, and MCA. He was represented for a number of years by Betsy Rosenfield Gallery in Chicago (now closed). AF

Vera Berdich

(Born 1915) Printmaker Vera Berdich is one of the deans of the Chicago art world: her innovative career stretches back to the immediate postwar years and continues to the present time. She was born in 1915 of Czech immigrants in Cicero, a south suburb of Chicago. While holding down jobs that included working as a retoucher at a postcard factory, Berdich attended SAIC part-time. After moving to live on her own in Chicago, she worked for the WPA at Hull House, where she first encountered the medium that she subsequently did so much to advance. She received her BA in 1946. A year after graduation, Berdich was hired by SAIC, where she set up the etching department and continued teaching until her retirement in 1979 as a professor emeritus.

From the beginning Berdich's techniques were highly experimental, utilizing a method of hand-applying various colored inks to the etching plate to create one-of-a-kind works (à la poupée). She was one of the first artists in the United States to use photographic techniques in printmaking, and in 1956 introduced a method of transferring photographic reproductions to canvas and paper, before Robert Rauschenberg's more famous, similar experiments. She also revived the use of a nineteenth-century technique, cliché verre, that involves the use of photographic materials without a camera. Throughout the 1950s, Berdich's Surrealist, dreamlike etchings won prizes in the annual C & V shows at AIC, and she showed throughout the United States and around the world in international print exhibitions. She developed the SAIC printmaking department into a significant force in the field, educating generations of young artists, and forming productive professional relationships with such fellow professors as Kathleen Blackshear and Whitney Halstead, who urged students to look beyond the classical Western tradition to the art of other cultures.

As a child, Berdich had lived for a time on a houseboat in a northern Wisconsin swamp, and she was profoundly affected by the isolation and the memory of images from this experience. Organic forms seem to float through her complex, often multilayered, etchings. Motifs associated with Surrealism—the eye, a hermetic interior crowded with oddly alive objects, and animals, especially cats—recur in her prints. Yet Berdich's imagery is more correctly seen as arising from her own mental world, rather than in homage to European artists such as Salvador Dali or André Masson, who utilized similar allusions.

In 1963 Berdich was the subject of a one-person exhibition at the San Francisco Museum of Art, in 1966 at AIC, and in 1967 at the Carnegie Mellon Institute in Pittsburgh. A retrospective was mounted at SAIC in 1979, and in honor of her eightieth birthday, at the Chicago Cultural Center in 1995. A large group of Berdich's works are in the print collection of AIC. LW

Fred Berger

(Born 1923) Fred Berger is one of Chicago's most admired "artist's artists"—a figure respected by generations of professionals but little known to the larger audience, despite a lengthy and distinguished exhibition history. The son of Romanian immigrants, Berger was born in Chicago. His father, a furniture dealer, moved the family to Grand Rapids, Michigan, when Berger was a small boy. After losing the business during the Great Depression, the family moved back to Chicago, where Berger showed early interest in pursuing a career in the arts. Urged to follow in the footsteps of his older brother, a commercial artist, Berger received a scholarship to a commercial art school. He applied instead to SAIC, though was forced to drop out after only six months when his older brother was drafted into the service and could no longer support the family.

Berger was largely self-taught as an artist. As a high-school student (and classmate of Seymour Rosofsky), he had taken a course at SAIC offered by Kathleen Blackshear that introduced him to the Field Museum. Objects from the New Ireland Islands and the Northwest American Indians were particular influences. Despite an abiding interest in the figure and in anatomy in particular, after seeing the work of Wassily Kandinsky in a book, Berger began to paint in a nonobjective style. He was also deeply impressed by László Moholy-Nagy, whom he heard lecture.

After working for the US Department of Treasury during the war, Berger was admitted on scholarship to ID, where he studied design and received his BS in 1952. While still in school, Berger received a one-person show at the prestigious Bordelon Gallery in Chicago (1949) and participated in AIC's C & V exhibitions starting in 1947 (and throughout the 1950s and early 1960s was a frequent prizewinner). Berger was also featured in the 1951 "American" Exhibition at AIC and participated in Exhibition Momentum in 1950, 1952, and 1953. He showed in 1953 at both Baldwin Kingrey and the Well of the Sea Restaurant at the Hotel Sherman, Chicago.

It was about this time that Berger became aware of Leon Golub's work, and greatly admiring his style, began figurative explorations again. He showed this work at the short-lived artists' cooperative Exhibit A in 1958. Through participation in these exhibitions as well as shows at HPAC in the late 1950s and early 1960s, combined with his subject matter of the human figure in strife-filled, mythological settings, Berger became associated with the first generation of Imagists, the "Monster Roster." When Franz Schulze included him in his seminal 1972 book *Fantastic Images*, this categorization became well established, although Berger's classical draftsmanship and choice of media—watercolor and ink on paper—set him well apart from painters such as George Cohen and Leon Golub or sculptors like Cosmo Campoli who are generally associated with this moniker. From 1953 to 1970 Berger worked in a commercial art studio; he also did occasional illustrations, most notably for *Playboy* magazine. He taught extensively, most importantly evening classes at ID shortly after he received his degree there and at the Chicago Academy of Fine Arts (1971–78) and American Academy of Art (1979–86). LW

Phil Berkman

(Born 1946) Phil Berkman embodies the tendency of many Chicago artists to produce challenging work—often years ahead of its time—while choosing to remain outside of the spotlight of success. Berkman was born in McKeesport, Pennsylvania, in 1946. He attended Syracuse University where he received his BFA in painting in 1968. Berkman spent two years in the Army (one year in Vietnam, the other in Germany) and moved to Chicago in the autumn of 1971. After two years in Chicago, Berkman became frustrated with the dearth of galleries for young contemporary artists in the city to show their work. With eight other artists (all, except for Berkman, students at SAIC), he founded N.A.M.E. Gallery in 1973.

Following the lead of artists such as Vito Acconci and Chris Burden, Berkman began by creating Conceptual works that incorporated performance, sculptural objects, and text to investigate art creation and appreciation. Besides exhibiting at N.A.M.E., Berkman performed or showed work at the Renaissance Society

in 1970 and at MCA in 1979. The latter would become, after N.A.M.E., his most important institutional affiliation; Berkman served as MCA's director of Security Services from 1975 to 1991. This position provided Berkman with much of his subject matter. His performance at MCA in 1979, *99 Bottles of Beer on the Wall*, featured Berkman guarding his $100 fee for performing—a critique of the appreciation of art according to its monetary value. Other particularly important works from this time are those created as part of the "Strike" series, in which Berkman fashioned "strike" signs, calling that sociopolitical act—and the political role of art—into question.

Berkman had one-person exhibitions at N.A.M.E. in 1981 and in 1993 and at Randolph Street Gallery in 1985. He cocurated the exhibition "Fa/eint" at Gallery 400 at UIC with three other artists (Leslie Bellavance, Michiko Itatani, and Paul Krainak) in 1995. His work through the 1980s and 1990s has remained committed to the use of Conceptual strategies to comment on the relation of art, the institution, and society. DM

Lyn Blumenthal

(1948–1988) Better known in Chicago for her efforts with colleague Kate Horsfield on behalf of video art, Lyn Blumenthal created a number of important works of video, installation, and sculpture during her career. Blumenthal was born in Chicago in 1948. She studied at Duke University in Durham, North Carolina (1966–67) and received her BA from Roosevelt University, Chicago, in 1969. Blumenthal went on to receive her MFA from SAIC in 1976. She began as a sculptor and gradually turned to video as her primary medium in the early 1970s. Having saved enough money from driving a taxi to buy an open-reel video portapak, and inspired by the growing power of the women's movement, Blumenthal began making tapes with Horsfield. Between 1974 and 1975, Blumenthal and Horsfield collaborated on six half-inch, unedited tapes of interviews with women artists.

In 1976, while still a graduate student, Blumenthal was selected to participate in MCA's "Abstract Art in Chicago" exhibition, a show that attempted to redress an often vocalized complaint that Chicago institutions supported only figurative art. Blumenthal's contribution was an ambitious video installation, *Ice Piece*. That same year, having now completed their graduate degrees, Blumenthal and Horsfield submitted a proposal to SAIC to oversee a collection of 125 videotapes of student work and visiting artist lectures at SAIC called the Video Data Bank. Establishing themselves as the codirectors of the institution, they con-

tinued to work on the video interviews with artists, expanding their focus to include a broader range of artists for the public record. This collection of taped interviews developed into the "On Art and Artists" series.

Blumenthal began to depart in the early 1980s from both the documentary-style videos that she had been creating with Horsfield and her own sculptural installations, and moved into the production of more personal video work. *Social Studies, Part 1: Horizontes* (1983) and *Social Studies, Part 2: The Academy* (1983–84) are reworkings of popular media elements to examine the political and entertainment uses of television. In these pieces Blumenthal took long sections of two examples of popular media (a Cuban soap opera in the first piece and part of the Academy Awards in the second) and overlaid text critiquing the politics that lie beneath the perceived situations. Her work with video artist Carole Ann Klonarides and painter Ed Paschke, *Arcade* (1984), is a highly collaged and layered stream of appropriated mass-media material and surveillance-style footage shot in the streets of Chicago.

In 1984 Blumenthal and Horsfield developed a project on behalf of the Video Data Bank called the Video Drive-in, designed to bring video art to a wider audience. The event, held at the Petrillo Music Shell in Grant Park in downtown Chicago, was a great success, with 10,000 people in attendance. Blumenthal, in the autumn of 1985, began work on "What Does She Want: Women With A Past," a series of six videotapes on VHS format compiling much of the most important work by women in film, performance, and video. The series, initiated as a strategy to promote the work of women artists usually overlooked by the art world, was completed shortly before Blumenthal's death in 1988 in New York. Her work has been screened at MOMA, the Whitney Museum's Biennial, The New Museum of Contemporary Art, and The Kitchen in New York, and at Documenta VIII in Kassel, Germany. She was the subject of a posthumous solo exhibition at Los Angeles Contemporary Exhibitions: "Lyn Blumenthal: Force of Vision" (1989). Soon after Blumenthal's death, Horsfield created the Lyn Blumenthal Memorial Fund for Independent Video at SAIC, which gives grants to video artists. DM

Phyllis Bramson

(Born 1941) Phyllis Bramson was born in 1941 in Madison, Wisconsin, of a first-generation Russian immigrant family. She received a BFA from the University of Illinois, Urbana-Champaign, in 1962, and returned to her home town to take an MA in painting from the University of Wisconsin in 1964. That same year she mar-

ried and traveled with her husband, who was in the Army. After settling on Chicago's North Shore in 1966, Bramson worked as a window-display designer for Marshall Field's department store and taught at the Chicago Academy of Fine Arts. Feeling out-of-touch with contemporary art, in 1971 she enrolled at SAIC, receiving her MFA in 1973. Her earlier training had been in painting and she had taken inspiration from figures as diverse as David Hockney, Joan Brown, and early Chicago figures such as Ellen Lanyon, June Leaf, and Seymour Rosofsky. Yet studying at SAIC at a time when painting had been declared "dead" caused her to turn away from the medium. She experimented with various media, including ceramic sculpture and drawings made with craypas, glitter, beads, and other materials, which she showed at Artemisia, where she was a founding member in 1973. In the late 1970s she achieved success with her work, showing in New York at Monique Knowlton Gallery and in Chicago at Marianne Deson Gallery.

In 1980, inspired by the exhibition of the late paintings of Phillip Guston that appeared at the MCA, Bramson again took up painting. Because of her use of the figure and her tendency toward bright color, Bramson was often labeled a "second-generation Imagist." Yet her themes are clearly Feminist; often the works depict women playing out exaggerated female roles, contorting their undulating bodies to accommodate traditional ideas of what women should be. The interiors in which these figures are set are theatrical, filled with rich color and detail. Her work in fact is much more sympathetic with that of artists associated with the first postwar generation in Chicago, including Robert Barnes and Irving Petlin (who are often called Magic Realists), than with the cartoony, linear style of Hairy Who artists such as Gladys Nilsson or Jim Nutt.

In 1985 Bramson began teaching at UIC, in an art department that emphasized the theoretical and conceptual aspects of art. Bramson began to explore the relation of her work to historical styles, such as Rococo, and experiment with the presentation of her paintings, including placing paintings within other paintings that function as frames, and collaging paint-by-number canvases and other found objects. Her themes became more expansive, but continue to express her philosophical views about life and the role of the artist as an observer and creator. Bramson has exhibited widely in Chicago and is in the permanent collections of the Hirshhorn Museum and Sculpture Garden, Washington, DC; the Madison Art Center; the Milwaukee Art Museum; and MCA. LW

(Born 1941) James Roger Brown was born in 1941 into a staunchly religious family in Alabama, where he lived until his high-school graduation. After taking a short trip to New York in 1960, Brown moved to Nashville to attend Bible school at David Lipscomb College with the intention of becoming a preacher. His interest in the ministry waned, and after taking life drawing classes at the University of Nashville, Brown decided that he wanted to attend art school. He was accepted at SAIC and moved to Chicago in 1962. After one semester Brown withdrew, choosing a more structured (and commercial) course of study at the American Academy of Design in Chicago. By 1965 a friend had persuaded Brown to return to SAIC; he received his BFA in painting in 1968 and an MFA in 1970. At SAIC, professors Ray Yoshida and Whitney Halstead were extremely influential on the development of Brown's work. With his close friends Christina Ramberg and Phil Hanson, Brown visited Joseph Yoakum at his South Side Chicago home. He began to amass what would become a significant collection of art by self-taught artists, including Yoakum, and popular culture memorabilia.

In 1968 at SAIC's annual fellowship show, Brown's work was noticed by HPAC Director Don Baum, who included him in the group show "False Image." In 1969 Brown was included in Baum's MCA show "Don Baum Says: 'Chicago Needs Famous Artists,'" the first museum showing for many of the artists who became known as the Chicago Imagists. Added to Phyllis Kind Gallery's roster after this exhibition, Brown received his first solo show at this influential gallery in 1971. By 1973, when his work along with that of many of his colleagues was included in the São Paulo Bienal, Brown was firmly associated with the "Chicago School."

About this time Brown began a long and close relationship with architect George Veronda. Veronda, who accompanied Brown on many of his travels, encouraged Brown's interest in utilizing architectural elements in his paintings and supported his ventures into three-dimensional painted constructions and theater-set design. Veronda's death from cancer in 1984 spurred Brown's series of paintings on illness.

Brown's cross-country road trips around the United States, and travels in Europe, Russia, South America, Mexico, and Egypt, have furnished images and inspiration for his paintings. Rural settings are reflected in his rolling hills dotted with identical, semicircular trees; stylized cloud forms fill an expansive sky. Urban settings feature patterns created

by repeated houses or skyscrapers, often with silhouetted figures at the boxy windows. Many of Brown's works are in the conventional rectangular format, although he has created some irregularly shaped canvases, including several in the form of the crucifix, and *Autobiography in the Shape of Alabama* (1976), a double-sided painting in the shape of his native state. To some extent always hortatory, Brown's work in the 1980s became increasingly politicized, featuring current events, American history, and commentary on the art world and homosexuality as subject matter investigated with wit and sarcasm.

Brown's work is in major collections around the world and has been featured in solo exhibitions at the Hirshhorn Museum and Sculpture Garden in Washington, DC (1987) and multiple showings at Phyllis Kind Gallery in Chicago and New York since the 1970s. He was the subject of a retrospective organized by the Montgomery Museum of Fine Arts in Alabama, which traveled around the United States in 1981, including an MCA venue. His work has been included in numerous group exhibitions including AIC, HPAC, MCA, and the Whitney Museum of American Art in New York. He has created theater sets for several Chicago productions, including Mozart's *Così Fan Tutte* at the Chicago Opera Theatre. Numerous public commissions include a mural-sized painting for the lobby of the NBC Tower in Chicago, a mosaic depicting Icarus and Daedalus on the 120 North LaSalle Street building in Chicago, and a mosaic at the site of the African Burial Ground at Foley Square in New York. AF

Harry Callahan

(Born 1912) Harry Callahan was born in Detroit in 1912. He did not have an early interest in photography, but rather he worked for the Chrysler Corporation and studied engineering at Michigan State College in 1931–33. In 1936 he married Eleanor Knapp, who would later serve as the subject of many of his photographic works. Callahan purchased his first camera in 1938 (a Rolleicord), and after attending a workshop taught by Ansel Adams in 1941, he began to devote himself to photography. During the years 1944–45, Callahan worked as a processor in the General Motors Corporation photo lab and continued his self-directed photographic studies.

Two major career developments occurred in 1946: Callahan was included in a MOMA exhibition "New Photographers," and László Moholy-Nagy hired him as an instructor in photography at ID. Callahan moved to Chicago, where he would spend the next fifteen years teaching at ID and shooting photographs. When Arthur Siegel resigned as head of ID's Light

Workshop (the photography department) in 1949, Callahan replaced him, holding this position until 1961, when he assumed the chairmanship of the photography department of the Rhode Island School of Design in Providence; he resigned in 1973. Callahan was an influential instructor and a role model for countless students, many of whom would become important photographers in their own right. His personal innovations and experimentations had a deep impact on ID's photography program; his legacy there included hiring Aaron Siskind in 1951.

Callahan's photos are intense and highly personal, yet he continues the tradition of Moholy-Nagy in his formalism and experimentation with the photographic medium. Prevalent in his work are elegant portraits of his wife, Eleanor, and daughter, Barbara, who was born in 1950; somber architectural scenes often of Chicago skyscrapers and rowhouses; bold landscapes which include striking beach scenes from Cape Cod; and textural nature studies of leaves, grasses, tree branches, and twigs. Often focusing on mundane images, Callahan infuses his photos of the ordinary with richness and elegance. Many of his experiments involve layered images, distortion, or manipulations of focus and contrast. Callahan was influenced by his travels, including a yearlong trip to Europe in 1956 funded by a grant from the Graham Foundation, trips to Mexico and New England, and other trips to Europe in later years.

Callahan was honored with a retrospective at MOMA in 1976. His photographs have been exhibited internationally. Important one-person shows in the United States include the Kansas City Art Institute in 1956; the George Eastman House in Rochester, New York, in 1958; his first one-person show in New York at the Hallmark Gallery in 1964; MOMA in 1967; and a touring exhibition organized by the Hallmark Photographic Collection in 1981–82, and most recently a major traveling retrospective organized in 1995 by the National Gallery of Art, Washington, DC. A variety of magazines have published his photographs, including *Life, Newsweek, The New York Times* and *Chicago Tribune* magazines, *U.S. Camera, Aperture,* and *Harper's Bazaar.* His photographs are included in many prominent collections. AF

Cosmo Campoli

(Born 1922) As one of the first postwar generation of artists in Chicago, sculptor Cosmo Campoli was an extremely influential member of the "Monster Roster." Born in South Bend, Indiana, in 1922, Campoli declared his vocation at the age of twelve after modeling a portrait of his sister from clay dug from the family farm's well. He first came to Chicago at age sixteen to take a summer course at AIC, and in 1942 began undergraduate study of painting and poetry at SAIC. Interrupting his education by three years of military service and spending two fellowship years in Italy, France, and Spain, Campoli eventually returned to Chicago and earned his BFA in 1950. In the same year he cofounded the Contemporary Art Workshop with sculptor John Kearney as well as developed and introduced casting techniques in Chicago, working with bronze, cement, lead, and plastic. Campoli taught sculpture at ID/IIT from 1953 to 1989.

Campoli has remained in Chicago since his student days, and his work has been remarkably self-contained with virtually no stylistic shifts. Its sense of mystery and fantasy has links with the introspective modes of painting prevalent during the same period, showing the artist's interest in expression rather than purely formal practices. Campoli prefers to model in clay, and the surfaces of many pieces have an earthy, pitted quality. He speaks of a need to have his "hands rooted in clay which gives sustenance to the sculptor's being and is the anchor that holds him to the earth from which all life springs." Campoli's sculptures are biomorphic, organic forms involved with the life processes of birth and death—eternally recurring themes formed from early memories watching chicks hatching and accompanying his father on his egg-delivery route, and the tragedy of his father's early death. Highly simplified forms of birds and eggs and the oozing, flowing lines often employed by Campoli frequently have erotic overtones and call to mind ancient fertility symbols. Campoli's elegant, sophisticated sculpture also recalls the work of Constantin Brancusi. Although such work was certainly familiar to Campoli, the similarities stem more from a shared interest in the mysteries of physical existence than from direct influence.

Campoli has exhibited internationally. He was a frequent participant in Exhibition Momentum, and was included in Peter Selz's significant "New Images of Man" exhibition at MOMA (1959); he had a thirty-year retrospective at MCA in 1971. His work is in such collections as MCA; The David and Alfred Smart Museum of Art, Chicago; and MOMA. His well-known public sculpture *Bird of Peace* (1962) was included in the Carnegie International Exhibition in Pittsburgh (1964). It was purchased in 1970 by the Hyde Park-Kenwood Community and installed at Kimbark Avenue and 54th Street in Chicago. MM

Rodney Carswell

(Born 1946) Rodney Carswell was born in 1946 in Carmel, California. Raised and educated in the Western United States, he grew up in Santa Fe, and received his BFA in 1968 from the University of New Mexico, Albuquerque, and his MFA from the University of Colorado, Boulder, in 1972. Carswell arrived in the Chicago area in the mid-1970s and began teaching at Illinois State University in Normal. He joined the faculty of UIC in 1983.

Carswell's style of geometric abstraction was introduced to Chicago in a 1973 C & V exhibition at AIC; he was picked up by the Roy Boyd Gallery, where he received his first local one-person show in 1976. His works of this era are irreverent constructions—unstretched canvases cut into geometric forms and painted—that feature seemingly casual means of display in their attachment directly to the wall.

In 1980 the artist moved to New York where he remained for three years, showing at Josef Gallery (1981), and continuing to show his work in Chicago. His paintings evolved into geometric abstractions rendered in a rich mixture of oil paint and wax (encaustic). Often featuring shaped or assembled canvases and usually offset from the wall by layers of wood, cross-braces, and other revealed support structures, the painting's surface is decorative and strangely devoid of meaning. The heart of the work lies in the interplay between the revealed support structures and the beautiful surfaces. After his return to Chicago in 1983, Carswell further explored this interplay, his works presenting possible middle grounds between painting and sculpture. Crosses, circles, and other geometric shapes make reference to both Suprematism and Constructivism of the early twentieth century and the more recent Minimalism of the 1960s—movements that sought to reduce the content and formal language of art to its most basic, universal forms. In interviews Carswell has acknowledged the legacy of Suprematism, but emphasized that his goal in his work—the highlighting of individual experience—diverges considerably from Suprematism's egalitarian, utilitarian goals of improving society.

Carswell was the subject of a retrospective at the Renaissance Society (1993), and was included in the "44th Biennial of Contemporary Painting" at the Corcoran Gallery of Art, Washington, DC (1995). Long associated with the Roy Boyd Gallery, Chicago and Los Angeles, he began showing at Feigen, Inc., Chicago, in 1995. He has shown in numerous area exhibitions exploring the topic of abstraction, including "Abstract: Chicago," Klein Art Works, Chicago (1993); "The Content of Abstraction," Illinois Art Gallery, Chicago, and Arts

Center of the College of DuPage, Glen Ellyn, Illinois (1994 and 1995); and "Chicago Abstract Painters," Evanston Art Center, Illinois (1995). LW

George Cohen

(Born 1919) George Cohen was born and raised in Chicago where he has been producing challenging and disturbing work for half a century. In 1946 he graduated from both Drake University, Des Moines, Iowa, and SAIC, where he had been taking classes since 1937. In 1942 he married Constance Teander, a painter, and in 1948 he received an MA and a PhD in art history from the University of Chicago. While a student, he worked at the Field Museum and spent time studying the ethnographic art collections that strongly influenced his painting. By that time Cohen, along with Leon Golub, June Leaf, and other Chicago painters, had developed a style consisting of direct, disturbing, rough-surfaced, neo-primitive images that earned them the name the "Monster Roster." Anticipating assemblage, Cohen often embedded other materials, including gold leaf, aluminum foil, and black lace, into the grainy, impasto surface of his paintings. His assemblages of the early 1950s that he later grouped under the title "The Phenomenology of Mirrors" explore real and imaginary space and the nature of time through distorted, repeated reflections. *Anybody's Self-Portrait*, an assemblage from the series that was included in MOMA's 1961 exhibition "The Art of the Assemblage," was purchased for the museum's permanent collection, acknowledging its importance as an early pre-Pop object.

Cohen, meanwhile, had committed full-time to painting and was working on a series that drew upon classic literary sources. Mirrors, eyes, and other references to ways of seeing continued to be prevalent in his crudely worked, content-rich canvases, as did disembodied limbs and the silhouette of a large, high-heeled woman. His work was included in a Surrealism show at MOMA in 1968. In 1984, after a long hiatus from publicly showing his work, Cohen displayed large, carefully rendered canvases full of art-historical allusions at Frumkin/Struve Gallery in Chicago. His technical style had changed radically from the stiff, hieratic symbols of the earlier paintings, but his use of mirrors and the intellectually challenging, surreal quality of his work continued.

Cohen participated in all of the Exhibition Momentum exhibitions from 1948 until 1957. He was in a number of AIC's C & V shows during the 1950s and 1960s, and had many shows at Feigen Gallery in Chicago throughout the 1960s. His work has been featured in galleries in New York, Los Angeles, and Paris, as well as at the Corcoran Gallery of Art,

Washington, DC (1959); Contemporary Arts Center, Houston (1960); San Francisco Museum of Art (1963 and 1964–65); The Arts Club of Chicago (1960 and 1962); and La Jolla Museum of Art, California (1965). Cohen participated in a two-person exhibition with his wife at Jan Cicero Gallery, Chicago, in 1994. He has taught in Illinois at the Evanston Art Center, ID, and Northwestern University, Evanston, where he was a professor of art from 1963 to 1984. LS

William Conger

(Born 1937) Born in Dixon, Illinois, in 1937, William Conger first studied art at SAIC, then at the University of New Mexico, Albuquerque, where he received his BFA in 1960. He pursued his education at the University of Chicago, earning an MFA in 1966. In addition to being a painter, Conger has taught art at the college level for over twenty years, beginning with a position at Rock Valley College in Rockford, Illinois (1966–71). From 1971 to 1984 Conger was a member of Chicago's DePaul University art faculty. In 1984 he became a visiting professor at Northwestern University in Evanston, Illinois, where the following year he became a professor and chair of the Department of Art Theory and Practice, a position he holds today.

Conger is a member of the group of Chicago artists known as the "Allusive Abstractionists," which included Frank Piatek, Richard Loving, and Miyoko Ito. Although he made some figurative works in the 1960s, Conger was influenced by the abstract style of his teacher Elaine de Kooning, with whom he studied at the University of New Mexico in the late 1950s. By the late 1960s and early 1970s, he had developed an abstract style featuring brightly colored, flat shapes against a lighter ground. In the mid-1970s, Conger deepened the color and further varied the shapes, producing dynamic works that juxtapose luminous hues and fractured, lively forms in a format sometimes resembling a stained-glass window. He introduced illusionistic space into his abstractions of the 1980s by overlapping the shapes and increasingly modulating the color. Although he paints in a nonrepresentational manner, Conger roots his works in everyday experience through his titles, which are descriptive, evocative, and metaphoric. Many of his works are based upon his youthful remembrances of Chicago.

Conger's work has been shown in numerous one-person and group exhibitions, including shows at the Krannert Art Museum, University of Illinois, Champaign (1976); in Chicago at Zaks Gallery (1978, 1980, and 1983) and Roy Boyd Gallery (1985, 1987, 1990, 1992, and 1994); and at Janus Gallery in Santa Fe (1992). Important Chicago exhibitions incorporating Conger's work include AIC's C & V shows (1963, 1971, 1973, 1978, 1981, 1984, and 1985); "Abstract Art in Chicago" at MCA (1976); "ART/WORK" at The Chicago Public Library Cultural Center (1980); "Chicago: Some Other Traditions" Madison Art Center, Wisconsin (1983); "Abstract/Symbol/Image," organized by the Illinois Arts Council, Chicago (1984); "Painting at Northwestern: Conger, Paschke, Valerio," Mary and Leigh Block Gallery, Northwestern University (1986); and "Chicago Abstract Painters," Evanston Art Center, Illinois (1995). MF

Jno Cook

(Born 1940) Jno Cook's humorous, offbeat, and often ingenious photography and kinetic sculpture are much in keeping with the deliberate "mis"-spelling of his name, taken from an Old English abbreviation of John. Born in 1940 in the Netherlands, Cook moved with his parents to Chicago in 1962. He attended IIT and received BS degrees in both electrical and industrial engineering (1963 and 1970, respectively). After years of working as an engineer, Cook attended SAIC, receiving his MFA in photography in 1983. He began exhibiting photographs whose construction was so complex and singular that it was necessary to construct cameras to take them. These cameras were exhibited in one of Cook's first solo exhibitions, "Reclaiming Technology" at Randolph Street Gallery, Chicago, in 1989.

Cook's recent sculptures make liberal use of found objects and projection devices. His work is focused upon the interrelationship of projected elements (such as sound, slide images, or light), the structure of the sculpture itself, and the message to be conveyed. Cook thus locates himself within the tradition of international kinetic sculptors such as Jean Tinguely and Rebecca Horn, and local artists such as Ben Pranger, Woody Haid, and Gary Justis.

Cook has taught photography at Columbia College in Chicago since 1983. He has written criticism for publications such as *Afterimage, Nit & Wit,* and *Exposure.* Cook's work has been included in various important group exhibitions such as "The Chicago Show" (1990) and "The Nature of the Machine" (1993), both at the Chicago Cultural Center, and "Recycled and Reassembled" at the Northern Illinois University Art Museum in DeKalb (1994). Cook's most quirky show, perhaps, was his exhibition for Beret International Gallery, Chicago, in 1994, entitled "Backyard Sale." For this exhibition, the last in Beret's space on Elston Avenue, he used the occasion of the gallery's move to hold a backyard sale, much in the same spirit of conventional yard sales that people hold when relocating. DM

Eldzier Cortor

(Born 1916) Eldzier Cortor has been painting for over fifty years. Born in 1916 in Richmond, Virginia, Cortor moved with his family to the South Side of Chicago within a year of his birth. From 1936 to 1938 he attended both night and daytime classes at SAIC, where he studied with Kathleen Blackshear, who introduced him to African sculpture during frequent visits to the Field Museum. While working for the WPA in 1938–40, he met an encouraging Archibald J. Motley, Jr., and was assigned to the South Side Community Art Center where he taught, organized exhibitions, and worked with other artists and writers, such as Elizabeth Catlett, Gordon Parks, Gwendolyn Brooks, and Richard Wright, to maintain Chicago's African-American art community. Cortor also attended ID in 1942, where he studied with László Moholy-Nagy. In 1946 Cortor moved to New York to study printmaking at Columbia University; he continued to maintain close ties with Chicago throughout the decade, exhibiting in C & V shows at AIC in 1948 and 1949.

Cortor's early works of the late 1930s and 1940s range from classic figure studies to genre paintings celebrating the life of blacks in Chicago (he was profoundly influenced by an exhibition of nineteenth-century French realist painters at AIC in the early 1940s). Two Julius Rosenwald Fellowships (1944 and 1945) enabled Cortor to travel through the Southeastern United States to conduct research for a series of paintings on the Gullah people living in the Sea Islands, off the coasts of South Carolina, Georgia, and northern Florida. Returning to Chicago he began executing the series from memory, as was his preferred manner of working. He continued the series, reworking some of the paintings, after his move to New York. At this time Cortor was interested in representing black racial types and exploring formal issues of color and composition. He specifically chose groups whose lifestyles were little influenced by Western ideas and accouterments, and attempted to portray them within their cultural milieus. Cortor characteristically places his figures, usually only partially seen, in the midst of an evocative and detailed background. Early works show romantic and mythic portraits of African-American women in homes or in landscapes, painted with rich colors. The setting later evolved into constructed spaces that combine both interior and exterior, whose design elements approach collage. Cortor is concerned with creating a harmonious balance between the figurative and the decorative components. Painted in the 1940s, the important "Room" series depicts African-Americans living in slum-like conditions. Presented—as always—with pride and integrity, these sinuous black nudes inhabit overcrowded rooms rendered with an abundance of texture and pattern formed by intersecting vertical, diagonal, and horizontal lines and planes. Cortor's later works include still lifes associated with memory, history, and black culture.

Cortor participated in AIC's C & V exhibition and Annual American Exhibition of Paintings in 1946 (he won prizes at both). His work has been shown in such places as the American Negro Exposition, Chicago (1940); South Side Community Art Center, Chicago (1941 and 1945); City College of New York (1967); Museum of Fine Arts, Boston (1970); National Center of Afro-American Artists, Boston (1973); the Studio Museum in Harlem, New York (1973); and Kenkeleba Gallery, New York (1988). His work is included in museums and collections nationwide. SB

Barbara Crane

(Born 1928) Barbara Crane has garnered an international reputation during her forty-year career as a photographer. In addition to her studio work, Crane is a renowned educator who has taught since 1964. Born in Chicago in 1928, Crane went to Oakland, California, to study art history at Mills College (1945–48). She completed her BA degree at New York University in 1950. Introduced to photography through her father who was an amateur photographer, Crane bought her first camera in 1947 while at college. After moving to New York in 1948, she got her first professional photography experience at Bloomingdale's portrait studio. Returning to Chicago in 1952, Crane put aside her commercial photography until 1960 when her youngest child entered preschool. She resumed doing portrait photography and enrolled in ID's graduate photography program in 1964, the same year she began teaching. Crane studied with Aaron Siskind and received her MS in photography from ID in 1966. In 1967 she became a professor of photography at SAIC, where she passed on to hundreds of students her ID legacy of technical excellence combined with constant experimentation; she was appointed professor emeritus in 1993.

A prolific artist, Crane works in two primary modes: abstraction and documentation. Excited by experimentation and chance, she has used a variety of formats and techniques, including multiple exposure and montage. Series titles reflect the range within her work as well as her vacillation between abstract experiments with the photographic medium and documentary photographs of people: "Petites Choses," "Combines," "Whole Roll" (which consisted of exposing and printing an entire roll of film as a single image), "Repeats," "Neon," "Human Forms" represent investigations into structures, patterns, and relationships. In her abstract work she often uses found objects to set up the compositions. Her documentary series reflect an almost sociological interest in human beings and attempt to catch them off-guard in order to capture their essence more accurately. The majority of her work is in black and white, though Crane began to explore color after being awarded a Guggenheim Fellowship in 1979 to pursue this investigation. Works range from tiny Polacolor pieces to giant murals. From 1972 to 1979 she was the official photographer for the Commission on Chicago Historical and Architectural Landmarks.

Crane has had two traveling retrospective exhibitions, one organized by the Center for Creative Photography, University of Arizona, Tucson (1981–82), and one organized by the Polaroid Corporation (1984–85). She has exhibited internationally in one-person shows; those in the United States include exhibitions at Catherine Edelman Gallery and Gallery 954 in Chicago; The Museum of Contemporary Photography, Columbia College, Chicago; and the George Eastman House in Rochester, New York. Her work has also been seen in numerous group exhibitions and is in many important collections including AIC; MCA; MOMA; Center for Creative Photography; Getty Museum in Malibu, California; and the National Museum of American Art, Washington, DC. AF

Tom Czarnopys

(Born 1957) Raised in the shadow of the vast woods of western Michigan, Tom Czarnopys as a young boy went hunting and fishing with his father and brothers. Continually faced with the forest's beauty and intricate ecosystem, Czarnopys found the woodlands to be a place of refuge and exhilaration. At an early age he feverishly drew and painted pictures of animals, attempting to interpret the character of the wildlife in its habitat, and seeking to sustain the experience once away from it. He was instinctively drawn to art by the experiences of his youth and by an unrelenting need to observe and respond to his natural surroundings.

Born in Grand Rapids in 1957, Czarnopys studied painting there in the late 1970s before earning his BFA degree from SAIC in 1982. One of his important artistic influences was Magdalena Abakanowicz, a fellow Polish Catholic artist who uses fiber weavings to construct her figures of despair and whose retrospective he saw at the MCA in 1982. His spiritual influence, however, has remained the woods: the dynamism of living systems,

growth and decay, is a recurrent theme through all of Czarnopys's work.

In the 1980s Czarnopys worked with faceless and distorted figures. He cast plaster gauze figures and added attachments of pine or birchbark, at times including natural creatures such as butterflies or grouse. An immediate success, these striking works were acquired by both museums and private collectors. In the early 1990s Czarnopys turned from the figure to abstraction. He presented entire, once-living systems implanted in assorted materials such as glycerin and plaster, or used his urine to accelerate fossillike etchings of the earth's plant and animal life onto bronze plates in order to bear witness to the cycle of life and death. In all of his work, Czarnopys attempts to reconnect to nature and to become a participant in its living theater.

Czarnopys has shown regularly in Chicago since his initial exhibition of the bark figures at ARC Gallery in 1984. His solo exhibition at the Grand Rapids Art Museum, Michigan, in 1987 traveled to the Contemporary Arts Center in Cincinnati in 1988. He was also featured as a solo artist in MCA's "Options" series in 1988, in an exhibition that traveled to the Virginia Museum of Fine Arts in Richmond. Czarnopys has participated in numerous group exhibitions nationally and is included in several public collections, including MCA and the Milwaukee Art Museum. L H

Henry Darger

(1892–1973) Henry Darger lived a solitary life far removed from the world of art. Born in 1892, by varying accounts in Brazil or Germany, Darger lived with his crippled father on the South Side of Chicago. At the age of eight, when his father could no longer care for him, Darger was taken to a Catholic boys' home where he was diagnosed as "feeble-minded." Sent to an asylum, by his own account he was cruelly mistreated and tried to escape. Darger finally left the asylum at the age of sixteen and began eking out a subsistence as a hospital janitor. In 1930 or 1932 he settled into rented rooms on Webster Avenue that he would transform into a shrine to his extraordinary inner life.

In 1972 a leg injury prevented Darger from climbing the stairs to his apartment. He was moved into an old-age home; he died six months later and was buried in a pauper's grave. When his former landlord, the photographer Nathan Lerner, came to empty Darger's rooms, he discovered an eleven-year weather log, a massive diary, and Darger's thirteen-volume, nineteen-thousand-page chronicle The Story of the Vivian Girls in What Is Known as the

Realms of the Unreal or the Glandelinean War Storm or the Glandico-Abbiennian Wars, as Caused by the Child Slave Rebellion (begun in 1911 or 1916). Most astonishing were eighty-seven huge watercolor-collages bound into three gigantic books—illustrations for his grand epic.

Realms of the Unreal takes place on a planet similar to Earth; the majority of characters are young children. The story revolves around a war between Abbiennia, a god-fearing Christian people, and Glandelinia, an evil child-enslaving nation. Led by seven "princesses," the blond-haired, spiritual Vivian sisters, the Abbiennians, with the help of Captain Henry Darger, eventually win the war. Darger was well read in Civil War history, and his descriptions of single battles go on for hundreds of pages in true epic style, yet the saga was more likely inspired by his own tortured psyche. Never married, Darger nevertheless prayed daily to be granted permission to adopt a child; frustrated by his unanswered prayers, he formed a "Children's Protective Society" with himself and his sole friend as members.

The double-sided artworks feature scroll-like narratives, packed full of figures (mostly little girls), flowers and trees, half-human creatures, crucifixes and other religious imagery, an occasional comic-book character, and, in the more violent scenes, explosions, storms, and carnage. A poor draftsman, Darger traced cutout images from children's storybooks, newspapers, religious ephemera, and coloring books; many of these images he had enlarged at the local drugstore. Occasionally images were collaged and embellished with watercolor and pencil, all pieced together on cheap construction paper. Often these embellishments are bizarre: his little girl figures are sometimes nude and feature male genitals; rams horns and serpentine tails are frequently added. Imaginary half-girl, half-butterfly creatures; dragonlike animals; mermaids with angel or butterfly wings fill his fantastical world.

Darger's work, like that of many other untrained artists, has fascinated Chicago artists and collectors. An important show at HPAC in 1977 featured not only Darger's books and artwork, but toys and religious kitsch from his room. His work has been included in many exhibitions, including solo shows at the Louisiana Museum of Modern Art in Humlebok, Denmark; the Musée des Arts Décoratifs in Paris; the Musée de L'Art Brut in Lausanne; and Phyllis Kind Gallery in Chicago and New York, as well as group shows of "outsider" art at MCA, the Los Angeles County Museum of Art, the Hayward Gallery in London, and the Whitney Museum of American Art in New York. AF

Barbara DeGenevieve

(Born 1947) Barbara DeGenevieve was born in 1947 in the small town of Wilkes-Barre, Pennsylvania, into a deeply religious, working-class family. After completing her art studies in Wilkes-Barre in 1969, DeGenevieve spent the next decade teaching art in a number of cities on the East Coast. Divorced in 1978, DeGenevieve changed her last name to a French translation of "of Genevieve," her mother's name. That same year she enrolled in the photography program at the University of New Mexico in Albuquerque. DeGenevieve and fellow-student Joel-Peter Witkin quickly made their mark with explosive content that challenged the status quo and extended the boundaries of the already progressive department. She received her MA in photography in 1979 (and her MFA later, in 1985), then fell under the unlikely influence of the Chicago Imagists, and moved in 1980 to the Chicago area. Though her work would not normally be associated with this group, DeGenevieve was fascinated by the raw, gritty, abject quality of the Imagist figures, particularly those of Jim Nutt, and was attracted as well to the autobiographical work of Hollis Sigler. During the 1980s DeGenevieve taught photography at the University of Illinois, Urbana-Champaign, and then spent five years teaching at California State University in San Jose. Returning to Chicago in 1994, DeGenevieve stepped into the role of chairperson of the photography program at SAIC, a tenured position vacated by Chicago photographer Barbara Crane.

DeGenevieve's early work attempted to demystify the male nude in a manner that paralleled the already socially affirmed demystification of the female nude. Strikingly honest and direct, her photographs (on large-format, photosensitized canvases) graphically address issues of sexuality and male/female relationships. DeGenevieve's work dramatically shifted immediately after she lost her mother to suicide in 1985. Withdrawing from her basic political agenda, DeGenevieve turned her focus inward, and her life and work became inextricably intertwined. Early in her career, DeGenevieve was a vehement opponent of pornography, believing it perpetuated negative images of women. In the 1990s, however, she has embraced pornography, using her work as a wedge to insert a female voice into a hitherto strictly male arena. This recent work concentrates on the politics of gender and female pleasure; she has also published erotic writings in magazines such as

P-Form, a Randolph Street Gallery publication, and Herotica 4, a Bay Area compilation of erotic writing by women.

In 1994, after initially being selected by the Photography Peer Review Panel for an NEA Fellowship, DeGenevieve's application, along with those of Andres Serrano and Merry Alpern, was rejected by the National Council on the Arts, an incident that attracted wide, national attention. DeGenevieve's work can be found in the Seattle Art Museum, the Tokyo Metropolitan Museum of Photography, and other significant collections. She participated in the 1990 "Photography: Inventions and Innovations" at AIC, and continues to show locally and nationally in a variety of solo and group exhibitions. LH

Dominick Di Meo

(Born 1927) Dominick Di Meo was born in 1927 in Niagara Falls, New York. He came to Chicago to pursue an art education at SAIC, receiving a BFA in 1952. While a student there, Di Meo helped found Momentum, the first of many artist groups in which he would be involved. He subsequently cofounded a cooperative gallery and art center, Gallery 5, in Iowa City, while a graduate student at the University of Iowa, where he obtained an MFA in 1953. Following a one-year postgraduate fellowship from the University of Iowa, Di Meo was given his first one-person show, at Lake Forest College, Illinois (1955), and was included in two consecutive "New Talent Show" exhibitions sponsored by Allan Frumkin, B.C. Holland, and Superior Street galleries in Chicago (1958 and 1959). Sensing his potential, a group of Chicago collectors sponsored Di Meo on a trip to Florence to further develop his art; he lived and worked in Italy from 1961 to 1963.

Di Meo early on established an iconography that consists of skulls, bones, appendages, and occasionally commonplace objects such as spoons and forks, which he impressed into his surfaces. His early small-scale relief paintings and sculptures were modeled out of taxidermist papier-mâché and plastic. The combination of symbolic imagery with very thick and textured materials, recalling the gritty, earthy works of Jean Dubuffet, resulted in small but substantial reliefs that resemble funerary slabs or fossilized pieces of earth or clay that have been uncovered through excavation.

The profusion of strange and mythical creatures and the exploration of Existentialist themes associate Di Meo's reliefs with the "Monster Roster" school. Figurative elements are often mingled with representations of the land to portray the cyclical nature of life, another

favorite subject of these artists, particularly Leon Golub and Cosmo Campoli. Also heavily influenced by Surrealism, particularly Joan Miró, Di Meo became interested in lyrical, yet sometimes melancholy, dreamlike landscape compositions filled with disembodied shapes hovering above and below the horizon line. In addition to acrylic transfers, he used objects such as dolls, egg cartons, and rope to texturize the surface of his assemblages of the mid-1960s.

After cofounding the organization PAC (Participating Artists of Chicago) in 1967 as well as participating in artist-initiated antiwar activities surrounding the 1968 Democratic Convention, Di Meo moved in 1969 to New York, where he resides today. His signature skulls, pared down to an elemental circle with three small holes for the eyes and mouth, remain an integral part of all of his work to date. He repeats them in rows and clusters to design studies for monuments, both sculptural and on paper.

Di Meo has had one-person exhibitions at Kendall College, Evanston, Illinois (1967) and P.S. 1, The Institute for Art and Urban Resources, Inc., Long Island City, New York (1982). He was associated with Fairweather-Hardin Gallery in Chicago from 1959 to 1973 and Westbroadway Gallery in New York from 1972 to 1977, where he had several solo shows. His work has been featured in numerous group exhibitions, including "Biennial of Prints, Drawings and Watercolors," AIC (1961–62, 1964, and 1966); "Chicago School 1955–1960," HPAC (1964); "Annual Exhibition of Contemporary American Painting," Whitney Museum of American Art, New York (1967); "Violence in Recent American Art," MCA (1968); "The Koffler Foundation Collection," National Collection of Fine Arts, Smithsonian Institution, Washington, DC (1979); and "American Drawings Since World War II," AIC (1990). SB

Jeff Donaldson

(Born 1937) A leader in the Trans-African art movement (a term synonymous with Pan-Africanism that the artist uses to describe an international aesthetic with its roots in the African experience), Jeff Donaldson has taken on the multiple roles of artist, educator, curator, activist, and writer. Born and raised in Arkansas, he graduated in 1954 from the University of Arkansas, Pine Bluff, with a BA in studio art. After serving in the Army, Donaldson moved to Chicago where he received an MS in art education and administration from ID in 1963. While serving as an assistant professor at Northeastern Illinois University, Chicago, Donaldson founded the Visual Arts Workshop of OBAC (Organization of Black American Culture) and partici-

pated in their Wall of Respect mural in Hyde Park (1967). In 1968, in the midst of political and social unrest and the Black Power movement, Donaldson and other activist artists, notably Wadsworth Jarrell, formed AfriCobra (African Commune of Bad Relevant Artists) to further the philosophy of a formally and thematically Afrocentric art. Donaldson's 1970 AfriCobra "manifesto" stressed the social responsibility of the artist while it defined the intrinsic qualities of the black aesthetic. In 1970, while pursuing a PhD in African and African-American art history at Northwestern University in Evanston, Illinois (received in 1974), Donaldson organized the seminal Conference on the Functional Aspects of Black Art (CONFABA). Later that year he moved to Washington, DC, to become the Art Department chairman as well as Art Gallery director at Howard University, where he is currently dean of the College of Fine Arts. Donaldson has also served as a director of the World Black and African Festival of Art and Culture, Lagos, Nigeria (1975–80); and as art director of the Jazz America Marketing Corporation, Washington, DC (1978–82).

Donaldson's early paintings are earth-toned, collagelike depictions of the African-American experience that are intended to motivate and uplift. They combine representations of the violence of the civil rights movement with strong graphic lettering from the urban landscape/battlefield and traditional symbols of the collective African heritage. The individuals Donaldson portrays, many of them symbolic of African gods and goddesses, are usually armed and ready for combat. The titles of his paintings refer to current events as well as mythologies from the past. Over the years Donaldson has turned to more vibrant, jazzy, abstract visualizations of African-American rhythms and music, many dedicated to important African-American cultural leaders.

Donaldson has been exhibiting with the AfriCobra artists since 1969, the year of their first shows at WJ Studio, Chicago; University of Notre Dame, Indiana; and AFAM Gallery, Chicago. The following year he participated in AfriCobra exhibitions at the Studio Museum in Harlem, New York; National Center for Afro-American Artists, Boston; South Side Community Art Center, Chicago; and at Black Expo-International Amphitheater, Chicago. Since 1970 Donaldson has exhibited with the AfriCobra group in over fifty-five different cities internationally, including the major "AfriCobra: The First Twenty Years" at the Nexus Contemporary Art Center, Atlanta (1990). As an independent artist, Donaldson has been given numerous solo exhibitions, and his paintings have been included in group exhibitions at Museo Civico D'Arte Contemporanea, Palermo,

Italy (1989); North Carolina Art Center, Charlotte (1990); National Black Art Festival, Atlanta (1991); and Corcoran Gallery of Art, Washington, DC (1992 and 1993). Donaldson is currently putting together an exhibition of AfriCobra artists to commemorate the group's forthcoming thirtieth anniversary. SB

Robert Donley

(Born 1934) Like that of many artists in the early 1960s, Robert Donley's work was informed by Abstract Expressionism; his Color-Field paintings from this time reflect an attention to surface and tone. However, beginning in the late 1960s, his paintings took on a Surrealist edge and in the 1970s he combined this with an interest in historical, mythological, and literary themes, producing works painted in a naive style and peopled by tiny, caricatured figures. In 1980 Donley opened his first one-person show in New York with a series of paintings dealing with the history of his own age. Exhibited at the Monique Knowlton Gallery, the paintings depict the great wars of the twentieth century as evidenced by their titles: *White Russia, Dedicated Resistance*, and *Stalingrad: The Turning Point*. Like his earlier paintings, these canvases are so saturated with figures that it is often difficult to decipher individual scenarios. However, upon close inspection miniature armies, trees, buildings, missiles, planes, and other war machines come into focus. Even though the subject matter is gruesome, Donley treats it somewhat whimsically. In the tradition of the Fauves, his landscapes and figures are arbitrarily colored: a moon is blue, animals anything from purple to yellow to black.

For the past fifteen years, Donley has been predominately concerned with what he calls "the total experience of the [modern] city," whether Chicago or a composite of several large cities, in terms of its historic, mythic, and sometimes fantastic manifestations. Although often depicted from a bird's-eye view, his cityscapes reflect a flaneur's interest in the street-level fabric of urban life. His cities are active and dense, filled with scores of miniature urbanites crammed into a grid of skyscrapers, apartments, monuments, and traffic. In typical Donley fashion, the relationships between some of the figures are often unlikely and ambiguous—such as the inclusion of Madonna and Stalin in the same picture—suggesting either a private joke or an overarching critique.

Born in Cleveland, Donley moved to Chicago in the 1940s and received both his BFA (1960) and MFA (1966) degrees from SAIC. He has been a professor of art at DePaul University, Chicago, since

1967, where he was also chairman of the department from 1984 to 1993. In 1977 his entry to AIC's C & V exhibition was awarded the Logan Prize. In 1990 he was asked by *U.S. News & World Report* to serve as a judge for a special issue of the magazine entitled "The Best of America," which honored individuals who had contributed significantly to the fields of education, science and technology, business, politics and government, and the arts. Donley's work has been exhibited throughout the United States and may be found in a variety of public collections, including the National Museum of American Art, Washington, DC; the First National Bank, Chicago; DePaul University; and Mobil Oil Corporation, New York. CES

Susanne Doremus

(Born 1943) Susanne Doremus has created a body of abstract paintings that evolved from a precise, pictographic style to a brightly colored, loosely painted manner. Born in Jersey City, New Jersey, Doremus showed an early interest in painting that was encouraged by private art lessons in New York. These lessons enabled Doremus to support herself as an undergraduate at Elmira College, New York, by painting portraits. After receiving a BA in 1965, she went on to the University of Wisconsin, Madison, receiving her MFA in 1968. At Wisconsin she abandoned figurative painting, and studied with visiting professor and abstract painter Milton Resnick, although most of her peers were painting in the Pop art and Minimal styles of the day.

Feeling at a loss for subject matter in a time when painting was not generally supported, Doremus stopped painting for eight years after leaving school. She relocated to DeKalb in 1968 with her husband, a history professor at Northern Illinois University, and they started a family. When her youngest child was four, she resumed painting. She received her first exhibition of works on paper at Artemisia Gallery, Chicago, in 1980, and showed at One Illinois Center that same year. When she was picked up by Zolla/Lieberman Gallery, then in one of the first huge converted loft spaces in the nascent River North district, Doremus increased the scale of her works, and showed paintings on canvas. She was affiliated with CompassRose Gallery, Chicago, during the mid-1980s, but returned to Zolla/Lieberman after the former gallery closed. During the 1980s she experimented with monoprinting on canvas to create images that would be similar, yet unique, across each painting or from painting to painting. Her most recent work involves a pouring technique. Because her main artistic interest lies in examining the process of painting and its

pictorial conventions, Doremus's work in spirit is closely aligned with the American abstract artists she admires, particularly Jackson Pollock and Willem de Kooning.

Doremus has received one-person exhibitions at Swen Parson Gallery, Northern Illinois University, DeKalb (1984) and Ruth Siegel Ltd., New York (1986), and she has shown widely in group exhibitions, especially in the Midwest. Important shows include the traveling exhibition "Chicago: Some Other Traditions," organized by the Madison Art Center (1982); "Painting and Sculpture Today," Indianapolis Museum of Art (1986); and "Surfaces: Two Decades of Painting in Chicago," Terra Museum of American Art, Chicago (1987). She began teaching at SAIC as an adjunct instructor in 1986, and currently is a tenured professor of painting. LW

Ruth Duckworth

(Born 1919) A ceramic sculptor of international stature, Ruth Duckworth was born in Hamburg, Germany, in 1919. Fleeing the Nazis in 1936, Duckworth went to live with her sister in Liverpool, England, where she learned to paint, sculpt, and draw at the Liverpool School of Art (1936–40). In 1940 she moved to Manchester, and spent the next two years traveling with an assistant performing puppet shows. Driven by the desire to fight Hitler, Duckworth worked in a munitions factory for a grueling two years, during which time she was profoundly moved by the vast three-dimensionality of the night sky. This fascination with the sky would become a recurring theme in her work. Duckworth moved to London and in 1945 attended Kennington School of Art to learn stone carving, which she put to use carving tombstones from 1947 to 1950. Primarily of women and undoubtedly influenced by Modernist Henry Moore, her carvings were first exhibited at Apollinaire Gallery, London, in 1953. Her cast-metal works of this period show a greater abstraction of the female form, resembling ancient fertility figures. Duckworth enrolled in Hammersmith School of Art in London in 1955 to learn glazing, but left in 1956 for the Central School of Arts, also in London, which had a less rigid attitude toward ceramics. In 1960 she began teaching at Central School, set up a studio with her husband, sculptor Aidron Duckworth, and produced ceramic sculpture. By challenging the traditional ideas of ceramics, she became an important figure in the English ceramics community. Invited to teach for one year at Midway Studios at the University of Chicago in 1964, Duckworth again relocated. A large-scale mural commission from the university convinced her to remain. She taught at

the University of Chicago until 1966, and again from 1968 to 1977.

In the early 1960s Duckworth began working in porcelain, producing small sculptures as well as large murals. Incorporating overlapping slabs of clay that partially conceal other design elements, the murals are biomorphic compositions of polished surfaces and rough edges. Her first mural, *Earth, Water, and Sky* (1968), commissioned by the University of Chicago, was critical in the transition of Duckworth's imagery from cycles of nature to forces of weather, which would later dominate her work. Duckworth's predominantly recognizable female forms eventually became more abstract and evolved into vessels with "womb-" and "vagina-" like openings. The artist is adamant, however, that the fecundity of the forms not be mistaken for specific sexual content—her forms are drawn from nature. Over the past fifteen years Duckworth's sculptures have become increasingly minimal, underscored by her largely monochromatic palette. Recent vessels continue to explore a recurring theme of "split" volumes, challenging the classical notion of the wholeness of a vessel, as well as opening up its interior.

Duckworth's first US exhibition was a one-person show at the Renaissance Society, Chicago (1965). Other solo exhibitions include those at Exhibit A, Chicago (1974, 1980, 1982, and 1984); Museum für Kunst und Gewerbe, Hamburg (1976); Museum Boymans-van Beuningen, Rotterdam (1979); and the Contemporary Art Center, London (1986). Duckworth's work is regularly exhibited and collected in the United States, Germany, The Netherlands, Britain, and Japan. She is represented by Thea Burger Associates, Inc., Geneva, Illinois. MM

Jeanne Dunning

(Born 1960) Born in Granby, Connecticut, Jeanne Dunning has lived in Chicago since 1982. She received her BA from Oberlin College, Ohio, in 1982, and her MFA from SAIC in 1985, where she studied sculpture and was active exhibiting while still a graduate student. Dunning received her earliest success in Chicago in 1986 when she coorganized and exhibited in "The Dull Edge" at Randolph Street Gallery. In her catalogue essay for this show, Dunning explored the influence of deconstructivist theory upon a new generation of SAIC-trained artists, which included her coexhibitors Tony Tasset and Hirsch Perlman. By 1987 Dunning had emerged as one of Chicago's leading and internationally focused Neo-Conceptual artists with her first exhibition at Feature gallery. She received widespread notice for a series of small black-and-white "Untitled Landscapes," that are in fact close-up views of the body.

After her initial exploration of black-and-white photography, Dunning began producing the large-scale Cibachrome photographs for which she is widely known. In her 1989–90 series "Heads," Dunning depicted the backs of women's heads, focusing on the seductive texture and luster of the hair and emphasizing the head's suggestive phallic shape. In 1990 Dunning began creating sexually charged photographs of glistening fruits and vegetables that both seduce and repulse. Although her visually ambiguous subject matter falls into traditional categories such as landscape, portraiture, still life, and the nude, Dunning radically transforms these genres to reveal jarring, sexual implications. Most recently she has been using video to explore issues of sexuality, control, and notions of the perverse. Blurring gender definitions and distinctions, Dunning's art fits within Postmodern concepts of sexual politics. Her vision is distinctly photographic, and much of its edge is derived from the implied veracity of the medium. Dunning's aesthetic is based on defamiliarizing her subjects by using such techniques as extreme close-up, scale manipulation, and differentiated focus. Her art is further enhanced by the rich, saturated colors of the Cibachrome process.

Throughout the late 1980s and 1990s, many national and international museums and galleries featured Dunning's work. She has had several one-person exhibitions at the following galleries: Feature, in both Chicago (1987, 1988, 1991, and 1992) and New York (1989–92 and 1994); Roy Boyd Gallery, Los Angeles (1990 and 1992); and Feigen, Inc., Chicago (1991, 1992, and 1994); and she has had one-person exhibitions at the University Galleries of Illinois State University, Normal (1991), and the Hirshhorn Museum and Sculpture Garden in Washington, DC (1994), which traveled to MCA. Dunning's photographs were included in the 1991 Whitney Biennial, and have been featured in numerous group exhibitions, including "The Photography of Invention: American Pictures of the 1980s," National Museum of American Art, Washington, DC (1989); "Vivid," Raab Galerie, Berlin (1993); and "Bad Girls," The New Museum, New York (1994). EKW

Stan Edwards

(Born 1941) Born in Joliet, Illinois, Stan Edwards moved to Chicago early in life. He studied painting and design at SAIC, receiving a BFA in 1964. While at SAIC, Edwards was influenced by Vera Berdich's printmaking classes, Betsey Rupprecht's color class, and Daniel Massen's design classes. After a brief stay in New York (1967–70), where he was pro-foundly shaken by the urban rioting and general upheaval of this time, Edwards returned to Chicago and later set up a studio in the Pilsen neighborhood.

Edwards is primarily a figurative painter whose work is informed by both Surrealism and Constructivism. Early hard-edge paintings from the mid-1960s feature a series of screaming babies set in brightly colored geometric environments. These works offer religious suggestions, as the infants are paired with ecclesiastical figures or presented atop an altar. Other protagonists of his series include dogs and faceless, silhouetted men. Recent paintings, which Edwards calls "Icons for a New Era: Assembled Art Imagery," feature iconic images composed of items from popular culture; witty titles often allude to the materials from which they are made. The found objects, vibrant colors, and slick presentation of his works indicate their relationship to and continuation of Pop art. Both humorous and sinister, Edwards's paintings reflect the psychological uneasiness associated with the close of the twentieth century.

Exhibitions include solo shows in Chicago at Fairweather-Hardin Gallery (1965, 1968, and 1973) and Carole Jones Gallery (1994). Edwards participated in such group exhibitions as "Momentum II" at the University of Chicago (1964); "The Sunken City Rises" at IIT (1964); the "29th Biennial Exhibition of Contemporary American Painting" at the Corcoran Gallery of Art, Washington, DC (1965); "Twelve Chicago Painters" at the Walker Art Center, Minneapolis (1966); "Violence in Recent American Art" at MCA (1968), as well as exhibitions at AIC, HPAC, and the Arts Club in Chicago. Permanent collections include the National Museum of American Art and the Corcoran Gallery of Art, Washington, DC. Edwards also works as a free-lance designer and illustrator. He writes criticism about art and against government subsidies for the arts for the magazines *Chronicles* and *PerformInk* and the publications of the Heartland Institute and the Lincoln Legal Foundation. Edwards has also taught for the International Academy of Merchandising and Design in Chicago; Columbia College, Chicago; and the Chicago Academy of Fine Arts. AF

Douglas Ewart

(Born 1946) Past president of the Association for the Advancement of Creative Musicians (AACM) and one of Chicago's premier free jazz musicians, Douglas Ewart has distinguished himself in both the sonic and visual arts with his compositions for and performance of woodwinds and saxophone and his unique sculpted flutes. Ewart was born in Kingston, Jamaica, in 1946. He immi-grated to the United States in 1963 and began studies in vocational training at Drake and Dunbar vocational schools. While developing the tailoring skills that would assert their presence in the costumes of his later performances, Ewart renewed his childhood interest in music, studying theory, composition, saxophone, and clarinet at the AACM School of Music from 1967 to 1977. He was named president of the AACM in 1978 and served until 1986.

Ewart now uses music as a bridge between cultural traditions, and between activities ranging from instrument building to managing his record label, Arawak Records, which he founded in 1983 and on which he has released *Red Hills* and *Bamboo Forest*. As a sculptor of wind instruments, he has progressed from small bamboo flutes to large totem flutes of up to seven feet in length. He incorporates elaborately carved designs using inlaid semiprecious stones, colored epoxy, and stainless steel and brass, sometimes leaving root stubs on the wood as a natural sculptural element. Ewart's workshops, lectures, and exhibitions have been presented at SAIC, the Field Museum, and the DuSable Museum of African American History in Chicago; the Contemporary Art Center, New Orleans; the National Museum of American History, Washington, DC; and internationally at venues such as the Museum of Contemporary Art in Stockholm and at the Institute of Contemporary Art, London. DM

Julia Fish

(Born 1950) Born in 1950 in Toledo, Oregon, Julia Fish received her BFA in 1976 from Pacific Northwest College of Art in Portland, and her MFA in 1982 from the Maryland Institute, College of Art in Baltimore. With her husband, sculptor Richard Rezac, Fish relocated to Chicago in 1985, the same time that she began to blur the distinction between representation and abstraction in her paintings. Fish has exhibited her work in Chicago for the past decade and become part of a new generation of Chicago artists drawn to abstraction.

Singular in its serenity, her work offers an interesting Conceptual departure. Consisting of biomorphic shapes rendered in muted hues with a deliberate and delicate touch, Fish's small, quiet paintings resonate with experiences of nature remembered from growing up in the verdant environment of the Pacific Coast. Her art relies on abstract implication and the suggestion of nature's forms and shapes—the crescent of the moon, branches, clouds, leaves—that fill her canvases, as well as natural phenomena, such as fog, frost on a windowpane, the shadow cast by a tree trunk, or snow. The compositions from the 1980s tend to be recollections of the landscape, weather, and atmospheric conditions of Oregon; while the specific locale may disappear in her work, a palpable sensation of place is always present. Fish's work of the 1990s reflects her residence in an urban environment, and while not abandoning nature, includes subject matter such as tile floors. Technically, the paintings appear deceptively simple, but close examination reveals a highly disciplined method of paint application built up from many layers. Fish's use of translucent oil paint creates subtle surfaces of muted tones.

Fish first exhibited in Chicago in 1987 at Robbin Lockett Gallery, which before closing in 1992 specialized in highly Conceptual new art. Fish's work was thus often reviewed as being part of Chicago's emerging Neo-Conceptual movement. Her drawings were the subject of a FOCI exhibition at the Illinois Art Gallery in 1995, and a retrospective was shown at the Renaissance Society in 1996. She has been included in numerous group exhibitions, notably "Surfaces: Two Decades of Painting in Chicago" (1987) at the Terra Museum of American Art, Chicago; "Korrespondenzen/Correspondences: 14 Artists from Berlin and Chicago" (1994–95) at the Berlinische Galerie, Berlin, and the Chicago Cultural Center; and "After and Before" (1994) at the Renaissance Society. Fish has been a professor of art at UIC since 1989. EKW

Tony Fitzpatrick

(Born 1958) A self-taught artist who defies the stereotype, Tony Fitzpatrick arrived in the art world through opening his own gallery in his home town of Villa Park, Illinois. Fitzpatrick was born in 1958 into a large, traditional Catholic family. The rebel of the eight children, he has been a boxer, bartender, cab driver, and gas pumper, but all along, he could always draw. When he was twenty-five, Fitzpatrick drove his car into a house. After recovering from the accident, he began to draw in earnest. Not afraid to expose the darker side of life or comment whimsically on taboo subjects, he uses sources as varied as tattoos, the macabre, Catholicism, comic books, and scientific illustrations.

Fitzpatrick's early works are small colored-pencil drawings executed on slate chalkboards or paper. His 1988 series "Bad Blood: Portraits of Murderers" features dark, monstrous portraits of mass murderers, circus freaks, strippers, and wild animals with backgrounds filled with symbols of the cruel and seedy side of life. Next he portrayed his favorite American heroes,

including Elvis Presley, but with references in the background to the darker side of fame. When these works were shown in New York's East Village in 1985 and film director Jonathan Demme purchased a number of them, Fitzpatrick's career was launched.

By 1992 Fitzpatrick's anger toward the world had subsided, and he turned toward more personal subject matter, including portraits of his wife and baby son. Around this time he was invited to produce prints at Chicago's Landfall Press, where he discovered etching, which was highly complementary to his drawing style. Prominent in his refined and comical etchings are anthropomorphic animal characters—crows, bulls, skunks, tigers, and dogs. Fitzpatrick has also perfected the difficult process of multicolored etching in elegant series of birds and flowers rendered in muted shades of red, yellow, and blue.

Fitzpatrick also is a poet, with volumes published in 1986, 1988, and 1992 that are illustrated with his drawings and etchings. He has hosted a radio talk show, has acted in movies (most notably in Demme's *Philadelphia*) and plays (winning a Jeff Award in 1990), written and illustrated for magazines such as *Playboy* and *Chicago*, and creates weekly comics for the Chicago *Reader*. He has also drawn album covers for recording artists, including the Neville Brothers.

Fitzpatrick's work has been featured in numerous one-person exhibitions, principally at Janet Fleisher Gallery in Philadelphia, and Carl Hammer Gallery in Chicago. He has been included in many group exhibitions and is in several public collections (including AIC and MOMA). Seeking to be as independent as possible, he founded the World Tattoo Gallery, which operated from 1990 to 1994 in Chicago's South Loop neighborhood. He continues to operate Big Cat Press, which he founded in 1992. AF

Nereida García-Ferraz

(Born 1954) A reluctant exile from Cuba, Nereida García-Ferraz struggles to preserve her identity and link different cultures through her art that combines visual symbols, image, and text. Born in Havana in 1954, García-Ferraz moved to the United States with her family when she was fifteen years old. She attended SAIC and received her BFA with a concentration in painting and photography in 1981. She lives and works in Chicago while continuing her world travels.

García-Ferraz's bright and colorful paintings, filled with Spanish words, are structurally complex compositions with narrative power. Sometimes political and

at other times autobiographical, her work echoes her concerns for the world around her and is always charged with spiritual values. Inspired by Santeria, an Afro-Caribbean religion that grafts Yoruba traditions with elements of Catholicism, García-Ferraz uses water as a recurring motif, as well as watermelons and animals. Boats are also a part of her personal iconography, appropriate for someone whose homeland is an island and who travels the globe. The highly developed symbolic vocabulary and immediacy of her style recalls "outsider" and folk-art traditions as well as many Chicago Imagists, whose early works García-Ferraz admires. Her work visually is situated somewhere between the brilliantly colored backdrops of Latino street theater with its roots in commedia dell'arte and illuminated manuscripts, both medieval in origin. Most recently, García-Ferraz has subdued her palette, incorporated text in a less bannerlike mode, and simplified the overall structure without losing the spiritual and magical qualities of her earlier work.

While a student, García-Ferraz was awarded the Ryerson Traveling Fellowship. She has also received numerous other awards and has served as a member of the Advisory Board on Cultural Affairs, City of Chicago (1984–89). With Kate Horsfield she coproduced a videotape on the life and work of the Cuban environmental sculptor Ana Mendieta, which was included in the Mendieta retrospective exhibition at The New Museum, New York (1987), and won Best Documentary Video, National Latino Film Festival, New York (1988).

García-Ferraz has had solo exhibitions at Arte Club, Sicilia, Italy (1989); Universitario del Chopo, Mexico City (1990); State of Illinois Art Gallery, Chicago (1991); Carla Stellweg Contemporary Latin American Gallery, New York (1995); and Hauss Gallery, Bradley University, Peoria, Illinois (1995). Selected group exhibitions include the C & V show, AIC (1984); "7 Artistas Latinoamericanos de Chicago," Museo de la Ciudad de Mexico, Mexico City (1986); "Urgent Messages," The Chicago Public Library Cultural Center (1987); "¡Adivina! Chicago Latino Expressions," Mexican Fine Arts Center Museum, Chicago, and Museo de Arte Moderno, Mexico City (1988); "Cuba-USA, The First Generation," MCA (1991); "American Voices: Latino Photography in the United States: FotoFest," Contemporary Arts Museum, Houston (1994); "Transnational Identities: Cultura en Proceso," DePaul University Gallery, Chicago (1995); "La Mano Viva," Gallery 312, Chicago (1995). MM

Gaylen Gerber

(Born 1955) Gaylen Gerber's work has put him at the forefront of a trend in painting heavily informed by Postmodernist theory and artistic practice, and often described as "Neo-Conceptual." Gerber was born in McAllen, Texas, in 1955. He attended The State University of New York at Brockport as part of the SUNY Independent Study program, receiving a BA in painting and drawing in 1977. After attending The New York Studio School of Painting, Drawing, and Sculpture in the summer of 1979, he moved to Chicago to attend SAIC, where he received his MFA in 1980.

Gerber's early work features views of his studio table rendered to suggest a blurred photograph or atmospheric haze. By the late 1980s, however, Gerber had developed what has become his signature style: repeated renderings of his studio table in barely discernible shades of gray, executed on small square canvases of equal dimension. In essence he has created the "same" painting for most of his career. There are subtle shifts in tone and color gradation among his canvases, however, calling into question the notion of what is "identical." Gerber's concerns place him in concert with his generational peers Tony Tasset, Joe Scanlan, and Mitchell Kane in a Postmodernist critique of painting's historic role as the dominant artistic medium.

Shortly after receiving his MFA, Gerber had a one-person show at Two Illinois Center, Chicago (1980). In 1987 he was included in the "Non-Spiritual in Art—Abstract Painting 1985-????" exhibition curated by Hudson and Kevin Maginnis, notable for its consolidation of various "Neo-Conceptual" artists under a single theme. He was also featured in the 1989 "Chicago Works: Art from the Windy City" exhibition curated by Joyce Fernandes at the Erie Art Museum, Pennsylvania, and The Bruce Gallery, Edinboro University of Pennsylvania, and in the "Prima Vision" section of the Milano Internazionale d'Arte Contemporanea (1990).

Gerber's exhibitions at Robbin Lockett Gallery in Chicago in 1988 and 1989 were notable for their nearly indistinguishable appearance. He exhibited with Lockett's gallery until its closing in 1992. That same year Gerber was featured in two very important exhibitions: Documenta IX in Kassel, Germany, and a solo exhibition at Chicago's Renaissance Society. He exhibited with Joe Scanlan at Nicole Klagsbrun Gallery, New York, in 1994 and in the group show "Being There" at Paolo Baldacci Gallery, New York, in 1995. Most recently, Gerber exhibited a work of sculpture in "Plane Speak: Contemporary Abstraction in Illinois," at the Chicago Cultural Center (1996). DM

gundersen clark ginzel—

ginzel

Roland **Ginzel**

(Born 1921) Roland Ginzel was born in 1921 in Lincoln, Illinois. One of the pioneering abstractionists in Chicago, he has quietly asserted himself as an important artist, teacher, and organizer in the city for nearly forty years. With his wife, painter Ellen Lanyon, Ginzel helped to create important arts organizations and exhibitions in Chicago. His art also serves as an early example of an abstract style not traditionally associated with Chicago's art history.

While attending SAIC, Ginzel was among the students from SAIC and ID (including Leon Golub, Irving Petlin, Robert Nickle, and Lanyon) who organized Exhibition Momentum in response to the exclusion of students by AIC from their C & V shows. Upon graduation from SAIC in 1948, Ginzel and Lanyon were married. They received their MFA degrees from the University of Iowa in 1950. After a year spent in London and Rome doing postgraduate work, Ginzel returned to Chicago and began teaching painting at UIC. In 1953 Ginzel founded (with Lanyon and others) the Graphic Art Workshop, a center for printmaking practice and exhibition. The workshop was damaged by fire in 1955 and closed in 1956.

During the three decades after Ginzel's return to Chicago in 1951, he was included in important shows of Chicago artists, including many of the Exhibition Momentum shows, and was part of the group that showed at the short-lived Superior Street Gallery from 1958 to 1961. He was featured in the "First Chicago Invitational" of 1962, sponsored by the Frumkin and Holland galleries; the Phalanx 3 exhibition of 1965; "Exhibition 150" at Barat College in Lake Forest in 1968 (celebrating the sesquicentennial of the State of Illinois); and "Abstract Art in Chicago" at MCA in 1976. Gallery 400 at UIC honored Ginzel's forty years as an artist and an instructor at the university with a retrospective in 1986. Ginzel continued to teach at UIC until 1985, when he retired and departed with Lanyon for permanent residence in New York that same year.

Ginzel's unique brand of abstract painting, using patterns of shapes, lines, and colors dispersed about the picture plane, has merited the exhibition of his work at The Metropolitan Museum of Art and MOMA in New York as well as showings throughout Europe and Japan. Many of his works are numbered variants under the title *Desbarats*, a word taken from the name of the Canadian island where he vacations in the summer. Ginzel has referred to his paintings with phrases like "lyrical formalism" and "soft geometry," suggesting a poetic use of abstract forms and a connection to Surrealism, respectively. Despite the strong figurative presence in Chicago, Ginzel has maintained an unwavering devotion to abstract painting. His long-term dedication to abstraction makes him one of the most singular and individualistic figures in the spectrum of postwar Chicago art. DM

Lee **Godie**

(1908–1994) In 1968 an unusual figure appeared on the steps of The Art Institute of Chicago. She appeared to be an eccentric bag lady in her late sixties, but was in fact what many called the "most collected artist in Chicago." A self-styled "French Impressionist," Lee Godie hawked her quirky, childlike paintings in the area around Michigan Avenue from AIC to the Drake Hotel and sold hundreds of paintings for five or ten dollars early on and up to $200 by the end of her career. Although she earned an income from her painting, Godie preferred to live on the streets. She stashed her belongings in lockers rented in bus terminals and made rounds every day to deposit quarters into them. She would sometimes paint her face with the same paints she used to make her art, applying big circles of rouge on her cheeks, large fake eyebrows, and thick eyeshadow. Many considered her to be severely mentally ill while others thought her an oddball character who had a peculiar kind of independence.

Little is known about Godie's early life. She claimed to have come from a wealthy family and spun inventive stories to support her assertion. She was born Jamot Emily Godee in Chicago in 1908; she had one daughter who died young and another daughter whom she abandoned at the age of three. By some accounts she wanted to be a nightclub singer; how she ended up on the streets is unknown. In 1988 Godie and her daughter were reunited; shortly thereafter, Godie fell and fractured her pelvic bone. This accident finally forced Godie's retirement from the streets. She was placed in a nursing home in the Chicago suburbs near where her daughter lived. She died in her daughter's home in March 1994, suffering from Alzheimer's disease.

Godie is best known for her paintings of "glamour girls" featuring 1920s, Gibson-Girl-style women with huge eyes and lush, caterpillarlike eyelashes. They often sport elaborate coiffures, chunky jewelry, and bright red lipstick. In later years Godie attached dime-store brooches to her paintings as well as photo booth snapshots of herself or postcards. Another figure recurrent in Godie's work is her "prince charming" or "prince of the city" image—a dashing young man, clean-cut and dressed in a tuxedo, also with oversized eyes surrounded by thick lashes. Godie also depicted famous people including Marilyn Monroe, Elvis Presley, Picasso, Barbara Walters, and Joan Crawford, which also double as self-portraits. Other subjects include still lifes of leafy branches, flowers, and birds. Particularly popular were her "piano hands" paintings, which she would cut to size for her customers: on long, scroll-like paper, numerous, identical hands sporting bright red nails, wristwatches, and brightly colored sleeves are arranged across a crude keyboard. Godie would sometimes sew paintings together to create diptychs or triptychs, sew several together along one edge to make painting "books," or sew two paintings back to back and stuff them with newspaper to make painting "pillows." As with other self-taught artists, she would trace her favorite images and make multiple paintings of the same thing.

Beginning in 1977 Godie's work was featured in shows of Chicago-based art and "outsider" art including those at the Chicago Cultural Center (1977 and 1992), MCA (1979), and the Massachusetts College of Art Gallery in Boston (1989). In 1989 she had her first solo exhibition at Carl Hammer Gallery in Chicago (also 1991 and 1993). The Chicago Cultural Center organized a retrospective of her work in November 1993, which closed just two months before her death. AF

Leon **Golub**

(Born 1922) Leon Golub has been a steadfast supporter of figurative imagery in the investigation of the human condition since his student days in Chicago in the 1940s. Committed to the potency and the durability of the human likeness and convinced that abstract painting approached "decoration," he knowingly relegated himself to a position outside the Abstract Expressionist mainstream. Only in the 1980s, with the increasing interest in figurative painting and social content, did Golub's work receive widespread critical acclaim.

Born in 1922 in Chicago, Golub as a child attended art classes at AIC as well as through the WPA program. Before enlisting in the Army during World War II, he received a BA in art history from the University of Chicago in 1942. Golub enrolled at SAIC on the GI Bill in 1946, and, perhaps because of his age, experience, and restless ambition, assumed a leadership role among the students. He was instrumental in initiating the protest against student exclusion from AIC's annual C & V shows, resulting in the formation in 1948 of Exhibition Momentum, a countersalon made up of students from SAIC and ID. Golub and his coworkers were able to secure such distinguished jurors from New York as artists Max Weber and Jackson Pollock and founding MOMA Director Alfred Barr. This early, dual role of artist and activist forms the basis of Golub's ideology to this day.

With a BFA and an MFA from SAIC completed and local opportunities for younger artists being scarce, Golub and artists Cosmo Campoli, John Kearney, Ray Fink, and John Alquith opened their own art school on Rush Street in 1950 called the Contemporary Art Workshop. Though Golub left after one year, the organization still survives today.

Golub's early artistic endeavors centered around the exploration of the human psyche. Profoundly affected by his war experiences, psychoanalysis, and Existentialism, he focused on his personal identity as well as his role as an artist. Rejecting the New York School as removed from reality, Golub was drawn to ancient African and Oceanic artifacts at the Field Museum as well as the art of untrained artists. Golub and many of his SAIC fellow students also found affinities with artists such as Dubuffet, Giacometti, Picasso, and the German Expressionists, who addressed the issue of man's anxiety.

Golub's paintings of the early 1950s feature simple, flattened figures worked in rough, earth-tone lacquers. One series depicts powerful priests, shamans, seers, and kings; another focuses on victims. Together these groups manifest the human dichotomies of strength and vulnerability, logic and intuition. In 1954 Golub began to depict the mythical sphinx, which for him represented the dualities of human nature: good and evil, reason and passion, the hunted and the hunter. His interest in this hybrid and often-times violent imagery was shared by other young artists in the late 1940s and early 1950s such as Campoli, George Cohen, Dominick Di Meo, and Joseph Goto. Critic Franz Schulze dubbed the group the "Monster Roster."

Golub had his first museum exposure in the "Younger American Painters" exhibition at the Solomon R. Guggenheim Museum in New York (1954). He continued to exhibit in both New York and Chicago. Golub and his wife, artist Nancy Spero (whom he had met at SAIC), spent 1956–57 in Italy, where Etruscan and Roman art inspired his "Heads" series. Golub returned to the United States in 1957 to teach at Indiana University in Bloomington. In 1959 Golub, Cohen, and Campoli were represented in MOMA's controversial "New Images of Man" exhibition organized by Peter Selz. That same year Golub moved to Paris, where he and his family spent the next several years, before settling permanently in New York.

Classical influences, primarily Hellenistic Greek sculpture, became Golub's primary source for imagery. After finishing his second "Burnt Man" series

and a group of "Combat" paintings, he began his Roman "Gigantomachies," a series he worked on throughout the 1960s. These multifigural, expressive compositions present tragi-heroic figures against virtually empty canvases. His work became more specifically political, with series such as "Vietnam," "Portraits of Power," "Mercenaries," and "Interrogators," based on current events and news photographs. Golub's powerful work is known internationally. He has had several retrospective exhibitions, as well as two-person exhibitions with Nancy Spero, the most recent organized by MIT's List Visual Arts Center (1994–95), which was also shown at the American Center in Paris. SB

Neil Goodman

(Born 1953) Born in 1953 in northwest Indiana, Neil Goodman grew up in an urban industrial landscape punctuated with steel mills. Not surprisingly, the material Goodman chose to use for his life's work is metal. Goodman received a BA from Indiana University, Bloomington, in 1977, completing postgraduate studies in sculpture at the Kansas City Art Institute the same year. After graduating with an MFA from the Tyler School of Art in Philadelphia in 1979, Goodman returned to his mill city roots when he accepted a teaching position at Indiana University in Gary, just a few miles southeast of Chicago. He continues to teach there today.

During his student years, Goodman grappled with philosophical issues that would eventually define him as an artist. Inspired by the writings of French philosopher Gaston Bachelard, especially *The Poetics of Space*, and the Jewish philosopher Martin Buber's humanistic approach to interactions with others in his work *I and Thou*, Goodman discovered the catalyst that fused his interest in religion and art. While his early readings spurred his intellectual curiosity, it was a later appreciation of Alberto Giacometti's modeling of his figures and the space surrounding them that crystallized the ideas that would drive Goodman's realization as a sculptor.

Goodman's sculptures of the early 1980s are intimate large and small bronze still lifes that blend figuration with abstraction, and possess a formal elegance that silently invites the viewer to circle and explore. In the 1990s his work took a dramatic shift when he created "Subjects/Objects," a group of wall objects that he arranged site-specifically and presented without the containing supports that characterize his earlier works. This act of separating, rather than combining, elements, was a profound shift for Goodman, who believed that this approach freed viewers to connect the works for themselves.

Goodman's work is unique in Chicago and though he was captivated by the

romantic quality of the work of earlier Chicago sculptors, particularly that of Cosmo Campoli, he is not identified with any particular group. He entered the Chicago scene in a two-person exhibition with sculptor Paul Slepak at The Chicago Public Libarary Cultural Center in 1980, and has participated in numerous group exhibitions, including "Chicago View, Selected Works from the 1980s" at the Indianapolis Center for Contemporary Art (1989). Goodman exhibited frequently at the Struve Gallery in Chicago until it closed in 1995. He also has completed several public sculptures, including a commission for the City of Chicago Public Art Collection and Temple Jeremiah in Northbrook, Illinois. LH

Joseph Goto

(1920–1994) Of Japanese heritage, Joseph Goto was born on the small Hawaiian island of Hilo in 1920. He relocated to Chicago in 1947 to study painting at SAIC, but the craft he had learned as a welder for Navy and Army engineers during World War II emerged as his artistic means as well. After studying painting at SAIC for two years and at Roosevelt University, Chicago, for one year, he discovered he had an allergy to turpentine, and turned his efforts to sculpture. His early works—small pieces created with welded steel rods—are extremely linear, and closely mimic the calligraphic drawing and painting style of his student years. Goto debuted his sculpture in the 1951 Exhibition Momentum juried by Jackson Pollock. The work, which was vaguely figural and featured myriad details suggestive of bone or cartilage, met with immediate success. Director Alfred Barr purchased *Organic Form I* (1951) for MOMA and collectors in Chicago also gave support. A frequent exhibitor at the annual C & V exhibitions, Goto, however, was dissatisfied with his work, and destroyed much of his early production in 1954. In the mid-1950s, moving away from the verticality that characterized his previous efforts, he began a series of horizontally spreading sculptures that suggested landscapes with organic growths "sprouting" from the horizontal plane. Although he was a colleague of artists such as George Cohen and Cosmo Campoli, who were dubbed the "Monster Roster" for their grotesquely distorted figurative painting and sculpture, Goto's expressive abstract style kept him from being aligned with this emerging Chicago School.

Goto began showing with Allan Frumkin Gallery in Chicago in 1956, and in New York when Frumkin expanded there in 1962. He then moved into working with slabs and rawly cut chunks of steel, creating the more massive composi-

tions for which he is best known. Because they utilized the same method of working, Goto was often compared with the better-known American sculptor David Smith, who also shared similar concerns for form and composition.

After leaving Chicago, Goto settled in Rhode Island and taught at the Rhode Island School of Design, Providence, which mounted his retrospective in 1971. He continued to show regularly in New York throughout the 1960s; his last one-person show in New York occurred at the Zabriskie Gallery in 1973. In 1981 and 1989 he showed in New York with his brother Byron, a painter, at the Sindin Galleries and the Virginia Lynch Gallery. Goto died in 1994. LW

Gundersen Clark

Bruce Gundersen (Born 1947) Bob Clark (Born 1948) Natives of Chicago, Gundersen Clark (their working title) became acquainted as art students in the late 1960s at Northern Illinois University at DeKalb (where they received their BFAs in 1969) and completed their first piece together in 1970. Both were born in Chicago (Gundersen in 1947 and Clark in 1948) and attended SAIC, receiving their MFAs in 1972. Their performances took place in an elaborate architectural installation and involved intense ritual and the incorporation of violent symmetrical body movement and obscure sounds.

Emerging from the sculpture department rather than the performance department of SAIC, under the tutelage of Jim Zanzi, Gundersen Clark created a stir at the school by winning its coveted graduate fellowship prize in 1972—the first ever for a work of performance art. They performed the piece *Scid Wa* at N.A.M.E. in the gallery's inaugural year of 1973. During the early 1970s N.A.M.E. was a central venue in Chicago for their outlandish performances. The titles of their works, such as *Rads Clubojer* (1973) or *Radma Wad* (1975–76) are cryptic and obscure; the refusal of the artists to comment upon their meaning enhances and heightens the mystery of their enigmatic work.

Dagar Ane (1977–79) took the form of a ritualistic altar or shrine, rendered in an amalgam of chain-link fence, wood, dirt, broken mirrors, and multicolored yarn. It was performed at The New Museum in New York as part of the "In a Pictorial Framework" exhibition, and at the Mickery Theater in Amsterdam in 1979. Gundersen Clark also performed at International Art '80 in Chicago in 1980. Gundersen Clark stopped performing in 1980 when Gundersen moved to New York where he currently lives. Bob Clark now resides in Arizona. DM

halkin– hoff

Theodore Halkin

(Born 1924) A Chicago native, Theodore Halkin received his BFA from SAIC in 1950, following this with an MS degree from Southern Illinois University, Carbondale, in 1952. He has taught at a variety of Midwestern colleges including Purdue University, West Lafayette, Indiana; Northwestern University, Evanston, Illinois; and Elmhurst College, Illinois, but his greatest teaching contributions have been at SAIC, where he has been associated since 1966 and currently holds the Frederick Lattimer Wells Professorship of Painting and Drawing. In 1960–65 Halkin worked as an exhibition designer for the Field Museum.

Halkin's paintings and plaster reliefs from the 1950s were widely shown as part of the group dubbed the "Monster Roster" for the often grotesque imagery and mythological subject matter they shared. Halkin in particular featured Mother Earth figures, astronomical references, and wild animals. By the 1960s he began to be associated with the group of artists Franz Schulze called the Imagists in his 1972 book *Fantastic Images,* and throughout Halkin's career he has been included in exhibitions of Imagist work as a first-generation figure. After series of detailed and textural organic abstractions, sculptures carved in wood, and small-scale houses, Halkin's style underwent a drastic change. He began doing still-life drawings and paintings and almost Impressionistic views of his garden in spring and summer featuring vibrant flowers and lush greenery.

Halkin's work has been shown in solo exhibitions at Jan Cicero Gallery and Phyllis Kind Gallery in Chicago, and Allan Frumkin Gallery in New York, and has been included in group shows including those at AIC, MCA, MOMA, and recently in "Chicago Imagism: A 25 Year Survey" at the Davenport Museum of Art, Iowa (1994–95). AF

Phil Hanson

(Born 1943) Born and bred in Chicago, Phil Hanson began painting in college, though he did not focus on his art until after he received a BA in humanities from the University of Chicago (1965) and spent one year studying architecture at UIC. Hanson then enrolled at SAIC, where he received an MFA in 1969. He was influenced by his studies with painting professor Ray Yoshida and formed friendships with fellow students who were to become associated with Imagism, particularly Roger Brown and Christina Ramberg, who later became his wife. Discovered by HPAC Director Don Baum while still at SAIC, Hanson was offered his first important show, at HPAC

with Brown, Ramberg, and Eleanor Dube. In the spirit of the earlier "Hairy Who" exhibitions also organized by Baum, this group called themselves "False Image" in two exhibitions in 1968 and 1969. This exposure led to Hanson's representation by Phyllis Kind Gallery and inclusion in numerous other Imagist exhibitions.

Hanson's paintings are vibrantly colored and intricately patterned and detailed. In contrast to that of many of his Imagist contemporaries, Hanson's work is often romantic and erotic in mood, and not punning, sarcastic, or ironic. His early works include paintings of hands holding sensual flowers in strangely decorated rooms and dresses created from various painted elements such as butterfly wings, valentine hearts, or tiers of fountains. In 1974 Hanson began a series of painted cloth constructions: shell-, leaf-, and flower-shaped wall sculptures made out of sewn bits of canvas and brightly painted.

After experimenting with three-dimensional works, Hanson returned to painting in 1975 with his dramatic "Vanity" series: stylized images of the backs of women dressed in ruffles and viewed sitting at vanity tables. These paintings address the concerns of the earlier works, concentrating on external appearances and decorative finery. In the early 1980s Hanson continued his interest in both garments and flowers. Turning to men's clothing and to Elizabethan costumes, Hanson painted bizarre jackets and codpieces composed of crystalline structures, flowery patterns, feathers, and other sorts of organic forms. The garments are depicted floating in space, suggestive of the human figure yet conspicuously lacking one; one can hardly imagine wearing this clothing. More recently he has utilized verdant, vegetative forms to create fantastical figures.

Hanson's work was featured in a solo exhibition at the Illinois State Museum in Springfield in 1985. He has been included in group shows at MCA (1969 and 1972); the Institute of Contemporary Art in Philadelphia (1969); the São Paulo Bienal (1973); and The Chicago Public Library Cultural Center (1977). Hanson has also been a professor at SAIC since 1973, currently serving as chair of the Painting and Drawing Department. His work is in the permanent collections of MCA, AIC, the National Museum of American Art, Washington, DC, and the Museum des 20. Jahrhunderts, Vienna. AF

Gene Hedge

(Born 1928) Gene Hedge was born in 1928 and grew up in Indiana. After military service, he attended Ball State University in Muncie, Indiana, for a brief period in 1948. There he came across writings by Lászlo Moholy-Nagy, the founder of ID, which prompted him to relocate to Chicago in 1949 to study at ID. Of particular influence on

Hedge were the instructor Eugene Dana, the collagist and designer Robert Nickle, and the photographer Aaron Siskind. Hedge received a BS in visual design in 1953. He also took courses at SAIC, and became involved with the Exhibition Momentum group of young artists, exhibiting his collages in the 1954 show. Picked up by Allan Frumkin Gallery in Chicago, Hedge soon began to show his distinctive collage-paintings in group shows around the United States, including the 1955 Carnegie International, Pittsburgh. In Chicago he showed at AIC in 1956, the year he relocated to New York.

The influence of Moholy-Nagy's emphasis on experimentation can be seen in Hedge's choice of materials. Utilizing industrial products such as the sisal-lined paper used in building construction, Hedge created expressive works that combine aspects of Minimalism with an Abstract Expressionist sensibility. Richly textured and often highly absorbent of light, these large-scale collages can appear battered and scarred as well as subtle and lyrical.

Hedge continued to show in Chicago at B.C. Holland Gallery and returned to the city to teach at UIC in 1980–86. Important shows for Hedge in the 1960s and 1970s include, in New York, "Contemporary American Painting" at the Whitney Museum of American Art (1963) and "Collage in America" at MOMA (1966); and in Chicago, "100 Artists, 100 Years" (1979) at SAIC. His works are in the collection of MCA and the Whitney Museum. LW

Robert Heinecken

(Born 1931) Robert Heinecken's long tenure as a professor at the University of California, Los Angeles (1960–94), where his work has functioned as an experimental edge in redefining the boundaries of photography as an art medium, made a major contribution towards Southern California's reputation as the laboratory of Postmodernism. Together with John Baldessari, Ed Ruscha, and Douglas Huebler, Heinecken has been a critical influence on the current generation of artists who manipulate photographic images. Born in 1931 in Denver, Heinecken received an AA in art from Riverside College, California, in 1951. He attended UCLA for two years before dropping out and enlisting as a naval aviation cadet. He received his pilot's wings in 1954 and was commissioned as a second lieutenant in the Marine Corps, serving as a fighter pilot and later as a flight instructor. Discharged as a captain in 1957, he reentered UCLA and received his BA in 1959 and his MA in 1960. Appointed an instructor in the Department of Art that same year, Heinecken initiated the photographic curriculum that was to become so influential.

Although chiefly associated with California, Heinecken began living every other year in Chicago. In the early 1980s he began guest-teaching at SAIC and formed a relationship with the photographer Joyce Neimanas. He became an integral part of Chicago's photography community, showing frequently; of particular importance was the 1988 video installation *Waking Up in News America* at AIC.

Although Heinecken is thought of as a photographer, he has never used a camera (except for brief experimentation with the Polaroid SX-70 "instant" camera). He is best described as an image scavenger. From the beginning of his career in the early 1960s, Heinecken has been interested in the mass media, with which he describes having a "love-hate relationship" because of its seductive and subversive power. This interest has resulted in several ongoing, interrelated bodies of work, including one utilizing photographic images culled from magazines to create three-dimensional "photo-sculptures," a form that Heinecken pioneered. The influential 1970 MOMA show "Photography into Sculpture" was directly influenced by Heinecken's ideas and teaching.

Another seminal contribution by Heinecken is his work in artists' books. His altered magazines were initially done in the 1960s as guerrilla actions. Cutting through advertisements and copy to create new juxtapositions and layouts, Heinecken placed these altered magazines back on magazine racks to be sold. This activity led to his well-known "Are You Rea" series of the 1960s, wherein magazine pages were used as "negatives" to create prints that merge images from both sides of the original magazine pages. Most recently Heinecken is using laser-jet printers to reproduce his elaborate color montages that employ advertising and pornographic photography to create modern versions of ancient gods, such as Shiva.

Heinecken has shown widely since the 1960s, with numerous solo exhibitions. A retrospective of his work was organized by the San Francisco Museum of Modern Art in 1978. He shows with Pace/MacGill Gallery in New York, and Vernon Ezell in Chicago, where he settled in 1994 after retiring from UCLA. LW

John **Henry**

(Born 1943) John Henry was born in 1943 in Lexington, Kentucky, where as a youth he worked in his father's construction business. In 1960, when he visited an exhibition of modern art at the University of Kentucky, Lexington, Henry decided to pursue a career as an artist. Painting was his first interest, primarily the bold Abstract Expressionist

work of Franz Kline and Willem de Kooning, an influence that can be seen in his graphic, linear sculptures. Henry studied at the University of Kentucky in 1961–65. Feeling unable to articulate himself sufficiently in paint, Henry took a stone-carving class with New York sculptor Kenneth Campbell in 1965 before coming to Chicago the following year to attend SAIC, from which he received a BFA in 1969. Taking advantage of the proximity of other local institutions, Henry attended IIT to study the science and technology of metals, and also spent time at the University of Chicago. A galvanizing force in the large-scale sculpture movement in Chicago in the late 1960s and 1970s (sometimes dubbed "The Prairie School" of sculpture), Henry was instrumental in promoting public sculpture by local artists. In 1968, while still a student at SAIC, he organized and participated in "Eight American Sculptors" at Pioneer Plaza (now Equitable Plaza), the first large-scale outdoor sculpture exhibition in the Midwest, which included, among other sculptors, Richard Hunt, Steven J. Urry, and Mark di Suvero, who was working in Chicago at the time. Henry served as an advisor for "Sculpture in the Park" at Grant Park (1974), and in 1978, with five other sculptors, founded ConStruct, an artist-run gallery designed to promote and exhibit monumental work nationwide. ConStruct closed in 1983, and in 1984 Henry moved to a studio outside Miami, where he began to sculpt in coral. He now divides his time between Florida and his native Kentucky.

Henry's early sculptures were in wood and stone, but he soon gravitated toward metal to create monumental cantilevered constructions consisting of welded beams and planes placed at many different angles. Sometimes crawling low along the flat land and other times bursting high into the air, these works offer a spatial complexity that changes with each view. Though echoing the industrially manufactured geometric forms of Minimalist sculpture, which was the dominant contemporary art movement during Henry's student days, his works are not prefabricated, and most are site-specific within the urban or natural landscape. Henry first preferred the intrinsic natural color of metal, but soon turned to painting the aluminum black, yellow, orange, or gray, depending on the circumstances of each sculpture's form and placement. Henry acknowledges that his works owe much to the Constructivists, with their emphasis on truth to materials, space rather than mass, and a scientific approach to making art.

Several of Henry's outdoor sculptures are in the Chicago area: at the Nathan Manilow Sculpture Park at Governors State University, University Park, Illinois; on Congress Avenue in Chicago's Loop;

and next to Chicago's Hyatt Regency at Stetson Street near Wacker Drive. *Bridgeport* (1984) was commissioned for the lobby of the James R. Thompson Center on Randolph Street. Henry's work has been exhibited and collected nationally; his public sculpture can be seen in numerous cities around the country. SB

Steven **Heyman**

(Born 1952) Though his style has changed over the years he has been painting in Chicago, Steven Heyman has remained true to abstraction. Born in Los Angeles in 1952, Heyman attended UCLA where he received his BA in 1976. During his student years, he spent a summer in Guadalajara, Mexico, where the light-suffused colors of the landscape impressed him. After moving to Chicago in 1978 to attend SAIC, Heyman traveled to Spain on a trip led by SAIC Professor Robert Loescher. The variety of Spanish decorative patterns and artistic traditions, as well as the bright colors, continued to push Heyman towards a style based on strong shapes and colors. He graduated with an MFA from SAIC in 1980, strongly influenced by painter and professor Ray Yoshida (a mentor of many of the Imagist painters of the late 1960s). That summer Heyman attended the Skowhegan School of Painting and Sculpture in Maine, where he worked with former Chicago painter Sarah Canright.

Debuting in Chicago with a one-person exhibition at Two Illinois Center (1980) and another the year after at Zolla/ Lieberman Gallery, Heyman continued in the Modernist tradition of a sharp-edged abstraction. Heyman, however, layered his planes, stripes, and spirals to add a spatial dimension to his canvases. His paintings refer to the cosmos as well as to landscapes (as is indicated in his early titles). As frantic as the random, intertwined shapes are the high colors Heyman employed to create jazzy, swirling patterns and splashes of dots. The vibrant energy of Heyman's early paintings evolved into the more organic, volumetric forms of his acrylic and pastel work from the late 1980s. Rounded projections of light and an abundance of anthropomorphic mechanical forms, rendered with a more diffused color scheme, fill the dynamic, yet mysterious and Surrealist-inspired landscapes of this period. In 1991–92 Heyman served for seven months as a visiting artist at the Staatliche Akademie der Bildenden Kunste in Karlsruhe, Germany. There he began his most recent body of work, which is characterized by a central orb of white light glowing against a saturated, monochromatic background. Linear markings, both cartoonish and scientific, swirl around the light source, which is sometimes recognizable as a figure. Heyman uses a staining technique

to achieve his radiant colors, and in some works combines multiple panels.

Heyman has had one-person exhibitions at Galerie Rohrbach, Obernberg, Germany (1990); Lichthof Galerie, Staatliche Akademie der Bildenden Kunste, Karlsruhe (1992); Chicago Cultural Center (1994); and regular exhibitions at Zolla/Lieberman Gallery, Chicago. His work has been included in several group exhibitions, such as the traveling "Chicago: Some Other Traditions" organized by the Madison Art Center, Wisconsin (1983–86); "Chicago Artists in the European Tradition" at MCA (1989); "Post 1960 Abstraction in America," Steensland Art Museum, St. Olaf College, Northfield, Minnesota (1995); and "Chicago Abstract Painters," Evanston Art Center, Illinois (1995). SB

Margo **Hoff**

(Born 1912) Margo Hoff was born into a large family in Tulsa in 1912. As a child she spent many hours playing outside, finding patterns in nature. She still finds patterns in life and now interprets them as bright, textural paintings.

Hoff graduated from Tulsa University in 1931. Three years later she moved to Chicago, enrolling in the National Academy of Art and later at SAIC. In 1939 she spent a few months in Europe traveling and looking at art, and has since traveled and worked in over twenty-five countries, including Brazil, Ethiopia, and Lebanon.

Hoff's early paintings usually feature a stylized figure in a flat, patterned, and often perspectively skewed space, evoking a sense of mystery or a dreamlike quality. She included images of children, holidays, animals, and seashores, still emphasizing design and geometry. With the protagonist usually absorbed in an activity, the viewer is left to construct a narrative to accompany the scene. Hoff's content is largely autobiographical, constantly changing with her environs and activities. The human figure remained an important component in her work until two pivotal moments encouraged an interest in abstraction: watching Sputnik I fly over the Earth (1957) and viewing an object through an electron microscope. Hoff became increasingly aware of the space surrounding the figures, rather than just the figures themselves. The human form eventually disappeared from her work, leaving abstract shapes of color in kaleidoscopic arrangements.

After moving to New York in the 1960s, Hoff began making collages of painted paper. In 1962 UNICEF chose one of her designs for their Christmas cards. In 1970 Hoff switched from paper to canvas collages, using vibrant colors to conjure up such sensations as the experience of a crowd, the rhythm of jazz, or the wail of night sirens. She also created lithographs, sculpture, stained-glass windows, wood block prints, and book illustrations. She has painted murals and designed tapestries and rugs, as well as stage sets and costumes.

Hoff showed in C & V exhibitions at AIC (1945, 1946, 1950, and 1953), winning several prizes. In addition to her long-standing association with Fairweather-Hardin Gallery, which began in 1955 with her first one-person exhibition in Chicago, Hoff's work has been shown often in New York, including Hadler-Rodriguez Galleries, Saidenberg Gallery, Babcock Gallery, Betty Parsons Gallery, and Banfer Gallery; and in Paris at Wildenstein Gallery. Her work can be found in the collections of major museums including The Metropolitan Museum of Art and the Whitney Museum of American Art, New York; Corcoran Gallery of Art and the National Museum of American Art, Washington, DC; Victoria and Albert Museum, London; and AIC. LS

Richard Hull

(Born 1955) Richard Hull's two-dimensional paintings are clearly influenced by the three-dimensionality of architecture. Calling to mind the bleakly surreal, metaphysical "landscapes" of Giorgio De Chirico, Hull's work combines personal narrative with formal abstract painting.

Since the late 1970s, Hull's richly surfaced oil and wax paintings have depicted abstracted architectural interiors where towers, gabled roofs, and arched doorways combine with geometric solids and intersecting planes to form a framework in which various figurative elements are situated. Color plays a significant role in creating this surreal environment. Hull tends towards deep rich hues, achieved by coating the canvas with melted beeswax before painting. By contrasting hot and cool colors, Hull skews perspective, creating a mysterious space in which to cast his characters. The overall effect is that of a theater set, but one in which a Lewis Carroll tale might be enacted.

However, the "players" in Hull's dramas are conspicuously absent, noticeable only by their residue. In many cases a lurking shadow offers the suggestion of a figure who, presumably, is just outside the picture frame. Sometimes wrapped, mummylike forms stand in for human actors but never reveal their true identity. Occasionally, disembodied hands, suspended in mid-air, point in conflicting directions, independent of human will. Even Hull's trademark mask faces are strangely decapitated. This quality of estrangement lends psychological depth to the paintings' spatial illusionism.

At the same time, Hull's obvious concern for surface—composition, pattern, and color relationships—derives from modern formalist painting. This is apparent in his more recent canvases, which have lost some of their spatial density due to his continuing fascination with pattern and line. His paintings from the 1990s are filled with lyrical, scroll-like patterns, reminiscent of chandeliers or Art Nouveau iron grillwork popular at the turn of the century.

Born in Oklahoma City, Hull received his BFA from the Kansas City Art Institute in 1977, and his MFA from SAIC in 1979. Shortly after graduating, he attracted the attention of dealer Phyllis Kind, who began exhibiting his paintings in both her Chicago and New York galleries. At Kind's gallery, Hull joined the company of well-known Imagists such as Roger Brown, Jim Nutt, Gladys Nilsson, and Ed Paschke. Besides a number of one-person shows at Phyllis Kind Gallery, Hull's work has been exhibited across the United States. His paintings may be found in many private and public collections, including AIC; the Milwaukee Art Museum; the Nelson-Atkins Museum, Kansas City; and the San Antonio Museum of Art, Texas. CES

Richard Hunt

(Born 1935) Richard Hunt was born in Chicago in 1935, and grew up in the South Side Woodlawn neighborhood. In 1953 he entered SAIC where he studied with the Chilean-born painter Matta during the Surrealist's three-week visiting artist stint in 1954. When he was a senior, Hunt gained national recognition when MOMA purchased one of his sculptures. Upon his graduation in 1957 with a BA degree in arts education, Hunt was awarded the James Nelson Raymond Foreign Travel Fellowship and studied in Europe for a year. Drafted into the Army in 1958, he maintained an active career through his discharge in 1960.

Hunt's work reflects his belief that artists are free to interpret nature; his expressionistic sculptures never fully depart from natural sources. Along with the linear forms of Matta, the welded metal sculptures of David Smith and especially Julio Gonzalez were early influences. The work of Hunt's colleague in Chicago, Joseph Goto, was also instructive. After teaching himself to weld in 1955, Hunt began to scour junkyards for materials (copper and iron in the 1950s, later aluminum and steel), fusing broken machine parts and discarded metals into abstract shapes that retain affinities to human, plant, and animal forms. His work of the 1950s into the mid-1960s is small, linear, abstract, and focused on biological forms. These works tend to have formally descriptive titles. Works since the mid-1960s are denser

and more monumental in both size and scale, and include a number of public works made of Cor-Ten steel. One of Hunt's signatures is the Modernist device of integrating the pedestal into the sculpture, but he breaks away from the purely monolithic by penetrating and displacing the surrounding space with planar extensions, inventing new forms and augmenting basic shapes found in nature.

Hunt has used his international status as a leading American sculptor to express his deep dedication to his native city. He has contributed significantly to Chicago's art history, not only as a teacher at SAIC and UIC in the 1960s and a role model to generations of apprentices that he has trained in his Lill Street studio, but through his over thirty public works in the area, including Eagle Columns (1989) in Jonquil Park on Wrightwood and Sheffield Avenues in Chicago; Slabs of the Sunburnt West (1973), a memorial to Carl Sandburg on the UIC campus; and a major work at the Ravinia Festival Park in Highland Park, Illinois. In the 1970s Hunt was a member of the selection committee of the S.W. and B.M. Koffler Foundation, which purchased significant works by local artists.

Hunt has had retrospective exhibitions at the Milwaukee Art Museum (1967), MOMA and AIC (1971), and the Indianapolis Museum of Art (1973). He has executed commissions for the City of New York, the Martin Luther King Memorial in Memphis, and Howard University in Washington, DC. His work can be found in numerous museum collections: in Washington, DC, at the Hirshhorn Museum and Sculpture Garden and the National Gallery; in New York at MOMA, The Metropolitan Museum of Art, and the Whitney Museum of American Art; in Vienna at the Museum des 20. Jahrhunderts; and in Jerusalem at the National Museum of Israel, among many others. Hunt served on the National Council on the Arts from 1968 to 1974, and numerous other boards, including the Illinois Arts Council (1970–75), MCA (1975–79), American Academy in Rome (1980–82), and the Institute for Psychoanalysis (1981–present). He has been awarded a Guggenheim Fellowship (1962) and a Tamarind Artist Fellowship through the Ford Foundation (1965), and honorary degrees at a number of colleges and universities, including SAIC in 1979. NW

Michael Hurson

(Born 1941) Michael Hurson was born in Youngstown, Ohio, in 1941. He attended SAIC receiving his BFA in 1963. He also took courses at SAIC's Oxbow Summer School of Painting, Saugatuck, Michigan (1960 and 1961), and Yale University's Summer School of Music and Art in Norfolk, Connecticut (1962). While at Oxbow, Hurson met Burr Tilstrom, the legendary Chicago puppeteer who originated "Kukla, Fran, and Ollie"; he subsequently spent several years as Tilstrom's assistant. Much of Hurson's irreverent imagery, which caused a stir when exhibited in AIC's annual C & V shows in 1961, 1963, and 1964, had its origins in his experience with the "Kuklapolitans." Hurson's charcoal-and-oil drawings of the time feature a "left-handed piano" and a ranch-style house. Hurson also gained considerable celebrity during his student years when Henry Geldzahler, then on the staff of New York's Metropolitan Museum of Art, acquired a drawing for the museum's permanent collection.

During Hurson's last year at SAIC, he took independent study with art critic Robert Pincus-Witten, then a young art historian just graduated from the University of Chicago. This unorthodox choice and the project Hurson submitted to the review committee—Oldenburgesque papier-mâché Barcelona chairs—caused even more notoriety. Hurson's cartoony drawing style and early success left him at odds with the majority of his peers. After a stint in the Army, travels in Europe, and touring the country with Tilstrom (including appearances at the Hollywood Bowl and on "The Tonight Show" with Johnny Carson), Hurson settled briefly in New York. His works of this period (1964–66) feature television imagery and associations, such as people watching TV. After his return to Chicago in 1969, he pioneered the use of silkscreen to make his paintings with imagery such as dancing eyeglasses and pencils (the pencils acting as directors who prompt the eyeglasses in their performances) and a series of swimming pools that feature Burr Tilstrom.

Hurson was the subject of a solo exhibition in 1972 at MCA featuring spare, balsa-wood constructions of interiors which were also exhibited in a solo exhibition at MOMA in 1974. In the mid-1970s he began showing in group exhibitions at Paula Cooper Gallery, New York. In 1978 Hurson was included in the seminal "New Image Painting" show at the Whitney Museum of American Art, New York. In Chicago he was affiliated with Michael Wyman Gallery and later with Dart Gallery, where he received solo shows in 1972 and 1978, respectively. In this latter show Hurson presented his signature portraits done in angular, vigorous strokes of pastels and featuring such Chicago collectors as Lewis Manilow and Gerald S. Elliott. He also showed portraits in a 1980 solo show at Daniel Weinberg Gallery, San Francisco. Hurson relocated to New York in the early 1980s. An exhibition of his drawings at The Clocktower, The Institute for Art and Urban Resources, New York (1984) traveled to AIC. LW

Yasuhiro Ishimoto

(Born 1921) Yasuhiro Ishimoto was born in San Francisco in 1921 to Japanese immigrant parents. His family returned to Japan in 1924, and he grew up in Kochi City, graduating from an agricultural high school. Ishimoto returned to the United States in 1939 to study agriculture at the University of California (1940–42). After being interned in a relocation camp in Colorado (1942–44), he attended architecture school at Northwestern University, Evanston, Illinois (1946–48). He continued his education in Chicago at ID, studying photography under Harry Callahan and Aaron Siskind and receiving a BS degree in 1952. His early work was included in Edward Steichen's hugely popular "Family of Man" exhibition at MOMA (1955). Returning to Japan in 1953, Ishimoto worked as a freelance photographer, photographing the Katsura Palace. He began to exhibit in Japan and in 1958 published the book *Someday, Somewhere*. He returned to Chicago in 1958 with his new wife, Shige, whom he had married in 1956. His subsequent street-photography series, "Chicago, Chicago," was featured in an exhibition and a book by the same name. After the publication of a book of his architectural photographs from Japan, *Katsura*, Ishimoto immigrated to Japan in 1961 and began focusing on Japanese culture and architecture. In 1977 he exhibited an important series on the Ryokai Mandala, an important Japanese cultural relic stored in a temple in Kyoto. He returned briefly to Chicago in 1982 through a grant from the Canon Company to shoot another series of Chicago images.

Formally, Ishimoto's stark portraits of the city and its people, with their abstract qualities and attention to technical details, reflect his training at ID. However, he has never lost sight of the subject matter that he is documenting. The dirt and grime of the city are emphasized in his photos of alleys and empty lots strewn with garbage. His architectural photos are concerned with form and line, but often include automobiles, billboards, and people to establish scale and context. Even in his figurative photos, Ishimoto stresses form and abstract qualities: the figures sometimes appear as black silhouettes against gray skies, or capture the emotions and moods of the city as they go about their daily life.

Ishimoto's solo exhibitions include MOMA (1953 and 1961); AIC (1960); "Chicago, Chicago," at Shirokiya Gallery, Tokyo (1962); Seibu Musueum of Art, Tokyo (1977); Photo Gallery International, Tokyo (1983 and 1986); and the Seibu Museum of Art, Funabashi, Japan (1984). Group exhibitions include "Photography in the 20th Century," National Gallery of Canada, Ottawa (1967); "New Japanese Photography," MOMA (1974); "The Photographer and the City," MCA (1977); "The New Vision," The Chicago Public Library Cultural Center (1980); and "The Art of Photography from the Art Institute of Chicago," National Museum of Art, Osaka, Japan (1984). Ishimoto's photographs are in major international collections. AF

Michiko Itatani

(Born 1948) Born in Osaka, Japan, in 1948, Michiko Itatani went through a traditional Japanese upbringing. As a child she studied calligraphy, an art form that later influenced her painting. While attending Kobe Joagkuin University, she majored in Japanese literature and philosophy, but was also involved with painting and drawing. Feeling restricted by the traditional way of life in Japan, Itatani came to the United States in 1970. Enrolling in SAIC, she received both her BFA and MFA degrees, in 1974 and 1976, respectively. She has had a prolific career as a painter, and was on the board of directors at N.A.M.E. Gallery (1976–83). Not only did she show her own works, but she curated several shows and coedited an anthology of artists' writings, *Art Book 2* (1980).

Itatani's early untitled paintings from the 1970s and early 1980s are subtle, geometric abstractions, heavily influenced by calligraphy and ritualistic practice. Itatani was one of the first artists to exhibit installation art in Chicago when, in the mid-1970s, her large rectangular canvases gave way to polygonal shapes that defied the gallery space by turning corners or spilling onto the floor. Infused with a Zen-like sense of meditation and order, these spare, often monochromatic painting installations were painstakingly crafted with a ruler and syringe of acrylic paint, resulting in grids of tiny painted lines that create shallow layers of shifting planes. In 1984 Itatani made an astounding shift in her work when she introduced bulky and muscular figures into her geometric abstractions. Painterly and gestural, these monochromatic figures contrast sharply with their vibrantly colored environments of grids, flat planes, and swirls of paint. Aimlessly tumbling within an unidentified space, they represent Itatani's identity as a foreigner: nonspecific, but a universal model of a strong and enduring humanity. The irregular shapes of the canvases, often overlapping and refusing to lie flat on the wall, contribute to the sense of tension and an unbalanced space.

Many of Itatani's figurative paintings are based on her writings. Her untitled paintings are qualified with subtitles such as *Forced Fit, High-point Contact, Flexible Couplings*, and *Blind, Floating, Counting*—alluding to a tough and turbulent world. These figurative paintings defy being classified as simply a blending of East/West concepts. They also defy any sort of label specific to Chicago, but are a unique balance between figuration and abstraction, East and West.

Itatani's work has been featured in numerous individual and group exhibitions including those at the Alternative Museum (1985) and Franklin Furnace (1991) in New York; Chicago Cultural Center (1992); and the University of Wisconsin Art Museum in Milwaukee (1992). She showed for many years at the Marianne Deson Gallery (now closed), as well as several galleries in her native Japan. Itatani is currently a professor at SAIC, where she has taught since 1979. AF

Miyoko Ito

(1918–1983) Miyoko Ito produced a singular body of work that hovers between figurative allusion and geometric abstraction. Born in 1918 in Berkeley to Japanese parents, Ito received a BA from the University of California, Berkeley, in 1942. Trained first by watercolorists, Ito early on was influenced by the synthetic Cubism of Braque and Picasso (she had seen Picasso's first large-scale retrospective while at college in Berkeley), as well as the planar geometry of Hans Hofmann. After a year of graduate study at Smith College in Massachusetts and time in an internment camp for Japanese-Americans, Ito arrived in Chicago in 1944, and accepted a graduate scholarship at SAIC. Her shift to oil painting came at the end of the 1940s at Oxbow, a summer art school in Michigan affiliated with SAIC, where she created work that could be described as "abstract impressionism"—a painterly surface of short brush strokes combined with the formal organization of Cubism.

Ito was awarded several prizes in AIC's annual C & V shows, and was included in AIC's "61st American Exhibition" in 1954, which featured such artists as Willem de Kooning, Joseph Albers, and Alexander Calder. Ito received the 1954 Cahn Prize for a painting by a Chicago artist. While concentrating on raising her two children during the 1950s, Ito sustained friendships with SAIC art historians Kathleen Blackshear and Whitney Halstead, and artists Evelyn Statsinger, Tom Kapsalis, Vera Berdich, and Ray Yoshida. Surrealism, one of their common interests, began to influence Ito's paintings. Landscapes and interiors became less recognizable as such. Images of land and water were evoked by intertwining organic forms and tubular bands. These tensions between surface and space and abstraction and representation became hallmarks of Ito's art.

As overt references to literal objects began to disappear, Ito's palette began to change from soft, subtle colors to glowing reds and oranges. A single biomorphic shape came to hover in front of horizontal bands that span the width of the canvas. Ito eventually brought back the poetic pastels of her early work, but intermittently used this dramatic palette. She continued to paint suggestions rather than depictions: arched forms for windows or mirrors, curved lines and rounded elements alluding to the body. These paintings of the 1960s and 1970s exemplify the link between Chicago Imagism and abstraction. Other series from the 1970s are characterized by cooler hues, references to furniture, and occasionally, figurative elements. The 1980s brought a return to a more hard-edged abstraction, related in this sense, as well as in their common use of evocative imagery, to the works of Chicagoans William Conger, Richard Loving, and Frank Piatek, who called themselves "Allusive Abstractionists." The metaphoric, dreamy stillness of Ito's paintings provokes a meditation on experience, memory, place, and time.

Though Ito was a mainstay of the Chicago art community, she also exhibited at Zabriskie Gallery in New York in 1961 and was represented by Phyllis Kind Gallery in both Chicago and New York. In 1971 Don Baum, Ito's long-time friend, organized a one-person exhibition at HPAC. Her work was included in the "1975 Biennial Exhibition: Contemporary American Art" at the Whitney Museum of American Art, New York. The Renaissance Society honored Ito with a major retrospective in 1980. She died three years later at the age of sixty-five. SB

Joseph Jachna

(Born 1935) Joseph Jachna was born in 1935 in Chicago, a city that would prove important to his artistic development. Jachna's interest in photography emerged while he was a student in electronics at Chicago Vocational High School. In the 1950s he began working at a portrait studio and, later, at an Eastman Kodak processing lab. He attended ID, where he received a BS in art education in 1958. Jachna decided to continue at ID, working with his mentor and strongest photographic influence, Aaron Siskind. He received an MS in photography in 1961. He began teaching at ID in the fall of 1961 and remained a full-time faculty member until 1969, when he accepted a teaching post at UIC, continuing as well at ID into the 1970s.

Unlike other Chicago and specifically ID photographers, Jachna concentrated primarily on landscape rather than urban themes. By his own admission he was never truly at ease in the city, but felt instantly comfortable in an unknown section of woods. His photographs reflect this affinity for the natural environment.

Two series of photographs of water encompass his love of nature, as well as the simplicity and reductivist aesthetics taught to him at ID. Throughout his career, but particularly in the 1970s, he found himself striving toward that ideal of simplified life and nature. In 1976 he completed a series in Iceland, funded through an NEA grant. These mysterious and strange vistas, full of shadows and unusual light effects, demonstrate Jachna's ability to capture the essence of even the most alien landscapes.

The year 1980 was important for Jachna's career. A Guggenheim Fellowship enabled him to make an extended trip to Wisconsin, where he had previously been inspired during trips to Door County in the summers of 1969 and 1970. He had a small show at AIC, and a large retrospective titled "Light Touching Silver" at The Chicago Center for Contemporary Photography at Columbia College. Among Jachna's numerous one-person exhibitions are those at AIC (1961); Friends of Photography, Carmel, California (1974); Chicago State University (1985); and Gallery 954, Chicago (1993). Group exhibitions include "Contemporary Photographers," AIC (1963); "Wider View," George Eastman House, Rochester, New York (1972); "Work by Former Students of Aaron Siskind," Center for Creative Photography, University of Arizona, Tucson (1983); "Iceland Sextet," National Museum of Modern Art, Kyoto, Japan (1986); "Josephson, Jachna and Siegel: Chicago Experimentalists," San Francisco Museum of Modern Art (1988); and "Vanishing Presence," Walker Art Center, Minneapolis (1990). KFK

Tom Jaremba

(Born 1938) Cofounder (with John Kurtich) of the Performance Department at SAIC, Tom Jaremba has made a lasting mark on the art of Chicago both as a performer and as an instructor. Jaremba was born in 1938 in Milwaukee. Having studied sociology and psychology at Marquette University (he received his BA in 1962), Jaremba became interested in dance and theater the last year of school. He moved to Chicago in 1962 to dance with Sybil Shearer, who had seen Jaremba perform and asked him to join her company. In 1964 he moved to New York where, supporting himself as a social worker, he studied with Alwin Nikolais and Murray Lewis and spent a short time with the Martha Graham Company. He returned to Chicago in 1966 and one year later was hired at The Goodman Theatre as a choreographer and to teach movement.

Having seen performance art listed in the CalArts catalogue in 1968, Jaremba tried repeatedly to fuse SAIC and The Goodman Theatre to yield a similar kind

of class. After joining SAIC as a part-time faculty member in 1970, Jaremba joined with Interior Architecture Professor John Kurtich to create a class called "expanded media" which integrated body movement, film, video, and slide projection. By the mid-1970s, the Performance Department at SAIC had emerged from the classes in movement taught by Jaremba in the "Design Communication" Department. He also ran a theater group called "The Fourth Force" with Ted Serantos as codirector.

During the mid-1970s Jaremba's loft-space, known as "Lodge Hall" and located in the Wicker Park artists' community, became a hub of performance activity for Jaremba and his students. Lodge Hall offered a space for experimentation to students such as Ellen Fisher, Jean Sousa, Christine Tamblyn, SAIC-alumni Gundersen Clark, and many others. Jaremba went on sabbatical in 1977, and performed *Dance Music* at Lodge Hall upon his return. During the mid-1980s, Jaremba's performances became group efforts in which he cast other local performance artists in the Jean Cocteau plays *Les Enfants Terribles* (1985) and *Orphée* (1986), the latter prefigured by his use of the play in his performance *At Sea* (1980). His work is characterized by its combination of dance and movement techniques and slide projections and sound. Jaremba presently lives in Chicago and continues to teach at SAIC. DM

Indira Freitas Johnson

(Born 1943) Born in Bombay in 1943, Indira Johnson is one of six daughters of the art director for the *Times of India* and a social worker who founded a large health and community development project in her native city. Reacting against cultural biases that favored boys, Johnson's parents encouraged all their daughters to pursue careers. Indira Johnson studied advertising at the Sir J.J. Institute of Applied Art in Bombay and simultaneously received a BA from the University of Bombay (1964). In 1965 she received a fellowship to study at SAIC, earning her MFA two years later. She met her future husband and the couple returned to India to marry; they remained for several years. After the birth of her first son, Johnson went to the Folk Universitet in Lund, Sweden, to master ceramics technique (1970–72). The family subsequently settled in Evanston, Illinois.

Constant themes in Johnson's work have been the integration of her experience as an Indian; as an immigrant to the United States; as an artist; and as a woman, wife, and mother. She uses such images as the torso, hand, foot, eye, and the wheel and cart, which are common in Indian folk culture, and about which Johnson has spoken eloquently: the hand traces life's pattern; the foot moves forward step-by-step; the eye sees the past, present, and into the future. After a series of polychromed ceramic torsos that focus on female archetypes, Johnson in the early 1990s began a series of ceramic vehicles (wheelbarrows, hand-drawn baggage carts). Her most recent series is "Process of Karma," in which she explores *Karma* (action), *jnana* (self-knowledge), and *bhakti* (devotion) from the historical perspective of Hinduism and from her own bicultural experience. These works currently take the form of floor installations that utilize traditional modes such as sand painting and the mandala motif.

Johnson has exhibited widely around the country and locally in group exhibitions focusing on Feminist themes and/or the medium of clay. Recent one-person exhibitions include "Storm Shelters and Other Works" at the Evanston Art Center, Illinois (1992); "Vehicles of Transformation " at the Chicago Cultural Center (1993); and a show at Clarion University of Pennsylvania (1994). Johnson is also the founder and director of Shanti: Foundation for Peace, which seeks to empower struggling populations, and thus achieve peace through economic and social development. A recent project was the "Getting Along: Peace Bus" which brought together the Chicago Children's Museum and the Chicago Transit Authority to transform a CTA bus into an intracity traveling exhibition of children's art and poetry. LW

Marva Lee Pitchford Jolly

(Born 1937) Marva Jolly was born one of eight children (and a twin) into a farming family in 1937 in Crenshaw, a small Mississippi town near the Tennessee border. Jolly moved to Chicago to pursue her education. In 1960 she received a BS from Roosevelt University, Chicago; fourteen years later she went back to school and took an MS in ethnic studies and political science from Governors State University, University Park, Illinois. Then, in 1982, after nearly twenty years as a teacher and social worker, Jolly struck out on a new career path as an artist. A self-taught potter, she used clay, which had great resonance for her because of her childhood on a farm, to tell stories about people, places, and situations that had left a mark on her imagination. In 1983 she founded Mudpeoples Studio at Chicago State University on the far South Side, where she is an assistant professor.

Jolly is perhaps best known for her "story pots"—globular ceramic works that express feminine energy. Many are inscribed with Jolly's private language of invented symbols, and are rakued, a firing process during which the black soot of a flammable material is fused with the surface of the clay. She then further embellishes the pots with bits of metal and cloth, or paints them. She is particularly interested in mining the rich legacy of African-American people, especially women, to express feelings of strength, caring, honesty, and love. In their sensitive depiction of strong, lived-in, black female faces, her portrait vases from the series titled "Spirit Women" typify this sensibility. As part of her project to celebrate black women and their creativity, Jolly was a founder of the Sapphire and Crystals artists' co-op, which meets as a discussion group and has held several exhibitions of members' works.

Jolly has participated in group exhibitions of ceramic artists, and in a number of the Museum of Science & Industry's annual "Black Creativity" exhibitions in Chicago. For years she was associated with Esther Saks and the Woodson galleries in Chicago, and now shows with Satori Fine Arts. In 1992 Jolly completed a major commission for Chicago State University, *Old People Say*, a frieze of faces and decorative elements inspired by the wise folk sayings she heard from her elders while growing up. Jolly's work is in the collection of the DuSable Museum of African American History, and she was the subject of a 1994 PBS documentary, "Mudpeoples," by Shuli Eshel. LW

Calvin B. Jones

(Born 1934) A Chicago native, Calvin Jones was born in 1934. He showed promising artistic talent as a child and was awarded a full scholarship to SAIC. Jones received his BFA in drawing and painting and illustration in 1957, though he now feels that he was "miseducated" by this system. He spent the next ten years in the advertising field, first in Kansas City, Missouri, as senior art director at Hallmark Cards, and then in his own company, Sales Graphic Advertising. In 1967 he relocated to Chicago, where he worked as senior art director at CNA Advertising Department and later as creative art director at Vince Cullers Advertising. Following his successful advertising career, Jones decided to concentrate on his own painting. He became codirector and owner of AFAM Gallery Studio and Cultural Center in Chicago, and has dedicated his paintings, murals, and illustration to documenting the African-American experience.

Committed to community outreach and education, Jones addresses issues of identity and culture. His philosophy defines his socially oriented objective: "My challenge and obligation is to document, sensitize, and relate to the black experiences of the societies and cultures in which we live and to be a responsible communicator in the projection and relation of my heritage—the mirror of my spiritual center." Combining traditional African symbols and mythologies with a bold abstract language of patterns and planes, Jones's paintings evoke his own deep spirituality and the significance of his cultural legacy. His imagery often combines masks, landscape elements, and vibrant designs reminiscent of African textiles. In addition to his more abstract paintings, Jones produces genre scenes celebrating contemporary African-American family life.

Jones's paintings have been featured in one-person exhibitions in Chicago at the South Side Community Art Center (1971–73); AFAM Gallery Studio and Cultural Center (1970–76); Museum of Science & Industry (1978); Isobel Neal Gallery Ltd. (1987 and 1988); and AIC (1992). His work has also been presented at Martin/Caraway Galleries, Dallas (1979); Bomani Gallery, San Francisco (1992); African World Festival, Detroit (1992 and 1993); and Howard University Gallery of Art, Washington, DC (1993). Group exhibitions include those at AIC (1955 and 1973); World's Fair, Black Art Pavilion, Spokane, Washington (1975); International Festac, Lagos, Nigeria (1977); Corcoran Gallery of Art, Washington, DC (1993); and Blaffer Gallery, University of Houston (1994). Jones is also an accomplished muralist, and since 1976 has created nine murals, seven of which are in Chicago. He has been honored with numerous awards, grants, and commissions from corporations around the country, including Motorola and Coca-Cola Company. SB

Kenneth Josephson

(Born 1932) Kenneth Josephson was born in Detroit in 1932 to Swedish-American parents. He purchased his first camera and darkroom equipment at age twelve with money saved from a paper route. This consuming hobby of photography, however, was for the young man only a means toward a possible commercial career, as he had little exposure to photography as a fine art. After a short stint as a lab technician at General Motors, Josephson entered the photography program at the Rochester Institute of Technology in New York, which in 1951 was completely focused upon the technical and commercial aspects of the field. After receiving his Associate in Applied Science degree in 1953, he was drafted and served in the US Army's mobile photolab in Germany. Upon discharge, Josephson returned to Rochester to receive in 1957 one of the school's first BFAs from the new fine-arts program, staffed by photography historian Beaumont Newhall and photographers Charles Arnold and Minor White, who taught his famous "zone system." In 1958, while working in various capacities as a photographer for Chrysler Corporation, Josephson learned about Harry Callahan's work as well as ID, where Callahan was teaching. This year also saw tragedy: Josephson's wife succumbed to a brain tumor. He then moved to Chicago where he received his MFA from ID in 1960. He married again this year and was hired as SAIC's first full-time instructor of photography, where he continues to the present day.

Josephson's earliest work shows the considerable influence of Callahan, and with a number of other Callahan students—Yasuhiro Ishimoto, Joseph Jachna, Ray Metzker, and Joseph Sterling—forms a recognizable school of Chicago street photography, recently examined in "Bystanders, The History of Street Photography" (1994) at AIC. By the mid-1960s, after travels abroad, Josephson began his characteristic work: classically oriented black-and-white photographs that explore various tenets of fine-arts photography, often with considerable humor and wit. His work enumerates and explores the artifices of the medium, often flouting its unwritten rules, which in the 1960s dictated that the photographer's presence must not be revealed and that photographs must be painstakingly seized from the environment and not consciously created. Josephson's work is an early example of the infusion of Conceptual ideas into the medium, which set the stage for the generation of Conceptual photographers of the early 1980s, such as Richard Prince, Sherrie Levine, and in Chicago, Jeanne Dunning.

Josephson has been the subject of over a dozen one-person exhibitions, including shows at AIC (1971); the Visual Arts Workshop, Rochester, New York (1971), which traveled around the United States; Photographer's Gallery, London (1979); and MCA (1983). He has received numerous awards and honors, and is a founding member of the Society for Photographic Education. He has served as a visiting professor at the Tyler School of Art, Philadelphia (1975) and UCLA (1981). LW

Gary Justis

(Born 1953) Gary Justis was born in 1953 in Maize, Kansas—a quiet, agricultural town that is a far cry from the clangorous, industrial environment of Chicago that influences Justis's work as an artist. Perhaps because of this small-town upbringing (or despite it), Justis was surrounded by ingenuity and innovation even though he felt aesthetically isolated. Raised by a father who was a plumbing contractor by trade but an inventor by passion, and a mother who painted as a hobby, Justis grew up tinkering with gadgets, building things, and making household repairs—

skills and interests that were valued in his practical, working-class surroundings. This background in mechanical fundamentals made for a natural transition to the aesthetics that Justis later embraced.

Justis received his BFA in sculpture from Wichita State University in 1977, and an MFA from SAIC in 1979. In his works, Justis attempts to reveal the utilitarian function of objects, transforming them into rich carriers of metaphors. His ideas proceed logically through combining light, movement, and sound with a variety of materials, most often aluminum, fluorescent lights, polypropelene (a translucent plastic), glass, bronze, steel, wood, wire, video imagery, motors, lasers, and/or electronics. The inner workings of his sculptures are always visible, as Justis never attempts to conceal the process or make the work less candid than its inherent properties. He describes his work as "hyper-functional," expanding the meaning of a utilitarian object by modifying it and allowing it to take on a life of its own.

Early in his career Justis pursued his interest in mythology by combining mythological subject matter with toollike and anthropomorphic forms in frenzied motion. In the 1990s the kinetic aspect in the work has become more subtle—at times nonexistent. Gestures and linear elements have evolved into investigations of forms with heavier masses. Shapes have grown more minimal while maintaining a command of the space. Justis's work can suggest comparisons to the Futurists of the early 1900s; it is distinctly a product of a generation immersed in a technologically sophisticated environment.

Justis's inclusion in "Opening New Doors" (1982) at Randolph Street Gallery, Chicago, was significant for his development. That same year he had a solo exhibition at Chicago's Museum of Science & Industry (where he worked as an audio-visual technician in 1980–84) titled "Object-Luminosus-Objectus: Electrokinetic Sculpture." Justis also participated in several group shows at MCA, including "Alternative Spaces" (1984) and "Chicago Artists in the European Tradition" (1989), and in New York in "Dimensions Variable" (1979) at The New Museum of Contemporary Art and "Modern Machines" (1985) at the Whitney Museum of American Art at Philip Morris. In early 1996 Justis's work was showcased in three Chicago locations simultaneously: Tough Gallery, The Lineage Gallery Project, and Klein Art Works, with whom he is currently affiliated. Justis has been both a lecturer in the Department of Art Theory and Practice at Northwestern University, Evanston, Illinois, since 1991, and a teacher of sculpture at SAIC since 1984. LH

Kartemquin Films

(Founded 1967) The steadfast, political-documentary filmmaking collective Kartemquin Films has provided rich and provocative insights into the political, social, and artistic history of Chicago. Founded in 1967 by University of Chicago graduates Stan Karter, Gerry Temaner, and Gordon Quinn (the name is a composite of their family names in homage to Sergei Eisenstein's classic film *The Battleship Potemkin*), Kartemquin grew out of Quinn and Temaner's work on a cinema verite–style documentary titled *Home for Life*. The 1966 film examined the lives of residents at the Drexel Home for the Aged. Quinn was later joined by Jerry Blumenthal, a graduate student in film at Northwestern University, Evanston, Illinois, and the two have remained the driving force behind Kartemquin.

Kartemquin's primary initiative has been to use documentaries as educational tools to show the need for (or breakdown of) certain social institutions. To fund much of their socially concerned work, they began making sports documentaries and educational films in the early 1970s. With solidified financial backing from their commercial ventures, Kartemquin expanded their staff to concentrate on the political aspects of the changing urban scene. In 1974 the collective added the name Haymarket to their title to represent their distributing branch, reflecting the political aspect of the new films (the title refers to the labor riot that occurred in Chicago in 1886). The name was eventually dropped in favor of Kartemquin Educational Films, one of the two parts (the other being Kartemquin Limited Films) of the Kartemquin collective.

Kartemquin's roster has changed often throughout their history. Peter Kuttner, a documentary filmmaker, became involved with the collective via his work with "Rising Up Angry," a group that worked with communities on the North and South sides of the city. The film that resulted from the combined efforts of Kartemquin and "Rising Up Angry," *Trick Bag* (1975), looks at white, working-class youth. Richard Schmiechen, whose 1984 documentary *Times of Harvey Milk* received national acclaim, was also associated with Kartemquin during the 1970s. In addition to films such as *Winnie Wright, Age 11* and *Now We Live on Clifton* (both 1974), Kartemquin produced *The Chicago Maternity Center Story* (1976), a provocative film about the closing of a maternity center on the North Side. This film became the center of controversy when WNET television in New York refused to broadcast it (the producers objected to the "biased" tone of the narrator) after it had been accepted for its program "Independent Focus."

During the early 1980s, Kartemquin focused upon the politics involved in labor strikes in the city. Their 1984 film *Golub*, an interpretive look at former Chicago-based artist Leon Golub, contextualized scenes of the artist working on immense, politically charged canvases with news footage of various recent world events. Kartemquin was thrust into the national spotlight in 1994 when *Hoop Dreams*, the documentary film they coproduced with KTCA-TV in Minneapolis-St. Paul, received rave reviews from major film critics across the nation. The film is the work of three Chicagoans, Steve James, Fred Marx, and Peter Gilbert, and centers on the hopes and tribulations of two high-school basketball players from Chicago's poverty-stricken inner city. *Hoop Dreams* aroused considerable controversy when it failed to receive an Academy Award nomination for best documentary, despite widespread popular and critical acclaim. DM

Jin Soo Kim

(Born 1950) Born in Seoul and raised in the difficult times following the Korean War, Jin Soo Kim knew early that she wished to pursue a path different from that encouraged by her traditional Korean upbringing. Even before she received her BS degree in nursing from Seoul National University in 1973, Kim was exhibiting art in Seoul galleries. In 1974 she immigrated with her husband to the United States, and while practicing as a nurse, took graduate-level art courses at Western Illinois University in Macomb (1976–77). She moved to Chicago in 1978, and went on to take an MFA from SAIC in 1983. While still in school, she began exhibiting widely, showing her poetic, finely worked paintings, and her more typical, ambitious installations of cast-off materials.

Kim's often room-sized installations were labeled "Environments" and titled *A* (at Randolph Street Gallery in 1983) through the artist's most recent work, *P* (for a group exhibition at the Sonje Museum of Contemporary Art, Kyongiu, Korea in 1991). Constructed from materials such as wires, bedsprings, and building scraps salvaged from excursions around Chicago, in these installations Kim created eerie, compelling monuments to modern man's reckless consumption and short attention span. In her work of the past several years, the artist has created free-standing sculptures by wrapping various salvaged materials with plaster-dipped gauze or cloth. Gradual oxidation stains the white plaster finish of the works, which Kim occasionally colors further or heightens with burns or patinas. She has also made free-standing works composed of steel grids wrapped with copper wire. In some works the wrapped and tied cloth pulls and shapes the rigid structures, merging the industrial and the organic and bringing her cast-off and new materials together to form interdependent wholes. The artist has recently spoken of coming to terms with her own history—a feeling triggered by visits to Korea after twenty years of living in the United States. The contrast between memory and experience is objectified in her work: memory in the found materials that form the infrastructure of the object and experience recorded in the folds and twists of the wrapped and tied cloth or wire; one shapes the other.

Kim's work has been exhibited widely throughout the United States, including the Southeastern Center for Contemporary Art, Winston-Salem, North Carolina, "Awards in the Visual Arts" exhibition, which traveled around the country (1986); "Sculpture Inside/Outside" at the Walker Art Center, Minneapolis (1988); and "Asia/America: Identities in Contemporary Asian American Art," organized by the Asia Society, New York (1994), which also traveled around the country. She has had solo shows at the Madison Art Center, Wisconsin (1991) and The Brooklyn Museum, New York (1992). Kim had a one-person exhibition at MCA in 1984, and participated in MCA's "Art at the Armory: Occupied Territory" group exhibition in 1992. LW

Wesley Kimler

(Born 1953) At the age of fourteen, Wesley Kimler left high school and the town where he was born, Billings, Montana, to embrace the life of a wanderer, traveling to San Francisco, as well as Canada, Iran, India, Pakistan, and Afghanistan. His art education included a year at the Laguna-Gloria School of Art in Austin, Texas (1976–77), and then the Minneapolis College of Art and Design (1978–80). From there Kimler made his way to SAIC, but was refused admission, perhaps because of the gaps in his formal education. He found a studio on the near West Side, and began to turn out large canvases dealing with monumental themes of man in harmony and in conflict with his environment. After a number of years in Chicago and notable success, Kimler moved to Los Angeles in 1988. He returned to Chicago in 1992 after the 1980s art boom had ended.

Kimler began painting his expressionistic canvases during the early 1980s, at a time when this style of painting was once again at the forefront of artistic activity internationally. Along with a number of other young painters, Kimler showed at Peter Miller Gallery and was a spokesperson for a painting style with little historical connection to Chicago. Kimler's work was notable for its sheer bravura, and his early work and lifestyle was often casually compared to that of great Modernist painters like Jackson Pollock and Willem de Kooning. Recently, Kimler has directed his energies into a closer study of classic Abstract Expressionists of the 1950s, as well as lesser-known figures such as contemporary British painters Frank Auerbach and Leon Kossoff or Bay Area painters Richard Diebenkorn, Joan Brown, and David Parks.

Kimler's latest work emphasizes traditional concerns in painting, such as techniques and the issues surrounding the relationship between painter and viewer. A conflict between abstraction and figuration is readily apparent: Hans Hofmann-like squares of saturated color compete with the cartoonish outlines of figures bearing a sword, a kite, or balloons. Kimler seeks to blend intellect and emotion to reveal the physicality of the painterly event as well as the literary meaning. The imagery at times recalls influences from the American literary tradition of Herman Melville, Jack London, and Ernest Hemingway, and most recently Kimler titled his works after the "dirty realist" short stories of Raymond Carver, who died in 1988 after a life of alcoholism. Created during a reflective period in his life, these huge, multipanel paintings are actually older canvases that Kimler has joined together and painted over, perhaps in a literal attempt to reconfigure his own past. The muddier palette of his recent paintings orchestrates a more sober response and demands a more thoughtful engagement than in the earlier work.

In 1995 Kimler had a solo exhibition at MCA. His work is in a number of private and public collections, including MCA and The Metropolitan Museum of Art in New York. Kimler was represented in Chicago from 1985 to 1995 by Struve Gallery (closed in 1995). MM

David Klamen

(Born 1961) Born in 1961, the young David Klamen was a loner in the small midwestern town of Dixon, Illinois (incidentally, Ronald Reagan's boyhood hometown), 100 miles west of Chicago. Perhaps he was shy because he grew up in one of the few Jewish families in town or because each social group thought he belonged to another. This sense of isolation—which continued as an undergraduate at the University of Illinois, Urbana-Champaign, where he earned a BFA in 1983, and through his graduate studies in painting at SAIC, where he acquired an MFA in 1985—was to become a compelling aspect of his work.

Klamen has always maintained an affinity with the Minimalists, particularly Donald Judd and Walter De Maria. He claims his greatest literary sources were Herman Melville's *Moby Dick* and his ongoing study of hermeneutics, the discipline that examines how we interpret images and text. In addition to Klamen's characteristic rational and methodical thought and analysis, his work also has a romantic side that is ripe with nostalgia, emotion, and personal history.

In 1985 Klamen began a series of signature black paintings that continue to define his work today. In these dark paintings Klamen meticulously, with laborious technical virtuosity, painted animals, still lifes, or interiors—the subject often a psychological self-portrait—and then nearly obliterated the image with layers of varnish that produce an impenetrable glassy surface. The result requires viewers to spend time with the evolving images which appear dark and elusive for the first several minutes of viewing. Klamen's subjects are most often solitary, graceful, and possess an innate silence and stillness. He frequently paints musical staves, white tubes, and other shapes on top of the varnished surface as a startling contrast to the paintings, to add psychological barriers and to establish a formal order.

Klamen exhibited in the 1985 C & V show at AIC, "A New Generation from SAIC" (1986) at MCA, and participated in the traveling exhibition "Unpainted to the Last: Moby Dick and American Art, 1930–1990" (1995), organized by the Spencer Museum of Art, University of Kansas, Lawrence. His work is included in the collections of The Metropolitan Museum of Art, New York, and the National Museum of Contemporary Art, Seoul, among others. In Chicago, Klamen showed in the mid-1980s at the Marianne Deson Gallery. In the early 1990s he became associated with Richard Gray Gallery. He also shows internationally, particularly in Italy. Klamen currently teaches at Indiana University Northwest in Gary. LH

Vera Klement

(Born 1929) Over the past thirty years during which Vera Klement has been painting in Chicago, she has consistently addressed themes of longing, expulsion, and memory. Born in 1929 in the Free City of Danzig, she and her family fled the Nazis and landed in New York. Klement graduated from the Cooper Union School of Art and Architecture in New York in 1950. Her early paintings were steeped in Abstract Expressionist concerns with gesture, spontaneity, and the tragi-heroic, which remain the basis of her art today. Chicago, where she arrived in 1965, afforded her the freedom to develop her own vision, and she moved toward an art of expressive figuration. Landscape and figural elements, though still rendered in a gestural, expressionist manner, began to take on a presence in her early Chicago works. Her all-over paintings changed into meditations on distinct, volumetric forms created with parallel brush strokes; the work gradually became more reductive and minimal, but with metaphoric and symbolic characteristics.

In the 1970s Klement was active in the founding of the women's cooperative gallery Artemisia. She was also a founding member of "The Five," a group of abstract artists (Ted Argeropolis, Larry Booth, Martin Hurtig, Larry Solomon, and herself) who exhibited together in 1971–76. Klement wrote a manifesto of sorts for their first showing, which protested against what "The Five" perceived as a regional and isolationist art climate in Chicago. These artists, who were working in an abstract mode in sharp contrast with the dominant figurative style of the Chicago Imagist painters, participated in an exhibition at the Michael Wyman Gallery called "The Other Tradition" (1975).

Klement's abstract structural forms reminiscent of trees or vessels are laden with symbolic meaning. Distinct elements share a pictorial space, seemingly infinite, which developed into mysterious pairings on two separate canvases. Inspired by musical composition, Klement divides her paintings into two registers, thereby allowing her motifs to coexist in separate yet related spaces. Expansive walls, windows, doors, and starry skies suggest the unknown; containers, floating figures, and landscape elements represent a certain physicality or the here and now. Through such seemingly opposite or unrelated images, Klement evokes a dialogue of desire for the unattainable.

Klement holds a significant position in the history of art in Chicago. From 1969 until her retirement in 1995, she was a professor of art at the University of Chicago. She has exhibited consistently throughout the United States, including a mid-career retrospective at the Renaissance Society in 1987 and several solo exhibitions at the Roy Boyd Gallery in Chicago. Her work was also included in "Surfaces: Two Decades of Painting in Chicago" at the Terra Museum of American Art, Chicago (1987). SB

Richard Koppe

(1916–1973) A pioneer of abstract art, Richard Koppe was born in St. Paul, Minnesota, in 1916. He studied at the St. Paul School of Art, one of the most avant-garde schools of its day, from 1933 to 1937, when he relocated to Chicago to study with László Moholy-Nagy at The New Bauhaus (later ID) and have direct contact with the European Modernist ideas he had been exposed to in his earlier education. In 1939 Koppe joined the WPA as one of its few abstract painters. During World War II, Koppe worked as an engineer for an aircraft corporation in Texas, but he returned to Chicago in 1946 to join the ID faculty, teaching the Foundation Course. In 1949 he was appointed head of the Visual Design Department. He was a frequent prize winner in AIC's C & V exhibitions throughout the late 1940s, 1950s, and early 1960s; he also participated in Exhibition Momentum. In 1963 Koppe became professor of painting at UIC, where he continued his considerable influence as a teacher.

Koppe's paintings of the late 1940s and 1950s consist of spiky, organic patterns that were derived from insect and animal forms. Cleanly executed and meticulously presented, the paintings show his training and interest in design. One of Koppe's best-known works of this period was a huge mural with sculptural elements for the Well of the Sea Restaurant at the Hotel Sherman in Chicago (now lost). His style evolved in the 1960s into a more geometric abstraction, featuring large circular or elliptical targetlike forms.

Koppe received wide exposure during his lifetime. He was the subject of a 1961 retrospective at ID, had over thirty one-person shows, and was featured in more than one hundred group exhibitions, some of which traveled internationally. He established an archive of his works at Syracuse University, New York, in 1965, and his paintings are in the permanent collections of the Whitney Museum of American Art, New York; AIC; and MCA, among others. Koppe is frequently included in publications on the Bauhaus. He also prepared several unpublished articles about the Chicago Bauhaus that are on deposit at UIC Library. After he committed suicide in 1973, his work was rarely seen in Chicago and became largely unknown. LW

Thomas Kovachevich

(Born 1942) Thomas Kovachevich is both a working artist and practicing physician. Born in Detroit in 1942, he received his BFA from Michigan State University, East Lansing (1965), and his DO from Chicago College of Osteopathic Medicine (1969). In the mid-1980s he was one of the founders of the Doctors by Phone project, the first 24-hour service offering practical medical advice by licensed physicians over the phone. Kovachevich's term "Conceptual Realism," coined as a reaction to the self-contained art world of the 1970s and 1980s, refers to ideas as solutions to real problems, instead of the Conceptualist

notion of art centered around pure idea. His early works are "watercolors" created by affixing clear tape on paper and applying a paint stroke to the tape, which beads and layers in relation to the ripples in the surface and the motion of the artist's hand. He also used gummed tape, cutting it into geometric shapes and sticking the pieces on a wall. Kovachevich is best known for his "Dancing Papers," staged performances involving paper and water, which he began in the late 1970s. Manipulating the hydrologic cycle, Kovachevich creates a metaphor for the human life cycle, fusing art and science. Inspired by an early fascination in medical school with cotton balls floating in bowls of water, Kovachevich staged performances in which tracing paper cut into simple geometric shapes was floated atop a semipermeable fabric (silk, rayon, or polyester) in various vessels filled with water. As the water evaporated through the fabric, the vapors seeped into the paper fibers and animated the shapes. Kovachevich calls this "K motion," "K" being the symbol for Konstant in physics, and the artist's initial. These hour-long performances in theatrically lit and darkened rooms were subtly manipulated, but not ultimately controlled, by the artist. Kovachevich determined the parameters by regulating water temperature and monitoring the humidity of the room, but he did not regulate the outcome, affected even by viewer presence. Paintings produced following the performances serve as records of the activities.

In the late 1980s Kovachevich created large-scale wood sculptures in the likeness of the paper shapes, which he calls portraits. He also produced drawings as investigations of geometry, time, and movement. In the 1990s he started creating large installations or "room portraits," fastening brown wrapping paper to gallery walls, ceiling, and floor, allowing it to curl naturally.

Kovachevich had his first solo exhibition at MCA in 1973, where he showed again in 1977. He has had one-person exhibitions at The Drawing Center, New York (1977); Kunstmuseum, Bern, Switzerland (1980); Betsy Rosenfield Gallery, Chicago (1981); Portland Center for Visual Arts, Oregon (1982); Albert & Vera List Arts Center, Reference Gallery, MIT, Cambridge, Massachusetts (1985); Dart Gallery, Chicago (1986); Farideh Cadot Gallery, New York and Paris (1987–89); Corcoran Gallery of Art, Washington, DC (1991); Curt Marcus Gallery, New York (1992); and Galerie Berggruen & Cie, Paris (1994 and 1996). His work has been featured in numerous group exhibitions throughout the United States and Europe. He is currently represented by Curt Marcus Gallery, New York, and Galerie Berggruen & Cie, Paris, and has lived and worked in New York since 1984. MM

Dennis Kowalski

(Born 1938) A Conceptual artist and sculptor, Dennis Kowalski was born in 1938 in Chicago, where he has spent most of his life. Originally intending to be an architect, he studied at UIC's School of Architecture in 1955–57, and later studied sculpture at SAIC, receiving his BFA in 1962 and his MFA in 1966.

Kowalski has been a central figure in the art of Chicago since the early 1970s, when he began making works informed by both the cool geometry of Minimalism and an anything-goes approach to media. Kowalski used raw plywood, roofing tar, and other low-grade materials to create complex geometric sculptures that reference their own origins as products of craftsmanship. The artist began showing these works in the mid-1970s in various group exhibitions including AIC's C & V shows, and mounted an important solo exhibition at N.A.M.E. Gallery in 1976 in which he created a large-scale installation— among the first in Chicago—that explored issues of interior space, architecture, and the nature of the art object and the art experience. Another important early project was *Seven Wedges for Crosstown Artworld* in which Kowalski published a cryptic advertisement in the *New Art Examiner* announcing the placement of seven crudely cast concrete wedges in front of important art-world institutions such as MCA, N.A.M.E., and the *New Art Examiner*.

A professor at UIC since 1970 and a founding board member of N.A.M.E. Gallery in 1973, Kowalski has been influential in the Chicago art community. At N.A.M.E., he supported efforts by artists exploring Conceptual art at a time when it commanded little interest in Chicago. In his work since the late 1980s, Kowalski has been less concerned with the status of the art object and more interested in ethical, philosophical, and political issues. Using sculpture objects, he often creates elaborate tableaus that evoke the horror of historical events, such as Kristallnacht, or refer to the exploitation of indigenous peoples in the post-Colonialist era. Even more recently, he has begun exploration of themes dealing with the natural world and man's relationship to and impact upon it by presenting natural objects alongside manmade simulations of the natural.

Kowalski has shown widely in Chicago and New York, including a 1995 solo exhibition at N.A.M.E. He was represented by Marianne Deson Gallery for over ten years amd is currently affiliated with Beret International Gallery. His work is in the permanent collections of MCA, AIC, and the Indianapolis Museum of Art. GS

Paul LaMantia

(Born 1938) Paul LaMantia was born in 1938 in Chicago, where he has remained. While a teenager, LaMantia met mechanical illustrator Jules Zinni, with whom he studied to prepare for a career as a commercial artist. Following this course, LaMantia attended the American Academy of Arts in Chicago in 1957–59 and worked as an advertising designer for five years (1958–60 and 1961–64). In 1960 he enlisted in the US Army Reserves, where his popular caricatures of officers allowed him to spend his basic training painting murals in the mess hall at both Fort Leonard Wood in Missouri and Fort Riley in Kansas. Once back in Chicago, LaMantia took night classes at SAIC and painted on his own, while still working in advertising. His increasing interest in painting led him to pursue a career in the fine arts. He exhibited early on in AIC's 1962 C & V show and participated in the important group exhibitions "The Sunken City Rises" (1964) and "Phalanx" (1965) at IIT. He enrolled at SAIC, receiving a BFA degree in 1966, followed by an MFA in 1968.

LaMantia was soon known for his erotic and often brutal paintings of groups of distorted, usually female, figures. Exploring the tensions between sexuality, violence, and emotion, these intense paintings explode with high-key colors, sharp abstract patterns, and multiple figures compressed within a tight interior space. Faces are grotesque or abstracted into partial features or misplaced appendages. Costumes and skin are often depicted or fused in such a way that they become both or neither, similar to the conflated imagery of Ed Paschke, Art Green, or Robert Lostutter, artists who emerged around the same time. These characteristic images reflect LaMantia's Surrealist tendencies and relate his work to the early "Monster Roster" painters, as well as the Imagists with whom he has been grouped on several occasions. The influence of popular culture and quotidian life is also evident in LaMantia's paintings, as telephones, televisions, mirrors, sexual devices, and, more recently, comic-inspired characters serve as symbolic elements, as well as reminders of reality. The combination of these seemingly commonplace items with horrific characters often presented in aggressive poses or engaged in shocking activities underscores the complexity of the psychosexual content of his art.

LaMantia has had one-person exhibitions at Alverno College, Milwaukee (1968); The Illinois Arts Council Gallery, Chicago (1970); Krannert Center for the Performing Arts, University of Illinois, Urbana (1977); and HPAC (1982); as well as at the Chicago galleries Deson-Zaks, Douglas Kenyon, and Zaks, his current representative. His paintings have been included in such group exhibitions as "Violence in Recent American Art," MCA (1968); "The Chicago Connection," E.B. Crocker Art Gallery, Sacramento (1976); "Masterpieces of Recent Chicago Art," The Chicago Public Library Cultural Center (1977); "Selections from the Dennis Adrian Collection," MCA (1982); "Recent Art from Chicago," Artists' Space, New York (1986); and "Chicago Imagism: A 25 Year Survey," Davenport Museum of Art, Iowa (1994); as well as numerous C & V shows at AIC. From 1967 until 1993 LaMantia taught art in the Chicago public schools. SB

Ellen Lanyon

(Born 1926) Ellen Lanyon was born in Chicago in 1926. From 1944 to 1948 she attended SAIC, where she was influenced by her study with the art historian Kathleen Blackshear and the collection of Early Renaissance Sienese paintings at AIC. In 1948 Lanyon and other students from SAIC and ID formed Exhibition Momentum in response to AIC's decision to bar students from participation in their C & V shows. Lanyon and her husband, painter Roland Ginzel, both received their MFA degrees from the University of Iowa in 1950; she attended the Courtauld Institute in London for a year on a Fulbright scholarship. The year after her return to Chicago in 1951, Lanyon began to teach at SAIC and started showing her work at Fairweather-Hardin, B.C. Holland, and later at Richard Gray and then Printworks Gallery, the last being her present Chicago representative.

Lanyon was an active organizer of art groups and exhibitions in Chicago. With Ginzel and others, she formed the Graphic Art Workshop in 1953 to promote printmaking through its facilities and the organization of exhibitions; it was damaged by fire in 1955 and closed in 1956. Lanyon was also part of Phalanx, the artists' support group that emerged in the mid-1960s and later became PAC (Participating Artists of Chicago). She participated in the RESPONSE exhibition held in reaction to the events of the 1968 Democratic Convention. Perhaps Lanyon's most significant creation as an organizer was W.E.B. (West East Coast Bag) in the early 1970s, an organization for women artists that spawned two important spaces for women's art in Chicago: Artemisia and ARC (Artists Residents of Chicago). In 1972 Lanyon, having taught at SAIC in 1960 and 1961, became the academic director of the Oxbow Summer School of Painting in Saugatuck, Michigan—a branch of SAIC. Having divided her time between New York and Chicago for a good part of the 1980s, Lanyon moved with her husband permanently to New York in 1985. Lanyon was honored in 1988 for both her artistic and activist achievements in Chicago by a retrospective exhibition at The Chicago Public Library Cultural Center.

Lanyon's penchant for "magical" transformations of mundane subject matter suggests the heavy influence that Dada and Surrealism have had on the artists of Chicago. Her works of the 1950s are primarily large, dreamy depictions of shadowy figures in atmospheric interiors. The 1960s brought a brighter palette and a shift to using family photographs and images culled from sports or circus magazines, yet retaining the fantasy of the mid-1950s works. Lanyon turned to drawing and acrylics after developing an allergy to turpentine in the late 1960s. Her work became more fantastic, featuring elements of animal and plant life in bizarre settings. DM

June Leaf

(Born 1929) June Leaf's almost fifty-year career as an artist began in Chicago where she became interested in city life on childhood trips downtown for ballet lessons. Born in 1929 and raised on the West Side, her training began in 1947 when she attended ID, but she left after three months to go to Paris where she was introduced to primitive art at the Musée de l'Homme. Returning to Chicago in 1949, Leaf began influential friendships with artists associated with SAIC, including Leon Golub, and showed her work in the Exhibition Momentum show of 1951. She became acquainted with artist Seymour Rosofsky, part of the SAIC circle, in 1952 during a short stint as a model in San Francisco, and became influenced by his work as well. In 1950–51 she taught at ID, while studying for her MA in art education there, which she received in 1954. She also taught at SAIC in the mid-1950s.

Leaf worked in Chicago through most of the 1950s. These early paintings and drawings have a very linear quality and somber palette, and the earliest works sometimes recall primitive goddesses or Mother Earth figures. Leaf combined these figures with an abstract space or architectural references. The figures in later paintings and drawings from the 1950s include grandmotherly women wearing wide-brim hats, and numerous portraits and self-portraits. Important to this time was Leaf's development of her personal mythology, worked out in her paintings and prolific sketchbooks. She began showing these works in Chicago at AIC's C & V exhibitions and at Allan Frumkin Gallery.

Leaf traveled to Europe in 1958–59 on a Fulbright scholarship. There she copied and sketched from Old Master paintings, including Goya and Vermeer. Upon her return in 1960, she settled in New York. There, around 1965, she translated the personal imagery she had developed in Chicago to scenes depicting New York urban life realized as mixed-media sculptural objects with free-standing figures. She also created some large pieces modeled after theater sets, including the monumental *Ascension of Pig Lady* (1969). These sculptures feature vibrant, almost circuslike, colors combined with roughly textured surfaces that Leaf acknowledges were influenced by childhood memories of Chicago's famous River View Amusement Park. This work was featured on the dust jacket for Franz Schulze's *Fantastic Images* (1972), and her inclusion in this influential book caused Leaf often to be referred to as one of the first generation of Chicago Imagists.

In 1970 Leaf moved to Mabou, Nova Scotia, with her future husband, photographer Robert Frank. There she began making small, more abstract sculptures and returned to painting. This caused a dramatic shift in imagery as Leaf began to combine her personal vision with the landscapes and birds she was seeing in nature. Since then, Leaf has continued to work on both paintings and sculptures.

Leaf has been featured in retrospectives at the Madison Art Center in Wisconsin (1973), MCA (1978), and the Washington Projects for the Arts in Washington, DC (1991); a retrospective showing of her prints took place at the Chicago Cultural Center (1995). Besides Frumkin gallery, she has been associated in Chicago with Young-Hoffman and Printworks galleries, and in New York with Terry Dintenfass and Edward Thorp galleries. She has been featured in over forty group shows all over the United States. Her work is in the collections of MOMA, AIC, MCA, and the Madison Art Center, Wisconsin. Besides her teaching in Chicago, Leaf taught at the Parsons School of Design in New York (1966–68.) AF

Nathan Lerner

(Born 1913) A designer, teacher, painter, and photographer, Nathan Lerner has lived the Bauhaus ideal, quietly making major contributions to the many fields he has explored. Born in 1913 to a Ukrainian family in the Maxwell Street area of Chicago, he began his study of art with Saturday children's classes at SAIC, subsequently continuing in Chicago at the National Academy of Art (1931), The Jewish People's Institute, at SAIC (1935–37), and most significantly, at The New Bauhaus (later ID; 1937–40).

Lerner began to make photographs in the early 1930s as a way to train his eye for painting; only decades later did he print most of his negatives. In 1935 he began his Maxwell Street series, an important photojournalism project that captures Depression-era Chicago. Two years later Lerner began more experimental studies at The New Bauhaus, working with László Moholy-Nagy, Gyorgy Kepes, and Henry Holmes Smith. With strong encouragement from Moholy-Nagy, Lerner became fascinated with the techniques of photography and invented the lightbox, which is widely used today as a means of isolating and controlling light in photographs. Lerner used the device to create a series of abstract, formal compositions of simple materials in which the main subject is light itself.

To avoid the draft during World War II, in 1943 Lerner accepted a civilian position in New York with the Navy as a light consultant and designer. His photography returned to recording daily life and street scenes, but retained the influence of his New Bauhaus training: instead of fabricating compositions, Lerner now discovered them, combining the inquisitive playfulness of Surrealism with the direct, uncontrived approach of his earlier work to create what he terms "natural Surrealism." When the war ended, Moholy-Nagy invited Lerner back to ID to become chairman of the Product Design Department and dean of faculty and students. After Moholy-Nagy died in 1946, Lerner served as acting educational director for a year, then continued in his prior positions. In 1949, when ID joined IIT, Lerner left to cofound with fellow ID faculty member Hin Bredendiek (also known as Hin Brandendieck) Lerner-Bredendiek Designs. Throughout the 1950s and 1960s, Lerner concentrated on product design, achieving national recognition; one of his most familiar creations is the "honey bear" plastic container.

From 1966 to 1971 Lerner taught a seminar in design philosophy at UIC, and in 1972 he was persuaded to have his first major exhibition of his New Bauhaus work, at Bradley University in Peoria, Illinois. Numerous exhibitions followed, including one-person shows at the Bauhaus Archiv in Berlin (1974); Institute of Contemporary Art in Boston (1979); The Chicago Public Library Cultural Center (1984); Milwaukee Art Museum (1995); and at galleries in Chicago, Washington, DC, and Tokyo. Inspired by the public success of his fine-arts work, Lerner again concentrated on photography. On his first trip to Japan in 1971, he shot a group of black-and-white photographs; in 1974 he returned and began an Abstract Expressionist series in color. He traveled to Mexico and Europe and continued to make trips to Japan into the 1980s, further developing both his black-and-white photographs and exploring formalist color photography as well. His photographs are in the collections of many major museums worldwide. LS

Robert Lostutter

(Born 1939) For over twenty-five years, Robert Lostutter has created fantastic, meticulous depictions of the human figure. Born in Emporia, Kansas, in 1939, Lostutter came to Chicago to attend SAIC (1958–62). There he was influenced by John Rogers Cox, an academic painter who stressed the importance of preliminary drawings and glazing methods. Lostutter first received attention in the late 1960s for his oil paintings, though he was also producing watercolors, both as studies and independent works. During the mid-1970s he began to concentrate on the watercolors, continuing his painstaking technique. The gemlike hues of his watercolors are built up through layers of tiny cross-hatches. Lostutter has worked in all sizes, from the early monumental oils and watercolors to the more recent miniatures.

Lostutter's early iconography consists of voluminous figures in profile, heavily influenced by the Pop images of artist Richard Lindner, placed against stylized, geometrically designed backgrounds. Lostutter subsequently developed a more personal vocabulary of individual or paired figures, sometimes masked, which seem to hang or float helplessly in an atmospheric, illusory space. The full and partial bodies experience a type of bondage, often constricted or pinched by ropes or straps. Their skin is often rendered as if scarred or even inflated, evoking painful psychological implications of being trapped and isolated within a damaged or artificial casing. In addition to acrobats, shrouded and ornamental bodies surrounded by other appendages (hands, legs) appear in these mysterious and erotic works. Initially inspired by the artist's trips to Mexico and his interest in tropical birds and plants, the new motif of hybrid bird-men entered Lostutter's watercolors in the mid-1970s, corresponding with his increasing attention to the watercolor medium. Exotic, multicolored plumage is fused with faces and torsos of nude figures, addressing the issue of man's coexistence with nature. Many of the tilted single heads with their leering eyes and sideways glances can be described as sinister or sullen, while the figures who are coupled sustain awkward postures and rarely meet each other's eyes, suggesting problems of intimacy. The sensuous opulence of the decorative surfaces contrasts sharply with the austere expressions of the faces, as well as the mechanical, obsessive painting process.

Lostutter's work has been featured in Chicago in one-person exhibitions at Deson-Zaks Gallery (1971, 1973, and 1975); Dart Gallery (1976, 1978, 1980, 1984, and 1987); the Renaissance Society (1984); Columbia College Art Gallery (1986); and Phyllis Kind Gallery (1992 and 1995), with whom he is currently associated; and at Monique Knowlton Gallery, New York (1981 and 1984). Numerous group exhibitions include C & V shows, AIC (1971 and 1973); "After Surrealism: Metaphor and Similes," John and Mable Ringling Museum of Art, Sarasota, Florida (1972); "Chicago: Some Other Traditions," Madison Art Center, Wisconsin (1983); "Currents," Institute of Contemporary Art, Boston (1984); "39th Corcoran Biennial," Corcoran Gallery of Art, Washington, DC (1985); and "Surfaces: Two Decades of Painting in Chicago," Terra Museum of American Art, Chicago (1987). Lostutter's paintings can be found in public collections nationwide. SB

Jim Lutes

(Born 1955) Jim Lutes was born in 1955 in Fort Lewis, which is in the Palouse area of eastern Washington. He attended Washington State University, Pullman, as an undergraduate. Drawn in part by the presence of the Imagists, he came to Chicago in 1980, receiving his MFA in 1982 from SAIC, where Ray Yoshida, Barbara Rossi, Christina Ramberg, and Suellen Rocca were teaching.

Lutes first gained national attention for his representational works which comment critically on popular and consumer culture. In paintings often described as "gritty" or "obsessive," the artist depicted, in an expressive, distorted figurative style, the streets of his crumbling Milwaukee Avenue neighborhood in Chicago; his studio filled with beer cans and overflowing ashtrays; his own morose flesh facing yet another trial—hangover, illness, sloth, depression. Inventive portraits, self-portraits, and cityscapes, many showing several different time-frames, explore the frustrations plaguing himself and others in a society flooded with meaningless, mass-produced consumer items. Human frailties, both physical and psychological, are shown in scathingly honest depictions—depression, ill health, sexual frustration, and obesity are provocative and disturbing subjects. Lutes achieved early success; his paintings were often described in catalogues and reviews as being in a lineage with the Imagist tradition of distorted figuration.

In the mid-1980s, Lutes's painting evolved into a more abstracted style that shows his increasing virtuosity with his medium. Swirls of color layer the canvas within larger, biomorphic forms that seem eerie remnants of figures. Yet even as the paintings became more abstract, recognizable images remained, typically embedded within matrices of abstract forms or floating within a maze of line and color. Indeed, each painting is structured around an underlying image that emotionally or psychologically inspired the work.

Lutes has shown at the Walker Art Center, Minneapolis (1985); Whitney Museum of American Art, New York (1987); Corcoran Gallery of Art, Washington, DC (1993); and locally at the Terra Museum of American Art (1987), the State of Illinois Art Gallery (1989 and 1991), and MCA (1989 and 1994). In 1993 he exhibited in Germany's prestigious "Documenta" in Kassel. He received a Southeast Center for Contemporary Art, Winston-Salem, North Carolina, "Awards in the Visual Arts" grant in 1988. LW

Iñigo Manglano-Ovalle

(Born 1961) Iñigo Manglano-Ovalle's work uses a decidedly Postmodern sensibility to comment upon complex issues of urban racial identity and community. Manglano-Ovalle was born in Madrid in 1961 and raised there and in Bogotá, shuttling for years with his family between Madrid, Bogotá, and Chicago before finally settling in the United States in the early 1970s. At Williams College, Williamstown, Massachusetts, he studied art, art history, Spanish, and Latin American literature, receiving his BA in 1983. Manglano-Ovalle began exhibiting in Chicago while attending SAIC. He participated in a number of group exhibitions at ARC, HPAC, and SAIC's Gallery 2 before receiving his MFA in 1989.

Manglano-Ovalle became exhibitions director at Randolph Street Gallery in 1989, a position he held until 1991. The *Assigned Identity Project* (1990), a collaborative effort that he undertook with the immigration amnesty program at the Emerson House Community Center in the West Town neighborhood of Chicago, focused upon the practices of the Immigration and Naturalization Services (INS) in granting amnesty. Manglano-Ovalle not only created works of art as part of the project, but provided immigrants with information on how the United States documents aliens and how they might be able to negotiate other forms of documentation, as well. The project thus fused together the creation of objects and active community service.

The *Assigned Identity Project* foreshadowed Manglano-Ovalle's next community-based project, *Street-Level Video*—a shifting video collaborative composed of Hispanic gang members. This project involved video-making by Latino youths in West Town to foster greater understanding of street culture and gang activity for both the participants and the audience. Video portraits of West Town residents were created as part of the project through Manglano-Ovalle's formation of the Westtown Vecinos Video Channel, a collaboration of the Community Television Network, Emerson House Community Center, Erie Neighborhood House, and Wells High School-within-a-School Program, all based in Chicago. Street-Level Video presented the related video installations *Cul de Sac* at the MCA and *Televecindario* as part of the "Culture in Action" program organized by Sculpture Chicago in 1993. Manglano-Ovalle continues to be involved with Street-Level Video.

Apart from his collaborative efforts, Manglano-Ovalle's work is characterized by its examination of how urban racial identity is constructed by social experience. Manglano-Ovalle employs a wide and unique array of materials, for example, green cards, gelatin-blocks for testing ammunition, huge car stereo systems, and DNA printouts, in elegantly minimal arrangements that are both didactically and aesthetically compelling. His work has been featured in numerous exhibitions in Chicago and abroad, with solo exhibitions at the Centre Gallery, Miami-Dade College (1991); New Langton Arts Center, San Francisco (1992); TBA Exhibition Space, Chicago (1994); and Feigen, Inc., Chicago (1995–96). Manglano-Ovalle was also featured in "Korrespondenzen/ Correspondences: 14 Artists from Berlin and Chicago," coorganized by the Chicago Cultural Center and the Berlinische Galerie, Berlin (1994–95). DM

Kerry James Marshall

(Born 1955) Kerry James Marshall was born in Birmingham, Alabama, in 1955, and raised in a housing project there and in the Watts section of Los Angeles, where his family moved when he was eight. Eventually, the Marshall family managed to move out of the projects and bought their own house. Marshall knew from an early age that he wanted to be a painter, and after finishing high school and city college, he enrolled in the Otis Art Institute, Los Angeles, receiving a BFA degree in 1978. Moving to Chicago in 1987, Marshall worked various jobs by day in order to paint at night. A major turning point in his career came in 1991 when he was awarded an NEA grant that allowed him to rent studio space and concentrate on his art.

Marshall's work from the late 1970s consists of large-scale, socially and politically conscious figurative drawings that gave way to experimentation with paper collage. He briefly abandoned the figure to investigate pure abstraction, but quickly returned to figuration when he began painting in 1980. The paintings focus exclusively on African-Americans, incorporating elements of both traditional folk art and Western European art history in compositions featuring stylized figures in flat pictorial settings. They fall into two categories: monumental works concerned with narrative content—an interest that stems, in part, from Marshall's extensive knowledge of film gained during work on several films as a production designer; and smaller, often confrontational, portraits. Many of Marshall's works combine painting and collage to create dense compositions juxtaposing stereotypical motifs with incongruous symbols that challenge the viewer to examine and dissect the stereotypes presented on the surface. The portraits are often concerned with blurring the boundaries between rich and poor, black and white. Marshall's most recent series is based on housing projects named after gardens, four in Chicago and the one in Los Angeles in which he lived with his family. These paintings utilize the loaded nomenclature to reveal the hopes, illusions, and complexities in these living situations. Marshall is able to be simultaneously a critic, a realist, and an optimist, as his paintings accentuate the humanity and the communal activities of the residents of these "gardens."

Marshall's work was featured in one-person exhibitions at Koplin Gallery, Los Angeles (1985, 1991, and 1993); the Studio Museum in Harlem, New York (1986), during his tenure as artist-in-residence; Chicago Cultural Center (1992); Jack Shainman Gallery, New York (1993 and 1995); and at the Cleveland Center for Contemporary Art (1994–95). Group exhibitions include the "43rd Biennial Exhibition of Contemporary Painting" at the Corcoran Gallery of Art, Washington, DC (1993); "Korrespondenzen/ Correspondences: 14 Artists from Berlin and Chicago" at the Chicago Cultural Center and the Berlinische Galerie, Berlin (1994–95); "Art at the Edge— Social Turf" at the High Museum of Art, Atlanta (1995); and "About Place: Recent Art of the Americas" at AIC (1995). His work is in numerous public collections. Marshall has been teaching at UIC since 1993. AF

Ray Martin

(Born 1930) Ray Martin, a Chicago native, was born in 1930, and grew up in the northern suburbs and in Florida. His father, an amateur painter who had emigrated from Norway, encouraged his son's interest in art, and Martin entered ID in 1949, studying with photographer Aaron Siskind and printmaker Misch Kohn. After receiving his BS in visual design in 1954, Martin began a career as a book designer and illustrator, first for the textbook publisher Scott-Foresman, and later for Edit, Inc., and also on a freelance basis. In 1956 he returned to ID to teach drawing, printmaking, and typographic design for a year before traveling to Paris on a Fulbright Fellowship. There he was influenced by the work of French artists Odilon Redon and Edgar Degas.

Martin began his influential career as a teacher of printmaking at SAIC in 1960, joining the department founded by Vera Berdich. Serving as chairman from 1968 to 1972, he reorganized and greatly expanded the department. Through a program that had the department act as a resource for artists wishing to produce editions, Martin served as master printer for Robert Natkin, Seymour Rosofsky, Ellen Lanyon, and others.

Martin is particularly known for his boxed sets of prints and writings, and for limited-edition and unique artists' books, such as *Acceptable Losses* (1983) or *At Issue* (1991). He originally was inspired to make artists' books after those produced by members of the Fluxus group, although his works are of a very different nature than the inexpensive, often crudely produced Fluxus products. Combining numerous types of imagery, some printed as lithographs, some hand-colored or drawn, with words, Martin's books are in the tradition of deluxe print editions. His works have been shown in print exhibitions around the United States and are in the collections of AIC, MCA, and the Cranbrook Museum of Art, Bloomfield Hills, Michigan. LW

Luis Medina

(1942–1985) Luis Medina was born in Havana in 1942. After leaving Cuba at age sixteen to finish his education in Spain, he traveled around Europe and finally settled in Miami in 1961, reuniting with his parents who had immigrated there after Fidel Castro rose to power. In Miami, Medina worked menial jobs and attended liberal-arts classes at Miami-Dade Junior College, graduating in 1967. Deciding that he wanted to be an artist, Medina came to Chicago in 1967 to attend SAIC, receiving his BFA in 1971 and MFA in 1973. Originally interested in becoming a sculptor, Medina soon switched to photography and was mentored by SAIC architectural photographer and professor Harold Allen and AIC photography curator Hugh Edwards. After graduating, Medina and his childhood friend José López, who had accompanied him to SAIC, began to collaborate on architectural projects, culminating in *Dreams in Stone* (1974), a two-year project photographing the University of Chicago. While working on commissioned projects, Medina started to expand his personal photography.

Investigating his position as an outsider in the United States, Medina began to concentrate on aspects of Latin-American life in Chicago. In the late 1970s he focused in on photographing

Chicago's gang graffiti and the youths responsible for it. Other subjects included altars and the people involved with the practice of Santeria, the Puerto-Rican motorcycle gang Sons of the Devil, local gay lifestyles, and weeds and trees in urban settings. Medina's photographs on the surface are documentary, yet they contain a deeper meaning often representative of his personal experience. Working with both color and black-and-white photography, Medina explored issues of marginalization and the grittiness of urban life. By focusing in on individuals or isolating specific objects, he encouraged viewers to expand upon the significance of his images.

Medina worked right up until his death in 1985 of a cytomegalovirus infection. His work has been featured in numerous national and international exhibitions, including two solo shows at AIC (1980 and 1993–94). Two-person shows with José López include those at the Amos Anderson Art Museum, Helsinki (1974); the National Gallery of Victoria, Melbourne, Australia (1976); and the Centre for Photographic Studies, Sydney (1978). Group shows include "The Photographer and the City," MCA (1977); "First Exhibition of Latin American Photography," Museo del Palacio de Bellas Artes, Mexico City (1978); "Traces: Three Chicago Photographers," Ukrainian Institute of Modern Art, Chicago (1981); "Harold Allen, Photographer and Teacher," AIC (1984); and "Cuba-USA: The First Generation," the Fondo del Sol Visual Arts Center, Washington, DC (1991). His photographs have been featured in such publications as *Aperture*, *Architectural Digest*, *Chicago Tribune*, *The New York Times*, and *Saturday Review*. Medina taught photography classes at Columbia College, Chicago; the College of DuPage, Glen Ellyn, Illinois; and Elmhurst College, Illinois. His estate is represented by Schneider Gallery, Chicago. AF

Adelheid Mers

(Born 1960) Adelheid Mers's spare, geometric light projections and sculptures prompt a meditation on the relation of the spectator to the space surrounding or covered by a work of art. Mers was born in Düsseldorf in 1960. She attended the universities of Düsseldorf and Cologne, studying literature, linguistics, and philosophy from 1980 to 1985. Mers concurrently studied under such artists as Tony Cragg, Klaus Rinke, and Günther Uecker at the Kunstakademie, Düsseldorf, receiving her MFA in 1986. In 1988 Mers moved to Chicago for postgraduate study in sculpture at the University of Chicago. That same year she received an award from the British Council and a DAAD grant from the German Academic Exchange Service.

Mers employs industrial-grade felt and plywood and draws on Minimalist sculpture and everyday experiences as models in her use of familiar organic forms. As with Minimalist sculptors Carl Andre and Donald Judd, her work is defined by its relation to the viewer and the surrounding space—in particular, the floor. She first exhibited this work in Chicago in a solo exhibition at Artemisia in 1989. In 1991 Mers exhibited at Ten in One Gallery with her husband, Patrick McGee, and Catherine Jacobi. It was the first of many exhibitions in the "Uncomfortable Spaces"—a group of galleries including Tough, Beret International, and MWMWM that focus upon younger or underrecognized Chicago artists. She was featured in a three-person exhibition at N.A.M.E. in 1992, and included in 1993 in "Real Small (Little Things)," organized by Randolph Street Gallery, which traveled to the Delta Axis Art Center, Memphis, and Art in General in New York.

In 1994, inspired by the work of James Turrell and Robert Irwin, Mers began working with spotlights fitted with shaped and colored cels that cast austere, geometric shapes and patterns on the floor. The viewer may become an active participant in these works, altering the shape of the projection. That same year she exhibited in a four-person show at N.A.M.E. with John Dunne, Carla Preiss, and Jessica Stockholder, and also began teaching at the American Academy of Art, Chicago. Mers was included in the "Radius" exhibition that was held concurrently with Art Expo 1995 and was important for displaying the work of many emerging Chicago artists. Since 1995 Mers has been the coeditor of *Whitewalls*, a journal devoted to artists' writings and projects. She created a site-specific light-projection installation for the "Plane Speak: Contemporary Abstraction in Illinois" exhibition at the Chicago Cultural Center in 1996. DM

John Miller

(Born 1927) Over the past forty years, John Miller has combined gestural abstraction with rich, intense color in his paintings. Miller was born in Princeton, Illinois, in 1927, and served in the US Army in Korea (1946–47). He returned to attend SAIC, where he received his BFA (1951), and obtained his MFA from the University of Chicago (1956). In 1953, with financial assistance from local benefactors Doc Walters and his wife, Shirley, a teacher in the Chicago Public School system, Miller founded the 414 Art Workshop Gallery, one of Chicago's earliest "alternative spaces." Miller worked on the workshop's faculty, teaching classes in painting, design, and jewelry-making, in addition to serving as director from 1953 to 1959. He has been a constant and influential

fixture on the Chicago art scene over the years, and has taught at SAIC since the late 1950s. He has also taught painting at Northwestern University, Evanston, Illinois (1956–63); HPAC (1957–58); UIC (1959–62); and Kendall College, Evanston (1965–67). Miller has been a frequent exhibitor in AIC's C & V shows since 1952, and although he continued to exhibit at these juried events, he was active on the board of directors of Exhibition Momentum in 1956–57. He served as chairperson of another important alternative space in Chicago, Superior Street Gallery Corporation (1959–61). Except for the year he spent living in Mexico (1970–71), Miller has lived in Chicago all his adult life.

Miller has devoted his career to exploring painterly issues, consistently combining a lush handling of paint with an investigation into compositional structure. From the mid-1950s to the late 1980s, Miller painted variations on the female nude, usually seated, in a Fauve palette. The figures eventually became increasingly abstracted and more integrated into the structural design. In the process of divorcing himself from the figure, Miller began to concentrate on a monumental architecture of abstract, largely geometric forms set in dynamic equilibrium with energetic passages of freely painted, gestural strokes. In addition to his large paintings on board (typically four-by-five-and-one-half feet), Miller has worked out his ideas on a smaller scale on paper. Following a brief period in the early 1990s during which Miller added collaged elements to his paintings, his work began to display a more cohesive overall tonal quality. Composed of a flurry of varying brush strokes and textures, the works reveal a subtle underlying organization of geometric forms and cause a shift in depth and perception.

Miller's solo exhibitions in Chicago include those at Superior Street Gallery (1960), Crane Gallery (1989), Three Illinois Center (1989), and Two Illinois Center (1992); and at Wolverhampton Polytechnic, England (1975). His work has been in such group exhibitions as "62nd Annual American Exhibition," AIC (1957); "The New Chicago Decade," Lake Forest College, Illinois (1959); "Annual Art Exhibition," HPAC (1959); "Exhibition Chicago," UIC (1965); "Phalanx 3: Prints, Drawings and Watercolors," Kendall College (1966); "Phalanx 4," IIT (1966); "Chicago Artists 1948–75," HPAC (1976); "Distinguished Alumni," SAIC (1976); and "Alternative Spaces," MCA (1984). Miller was affiliated with Richard Gray Gallery, Chicago, during the late 1970s, and since 1989 has been represented by Jan Cicero Gallery, where he exhibited with his wife, photographer Barbara Crane, in 1996. MM

mers— mers motley

Konstantin Milonadis

(Born 1926) Konstantin Milonadis, a Constructivist sculptor, was born in 1926 in Ukraine. After immigrating to this country in 1951, he served two years in the US Army. He received his BAE from SAIC in 1957, followed by his MFA from Tulane University in New Orleans in 1959.

Milonadis states that his work belongs to the Constructivist tradition forged by Naum Gabo and Antoine Pevsner, and brought to this country by László Moholy-Nagy and the Bauhaus School. Milonadis, however, does not fall strictly in line with the traditional utilitarianism of the Constructivists. He instead is concerned with the concept of sculpture emphasizing space rather than the traditional emphasis on mass. Milonadis was most closely influenced by his sculpture professor at Tulane University, George Rickey, who was in turn taught by Alexander Calder.

Milonadis employs thin stainless-steel wire, occasionally accented by small pieces of sheet steel. Movement is fundamental to his work. Small tight springs ensure that a light touch or breeze can trigger clockworklike motion that serves to make the viewer extremely aware of the physical space that the object occupies. Although they take up little space in the traditional sense, in motion, the pieces define a distinct volume over time. They are, in effect, four-dimensional sculptures. The most notable aspect of Milonadis's work is its precision. A row of his sculptures in motion invokes the feeling of a clockmaker's workshop. With no apparent purpose, they seem to exist equally for their mechanical precision as well as their physical beauty and sense of lightness and airiness. At rest, the pieces suggest a fascination with technology, perhaps bringing to mind an image of television antennae sticking up over the rooftops of an urban landscape.

Milonadis's work has been represented in group exhibitions in various institutions throughout the country, including AIC (1958, 1959, 1961–65, and 1967); the Isaac Delgado Museum of Art in New Orleans (1958 and 1959); and the Indianapolis Center for Contemporary Art, Herron Gallery (1963, 1964, and 1967). He has been featured in one-person exhibitions at the Lexington Gallery at the University of Chicago (1962), the Snite Gallery of Art at the University of Notre Dame, Indiana (1965 and 1967), and at the Fort Wayne Art Museum in Indiana (1968). His work has earned him numerous awards, including the Palmer Prize and the Linde Award from AIC. Milonadis is also well regarded as a teacher. He has taught sculpture at several institutions, including Newcomb College at Tulane University, and Valparaiso University.

He held the position of Distinguished Professor and Sculptor-in-Residence at Notre Dame until 1974. The subsequent whereabouts and activities of the artist are unknown. JK

László Moholy-Nagy

(1895–1946) László Moholy-Nagy was born in 1895 and raised in the small village of Bacsbarsod in southern Hungary. At the gymnasium (prep school) in Szeged, he studied law until he was drafted in 1914 to serve in World War I. Hospitalized twice during the war, he spent his recovery reviving his childhood interest in drawing. Moholy-Nagy resumed his legal studies at the University of Budapest after the war, but dropped them, returned to Szeged, and began working as an artist. In 1920 he moved to Berlin, where he met his future wife and frequent collaborator, Lucia Moholy (née Schultz); they were married the next year. With the leader of the Hungarian political and artistic avant-garde, Lajos Kassák, Moholy-Nagy coedited and designed the *Buch neuer Künstler* (*Book of New Artists*). In 1923 Walter Gropius asked Moholy-Nagy to teach at the Bauhaus, which Gropius had founded in Weimar, Germany, four years earlier.

Moholy-Nagy replaced Johannes Itten in teaching foundation courses; he remained at the Bauhaus until 1928. His marriage to Lucia ended in 1929 and, in 1931, he married Sibyl Pietzsch. Returning to Berlin, Moholy-Nagy continued making his art and worked as a designer. Around 1928 he began using plastics to create dynamic sculptures in which the interaction of light is a crucial element—especially in the Light-Space Modulators that he began to construct in 1930. Meanwhile, his work in graphic design grew out of his collages of the 1920s and 1930s, in which he cleverly combined photography, text, and formal elements of his "fine-arts" work.

The Nazis' growing hostility towards modern artists forced Moholy-Nagy's flight to Amsterdam in 1934, London a year later, and across the Atlantic to Chicago in 1937. The Association of Arts and Industries invited Moholy-Nagy (on the recommendation of Gropius) to direct a design school in Chicago called "The New Bauhaus." Moholy-Nagy accepted the position. While the school lasted only one year, Moholy-Nagy opened his own "School of Design" in Chicago in 1939, retaining most of the original teaching staff. The name was subsequently changed to Institute of Design (ID) in 1944.

Moholy-Nagy continued to work at design as well as painting while directing the school in Chicago. His art always embodied the principles of the Bauhaus in its use of industrial materials and emphasis on geometric abstract form. He did paintings on Plexiglas while in Chicago which were mounted in front of a white background, as well as abstract sculptures in which the artist would combine Plexiglas and steel rods.

Moholy-Nagy died in Chicago in 1946 of leukemia. *Vision in Motion*, a collection of various texts, published posthumously by Sibyl Moholy-Nagy, presents the most comprehensive articulation of Moholy's belief in the inseparability of art and life, a pedagogical philosophy that has had a far-ranging impact. Retrospective exhibitions of his work were held at AIC in 1947, at MCA A New Vision for Chicago" at the Illinois State Museum in Springfield and Chicago in 1991. An archive of his papers is located in Berlin. DM

Keith Morrison

(Born 1942) Born in Linstead, Jamaica, in 1942, Keith Morrison has been profoundly influenced by African and Caribbean cultures. After graduating from high school in Jamaica, he studied liberal arts at the University of Chicago (1959–63); painting at SAIC, where he obtained his BFA (1963) and MFA (1965); and education at DePaul University (1965–67) and Loyola University (1967), both in Chicago. He has served as chairman of the Department of Art, DePaul University (1969–71); associate dean of the College of Architecture and Art, UIC (1971–75); and chairman of the Department of Art, University of Maryland, College Park (1988–92). Morrison has been dean of the College of Creative Arts at San Francisco State University since 1994.

As a student in the mid-1960s, Morrison painted in the current Abstract Expressionist style. The artist has said, "as a black person in art school during that time there was no room or receptive audience for your kind of experiences to play themselves out in painting." The violent events at Chicago's 1968 Democratic Convention and the assassination of Martin Luther King, Jr., angered Morrison to a point where he felt that abstraction was too limited to express his ideas. Morrison's work from 1968 to 1972 concentrates on the black urban experience and combines figurative elements with curvilinear planes of abstraction, offering unusual vantage points. Once the immediacy of the "moment" had passed for Morrison, he returned to abstraction, but this time from a point of view inspired by painters such as Richard Diebenkorn, Gene Davis, Frank Stella, and especially Ellsworth Kelly. Morrison's large dynamic canvases with diagonal rectangles are not related to the decorative concerns of the pattern painters of the 1970s, but manifest a rhythmic tension based on musical structure. By the mid-1980s, feeling he had exhausted abstraction, Morrison returned to figural paintings dealing with African and Caribbean themes. The patterns and colors of his earlier work now comprise a world of tropical settings filled with representations of African legends and myths reconstructed from the artist's childhood memories of village life and religious practice. These later works blend Morrison's sensibilities: forms are interpreted literally, but the ideas are reinforced by abstract principles.

Morrison's solo exhibitions in Chicago include Harper Gallery (1967); Illinois State Arts Council (1975); South Side Community Art Center (1975); DePaul University Gallery (1976); and Chicago State University (1978). Additional one-person shows were at Fisk University, Nashville (1975); Organization of African Unity, Monrovia, Liberia (1979); The University of Michigan Museum of Art, Ann Arbor (1990); and Alternative Museum, New York (1990). Morrison has participated in numerous group exhibitions, including "Phalanx IV," IIT, Chicago (1966); "Keith Morrison and Othello Anderson," N.A.M.E. Gallery, Chicago (1978); "Chicago Abstraction," Galerie Tillie Hardek, Karlsruhe, West Germany (1980); "East/West: Afro-American Contemporary Art," California Afro-American Museum, Los Angeles (1984); "Myth and Magic in the Americas: The Eighties," Museo de Arte Contemporaneo de Monterrey, Mexico (1991); "Free Within Ourselves," National Museum of American Art, Washington, DC (1992); Caribbean Biennial, Santo Domingo (1994). Morrison has curated several exhibitions of African-American art. His work is in numerous public collections around the world. MM

Archibald J. Motley, Jr.

(1891–1981) Archibald J. Motley, Jr. was born in 1891 in New Orleans. His family moved to Chicago in 1893, and his childhood was spent in the Englewood neighborhood on Chicago's South Side where he graduated from high school. Motley went on to attend SAIC from 1914 to 1918. In 1924 Motley, an African-American, married Edith Granzo, a white woman from his neighborhood, and the next year received the Frank G. Logan prize from AIC for his painting *A Mulatress*.

He had a successful one-person exhibition in 1928 at the New Gallery in New York that featured portraits of family members, mulatresses, and octoroon women, as well as fantastic paintings derived from African folklore. On the strength of this and other exhibitions, Motley was awarded the Harmon Foundation Prize in 1928 (for his painting *Octoroon Girl*) and a Guggenheim

Fellowship in 1929, which took him to Paris to study the Old Masters at the Louvre and to observe the interactions between blacks and whites in a foreign urban environment.

Upon his return to Chicago, Motley began depicting the street scenes and club life of the "Black Metropolis" area of Chicago's South Side. His sympathetic and keen depictions of life and culture reflect Motley's desire to create a more veristic image of the African-American in opposition to the denigrating stereotypes circulated by the mass media of the time. Motley's paintings were featured in the Century of Progress exhibitions in Chicago of 1933 and 1935. In 1933 his son, Archibald Motley III, was born, and two years later, owing to his growing reputation, Motley earned a visiting professorship at Howard University, Washington, DC. As part of the WPA of the 1930s, Motley was commissioned to paint a mural for the Wood River, Illinois, post office. During the 1940s, Motley would continue to work on various WPA projects, including the South Side Community Art Center (f. 1941). Although frequently included in AIC's juried group shows during the 1920s and 1930s, Motley was shown only once in the 1940s.

After the death of his wife in 1948, Motley worked for two hand-painted shower curtain companies, putting his painting largely on hiatus during the 1950s. The paintings made during this time were based primarily on the two years (1953–54) that he spent in Mexico. Motley returned to themes of life in Chicago in his work of the 1960s and 1970s. He received an honorary Doctorate of Fine Arts from SAIC in 1980 and was one of ten black artists honored by President Jimmy Carter at a White House reception that same year. Motley died the following year. He was the subject of a one-person exhibition at the Chicago Historical Society in 1992, which traveled to museums in New York, Atlanta, and Washington, DC. DM

(Born 1930) Robert Natkin was born in Chicago in 1930 into a Russian Jewish family. As a young child, he accompanied his grandmother to the Museum of Science & Industry and AIC. When he was fifteen, the family relocated for about a year to Oak Ridge, Tennessee. Being transplanted to a pleasant, rural area from the grimy, working-class neighborhoods of his childhood had a major impact on Natkin: he decided to become an artist. Returning to Chicago, he took youth classes at SAIC, and went on to receive his BFA in 1952, becoming part of the postwar generation of artists that was to have such a great impact on Chicago's art world. Natkin was particularly influenced by art-history professor Kathleen Blackshear, and with other students studied ethnographic materials at the Field Museum. Natkin's special interest was textiles, which were to emerge as a major motif in his paintings.

After traveling to New York and San Francisco in search of a better artistic climate and instead finding himself confused and unsettled, Natkin returned to Chicago, where he got a job at The Newberry Library packing books. Although he had been active in the artist-organized Exhibition Momentum even while in school and counted as friends many of the "Monster Roster" artists (particularly Leon Golub), Natkin was of a slightly younger generation, and was drawn to Abstract Expressionism and not the grotesque figurative style of that group. Willem de Kooning's *Excavation* (1950) especially impressed Natkin when he saw the work in an American show at AIC. The mid-1950s were formative years for Natkin, with great variation in his painting style; in 1957 he began a series of confident Abstract Expressionist canvases in bright colors that are very different from the later, highly textured and subtly colored painting for which he is best known. Also in 1957 Natkin met his wife and frequent coexhibitor, Judith Dolnick. Together with several other artists, they opened the Wells Street Gallery that same year to considerable press attention. Devoted to exhibiting Abstract Expressionism, the gallery gave sculptor John Chamberlain his first show and served as a focal point for young artists interested in the New York School. Natkin, however, felt restless in Chicago: he closed the gallery in 1959 and relocated with his wife to New York.

Natkin executed a major mural for Baxter Laboratories corporate headquarters in Chicago in 1975. His distinguished exhibition record includes a retrospective at the San Francisco Museum of Art (1969), and solo exhibitions at AIC (1975) and the Seattle Art Museum (1990). He currently lives in Redding, Connecticut, and is associated with Gimpel Fils Gallery, London; Gimpel & Weitzenhoffer Gallery, New York; and Thomas McCormick Works of Art, Chicago. His work is in the collection of most major US museums. LW

Joyce Neimanas

(Born 1944) Joyce Neimanas was born and raised in Chicago, and received a BAE and MFA from SAIC, in 1966 and 1969, respectively. She began teaching at SAIC in 1971, serving as the Photography Department chairman at various times during her tenure, and working alongside fellow photography professors Kenneth Josephson and Harold Allen, with whom she had studied as a graduate student. Neimanas's work of the late 1960s and early 1970s was highly experimental for the times, which were dominated by the classical ideas promulgated by such masters as Ansel Adams and Edward Weston. Often dealing with gender roles and erotic themes, Neimanas was an early practitioner of using pornography, advertising images, and other found photographic visuals in her work, often juxtaposing these images with texts. Her frequently provocative images consistently tested the veracity of photography as a communication device. These early experiments led to a body of work in the late 1970s that freely mixes media (photographic and nonphotographic) as well as source materials. Her partner, photographer Robert Heinecken, appears in some of her work.

In the 1980s Neimanas began living part of the year in Los Angeles, where she would often teach at various universities, and part of the year in Chicago. After buying a Polaroid SX-70 camera in a pawnshop in 1980, she began a series that brought together sometimes as many as 200 Polaroids to create large-scale montages. This manner of working is most commonly associated with David Hockney, who began his explorations several years after Neimanas. Neimanas has continued her wide-ranging experimentation that continually broadens the definition of contemporary photography. During the 1980s and 1990s, she has made large-scale works created by contact-printing found imagery; light drawings; sculptures that combine photography and objects; and intricate, highly-colored, computer-generated inkjet prints.

Neimanas has been the subject of over twenty solo exhibitions at various museums and university art galleries, including the Tyler School of Art, Temple University, Philadelphia (1977); Center for Contemporary Photography, Columbia College, Chicago (1979); Rhode Island School of Design, Providence (1985); and California State University, Sacramento (1989). She has also been featured in over thirty group exhibitions in the United States and abroad, many of which traveled, including "BIG Pictures by Contemporary Photographers," MOMA (1983); "Photography and Art: Interactions Since 1946," Los Angeles County Museum of Art (1987); and "Recorded and Revealed," AIC (1987). Her work is represented in numerous public collections, including MCA; AIC; International Museum of Photography at George Eastman House, Rochester, New York; Center for Creative Photography, University of Arizona, Tucson; San Francisco Museum of Modern Art; and the Museum of Fine Arts, Houston. LW

Elizabeth Newman

(Born 1952) Elizabeth Newman is interested in the inherent symbolic qualities of natural and discarded materials. An ardent collector, Newman grew up in Grand Haven, Michigan, where she scavenged the shores of Lake Michigan for keepsakes to sort and examine. She attended Michigan State University in East Lansing, receiving a BFA in 1978 before moving to Chicago to attend SAIC. Though usually thought of as a sculptor or installation artist, Newman studied with painters Ray Yoshida and Michiko Itatani, and graduated with an MFA from SAIC's Fiber Department in 1984.

Through the process of collecting, altering, and combining found objects, Newman involves herself in a ritualistic process of rebirth. Mundane objects as well as manufactured structures that have a worn feel are transformed into assemblages that are at once familiar and fantastic, addressing such personal and humanistic concerns as memory, history, family, and sexuality. Her works stand alone as discreet objects as well as work together in an installational form. An early construction took the form of a rusty swing set peopled by odd podlike sculptures, recalling organic or biomorphic forms. Wire baskets, farm and medical instruments, toys, natural and synthetic fibers, eggs, beeswax, talcum powder, and fluids are some of the evocative materials Newman combines with her handmade creations to produce unique artifacts, which she displays on shelves as well as placed strategically on the floor.

Ironic and witty, as well as meditative and spiritual, Newman's curious constructions reflect a certain Feminist ideology while displaying Surrealist absurd forms. Life cycles are constantly addressed as forms are presented in several generative states. Newman tends to recycle components from her sculptures and her installations. The changing character of her special objects and their ability to take on new meaning when juxtaposed with other memorabilia reflect her interest in time and process. A sense of the past is always present.

While she was living in Chicago during the mid- and late 1980s, Newman's work was included in such group exhibitions as "A New Generation from SAIC" at MCA (1986); "Fetish Art: Obsessive Expressions," at the Rockford Art Museum, Illinois (1986); and "Present at the Creation" at The Chicago Public Library Cultural Center (1989). She has had solo exhibitions in Chicago at Marianne Deson Gallery (1986) and CompassRose Gallery (1990), and in Geneva at Galerie Eric Franck (1989). Since leaving Chicago in 1991, Newman has lived in Connecticut and participated in several site-specific exhibitions. In these poetic and haunting installations, she has attempted to reconcile the history of the place with contemporary social concerns. She participated in the 1991 Spoleto Festival in Charleston, South Carolina, with a work called *Honey in the Rock (Got to Feed God Children)*, and in MCA's 1992 exhibition "Art at the Armory: Occupied Territory" with an installation titled *Histories of Human Flesh*. She was recently included in the 1995 exhibition "The Pervasiveness of Memory" at the Corcoran Gallery of Art, Washington, DC. Newman shows regularly at Galerie Lelong in New York. SB

Robert Nickle

(1919–1980) Robert Nickle began to work in collage in 1946, the year he first came to Chicago from Michigan, and he continued in that medium over the course of his thirty-four-year professional career. Remarkably consistent in appearance over the years, his works are tidy, carefully balanced compositions made up of layered scraps of paper from Chicago's streets. They are often untitled or titled only descriptively; Nickle wrote that he preferred his works to speak for themselves and for him.

Nickle came to Chicago to study with László Moholy-Nagy at ID. As he trained in graphic design, he began to make collages; his artwork was shown publicly as early as 1947, when one of his collages was included in the "New Realities" show in Paris. After he finished his studies at ID, Nickle accepted a teaching position in design there from 1949 to 1952. He subsequently took a job at UIC, where he remained for the rest of his career.

Nickle admired Piet Mondrian, and like him, devoted painstaking attention to the subtle adjustments required to achieve balance in his art, sometimes taking years to complete a single work. Nickle would spread up to fifty collages at a time on the work tables of his studio, each one sandwiched in glass to preserve its arrangement. Moving from one work to another, he would scrutinize and make adjustments in a process he described as being akin to playing simultaneous chess games. A finished work would be signed on the back next to a photograph of the artist (he did not want his signature to disturb the collage), and framed between two pieces of glass in a stainless-steel frame of his own construction.

The works range in size from one to eight square feet. Most are at the smaller end of this range, because Nickle liked to see a collage in its entirety as he worked on it. He made use of texture, overlapping, and variations in edges of the scraps as well as shape and size to achieve a remarkable richness and range of effects. Although he used predominantly subdued tones, at times he would include a brightly colored element in a composition or assemble together several pieces of colored paper, creating interest from their variations in tone as well as shape. Like Paul Klee, another artist he admired, Nickle would sometimes include a letter or word as an element of visual interest in his compositions.

Nickle exhibited extensively during his career. He had one-person shows at AIC (1978); Cranbrook Academy Museum in Bloomfield Hills, Michigan (1979); and UIC's Gallery 400 (1994); and numerous solo shows at his long-time gallery, Richard Gray, Chicago, and at the Acquavella Contemporary Art Gallery in New York. He participated in MOMA's "Assemblage" (1961) and MCA's "Abstract Art in Chicago" (1976). His works are in the collections of several museums, including AIC, MCA, and The David and Alfred Smart Museum in Chicago; the Whitney Museum of American Art in New York; National Gallery in Washington, DC; and the Albright Knox Museum in Buffalo. MHM

Gladys Nilsson

(Born 1940) Gladys Nilsson was born in 1940 in Chicago, where she has lived and worked for most of her life. Her artistic ability was recognized early: she won a scholarship to attend lectures and drawing classes at SAIC before she reached her teens. In 1958 Nilsson entered SAIC's undergraduate program, where she became good friends with art-history professor Whitney Halstead. On Halstead's field trips to the Field Museum, Nilsson was particularly influenced by Egyptian art, Australian Aboriginal bark painting, and Indian miniatures. She received her BFA in 1962. At SAIC, Nilsson met fellow student Jim Nutt; they married in 1961. The pair exhibited together in shows coordinated by Chicago artists, such as "Eye on Chicago" (1964) and "Phalanx" (1965), both at IIT. They also taught children's art classes at HPAC. When HPAC's director, Don Baum, asked Nutt for suggestions for exhibitions, Nutt recommended five artists (Nilsson, James Falconer, Art Green, Suellen Rocca, and himself). These five plus one of Baum's choosing (Karl Wirsum) became the Hairy Who, a group who showed together in three separate exhibitions at HPAC in 1966, 1967, and 1968. All SAIC students or former students, these artists were interested in figurative art and popular imagery, including images from comic books and advertising. After winning the prestigious Logan Medal in AIC's 1967 C & V show, Nilsson moved with Nutt and their young son, Claude, to Sacramento, California, where Nutt had found a teaching position. They lived there from 1968 to 1976, when they returned to Chicago, dissatisfied with life in California.

Nilsson's works are distinctive in their playful mood and watercolor medium, although early on she experimented with acrylic on Plexiglas and silver pencil on paper. Her paintings present her insightful and humorous perspective on familiar subjects from sex and desire to art, television, and shopping; her titles reveal her delight in wordplay, a characteristic she shares with the other Hairy Who artists. Figures and fantastic creatures sometimes too numerous and complexly entwined to count crowd her lyrical compositions. Nilsson's source material spans a wide range, from popular culture (in 1969–70 she produced a series of watercolors loosely based on the TV show "Star Trek") to art history (in 1974 she began a "Bottacellee" series, inspired by seeing Botticelli paintings in Florence in 1972). Whether the references in the work are vernacular or traditional, her themes often address male/female relations. In 1982–83, inspired by Clare Booth Luce's play *The Women*, for which she also produced a poster, Nilsson created several amusing works showing women in various stages of life, a series called "Luce Women," illustrating another frequent topic—women's sexuality.

Nilsson has exhibited extensively over the course of her career. She is represented by the Phyllis Kind Gallery in Chicago and New York and has had several one-person shows at each location since 1970. Additional solo exhibitions include the Whitney Museum of American Art in New York (1973); the Portland Visual Arts Center, Oregon (1979); and Randolph Street Gallery in Chicago (1984). Her works have been featured in group exhibitions at MCA (1969, 1972, and 1984), AIC (1976 and 1990), the Whitney (1969–70 and 1986), and the Los Angeles County Museum of Art (1992). MHM

Jim Nutt

(Born 1938) Born in Pittsfield, Massachusetts, Jim Nutt grew up in the Midwest and received his BFA degree in 1965 from SAIC. Important to his artistic development were classes with art historian Whitney Halstead, who introduced Nutt to self-taught artists and ethnographic art. He also took classes with Ray Yoshida and was influenced by the self-taught Chicago artist Joseph Yoakum. While a student, Nutt gained additional experience in the art world working at Allan Frumkin Gallery and the Arts Club. At SAIC, Nutt became friends with other artists who were working in similar styles, including Gladys Nilsson, whom he married in 1961. Nutt accepted a teaching position at Sacramento State College and the two artists moved to California in 1968 with their son, Claude. Dissatisfied with life in California, they returned to Chicago in 1976.

Nutt's early work (1966–69) is highly informed by comics and popular culture. Often featuring mutilated bodies, acne-covered faces, and all sorts of scatological and sexual imagery, these works—many of which are acrylic reverse paintings on Plexiglas—poke fun at the world. The titles of these (and later) paintings often feature puns and creative spellings in the painting itself as labels or sideline commentary. It was this work that Nutt showed in the legendary "Hairy Who" exhibitions of 1966, 1967, and 1968. Along with Gladys Nilsson, the group included fellow SAIC students and alumni James Falconer, Art Green, Suellen Rocca, and Karl Wirsum. With unusual installations that featured flowered linoleum as wallpaper and comic books as catalogues, these shows marked the emergence of a style that soon became known as "Imagism." Nutt's work in particular became a prime example of Chicago's unique art through a 1974 MCA retrospective that traveled to Europe.

By 1970, having developed an artistic vocabulary of bizarre tableaus featuring strange and disquieting situations between often tiny male and oversized, wildly distorted female figures, Nutt began painting on more conventional surfaces. In 1973 he started his so-called "theater" paintings (including some three-dimensional constructions), distinguished often by painted stage curtains at the edges and a heightened sense of narrative. Nutt's work is generally vibrantly colored, though he has done a small number of black-and-white, and toned-down drawings. His earlier works feature elaborate, decorative frames. Since 1987 he has concentrated on bust-length portraits of imaginary women with jarringly odd hairstyles and prominent noses, meticulously painted with multiple layers of acrylic glazes. They were featured in a 1994 retrospective organized by the Milwaukee Art Museum that traveled to Washington, DC; Seattle; and Cincinnati.

Besides numerous shows at his longtime gallery, Phyllis Kind, Nutt's work has been featured in solo exhibitions at the Whitney Museum of American Art in New York (1974), the Walker Art Center in Minneapolis (1974), the San Francisco Art Institute (1975), and Rotterdamse Kunststichting in the Netherlands (1980). Nutt has appeared in close to 200 group exhibitions, including "Made in Chicago," at the XII Bienal de São Paulo, which toured South America in 1973 and appeared subsequently in Washington, DC, and at MCA; and "Who Chicago," which traveled in Great Britain in 1980 and appeared in Boston and New Orleans. His work can be found in a number of national and international collections. Since 1990 Nutt has taught in the Painting and Drawing Department at SAIC. AF

Lorenzo Pace

(Born 1943) Lorenzo Pace, one of the architects of a new black aesthetic vocabulary in art in the 1970s and 1980s, was born in Birmingham, Alabama, in 1943, the seventh son and one of thirteen children of a Pentecostal preacher. Pace relocated to Chicago to attend SAIC, receiving his BFA in 1974 and his MFA in 1976. While in school, he served as art director for the Black Center for Strategy and Community Development, and later as assistant director for the Chicago Youth Centers. He went on to receive a PhD in art education and administration from Illinois State University, Normal, in 1978. While he was attending SAIC and ISU, Pace was also an instructor at Kennedy King College in Chicago.

Pace's first artistic medium was wood: a musician as well as an artist, he would carve his own flutes from driftwood retrieved along Lake Michigan's shores. As a graduate student he experimented with metal-working, film, and video, all of which put him in good stead in his early experiments in what was then called "expanded media" and later became known as multimedia installation art. Pace was one of the first in Chicago to venture into this area, mounting an extraordinary series of body art performances called the "Mummification Series" in which he wrapped himself or other subjects as "mummies" during ritualistic performances that featured music, movement, and carefully conceived and designed sets. His first *Mummification* was done at SAIC in 1980; a second was enacted at UIC in 1981; a third was at Real Art Ways in Hartford, Connecticut, in 1982. Pace also produced a 1981 work called *Sacrifices* as part of an exhibition at N.A.M.E. Gallery, Chicago, where he was also active as a curator. All these works looked to the African heritage of the black American, as well to the black experience in the South both as a slave and later as a second-class citizen. As a professor in UIC's Black Studies Program from 1979 to 1982, Pace was also a seminal force in Chicago's academic community, focusing on African-American art history and the developing philosophy of Pan-Africanism, in which black artists looked to their African heritage in both the method and materials of their works.

Pace left Chicago to teach at Medger Evers College, New York, from 1983 to 1988. He currently is director of the Montclair State University Art Galleries in Upper Montclair, New Jersey, and resides in Brooklyn, New York. He has exhibited widely around the United States, and most recently was featured in a one-person exhibition entitled "Honor Thy Father and Mother" at the Birmingham Museum of Art (1994). LW

Tom Palazzolo

(Born 1937) Tom Palazzolo has been so intent on creating a style and feeling capturing the craziness and eccentricity characteristic of Chicago, that he has on occasion used the pseudonym "Tom Chicago" in the credits for his films. Palazzolo was born in St. Louis in 1937. After studying at the John and Mable Ringling School of Art in Sarasota, Florida (1958–60), he attended SAIC, where he studied photography and painting and exhibited with the Hairy Who. Palazzolo received his MFA from SAIC in 1965, and began to make films that same year. He was involved with some of the small collectives presenting experimental film at this time in Chicago, such as the Floating Cinematheque (with fellow underground filmmaker John Heinz) and the Center Cinema Co-op. During the late 1960s, Palazzolo became well known in what was then called "underground" film; in 1969 he traveled in the Middle East with a program of American experimental films under the auspices of the United States Information Agency, and in 1970 he received a grant from the American Film Institute.

Palazzolo's films of the late 1960s are alternately political and comedic. *Campaign* (1968), for example, is a highly personal use of footage taken of the 1968 Democratic Convention and the riots that resulted, while *Venus and Adonis* (1965/66) humorously re-creates the Greek myth on Chicago's North Avenue Beach. His film *Love It/Leave It* (1970) was shown at the Whitney Museum of American Art's New American Filmmakers series in 1973. In the early 1970s, Palazzolo began to experiment with forms of cinema-verite documentary, and for the next ten years his films focused on the people and events of working-class Chicago. One series of films concerns the rituals surrounding marriage: prom night, showers, bachelor parties, weddings, receptions, and anniversaries.

During the 1980s Palazzolo shifted his style and focus once again, using local performance artists as actors in two bizarre and semi-autobiographical narrative films, *Caligari's Cure* (1982)—featured in 1983 as part of the Whitney Museum's New American Filmmakers series—and *Added Lessons* (1990). Recent films have marked a return of sorts to his work of the late 1960s—bringing quirky personal views to documentary filmmaking. *I Married a Munchkin* (1994), about Mary Ellen St. Aubin who ran a midget bar on Chicago's South Side, takes its place beside his unusual films from the 1960s and 1970s of a tattooed lady, a wet

T-shirt contest, and other offbeat people and events.

Palazzolo is represented in the film collection of MOMA. In addition to filmmaking, Palazzolo has continued to work in photography and painting. He has taught film at SAIC and is an associate professor in the Department of Human and Public Services at Richard J. Daley College, where he teaches art history and photography. Palazzolo currently lives and works in Oak Park, Illinois. DM

Esther Parada

(Born 1938) Born and raised in Grand Rapids, Michigan, Esther Parada received an MFA from The Pratt Institute in Brooklyn, New York, in 1962. She served as a Peace Corps volunteer art instructor in Bolivia from 1964 to 1966, which fostered a special interest in Latin America.

Returning to the United States, she enrolled in the photography program at ID at IIT, receiving her MS degree in 1971. The next year she began teaching at UIC, where she continues today as a professor of photography.

In 1976, along with Jane Wenger and other women photographers, Parada founded the photography gallery within the Feminist cooperative Artemisia. Although short-lived (it closed after only a year), this gallery was one of the first efforts in Chicago to present in a serious, professional context the work of women photographers. This involvement and the subject matter of her work has led some to label Parada as a political artist. Her photographs, however, have multiple levels of meaning, and focus on the humanity of individuals within the modern global culture. Her works of the mid-1970s, for example, seek to unmask the historical contradictions between what is presented and perceived as "fact" and as "propaganda" in a given cultural context. Her "Overview" series of 1975 shows aerial views of excavated Indian burial sites in the Dickson Mounds in southern Illinois. Not only were these sacred places turned into sites for Western scientific research, they were opened to the public as a tourist attraction. In examining such complex, multicultural situations, Parada's approach in these artworks positions her as a early practitioner of the now widespread contemporary practice of deconstructivism.

Since 1986 Parada has worked almost exclusively with a Macintosh computer, using digital technology to create a number of photo/text or photo/collage works that present a revisionist historical perspective. *Monroe Doctrine, Part One: Theme and Variations* (1987), for example, was generated from a single digitalized image: a 1927 historical photograph of the US Marine Corps officers review-

ing members of the newly formed Nicaraguan National Guard. Embedded in a map of North and South America, this photograph epitomizes the irony of the Monroe Doctrine—our government rejecting old world domination while flexing its own military muscle in this hemisphere.

In 1991 Parada was one of eight artists invited to create a site-specific public artwork at the Königsplatz in Munich. In Chicago in 1993 she participated in Randolph Street Gallery's exhibition "Backtalk" with her project *Who Dis/covers-Who/Discolors*, which uses photographs, video, and printed texts to reveal the efforts of an African-American women's group to honor Jean Baptiste DuSable (founder of Chicago) at the 1933–34 Century of Progress World's Fair, despite the realities of racism. Parada was included in an exhibition of digital photography in Paris in 1992 and has exhibited worldwide between 1990 and 1994. Her work is included in the permanent collections of AIC, MCA, MOMA, and the Museum of Fine Arts in Houston. SK

Ed Paschke

(Born 1939) Ed Paschke is one of the most celebrated artists from Chicago, the city of his birth in 1939 and his home thereafter. After receiving his BFA from SAIC in 1961, Paschke worked as a psychiatric aide and sold spot illustrations to *Playboy* magazine. Drafted into the Army in 1962, Paschke spent two years illustrating weapons manuals and pursuing AWOL soldiers in Louisiana. Following a brief trip to Europe, he returned to Chicago and in 1965 joined a team of draftsmen at the Wilding Studio rendering a map to be used in training astronauts for the Apollo moon mission. Paschke then began work for Silvestri, a display company, painting a Piranesi-style scene on a temporary, first-floor facade of the Carson, Pirie, Scott and Company department store. In 1967 Paschke quit working to have more time to paint; on the GI Bill, he enrolled at SAIC, receiving his MFA in 1970.

At the first "Hairy Who" exhibition at HPAC in 1966, Paschke saw several of his former SAIC colleagues professionally engaged and organized. He assembled his own group of SAIC alumni (Sarah Canright, Edward C. Flood, Robert Guinan, and Richard Wetzel) and exhibited at HPAC in 1968 as the "Nonplussed Some." In 1969, dropping Guinan and Wetzel and adding Don Baum, they exhibited as "Nonplussed Some: Some More"; in 1970 they merged with some Hairy Who artists as "Marriage Chicago Style"

(Wirsum, Rossi, Paschke, Rocca, Flood, Canright); and in 1971 the same three couples exhibited as "Chicago Antigua." Although this exhibition history often has associated Paschke with the Chicago Imagists, his subject matter and almost Photorealist style sets him apart from this group.

Like many Pop artists of the 1960s, Paschke worked from various media images, though culled from tabloids, sports papers, and pornographic magazines, to portray inhabitants from the fringes of society that were subjects rare to Pop art. With the aid of an overhead projector, Paschke combined disparate elements into one composition, painted first in black and white and then in color to achieve the luminous, almost electrified, look still characteristic of his canvases. In the early 1970s, Paschke's focus shifted from complex, composite images to solitary figures. A group of object "portraits" feature bulging leather shoes and purses sprouting hair or warts, thereby asserting their origin as skin. Continuing his fascination with bodily embellishments, especially tattoos and fantastical costumes, Paschke began to concentrate on elaborately costumed figures against richly patterned backgrounds, which culminated in a series of fabric abstractions painted in 1976. In the late 1970s, Paschke's work underwent a radical shift from realistic, recognizable individuals to anonymous dandies and elegant women seemingly from the glamorous entertainment world. Spectral bands of color cut through both figure and background, recalling images on a malfunctioning color television. Masked characters with black holes for eyes and mouths point to the spiritual emptiness behind these celluloid images. In the 1980s the electronic disturbances eventually disintegrated Paschke's images, leading him back to more solidified forms with psychological presences and toward an investigation of religion, violence, and sexuality.

Paschke is currently a professor of drawing and painting at Northwestern University, Evanston, Illinois, where he has taught since 1977; he served as chairman of Northwestern's Department of Art Theory and Practice (1980–85) and as acting chairman of their Art Department (1993). His distinguished teaching career began at Meramac College, St. Louis (1970–71); Barat College, Lake Forest, Illinois (1971–77); SAIC (1974–76); and Columbia College, Chicago (1977–78).

Paschke's first retrospective exhibition (1982) was at the Renaissance Society and traveled to the Joslyn Art Museum, Omaha, and the Contemporary Arts Museum, Houston. AIC gave Paschke his second retrospective (1989), which traveled to the Centre Georges Pompidou in Paris and the Dallas Art Museum.

He has also been featured in numerous group exhibitions at MCA, MOMA, and the Whitney Museum of American Art, New York. His work is represented in major American and European museums. He has been represented by Phyllis Kind Gallery since 1977. MM

Jerry Peart

(Born 1948) Jerry Peart was born in Winslow, Arizona, in 1948. He received his BFA from Arizona State University, Tempe, in 1970 and his MFA from Southern Illinois University, Carbondale, in 1972. In that year he moved to Chicago, attracted by the city's thriving community of sculptors, which included John Henry, Richard Hunt, and Steven J. Urry. Asked by Urry to assist on the fabrication and installation of a project, Peart decided to stay in Chicago. He became involved in the sculpture community, and in 1978 helped found ConStruct Gallery, which promoted large-scale public sculpture through exhibitions until its 1983 closing.

Peart works on a monumental scale, frequently outdoors, and often in an urban setting. His large welded and painted sculptures are site-specific. Frequently figurative in subject, the sculptures suggest, through the juxtaposition of materials and form, the industrial and the organic. Peart has allied his work with that of West Coast Funk ceramists like Rudy Autio, David Gilhooly, and Peter Voulkos.

Formally Peart's sculptures unite geometric and organic forms to create energy and movement. The asymmetrical closed and open shapes weave complex compositions that shift with each vantage point. Light bounces off the smooth surfaces to enhance the effect of dynamism. Color may be monochrome or polychrome; Peart frequently combines colors to establish a mood and animate the subject. He places his sculptures directly on the ground to eliminate any barrier between the observer and the artwork. People climb, play, or simply repose upon many of his public pieces.

Peart lives and works in Chicago. He has executed sculptures for numerous sites in the United States, including public commissions for the Illinois Center in Chicago; the City of Toledo, Ohio; Arizona State University, Tempe; and the City of Albuquerque. Peart has been the subject of solo shows at the Mitchell Gallery in Carbondale, Illinois (1972); and in Chicago at the Triforum Gallery (1972), the Walter Kelly Gallery (1974 and 1976), ConStruct (1979), and Richard Gray Gallery (1988 and 1992). His sculptures are in the collections of the Virginia Museum of Fine Arts, Richmond; the

Marion Perkins

Palm Springs Desert Museum, California; the Museum of New Mexico, Albuquerque; and the University of Arizona Museum, Tucson. MF

(1908–1961) Born in 1908 in Charme, Arkansas, Marion Perkins came to Chicago as a young child after the death of his parents. He eventually married, had three children, and took odd jobs to support his family. In the early 1930s, he began his art career under the federally sponsored WPA program. Along with a number of African-American artists and writers, such as Margaret Burroughs, Eldzier Cortor, Charles White, and Richard Wright, Perkins was involved in the founding of the South Side Community Art Center.

Perkins, largely self-taught, became known for his direct carving in stone, though he also used clay and wood. His subject matter remained figurative throughout his career and was steadfastly devoted to the black experience. Most works are of a small or medium size and are generalized depictions of African-American people, some with eyes closed, some with eyes staring directly at the viewer. Though many seem to contain their emotions proudly, a few express suffering through clenched fists or gaping mouths with heads tilted upward. A social advocate, Perkins spoke out in favor of the importance of reconnecting with Africa and the creation of a black aesthetic that consciously eschewed Western standards. He lectured around the nation, in places such as the first Black Artists Conference at Atlanta University (c. 1960), about the social responsibility of the artist and the necessity of expressing the unique black cultural heritage.

Perkins's sculptures were included in a number of AIC's C & V shows (1948, 1949, 1951, and 1952), at which he won several prizes. His poignant marble head *Man of Sorrows* (1951) won the Pauline Palmer Purchase Prize and is now in the collection of AIC. In 1956 he was awarded the New Talent Award sponsored by *Art in America* and won first prize at the "Atlanta University Art Exhibit." Perkins's sculptures were shown numerous times in Chicago at the South Side Community Art Center and at the DuSable Museum of African American History, as well as at the Contemporary Art Workshop (1959) and the Second and Third Annual Exposition, Negro in Business and Culture (1960 and 1961), among many others. Perkins died in 1961. SB

Hirsch Perlman

(Born 1960) Hirsch Perlman's work analyzes the rupture between language and image and the resultant breakdown of representation. Born in Chicago in 1960, Perlman attended Yale University, receiving a BA degree in architecture in 1982. Two of Perlman's most important early exhibitions were the "Dull Edge" group show at Randolph Street Gallery and a pairing with Los Angeles artist Charles Ray at Feature, both in Chicago in 1986. The former was one of the first exhibitions in which Perlman was shown with artists such as Tony Tasset and Jeanne Dunning, who were working in a comparable Conceptual idiom. Perlman's exhibition at Feature marked the beginning of a long association with the gallery.

Reading Modernist architecture through various strains of critical theory, Perlman in his early work used elements of photography, sculpture, and text to question the relationship between language, image, and representation in our reception of the "International Style" of the twentieth century. His 1988 installation at the Renaissance Society, for example, centered on representations of the house designed by the philosopher Ludwig Wittgenstein in 1928. Subsequent works introduced video to represent people speaking from varied texts, intensifying the disparity of language, image, and text in Perlman's work and, by extension, in the world outside. In the 1994 exhibition at MCA "Radical Scavenger(s): The Conceptual Vernacular in Recent American Art," Perlman showed a series of works based on the practice and techniques of interrogation.

Perlman continues to exhibit at Feature in New York as well as at Donald Young Gallery in Seattle—both galleries having represented Perlman when they were located in Chicago. His work was presented in the Whitney Biennial, New York (1989); "The Photography of Invention: American Pictures of the 1980s," National Museum of American Art, Washington, DC (1989); and in the Venice Biennale in the "Aperto" exhibition (1993). Perlman has shown frequently in Europe—in keeping with the internationalism of this generation of Chicago artists—with solo exhibitions at Galerie Claire Burrus in Paris (1988, 1991, and 1993), the Shedhalle in Zurich (1990), and at Monika Spruth Galerie in Cologne (1991 and 1994). Perlman relocated to Los Angeles in 1995. DM

Dan Peterman

(Born 1960) Dan Peterman is one of the key members of the group of internationally focused, Chicago-based Conceptual artists of the 1980s. Peterman was born in 1960 in Minneapolis. He received his undergraduate degree at the University of Wisconsin-Eau Claire, and moved to Chicago in 1983 to study with Robert C. Peters at the University of Chicago, where he received his MFA degree in 1986.

Peterman works with ideas about recycling systems and recycled materials. Since his student days, he has kept a studio within The Resource Center, a recycling center on the border of Chicago's Hyde Park and Woodlawn neighborhoods. Although Peterman is often written about as an "environmental artist," his intent is far more encompassing than a simple condemnation of man's folly; he seeks to reveal processes. Particularly fascinating to the artist are the discrepancies between the complex systems of design, manufacturing, and distribution that characterize consumer products, and the much less sophisticated efforts to deal with the waste that these products all too quickly become. The artist takes a nonjudgmental approach; human efforts to deal with human problems form a rich resource for the artist to engage the viewer personally in "real world" Conceptual art.

Peterman often uses modest objects to elucidate interlocking social, political, and personal systems that make up life in the modern world. Aluminum, plastics, glass, and recycling systems including composting, water purification, and the removal of toxic contaminants have all been the subject of works or series. Aluminum cans, for example, inspired a number of works. For *Medium of Exchange* (1987), Peterman melted aluminum cans to make simple castings that were placed in various sites around the city and tracked, via a numbering system, when they were brought into recycling centers. For *Composition en plein air/Composition Out of Doors* (1989), Peterman placed 800 pounds of crushed aluminum cans on a shipping pallet for an exhibition at SAIC. The piece's French title and glistening surface were droll references to the famous Impressionist collections of the adjacent AIC. *Model Efficiency* (1989) was a "model" homeless shelter constructed from blocks of crushed aluminum cans. Recycled plastics have provided a rich source of material for Peterman in the early 1990s, and more recently he has begun explorations of the way in which gaseous emissions, such as sulfur dioxide, are recycled.

Peterman has exhibited extensively in Europe, New York, and Chicago, especially at Randolph Street Gallery, where he has also participated in organizing exhibitions. He was featured in the 1989 Sculpture Chicago and was included in the 1993 Venice Biennale. He received a one-person exhibition at MCA in 1995. LW

Robert C. Peters

(Born 1938) Robert Peters has developed a densely layered and esoteric variety of Conceptual installation and performance art in Chicago since the early 1970s. Born in 1938 in Oakland, California, Peters received his BS in forestry from the University of California at Berkeley in 1960 and his MS in forestry, with a concentration in biometrics, from Yale University the following year. Peters returned to get his BFA from the University of Washington at Seattle in 1967, and his MFA in painting and sculpture from the University of California at Santa Barbara in 1970. He moved to Chicago in 1971 to teach at SAIC, and in 1974 went to England on a Fulbright Grant and taught art in Manchester.

Upon his return to Chicago the following year, Peters took a teaching position in the Art Department at the University of Chicago, where his Protean, Conceptual style has influenced a generation of artists currently working in Chicago. His work has been heavily informed by Dada, Fluxus, and the writings of Bertolt Brecht, Allan Kaprow, and John Cage. A major early work for Peters was a proposal for a "memorial garden" to commemorate the mayor for the 1978 exhibition "Daley's Tomb," curated by Jerry Saltz at N.A.M.E. Gallery. It provided an implicit critique of Daley's powerful sway over city politics. Peters's first collaborative performance of 1978, *The Complete and Unabridged History of All Art* (with Nick Despota and Bob Gottlieb), explored systems of classification through events such as asking an audience member on arrival whether he/she wished to sit on the men's or women's side. In *A Pinewood Derby* (1980), also performed at N.A.M.E. with Despota and Tom Mapp, the artists put their $100 honorarium on the wall for the audience to take, putting the "performance" into the hands of the audience.

Peters's most complex and extravagant work to date is *CHICAGO: Although Marco Polo Never Heard of Chicago Its Story Really Begins With Him*, an installation/performance at MCA in 1982. This work incorporated sound, text, images, and various artifacts from around the city and dealt with the perceptions and reality of how the diversity and distinct flavor of the city are constructed by the social, political, and cultural "contracts" entered into by both residents and outsiders. The museum patron viewed such "icons" as samples of bread from bakeries in different ethnic neighborhoods

or heard a tape of a linguist pronouncing words in the Chicago dialect. *Money*, a smaller-scale multimedia installation done in a Chicago storefront at State and Hubbard streets, confronted pedestrians on the street, involving them in a meditation on money and its curious position in our culture.

Peters has exhibited in various group shows, including "Images for Human Conduct" at MCA in 1987 and "Present at the Creation" at The Chicago Public Library Cultural Center in 1989. Peters also participated in the 1993 Sculpture Chicago project "Culture in Action." In this work, titled *Naming Others: Manufacturing Yourself*, Peters investigated the limits of verbal interaction between communities in Chicago by creating an 800 number to talk to people about certain politically charged words or phrases regarding their cultural identity. DM

John Phillips

(Born 1953) John Phillips takes into account the history of abstract painting and infuses it with his passion for 1950s rhythm-and-blues. Born in Chicago in 1953, Phillips was raised in the suburbs and grew up with a love for chess, sailing, and music. He attended the University of Colorado, Boulder, and was pre-med for three years before changing his major to art and receiving his BFA in 1975. Phillips returned to Chicago and obtained his MFA from SAIC in 1979. He spent a year in New York as a fellow with the Independent Study Program of the Whitney Museum of American Art (1978). Back in Chicago, Phillips hosted one of the first huge "art parties" in his loft following HPAC's "Non-Naive" exhibition in 1980. He was one of eight artists working with day-glo paint and black or ultra-violet light included in the privately organized, and infamous, "Black Light-Planet Picasso" exhibition in 1981. Phillips continues to live in Chicago, where he also works as an architectural restorer with his wife, artist Jo Hormuth. He is a serious collector of postwar music and has played his collection in clubs as a disc jockey for fifteen years.

From 1978 to 1986 Phillips created ambitiously sized acrylic paintings (up to ten-by-sixteen feet) of geometric abstractions. His canvases of odd-shaped geometric forms rendered in bright, solid colors have funky titles like *Zombie Dance* (1981) and *Heebie Jeebies* (1982), and reveal the artist's concern with issues of color, form, and composition. By the mid-1980s the number of formal elements, along with the scale, had been reduced. The glossy color of these works was achieved by incorporating

acrylic, enamel, encaustic, oil, and industrial paints on panels. Phillips's interest at the time was balancing the component parts, mostly ovals, sweeping commalike arcs, and wide bands of color, into a compact space. A fusion of Pop and Cubist rhythms, Phillips's arrangements are fixed, yet seem in constant flux.

Renovating a building in 1987 gave Phillips time off from his art-making. He returned with the "scroll" or ribbon motif that continues to dominate his work. The scrolls began as ready-made computer "clip art." Transformed into paintings, usually with at least four layers of paint, the undulating scrolls snake, knot, and unfurl over the surface, taking on a life of their own and becoming figurative elements dancing through the composition. The artificial color, black outlines, and cartoonish Abstract-Expressionist gestures recall Pop art, especially the works of Roy Lichtenstein. In reference to his most recent work, Phillips stated, "if Barnett Newman had a lava lamp, it might look like one of my paintings."

Since his first solo exhibition, at Barbara Balkin Gallery, Chicago, in 1981, Phillips has had one-person shows in Chicago at One Illinois Center (1983 and 1992); Marianne Deson Gallery (1987); Dart Gallery (1992); and The University Club (1993). Group exhibitions include "Critical Perspectives," P.S. 1, New York (1982); "Emerging," the Renaissance Society, Chicago (1983); "Formal Abstraction," N.A.M.E. Gallery, Chicago (1984); C & V show, AIC (1985); "In Full Effect," White Columns, New York (1991); "Chicago Abstract Painters," Evanston Art Center, Illinois (1995); and "Plane Speak: Contemporary Abstraction in Illinois," Chicago Cultural Center (1996). MM

Frank Piatek

(Born 1944) A native Chicagoan, Frank (Francis) Piatek has played a crucial role in the development and refinement of abstract painting in Chicago. His carefully rendered, biomorphic compositions illustrate the dialectical relationship that has continued to exist between abstraction and figuration—styles that have very distinct and idiosyncratic traditions in Chicago. Displaying neither the formal Modernism associated with The New Bauhaus nor the figurative expressiveness of the Imagists, Piatek's paintings are more like a synthesis of both, prompting critic Andy Argy to remark that "they are not quite non-objective, since they resemble objects; not quite abstract, since they do not derive from anything else, and not quite representational, since they exist as independent entities."

While he was still an undergraduate, Piatek's work met with critical approval. He received his BFA from SAIC in 1967; that same year SAIC awarded him the

Francis Ryerson Traveling Fellowship, which he used to study in Europe. In 1968 his work was exhibited in the Whitney Museum of American Art Annual in New York, and in 1969 he had a one-person show at HPAC. During this time he also established a relationship with the Phyllis Kind Gallery, where he subsequently had a solo exhibition in 1972.

Piatek's first paintings done as a student at SAIC feature bending stripes, precursors to the writhing tubular forms that have become his trademark. These early pieces, painted in acrylic on shaped canvases, were made in direct response to the stripe paintings of Frank Stella; however, whereas Stella's lines were meant to emphasize the flatness of the picture plane and thereby its "objectness," Piatek's tubular forms affirmed painting as an illusionistic process. That his images alluded to objects in the real world, such as worms, phalluses, or metal tubes, was due to his disenchantment with the Minimalist credo that art should be pure and devoid of content, and a result of his interest in traditional pictorial modeling. In the early 1970s Piatek temporarily interrupted the illusionistic abstraction for which he had become well known, in order to concentrate on his drawing skills. During this time he also severed his ties with the Phyllis Kind Gallery. In 1973–74 he received a one-year teaching appointment at Washington University in St. Louis, where he not only taught drawing but focused more on his own craft. As he honed his skills, Piatek also became intrigued by the history of myth and the collective unconscious, particularly the writings of Carl Jung. This interest spawned a body of work featuring drawings of spiders and trees, as well as carvings of snakes and podlike sarcophagi, which he exhibited at N.A.M.E. Gallery in 1975.

Since 1976 Piatek has taught at SAIC, where he has developed a course in the materials and techniques of painting. In 1981 he joined three other nonfigurative painters, William Conger, Miyoko Ito, and Richard Loving, to form a group, often called the "Allusive Abstractionists," that sought to explore and support their common interest in form as metaphor. CES

Kerig Pope

(Born 1935) Born in Waukesha, Wisconsin, Kerig Pope attended college at SAIC, receiving his BFA in painting in 1958. While at SAIC, Pope was influenced by art-history professors Kathleen Blackshear and Whitney Halstead, drawing professor Tom Kapsalis, and painting professor Boris Margo. He also cultivated friendships with fellow artists Richard

puryear—raya puryear—

Hunt, Irving Petlin, Robert Barnes, Ray Yoshida, and H. C. Westermann.

Heavily influenced by Surrealists such as Matta, Pope was part of the Imagist movement in Chicago. Concerned with bringing abstract shapes to life, Pope's oil paintings feature oddly constructed, biomorphic characters in whimsical settings. His imagery is largely based on growing forms such as roots, stems, and buds. Carefully chosen, often humorous titles allude to the extended metaphors of the images.

Pope's work has been included in group shows at MCA, the Bienal de São Paulo of 1973, the Whitney Museum of American Art in New York, HPAC, and the Museo de Arte Moderno in Mexico City. The Evanston Art Center, Illinois, hosted a retrospective of his work in 1971. Permanent collections include AIC, MCA, the National Museum of American Art in Washington, DC, and the Smart Museum in Chicago. Pope has been the managing art director at *Playboy* magazine in Chicago for the past thirty years. AF

Martin Puryear

(Born 1941) Martin Puryear was born in 1941 in Washington, DC. In 1963, after receiving a BFA from The Catholic University of America in his native city, he spent two years in the Peace Corps in Sierra Leone. Subsequently he studied printmaking for two years at the Swedish Royal Academy of Art in Stockholm. In 1971, after study with such major American painters and sculptors as Al Held, Robert Morris, and Richard Serra, Puryear received an MFA in sculpture from Yale University. He subsequently taught at Fisk University, Nashville, and at the University of Maryland, College Park, before moving to Chicago in 1978 (after a fire destroyed the Brooklyn studio he had kept since 1973) to teach at UIC. Upon his departure in 1990, Puryear left behind an extraordinary legacy as a teacher and role model. It was during Puryear's tenure that UIC's graduate program began to attract deeply committed students from around the nation.

Puryear gained international recognition as a sculptor during his years in Chicago. Combining lessons learned from such disparate sources as printmaking, the traditional arts of West Africa, modern Danish furniture, and the severe formalist aesthetics of his Yale education, Puryear created a complex and highly personal sculptural vocabulary. Building works by hand—as opposed to carving or casting his sculpture—Puryear integrates the often sharp distinctions made between arts and crafts by utilizing primary forms but emphasizing the tangible evidence of his working process. The precision of his craft and the discipline of his process lend an extraordinary integrity to his works, which range in scale from small, gallery pieces to large installations and public works, such as *Bodark Arc* (1982) in The Nathan Manilow Sculpture Park at Governors State University, University Park, Illinois, or *Knoll for NOAA* (1983) at the National Oceanic and Atmospheric Administration building in Seattle. His materials range from numerous kinds of wood, both natural and milled, to metals, especially copper and steel mesh, to leather, rattan, and gourds—and often dictate not only his method for a particular work, but the look of the piece as well.

Puryear's subject matter reveals a personal identification with heroic figures or forms. In 1980 Puryear installed the ambitious *Equation for Jim Beckwourth* at MCA. James Beckwourth, a mid-eighteenth-century emancipated slave, had a colorful history: he made expeditions to California during the Gold Rush, participated in the Mexican War of 1846–48 and the Cheyenne War of 1868, married a Crow Indian woman, and was made a chief. Beckwourth's journey from servitude to leadership intrigued Puryear, who selected natural materials to create a powerful installation that referred to origins, transitions, and destinations. The elements used in this important early work reappeared in subsequent exhibitions, such as Puryear's 1991 retrospective at AIC.

Themes of migration and survival through flight occur frequently in Puryear's work, expressed particularly by his use of a yurt (a nomadic tent) and a falcon. Metaphorically, the yurt can indicate both mobility and security, while the bird symbolizes freedom, and personally for the African-American artist, racial difference as it ranges in shade from black to white according to the regions it inhabits. These symbols stand in many ways as metaphors for the artist's own experiences.

Puryear has received numerous public commissions, awards and honors, and exhibitions. His work is included in such museum collections as AIC; MCA; the Milwaukee Art Museum; the St. Louis Art Museum; the Solomon R. Guggenheim Museum and the Whitney Museum of American Art, New York; and the National Gallery of Art, Washington, DC. His public works include pieces at the River Road station on the O'Hare Rapid Transit Line in Chicago and at the Walker Art Center Sculpture Garden, Minneapolis. He received a John D. and Catherine T. MacArthur Foundation Fellowship in 1989, a Louis Comfort Tiffany Grant in 1982, and a John S. Guggenheim Memorial Foundation Grant, also in 1982. Puryear was the sole US representative to the 1989 São Paulo Bienal and was awarded the grand prize. NW

Carmela Rago

(Born 1953) Carmela Rago has been one of the stalwarts of the Chicago performance art scene, both as an artist and as a critic. Rago was born in Chicago in 1953. Her family life was divided between the literary world of her father, Henry Rago, poet and editor of *Poetry* magazine, and the working-class life of her Italian relatives on the West Side of the city. After graduating from Francis Parker Grammar and High School in Chicago, she attended Bennington College in Vermont (1973–75). Rago subsequently traveled and worked in Southern California, returning to Chicago to attend SAIC, where she received her BFA in 1979. She began performing in public with her 1977 piece *I Am, I'm Jealous* at N.A.M.E. Gallery, a collaboration with James Byrne incorporating performers and video.

Rago performed frequently from the late 1970s to the early 1980s. Early performances consisted of both solo and collaborative efforts, the latter with friends and colleagues such as Kate Cormack, Harvey Weiss, and Philip Yenawine. Rago's work at this time was a combination of literary elements and dance and movement techniques. Eventually, character-based monologues began to dominate her performances, culminating in *Living in the Midwest* (1984). Creating the character Carla Bulgari from various models in her family background, Rago aimed to investigate the existence of a lonely Italian housewife with a curious and unexpectedly enlightening view of life. Rago debuted *Living in the Midwest* at MoMing in Chicago and took the show to New York and Cleveland. She toured often with James Grigsby, the duo billing themselves as "A Couple from Chicago."

During the mid-1980s, Rago took a position as the director of communications for a large insurance association. Having grown tired of the rigors of performing and working her day job, in 1988 she stopped performing. She returned to the stage in 1991 with her performance *Real Life—Stories from the Real World*, based largely on her experiences in the corporate world. Since 1992 Rago has written performance criticism for the *Reader* and the *Chicago Tribune*. She teaches both in the division of Continuing Studies at SAIC and at various elementary schools in Chicago. DM

Christina **Ramberg**

(1946–1995) Although she never identified herself closely with any group, Christina Ramberg was associated with the Chicago Imagists ever since she first exhibited at HPAC in 1968 in the first "False Image" exhibition with Roger Brown, Philip Hanson, and Eleanor Dube. Ramberg is best known for her meticulously finished paintings focusing on the psychological exploration of women's perceptions of their own bodies. She was born in Fort Campbell, Kentucky, in 1946 and attended SAIC, receiving her BFA in 1968 and an MFA in 1973. She was married to Hanson, and her early paintings shared a visual affinity with his work. Ramberg was chairperson of SAIC's Painting and Drawing Department from 1985 to 1989, and taught there for many years until a debilitating illness prevented her from working and eventually resulted in her death in 1995.

Throughout her career Ramberg produced technically proficient paintings of fragmented figures. Her paintings from 1968 through the mid-1970s are small-scale, bluntly cropped, partial views of female anatomy, showing body parts tightly corseted or bound. Her initial focus was on the head seen from the back or partially veiled with elaborate hairstyles, but by 1971 her interest had shifted to the upper torso, attired in assorted shaping or constraining undergarments, perhaps inspired by her collection of advertisements for underwear foundations. Ramberg's figures suggest stereotypical images from girlie magazines, often becoming sinister fetishes obliterating the individual. But to construe Ramberg's work as strict Feminist abhorrence of the subjugation of women is to deny its multiplicity of interpretive possibilities. By 1972, as the size of her paintings increased, the garments and accessories decreased, and the figure metamorphosized into a more structural component. A series of large figure paintings from 1974–81 show the body tightly wrapped and bound. During this time she also experimented with different objects, such as chair backs, lamps, vases, and outer clothing, whose forms are structurally analogous to parts of the body. The figures became more androgynous, and the focus shifted to patterns in hair braiding and wood graining. Ramberg experienced a major shift in the early 1980s when she investigated pattern in dazzling, large-scale quilts, later returning to small panel painting. She restricted herself to a grisaille palette, and switched from painting acrylic on Masonite to canvas, which allowed for a brushy, more atmospheric, background. Although these symmetrical compositions of geometric and linear structures recall schematic torsos, they are less legible as anatomy and more open-ended, both formally and conceptually.

Ramberg's work was included in "Don Baum Says: `Chicago Needs Famous Artists,'" MCA (1969); "Spirit of the Comics," Institute of Contemporary Art, University of Pennsylvania, Philadelphia (1969); C & V exhibitions, AIC (1969, 1974, and 1977); "Made in Chicago," XII Bienal de São Paulo (1973); the 1973 and 1979 biennials at the Whitney Museum of American Art, New York; "The Figurative Tradition in American Art," Whitney Museum (1980); the traveling exhibition "Who Chicago?," Ceolfrith Gallery, Sunderland Arts Centre, England (1980); and "Chicago Imagism: A 25 Year Survey," Davenport Museum of Art, Iowa (1994). Ramberg was given a retrospective at Chicago's Renaissance Society in 1988. Her work has been represented by Phyllis Kind Gallery, Chicago and New York, since 1974. MM

Daniel **Ramirez**

(Born 1941) Chicago native Daniel Ramirez, also known since the 1980s by the name Daniel Smajo-Ramirez, which honors his mother, has been one of the city's leading champions of abstract painting since the mid-1970s. Along with artists as disparate as Miyoko Ito, Frank Piatek, and William Conger, Ramirez upholds a tradition of nonrepresentational painting that has flourished in Chicago alongside its better-known figurative counterpart since the 1950s. After a short stint as a truck driver hauling steel at a mill, Ramirez at age thirty-two enrolled at UIC to study art. Immediately after receiving his BA in painting in 1975, he pursued an MFA from the University of Chicago (1975–77). He emerged from graduate school with a taut visual language of severely geometric forms, a Minimalist treatment of color, and a compositional tendency toward Chicago Bauhaus Constructivism.

In his paintings Ramirez is always careful to maintain an equilibrium of color, line, shape, and tone. As his work evolved, black, blue, green, and orange modulated lines began to divide and define the compositions, serving both as borders that enclose the larger shapes within the painting and as narrow, tapering demarcations that separate the canvas into vertical rectangles. By 1976 the paintings had increased dramatically from three feet square to eight-by-twelve feet. Ramirez also began to combine canvases, adding triangular sections to create trapezoidal paintings as well as graduated graphite panels to his painted canvases.

Contrary to his aloof and cerebral aesthetic, however, Ramirez's paintings reflect his personal responses to the world and express extreme emotions such as anguish, tragedy, or spiritual rapture. For Ramirez, form, line, and color convey a visual harmony in their relationships, but they must also reveal the experiences of the soul. He often takes his inspiration from music or philosophy. His paintings from the late 1970s entitled *TL-P* are a direct response to the writings in Austrian philosopher Ludwig Wittgenstein's *Tractatus Logico-Philosophicus*. A 1980 series of etchings is a response to the music of French composer Olivier Messiaen: the rich purples are meant to reveal the extent of the artist's soul and to evoke religious convictions. Ramirez's most recent works, completed since he relocated to Wisconsin in 1988, combine his characteristic formalism with expressively crafted sculptural elements.

Ramirez taught at UIC from 1978 until 1988; he now teaches at the University of Wisconsin, Madison. For over two decades his work has been widely exhibited, including a number of one-person shows at Roy Boyd Gallery in both Chicago and Los Angeles. Chicago's Renaissance Society held a one-person exhibition of Ramirez's paintings in 1979, and AIC featured a suite of Ramirez's intaglio prints in "Twenty Contemplations on the Infant Jesus: An Homage to Olivier Messiaen" in 1981. Ramirez's group exhibitions include "Recent Masterpieces of Chicago Art" at The Chicago Public Library Cultural Center (1977); C & V show at AIC (1978); "Chicago: Some Other Traditions," Madison Art Center, Wisconsin (1983); "Abstract/ Symbol/ Image: A Revision" at HPAC (1984); "¡Adivina! Chicago Latino Expressions" at the Mexican Fine Arts Center Museum, Chicago, and Museo de Arte Moderna, Mexico City (1988); and "Post-Minimalism and the Spiritual: Four Chicago Artists" at The Museum of Contemporary Religious Art, St. Louis University (1994). EKW

Ed **Rankus**

(Born 1953) The solo and collaborative work of video artist Ed Rankus has received critical attention both in Chicago and internationally, confirming his status as one of the premier video artists in the city.

Rankus was born in Chicago in 1953. As a teenager he began to experiment with his father's darkroom, still cameras, and 8mm filmmaking equipment. Rankus and his friends developed a small film club, creating numerous short dramatic films. He developed his interest in film and other media in college, receiving his BA in photography, filmmaking, and video production at UIC in 1975, and his MFA in video and audio production at SAIC in 1977.

Rankus's first major video project was *AlienNATION* (1979), a collaborative piece with fellow video artists Barbara Latham and John Manning. Noted critical theorist Frederic Jameson devoted a significant amount of attention to the work in the "video" chapter of his 1991 text *Postmodernism, or the Cultural Logic of Late Capitalism*. The video was screened at MCA and MOMA, and is in the permanent collection of the Musée National d'Art Moderne, Paris. It has been described as a "hipster's Star Trek" by the *Village Voice* for its irreverent reworking of found footage from science-fiction movies. Rankus's solo video projects of the 1980s, *Naked Doom* (1983) and *She Heard Voices* (1986), are haunting, *film-noir* visualizations of psychological torment and duress. Both were screened internationally in various museums and film and video festivals.

In recent years Rankus has devoted much of his time to working as an instructor in video production at DePaul University, Chicago, and SAIC. With filmmaker Hans Schaal, he has worked since 1989 as a video producer associated with the Center for Instructional Support at DePaul University. In 1995 Rankus released his video work *Nerve Language*, an eerily surreal piece whose juxtapositions of objects, bodies, and visual effects are psychologically suggestive and create an overall sense of dread. It was screened at the 14th American Film Institute National Video Festival in Los Angeles and at Chicago Filmmakers in the autumn of 1995. DM

Marcos **Raya**

(Born 1948) Since immigrating to the United States in 1964, Marcos Raya has worked as an activist in the Chicano movement, a muralist, an arts educator, and a studio artist. Born in the village of Irapuato in the rural Guanajuato region of Mexico, Raya was sixteen when he came to live with his mother, a Springfield, Illinois, native who had moved to the Little Italy neighborhood on Chicago's Near South Side after leaving Raya's father. As a child in Mexico, Raya had been deeply impressed when he met Jose Chavez Morado, one of the muralists of the great period of Mexican muralists that included Diego Rivera, Jose Clemente Orozco, and David Alfaro Siqueiros. In high school in Chicago, an art teacher further sparked Raya's interest in art and he began taking courses at SAIC. Chosen in 1967 for a scholarship to the Windsor Mountain preparatory school in Lenox, Massachusetts, through Upward Bound, a program for disadvantaged inner-city youth, Raya was able to study painting and visit New York's great museums regularly. Facing the draft, he left the United States in 1968 and returned to Mexico, where he became involved in the student protest movement that was sweeping that country. A year later he returned to the United States, and after a year's residence in Santa Fe, he moved back to Chicago where he painted his first mural, *We Shall Overcome the Ruins of Fascism*, inside a barbershop on the corner of Taylor and Racine streets in 1970. Active now in the Chicano political movement, Raya took a studio in West Pilsen, a predominantly Mexican-American neighborhood on Chicago's Near South Side, and became involved with Casa Aztlán, a community center.

While heavily involved in painting community murals such as *A la esperanza (Towards Hope)* (1979), with Jaime Longoria, Malú Ortego y Alberro, José Oscar Moya, and Salvador Vega (on the Laflin Street wall of Benito Juárez High School), and *Prevent World War III* (1980), with members of the Chicago Mural Group and Aurelio Díaz Alfaro and Carlos Cortéz (on the Burlington Railroad abutment on 18th Street and Western Avenue), Raya was also leading a self-destructive, dark existence that he taps in his powerful studio works. Illness, alcoholism, and street people are often-repeated themes, and unusual self-portraits, painted as if from within the artist's skull looking out through his eyes or as a dog (referring to what the artist calls his "dog days"), are also common motifs. The artist additionally works in an assemblage method, creating installation works that combine altered furniture, objects, paintings, and items that serve as *retablos*.

Raya has exhibited his studio works extensively, including in the traveling exhibitions "Chicano Art: Resistance and Affirmation" (1990), organized by the Wight Art Gallery, University of California, Los Angeles; "Chicano Codices" (1992) and "Ceremony of Spirit" (1994), organized by The Mexican Museum, San Francisco; and "Art of the Other Mexico" (1993), organized by The Mexican Fine Arts Center Museum, Chicago. He has also exhibited locally in numerous group exhibitions, and had a solo exhibition at The Mexican Fine Arts Center Museum in 1989. His mural work has been featured in shows in Germany, France, and locally, most recently in the "Healing Walls" exhibition at the Illinois Art Gallery, Chicago, in 1995. LW

Richard Rezac (Born 1952) Sculptor Richard Rezac was born in 1952 in Lincoln, Nebraska. After receiving his BFA degree from Pacific Northwest College of Art, Portland, in 1974, he joined the area's expanding art scene, cofounding and exhibiting at the alternative space Blackfish Gallery in Portland. In 1980 he returned to school, receiving an MFA in 1982 from the Maryland Institute, College of Art in Baltimore. He returned to Portland to teach and exhibit for two years. In 1985, with his wife, Julia Fish, a painter he had met in Portland, Rezac decided to relocate to Chicago, where he began exhibiting alongside such as-yet-unknown figures as Jeff Koons, Charles Ray, and Tony Tasset in the newly established and influential Feature gallery.

This exhibition context colored the initial reception of Rezac's work: he was often shown in contexts with Chicago's Neo-Conceptual artists emerging in the mid-1980s. Rezac, however, acknowledges his debt to such mid-century movements as Minimalism, and he extends this vision without ironic or theoretical commentary, common features of Neo-Conceptualism. "Balance" is the essential word in any description of Rezac's sculpture, and the artist describes the search for balance as his primary motivation. Reflecting his interest in Minimalism, Rezac has utilized all aspects of the exhibition space—the so-called "white cube"—the floor, the wall, the corners. Among his early works, which were often realized in such fragile materials as plaster, is the often-exhibited and reproduced work *Departure* (1983), which features two stylized foot shapes atop one another and lying sideways on the floor. Later works feature an extraordinary range of sculpture materials—from the traditional, such as cast iron and bronze, steel, and wood—to the less typical ceramic tile, silk, and cast concrete. Rezac's work is human-scale and has its origins in often-recognizable human forms, such as body parts, and in other natural forms, such as the course of a river. A quiet humanity characterizes the work.

Rezac has earned considerable national stature. He has shown widely, especially on the Northwest Coast, having been the subject of a traveling solo exhibition organized by Washington State University Museum of Art in Pullman in 1976. He also has received one-person exhibitions, in 1989 at Artgarden in Amsterdam, and in 1990 at MCA. LW

Suellen Rocca (Born 1943) Suellen Rocca received her BFA from SAIC in 1964, which put her career a few years ahead of those of her fellow Hairy Who artists (Art Green, Gladys Nilsson, Jim Nutt, and Karl Wirsum), who burst onto the scene in 1966 in the first of three lively, irreverent exhibitions at HPAC. Rocca's early work was also featured in the 1965, 1967, and 1968 C & V exhibitions at AIC.

Rocca's paintings of the 1960s were seminal in establishing the formal aspects of what would become popularly known as Chicago Imagism: an exacting yet eccentric drawing style; personal imagery; the overlaying of elements within complex, flattened spaces; high color; and objectlike paintings or actual painted objects, such as mattresses. Particular to her own work is her personalized vocabulary of images related to women, and in specific, adolescent girls—wigs, purses, jewelry, plants, poodles, female models, dancing figures, and so on, often adapted directly from popular magazines. Her dancing couple motif was from an advertisement for the Arthur Murray Dances Studios; jewelry was drawn from jewelers' catalogues. Rocca's early work has a startling freshness and vitality, particularly in light of present concerns in the contemporary art world relating to Feminism, gender roles, and the common use of advertising and popular cultural imagery in art.

Rocca left Chicago in 1972, when her work was becoming widely known through exhibitions such as "What They're Up to in Chicago," organized by the Extension Service of the National Gallery of Canada, Ottawa (1972), which toured Canada. Living in Walnut Creek, California, in the East San Francisco Bay area, she stopped working as an artist for almost a decade. Her early achievements became increasingly overshadowed by the continuing production of her fellow Imagists. In 1981, the year her work was included in "Who Chicago?," organized by the Ceolfrith Gallery, Sunderland Arts Centre, England, which toured the British Isles, Rocca returned to Chicago and again took up her career, concentrating primarily on drawings. She became an instructor at SAIC's Division of Continuing Studies and Special Programs, where she still teaches. She also worked as an instructor at Elmhurst College, Illinois, from 1983 to 1995. Rocca was hired as a teaching artist for Art Resources in Teaching (ART), an organization begun in 1894 as a program of Jane Addams's Hull House which sends professional artists primarily into Chicago public elementary schools; in 1993 Rocca became ART's program director. Rocca has been represented by Phyllis Kind Gallery, Chicago, since its founding. Most recently she was included in the 1994 "Chicago Imagism: A 25 Year Survey" at Davenport Museum of Art, Iowa. LW

Arnaldo Roche Rabell (Born 1955) Arnaldo Roche Rabell, known as Roche, although variously published as "Roche-Rabell" or simply "Arnaldo Roche," was born in 1955 in Santurce, Puerto Rico. He studied architecture at the University of Puerto Rico before moving to Chicago to attend SAIC, where he received both his BFA and MFA degrees, in 1982 and 1984, respectively. At SAIC he found a sympathetic supporter in Robert Loescher, a noted historian of Hispanic art, and perfected his painting style in study with Ray Yoshida, a figure associated with the Imagists. While still in graduate school he was recognized as an important talent. His large-scale, abstracted figurative works were associated with the Chicago Neo-Expressionism that had emerged in the early 1980s. An important early showing was in HPAC's "The Big Pitcher: 20 Years of the Abstracted Figure in Chicago Art" (1983), which also featured such established Chicago figures as Phyllis Bramson, Paul LaMantia, and Karl Wirsum.

Roche, however, defies labels such as "Expressionist." His early technique included *frottage*—a rubbing process favored by the Surrealists—yet Roche used the human body as the frottaged object. The result was outsized, strangely flattened figures that bear superficial similarity to Jean Dubuffet's "l'art brut" style, thus perhaps explaining Roche's immediate success with Chicago's collectors. Living half the year in Chicago and half the year in his native Puerto Rico, Roche quickly established himself nationally as a leading Hispanic painter. He has been included in such major surveys as MOMA's "Latin American Artists of the Twentieth Century" (1992). Roche's heritage is indeed an important part of his iconography. He refers to Puerto Rico and his upbringing through symbols, titles, and by using dreams and myths as subject matter, interweaving the frottage portraits and his self-portraits with lush vegetation.

In the 1990s Roche, who had always used instruments other than brushes to apply his paint, began exposing underlying layers of paint through a scraping technique similar to that used by Leon Golub. The result is a toned-down palette and a more graphic image similar to a woodblock print. He has also moved from the personal to more universal themes, as evidenced by an ambitious series called "El Legado/The Legacy," which explores world events that focus on the relationship between the United States and the cultures of Latin America.

Roche received the James Nelson Raymond Travelling Fellowship upon his graduation from SAIC and was the recipient of the Southeast Center for Contemporary Art, Winston-Salem, North Carolina, "Awards in the Visual Arts" in 1991. He has had over two dozen solo exhibitions, including a 1992 exhibition at the Museo de Arte Contemporaneo, Monterrey, Mexico. He is featured in the collections of AIC; the Hirshhorn Museum and Sculpture Garden, Washington, DC; The Metropolitan Museum of Art, New York; the Museum of Contemporary Art of Puerto Rico, San Juan; and the Museum of Fine Arts, Houston, among others. LW

Miroslaw Rogala

(Born 1954) An internationally known artist based in Chicago, Miroslaw Rogala was born in Poland in 1954 and came to the United States in 1979 after completion of his Master's degree at the Academy of Fine Arts in his native Cracow. He studied video and performance at SAIC, and graduated in 1983 with an MFA. Originally trained as a musician, while still in school Rogala embraced video as a universal medium of expression and communication. In fact, a dominant theme in Rogala's work is the construction of a type of universal communication. This tendency no doubt is fueled by his experience of growing up in a Communist country where communication was difficult, guarded, and controlled.

Rogala's art is situational, and after early efforts, highly collaborative. Some of his earliest works are photographs of his native Polish landscape seared by the ruby light of a laser. They are poignant in their palpable absence of others—the collaborative team of performers, dancers, singers, musicians, and image- and sound-makers that Rogala more typically brings together to create works such as the 1989 video theater *Nature Is Leaving Us*, presented in Chicago at The Goodman Theatre. In this work, fairly simple images—such as a baby or a tree—were elaborated with vocal, instrumental, and electronic music both recorded and live; movement, recorded and live; and electronic effects. Thus these basic images were amplified into multiple senses.

In the 1990s Rogala began using hypermedia, bringing both the collaborative aspect of his work and the need for image (often photographically derived) firmly to the forefront. The 1995 interactive work *Lovers Leap* was presented in Karlsruhe, Germany, at the Zentrum für Kunst und Medientechnologie's fourth "Multimediale" festival. Through a site on the World Wide Web, Rogala is initiating new collaborative contacts, including a recent effort with the group (Art)^n.

Rogala has worked with such figures as performance artist and filmmaker Carolee Schneemann, word-jazz composer Ken Nordine, vocalist Urszula Dudziak, and pianist Frank Abbinanti, and created multimedia sections for such theatrical productions as The Goodman Theatre's *A Sunday in the Park with George* (1986) and the Piven Theater's *MacBeth* in Evanston, Illinois (1988). Rogala was featured in MCA's exhibition "A New Generation from SAIC" (1986) and in "Performance Chicago" at the State of Illinois Center in 1986. LW

Alejandro Romero

(Born 1948) Born in Tabasco, Mexico, Alejandro Romero began his study of art in 1967 at the Academia de San Carlos of the Escuela Nacional de Artes Plasticas in Mexico City. He spent a year studying mural art at the workshops of Juan O'Gorman and David Alfaro Siqueiros, ending in 1970. From 1971 to 1974 Romero was a freelance photographer and art director for an advertising agency. He subsequently furthered his study of the fine arts at the Université de Vincennes outside Paris and the Artists' Collective in Taos, New Mexico. After relocating to Chicago in 1976, he attended SAIC, where he made contact with Latin American art-history scholar and chairman of the Art History and Criticism Department, Robert J. Loescher, whose expertise in and enthusiasm for the art of Latin America was of particular help in the artist's transition to the United States.

Romero's life as an artist is fully integrated into his life as a leading figure in his Pilsen neighborhood for over twenty years. An expert lithographer and poster artist, Romero has worked tirelessly to further social causes in the Mexican-American community while exhibiting his artworks in museums and galleries worldwide. He has also completed a number of murals in Mexico City and Chicago, and done set designs for Chicago's Victory Gardens Theatre Center. Combining cultural, political, and artistic aspects of his Mexican heritage with his identity as a Chicagoan, Romero creates paintings that hold within their confines the sweeping ambition and scope of murals. Bright lush color, layering of images, and dynamic compositions characterize his work. Figures from Mexican history and political life combine with Chicago figures and landscapes, creating rich commentary on both cultures.

Romero has been the subject of over sixty-five solo exhibitions since his first at the Universidad de Chiapas, Mexico, in 1972. In the Chicago area he received exhibitions at the Beverly Art Center (1979); the Dittmar Memorial Gallery at Northwestern University, Evanston, Illinois (1981); The Chicago Public Library Cultural Center (1984); and the Latino Arts Coalition Gallery (1988). In Mexico he received solo exhibitions at the Museo Carlos Pellicer, Tabasco (1982); El Palacio Nuevo de los Camara de Diputados, Mexico City (1985); Museo de la Cuidad de Mexico (1989); and Museo Nacional de la Estampa, Mexico City (1990). He was also featured in a retrospective at the Museum of Modern Latin American Art, Washington, DC, in 1987. Romero has been included in

numerous group exhibitions in Japan, Germany, Spain, Mexico, Canada, and the United States. He is represented in the permanent collections of AIC, Museo Nacional de la Estampa, and the Hermitage, St. Petersburg. LW

Kay Rosen

(Birthdate undisclosed) Kay Rosen has received international attention for her Minimalist paintings that play clever, meaningful games with words, phrases, and names. Rosen was born in Corpus Christi, Texas. She attended Newcomb College of Tulane University, New Orleans, receiving her BA in Spanish, linguistics, and French. Rosen moved back to Texas and subsequently to Evanston, Illinois, to attend Northwestern University, where she received her MA in Spanish, linguistics, and French.

Rosen had three early solo exhibitions at ARC Gallery, Chicago. Her work of the mid-1970s combines serial photography of performances and diagrams in various geometric patterns and shapes. She had a solo exhibition in New York in 1979 at Bertha Urdang Gallery, with subsequent shows at the gallery in 1981 and 1983. Her time-based photographic work was included in the group exhibition "New Dimensions: Time," at MCA (1980).

In 1983 Rosen's concentration shifted to language-based paintings, a return to the type of work she had produced following her student years. Her first solo exhibition of these works was in 1984 at Feature gallery in Chicago. That same year she presented a window installation at The New Museum of Contemporary Art, New York. Following her 1984 show, Rosen was associated with Feature gallery, both in Chicago and New York, for the next ten years, with one-person exhibitions in 1987, 1988, 1989, 1990, 1992, and 1993. Her art since this period presents a sophisticated and often humorous restructuring of familiar phrases, names, and words in varying colors and typefaces. Her work reflects the influence of Feminist theory and linguistics-based philosophy on the art of the past decade.

During the early 1990s, Rosen steadily gained international recognition with solo exhibitions at the Witte de With, Rotterdam (1990); Victoria Miro Gallery, London (1990 and 1993); and the Shedhalle, Zurich (1991). Her 1994 show "Kay Rosen: Home on the Range" at MCA was one of a series of solo exhibitions devoted to locally based artists. Also in 1994 were solo exhibitions at Galeria Massimo de Carlo, Milan; Richard Telles Fine Art, Los Angeles; and the Indianapolis Museum of Art. Rosen participated in the 1994–95 "Korrespondenzen/Correspondences:

14 Artists from Berlin and Chicago," coorganized by the Chicago Cultural Center and the Berlinische Galerie, Berlin. That same year, she exhibited at Galerie Erika & Otto Friedrich, Bern, Switzerland. Rosen lives and works in Gary, Indiana. DM

Paul Rosin

(Born 1957) A life-long Chicagoan, Paul Rosin was born in 1957. He received his BFA in 1981 from SAIC, where even as an undergraduate, his work showed remarkable individuality and maturity. With black-and-white Polaroid 665 positive/negative stock images Rosin creates a world of stylized beauty, passionless lust, inexplicable attitudes and acts, and a disturbingly attractive decadence that is compelling yet difficult. The hallucinogenic reality of Ralph Meatyard, the unsettling freakishness of Diane Arbus, and the jaded sensuality of Brassaï are all present in varying degrees in Rosin's work. He puts forth a strong lyrical expression of a cynical urban romanticism; the photographs could be stills from a modern film noir. Rosin's photographs generally exclude anything, such as recognizable clothing styles or objects, that would easily date them, and the artist purposefully works toward a mottled, tintypelike appearance with a coarse, dull grain and scratched emulsion. He sometimes tones or hand-colors the photographs, or overpaints with enamel paints. Rosin's is a world where there is no time, but more disconcerting, there is no verdict on its lack of tradition and hope for the future.

Rosin typically creates ongoing series. Images shot early in his career resurface in the context of new series; exhibitions are not opportunities to show a new body of photographs so much as to integrate new images into the overall context of his work, showing photographs from the early 1980s alongside works from the mid-1990s.

Early in his career Rosin was close to the punk music scene in Chicago and New York. He often worked with performance artists, musicians, and individuals he met in nightclubs and bars to create his images, which despite their seeming spontaneity, are for the most part carefully staged. He also showed often in clubs such as Limelight, which was located in a former ID site, and other venues outside of the gallery-museum mainstream, participating in the notorious 1983 "The Sex Show" held in a Clark Street penthouse. He also showed with New York clubs active in the 1980s, such as Area X.

Rosin has received considerable attention from galleries, museums, and collectors. He has exhibited at Edward Thorp Gallery in New York and in a number of group photography shows in Europe; and was the subject of a one-person exhibition at MCA in 1985 and at the University Galleries of Illinois State University, Normal, in 1993. LW

Seymour Rosofsky

(1924–1981) For the painter Seymour Rosofsky, Chicago remained not only his life-long home, but an integral part of his work. The lake, the buildings, the people, and the raw and insular character he associated with his hometown found their way into his strange and often autobiographical narratives. Born in 1924 to Jewish immigrants on the West Side of Chicago, Rosofsky received his BFA in 1949 (after a military hiatus from 1944 to 1946), and his MFA in 1951 from SAIC, while simultaneously completing humanities courses at the University of Chicago and at Northwestern University, Evanston, Illinois. At SAIC he studied with Boris Anisfeld, a former student of Chagall, known for his traditional painting techniques and classical figure study.

Rosofsky's early work was associated with that of the "Monster Roster" artists; his expressive, gestural renderings of distorted figures were in part informed by the non-Western art he studied with his classmates at the Field Museum, by German Expressionism, and by his wartime experiences. Important events, such as AIC's 1951 Edvard Munch exhibition and the 1951–52 Dubuffet exhibition at the Arts Club, also inspired Rosofsky's penetrating series of grotesque characters, which paralleled the Existentialist leanings of the period. Around 1956 his emphasis began to shift toward faceless men, sometimes in hospitals or in wheelchairs. Vulnerable and often in uncomfortable situations, these invalids are depicted alone in an empty space constructed by agitated lines reminiscent of Giacometti. Figures immobilized in circumstances beyond their control remained an important component in Rosofsky's later works. His formal concern with organizational structure surfaced during his 1958 stay in Rome on a Fulbright Fellowship: perspectival grids began to appear in a dramatic and theatrical manner in works undoubtedly influenced by his friend and fellow painter June Leaf.

A Guggenheim Foundation Grant brought Rosofsky and his family to Paris in 1962. Through an introduction to the Surrealist-oriented Galerie du Dragon by his friend the expatriate Chicago painter Irving Petlin, Rosofsky's predilection toward the absurd was fostered. He began to develop a vocabulary of fantastic, sometimes frightening, personages: laughing clowns, indifferent children, a variety of menacing faces. Intense col-ors and dramatic fervor added to their urgency. His sources ranged from Goya and Velásquez to his own life and endless imagination. In addition to constant examination of the power and/or impotence of the artist, Rosofsky's autobiographical themes were most overt when referring to his failing marriage. In the 1970s he concentrated on the domestic roles of women and men. The content was often caustic and the figures depicted as cardboard cutouts in stage settings or puppets whose actions seem predetermined. The culminating series from the late 1970s are violent, and sometimes actively spiteful, images of couples and women in general.

Rosofsky's last works, done after discovering he had congenital heart disease, illustrate the artist in a more contented, though sometimes detached, state. One of his final projects was the "commedia dell'arte" drawings requested to accompany the 1982 Venice Biennale's Carnevale del Teatro, which encompassed many of his signature characters.

Rosofsky taught at the Chicago Loop College (now the Harold Washington Community College) from 1964 until his death in 1981. Throughout his life he was associated with the most international Chicago galleries: Richard Feigen, B.C. Holland, and Richard Gray, and several galleries in Europe. His work was shown in numerous C & V shows at AIC from 1950 to 1981, and was included in Franz Schulze's 1972 book Fantastic Images. The Krannert Art Museum, University of Illinois, Champaign, organized a retrospective in 1984. Rosofsky's work can be seen in the collections of MOMA; the National Museum of American Art, Washington, DC; the Los Angeles County Museum of Art; and MCA, among others. SB

Barbara Rossi

(Born 1940) Chicago native Barbara Rossi received her MFA in 1970 from SAIC, where she was deeply influenced by her introduction to art of the insane and self-taught and by professors Ray Yoshida and Whitney Halstead. Halstead introduced Rossi to the work of self-taught Chicago artist Joseph Yoakum, an experience that reinforced her experiments with automatic drawing. Becoming deeply interested in folk art, she traveled widely to sites in the United States and then to Europe with her SAIC colleagues Roger Brown, Christina Ramberg, and Phil Hanson to see major collections of "outsider" art there. Three trips to India in the 1980s influenced her painting and led her to curate an exhibition of Indian art at The David and Alfred Smart Museum of Art in Chicago in 1995.

Although associated with the Hairy Who artists who debuted at HPAC in 1966, Rossi emerged later, first in HPAC's "Marriage Chicago Style" (1970), which featured artists from the Hairy Who group as well as those who had emerged as the "Nonplussed Some" (Ed Paschke); she also took part in HPAC's 1971 show "Chicago Antigua." Rossi's work tends to reflect inward to the spiritual rather than promote a critical view of the outside world. Her early paintings and drawings feature headline organic abstractions composed of misplaced body parts and rendered in a spontaneous manner. Most of her work is painted in flat, muted but glowing colors. In a trait shared by others in her artistic circle, including Jim Nutt and Gladys Nilsson, Rossi's works feature titles with inventive spelling and word play. She also experimented with reverse painting on Plexiglas, as did many of her colleagues; her later paintings are on Masonite or occasionally canvas. In addition to painting and drawing, Rossi has produced prints, including a series from the early 1970s of etching and aquatint on satin, which she then made into quilts that are embellished with beads, buttons, and fringe. In the late 1970s Rossi began to move away from exclusive references to the figure, incorporating architectural scenes with forms suggestive of furniture. These paintings began to project more of a traditional pictorial space. Her Indian-influenced work since 1983 features images adapted from Indian folk art and Indian and Persian miniature painting.

Rossi has been featured in numerous group exhibitions that introduced the art later known as Chicago Imagism, including "Don Baum Says: 'Chicago Needs Famous Artists'" at MCA (1969) and the 1973 São Paulo Bienal. She was the subject of solo exhibitions at the Renaissance Society in Chicago (1991) and at her long-time gallery, Phyllis Kind, in Chicago and New York. She has also been included in numerous group exhibitions at AIC, HPAC, and MCA; and at the Whitney Museum of American Art in New York (1970, 1973, and 1975); the Madison Art Center in Wisconsin (1970, 1975, and 1989); the Terra Museum of American Art in Chicago (1987); and the Los Angeles County Museum of Art (1992). She is included in many museum collections, including MCA and AIC. Rossi has taught in the Painting and Drawing Department at SAIC since 1971. AF

Tom DeFanti Dan Sandin

Dan Sandin (Born 1942)
Tom DeFanti (Born 1948)
Two of Chicago's true pioneers for nearly twenty-five years, Dan Sandin and Tom DeFanti have revolutionized the use of advanced computer technology in art. Sandin, born in 1942 in Rockford, Illinois, received his BS in physics from Shimer College, Waukegan, Illinois, in 1964, and his MS in physics from the University of Wisconsin, Madison, in 1967. While continuing on for his PhD, he became fascinated by the intense televised imagery of the times. Sandin was interested, moreover, in how those images were produced—the optical and chemical processes used to transform existing images into radically different images. It became clear to him that he could perform these transformations with electronic video image processing and computer image generation techniques.

Sandin gained recognition exhibiting highly processed photography, configured electronically controlled light shows, and computer-controlled environments. On the strength of this work, UIC invited him in 1969 to join its art department and develop a cybernetic curriculum. Sandin became involved with video during the 1970 student protests following the Kent State killings. Using video to transmit the protests, he became fascinated by the ability to produce images in real time, as well as the visual effect of the video screen. With a grant from the Illinois Arts Council, Sandin developed and finished his first Image Processor, a highly programmable analog computer for processing video images, in 1973. The first performance involving the Image Processor was *The Inconsecration of New Space* that same year, with Sandin processing black-and-white images, which Jim Wiseman then "colorized" through the use of a Paik/Abe Synthesizer.

Sandin was joined at UIC by Tom DeFanti in 1973. DeFanti was born in 1948 in New York and received his PhD from Ohio State University, Columbus. He had already developed the GRASS system—a user-friendly, interactive computer-graphics system—with Charles Csuri prior to joining Sandin at UIC. (An interesting footnote in DeFanti's history at UIC is his development of the graphics for the "Death Star" model used in the science-fiction film *Star Wars*.) With their students, Sandin and DeFanti combined the power of Sandin's Image Processor with DeFanti's newly developed computer graphics system to create Electronic Visualization Events, a series of live performances in which images were computer-generated and color-processed in real time. Sandin made the plans for the Image Processor public, allowing those willing to learn how to build one, the free use of its technological advances.

Sandin and DeFanti developed the Circle Graphics Habitat between 1973 and 1975, which subsequently evolved into the Electronic Visualization Laboratory—the oldest formal collaboration between schools of engineering and art in the country. During the 1980s Sandin created computer animation projects such as *Air on the Dirac Strings* and *A Volume of Stacked 2D Julia Sets*. Sandin and DeFanti have also been involved with the art collaborative (Art)^n, whose sculptural, three-dimensional images have been widely exhibited across the country. In 1991 Sandin and DeFanti conceived the CAVE virtual-reality theater, which still operates today, continuing their interest in using computer graphics in "real time." DM

Joe Scanlan

(Born 1961) Joe Scanlan emerged at a point in Chicago's art history when the long-dominant pictorial mode of the city was being challenged by young, Conceptually oriented artists. Scanlan was born in 1961 in Stoutsville, Ohio. He received his BFA from the Columbus College of Art and Design, Ohio, in 1983, and attended SAIC for the 1985–86 school year, choosing not to finish the MFA program. Scanlan served as assistant director and editor at the Renaissance Society during the late 1980s and early 1990s and has written criticism for a number of journals, including *Frieze, Art Issues*, and *Artscribe*.

An air of controversy surrounded a 1989 project of Scanlan's for a group show titled "The Size of Chicago" at the now-defunct Ricky Renier Gallery in Chicago. Scanlan exhibited candles in the shapes of cereal boxes and milk cartons both at the gallery and in a low-cost furniture store downstairs. The candles were priced to fit the "venue"—hundreds of dollars apiece at the gallery and from $4 to $30 in the furniture store. When the piece began to "operate," with people preferring to buy the "cheaper" candles downstairs rather than the art in the gallery, Renier removed Scanlan's work from the show. Arguments ensued within the local art world over the incident— some supporting Scanlan's intention to disclose the commodified nature of the artwork, others denouncing him for a willful breach of business faith with a dealer committed to young artists' work.

The intention of the project, to lay bare the commercial underpinnings of the work of art, has been a fixture of Scanlan's work throughout his career. His use of household refuse in his sculptures and his creation of essentially functional pairs of underwear (able to be worn for four days), bookcases, and benches led many critics to find in his work an update of Marcel Duchamp's readymade sculptures or an underlying concern for the environment. What Scanlan's work ultimately points out is the peculiar place that the work of art occupies in our society. Exemplary of the international appeal and character of the art of Chicago in the 1980s and 1990s, Scanlan's work has been featured in the Documenta exhibition in Kassel, Germany, in 1992, and has been exhibited numerous times throughout Europe. He had his first solo exhibition in Chicago at Robbin Lockett Gallery in 1991, and is currently represented by Christopher Grimes Gallery in Santa Monica, California. DM

David Sharpe

(Born 1944) David Sharpe is a prolific painter whose work has evolved from vibrant abstraction to naturalistic figuration to stylized realism. He was born in Owensboro, Kentucky, in 1944. Possessing a maturity unusual for a young painter, Sharpe was exhibiting as early as 1964 while still an undergraduate at SAIC; he received his BFA in 1966 and his MFA in 1968. Although he remained in Chicago for only two years following his graduation, Sharpe's presence in the Chicago art world has been considerable. A huge, mural-sized painting, *Universe* (1968), executed for his graduate fellowship competition, has been on display at The David and Alfred Smart Museum for a number of years. Consisting of various abstract and organic shapes within a black ground, this painting was a precursor to an important body of abstract work completed in Chicago at a time when Imagism was emerging as the predominant painting style. Painted in bright, clear colors, these works feature various biomorphic shapes that energetically explode across the canvas and share characteristics of both Imagism and the Pop art that was emerging in New York in the late 1960s and early 1970s.

After he ceased exploring abstraction, his wife, painter Ann Abrons, became a frequent subject for Sharpe. He also explored mythological subjects, depicting male and female nudes with angular, outlined bodies. In the 1980s he executed a number of tropical-island scenes that feature objects and figures rendered in a faux naïf style within expert compositions and a sophisticated palette.

Sharpe has appeared in numerous group exhibitions in Chicago, including SAIC's "Visions/Painting and Sculpture: Distinguished Alumni, 1945 to the Present" (1976); The Chicago Public Library Cultural Center's "Masterpieces of Recent Chicago Art" (1977); MCA's "Selections from the Dennis Adrian

Collection" (1982); and HPAC's "The Big Pitcher: 20 Years of the Abstracted Figure in Chicago Art" (1983). Sharpe showed at Douglas Kenyon, Chicago, in the mid-1970s, and has been associated with Sonia Zaks Gallery, Chicago, since 1978. His paintings were featured in a twenty-year retrospective in 1990 at the UWM Art Museum of the University of Wisconsin, Milwaukee. Sharpe currently · lives in New York. LW

Arthur Siegel

(1913–1978) Arthur Siegel was born in Detroit in 1913. He studied sociology at the University of Michigan, Ann Arbor (1931–33), and at Wayne State University, Detroit, receiving a BA degree in 1936. Siegel moved to Chicago to study photography at The New Bauhaus (later ID) in 1937–38 as a member of the first class. He had begun taking photographs in 1927, but it was in 1937, in classes at ID with László Moholy-Nagy, that he started to experiment with abstraction and the photographic medium. Siegel subsequently returned to Detroit to work as a commercial photographer, incorporating experimentation into his commercial work. Invited by Moholy-Nagy in 1946 to head ID's Photography Department, Siegel developed courses that would influence several generations of students. He left ID in 1950 to pursue his freelance career, but returned occasionally to teach in the 1960s. In 1967 Siegel abandoned professional photography to concentrate again on teaching; he chaired ID's Photography Department for a second time (1971–78). He concentrated not only on the technical side of photography, but also emphasized a knowledge of the history of photography and attention to intellectual content.

Siegel is known primarily as a documentary photographer. His *Right of Assembly* (1941), showing a huge crowd of autoworkers during a strike in Detroit, has become an icon of American photography. However, early on he experimented with photograms, playing with varying qualities of light and dark and overlapping abstract forms. He was a pioneer in the use of 35mm color photography, stressing strong colors and attention to forms and patterns. In 1965 he published an important book of photographs of Chicago architecture, *Chicago's Famous Buildings*. He has photographed such subjects as automobiles, window displays, neon signs, and pedestrian traffic. In addition to his teaching appointments at ID, Siegel also taught photography at Wayne State University in the Department of Visual Education (1934–37). He worked as a photographer for such publications as *The New York Times*,

Time, Life, Sports Illustrated, and the Associated Press Photo Bureau. He served as a photographer for the Office of War Information, Washington, DC (1942–43) and in the US Air Corps Aerial Photography Department in Rantoul, Illinois (1944–46).

Siegel has had one-person exhibitions at AIC (1954 and 1967); George Eastman House, Rochester, New York (1955); Chicago Historical Society (1981); and a retrospective at Edwynn Houk Gallery, Chicago (1982). Other important shows include "Abstract Photography," with Harry Callahan and Aaron Siskind, American Federation of Arts, New York (1957); "2 Illinois Photographers," with Aaron Siskind, HPAC (1967); and "Josephson, Jachna and Siegel: Chicago Experimentalists," San Francisco Museum of Modern Art (1988). Group exhibitions include "Photography in the 20th Century," National Gallery of Canada, Ottawa (1967); "Photography in America," Whitney Museum of American Art, New York (1974); "The Photographer and the City," MCA (1977); "The New Vision," The Chicago Public Library Cultural Center (1980); "Counterparts: Form and Emotion in Photographs," The Metropolitan Museum of Art, New York (1982); and "Photography and Art 1946–86," Los Angeles County Museum of Art (1987). AF

Paul Sierra

(Born 1944) Paul Sierra was born in Havana in 1944. Growing up, he dreamed of being a filmmaker, and after immigrating with his family to the United States shortly after the failed Bay of Pigs invasion in 1961, he took a course in film at the University of Chicago. Painting, however, seemed more feasible, and he studied at SAIC from 1963 to 1967. There he was influenced by Puerto Rican painter Rufino Silva, and was a peer of students such as Jim Nutt and Roger Brown who would later be known as the Imagists, but Sierra left before taking a degree. He also took courses at the more commercially oriented American Academy of Art in Chicago. Subsequently he worked as an art director for a Hispanic advertising agency now known as Unimar. He briefly worked in a Minimalist style, but after an inspiring trip to Puerto Rico in 1975, began painting in an expressive, magical realist style for which he is primarily known.

Sierra's lushly colored canvases often depict remembered or symbolic landscapes of his native country, self-portraits, or interiors. His themes include Greek mythology; the exploration of psychological states, especially dramatic or painful situations; and the artist's journey through life. Sierra's interest in film

is recognizable in his works of the early 1980s, whose compositions display painterly interpretations of cinematic devices: doors open to present "clips" — landscapes and scenes different from that of the primary image and images "cut" from one to another by ending in mid-stroke to reveal a different image behind. In the late 1980s, perhaps finally coming to terms with the fact that he would never be able to return to Cuba (which had been his family's intention when they fled Fidel Castro's regime), Sierra began to juxtapose images representing his past, such as palm trees, Cuban musicians, or landscapes, with those from his present existence in the Midwest, such as elm trees, rolling farmland, and Chicago architecture. These paintings convey an apocalyptic feeling with central figures falling, ducking, and fainting, surrounded by fire and black clouds.

Sierra has been widely included in traveling exhibitions that feature Latino and Cuban artists, including "Hispanic Art in the United States," organized by the Corcoran Gallery of Art, Washington, DC (1987); "¡Mira!," an independently organized show which traveled to the Terra Museum of American Art in Chicago (1988); and "Cuba/USA," organized by the Fondo del Sol Visual Arts Center, Washington, DC, which traveled to MCA (1991). In 1990 Sierra had a solo exhibition at the Evanston Art Center, Illinois, and in 1995 at The Snite Museum of Art at the University of Notre Dame, Indiana. Sierra has been associated for a number of years with the Frederic Snitzer Gallery in Miami. He showed with Gwenda Jay Gallery in Chicago in the early 1990s, and currently shows with Phyllis Kind Gallery, Chicago and New York. Sierra's paintings are included in numerous area public collections, including MCA and The Harold Washington Library Center. LW

Hollis Sigler

(Born 1948) Hollis Sigler was born in Gary, Indiana, in 1948. She received a BFA in 1970 from Moore College of Art in Philadelphia, where she produced Abstract Expressionist paintings. Sigler moved to Chicago in 1971 to study at SAIC, receiving her MFA in 1973. Chicago allowed her the freedom to develop her own personal style, away from the influence of the New York School that permeated the East Coast. Gravitating toward the figure, she began to create large-scale paintings and watercolors of underwater swimmers. Around 1974 Sigler turned inward and, recalling her childhood delight in drawing, began to make small sketches in a notebook that dealt with her memories, desires, and fantasies. The graphite and oil-pastel drawings became a visual diary of interior spaces laden with emotional and symbolic objects. Encouraged to show these very intimate works in public, Sigler exposed herself—her female-oriented, small-scale, narrative drawings stood in opposition to the grand heroics of the male-dominated art world.

As it developed, Sigler's work increased in size around 1980, when she began to paint with oils, while still continuing her pastels. The emotional titles of the works, inscribed on the canvas in a delicate script, are poetic and describe the fictitious, though often autobiographically based, experiences of "the lady," a figure absent from the compositions. Private interior spaces of homes and backyards containing personal items, such as housewares, furniture, and clothing, bear traces of recent female presence, as if "the lady" had exited hastily. Sigler's psychologically complex images are depicted in what has been called a "faux naïf" style—they are not realistically rendered and the perspective of the space often seems skewed. The jewellike colors are lyrical and seductive, but often contrast with the serious and even violent nature of many of the intense scenes, especially in her work dealing with breast cancer. In 1985 Sigler was diagnosed with the disease, which has since spread to her bones. Although her work dealt with the emotional effects of the diagnosis, it was not until "The Breast Cancer Journal" series of 1992 that Sigler publicly revealed the cause.

Sigler has had one-person exhibitions at the Akron Art Museum, Ohio (1986); Rockford College Art Gallery, Illinois (1993); National Museum of Women in the Arts, Washington, DC (1993); and MCA (1994). She was previously associated with Nancy Lurie Gallery, Chicago, and Barbara Gladstone Gallery, New York; her current galleries are Printworks and Carl Hammer in Chicago; Susan Cummins in Mill Valley, California; and Steven Scott in Baltimore. Sigler's work has been presented in many contexts including Feminist, Chicago Imagist, narrative, and political, and since 1973 has been featured in numerous group exhibitions at, in Chicago, Artemisia Gallery; AIC; MCA; Chicago Cultural Center; and Terra Museum of American Art; as well as at the Whitney Museum of American Art, New York; Walker Art Center, Minneapolis; Kunstmuseum, Lucerne; Museo Rufino Tamayo, Mexico City; and The Drawing Center, New York. In addition to her paintings and pastels, Sigler has recently published a book and has begun to use the fragile process of paper cut-outs in her work. She has been on the faculty of Columbia College in Chicago since 1978. SB

Diane Simpson

(Born 1935) Diane Simpson's highly crafted and elegant sculptures examine the architecture of apparel design using unconventional materials and processes. Simpson was born in Joliet, Illinois, in 1935, and at age ten began her long history with SAIC, commuting to its junior school, where she and Richard Hunt were classmates. Simpson received both her BFA (1971) and MFA (1978) from SAIC. Since 1978 she has been a visiting artist and guest lecturer at SAIC, UIC, Midway Studios at the University of Chicago, and Barat College, Lake Forest. Simpson currently lives and works in Evanston, Illinois.

With such diverse sources as Japanese roof shapes, silos, kilns, water tanks, and garden structures, to Japanese armor, seventeenth-century undergarments, bodice and sleeve design, and most recently bonnets or other headgear, Simpson transforms nontraditional materials into objects of personal shelter that are at once formally striking and rich in metaphor. Beginning with the armor of a Samurai warrior, the pleats of a skirt, or the design of a bonnet as the core, Simpson permutates the source through drawings, which have always played a crucial role in her work and have often been displayed alongside the sculptures. These garment-inspired patterned sculptures, which at times Simpson literally sews together, with their large scale and minimal form, suggest a Feminist viewpoint. Simpson's sculptures waver between flatness and volume, showing the artist's early interest in eroding the distinction between two-dimensional and three-dimensional space. Because she builds isometric drawings in three-dimensional space, a sense of flatness prevails and the volume usually associated with sculpture becomes illusory. Simpson often applies this system of drawing directly onto the flat surfaces of the constructions; a curious flattening results, the antithesis of a clothing pattern resulting in a volumetric form.

In addition to the diversity of forms, Simpson is known for her eclectic and inventive use of materials. Her earliest sculptures were made primarily of corrugated cardboard, but by 1983 she had replaced cardboard with wood. With an increased attention surface, Simpson continued to allow patterns to grow from peculiarities of the material, but now through painting, staining, drawing, scoring, and sanding. Eventually she began to combine industrial materials (fiberboard, metal grid, and tubing) with more "domestic" materials (cotton mesh, needle-point backing, waxed thread, upholstery webbing, and braided cords). Regardless of medium, Simpson has always shown respect for materials and craftsmanship and eschewed commercial fabrication.

Simpson has had solo exhibitions at ARC Gallery, Chicago (1974); Artemisia Gallery, Chicago (1979); Illinois Wesleyan University, Bloomington (1981); College of DuPage, Glen Ellyn, Illinois (1995); and Chicago Cultural Center (1995). Her work has been included in C & V shows, AIC (1978, 1980, 1981, and 1985); "100 Artists, 100 Years," AIC (1979); "New Dimensions: Volume and Space," MCA (1979); "Ten Years Later: An Exhibition of Women Artists," Ukrainian Institute of Modern Art, Chicago (1982); "Alternative Spaces: A History in Chicago," MCA (1984); "Chicago Works: Art from the Windy City," Erie Art Museum, Pennsylvania (1989); "Architectural Fiber," Textile Arts Center, Chicago (1993); "RADIUS," 213 West Institute Place, Chicago (1995); and "16 Chicago Sculptors," Cultural Center, Zalaegerszeg, Hungary (1995). MM

Art Sinsabaugh

(1924–1983) Though associated, almost synonymously, with the midwestern landscape, Art Sinsabaugh was originally from the East Coast. Born in 1924 in Irvington, New Jersey, Sinsabaugh had an early interest in photography and commuted to New York to attend a photography trade school while simultaneously working as a junior photographer for the War Department. Drafted into the Army Air Force, he served as a sergeant-photographer in the Far East in 1943–45, before relocating to Chicago to study at ID with László Moholy-Nagy and Harry Callahan. Sinsabaugh received a BS from ID in 1949 and remained in Chicago, teaching at ID from 1951 until 1959, when he moved to Urbana-Champaign to begin a long academic career at the University of Illinois, lasting until his death in 1983.

Sinsabaugh considered his photographs of urban and rural vistas to be landscapes above all. The horizontal lines of the Chicago streets, rather than the verticality of its many skyscrapers, as well as the vast, flat prairie of Illinois and Indiana, attracted him. While in Urbana, Sinsabaugh discovered the unwieldy banquet camera, whose 12-by-20-inch negatives are designed to shoot large groups of people. The wide format suited the horizontal perspective that is accentuated in his signature midwestern landscape compositions of the 1960s. He often cropped the height of the negatives, sometimes down to one inch, but left the full width to emphasize the prairie aspect. Sharp tonal contrasts between foreground elements and the background, usually a monotone sky, produce a flatness that approaches silhouette. Sinsabaugh focused on the rhythmic quality of such structures as telephone poles, trees, and houses situated at certain intervals along the persistent horizontal landscape, illustrating his interest in both documentation and abstraction. In 1964, while again studying at ID, this time with Aaron Siskind, Sinsabaugh began a three-year project photographing the city of Chicago. These descriptive, detailed works, usually utilizing the full 12-by-20-inch frame, are studies in abstract arrangements and geometric patterns, which Sinsabaugh found in abundance in Chicago's numerous architectural structures.

Sinsabaugh was given a one-person exhibition at AIC in 1963, the same year he was included in "The Photographer and the American Landscape" at MOMA, where he later had a solo exhibition in 1978. His work has been featured worldwide in numerous exhibitions chronicling postwar American photography, as well as histories of ID. Sinsabaugh wrote several articles on Chicago and midwestern landscapes, and published a book entitled 6 Mid-American Chants/11 Midwest Landscapes with writings by Sherwood Anderson (1964). In keeping with his long-time devotion to education (he taught a number of important artists at the University of Illinois, including Robert Cumming, Eve Sonneman, and William Wegman), Sinsabaugh was a founding member of the Society for Photographic Education. The Art Sinsabaugh Archive is located at the University of Indiana, Bloomington. SB

Aaron Siskind

(1903–1991) Born in New York in 1903 to poor immigrant parents from Ukraine, Aaron Siskind grew up on the Lower East Side. His mother raised five children while his father managed a number of neighborhood stores. Siskind received his BSS from the College of the City of New York in 1926, and then taught English in public elementary schools in New York until 1949. A self-taught photographer who originally considered his art a hobby, Siskind did not begin his career as a documentary photographer until the 1930s. In the latter part of the decade, he concentrated on a series documenting areas of Harlem; he became involved in the Photo League of New

York, a circle of individuals dedicated to using photography for social betterment. In 1951 the photographer Harry Callahan invited Siskind to join the staff of Chicago's ID, where he became an influential teacher to many serious photography students, such as Barbara Crane, Joseph Jachna, Kenneth Josephson, and Ray K. Metzker. Siskind was head of the Department of Photography from 1959 until 1971, when he accepted a position as professor of photography at the Rhode Island School of Design, Providence (which later named its museum's photography study center after him). He remained at RISD until 1975. He was also a visiting lecturer at the Carpenter Center for the Visual Arts at Harvard University, Cambridge, Massachusetts, and lived and worked in Providence and Martha's Vineyard, Massachusetts, until his death in 1991.

In 1943–44 Siskind developed his trademark style of using close-up, abstracted forms. He moved from photographically documenting social problems in a conventional way to an abstract expression of a similar idea. By the 1950s his work was entirely abstract. Though he was still photographing the commonplace and neglected, Siskind's subjects became less recognizable and his style more personal. Moving away from Social Realism, Siskind used fragments of walls, isolated objects, pavements, weathered wood, peeling paint, torn posters, graffiti, concrete remnants, and other documents of urban chaos and decay to create collage-like images on a flat plane. He is often viewed as an Abstract Expressionist photographer because of his devotion to gestural markings, flat surfaces, and his close association with abstract painters. He had long-term friendships with many of the Abstract Expressionists of the time, especially the painter Franz Kline. Siskind's later work was influenced by his travels, particularly by trips to Mexico, South America, and Italy.

Siskind is considered a pioneer in the field of photography. Egan Gallery in New York (which also first supported the Abstract Expressionists) gave Siskind his first major exhibition in 1947. He was given a one-person exhibition at AIC in 1955 and at MOMA in 1965, and subsequently had numerous solo exhibitions throughout the United States, Europe, and Japan. In 1966 he was awarded a Guggenheim Fellowship and in 1971 was given an Honorary Doctor of Arts degree from Columbia College, Chicago. Siskind has been the subject of numerous publications and monographs, and his photographs can be found in the collections of most major museums. Siskind's archives are located at the Center for Creative Photography at the University of Arizona, Tucson. LH

Bob Snyder

(Born 1946) Working in both video and sound, Bob Snyder has been important as an artist and an instructor for the time-arts community in Chicago. Born in Kalamazoo, Michigan, in 1946, Snyder studied piano at the American Conservatory of Music in Chicago beginning at age four. He attended the Interlochen National Music Camp of the University of Michigan School of Music, playing solo bass clarinet and second B-flat clarinet in the touring orchestra. Snyder attended Indiana University, Bloomington, and received his BM degree in 1969 and an MM with honors in 1971 from Roosevelt University, Chicago. His Master's thesis was the first in the history of Roosevelt that existed only on magnetic tape.

Snyder became involved in video through his study of video synthesis with Dan Sandin at UIC in 1974. He later provided the musical accompaniment for the groundbreaking EVE (Electronic Visualization Events) I and II (1975 and 1976), collaborating with Sandin, Tom DeFanti, and Phil Morton. Snyder began teaching at SAIC in 1975 and started to combine video and sound synthesis in his work the next year. The use of Sandin's Image Processor is apparent in early videos such as *Winter Notebook* (1976) and *Icron* (1978). In 1979 Snyder used the money he received from an NEA fellowship to design a specialized interface that connects a sound synthesizer to the Image Processor.

One of Snyder's most important works, *Trim Subdivision* (1981), is characterized by its lack of sound and its manipulation of camera images of tract houses in a small Indiana town through digital effects and editing. Snyder was featured in the video sections of the 1981 and 1983 Whitney Biennials, New York; performed a lecture-demonstration at MOMA in 1985; and was featured in the 1987 São Paulo Bienal. He was also included in "Chicago Works: Art from the Windy City," a 1989 exhibition sponsored jointly by the Erie Art Museum, Pennsylvania, and the Bruce Gallery, Edinboro University of Pennsylvania. Snyder released a videodisc compilation of his work from 1975 to 1990, from the early work on the Image Processor, to *Hard and Flexible Music* (1988), a piece that exemplifies his interest in combining improvisational music and video images into an integrated whole. DM

Buzz Spector

(Born 1948) Buzz Spector's unique, object-driven Conceptual art combines the use of text and theory with his penchant for collecting books and postcards. Spector was born in Chicago in 1948. He received a BA in art from Southern Illinois University, Carbondale, in 1972, and an MFA from the University of Chicago in 1978. From 1978 to 1987, Spector was the publisher and editor of *Whitewalls*, a Chicago-based magazine featuring writings by artists. He has been a frequent contributor to *Artforum, Art Issues, New Art Examiner*, and other journals, and has written essays for several exhibition catalogues since 1977. His critical writings provide an early indication of the shift towards Conceptual art that would dominate Chicago's art scene starting in the late 1980s.

Spector was a poet before turning to art, much like the Belgian artist Marcel Broodthaers, who has been a steady influence on his work. Following Broodthaers's first gesture as an artist—encasing his complete works of poetry in plaster—Spector makes use of books in his art. He manipulates books in various ways, letting meaning emerge from the interplay between their organization or mutilation and the information they contain between their covers. Postcards that Spector collects find their way into his work as well, juxtaposed to create humorous and witty narratives and statements. Spector's art often makes conscious reference to archetypal works of modern art and thought, such as a reconstruction of Kasimir Malevich's *Suprematist Composition* using red books, or an investigation of the work of Sigmund Freud in which the standard edition of his writings are encased, volume by volume, in blocks of ice. Moving freely from medium to medium throughout his career, Spector has used books, postcards, and other prefabricated objects based on their relation to the subject or concept that he wishes to address.

At AIC in 1988, Spector installed *The Library of Babel*, an allusion to the story of the same name by the Argentinean author Jorge Luis Borges. Spector had a solo exhibition at the Newport Harbor Art Museum in Southern California and was paired with Donald Lipski in an exhibition titled "Transgressions" at the Corcoran Gallery of Art in Washington, DC, both in 1990. He has had various residencies as a visiting artist or professor at universities in Chicago, downstate Illinois, and California. Spector moved to Southern California in 1988, but returned to Illinois in 1994 to teach at the University of Illinois, Urbana-Champaign. DM

Nancy Spero

(Born 1926) Nancy Spero has devoted her forty-five-year career as an artist to presenting images of women and examining their plight in a male-dominated society. Born in Cleveland in 1926, Spero moved with her family to suburban Chicago. She pursued an art education at SAIC, receiving a BFA in 1949. Friendly with the vocal and politically active students at SAIC, Spero participated in the first Momentum exhibition (1948), and continued to show her work in these salons until 1958. After graduation she spent two years studying at the Ecole des Beaux-Arts and Atelier André l'Hote in Paris and working in New York. She relocated to Chicago in 1951 and married fellow SAIC alumnus Leon Golub.

Spero's early paintings center around the theme of mother and child, perhaps partially influenced by the birth of two sons in the early 1950s. Ghostly silhouetted figures seem almost to dissolve into the mysterious blue or earth-toned atmosphere of an undefined space. The art manifests an Existential leaning along with an adamant figurative bias—characteristics of the "Monster Roster" art of Spero's peers (including her husband), who defiantly countered the prevailing Abstract Expressionism. While she was living in Italy (Ischia and Florence) with her family in 1956–57, Spero's iconography broadened to include reclining figures and ancient Egyptian Canopic jars. While living in Bloomington, Indiana, during the following two years, her subjects were derived largely from tarot cards. The occasional inclusion of text in the paintings signals what would become a major component in her later work.

Spero relocated with her family once again, this time to Paris (1959–64), where she worked on a series examining the sexual and emotional dilemma of lovers. In 1964 she settled permanently in New York, becoming overtly political and championing the antiwar and Feminist movements in what has become her signature work. Rejecting the traditional oil-on-canvas formula in 1966 for gouache on paper, Spero soon developed her unique collaged and printed images and text scrolls, recalling medieval manuscripts and the Egyptian Book of the Dead. The repeated, fragmented, and often violent imagery, after 1974 consisting exclusively of women, blatantly exposes the repression and victimization of women from all cultures. Spero joins images from ancient and contemporary sources to connect the past with the present and reclaim women's history.

Spero exhibited her work at a few small galleries in Chicago during the early 1950s, and had a two-person exhibition with Leon Golub at Indiana University, Bloomington (1958). Galerie Breteau in Paris gave Spero one-person exhibitions in 1962, 1965, and 1968. She exhibited some of her major series at A.I.R., New York's first all-women's gallery, which she helped found in 1972. Retrospectives have been organized by the Institute of Contemporary Art, London (1987); Everson Museum of Art, Syracuse, New York (1987); Haus am Walsee, Berlin (1990); and a joint retrospective with Leon Golub at The American Center, Paris, and MIT List Visual Arts Center, Cambridge, Massachusetts (1994). Her work has also been featured in hundreds of group exhibitions worldwide. Since 1988 Spero has printed directly onto walls, including a permanent ceiling installation at The Harold Washington Library Center, Chicago (1991). She was previously associated with Josh Baer Gallery, New York, and is currently represented by Rhona Hoffman Gallery and Printworks Gallery, Chicago. SB

Evelyn Statsinger

(Born 1927) Originally from Brooklyn, where she was born in 1927, Evelyn Statsinger came to Chicago in 1947 and stayed. She had previously attended the Art Students League, New York, and the University of Toledo, Ohio, for brief periods. Once in Chicago, she studied at the University of Chicago for a year and received her BAE from SAIC in 1949. Statsinger's first mature work, exhibited in her first one-person show at Chicago's 750 Gallery in 1949, was a group of obsessively detailed ink drawings. Surrealist in their strange collection of archetypal characters as well as their overall pattern of abstract shapes and enigmatic symbols, the black-and-white drawings are punctuated by areas of colored crayon. Associated with the "Monster Roster" painters because of the distorted figures, Statsinger's works were actually inspired by sources ranging from Franz Kafka, her own job on a telephone switchboard, to an interesting pattern of mold growing in her refrigerator. Quite large in scale for ink-on-paper works, some reach a length of seven feet.

In 1951, on a fellowship from the Huntington Hartford Foundation, Statsinger traveled to Los Angeles where she continued her student experiments with the photogram process, using bits of wire, paper, fabric, and leaves. These complex, magical works would serve as a precursor to her Xerox collages of the 1980s. Statsinger then returned to painting and abruptly changed her direction. She eliminated the figure, relying solely on compositions of floating abstract shapes, many evoking natural forms, enlivened by varied textures. These were executed in pastel, charcoal, and graphite. Introducing a new element of color, Statsinger was drawn to a palette of quiet earth tones accented by other hues. Her later works include oil paintings, collages, drawings, sculpture, and prints, which continue to reveal Statsinger's interest in texture and organic form. Organizing her imaginative shapes into rectilinear compartments, she is able to create a variety of spatial illusions. Many of the biomorphic forms in her works suggest male/female references, as well as other elements from nature.

Statsinger participated in the first Exhibition Momentum (1948) as well as later ones in 1950 and 1952. At age twenty-five, she was given a one-person exhibition at AIC (1952) and again in 1957. Her many other solo exhibitions include those at Paul Kantor Gallery, Los Angeles (1952); and in Chicago at the Chicago Public Library (1958), Superior Street Gallery (1961), Artemisia Gallery (1978), and several at Jan Cicero Gallery, the most recent in 1995. The Whitney Museum of American Art, New York, exhibited her work in their 1954 Annual, as did AIC in numerous C & V shows, where she won several prizes. Statsinger's work has been in such group exhibitions as "Reality and Fantasy," Walker Art Center, Minneapolis (1954); "Chicago Imagist Art," MCA (1972); "Chicago Currents," National Museum of American Art, Washington, DC (1979); "Chicago: Some Other Traditions," Madison Art Center, Wisconsin (1983); and "Chicago Abstract Painters," Evanston Art Center, Illinois (1995). SB

Lawrence Steger

(Born 1961) Emerging from the cabaret performance art scene that developed around Club Lower Links during the late 1980s, Lawrence Steger has consistently created performance and video works around transgressive situations or historical figures. Born in St. Louis in 1961, Steger received his BFA in performance from Antioch College in Yellow Springs, Ohio, in 1984. During his undergraduate years, Steger interned with eminent dance instructor Alwin Nikolais in New York and performed at various New York performance clubs such as 8BC, Doorinka, and Pyramid. He began performing in Chicago in 1985, a year after he had moved to the city to attend SAIC, from which he received his MFA in performance in 1986.

Steger's first major performance in Chicago, *The Marriage or Story of Sisters*, was presented at Randolph Street Gallery in 1986. It provided early signs of traits that would reappear in Steger's work: recorded music (culled from both popular and classical sources), the self-analysis of the performance as part of its structure, and an examination of morality pushed to its limits in specific situations. The next year Steger collaborated with video artist Suzie Silver on *La Vida Loca (The Crazy Life)*, a piece that incorporated both video and live performance in focusing upon the relationship between a Russian-Polish immigrant and a Hispanic street gang. Silver would remain a crucial collaborator for Steger, providing video assistance for many of his performances.

Steger's solo performances *Rented Movies* (1988) and *Worn Grooves* (1990) are exemplary of his adaptation to the cabaret format that Club Lower Links demanded. In the former, Steger dealt with his identity as part of the gay community, ironically lip-synching Marlene Dietrich and Lou Reed songs or delivering self-consciously "bad" comedy routines. *Worn Grooves* featured a similar switching of personae, showing Steger changing from a mock-Arab costume to a contemporary outfit, with acidic observations on relationships and sex. The denouement of the performance featured Steger reading from a Rolodex with cliché phrases uttered in the various stages of relationships, break-ups, and one-night stands. In 1991 Steger collaborated once again with Silver on the video *Peccata Mutum*, a fantasy on the lesbian sexual life of a group of nuns.

Steger has performed overseas, sharing the bill with other Chicagoans such as the performance collective Goat Island and the Ethnic Heritage Ensemble. He performed *Rough Trade* with frequent collaborator Iris Moore at the Center for Contemporary Art in Glasgow in 1993. Steger's latest work includes the video *It Never Was You* (1993), created with Patrick Siemer, and perhaps his most ambitious project to date, *The Swans* (1995), a performance focusing upon a proposed film about two outrageous historical figures: Gilles de Rais, a sadistic medieval French military figure, and King Ludwig II of Bavaria, the most eccentric monarch of the nineteenth century. Performed with Douglas Grew and Laura Dame, Steger's performance-about-the-performance demonstrated his continuing interest in investigating morality through the theoretical framework of writers such as Jean Genet and the Marquis de Sade. DM valerio **sykes-dietze—**

Barbara **Sykes-Dietze**

(Born 1953) As an artist, curator, and instructor of video art, Barbara Sykes-Dietze has made a unique contribution to the medium during her long career in Chicago. She was born in Chicago in 1953 and studied at UIC with video pioneers Dan Sandin and Tom DeFanti from 1975 to 1979. Sykes-Dietze participated in some of the first EVE (Electronic Visualization Events) "real time" video and performance events held by Sandin and DeFanti beginning in 1975. She was accepted into the video program at SAIC on the strength of her work and experience at UIC's Electronic Visualization Laboratory, and received her MFA in 1981.

The work that Sykes-Dietze produced during the 1970s displayed the strong influence of the experience with Sandin's and DeFanti's combination of the "real time" possibilities of video and the image-processing capabilities of computer technology. She gradually moved into creating more personal expressions with the medium, reflecting her interest in female mythological figures, rituals, dance, art, and music of other cultures as well as depicting dream states and fantasied visions. *Electronic Masks* (1978) is an early indication of this shift, with its use of computer graphics to create pulsating masks reminiscent of the totem poles of the Northwest Native American peoples. Sykes-Dietze's work of the late 1970s and early 1980s is marked by an interest in combining elements of performance and dance with computer-imaging techniques. Her most recent work has focused on the sacred rituals of Eastern cultures in a combination of documentary and personal reflection, based on her experiences in Nepal and the Middle East.

During the 1980s Sykes-Dietze was an active promoter and curator of Chicago video art. From 1982 to 1988 she was the video coordinator at Columbia College in addition to teaching experimental and advanced production courses for their television department and organizing numerous visiting artists and lecture series and exhibitions of video art. During a sabbatical, sponsored in part by a Chicago Artists Abroad award, she exhibited in a number of one-person shows in Japan, Spain, Australia, and in China, where she was the first woman video artist to present her work. Sykes-Dietze is currently professor of television at Columbia College. DM

Tony **Tasset**

(Born 1960) Tony Tasset's art has investigated the ways in which art is presented, protected, collected, and, of late, created. Tasset was born in 1960 in Cincinnati, Ohio, and attended the Art Academy of Cincinnati, receiving his BFA in 1983. He moved to Chicago that same year and attended Northwestern University and SAIC, receiving his MFA from the latter in 1985. Originally trained as a painter, Tasset turned to sculpture in order to enter an artistic dialogue with Marcel Duchamp, expanding upon the latter's analysis of the institutionalization of the art object. He has often exhibited with or curated exhibitions of the group of young Conceptual artists who emerged with him during the mid-1980s, such as Jeanne Dunning, Hirsch Perlman, and his wife, painter Judy Ledgerwood.

Tasset's breakthrough works are the "Domesticates," stemming from his experience working for Rhona Hoffman Gallery (who has represented Tasset in Chicago since 1989) as a graduate student. These works examine the trophy status of art in the home of the collector, with their framed animal hides bearing a striking resemblance to the work of the Abstract Expressionists. Exhibited in 1984 at his one-person show at Feature (then in Chicago), they exemplify his citation of Modernist styles and philosophies to question the social, economic, and political structures forming the context for the work of art. Tasset's subsequent works—including display cases and manipulated materials used for packing or protecting works of art—are Minimalist meditations on the presentation and preservation of precious objects. Recent works adopt the process-oriented strategies of Post-Minimalist artists such as Bruce Nauman and Robert Smithson, performing a simultaneous homage to and interrogation of their presentation of the "making" of art object as its essence and endgame.

Tasset's contributions as an artist have been complemented by the exhibitions he has organized for local galleries. "Dull Edge," curated with Jeanne Dunning for Randolph Street Gallery in 1986, was the first group presentation of the aforementioned "Neo-Conceptual" artists. His most notorious curatorial effort was "Sex, Death, and Jello" (1988) at Randolph Street Gallery, with a performance by Susan Wexler in which she and two other women wrestled nude in day-glo jello. Tasset, more importantly, has made a significant contribution to art in Chicago as a tenured professor at UIC. He exhibited at the Shedhalle in Zurich in 1992, has had one-person shows in Los Angeles and London, and participated in an installation of Robert Smithson works at MCA titled "Smithson: Site/Non-Site" in 1995. DM

Bob **Thall**

(Born 1948) For over twenty years, Bob Thall has explored and investigated Chicago and its environs. Born in the Chicago suburb of Evanston in 1948, Thall studied architecture at UIC, where his interest in urban forms began. Taking a photography course as part of the required curriculum, Thall switched his focus, obtaining his BA in photography in 1972, and his MFA in photography in 1986. He has been a professor of photography at Columbia College, Chicago, since 1976, and also works as a freelance architectural photographer.

Chronicling the landscape of urban Chicago with an unwieldy view camera, Thall's sharply contrasting black-and-white photographs illustrate the often hidden, picturesque elements of brutal city forms. However, Thall has not limited his work to Chicago. His photographs of American county courthouses, published in a critically acclaimed book entitled *Court House* (1978), were exhibited at MOMA (1977) and AIC (1978). A 1995 exhibition at Ehlers Caudill Gallery, Chicago, "Place: Photographs of the Midwest, 1972–1995," consisted of Thall's depictions of small midwestern towns along the Mississippi and Ohio rivers, as well as photographs taken in Southwest Chicago. Thall is particularly interested in recording changes that inevitably occur within a landscape, whether rural or urban. He emphasizes the collision between old and new, between peculiar and banal. The images resulting from this sort of intersection are prevalent in his 1994 book *The Perfect City*, which served as the catalogue for his AIC show. In it Thall said, "Chicago is never meant to be finished; like any landscape, it is predicated on continuous, sweeping change."

Thall's subject matter leads to frequent connections between his work and that of late nineteenth-century American landscape photographers. In the same way that William Henry Jackson's photographs document exploration in the American West, Thall's work functions as cultural and topographic "maps" of the areas he investigates. The viewer is informed on a variety of levels, from strict geographic recording to the footprints left behind by inhabitants of the landscapes.

Thall has had one-person exhibitions at the Evanston Art Center, Illinois (1980); MoMing Art and Dance Center, Chicago (1981); Swen Parson Gallery, Northern Illinois University, DeKalb (1982); Chicago Center for Contemporary Photography, Columbia College (1983); Illinois State Museum, Springfield (1984); Edwynn Houk Gallery, Chicago (1984); and AIC (1994). His work has been featured in several group exhibitions, including "Landscape Starts Here," Visual Studies Workshop, Rochester, New York (1983); "Chicago, the Architectural City," AIC (1983); "Road, Roadside," AIC and Illinois State University, Normal (1987); "Changing Chicago," The Chicago Public Library Cultural Center and AIC (1989); "Site Work," Photographers' Gallery, London (1991); and "New Photography from Wisconsin, Illinois, and Minnesota," Madison Art Center, Wisconsin (1995). SKM

Julia Thecla

(1896–1973) Born Julia Thecla Connell in 1896 in the rural town of Delavan, Illinois, Thecla showed an early predilection for making art, but only when she was old enough to pay for her own classes was she able to pursue an art education. After studying at Illinois State University at Normal for a summer and a short stint teaching in a rural high school, Thecla began her dream of becoming an artist. By 1920 she was living in Chicago and attending courses at SAIC which she financed through art and antique restoration work. Establishing herself as a professional artist, Thecla exhibited her first work at one of AIC's Watercolor exhibitions. She went on to participate in many shows, including Chicago's first outdoor art fair held in Grant Park. She also joined many artists' associations, including the Chicago Society of Artists and the Neoterics. Thecla's paintings of this period reveal a dramatic shift in the thematic content of her works. Fairy-tale-like images of children and animals gave way to increasingly arbitrary and unusual subject matter. During the 1930s Thecla was quickly absorbed into the dynamic community of Chicago artists. She met such influential individuals as Ivan Albright and Gertrude Abercrombie, and aligned herself with the emerging Chicago tradition of art based on fantasy and imagination.

During the Depression, Thecla was employed by the WPA, producing paintings that tended to explore more prosaic themes of everyday life. Many of these early paintings are self-portraits, a theme of self-examination throughout her life. Enigmatic, whimsical, and spiced with mystery, Thecla's work eludes easy classification. Her fantastic visions of private landscapes, wherein intimate figures and surreal imagery float unyielding to gravity, imitate the disjunctive state of dream. The small scale and refined execution of the paintings elicit the viewers meditative immersion within the murky world of the artist's expansive imagination. Color plays a crucial role in Thecla's work; expressive and evocative, it sets the emotional tone of her paintings.

Thecla's one-person exhibitions include a retrospective at the Illinois State Museum in Springfield (1984), which traveled to the State of Illinois Art Gallery, Chicago; and shows in Chicago at Albert Roullier Art Galleries (1937 and 1944), Ten-Twenty Art Center (1956), and Findlay Galleries (1961). Group exhibitions include those at The Arts Club of Chicago, AIC, and the Renaissance Society, in Chicago; and at MOMA and the San Francisco Museum of Art. Thecla designed scenery and costumes for three ballets during 1945–46, all choreographed by her friend Berenice Holmes. She served as secretary of the Women's Artists' Salon of Chicago, Inc. in 1942, and as secretary of the Chicago No-Jury Society of Artists in 1934 and 1936. AB

Ruth Thorne-Thomsen

(Born 1943) Ruth Thorne-Thomsen was born in New York in 1943 and raised in Berkeley, California, and Lake Forest, Illinois. In 1961–63 Thorne-Thomsen studied dance at Columbia College, Missouri, then trained as a painter and printmaker at Southern Illinois University in Carbondale, where she received her BFA in 1970. It was there that she began exploring photography, which she continued to study at Chicago's Columbia College, receiving her BA in 1973. She received her MFA in photography from SAIC in 1976. Since her final year in graduate school, Thorne-Thomsen has used pinhole photography as a vehicle to explore the realm of the imagination and the unknown worlds of the unconscious. Her pinhole photographs were first exhibited in Chicago in 1980 at Allan Frumkin and Randolph Street galleries. Her photographs have dramatically transformed the genre and have made her one of the most celebrated contemporary pinhole photographers.

Employing symbols that suggest Jungian notions of the collective unconscious, Thorne-Thomsen constructs imaginative landscapes and whimsical locales that link contemporary culture to the past. She draws inspiration from such varied sources as ancient Greek sculptures and ruins, Renaissance portrait paintings, and the Italian landscape. Her work is also strongly influenced by the nineteenth-century exotic travel photography of Francis Frith and Maxime Du Camp.

Thorne-Thomsen's use of the pinhole camera imbues her photographs with a dreamlike aesthetic that is marked by a delicate soft-focus haze, an infinite depth of field, and a diminutive size (some prints are as small as three and one-half by four and one-half inches). The figures and objects in her photographs are typically cutout images made in her studio or simple objects placed in the environment and rephotographed close-up so as to achieve a surreal distortion of scale. Thorne-Thomsen's use of the pinhole technique, along with her extensive use of collage, allows her to combine symbols and scenes from other cultures with American landscape to create enchanting views of imaginary lands and surreal fantasy.

Thorne-Thomsen served on Chicago's Columbia College faculty from 1974 to 1983 and went on to become assistant and associate professor at the University of Colorado at Denver (1983–89). Thorne-Thomsen's work has been exhibited in several group shows, including: "Extending the Perimeters of Twentieth Century Photography," San Francisco Museum of Modern Art (1985); "Poetics of Space," The Museum of Fine Arts, Santa Fe (1987); and "Fantastic Voyages," Houston Center for Photography (1992). She has had over two dozen national and international solo exhibitions, including a 1993 mid-career retrospective at Chicago's Museum of Contemporary Photography. She currently resides in Philadelphia and Moab, Utah, with her husband, photographer Ray K. Metzker. EKW

Steven J. Urry

(1939–1993) Steven J. Urry was born on the South Side of Chicago in 1939. His father was a distinguished organic chemist at the University of Chicago, who later aided the artist in his mastery of materials. Urry studied welding in high school, but spent a great deal of his training as a painter. He attended SAIC in 1957–59 and received his BA from the University of Chicago in 1959. After graduation he traveled to the West Coast to study at the Art Institute of San Francisco and the California College of Arts and Crafts in Oakland before being lured back to his native city by the availability of metal-manufacturing facilities.

Throughout the 1960s Urry was one of a few sculptors in Chicago doing large-scale works, predating the monumental works of Richard Hunt and the arrival of fellow sculptor John Henry. Urry's forms are organic and almost free-flowing, as if he were making continuous doodles in metal. Splashes, drips, and puddles often refer to the human body, evoking its shapes as well as its functions, as illustrated by their designation as "Dribblescapes," Urry's own title for his works. Many of his titles (*Oop-Zig*, *Blat*) as well as his graphic abstract forms seem to be influenced by comic books and cartoons, as were the paintings of Chicago Imagists Jim Nutt and Karl Wirsum, alongside whom he had exhibited at the Phalanx shows of the mid-1960s. Often polished to a shimmering silver finish, Urry's sculptures are at once precious and playful. Urry cast and welded such materials as iron, steel, aluminum, and polyurethane, which he occasionally painted. He worked in a scale just small enough to be shown indoors, though many sculptures are monumental and require a public or corporate setting.

Urry was the first sculptor to have a one-person exhibition at MCA (1969), after showing his work at Royal Marks Gallery, New York (1967), the University of Chicago (1966 and 1968), and Dell Gallery, Chicago (1966). He was given solo exhibitions at Zabriskie Gallery, New York (1970, 1972, and 1976) and at Phyllis Kind Gallery, Chicago (1972 and 1974). His work was featured in several C & V shows at AIC (1967 and 1969–71), for which he won numerous prizes, and was included in such group exhibitions as "Eight American Sculptors," in Pioneer Plaza (1968, now Equitable Plaza), Chicago; and "Sculpture Off the Pedestal" in Grand Rapids, Michigan (1974). Urry's works are in public and private collections nationwide. He ceased being active toward the end of his life and died in 1993. SB

James Valerio

(Born 1938) James Valerio was born in Chicago in 1938 and became interested in art in grammar school. After graduating from high school in 1956, Valerio relegated his interest in art to night classes at Wright Junior College in Chicago. There, he studied with Seymour Rosofsky, who recognized Valerio's talent and encouraged him to enroll full-time at SAIC, where he received his BFA in 1966 and MFA in 1968. While at SAIC, Valerio was influenced by the AIC collection of Old Master paintings (especially *The Chastisement of Love* by Bartolomeo Manfredi) as well as modern works by Ivan Albright. After graduating, Valerio spent time traveling in England and studying Old Master paintings in the National Gallery, London. After his return, he spent two years teaching in Rockford, Illinois, and then moved to Los Angeles to teach in UCLA's art department. In Los Angeles, Valerio began to use photographic transparencies as source material in addition to actual objects and models. While on sabbatical in 1977, he had the opportunity to study Baroque painting in Italy and France. A major turning point in Valerio's career occurred in 1978 when he was invited to participate in a group exhibition, "The Big Still Life," at Allan Frumkin Gallery, New York. The painting he showed, *Still Life #2*, became widely reproduced, leading to Valerio's inclusion in a large number of shows. In 1979 he moved to Ithaca, New York, to teach in the graduate art department of Cornell University, then moved back to Chicago in 1985 to teach in Evanston, at Northwestern University's Department of Art Theory and Practice.

While Photorealistic in appearance, Valerio's paintings are in fact constructed from drawings, transparencies, and his own observations. Dramatic lighting and an intense attention to detail make his paintings visually lush, even when the subject matter is mundane. Valerio's wife, Pat, and his son, Paul, often appear in the paintings, which range from portraits to genre to still life, often with underlying narrative or psychological content. Inherent in his work is a commentary on the Old Master paintings from which he draws so liberally, as Valerio manipulates and updates traditional themes.

Valerio's work has been featured regularly in solo exhibitions at Frumkin and Struve Gallery, Chicago, and Frumkin/Adams Gallery, New York. He received solo shows at the Delaware Art Museum, Wilmington (1983), and the Museum of Art, University of Iowa, Iowa City (1994). He has been widely featured in group shows that explore contemporary realism, including "Painting and Sculpture in California: The Modern Era," San Francisco Museum of Modern Art (1977); "Reflections of Realism," Albuquerque Museum of Art (1979); "Real, Really Real, Super Real," San Antonio Museum of Art (1981); "American Still Life 1945–1983," Contemporary Arts Museum, Houston (1983); "American Realism," Itesan Museum, Tokyo (1985); and "Exquisite Painting," Orlando Museum of Art, Florida (1991). Other important group shows include "Painting at Northwestern: Conger, Paschke, Valerio" Mary and Leigh Block Gallery, Northwestern University (1986), and "Surfaces: Two Decades of Painting in Chicago" Terra Museum of American Art, Chicago (1987). AF

Kazys Varnelis

(Born 1917) Kazys Varnelis is regarded by *Encyclopedia Lituanica* as the first Lithuanian abstract painter. His unique style has been influenced by prominent twentieth-century art movements, especially Cubism and Op art.

Varnelis was born in Alsedziai, Lithuania, in 1917. His father carved religious statues and crucifixes as well as decorating church interiors for a living. This influence most likely contributed to Varnelis's decision to attend the Institute of Fine Arts in Kaunas, where he became an instructor after graduation in 1941. At this time he was also director of the Museum for Ecclesiastical Art in Kaunas. When World War II began, Varnelis left Lithuania for Vienna, where

he attended the Akademie der bildenden Künste. He received his degree in painting in 1943 and immigrated to Chicago in 1949. From 1951 until 1963, Varnelis worked in his own ecclesiastical-art studio where he designed several church interiors. At the same time he was active as a painter; he has devoted himself exclusively to painting and sculpture since 1963.

Varnelis has said that his works belong "to Constructivism and show optical as well as minimal trends." His work is generally monochromatic, with contrasting forms gradually shading from light to dark. Through repeated forms he creates the illusion of three dimensions such as curved surfaces or hollowed-out spaces. These forms are subject to sudden reversals of perspective so that cuplike depressions quickly change into a field of rounded forms or vice-versa. This duality of form sets up tension and makes the viewer an active participant in the experience of the art. Varnelis's technique, which gives brushed acrylic the illusion of airbrushed paint, only serves to strengthen this dynamic tension. Despite the modern character of his work, elements of his repeated patterns draw from both Lithuanian folk-art woodcarving as well as industrial forms gleaned from the urban landscape of Chicago.

Varnelis's work was not ignored in Chicago. He was included in several of AIC's C & V shows in the late 1960s and early 1970s, and was the recipient of AIC's Vielehr Award in 1969. He was given solo exhibitions at the MCA (1970) and the Milwaukee Art Center (1974–75), and participated in the group exhibitions "Twelve Lithuanian Artists in America" at the Corcoran Gallery of Art in Washington, DC (1973) and "Abstract Art in Chicago" at MCA (1976). In 1976 Varnelis exhibited in Chicago with the abstract painters known as "The Five." More recently his paintings have been exhibited in Lithuania at the Vilnius Museum of Fine Arts (1986) and the Exhibition Palace in Budapest (1995). His works are represented in a number of private collections and museums in the United States, including MCA, AIC, and the Solomon R. Guggenheim Museum in New York. Among Varnelis's other interests are teaching and cartography. He was a professor in the Art Department at the Chicago City Colleges from 1968 until 1982. His collection of maps, books, and antiques pertaining to Lithuanian history is considered to be among the best outside of Lithuania. Varnelis currently resides in Stockbridge, Massachusetts. JK

Gregory Warmack

(Mr. Imagination; born 1948) For Gregory Warmack, trauma gave rise to an artistic breakthrough: a nearly fatal mugging caused his transformation from a talented, self-taught community artist to the inspirational, nationally known Mr. Imagination. Born on Chicago's West Side in 1948, Warmack was the third of nine children in a spiritually dedicated Baptist family where his talent was recognized and encouraged by his mother. In the early 1960s his family moved to the South Side, where Warmack continued to reside until 1985, when he took an apartment and studio near Wrigley Field on the North Side.

Warmack peddled his jewelry and other crafts on the streets. Working on his back porch, with scavenged materials, he captured the attention of neighborhood kids; his impromptu workshops for these children were a precursor to his later, more organized community teaching efforts. In 1978 Warmack was shot twice at point-blank range in the chest during a robbery near his South Side apartment. During the six-week coma that followed, Warmack had an out-of-body experience that shaped his future: bathed in a bright light, he envisioned himself as several African kings and an Egyptian pharaoh. After a long recovery, he returned in 1979 or 1980 to scavenging for art materials. He came across a lot where chunks of easily carved industrial sandstone, a by-product of the steel industry, had been dumped. The totemic ancestral heads he carved earned Warmack the nickname "Mr. Imagination." It was another tragedy—a devastating fire at his apartment—that ironically introduced him to the mainstream art scene: the salvaged, blackened sandstone heads caught the eye of gallery owner Carl Hammer, who gave Mr. Imagination his first show in 1983.

Much of Mr. Imagination's work is based on hoards of things he has happened upon or collected, including bottle caps from which he has made hats, neckties, staffs, and the extraordinary *Throne and Footstool* (1992). His numerous figures made from worn-out paintbrushes gave rise to larger, similar figures made from broom heads. A recent series, begun in 1992, features "totem poles" made from wood putty applied to the outside of large cardboard tubes. These sometimes quite large works feature sculptural heads piled one on top of another and embellished with found objects.

Along with his regular exhibitions, Mr. Imagination is active in youth projects, including a recent collaboration with neighborhood children on the creation of a grotto for a park adjacent to the Donnelly Youth Center on South

biographies

wharton varnelis—

Michigan Avenue. Since his debut, Mr. Imagination has had numerous solo and group shows at galleries in New York, Boston, San Francisco, Dallas, and Philadelphia. In 1992 he had a one-person show at the Illinois State Museum in Springfield, and in 1994 was featured in an exhibition at the Terra Museum of American Art in Chicago with David Philpot and Kevin Orth. AF

Ken Warneke

(Born 1958) Born in Milwaukee in 1958, the painter Ken Warneke has made Chicago his home since 1981, when he received his BFA from Northern Illinois University, DeKalb. He began showing early in his career, often with a group associated with club life and punk music, especially figures involved with the short-lived "black light party" phenomenon of the late 1970s and early 1980s. He participated in 1983's notorious "The Sex Show" held in a Clark Street penthouse. In the same year he was also featured in HPAC's "The Big Pitcher: 20 Years of the Abstracted Figure in Chicago Art," which grouped established Chicago figures from the 1970s with talents emerging in the 1980s. In 1985 Warneke received a one-person exhibition at MCA. In 1986 he was included, along with such figures as Don Baum, Paul LaMantia, Jim Lutes, and Wesley Kimler, in an important exhibition at New York's Artists Space organized by Renaissance Society Director Susanne Ghez and titled "Recent Art from Chicago." He was included in several press features of "artists to watch." Despite this considerable early success, by the late 1980s Warneke had become less visible and more of what is often described as "an artist's artist." He reemerged in 1993 with a striking body of work that displays a new command of painterly technique and a refinement of his characteristic subject matter of anonymous people mutely trapped in enervated environments.

Some of Warneke's earliest mature works, created in 1984, consist of untitled huge plaster heads, their features painted in a rudimentary, almost comic-book, style—black-outlined lips, lines marking the folds of the face. The artist then turned exclusively to painting, creating a series of monochromatic purple (a color Warneke often uses and associates not only with royalty but bruised flesh) "cave paintings," which show his typical figures in cave settings with legs and arms cleanly severed. These figures display a complete lack of either physical or psychological trauma, a powerful statement on the numbness of modern society and the emotional bankruptcy of modern art.

Warneke's recent art deftly combines various features from individual faces to create startling portraits. These precisely and expertly painted features—a female-appearing blue eye with light skin and a blonde brow and lashes; a brown, snub nose; seemingly male set of olive-skinned lips—are set within a painted matrix of roughly applied, often fleshy color. Warneke's bleak vision has deep roots in the Nihilist philosophy of the 1950s (the same Existential philosophy that inspired Leon Golub and his generation to create a deeply humanistic vision). It sets him firmly in the figurative tradition of Chicago inaugurated by Ivan Albright. LW

Jane Wenger

(Born 1944) Jane Wenger was born in New York and received her BFA in ceramics from Alfred University, New York, in 1966. After moving to Chicago in the late 1960s, Wenger attended ID, where she completed the experimental but rigorous coursework developed by Harry Callahan, Aaron Siskind, and others, receiving an MS degree in 1969; she later received an MFA from UIC in 1980. Wenger was a cofounder of the short-lived but influential photography gallery within the Feminist co-op Artemisia from 1976 to 1977. In 1985 Wenger bronzed her camera and retired from photography, although she continues to explore other media.

Through black-and-white photographs focusing on the human body, Wenger expressed themes of physical and psychological tension and ambiguity. Among other sources of influence, Wenger cites fashion photography, which helped her to develop a sense of beauty and the controlled use of light and dark in her work. Her use of ambiguous space and elimination of references to scale add abstract and surreal elements to her photographs, similar to the qualities found in the paintings of René Magritte, an artist whose work influenced Wenger. She attributes her choice of the body as landscape and her use of radical cropping to the work of British photographer Bill Brandt. Wenger's various series include "Extended Arms" (1974–76), "Self-Portraits" (1976), and "Bald Heads" (1977) that present bodies and body parts manipulated by various photographic techniques to create intense and disturbing images. In the "Self-Portraits" series, Wenger transformed her nude body into a primal monument in a bleak landscape of sky and horizon line. These explorations culminated in the series "Faces" (1978–79), which feature severely cropped faces, often caught in grimaces that seem about to burst out of the confines of the picture. Sharp contrasts of intense light and dark heighten the drama of the works. This series was additionally manipulated in Wenger's 1981 environmental installation at the MCA, for which ten works were enlarged to four-by-six feet and displayed in an entirely black space. The sense of disorientation was augmented by an enigmatic soundtrack of the grunts and groans of body builders working out.

Wenger's solo exhibitions include those at MCA, the Milwaukee Art Museum, Foto Gallery and P.S. 1 in New York, and Artemisia and Allan Frumkin galleries in Chicago. Her work was included in group shows at HPAC, Chicago Cultural Center, and N.A.M.E. Gallery in Chicago; and the Lakeview Museum of Arts and Sciences in Peoria, Illinois. Wenger's photographs are in prominent public collections. EV

H.C. Westermann

(1922–1981) Horace Clifford Westermann was born in Los Angeles in 1922, the son of an accountant. As a young man he worked in the Pacific Northwest in the lumber industry, where he perhaps first began his love affair with the medium of wood, which primarily defines his oeuvre. Enlisting in the Marine Corps upon the outbreak of World War II, he served in the South Pacific as a gunnery mate aboard the USS *Enterprise* where he was injured in a kamikaze attack and witnessed the devastation of the USS *Franklin*. After his discharge he toured the East as part of an acrobatic act for the USO. In 1947, utilizing the GI Bill, Westermann enrolled at SAIC, but his studies in advertising and design were interrupted by his reenlistment in the Marines during the Korean War. After serving in Korea, he reentered SAIC in 1952 to study painting. Older than many of his fellow students and profoundly affected by the horrors he had witnessed during his military service, Westermann went his own way. He supported himself as a handyman and carpenter. Yet after the idiosyncratic artist made his first sale, in 1955 to Mies van der Rohe, Westermann began to be regularly shown in Chicago and associated with the Chicago School of figurative art. His first show was at fellow-artist John Miller's 414 Art Workshop, but he was soon picked up by dealer Allan Frumkin, who gave him a one-person show in 1958, out of which many important collectors (including Joseph Randall Shapiro, Edwin Bergman, and Lewis Manilow) purchased pieces. He was included along with fellow-SAIC-alumni Cosmo Campoli and Leon Golub in Peter Selz's important 1959 exhibition, "New Images of Man" at MOMA. Although the show generated positive as well as negative publicity, Westermann was singled out by New York critic John Canaday for a particularly brutal assessment.

Often labeled a "neo-Dadaist," Westermann was a maverick with a highly individual approach to his work and an aversion to art theory, fad, and fashion. Although much of his work refers to personal experience, it is ultimately concerned with the unpredictability and danger of universal human existence and the absurdities of modern life—including the art world. Themes include war, particularly the motif of the "death ship," which appears in numerous works; the house; and the human figure, often transformed into architecture. The harshness of his often pessimistic view was softened by Westermann's subtle humor; he often incorporated visual puns. Although his primary medium was wood and his technique that of a master woodworker—constructing, laminating, and embellishing his pieces rather than carving them—Westermann also created works from metal, found objects, and such unlikely materials as Astroturf.

After his marriage to the artist Joanna Beall, Westermann left Chicago in 1961 for Brookfield Center, Connecticut, where he resided until his death in 1981. He received a retrospective of his work in 1969 at the Los Angeles County Museum of Art which traveled to MCA, and in 1978 at the Whitney Museum of American Art in New York. He is represented in depth in the collection of MCA and has works in the collections of AIC, the Whitney, and the Walker Art Center, Minneapolis. LW

Margaret Wharton

(Born 1943) Margaret Wharton was born in Portsmouth, Virginia, in 1943. She studied advertising at the University of Maryland in Baltimore, graduating with a BS degree in 1965. After marriage and several years in Bethlehem, Pennsylvania, she relocated in 1971 to Glenview, on Chicago's North Shore, where she still lives. Inspired by the Feminist movement to explore more fully her own potential, Wharton enrolled in SAIC, receiving her MFA in 1975. While still a student, she became involved with a group of women interested in Feminist ideas and exhibition opportunities for their work. They went on to found the co-op Artemisia, where Wharton showed in 1973–75 as Margaret Harper. She was soon being hailed as one of the most innovative artists to emerge in Chicago in years; a retrospective at MCA in 1981 showed her signature reworked chairs. When Wharton's retrospective traveled to Texas, Florida, and South Carolina, her success prompted Chicago artists to hope that national careers might be more easily launched from this city—a promise that unfortunately was not fulfilled for many of Wharton's peers.

Because of the extremely refined craftsmanship and intricate surface qualities of Wharton's sculptures, which in her early career featured old wooden kitchen chairs sliced and reassembled into various configurations, she was seen in the lineage of H.C. Westermann and as an inheritor of Chicago Imagism. This perception was strengthened when Wharton was picked up immediately after her graduation from SAIC by Phyllis Kind Gallery, which represented most of the Imagists. Wharton, however, credits her father, a zoologist, with inspiring her analytic method of selecting, dissecting, reassembling, and ultimately transforming her original materials. The New York artist Lucas Samaras, who creates decorative, obsessive variations on boxes and chairs, was her aesthetic inspiration. After a number of years of using chairs both as raw material and motif, Wharton began to explore the use of other common objects, particularly books, investigating their forms and properties as she has continued to do inventively with chairs.

Wharton left Phyllis Kind Gallery in the early 1990s and most recently has been showing in Chicago with Jean Albano Gallery. She has shown widely around the United States in group exhibitions such as "Chicago Works," organized by the Bruce Gallery at the Edinboro University of Pennsylvania (1987); the traveling exhibition "Making Their Mark: Woman Artists Move into the Mainstream 1970–1985," organized by The Cincinnati Art Museum (1988); and "Assemblage" at the Southeastern Center for Contemporary Art (SECCA), Winston-Salem, North Carolina (1992). She was the recipient of a SECCA Awards in the Visual Arts grant and traveling exhibition in 1984. LW

Frances **Whitehead**

(Born 1953) Frances Whitehead's work is at once enigmatic and bizarre, scientific and scholarly. Born to two artists in Richmond, Virginia, she learned a respect for mathematics and a curiosity about the physical world from her mother and the desire to define the intangible and pursue the metaphysical from her father. With clean lines and exact measurements, Whitehead's own work layers meanings, references, and materials; Shakespearean allusions with Latin roots; gold leaf on oriental paper; chemical natures and cultural histories; plant oils with steel mesh.

Whitehead received her BFA from East Carolina University, Greenville, North Carolina (1975) and her MFA in printmaking from Northern Illinois University, DeKalb (1978). Her precise prints and drawings dissect paradigmatic shapes and organic objects to reveal their intrinsic geometric structures. Whitehead's early formalist sculptures explore the chemical properties and implications of different types of metals, such as steel, copper, and zinc. During the late 1980s, the introduction of shellac, an insect secretion, as a major component in her sculpture, marks Whitehead's transition from industrial to organic materials. In 1986 Whitehead received an NEA grant that she used to raze the building adjacent to her own and, in what she thought at the time was an attempt to create a pastoral setting in urban Chicago, planted a garden. Instead of simply providing an escape from the city, Whitehead instead found herself working to bend the will of the living plants as she had earlier bent tin and steel rod. She coerced gourds into growing within metal frames that forced them into the shape of Platonic solids. She exhibited them alongside her failed attempts: gourds that had not conformed and hence withered. She also became interested in toxic plant species, such as *Atropa belladonna* (deadly nightshade) and *Datura stramonium* (jimsonweed), and the allegorical or mythological derivations of their names. Whitehead incorporated these symbolic elements into her art, making references to medicine, desire, excess, and death. The juxtaposition of evocative natural materials with mathematical structures is a hallmark of her sculptural installations.

Whitehead was represented for many years by Dart and Marianne Deson galleries in Chicago, and in 1996 alone had solo exhibitions at The Laumeier Sculpture Park in St. Louis, The Herron School of Art in Indianapolis, and Tough Gallery in Chicago; as well as group shows at the National Gallery of American Art in Washington, DC, The American Academy of Arts and Letters in New York, Northern Illinois University Gallery in Chicago, and ARCO in Madrid. Her work has been featured in other group shows, including "Standing Ground: Sculpture by American Women," Contemporary Arts Center, Cincinnati (1987); "Artful Nature," Evanston Art Center, Illinois (1992); "The Return of the Exquisite Corpse," The Drawing Center, New York (1993); and "The Nature of the Machine," Chicago Cultural Center (1993). Whitehead has taught at Texas Tech University, Lubbock (1979–80); Illinois State University, Normal (1980–81); Indiana University, Bloomington (1981–84); and has been a professor of sculpture at SAIC since 1984, serving as chairperson of the Sculpture Department a number of times. LS

Richard **Willenbrink**

(Born 1954) Rendering nude figures in lush, colorful backgrounds, Richard Willenbrink has created an exclusive space for himself in the history of painting in Chicago. Willenbrink was born in Louisville, Kentucky, in 1954. He received his BFA from the University of Notre Dame, Indiana, in 1976, and his MFA from Northern Illinois University, DeKalb, in 1979. In 1979 he taught at Sauk Valley College in Dixon, Illinois, and moved to Chicago later in the year. Willenbrink quickly established himself in Chicago with a solo exhibition at Two Illinois Center (1981) and as part of the "Emerging Artists" group exhibition at the Renaissance Society (1983). Recognized by critic Dennis Adrian for filling a gap left open for many years in Chicago as a realist painter of the human figure, Willenbrink was featured in "Chicago: Some Other Traditions," a 1983 exhibition organized by the Madison Art Center, Wisconsin, that traveled to several venues across the Midwest through 1986.

Willenbrink's large paintings present nude figures of both sexes surrounded by allegorical situations and props. Reflecting his classical training in art, the paintings often present subjects from ancient mythology yet feature an intense, modern palette and unmistakably contemporary interiors, props, hair and body styles. This depiction of classic themes is often startling until one remembers that the "classics" were painted in the conventions and styles contemporary to their own times as well. Willenbrink is also known for his nude self-portraits and representations of local art figures.

Willenbrink taught at SAIC for the 1986–87 school year. He rejoined the SAIC faculty in 1992, where he continues to teach. He has been a visiting artist at Northwestern University, Evanston, Illinois; UIC; and the University of Notre Dame. Willenbrink is often featured in group exhibitions focusing on figure painting. In 1984 he exhibited in such a show at N.A.M.E. Gallery. In 1987 he was included in "Figurative Painting in Chicago" at Northern Illinois University. In 1992 Willenbrink had a retrospective at the Rockford College Art Gallery, Illinois. His paintings were most recently the crux of the 1995 "Seeing the Figure Now" exhibition at the Betty Rymer Gallery at SAIC. DM

Anne Wilson

(Born 1949) In 1979 Anne Wilson arrived in Chicago to serve for a year as a visiting artist in the Fiber Department at SAIC; she remained and is now a tenured professor. Her own labor-intensive work, made of fibrous materials and found objects, extends the boundaries of what is traditionally thought of as fiber art. She positions her work not as craft, but as part of the contemporary art dialogue, dealing with issues such as simulation, materials, process, Feminism, and the body.

Born in Detroit in 1949, Wilson attended the University of Michigan in Ann Arbor and later the Cranbook Academy of Art in Bloomfield Hills, where she received a BFA in 1972. After studying at the Haystack Mountain School of Crafts in Deer Isle, Maine, with European artists Peter and Ritzi Jacobi, Wilson moved to Oakland to attend the California College of Arts and Crafts, which emphasized experimentation, process, and interdisciplinary studies between fiber, sculpture, and painting. During the late 1970s, Wilson produced Minimalist hanging grids made of netting, ink-soaked paper, or abaca fibers.

In Chicago, after her move from the Bay Area to the urban environment, Wilson began her series of "urban furs." She calls these works of the mid-1980s her "hair paintings." Wilson stitched acrylic-painted synthetic and linen fiber through a base of painted felt. These furry tufts produce subtle designs reminiscent of animal pelts as well as Abstract Expressionist markings. Parts are dyed bright colors to accentuate the tension between the natural and the artificial. The shape of these works became increasingly regular and geometric, suggesting easel-size paintings, commenting perhaps on the painted surface as a sort of skin.

During the 1990s Wilson's work moved in a related direction, concentrating on the associations of human hair. When offered the gift of a student's recently cut tresses, Wilson began to investigate how hair contributes to cultural and sexual identity. She continued to "fake it" by sandwiching manipulated real and synthetic hair between pieces of glass in her "Specimen Cases" (1991) and "I Cut My Hair" (1993) series. In her most recent work, real hair and thread are obsessively stitched around holes and stains already present in worn linens to accentuate areas of ruin or loss. Unruly hair and body references are coupled with domestic symbols and elegant formal arrangements on shelves in series entitled "Areas of Disrepair" (1993) and "Mendings" (1995).

Wilson's 1995 solo exhibition at Illinois Wesleyan University in Bloomington was accompanied by an artist's book she produced with Sally Alatalo called *Imperfect Sutures*. Other important exhibitions were at the Madison Art Center, Wisconsin (1993–94); the Halsey Gallery, School of the Arts, College of Charleston, South Carolina (1992); The Chicago Public Library Cultural Center (two-person show with Dann Nardi, 1988); Roy Boyd Gallery, Chicago (1991 and 1994), as well as other galleries in San Francisco and Berkeley. Her work has been included in numerous group exhibitions. Wilson has lectured extensively around the United States since 1978 and has served as a guest curator on several occasions. SB

Charles Wilson

(Born 1937) In large-scale Conceptual installations, Charles Wilson investigates historically charged political and sporting events from the last fifty years. Wilson was born in New Orleans in 1937. He received his BA in 1959 from Louisiana State University, Baton Rouge, and followed with a year at the University of Alabama, Tuscaloosa. He received a BFA from Yale University, New Haven, Connecticut, in 1962, earning his MFA there the next year. Wilson studied closely with the sculptor Naum Gabo while at Yale, and continued to teach there after completing his graduate scholarship. In 1965 he had his first solo exhibition, at the Kanegis Gallery in Boston, and was included in the Whitney Museum of American Art, New York, Biennial. He continued to exhibit at Kanegis and other spaces on the East Coast through the late 1960s.

Wilson moved to Evanston, Illinois, in 1972, and the following year began teaching at UIC, where he still teaches. He rewrote the traditional undergraduate curriculum to deemphasize drawing and was instrumental in starting the graduate school of art. His first exhibition in Chicago was in a group show at DePaul University in 1972. In 1978 Wilson had his first local solo exhibition at N.A.M.E. Gallery. He was represented in *N.A.M.E Book 2*, a book of artists' projects compiled in 1980. His work was exhibited in the "City Sculpture" exhibition (1981) at The Chicago Public Library Cultural Center. Wilson's work of this period consists of subdued, Conceptually oriented photographic essays and sculpture, much in keeping with the Chicago Conceptualism of artists such as Phil Berkman and Dennis Kowalski. His primary interests were the photographic construction of reality, language and labeling, and the documentation of time. Wilson was featured in N.A.M.E.'s tenth anniversary exhibition (1983), a testimony to his involvement with the gallery during the 1970s and early 1980s.

In the early 1980s Wilson developed the large, mixed-media installations for which he is currently known. He incorporated the fuselage of a World War II B-17 bomber with drawings and bright red neon text in his installation at Marianne Deson Gallery in 1983. The use of neon inscriptions and theatrically scaled elements that came to characterize Wilson's work reflects his interest in the contemporary history of European and American relations. His work has always possessed a debt to the Constructivism of his mentor Gabo. An expert on Gabo, Wilson coorganized the 1986 retrospective of his work at the Museum of Fine Arts, Dallas, which then traveled to Düsseldorf. In 1989 Wilson was included in both "Encontros: Portuguese-American Meetings on Art, Contemporary American Sculpture" at the Fundação Calouste Gulbenkian, Lisbon, and the "Awards in the Visual Arts 7" exhibition at the High Museum, Atlanta. His works for the "New Generations: Chicago" exhibition at the Carnegie Mellon Art Gallery, Pittsburgh, in 1990, examined military devices and the historical context of war, specifically the Cold War between the Soviet Union and the United States. Wilson's recent work—exhibited in the "Korrespondenzen/ Correspondences: 14 Artists from Berlin and Chicago" exhibition held at the Chicago Cultural Center and the Berlinische Galerie, Berlin (1994–95)—features documentation from the lives and crucial matches of prizefighters Joe Louis and Benny Paret. DM

Maurice Wilson

(Born 1954) Born on the South Side of Chicago in 1954 to an artistic family, Maurice Wilson early on displayed extraordinary talent. Active as an artist even while in high school, he showed in youth fairs such as the Buckingham Foundation Art Fair where he won prizes and made contact with important figures in the arts. As an undergraduate at SAIC, Wilson exhibited in AIC's C & V exhibitions, and after a eight-month sojourn in Italy in an independent study program, he received his BFA (1979). He went on to receive an MFA from Yale University in New Haven, Connecticut (1981). Although he came of age in the turbulent late 1960s, Wilson consistently looked toward ancient and classical sources as the measure of his own production, in technique as well as concept.

Wilson's early work consists of classically rendered female nudes, often drawn from memory and inspired by his admiration of such Modernist masters as Picasso and Balthus. He showed these works in a solo exhibition at Chicago State University (1983) and at Chicago alternative spaces such as Artemisia, as well as at the South Side Community Art Center and in the exhibition "Midwest Realists," which traveled to the Center for the Visual Arts at Illinois State University, Normal; the Burpee Art Museum, Rockford, Illinois; and The Paine Art Center and Arboretum, Oshkosh, Wisconsin (1985). In the mid-1980s he became affiliated with Peter Miller Gallery in Chicago, where he showed a body of work called "The Pink Room Suite" (1987), and participated in the "5 + 5: Ten Perspectives in Black Art" exhibition at The Chicago Public Library Cultural Center (1985). Believing that Chicago art institutions have failed in the area of supporting artists, especially African-American artists, Wilson founded Plum Studio Ltd. in 1989 to allow himself independence in producing and marketing his art.

At about this time Wilson began utilizing burlap as a painting surface, choosing it for its raw, natural beauty and its positive associations with the historical African-American experience of making do with meager resources. He began using tar as a painting medium, frequently depicting plums, which for Wilson are complex symbols referring to folk expressions such as "the darker the berry (or plum), the sweeter the juice" and to the appearance and sensual quality of black skin. Other recent works divide the canvas into various areas that feature disparate images: an impishly grinning black female nude Wilson dubs "Shock-o-late," a looping "S" form, and a four-pointed flower symbol adapted from the Benin culture of West Africa. He also sharply contrasts the coarse qualities of the burlap canvas with gold leaf and elegantly rendered images of classical Egyptian heads. These works were shown in a 1993 solo exhibition at the Chicago Cultural Center. LW

Karl Wirsum

(Born 1939) Karl Wirsum's paintings and sculptures match skillful technique to a frenzied display of elements from popular culture and ordinary life. Born in Chicago in 1939, Wirsum has lived in the city for all but the three-year period he spent teaching at Sacramento State University, California, in 1971–73. He received his BA from SAIC in 1961, and spent five months in Mexico after graduation. Soon after his return to Chicago, he exhibited in such important group shows as "The Sunken City Rises" (1964) and "Phalanx 3" (1965), both at IIT. He was already beginning to develop the cartoonlike style for which he would later become known. Crucial for Wirsum was the "Hairy Who" exhibition of 1966 at HPAC, in which his work appeared with that of a group of artists (James Falconer, Art Green, Gladys Nilsson, Jim Nutt, and Suellen Rocca) who shared

Ziolkowski woelffer—Woelffer

a similar style, attitude, and subject matter. Wirsum and the rest of the Hairy Who quickly became dominant forces in Chicago art during the 1960s among the various artist factions working in the figurative mode—later dubbed "Imagists" by Franz Schulze.

An animated and often outrageous treatment of the figure characterizes Wirsum's painting and sculpture. Using vibrant colors, dynamic line, and puns of all sorts, Wirsum adopts the logic and strategies of popular culture to create a bizarre fantasy world of odd characters and improbable situations. An exacting formal polish tempers with irony and offsets the fantastic life found in Wirsum's art.

Wirsum's activities in Chicago during the 1970s and 1980s included his participation in the "Made in Chicago" exhibition, the US entry to the São Paulo Bienal exhibition in 1973; a part-time teaching position at SAIC beginning in 1974; and a 1980 exhibition at MCA titled "Hare Toddy Kong Tamari," which presented Wirsum's hitherto overlooked sculptural objects. The primary inspiration for the three-dimensional works was most likely Wirsum's home, described by Franz Schulze as "an environment affectionately heaped with memorabilia of 1930s, lower-class America." The Krannert Art Museum, University of Illinois, Champaign, gave Wirsum a retrospective in 1991. His most public presentation in Chicago is the large mural *Plug Bug* (1991) he created for the Gallery 37 space in the Loop. He is represented in Chicago and New York by Phyllis Kind Gallery, with whom he has shown since 1974. DM

Emerson Woelffer

(Born 1914) A Chicago native, abstract painter Emerson Woelffer was born in 1914. He studied at SAIC in the mid-1930s, serving also as an assistant in the Katherine Kuh Gallery, where he was exposed to works by Modernist masters. He joined the WPA in 1938, working in both Chicago and St. Louis. He joined the US Army Air Force (1939–42) and worked as a topographical draftsman. In 1945 he was hired by László Moholy-Nagy as an ID faculty member, teaching drawing, design, sculpture, and photography until 1949, when Buckminster Fuller invited him to teach a summer course at Black Mountain College in the mountains of North Carolina. Away from an urban area for the first time in his life, Woelffer experienced a desire to travel, and spent a number of months with his wife, Diana, painting in Campeche in the Yucatan Peninsula in Mexico. Upon his return, he founded a short-lived art school in Chicago, but left the city in 1950 to take a position as a painting instructor at the Colorado Springs Fine Art Center.

Although Woelffer went on to spend most of his career on the West Coast, his impact on the Chicago art world of the 1940s and into the 1950s as he continued to show actively in the city was significant. The Krannert Art Museum at the University of Illinois in Champaign organized a major show in 1950, and AIC mounted a one-person show in 1951. At ID, Woelffer was a focal point. A great lover of jazz and dedicated amateur "scat" drummer, Woelffer held forth in his studio beneath Stuart Brent's just-founded Seven Stairs Bookshop on Rush Street, where artists, musicians, and writers would spontaneously gather. He held legendary parties, some in his studio in Cyrus McCormick's former carriage barn (which still contained McCormick's abandoned carriages), where he would hang works of his students and fellow-ID instructors in informal exhibitions. As one of the few Chicago-based painters exploring Abstract Expressionism, Woelffer was well received in New York: he was included in group exhibitions at the Solomon R. Guggenheim Museum several times in the mid- and late 1940s, and had a critically acclaimed solo exhibition at The Artists Gallery in 1949. In Chicago he showed his work in C & V exhibitions at AIC, often winning prizes. His work of the 1940s is characterized by energetic, rhythmic forms; bright colors against darker backgrounds; and, in the late 1940s, pictographic forms. He also produced drawings and experimented with collage.

Woelffer has had numerous one-person shows in galleries and museums around the United States and in Europe. The Pasadena Art Museum, California, mounted a retrospective exhibition in 1962. Another retrospective was organized in 1992 by the Otis Parsons Art Institute, Los Angeles (where he was chairman of the Painting Department for many years). Woelffer currently resides in Los Angeles. LW

Joseph E. Yoakum

(1886/88–1972) One of the most significant self-taught artists to come out of Chicago and an important influence on the Imagists, Joseph Yoakum began his art-making late in life. In only ten years he produced a tremendous number of works, primarily drawings of landscapes culled from memories of his youthful travels. Although his early history may in part be legend, this son of a former slave claimed to have been born on Arizona's Window Rock Navajo Reservation in either 1886 or 1888. While he was still a child, his family moved to a farm in Missouri. At age fifteen, with little formal education,

Yoakum ran away with the Adams Forpaugh Circus. Yoakum claimed that after working for Buffalo Bill's Wild West Show and the Ringling Brothers' Circus, by 1911 he had visited every continent except Antarctica. After being stationed in France during World War I, he married for the second time. Eventually Yoakum settled in Chicago, where he supposedly ran an ice-cream store until he retired; after being inspired by a dream, he began drawing only ten years prior to his death in 1972.

Staunchly religious and committed to reading his Bible every day, Yoakum described his drawings as "spiritual unfoldment." Blending memories of natural settings with scenes found in *National Geographic,* Yoakum created imaginative and idiosyncratic works in a flattened, stylized pattern of ballpoint-pen lines and watercolor washes. This technique, which included tracing from favorite works, resulted in images of fantastical places that seem not of this earth, despite the elaborate, specific place-names Yoakum would prominently assign each drawing. Later he switched to using colored pencils, which he would scrub to achieve an effect similar to pastels. However, the bold, serpentine outlines of natural forms that Yoakum filled in with intricate patterns dominate the compositions. Although the majority of Yoakum's works are landscapes, he made portraits of African-American movie stars, recording artists, and sports figures. He also believed in the existence of UFOs, which he portrayed in his "Flying Saucer" pictures, and occasionally drew trains and boats.

Yoakum hung his drawings in the window of his South Side storefront apartment, where he sold them for as little as twenty-five cents. A passerby, John Hopgood, an instructor at Chicago State College, was captivated by the works and arranged for an exhibition at the nearby Whole Cafe. Artist Tom Brand, who saw the exhibition, introduced the work to art dealer Edward Sherbeyn. The "first gallery showing of Chicago's own primitive" opened at Sherbeyn's North Clark Street gallery in 1968 with some fanfare. It was here that Karl Wirsum came in contact with and eventually collected Yoakum's drawings. Others of Wirsum's circle, such as artists Roger Brown, Phil Hanson, Gladys Nilsson, Jim Nutt, Christina Ramberg, Barbara Rossi, and Ray Yoshida and SAIC art-history professor Whitney Halstead became enthusiastic about Yoakum's work. In particular, Halstead cultivated a close relationship with the artist, amassing a large collection of his work, which he bequeathed to AIC in 1979 and which formed the basis for Yoakum's one-person AIC show in 1995.

Yoakum has been featured widely in exhibitions of works by self-taught artists, including shows at MCA and the

National Museum of American Art in Washington, DC. His work was included in "Parallel Visions: Modern Artists and Outsider Art" (1992), organized by the Los Angeles County Museum of Art, which traveled nationwide and to Europe and Japan. Solo exhibitions have included those at the Whitney Museum of American Art in New York (1972); Carl Hammer Gallery in Chicago (1982); and Janet Fleisher Gallery in Philadelphia (1989). AF

Ray Yoshida

(Born 1930) Ray Yoshida has made important contributions to the Chicago art scene both as a painter and as a long-time teacher at SAIC. Yoshida was born in Kapaa, Kauai, Hawaii. His artistic talent was recognized and cultivated at an early age. After two years at the University of Hawaii, he was urged by an older sister in nursing school in Chicago to enroll at SAIC, where he received his undergraduate degree in 1953. After receiving an MFA in 1958 at Syracuse University in New York, he immediately returned to teach at SAIC; he was appointed Frank Harold Sellers Professor in 1971, and continues to be an influential painting teacher. Along with SAIC art-history professor Whitney Halstead, Yoshida was especially important for the group of artists introduced by HPAC's "Hairy Who" and "False Image" exhibitions, including Roger Brown, Philip Hansen, Gladys Nilsson, Jim Nutt, Christina Ramberg, Barbara Rossi, and Karl Wirsum.

Yoshida's early works feature painterly geometric forms and occasionally a lone, red heart. In 1968 and 1969, in a series that marked an important development, Yoshida created collages of ordered rows of text and images cut from comic books. Yoshida's "Bathrobe" series followed in the early 1970s—paintings of cartoonish, faceless figures in dizzyingly striped robes that seem simultaneously to blend into and fight with their similarly striped environments. In 1973 Yoshida returned to collage in another series, which features rocklike forms drawn in a comic-book style also arranged in horizontal rows. An avid collector of eccentric objects and folk art, Yoshida likely found inspiration in his collection for the odd, abstract objects depicted in these works.

In the late 1970s Yoshida's work began to make large paintings filled top-to-bottom with tall, vertical objects. By 1980 these totemic images translated into figures that became increasingly more colorful. Yoshida's paintings since the late 1970s generally feature busy surfaces where every form is filled in with textural scribbles, dots, and tiny lines. These paintings emphasize figure/ground relationships and the interaction of color and pattern.

Yoshida's work has been featured in numerous national and international group exhibitions where it is often shown as part of the Imagist tradition. These include exhibitions at MCA (1969, 1972, 1984, and 1985); the São Paulo Bienal (1973); the National Collection of Fine Arts, Smithsonian Institution, Washington, DC (1979); and the Whitney Museum of American Art, New York (1983). He has been associated with Phyllis Kind Gallery, Chicago and New York, since 1975 and was the subject of a solo exhibition at N.A.M.E. Gallery, Chicago, in 1984. His work is included in the permanent collections of AIC, MCA, Museum des 20. Jahrhunderts in Vienna, and the National Museum of American Art, Washington, DC. AF

Claire Zeisler

(1903–1991) Claire Zeisler was born in 1903 in Cincinnati. In the mid-1940s, Zeisler's studies with Russian sculptor Alexander Archipenko and avant-garde Hungarian artist László Moholy-Nagy at Chicago's ID sparked her interest in three-dimensional forms. However, it was Chicago weaver Bea Swartchild who taught Zeisler how to weave and encouraged her artistic pursuits in the fiber arts. Although Zeisler's career as a fiber artist began relatively late in her life, her innovative style and experimental working methods gained her international recognition and established Chicago as an important center for fiber art. Zeisler was also a major collector of Modernist art, which she began acquiring in the 1930s, and eventually put together a collection of distinction that included tribal art, antiquities, and contemporary art.

Moving from making traditional and functional loom weavings in the 1950s, Zeisler began making off-loom experimental pieces in 1962, which evolved into free-standing three-dimensional structures. In 1962, at the age of fifty-nine, Zeisler had her first solo exhibition, at The Chicago Public Library, and later that same year she had another one-person show at the Renaissance Society. The inclusion of her work in the 1963 landmark exhibition "Woven Forms" at the Museum of Contemporary Crafts in New York established her as one of the country's leading fiber artists. A new generation of fiber artists in the 1960s, led by Zeisler, Sheila Hicks, and Lenore Tawney, elevated this traditional craft beyond function and decoration to the status of fine art.

Using alternative techniques of knotting, braiding, and wrapping, Zeisler created large, free-standing sculptures. Her monumental pieces of the 1960s (often six to eight feet high) marked the emergence of her signature style of bold shapes that frequently suggest distinctly female forms with an emphasis on elegant, cascading strands of bristly natural fiber, contrasting textures, and brilliant primary colors of blue, red, yellow, black, and white. These formal concerns continued throughout her career and were enhanced by her explorations in the 1970s in pieces made of folded leather as well as long coiled wires wrapped with brightly colored cotton threads.

In addition to her artistic innovations, Zeisler spent her career conducting workshops and teaching several generations of fiber artists. She consistently showed her work at the Richard Feigen Gallery in Chicago and New York, as well as at the Museum of Contemporary Crafts of the American Craftsmen's Council, also in New York. Her work was celebrated in a retrospective at AIC in 1979 and at the Whitney Museum of American Art, New York, in 1984. Claire Zeisler died in 1991. EKW

Zhou Brothers

(Shan Zuo Zhou, Born 1952; Da Huang Zhou, Born 1957) The Zhou Brothers, who have painted as a collaborative team throughout their career, were born in the Guangxi province in southern China to a family of educators, scholars, and poets. Their father, the headmaster of a college, became a victim of the Cultural Revolution of 1966–76, and was exiled to a mountainous farming region. The two brothers were separated, one cared for by their mother, the other by their grandmother. Despite the current pressures against artists and intellectuals, the Zhou Brothers studied music, poetry, and traditional Chinese calligraphy. They learned Western art from books obtained by a sister who was attending an art school. Reunited in 1976, the two brothers traveled in China and enrolled in the Shanghai Drama and Art College, receiving their BFAs in 1980. After winning considerable recognition, they enrolled in the Central Institute of Art and Graphics, studying mural and fresco techniques, and received their MFAs in 1984. They continued to receive more honors, and their work was exhibited at prestigious venues, including the National Museum of Art, Beijing. Although the new openness of the Chinese government allowed them freedom to paint as they wished, and they were proclaimed leaders of a "new Chinese renaissance," the Zhou Brothers were wary that this freedom might end at any time. In 1986 they relocated to Chicago, where they have continued their international success, showing widely in Chicago, Europe (especially Germany), and Hong Kong.

The abstract style of the Zhou Brothers has numerous sources, chief of which are the ancient art and mythology of China. The neolithic Huashan pictographs of their native province (which the brothers visited as children with their father) were particular influences; pictographic figures and symbols often dominate their large-scale canvases and huge mural works. The influence of ink brush painting and calligraphy can also be seen, especially in the bold forms and palette of grays, black, and white that the artists prefer. The surfaces of the paintings are often richly textured, with vigorous, scrubbing brush strokes bisected by lines of blood red. The frequently poetic titles given to their works indicate concerns with the artistic process, philosophical inquiry, and natural forces and rhythms, such as the wind and sunrise and sunset. The Zhou Brothers were affiliated with East West Contemporary Art in Chicago in the late 1980s, and currently show with Oskar Friedl Gallery, Chicago, and Nahan Galleries, New York. They have been the subject of over fifty solo exhibitions around the world, including a retrospective at Kunsthalle Darmstadt, Germany, and have been included in numerous group exhibitions. LW

Joe Ziolkowski

(Born 1960) The stark representation of daringly posed, muscular male nudes against a white background has become the signature style of photographer Joe Ziolkowski. Exhibitions of his work are often accompanied by controversy, because of his frank depiction of homoerotic themes. Joe Ziolkowski was born in 1960 in Jacksonville, Florida, and received his BA in photography in 1982 from Southern Illinois University, Carbondale. In 1980, while studying at SIU, he began photographing the nude male figure. Ziolkowski moved to Chicago in 1983 and received his MFA in photography from SAIC in 1987. His photographs are informed simultaneously by Greek sculptural ideals of perfection in the male body, the crisp photography of predecessors such as Minor White and Edward Weston, and the persistent threat of the AIDS virus in the gay community and the world at large.

In 1988 two of Ziolkowski's images were featured in a SAIC alumni exhibition at 200 North LaSalle Street, curated by Joe Cavalier and Tony Tasset. The exhibition could be seen from both the street and the lobby, prompting complaints from tenants regarding his work *Beyond Boundaries #3*, in which two male nudes embrace. During an ensuing controversy, a compromise was reached between Ziolkowski, the curators, and the building's management, resulting in the covering of the photograph with paper, with the note "covered from the public view by request of the management" placed beside it. Ziolkowski's concurrent exhibition at N.A.M.E., "A Year in the Life of Joe Z.," which documented his daily routine, proceeded without incident.

Ziolkowski moved to New York in 1990. Conflict followed him to his 1991 exhibition at Lycoming College in Williamsport, Pennsylvania, where a number of people expressed their displeasure with the exhibition. The exhibition featured Ziolkowski's "The Numbered" series, a numerically titled series of portraits of male and female nudes shown hanging upside down from torso to head. Begun in 1988, the series metaphorically represents the anxiety experienced by those awaiting the results of HIV tests. In 1992 Ziolkowski completed "The Pressure" series, consisting of images of nude males taken from beneath a pane of glass, demonstrating Ziolkowski's desire to experiment with the physicality and malleability of the body. He returned to Chicago in 1994 and created "The Silence," a series that marks a further departure from his earlier photos in the use of a studio environment and props, with the ubiquitous male nudes testifying to the silence maintained within our society on various levels and subjects.

Ziolkowski has published a book of his photographs titled *Walking the Line* (1992). A successful freelance photographer, he served as the MCA staff photographer from 1987 to 1989, and rejoined the staff in 1995. He currently teaches at both SAIC and the American Academy of Art in Chicago. DM

(Art)ⁿ Laboratory

(Founded 1983) Comprised of a shifting set of collaborative artists, (Art)ⁿ creates visually stimulating work through the use of computer technology. Founded by Ellen Sandor in 1983, (Art)ⁿ Laboratory is a collective of artists, scientists, mathematicians, and computer experts who invented PHSColograms®—museum-quality photography of virtual reality and three-dimensional computer graphics—that can be viewed in a light box or reflectively. Their technologically advanced work was inspired by the process-oriented works of the modern artists Man Ray, László Moholy-Nagy, and Marcel Duchamp. (Art)ⁿ original members included Jim Zanzi, professor of sculpture at SAIC, sculptors Gary Justis and Randy Johnson, video artist Mark Resch, and fashion photographer Gina Uhlmann.

Their early work explores the effect of technology on society and consists of large-scale sculptures that combine holography, three-dimensional photography, video, and occasionally sound. (Art)ⁿ utilizes its innovative technologies to produce works that address scientific, political, social, and aesthetic issues, including AIDS, chemical warfare, fractals, and architecture.

In 1985 (Art)ⁿ collaborated with Dan Sandin and Tom DeFanti of the Electronic Visualization Laboratory (EVL) at UIC and Larry Smarr and Donna Cox of the National Center for Supercomputing Applications (NCSA) at the University of Illinois at Urbana-Champaign to create a digital process for producing PHSColograms. Their first images were Romboy Homotopies—computer-generated, four-dimensional, complex mathematical structures—that were shot off of a computer monitor using a video camera. The collaboration between (Art)ⁿ, EVL, and NCSA produced a significant collection of digital scientific visualization virtual three-dimensional hard copy. In 1988, with the efforts of Stephan Meyers, currently associate director of (Art)ⁿ, hardware selection and software development occurred, resulting in the first all-digital PHSColograms.

In 1991 Sandor coined the term "virtual photography" to describe the PHSColograms, and a patent for the PHSCologram process was awarded the following year. (Art)ⁿ has produced over 250 digital works that have been exhibited internationally. Selected exhibitions include "The Interactive Image," Museum of Science & Industry, Chicago (1987); "Matter Over Mind=Sculpture," Fermilab, Batavia, Illinois (1991); "The New Images, Montage '93," George Eastman House, Rochester, New York (1993); "(Art)ⁿ Laboratory: Virtual Photography/PHSColograms," Gahlberg Gallery, Arts Center, College of DuPage, Glen Ellyn, Illinois (1994); "The Role of Computer Graphics Technology in the Human Perception of Reality," The Wexner Center for the Arts, Ohio State University, Columbus (1995); and "Beyond the Global Village, Triennale di Milano," Palazzo della Triennale, Milan (1995). Currently represented by Oskar Friedl Gallery in Chicago, (Art)ⁿ was formerly associated with Feature, New York, and Rhona Hoffman Gallery, Chicago. In addition to creating works of art, (Art)ⁿ uses the PHSCologram process for commercial purposes as well. (Art)ⁿ Laboratory is based at the Basic Industrial Research Laboratory at Northwestern University, Evanston, Illinois. DM

checklist
of the exhibition

dimensions indicated in inches;
height precedes width precedes
depth

Gertrude Abercrombie
(American, 1909–1969)

The Courtship
1949
Oil on Masonite
21 3/4 x 25 1/4
Museum of Contemporary Art, Chicago,
Gift of the Gertrude Abercrombie Trust
plate 13

Mary Ahrendt
(American, born 1940)

A Guest
1982
Pigment on chromogenic color print
Three parts, overall 90 x 27 3/16
Museum of Contemporary Art, Chicago,
Gift of Charles S. Panozzo
plate 114

Ivan Albright
(American, 1897–1983)

*The Temptation of
St. Anthony*
1944–45
Oil on canvas
50 x 60
The Art Institute of Chicago,
Gift of Ivan Albright
plate 1

Harold Allen
(American, born 1912)

Church, Chilili, New Mexico
1955
Gelatin silver print
13 3/4 x 10 7/8
Museum of Contemporary Art, Chicago,
Illinois Arts Council Purchase Grant
plate 26

Edith Altman
(American, born Germany 1931)

Obuli #23
1970
Birch wood
Twenty-four parts, each 23 x 8 x 1;
overall dimensions variable
Courtesy the artist, Chicago
plate 70

Othello Anderson
(American, born 1944)

Fern Shaffer
(American, born 1944)

*Winter Solstice/Crystal Clearing
Ceremony* (detail)
1985
Documentary color photographs
Three parts, each 20 x 30
Courtesy the artists, Chicago
plate 128

Effigy Mounds (detail)
1987
Documentary color photographs
Three parts, each 20 x 30
Courtesy the artists, Chicago
Not illustrated

Don Baum
(American, born 1922)

The Babies of della Robbia
1965
Plastic dolls, nylon, paint, wood, cloth,
and paper
29 5/8 x 46 1/2 x 9 5/16
Museum of Contemporary Art, Chicago,
Gift of Joseph and Jory Shapiro
plate 58

Chinatown
1980
Wood, crushed metal cans, rulers, and
glue
14 1/2 x 9 1/2 x 14 3/4
National Museum of American Art,
Smithsonian Institution, Washington, DC,
Gift of S.W. and B.M. Koffler
plate 107

Vera Berdich
(American, born 1915)

Things to be Remembered
1949
Soft ground and photo etching with
aquatint on paper
18 1/2 x 14 3/4
Courtesy the artist and
Printworks Gallery, Chicago
plate 14

Fred Berger
(American, born 1923)

A Flower; A Child; Will They Grow?
1971
Charcoal and crayon on paper
79 1/2 x 67 1/2
Museum of Contemporary Art, Chicago,
Restricted gift of Ruth Horwich,
Samuel W. and Blanche M. Koffler,
Audrey and Robert Lubin, Susan and
Lewis Manilow, Joseph and Jory Shapiro,
and Lynn and Allen Turner
plate 75

Phil Berkman
(American, born 1946)

City security: Chicago
1973
Xeroxes on board
Eleven parts, each 8 1/2 x 11
As published in "Anti-Object Art" issue,
TriQuarterly 32 (winter 1975)
Private collection, Chicago
plate 81

Phyllis Bramson
(American, born 1941)

Winter (again)
1992
Oil on canvas
68 x 68
Melynda Lopin Ehrlich
and Sheila Lopin Goode, Chicago
plate 157

Roger Brown
(American, born 1941)

*Autobiography in the Shape of
Alabama (Mammy's Door)*
1974
Oil on canvas, mirror, wood, hardware,
Plexiglas, photographs, postcards,
and cloth shirt
89 3/4 x 48 3/4 x 18
Museum of Contemporary Art, Chicago,
Gift of Maxine and Gerald K. Silberman
plate 83

Buttermilk Sky
1974
Oil on canvas
72 1/4 x 72 1/2
Dr. and Mrs. Peter W. Broido, West Chicago
plate 84

*The Entry of Christ into Chicago
in 1976*
1976
Oil on canvas
72 x 120
Whitney Museum of American Art,
New York, Purchase with funds from
Mr. and Mrs. Edwin A. Bergman and the
National Endowment for the Arts, and
Joel and Anne Ehrenkranz, by exchange
plate 90

*The Race to Make the World's
Largest Painting*
1988
Oil, straw, and pottery on canvas
48 x 72
Lynn and Allen Turner, Chicago
plate 134

Harry Callahan
(American, born 1912)

Eleanor
1947
Gelatin silver print
4 1/2 x 2 5/8
Courtesy PaceWildensteinMacGill,
New York, and Ehlers Caudill Gallery,
Chicago
plate 7

Chicago
c. 1949
Gelatin silver print
6 x 6
Courtesy PaceWildensteinMacGill,
New York, and Ehlers Caudill Gallery,
Chicago
plate 12

Collage, Chicago
1957
Gelatin silver print
7 5/8 x 9 5/8
Center for Creative Photography,
The University of Arizona, Tucson,
Harry Callahan Archive
plate 30

Cosmo Campoli
(American, born 1922)

Birth of Death
1950
Bronze, rock, wax, and steel
70 x 18 3/4 x 24 1/2
Museum of Contemporary Art, Chicago,
Gift of Joseph and Jory Shapiro
plate 15

Rodney Carswell
(American, born 1946)

*Tri-Color Cross, Encircled in 3 Gray
Panels*
1988
Oil and wax on canvas on wood
88 x 88 x 4 1/2
Courtesy Feigen, Inc., Chicago
plate 135

George Cohen
(American, born 1919)

Emblem for an Unknown Nation #1
1954
Oil on Masonite
68 1/8 x 51 1/4
Museum of Contemporary Art, Chicago,
Gift of Muriel Kallis Newman
plate 21

William Conger
(American, born 1937)

South Beach
1985
Oil on canvas
60 x 72
Elmhurst College, Illinois
plate 127

Jno Cook
(American, born 1940)

35mm Cockroach Camera
1978
Reclaimed materials
7 1/2 x 8 x 7 1/4
Courtesy Beret International Gallery,
Chicago
plate 98

Eldzier Cortor
(American, born 1915)

Room No. 6
c. 1946–49
Oil on gesso on board
31 1/2 x 42
Private collection, New York
plate 5

Barbara Crane
(American, born 1928)

Human Form
1965–66/1993
Gelatin silver print
7 1/4 x 10 3/4
Courtesy the artist and Ezell Gallery,
Chicago
plate 55

Tom Czarnopys
(American, born 1957)

Untitled
1984
Oak and maple bark, poplar branch, and
acrylic paint and matte medium on
plastered gauze
66 3/4 x 21 1/2 x 48
Museum of Contemporary Art, Chicago,
Restricted gift of MCA Collectors'
Group; and Illinois Arts Council Partners
in Purchase Grant
plate 121

Henry Darger
(American, 1892–1972)

*At Jennie Richee—Mabel introduces
her Blengin sisters (three of them)
to the little Vivians one p.m.
(recto and verso)*
Date unknown
Carbon ink, pencil, tempera, and collage
on paper
24 x 108 1/2
Museum of Contemporary Art, Chicago,
Gift of Nathan Lerner
plate 85

Barbara DeGenevieve
(American, born 1947)

Folie à Deux
1984
Photolinen
Two parts, overall 104 x 36
Courtesy the artist, Chicago
plate 118

Dominick Di Meo
(American, born 1927)

Excavation
1959
Papier-mâché
18 x 23
Theodore Halkin, Evanston, Illinois
Not illustrated

Torso/Landscape
1962
Plastic
20 x 14
Courtesy the artist, New York
plate 44

Jeff Donaldson
(American, born 1937)

A La Sango
1968
Mixed media on canvas
28 x 23
South Side Community Art Center,
Chicago
plate 63

Robert Donley
(American, born 1934)

Invasion of the Continent
1978
Oil on canvas
66 x 72
Courtesy the artist and
Gruen Galleries, Chicago
plate 100

Susanne Doremus
(American, born 1943)

Chicago
1994
Oil and linocut on canvas
78 x 84
Courtesy the artist and
Zolla/Lieberman Gallery, Chicago
plate 166

Ruth Duckworth
(American, born Germany 1919)

Untitled
1972
Glazed stoneware
17 1/4 x 19 x 3
The David and Alfred Smart Museum
of Art, The University of Chicago,
Gift of Margaret Fisher
plate 79

Jeanne Dunning
(American, born 1960)

Neck
1990
Silver-dye bleach print mounted
to Plexiglas
33 x 28
Edition 2/3
Refco Group, Ltd., Chicago
Not illustrated

Detail 8
1991
Laminated silver-dye bleach print
21 1/2 x 17
Edition 1/2
Lance Kinz and Susan Reynolds, Chicago
plate 149

Stan Edwards
(American, born 1941)

Infant in Altar IV
1964
Oil and acrylic on canvas
60 x 60
National Museum of American Art,
Smithsonian Institution, Washington, DC,
Gift of Mr. and Mrs. David K. Anderson,
Martha Jackson Memorial Collection
plate 50

Douglas Ewart
(American, born Jamaica 1946)

Wind Song
1983
Bamboo, steel, redwood, acrylic flutes,
and brass chimes
96 x 96 x 96
Courtesy the artist, Minneapolis
plate 115

Julia Fish
(American, born 1950)

Cumulous
1990
Oil on canvas
30 1/16 x 27 1/16
Museum of Contemporary Art, Chicago,
Gift of Mr. and Mrs. E.A. Bergman and
Mr. and Mrs. Richard L. Feigen by
exchange; and Illinois Arts Council
Partners in Purchase Grant
plate 144

Tony Fitzpatrick
(American, born 1958)

Dandelion
1995
Chine collé etching on paper
8 x 6
Courtesy the artist, Chicago,
and Janet Fleisher Gallery, Philadelphia
Not illustrated

Immigrant Flowers
1995
Chine collé etching on paper
8 x 6
Courtesy the artist, Chicago,
and Janet Fleisher Gallery, Philadelphia
plate 173

Nereida García-Ferraz
(American, born Cuba 1954)

Todo o nada
1990
Oil and wax on paper
38 x 50
Joan Golden, Chicago
plate 142

Gaylen Gerber
(American, born 1955)

Untitled
Not dated
Oil on canvas
33 x 38
Howard and Donna Stone, Chicago
plate 154

Roland Ginzel
(American, born 1921)

Untitled
1963
Oil on canvas
44 x 40
Patricia F. Sternberg, Chicago
plate 48

Lee Godie
(American, 1908–1994)

Untitled (Prince of a City)
Date unknown
Oil on window shade
56 1/8 x 23 1/4
Larry and Evelyn Aronson,
Glencoe, Illinois
plate 116

Leon Golub
(American, born 1922)

Hamlet
1954
Lacquer on Masonite
52 x 24
Peter Selz, Berkeley, California
plate 23

Siamese Sphinx II
1955
Lacquer on Masonite
48 x 48
Ulrich Meyer, Chicago
plate 25

Head (XIII)
1958
Lacquer and oil on canvas
32 x 24
Museum of Contemporary Art, Chicago,
Gift of Joseph and Jory Shapiro
Not illustrated

Reclining Youth
1959
Lacquer on canvas
78 3/4 x 163 1/2
Museum of Contemporary Art, Chicago,
Gift of Susan and Lewis Manilow
plate 40

Neil Goodman
(American, born 1953)

Triptych
1991
Bronze
75 x 77 x 7
Courtesy the artist, Chicago
plate 153

Joseph Goto
(American, 1920–1994)

Organic Form I
1951
Steel
Two parts, overall with base
136 1/4 x 21 1/4 x 12
The Museum of Modern Art, New York,
Purchase
plate 18

Family Tree
1954
Stainless steel
128 x 21 1/2 x 18 3/4
The Art Institute of Chicago, Watson F.
Blair Purchase Prize
Not illustrated

Untitled
c.1956
Steel
12 x 61 3/4 x 9
Museum of Contemporary Art, Chicago,
Gift of Mr. and Mrs. Allan Frumkin
plate 27

Theodore Halkin
(American, born 1924)

Lunar Perigee
1962
Mixed media on plywood
63 x 48 x 3
Courtesy the artist, Evanston, Illinois
plate 45

Phil Hanson
(American, born 1943)

Rousseau's Lily
1972
Acrylic on board
28 1/4 x 27
Museum of Contemporary Art, Chicago,
Gift of Albert J. Bildner
plate 77

Gene Hedge
(American, born 1928)

Untitled
1964
Sisal lined industrial paper
48 x 42
Jim Glasser, Tucson, Arizona
plate 54

Robert Heinecken
(American, born 1931)

Waking Up In News America
1984
Photolithograph on paper
26 x 38
Center for Creative Photography,
The University of Arizona, Tucson,
Gift of the artist
plate 123

John Henry
(American, born 1943)

Lafayette '61
1981
Polished aluminum
93 x 80 x 108
Robert Vogele, Chicago
plate 110

Steven Heyman
(American, born 1952)

Siblism
1995
Acrylic on canvas
Eighteen parts, each 23 x 19;
overall 72 x 120
Courtesy the artist, Chicago
plate 169

Margo Hoff
(American, born 1912)

Murder Mystery
1946
Oil on casein on canvas board
30 x 20
The Art Institute of Chicago,
Walter M. Campana Memorial Prize
plate 4

Richard Hull
(American, born 1955)

The Piano
1979
Oil on canvas
30 x 26
Lolli Thurm, Chicago
plate 105

Richard Hunt
(American, born 1935)

Construction D
1956
Cottonwood and steel
61 x 18 1/2 x 16
Courtesy the artist, Chicago
Not illustrated

Construction N
1956
Cottonwood and steel
55 x 27 x 22
David and Sarajean Ruttenberg, courtesy
Ruttenberg Arts Foundation, Chicago
plate 29

Hero Construction
1958
Steel
69 1/4 x 23 3/4 x 15
The Art Institute of Chicago,
Gift of Mr. and Mrs. Arnold H. Maremont
plate 38

Michael Hurson
(American, born 1941)

Ballet of the Left-Handed Piano
1962
Charcoal and oil on canvas
88 3/16 x 69 3/4
The Art Institute of Chicago,
Joseph N. Eisendrath Purchase Prize
plate 47

Yasuhiro Ishimoto
(Japanese, born 1921)

Untitled from the series "Chicago,
Chicago"
1960
Gelatin silver print
10 x 7
The Museum of Contemporary
Photography, Columbia College Chicago,
Gift of Jack A. Jaffe
plate 41

Michiko Itatani
(American, born Japan 1948)

Untitled
1980
Acrylic on canvas, wood, and
metal hinges
Four sections, each 63 1/4 x 21 x 4
Museum of Contemporary Art, Chicago,
Partial gift of Marianne Deson
plate 109

Miyoko Ito
(American, 1918–1983)

Monnongahela
c. 1961
Oil on canvas
52 x 48
FMC Corporation, Chicago
plate 42

Sea Chest
1972
Oil on canvas
47 x 45
Cole Taylor Bank, Chicago
Not illustrated

Joseph Jachna
(American, born 1935)

Door County, Wisconsin
1970
Gelatin silver print
8 x 10
Museum of Contemporary Art, Chicago,
Gift of Arnold M. Gilbert
plate 71

Indira Freitas Johnson
(Indian, born 1943)

Transformation from the "Process of
Karma" installation
1995
Bark, stones, and plastic containers
6 x 48 x 48
Courtesy the artist, Evanston, Illinois
plate 170

Marva Lee Pitchford Jolly
(American, born 1937)

Alice from the series "Spirit Women"
1993
Pit-fired clay
16 x 11 x 8
Courtesy the artist and
Satori Fine Art, Chicago
plate 158

Bessie from the series "Spirit Women"
1993
Pit-fired clay
15 x 19 x 6
Courtesy the artist
and Satori Fine Art, Chicago
Not illustrated

Calvin B. Jones
(American, born 1934)

*Brilliant•as•the•Sun•Upon•the•World
(Egungun)*
1994
Mixed media on canvas
48 x 54 x 6
Courtesy the artist, Chicago
plate 167

Kenneth Josephson
(American, born 1932)

Chicago, 1964
1964
Gelatin silver print
9 x 9
The Museum of Contemporary
Photography, Columbia College Chicago,
Gift of David and Reva Logan Foundation
plate 53

Stockholm, 1967
1967
Gelatin silver print
8 x 12
Museum of Contemporary Art, Chicago,
Illinois Arts Council Purchase Grant
Not illustrated

Gary Justis
(American, born 1953)

Untitled
1993
Aluminum, brass, and motors
39 x 108 x 37
Courtesy the artist and Klein Art Works,
Chicago
plate 165

Jin Soo Kim
(American, born Korea 1950)

Untitled, amputated
1988
Mixed media
50 x 30 x 40
Daryl Gerber, Chicago
plate 136

Untitled
c. 1989
Copper wire and mixed media
32 x 18 1/2 x 24
Ruth Horwich, Chicago
Not illustrated

Wesley Kimler
(American, born 1953)

Egmont
1995
Oil on canvas
99 x 120
Museum of Contemporary Art, Chicago,
Gift of the artist
plate 172

David Klamen
(American, born 1961)

Untitled (Vase)
1993
Oil on linen
86 x 66
Ronald and Meta Berger, Chicago
plate 159

Vera Klement
(American, born Free City of Danzig,
Germany 1929)

Door to the River
1989
Oil and wax on canvas
Two parts, overall 78 1/4 x 126 1/4
Museum of Contemporary Art, Chicago,
Gift of artist and Fassbender Gallery
plate 141

Richard Koppe
(American, 1916–1973)

Wall
c. 1947
Oil on canvas
20 x 26
Tom Talucci, Chicago, courtesy Adams
Fine Art, Chicago
plate 6

Thomas Kovachevich
(American, born 1942)

Caressing You
1977/1996
Tracing paper and polyester
Dimensions variable
Courtesy the artist and Curt Marcus
Gallery, New York
plate 92

Dennis Kowalski
(American, born 1938)

Wedges
1976
Graphite on concrete and *New Art
Examiner* magazine advertisement
Seven wedges, each 8 x 36 x 10;
Public installation
As documented by seven photographs,
one wedge, and magazine advertisement
Courtesy the artist and Beret
International Gallery, Chicago
plate 89

Paul LaMantia
(American, born 1938)

Sorry Wrong Number
1972
Oil on canvas
73 3/8 x 84 1/2
The David and Alfred Smart Museum
of Art, The University of Chicago,
Gift of Naomi and Richard Vine
plate 76

Ellen Lanyon
(American, born 1926)

Fregene
1962
Oil on canvas
69 x 66
Courtesy the artist, New York
plate 46

June Leaf
(American, born 1929)

Red Painting
1954
Oil on canvas
72 x 108
Stuart Katz, Laguna Beach, California
plate 22

Arcade Women
1956
Oil on canvas
71 11/16 x 100 5/16
Museum of Contemporary Art, Chicago,
Gift of Allan Frumkin
plate 28

Nathan Lerner
(American, born 1913)

Eye on Window
c. 1945
Gelatin silver print
13 x 14 1/2
Courtesy the artist and
Ehlers Caudill Gallery, Chicago
plate 2

Robert Lostutter
(American, born 1939)

Red-Throated Bee-Eater
1978
Watercolor and graphite on paper
12 1/2 x 13 7/8
Jorge and Martha Schneider, Chicago
plate 101

Jim Lutes
(American, born 1955)

The Evening of My Dysfunction
1985
Oil on canvas
55 x 44 1/2
Museum of Contemporary Art, Chicago,
Gift of Ralph I. and Helyn D. Goldenberg,
Ruth Horwich, and Illinois Arts Council
Partners in Purchase Grant
plate 126

Iñigo Manglano-Ovalle
(American, born Spain 1961)

Assigned Identities (Part 1)
1990
Laminated chromogenic color prints
Eleven parts, each 13 x 20
Susan and Lewis Manilow, Chicago
plate 147

Kerry James Marshall
(American, born 1955)

Untitled (Altgeld Gardens)
1995
Acrylic and collage on canvas
78 x 100
Johnson County Community College,
Overland Park, Kansas
plate 171

Ray Martin
(American, born 1930)

Acceptable Losses
1983
Cloth-bound book with lithographs,
graphite, watercolor, and ink on paper
Book closed 12 5/8 x 9 7/8 x 3/4
Museum of Contemporary Art, Chicago,
Gift of Printworks, Ltd. and
Illinois Arts Council Purchase Grant
plate 117

Luis Medina
(American, born Cuba, 1942–1985)

Sons of the Devil, Chicago
1978
Silver-dye bleach print
10 3/4 x 10 3/4
Richard and Ellen Sandor, Chicago
plate 97

Dead Gang Member, Chicago
1979
Silver-dye bleach print
11 x 14
Richard and Ellen Sandor, Chicago
Not illustrated

Adelheid Mers
(German, born 1960)

American Beauties #19 (Flame)
1994
Ellipsoidal light fixture,
aluminum templet, and color gel
Dimensions variable
Irene Tsatsos and Mitchell Kane,
New York
plate 168

John Miller
(American, born 1927)

Seated Figure II
1957–58
Oil on canvas
64 x 48 1/4
Donn Shapiro, Glencoe, Illinois
plate 34

Konstantin Milonadis
(Ukrainian, born 1926)

Wave-Goer
c. 1964
Stainless steel and stone
30 1/2 x 17 x 5
Ruth Horwich, Chicago
plate 51

László Moholy-Nagy
(Hungarian, 1895–1946)

Nuclear II
1946
Oil on canvas
49 3/4 x 49 3/4
Milwaukee Art Museum,
Gift of Kenneth Parker
plate 3

Keith Morrison
(American, born Jamaica 1942)

Under the El
1972
Oil on canvas
72 x 132
Cole Taylor Bank, Chicago
plate 78

Archibald J. Motley, Jr.
(American, 1891–1981)

Gettin' Religion
1948
Oil on canvas
31 7/8 x 39 1/4
Archie Motley and
Valerie Gerrard Browne, Evanston,
Illinois
plate 8

Robert Natkin
(American, born 1930)*

Honeymoon
1957
Oil on canvas
60 5/8 x 79 1/8
Paul R. Campagna, Chicago, courtesy
Thomas McCormick Works of Art,
Chicago
plate 32

Joyce Neimanas
(American, born 1944)

Don't Touch
1978
Ink, colored pencil, paper, staples, and
safety pins on gelatin silver print
28 11/16 x 24 5/8
Museum of Contemporary Art, Chicago,
Illinois Arts Council Purchase Grant
plate 99

Elizabeth Newman
(American, born 1952)

Untitled
1987
Cocoon jar, test tubes, test-tube rack,
scissors, garden tool, root, calf-weaning
device, hair, eggs, weighted cord, and ball
Seven parts on four shelves,
overall 65 x 32 x 5 1/2
John and Wendy Cartland,
Lake Bluff, Illinois
plate 131

nickle—siskind

checklist

Robert Nickle
(American, 1919–1980)

Untitled
1961
Paper collage
9 x 13 1/2
Richard and Mary Gray, Chicago
plate 43

Gladys Nilsson
(American, born 1940)

The Enterprize Encounterized By The Spydar People
1969
Watercolor on paper
22 1/4 x 30 1/2
Courtesy the artist, Wilmette, Illinois
plate 66

Jim Nutt
(American, born 1938)

Miss E. Knows
1967
Acrylic on Plexiglas, aluminum, rubber, and enamel on wood frame
75 5/8 x 51 5/8
The Art Institute of Chicago, Twentieth Century Purchase Fund
plate 59

Summer Salt (recto and verso)
1970
Vinyl paint over plastic and enamel on wood and Masonite
62 x 36 1/4 x 6 1/2
Museum of Contemporary Art, Chicago, Gift of Dennis Adrian in honor of Claire B. Zeisler
plate 68

I'd Rather Stay (on the Other Hand)
1975–76
Acrylic on canvas and wood frame
49 x 43
Private collection, Chicago
plate 86

Moat
1992
Acrylic on linen and particle-board frame
28 3/8 x 27 3/8
Mr. and Mrs. Daniel Olswang, Chicago
plate 156

Lorenzo Pace
(American, born 1943)

Mummification Series VIII
1978
Wood, cord, sand, tape, and gauze
Installation, overall 120 x 72 x 48
Courtesy the artist, Brooklyn, New York
plate 96

Esther Parada
(American, born 1938)

Overview #1 and *Overview #2* from the series "Site Unseen"
1976/79
Graphite and van Dyke brown emulsion on Arches paper
Two parts, each 11 x 13 7/8
Museum of Contemporary Art, Chicago, Gift of the artist; and Illinois Arts Council Purchase Grant
plate 93

Ed Paschke
(American, born 1939)

Hophead
1970
Oil on canvas
45 x 60
Dennis Adrian, Chicago
plate 67

Adria
1976
Oil on canvas
98 x 75 11/16
Museum of Contemporary Art, Chicago, Gift of Susan and Lewis Manilow in honor of Dennis Adrian
plate 87

Fumar
1979
Oil on linen
60 x 46
Richard and Ellen Sandor, Chicago
plate 103

The Decision
1993
Oil on linen
40 x 70
Private collection, Florence, Italy
plate 161 (not in exhibition)

Jerry Peart
(American, born 1948)

Escape
1973
Painted aluminum
37 x 48 1/4 x 24 1/4
Museum of Contemporary Art, Chicago, Gift of Larry N. Deutsch in honor of Julie R. Deutsch and their children, Loren, Cathy, and Leigh
plate 82

Marion Perkins
(American, 1908–1961)

Man of Sorrows
1950
Marble
17 1/2 x 9 3/4 x 9 1/4
The Art Institute of Chicago, Pauline Palmer Purchase Prize
plate 16

Hirsch Perlman
(American, born 1960)

Untitled (Armory)
1988
Chromogenic color print, Cor-x, frame, Plexiglas, laminated gelatin silver print, honeycomb board, and Sintra
Two parts, overall 26 x 72
Courtesy the artist, Los Angeles, and Donald Young Gallery, Seattle
plate 137

Dan Peterman
(American, born 1960)

Small Change
1989
Densified, recycled aluminum cans
Three parts, each 40 x 40 x 8
Museum of Contemporary Art, Chicago, Gift of Maremont Corporation by exchange
plate 140

Robert C. Peters
(American, born 1938)

Chicago: Although Marco Polo Never Heard of Chicago, Its Story Really Begins with Him
1982/1996
Loaves of bread, map, and text panels
Installation, dimensions variable
Courtesy the artist, Lake Forest, Illinois
plate 112

John Phillips
(American, born 1953)

Space Shuttle
1981
Acrylic on canvas
112 x 94
Courtesy the artist, Chicago
plate 113

Frank Piatek
(American, born 1944)

Herosagamos II (347th tube painting)
1967
Oil on canvas
77 7/8 x 69 5/8
Ruth Horwich, Chicago
plate 61

Kerig Pope
(American, born 1935)

Two Children Observing Nature
c. 1965
Oil on canvas
68 1/2 x 84
Ruth Horwich, Chicago
plate 56

300

Martin Puryear
(American, born 1941)

Greed's Trophy
1984
Steel rods and wire, hickory, ebony,
rattan, and leather
153 x 20 x 55
The Museum of Modern Art, New York,
David Rockefeller Fund and Purchase
plate 119

Old Mole
1985
Red cedar
61 x 61 x 32
Philadelphia Museum of Art, Purchased:
The Samuel S. White, 3rd, and Vera
White Collection (by exchange) and
Gift of Mr. and Mrs. C.G. Chaplin
(by exchange), and funds contributed
by Marion Stroud Swingle, Mr. and Mrs.
Robert Kardon, Mr. and Mrs. Dennis
Alter, and funds contributed by
friends and family in memory of Mrs.
H. Gates Lloyd
plate 125

Christina Ramberg
(American, 1946–1995)

Black Widow
1971
Acrylic on Masonite
31 x 18 1/2
Illinois State Museum, Springfield
plate 73

Daniel Ramirez
(American, born 1941)

TL-P 6.421
1976–77
Acrylic on canvas
95 3/8 x 120 3/16
Museum of Contemporary Art, Chicago,
Gift of Marianne Deson and the artist
plate 94

Marcos Raya
(Mexican, born 1948)

Night Nurse
1993/1996
Acrylic on canvas, cabinet, surgical
instruments, mannequin, and found
objects
Installation, overall 94 x 204 x 48
Mexican Fine Arts Center Museum,
Chicago, Gift of Dr. Merilyn M. Salomon
and the artist; additional objects
courtesy the artist, Chicago
plate 162

Richard Rezac
(American, born 1952)

Untitled
1986
Vermilion ink and acrylic medium on wood
6 1/2 x 24 x 4
Museum of Contemporary Art, Chicago,
Restricted gift of Robert H. Bergman,
Douglas and Carol Cohen,
Gerald S. Elliott; and Illinois Arts
Council Partners in Purchase Grant
plate 129

Suellen Rocca
(American, born 1943)

Suellen's Corness Painting
1965
Oil on canvas
73 x 59 3/8
Dennis Adrian, Chicago
plate 57

Arnaldo Roche Rabell
(Puerto Rican, born 1955)

You Have to Dream in Blue
1986
Oil on canvas
83 7/8 x 59 7/8
John Belk and Margarita Serapión,
Hato Rey, Puerto Rico
plate 130

Miroslaw Rogala
(Polish, born 1954)

Trees are Leaving #2
1993
Chalk on paper, LCD-display color
monitor, wood frame, videotape, and VCR
Frame 60 3/8 x 48 3/8
Museum of Contemporary Art, Chicago,
Gift of Oskar Friedl Gallery
plate 160

Alejandro Romero
(Mexican, born 1948)

Procession
1991
Acrylic on canvas
108 x 156
Dr. Alfredo Cisneros, Elburn, Illinois
plate 151

Kay Rosen
(American, birthdate undisclosed)

Various Strata
1985/1996
Sign paint on wall
100 x 96
Courtesy the artist, Gary, Indiana
plate 124

Paul Rosin
(American, born 1957)

Birth
1993
Oil on gelatin silver print
20 x 16
Courtesy the artist, Chicago
plate 164

Seymour Rosofsky
(American, 1924–1981)

Unemployment Agency
1958
Oil on canvas
52 x 71
The Estate of Seymour Rosofsky,
Chicago
plate 39

Officer and Lady
1979
Oil on canvas
36 x 48
Mildred Armato, Winnetka, Illinois
plate 104

Barbara Rossi
(American, born 1940)

Brr'd and Baa'd
1972
Acrylic on Plexiglas, satin, human hair,
and oil on wood frame
41 3/4 x 33 1/2 x 2 1/4
Lois Craig and Stephen Prokopoff,
Iowa City
plate 80

Joe Scanlan
(American, born 1961)

Untitled Candle (8 oz. milk)
1988
Paraffin wax and cotton wick
4 1/2 x 3 1/2 x 3
Patricia A. Scott, Riverdale, Illinois
plate 138

Untitled Candle (meat tray)
1988
Paraffin wax and cotton wick
1 x 6 x 8
Kathryn Hixson, Chicago
Not illustrated

Untitled Candle (Pop Tarts)
1988
Paraffin wax and cotton wick
6 x 3 1/2 x 2 5/8
Gaylen Gerber, Chicago
Not illustrated

David Sharpe
(American, born 1944)

Untitled
1970
Oil on canvas
78 x 100
Mr. and Mrs. Jerome Torshen, Chicago
plate 69

Arthur Siegel
(American, 1913–1978)

Untitled
c.1952
Color photograph
16 x 20
Blanche M. Koffler, Chicago
plate 19

Paul Sierra
(Cuban, born 1944)

Passing Storm
1987
Oil on canvas
80 x 60
Dr. Alfredo Cisneros, Elburn, Illinois
plate 132

Hollis Sigler
(American, born 1948)

*She Wants To Belong To The Sky,
Again*
1981
Oil on canvas with painted wood frame
43 1/8 x 61 1/4
Museum of Contemporary Art, Chicago,
Illinois Arts Council Purchase Grant
and matching funds
plate 111

Diane Simpson
(American, born 1935)

Ribbed Kimono
1980
Colored pencil and crayon on
corrugated archival board
84 x 60 x 40
Courtesy the artist, Wilmette, Illinois
plate 106

Art Sinsabaugh
(American, 1924–1983)

Chicago Landscape #58
1964
Gelatin silver print
5 7/8 x 19 5/8
Indiana University Art Museum,
Bloomington, Art Sinsabaugh Archive
plate 52

Aaron Siskind
(American, 1903–1991)

Chicago 30
1949
Gelatin silver print
13 7/8 x 17 5/8
International Center of Photography,
New York, Gift of Mr. and Mrs.
Edgar B. Howard
plate 11

Chicago 42
1952
Gelatin silver print
13 3/4 x 16 1/2
The Art Institute of Chicago,
Gift of Mr. Noah Goldowsky
plate 20

Buzz Spector
(American, born 1948)

Library
1984
Altered book pages, rocks, and wood
11 x 61 3/4 x 12 3/4
Museum of Contemporary Art, Chicago,
Gift of Howard and Donna Stone
plate 122

Nancy Spero
(American, born 1926)

At Their Word (The Sick Woman)
1957–58
Oil on canvas
60 x 40
Courtesy the artist, New York
plate 37

Evelyn Statsinger
(American, born 1927)

In the Penal Colony
1949
Pen, ink, and crayon on paper
31 x 58
Courtesy the artist, Chicago
plate 10

Tony Tasset
(American, born 1960)

Abstraction with Wedges
1990
Plexiglas and poplar
5 3/4 x 44 1/4 x 43 1/4
Museum of Contemporary Art, Chicago,
Bernice and Kenneth Newberger
Purchase Fund; and Illinois Arts Council
Partners in Purchase Grant
plate 145

Bob Thall
(American, born 1948)

*Clark Street near Randolph Street,
view west through State of Illinois
Building construction site*
1980
Gelatin silver print
16 x 20
Courtesy Ehlers Caudill Gallery, Chicago
plate 108

Julia Thecla
(American, 1896–1973)

Confusion of Christmas
1948
Gouache with incising, graphite, and
charcoal on cardboard
17 7/8 x 11 3/4
The Art Institute of Chicago,
Olivia Shaler Swan Fund
plate 9

Ruth Thorne-Thomsen
(American, born 1943)

Plane Crash
1977
Gelatin silver print
50 7/16 x 41
Museum of Contemporary Art, Chicago,
Purchase
plate 95

Steven J. Urry
(American, 1939–1993)

Blat
1967
Steel
83 x 78 x 42
Richard Brown Baker, New York
plate 62

James Valerio
(American, born 1938)

Night Fires
1984
Oil on canvas
92 x 100
Union League Club of Chicago
plate 120

Kazys Varnelis
(American, born Lithuania 1917)

Untitled
c. 1971
Acrylic on canvas
60 x 40
Inez and Raymond Saunders,
Chicago
plate 72

**Gregory Warmack
(Mr. Imagination)**
(American, born 1948)

Throne and Footstool
1992
Bottle caps, velvet, buttons, and
mixed media
Throne 81 x 42 x 23 1/2
Footstool 9 1/2 x 18 3/8 x 11 3/4
Courtesy the artist and
Carl Hammer Gallery, Chicago
plate 155

Ken Warneke
(American, born 1958)

The Tyranny of Everyday Life
1990
Oil and acrylic on Masonite
52 3/4 x 46 11/16
Museum of Contemporary Art, Chicago,
Gift of Mr. and Mrs. M. A. Lipschultz,
Mr. and Mrs. E.A. Bergman,
Nathan Cummings, Grace and Edwin
Hokin, and Mr. and Mrs.
Richard L. Feigen by exchange
plate 143

Jane Wenger
(American, born 1944)

Untitled from the "Self-Portrait" series
1976
Gelatin silver print
4 3/4 x 3 1/8
Museum of Contemporary Art, Chicago,
Illinois Arts Council Purchase Grant
plate 88

H.C. Westermann
(American, 1922–1981)

The Old Eccentric's House
1956–57
Fir lath, birch-veneer plywood,
and mirrors
18 1/2 x 18 7/8 x 33 1/4
Museum of Contemporary Art, Chicago,
Gift of Dennis Adrian in honor of
Mr. and Mrs. Joseph Randall Shapiro
plate 33

Death Ship of No Port
1957
Pine, brass, metal wire, and enamel on
fabric
24 1/4 x 30 1/2 x 3 5/8
Museum of Contemporary Art, Chicago,
Gift of John Miller
plate 31

Mad House
1958
Douglas fir, metal, glass, and enamel
69 5/8 x 23 3/4 x 25 3/16
Museum of Contemporary Art, Chicago,
Gift of Joseph and Jory Shapiro
plate 35

*Memorial to the Idea of Man
If He Was an Idea*
1958
Pine, bottle caps, metal, glass, enamel,
and toys
Open 75 1/4 x 39 1/2 x 20 1/2
Museum of Contemporary Art, Chicago,
Gift of Susan and Lewis Manilow
plate 36

Margaret Wharton
(American, born 1943)

Morning Bed
1978
Painted wood chair, epoxy glue, glass,
wire, and wood dowels on concrete base
65 x 37 1/2 x 50 1/8
Museum of Contemporary Art, Chicago,
Illinois Arts Council Purchase Grant
plate 102

Frances Whitehead
(American, born 1953)

Cigale
1989
Shellac on steel
60 x 60 x 24
Courtesy the artist, Chicago
plate 139

Richard Willenbrink
(American, born 1954)

Bacchus and His Attendants
1991
Oil on canvas
80 x 102
William and Virginia Gordon,
Burr Ridge, Illinois
plate 152

Anne Wilson
(American, born 1949)

Running in White Circles
1987
Synthetic felt, linen, and acrylic paint
72 x 72 x 3
Courtesy the artist, Evanston, Illinois
plate 133

Charles Wilson
(American, born 1937)

Les Feux des Joie
1977
Chromogenic color prints and text on
paper
Installation, dimensions variable
Courtesy the artist, Evanston, Illinois
plate 91

Maurice Wilson
(American, born 1954)

Shock-O-Late and Nubian Head
1993
Acrylic and tar on burlap
48 x 48
Eric McKissack, Chicago
plate 163

Karl Wirsum
(American, born 1939)

Armpits
1963
Oil and fur on canvas
28 x 26
Larry and Evelyn Aronson, Glencoe,
Illinois
plate 49

Screamin' J. Hawkins
1968
Acrylic on canvas
48 x 36
The Art Institute of Chicago,
Mr. and Mrs. Frank G. Logan Prize Fund
plate 64

Emerson Woelffer
(American, born 1914)

Untitled
1951
Oil and enamel on linen
20 1/8 x 24
Jo Hormuth and John Phillips,
Chicago
plate 17

Morning Earth
1955
Oil and collage on canvas
36 x 28
Courtesy Manny Silverman Gallery,
Los Angeles
plate 24

Joseph Yoakum
(American, 1886–1972)

Mt. Sadlerock near Packard Maine
1965 (?)
Watercolor and ink on paper
12 x 18
Roger Brown, Chicago
Not illustrated

Mt. Baykal of Yablonvy Mtn. Range
1969 (?)
Ballpoint pen, colored pencil,
and ink on paper
19 1/16 x 12 1/8
Jim Nutt and Gladys Nilsson,
Wilmette, Illinois
plate 60

Ray Yoshida
(American, born 1930)

Jizz and Jazz
1971
Acrylic on canvas
50 1/4 x 40 1/8
Harold and Barbara Klawans,
Munster, Indiana
plate 74

Claire Zeisler
(American, 1903–1991)

Red Preview
1969
Dyed jute
96 x 72 x 40
The Art Institute of Chicago,
Gift of Claire Zeisler
plate 65

Zhou Brothers
(Chinese, Shan Zuo born 1952;
Da Huang born 1957)

Childhood Dream
1990
Oil and mixed media on canvas
Triptych, overall 30 x 78 1/2
Peter and Lilian Vardy, Chicago
plate 148

Joe Ziolkowski
(American, born 1960)

No Title
1990
Gelatin silver print
14 1/4 x 14 1/4
Edition 4/25
Museum of Contemporary Art, Chicago,
Gift of the artist
plate 146

(Art)ⁿ Laboratory
(American, Stephan Meyers, born 1968;
Ellen Sandor, born 1942)
Founded 1983
Special thanks to Jim Zanzi and Richard
Sandor

*The Equation of Terror: Chemical
Terror, Arithmetic Operators I,
Biological Terror, Arithmetic
Relations, Economic Terror*
1991
PHSColograms®
Virtual photography installation
Five parts, three *Terror* panels,
each 24 x 20; two *Arithmetic* panels,
each 14 x 11
Courtesy the artists and Oskar Friedl
Gallery, Chicago
plate 150

index

to the catalogue